to my good fr[ie]

(Rev- Prof. Dr J. [?]

with many blessings

George

Jewish Messianic Movements

From AD 70 to AD 1300:
Documents from the Fall of Jerusalem to the End of the Crusades.

Introduction, Translation, Conclusions and Notes
By George Wesley Buchanan,
Professor Emeritus of New Testament at Wesley Theological Seminary

Wipf and Stock Publishers
EUGENE, OREGON

Wipf and Stock Publishers
199 West 8th Avenue, Suite 3
Eugene, Oregon 97401

Jewish Messianic Movements from AD 70 to AD 1300
Documents from the Fall of Jerusalem to the End of the Crusades
By Buchanan, George Wesley
Copyright©1978 by Buchanan, George Wesley
ISBN: 1-59244-382-6
Publication date 10/7/2003
Previously published by Western North Carolina Press, 1978

To
My Teachers at Hebrew Union College

Norman Golb
Alexander Guttmann
William Hallo
Aryeh Kahana
Robert Katz
Julius Lewy
Eugene Mihaly
Elisha Nattif
Jakob Petuchowski
Samuel Sandmel
Ezra Spicehandler
Mattatiyahu Tsevat

TABLE OF CONTENTS

PREFACE

During the year 1956-57 the graduate faculty seminar at Drew U. studied the theology of Rudolf Bultmann, much of which was concentrated on his eschatology. The more Bultmann's eschatology was discussed, the more I became convinced that it was not biblical. To support this conviction I set out to discover what biblical eschatology really was. I began at that time the research that has continued ever since as necessary background for a commentary on the Book of Revelation. The first step was to write a Ph.D. thesis, *The Eschatology of the Qumran Community* (Madison: Drew U., 1959). Research for this thesis convinced me that there was no teaching in the Dead Sea Scrolls or the OT that expected an otherworldly end. The ancients only anticipated the end of the current evil era when the Gentiles controlled the promised land. "Eschatology and the 'End of Days,'" *JNES* 20 (1961), 188-93, showed that the expression "end of days" in the Bible never anticipates a non-temporal state. The composition of the introduction for the reprinting of R.H. Charles, *Eschatology* (New York: Schocken Books, 1963), analyzed the various biblical, ethical, and philosophical eschatologies that had been proposed by scholars up to that time, showing the difficulties scholars have had in trying to understand that concept in nonpolitical terms. Research for *The Consequences of the Covenant* (Leiden: E.J. Brill, 1970) taught me the close relationship between eschatological anticipations of the OT, NT, and rabbinic literature and sabbatical and jubilee justice. By this time I was no longer merely challenging the eschatology of Bultmann as unbiblical, but also the views of Johannes Weiss, Dodd, Althaus, and most other popular eschatologies. The only biblical eschatology I could find was national, the end of the Gentile control over the promised land. I called this "sabbatical eschatology." This had been proposed before without that title by H.S. Reimarus, whose book was seldom read. I translated his thesis, *The Goal of Jesus and his Disciples* (Leiden: E.J. Brill, 1970) into English to make it available to many scholars who had never read it. Preparation of this translation and the research required for the introduction convinced me that Reimarus had been condemned as a heretic but never answered by sound scholarship.

Reviewers of *The Consequences of the Covenant* have not argued that the conclusions made on the basis of primary data given were unsound. Those who appraised the conclusions among the reviewers and other friends who read the book said they believed that Jews and Christians changed their eschatological views in NT times. It was against that claim that I began the research that resulted in this collection. All the materials I could find and read taught me that in Judaism from the time of Jesus to the end of the Crusades the only eschatological expectation shown was closely related to the reestablishment of the promised land to the Jews under Davidic rule which would be extended to the end of the then civilized and known world. I did not think it was enough to read this material and report the conclusions to NT scholars for them to believe or disbelieve. I chose to translate some of the most important materials and make them available to scholars to read in English for themselves. In the process I learned the close relationship between apocalyptic literature and the doctrine of redemption. I also learned the centrality of this eschatological longing for redemption among medieval Jews and the excellent literary ways they had of expressing it. The literature collected is by no means an exhaustive collection, but only a sampling. The collection could be reduced still further and be representative, but the extent and depth of this doctrine will not receive its full impact with only a quick survey. These eschatological hopes found expression in every walk of life and were kept in mind through prayer, song, and catechism. This literature should not be read only by NT scholars to learn the nature of eschatology in ancient Judaism and Christianity, but it should be read for its own sake, just to appreciate the feelings of a people and their artful literary skills, whether or not the reader agrees with the composer's convictions. They represent an important part of the world culture that should be preserved and known.

I am grateful to Bultmann for stimulating me to search the Bible and associated literature to learn the real nature of biblical eschatology. The goal of correcting Bultmann was given up as a main motivation long ago and replaced by a positive desire to learn the correct thought forms and drives of our religious ancestors, particularly as they were dominated by eschatology.

The book is dedicated to my excellent teachers at Hebrew Union College-Jewish Institute of Religion, where I was enrolled in pre-doctoral and post-doctoral studies (1957-60). Without their inspiration, patience, and interest in introducing me to the languages and literature of Judaism it would have been impossible for me to do the research or translation necessary for this volume. Each of these has made a distinctive contribution to my education: With Dr. Golb I continued my studies in the Dead Sea Scrolls and enjoyed many discussions. I also appreciate his kindness in letting me use his office and books. From Dr. Guttmann I learned to study rabbinic literature generally, and the Tosephta in particular. The hours spent with him have enabled me to think midrashically and rabbinically. I still study and learn from material to which he introduced me, and I still find support and encouragement from his mature scholarship. Dr. Hallo taught me to read biblical Hebrew and Aramaic. With him I studied the Psalms and sharpened my research skills. Dr. Kahana was my professor of Mishnah. With Dr. Katz I studied commentaries. Dr. Lewy taught me beginning Syriac and reviewed with me all the languages I had previously studied. With Dr. Mihaly I studied Midrash Rabba and Mekilta. Rabbi Nattif was my language laboratory instructor. I took no courses with Dr. Petuchowski or Dr. Tsevat but spent many fruitful hours with them, discussing scholarly topics. Dr. Sandmel was a helpful counsellor, stimulating teacher, and meaningful friend. With him I studied Hellenistic literature, Philo, and NT backgrounds. I tested many new ideas against his judgment and found him always interested, imaginative, and judicious. I am still working on research projects I began under his guidance. Dr. Spicehandler was a patient but hard taskmaster in modern Hebrew. I learned more Hebrew in one year under the combined direction of Dr. Spicehandler, Dr. Hallo, and Rabbi Nattif than I ever thought was humanly possible. It was a real privilege to be a part of the language program at HUC at that time. I take pride in Hebrew Union College; I am very happy for my opportunity to study there; and I continue to cherish my relationships with the faculty there.

Research in Jewish studies that received a strong impact at Hebrew Union College has been further strengthened with the aid of Dr. Lawrence Marwick and Mr. Myron Weinstein of the Hebraic section of the Library of Congress. These two experts in rabbinic studies and Arabic literature have been very helpful to me in many ways, only one of which has been finding the literature I needed for research. I alsc appreciate the many kindnesses extentended to me by the librarians at Hebrew University and the Schocken Library in Jerusalem and the university library at Göttingen, Germany. Dr. Ibn Shmuel, a pious Israeli scholar who is

about ninety years old and who prepared an important collection
of apocalyptic documents in Hebrew (*Midrashim of Redemption* =
מדרשי גאולה) , was very helpful to me in Jerusalem. He met with
me several times and suggested places where I might find certain
documents.

All the translations have been checked either by Dr. and Mrs.
Pinḥas Lapide or Dr. S.M. Lehrman. These scholars have
improved my translations very much. The reader may learn which
scholars read which manuscripts by the initials: RPL for Ruth and
Pinḥas Lapide and SML for Dr. Lehrman. Rev. James McGinnis
and Rev. William Summerhill have carefully checked the
manuscript for accuracy of biblical references. My wife, Harlene,
not only read the entire manuscript for typographical errors, ac-
cidental omissions, and grammatical mistakes, but she supports,
assists, and encourages me in all of my research.

My next project in eschatology is one on which I have worked
for many years: the commentary on the Book of Revelation which
required this background research before the text could be interpreted accurately.

ABBREVIATIONS

Any rabbinic tractate that has only a chapter and verse designation (Berakoth 2:3) is from the Mishnah. The same reference with a T in front of it (TBer 2:3) is from the Tosephta. If the tractate is followed by a number and a small Arabic a or b, it is from the Babylon Talmud on the page given (Ber 12a). If a J precedes such a tractate passage, the reference is from the Jerusalem or Palestinian Talmud (JBer 5a). Any scriptural book followed by R is from Midrash Rabba (GenR 3:4). Sometimes further specification of paragraph or division is also given. Some editions of the Jerusalem Talmud have two columns to a page, so there are not only a and b, but also c and d, given in references. Other references are given in the following list alphabetically:

Ant.	Josephus, *Antiquities of the Jews*
AZ	Abodah Zarah
Ber.	Berakoth
BA	*Biblical Archaeology*
BJ	Josephus, *The Wars of the Jews*
BK	Baba Kamma
BM	Baba Metzia
DtR	Deuteronomy Rabba
EstR	Esther Rabba
ExR	Exodus Rabba
GenR	Genesis Rabba
Ḥag.	Ḥagigah
HE	Eusebius, *Ecclesiastical History*
JE	*Jewish Encyclopaedia*
JGit	Jerusalem Talmud Gittin
JNES	*Journal of Near Eastern Studies*
JTaan	Jerusalem Talmud Taanith
Ket.	Ketuboth
Kid.	Kiddushin
Mac.	Maccabees
MPG	Migne Greek Text of the Church Fathers
Ned.	Nedarim
NT	The New Testament
OT	The Old Testament

PR	Pesikta Rabbati
PsJ	Targum Pseudo-Jonathan
Ps. Sol.	Psalms of Solomon
1QM	Qumran Cave 1, The War Scroll
1QS	Qumran Cave 1, The Order of the Community
REJ	*Revue Etudes Juives*
RPL	Dr. and Mrs. Pinhas Lapide
RQ	*Revue de Qumran*
Shab.	Shabbath
SML	Dr. S.M. Lehrman
SO	Sibylline Oracles
SSR	Song of Songs Rabba
Suk.	Sukkah
Tanak	The Torah, Prophets, and Writings
Tanh.	Tanhuma
Zeb.	Zebahim

INTRODUCTION

Literature and Doctrine

The doctrines of redemption and relevation have been very important, both in understanding and in shaping Jewish and Christian history and literature. On the basis of divine revelation, Israelites left Egypt, accepted the ten commandments, engaged in various battles with the peoples of the land of Canaan, and erected the temple. Sometimes revelation came unsolicited, and at other times it came as a result of studying earlier history of the people of the literature covenanters had accepted as authoritative. For example, it was Jeremiah's familiarity with Deuteronomy and Leviticus that motivated him to predict the Babylonian Captivity. It was Daniel's familiarity with Jeremiah's prophecy that prompted him to interpret the "seventy years" in terms of further prophecy (Dan 9:1—27). This was considered revelation. It was also called apocalyptic. Apocalyptic literature received its name from the Greek ἀποκάλυψις which means to uncover, open, or unroll. Anyone who unrolled a scroll, "uncovered" its contents, so that they were no longer hidden. Even after apocalyptic literature had been unrolled or opened, however, it remained a puzzle whose solution was still hidden except for the few who understood the concepts and the allusions included. A knowledge about the life of the people to whom the literature was written will explain why the content of the material had to be "covered." The most important apocalyptic book of the NT is called "The Revelation of John." It is also sometimes called "The Apocalypse." The same type of apocalyptic literature in medieval Judaism is called "Redemption Literature," because the revelation or unveiling involved Israel's past and future redemption. This whole theological structure has been patterned after the economic system that was practiced in the ancient Near East at the time the theology of revelation and redemption was formulated.

The Treasury of Merits

The economic structure. — One of the economic patterns that formed a basis for theology was the banking structure that enabled

1

individuals to invest their money in a certain place where it could accumulate and be drawn on later, or they could borrow money from this accumulated supply when they needed it and pay it back later. Any such system requires some understood rules related to interest, sanctions, and the protection against exploitation. It is only after such a program has become firmly established and accepted as authoritative that the same rules can be extended into an understanding of God's way of administering justice. The treasury of merits doctrine presumed that good deeds could be stored up for future use just as money could. It also assumed that the lender could "foreclose" whenever the account was overdrawn, and there was no immediate resupply. This doctrine occurs frequently in the scripture.

Merits in the OT. — In some places the accumulation of merits or sins is directly described as such, but in other cases history was interpreted in a way that just took this for granted. One illustration of the latter is the exodus of the Israelites from Egypt. Israel was required to suffer severely in Egypt because God hardened the heart of Pharaoh (Ex 4:21). This act accomplished two functions: 1) It cancelled Israel's sins so she deserved liberty, and 2) it filled up the measure of Pharaoh's sin so that he deserved the punishment necessary to set the Israelites free, but this is not clearly stated in Exodus.[1] In Genesis, however, the reason given for Israel's failure to enter the promised land right after leaving Egypt was that the sins of the Amorites had not yet been completed, so the Israelites would have to wait until the Amorites had sinned more and deserved the punishment they were destined to receive at God's hand through the agency of the Israelites (Gen 15:16). Gabriel told Daniel that the Jews had been required to suffer in the exile because of their sins. Their treasury of merits had been depleted, so a sentence of "seventy weeks was decreed over" Israel and over "her holy city, to cancel the transgression, seal up sins, and atone for iniquity" (Dan 9:24). These were not three different events, but an emphatic and repetitious way of saying the same thing. The *sin* was the wicked activity committed by the Israelites which was also considered *transgression* of divine laws or rebellion against God. The record which God kept of these activities was the *iniquity* or negative mark in the balance of merits and demerits.[2] Whenever the iniquity was atoned or "covered up,"

---

[1] But see Ned 32a; EstR 1:1; SSR 7:14; MidPs 31:7; DtR 7:10. For a lengthy discussion, see A. Marmorstein, *The Doctrine of Merits in Old Rabbinic Literature* (New York, c1968), 91, 99, 152-153.

[2] See further *The Consequences of the Covenant* (Leiden, 1970), 156-159.

the sin was sealed, and the transgression was completely paid up or cancelled, so that the sentence Israelites had been required to serve would have reached its end and could be removed.

Merits in the NT. — Because God kept records of good deeds in his treasury, Christians were urged to "treasure up" for themselves "treasures in heaven, where neither moth nor rust destroys and where thieves do not break in and steal" (Mt 6:20). Those who were rich in this age were encouraged to "do good, become rich in good works, generous, [and] sharers, treasuring up for themselves a good foundation for the time to come" (I Tim 6:18-19). One early Christian claimed that there was laid up for him a crown of righteousness because of his good works (II Tim 4:7-8). The Jews, however, who killed the Lord and the prophets, persecuted the Christians, and prohibited Christians from sharing the gospel with the Gentiles, were "filling up their [quota] of sins" before God's wrath would come upon them (I Thes 2:14-16). Their condition was like that of the Egyptians just before the exodus and the Amorites just before the Israelite conquest of Canaan. Later rabbis and church fathers took the treasury of merits for granted and discussed details of justice on the basis of its implications.[3]

The treasury of merits was clearly a doctrine that developed out of an understanding of community economic and banking practices. A further extension of borrowing and lending customs developed the theological doctrine of national eschatology, basic to all apocalyptic or redemption literature.

Sabbatical Eschatology[4]

Sabbatical rules. — The ancient Israelite who loaned money to his fellow covenanter received no interest. The only protection he had for his investment was the right to force the borrower who could not repay his debt in cash to work for him at half wages until the debt was paid (Dt 15:12-13, 18). Should the sabbatical year come around, however, before the debt was paid, the creditor was required to release the debtor anyway, because he had worked at half wages, or paid twice the amount of money he borrowed (Dt 15:12-13, 18). If a man owned property and needed money, he could sell it, but on the jubilee year, the man who bought it was required to return it to the seller or his heirs, so that the land could not finally be taken from the family. At the jubilee, which happened

---

[3] B.L. Conway, *The Question Box* (New York, 1929), 225-228; Marmorstein, *The Doctrine of Merits.*

[4] This entire discussion on sabbatical eschatology has been explained more thoroughly in *Consequences,* 12-18.

every forty-nine years, not only were the debtor-captives set free, but the land was restored to the original owners (Lev 26:8-10). These were rules of economic justice that enabled covenanters to borrow and lend, but protected both borrower and lender from extensive exploitation. This concept was later transferred to national theology.

The national debt. — Just as the individual Israelite was obliged to work off his debt at half wages, so Jeremiah warned that the nation, which had accumulated a large debt of sin that it could not repay, would also go into captivity until she had paid double for all her sins (Dt 15:18; Jer 16:18). Jeremiah's original prophecy, however, was made in terms of sabbath years and jubilees,[5] it was finally made to cohere with the facts—ten sabbath years from 587 B.C., when the captivity began, to 516 B.C., after the Jews had been restored to the land and the temple was completed. Before this took place, II Isaiah in Babylon foresaw deliverance just ahead, probably just before the end of the forty-ninth year in Babylon, which coincided with Cyrus' victory over Babylon. It was time to proclaim release to the captives! This meant their term of servitude as debtor-captives had been completed. They had paid double for all their sins (Dt 15:18; Jer 16:18; Isa 40:1; 61:1-3).

The National jubilee. — The earliest recorded interpretation of exile and return in terms of debtor-captives and jubilee justice was probably written nearly a jubilee of years after the Assyrian captivity of North Israelites. The Isaianic apocalyptist anticipated the trumpet blast, as in jubilee, when the exiles from Assyria and Egypt would return to their land (Isa 27:13). That prophecy was not fulfilled, but in the opinion of some Jews, another prophecy was. After the Maccabean victory, some ingenious eschatologist who believed that this was the real fulfillment of Jeremiah's prophecy, was not perplexed by the delay. He noticed that instead of seventy years, about seven times seventy years had elapsed since the captivity in Babylon. With only slight adjustments the scheme worked out perfectly: seven weeks of years was spent in Babylon, sixty-two weeks of years intervened from the return until a certain covenant was made: sixty-two plus seven equals sixty-nine—only one more week of years until the tenth jubilee! One half week of years later the temple was defiled and the sacrifice, stopped (Dan 9:24-27). Before the second half week of years was over, Judas had cleansed the temple (Dan 7:25; 8:14; 9:27; 12:7).

---

[5] Jeremiah may originally have predicted seven years or forty-nine years, since he also bought land in the promised land as if he expected to reclaim it during his lifetime.

The end that Daniel had "predicted" was the end of foreign control of the temple and the land. This was the national jubilee when the promised land was restored to its "original" owners, the Jews. With the Maccabean victory, the land had "rest," and freedom was proclaimed throughout the land. Pseudo-Jonathan and Jubilees narrated the history of Israel from creation until the "anticipated" entrance into the promised land in terms of jubilees. The Assumption of Moses, *mutatis mutandis*, followed the same type of eschatology (see also I Mac 1:45-54; 4:54). Zechariah announced that Israel's enemies would be defeated and her king ride in procession when the Lord sounded the trumpet, when he set the captives free, and when he restored them double, as at jubilee (Zech 9:1-14).

In the Dead Sea Scrolls (1QS 10:3-4, 7-8; 11Q Melch), Apocryphal and Pseudepigraphical literature (IV Ezra 6:23; Apocalypse of Abraham 31; SO 7:174; Ps Sol 11:19; *et passim*), the NT (Mt 13:39-40; 24:3; 28:20; I Cor 15:51-52; I Thes 4:16; Heb 3:11, 18; 4:1, 3, 5, 10, 11; Rev 11:2, 3, 15; 12:6, 14), and rabbinic literature, terminology related to the expected end of the age and the restoration of the land in terms of sabbath rest, jubilee trumpets, release of debtor captives, the prison terms occur over and over again. Those medieval Jewish rabbis and poets who calculated the end-times usually did so according to the sabbath years and jubilees. In this they were consistent with biblical eschatology which is always reasoned in terms of sabbatical years and jubilees or else in other real time-span terms related to Israel's history, such as the length of time Israelites spent in Egypt or Babylon. Their hope was consistently related to chronological years and ages and real restoration of the promised land to the chosen people. Because their eschatology was related to the economic defense of the borrower, they believed God, as the creditor, was required to restore their land at the end of a certain term. When they calculated that the defined term was completed, they made plans to return to the promised land. When their plans were frustrated, they complained bitterly, but returned to their desks and began to recalculate the prison term of debtor slaves.

NT scholars who have become comfortable with the eschatological interpretations of such non-biblical eschatologists as Bultmann, Dodd, and Althaus,[6] will need to be prepared to reorient themselves to sabbatical eschatology in order to

---

[6] For a further analysis of these positions, see the introduction to the reprinting of R.H. Charles, *Eschatology* (New York, c1963), vii-xxx.

understand the views of the medieval Jews whose works are here translated. Medieval Jews were not trained in philosophical existentialism, but they knew the temporal monetary structure of debtors in relationship to creditors, sabbath years, and jubilees, just as biblical authors did. Both agreed in transferring a local economic structure to a national, theological doctrine, but since sins were considered debts in relationship to God, the creditor, it seemed reasonable to extend the doctrine still further to deal with the abolition of sins according to the same structure. This is the rationale for the doctrine of redemption.

The Doctrine of Redemption

Shortening the term. — Once a covenanter found himself a debtor captive to his fellow Israelite, it was not a foregone conclusion that he had to serve out his full term or even work until the sabbath year or jubilee. At any point after he had begun to work off his debt, he was free to pay off his debt in silver or goods. Although he had no money to pay his debt, his brother, uncle, or cousin might be able to pay it for him and release him from further captivity (Lev 25:47-49). If no relative volunteered to pay his debt, but his own economic condition changed favorably, then he might pay his own debt and thus be released from it and from his debtor-captivity (Lev 25:49). The act of buying back the remainder of a debt so as to release someone from debtor-slavery was called "redeeming" (גאל). Just as the debtor captive could be redeemed before the sabbath, so also his land might be redeemed with money before the jubilee (Lev 25:25-26).

If one man injured another, the injured party had to be compensated for his injury. If he had been killed, then a near relative was expected to avenge him by killing the murderer. One who did this for another was called the other's avenger or redeemer. He redeemed his kinsman by paying back the injury (Num 35:19-27; Dt 19:6; Josh 20:3, 5; 20:9; II Sam 14:11; I Kgs 16:11; Job 19:25). A person who owed God a tithe, offering, or sacrifice, such as a lamb which he really wanted to keep for himself, might compensate the priest with money for the value of the lamb plus a twenty-percent surcharge (Lev 27:13, 31). The act of buying off the obligation with money was called redemption. The covenanter might also redeem a devoted house or field under the same terms (Lev 27:15, 19, 27-28). If a person was forced to sell a field, close relatives had first opportunity to buy it and keep it in the family. This was called redeeming the property (Jer 32:7-8; Ruth 2:20; 3:9, 12, 13;

4:1, 3, 4, 6, 7, 8, 14). The same word took on an extended meaning to include deliverance or salvation which did not literally involve the expenditure of money, but deliverance from enemies, violence, or evil (Gen 48:16; Ps 69:18; 72:14; 106:10; 107:2; Jer 31:11[10].

God as a redeemer.— The Torah does not say that the creditor might himself act as redeemer and freely cancel the debt, allowing the debtor to go free, but hypothetically, that might occur. When *the Lord* was the creditor, however, Israel expected him also to act as redeemer (Ps 19:14; 77:15-16; 78:35; Prov 23:11; Isa 41:14; 43:14 44:6, 24; 47:4; 48:17; 49:7, 26; 54:5, 8; 59:20; 60:16; 63:16; Jer 50:34; Lam 3:58; Micha 4:10). When the Lord had redeemed Israel in the past, he forgave her sins (Isa 44:22) and delivered her from Egypt (Ex 6:6; 15:13; Isa 51:10) or from Babylon (Isa 35:9; 43:1; 44:23; 48:20; 52:3, 9; 62:12; 63:9) where, according to Jeremiah and II Isaiah, Israel was serving time as a debtor captive, working off twice the amount of her debt of sin to the Lord. The redemption to which medieval Jews looked longingly also anticipated the restoration of the promised land to the Jews under the independent rule of their own Davidic king. This means that Israelites related their eschatology to deliverance or redemption, and both of these concepts were theological applications of economic structures.

Bringing up the balance.— Whenever Jews were away from the promised land and the land was not under the independent rule of a Jewish king, they considered themselves to be "captive debtors" regardless of their status in the diaspora, economically, politically, or socially. When they were in this situation, they believed they would be restored to the promised land in due time, regardless of their behavior, whenever the true jubilee arrived so that the captives would be set free and the land restored. There was always the possibility that the Lord would shorten the sentence for good behavior or just out of his mercy as a redeemer who was willing to cancel the remaining debt of sin, even though it was not completed, and the jubilee had not yet arrived (Mt 24:22). There was the other possibility that the covenanters themselves might work to pay off their debt. In this case they might redeem themselves just as a debtor slave who had become prosperous. This was done by turning the other cheek, walking the second mile (Mt 5:39-41), giving food and drink to enemies (Rom 12:19-20), and performing other extraordinary deeds which would enable the believers to lay up treasures in heaven (Mt 6:19-20). There was always the other possibility that some other human being or human beings would

have laid up enough treasures in heaven to cancel the sins of the
other covenanters. Some who were believed to have been excep-
tionally virtuous were the patriarchs.[7] Christians believed Jesus,
by his suffering, had cancelled the sins of all, or nearly all (Col
1:24), believers. Jews believed a messiah, son of Joseph or
Ephraim, was currently in hiding, suffering unendurable agony to
cancel the sins of all Israel. In these cases, Jesus and the Messiah of
Ephraim were considered to be redeemers. Any method that
brought about redemption would also put an end to the contemporary political situation under foreign rule and thus achieve the
goal of their eschatology. It would be their redemption; and it
would restore the Jews to the promised land under the rule of a
Davidic king. These all would take place together or not at all. The
firm belief in these doctrines by Jews and Christians was not only
reflected in medieval history, but it helped to shape the history itself.

The Enterprise of the Elect

The elect among the non-elect. — Wacholder's calculations agree
with those of Maimonides that A.D. 70 was a sabbatical year.[8]
The Jewish war with Rome had gone on for three and a half
years—a time, two times, and half a time—as Daniel had
promised would occur before the temple would be cleansed of
foreign influences and the land restored to the Jews (Dan 12:7).
Jews, and probably many Christians, had fought strenuously in
the confidence that history would repeat itself. Rome learned that
eschatological expectations of the Jews provided a strong
motivating factor that could not be easily suppressed. Rome also
knew that Jews and Christians would soon become a threat to
Rome itself if this movement were not completely overcome.
There were Jews and Christians all over the Roman Empire, so that
even after the destruction of Jerusalem revolts had to be put down
(*BJ* VIII [407-416; 437-450]). Hegesippus said Vespasian,
Domitian, and Trajan hunted down and executed all Jews of the
house of David in order to root out the hope on which the Jews
relied (*HE* III.12, 19-20; XXXII.3-4). The Fragments of Tacitus (2)
report that people encouraged Titus to destroy the temple so as to
annihilate the religion of the Jews and Christians; for they urged

[7] JBer 9b; JTaan 63d; Tahn II, p. 32. There were also individuals such as R. Shimon ben
Yohai (Suk 45b; JBer 13d; GenR 35:2).
[8] Maimonides, הלכות שמיטה ויובל X.4. See B.Z. Wacholder, "The Calendar of
Sabbatical Cycles during the Second Temple and the Early Rabbinic Period," *HUCA*. 44
(1973), 153-196.

that "these religions, granted that they are in conflict with each other, nevertheless, they came from the same origins; the Christians had emerged from the Jews; if the root were destroyed, the stock would easily perish." Apparently Christianity and Judaism were both believed to be fifth columnist movements at the time, but it took only the Bar Cochba Revolt of A.D. 132-35 to convince Rome that these factions would not evaporate the instant the temple was burned. After this complete defeat, Jews and Jewish Christians were forbidden to enter any of the area near Jerusalem. Jerusalem was plowed like a field (Micah 3:12), but Jews and Christians continued to exist in the diaspora, and the intensity of the persecution they suffered suggests that Jews and Christians had worked themselves into positions of influence and power where their activity had become a threat to the government. Although Jews and Christians treated one another with hostility, their basic convictions were very similar; they both originated from the same sects of earlier Judaism; they both followed similar practices of behavior, worship, and attitudes towards themselves and others. They both had the same basic goals. These were both exclusive groups that believed they were the only elect of God. They alone were God's chosen people, segregated from all other peoples to be the Lord's royalty. Each group believed it was destined to rule, not only Palestine, but unlimited territories of Europe, Africa, and Asia. They believed that the Gentiles, on the other hand, were created to be their slaves, to tend their flocks and care for their vineyards, while they themselves enjoyed the luxury that came from wealth, prosperity, social position, and political power (Isa 61:1-22). The Bar Cochba defeat did not put an end to these beliefs and hopes. It only entrenched them deeper and made Jews and Christians work still harder underground. This behavior prompted various Roman emperors and local leaders to use force to put down these fifth columnists. Some were burned alive; others were thrown to lions; still others were imprisoned. Churches were destroyed. Christians and Jews called these movements persecution and martyrdom, but Romans considered them necessary ways of tightening their security and protecting themselves against sabotage. All this time Jews and Christians were fighting also among themselves, because each considered the other to be the worst kind of heretics, maliciously competing for its own true position.

Christian success. — Evidently Christians were successful in this endeavor, at least in the fourth century, but their maneuver

was probably nothing new to Jewish history. II Isaiah hailed
Cyrus as the Lord's Messiah before Cyrus entered Babylon.
This probably means that Babylonian Jews had used their
diplomatic skill and power to negotiate with Cyrus, agreeing to
assist Cyrus in overthrowing Babylon from within, if Cyrus, in
turn, enabled them afterwards to return to the promised land.
Centuries later, Christians made some agreements with Constantine to provide him with inner preparations and also military support in his battles to gain control of Rome. In turn Constantine
agreed to make all of his territories Christian. When this actually
happened, Christians interpreted the action as God's will. This
was the new exodus (*HE* IX.iv.3-10; X.i.4ff.; iv.49ff.; viii.16ff.),
the resurrection of the dead (*HE* X.iv.10-12), and the reestablishment of Solomon's temple (*HE* X.iv.2-7). This was the beginning
of the goal both Christians and Jews had in mind, and it proved to
Christians that they were really the elect of God in contrast to the
Jews, who clearly were not. Jews, of course, did not concede this
point, and the hatred between these two self-appointed groups of
chosen people increased.

The chances of the chosen. — When Christianity suddenly
became an openly strong controlling power in the government, the
relative positions of Christianity and Judaism changed radically.
When Christianity moved from a minority, subversive power
within Rome to a majority, controlling force, it grew in political,
external power and numbers, but rapid growth and mass conver-
sions weakened it per capita in training, leadership, and wealth.
Although it held external evidence that it had begun its destined
rule, administrative details prevented Christianity from maintaining its religious and leadership ability. Judaism, on the other
hand, continued to maintain its subversive position as a strong
minority movement of wealthy, upper class, well-educated,
political, economic, and military leaders whose ability could not
be neglected or overlooked by the ruling powers. In many ways
Judaism was a thorn in the flesh of Christianity. Christians were
convinced that Jews were destined to serfdom. Therefore it was
the obligation of Christians to keep them in this lowly position,
but it could not be done. Jews appeared everywhere the most
wealthy people in each nation. Those destined, in Christian judgment, to be slaves, themselves owned Christian slaves who were
required to be circumcised.[9] They also hired Christian servants to
work on Sunday and abstain from work on the Jewish sabbath.

---

[9]M.L. Margolis and A. Marx, *A History of the Jewish People* (London, 1927), 350.

One Jew was king of Himyara; another was acting ruler of Granada; many were ministers of finance or leading physicians. They were bankers or moneylenders and leading international merchants. Many times Christians were threatened by Jewish power and were injured by Jewish ability to exploit Christians from their positions of economic, military, or political power. Sometimes this resulted in retaliatory armed rebellion and mass slaughter. At other times ruling powers needed the wealth which Jews possessed. At such times, Jews were threatened with expulsion or death, and Jews usually responded with offers of bribes which fulfilled the emperor's need and intended goal, so the threat was not carried out. It would have seemed more fair to have levied a tax on the upper class generally without discrimination to meet the needs of the national economy, but no ruler had the strength to do so, even if he were so motivated. There was open conflict between Jews and Christians as each tried to prove that it alone constituted the chosen people.

Christians were limited in their retaliatory power. If they expelled the Jews from their country, as they sometimes did, the Jews would migrate to the country of their enemies and use their power to injure the country from which they fled. So many Jews were engaged in international commerce that they were acquainted with languages and customs of several countries, making migration less formidable than for most people. Jews, far from believing that Christian victory by association with Constantine proved they were the only elect, believed instead that Christians were really only antichrists who prevented the Messiah from establishing the Jews in the positions of superiority that they clearly deserved, in their own judgment.

If only. — It is sometimes interesting, but never completely convincing, to speculate about the way things would be if certain events had turned out differently. This is less hazardous, however, when the people involved in the history were governed by certain rules and attitudes requiring them to behave in a specific way to a given set of circumstances. This kind of pattern-behavior is somewhat predictable. Since both Jews and Christians were controlled by the same kind of drives and beliefs, what would have happened if, instead of Christians, Jews had got to Constantine first and successfully negotiated with him? In such a case, the whole pattern might have been reversed. Jews, while becoming an administrating majority may also have become an "all class" society rather than an upper class minority. Christians, then, unimpeded by political responsibilities might have continued as a powerful, upper class minority which could use the skills employed to make Constantine succeed in order to overthrow the power of the Jewish government. Jews, then, might have become threatened by the mobile Christian minority the same way Christians actually did feel threatened by the powerful Jewish minority. Using minority forces, Christians might have exploited Jews in the same way Jews actually exploited Christians, and Jews, in response, may have used physical force the way Christians did. Of course, this is only imaginative speculation, but the basis for this rests on the beliefs that both groups really held and their religious antipathy against one another had a lot to do with the events of history during the Middle Ages.

It may not follow that anyone who wanted to conjecture how Jews would have acted as the majority and Christians as the minority had only to observe the behavior of the other group. It is possible, however, to learn how each group actually did behave during the Middle Ages, and the person who wishes may imagine the situation reversed. These were not just helpless victims of historical fate. Both groups were religious, and both groups acted to change the course of history as well as to respond to the events that confronted them. Since this book is concentrated primarily on Jewish literature, the history discussed will be primarily Jewish history, but it did not take place in a vacuum. Christians and Moslems were closely related to many situations that effected Jewish faith and history. The behavior both of Jews and Christians, in many cases is embarrassing to sensitive, non-militant Christians and Jews of today, but the extent to which this is true is a good measure of the extent to which Judaism and Christianity have changed in the meantime. Some of the conflicts between Jews and Christians would have happened in almost any society where there is a great financial and social difference between classes, but some of the conflict was religiously instigated or at least made more intense because each group believed that the other was the enemy of God and deserved to be destroyed.

Religious apartheid.— None of the prevailing religions— Judaism, Islam, and Christianity—made any attempt to provide equal justice for all people before the law. In Moslem countries, Jews and Christians had to pay special poll taxes from which Moslems were exempt, had to wear distinctive clothing, and were not permitted to ride on horses as upper class citizens did.[10] If

---

[10] H. Graetz, *History of the Jews* (5 vols.; Philadelphia, 1902), vol. III, 145.

a Jew killed a Christian, he was not likely to be tried for guilt in a court. Instead, a mob usually took over, killed many Jews, and burned Jewish homes and synagogues.[11] When the situation was reversed, however, and a Jew was king in Himyara, he acted in exactly the same way, avenging the deaths of two Jews by massacring three hundred, forty Christians and throwing their bodies into a river.[12] There was an open conflict for privilege rather than any attempt to provide equality for all. Spinoza said Jewish isolation practices of his day were strengthened as much by hatred for Christians as by a Jewish desire to do God's will.[13] Religious hostilities of Jews were not limited to Christians or vice versa. Byzantine Christians treated Jews better than Christian heretics, and rabbinic Jews showed no special kindness toward Karaites or Samaritans. Jews in the Diaspora continued catechetically to maintain their highest loyalty to Palestine rather than to the countries in which they lived, thus maintaining an unwillingness to identify themselves with the countries in which they resided. This was carried to the extent of forbidding Jews to pray for rain if rain was not also needed at that very time in Palestine as well as in the country in which they lived. To do so would be to show a greater concern for the countries in which they lived than in Palestine which was their promised and lasting destiny.[14] Especially in times of persecution, Jews prayed loudly the 'Alenu prayer, praising God because "he has not made us like the Gentiles, nor placed us on a par with the clans of the earth. He has not set our fate with theirs nor cast our lot with all their multitude."[15] It is not fair at this distance to blame one group more than another for these interreligious tragedies or expect them to have acted on the basis of modern, desegregation ethics. They were all controlled by the same apartheid policies and did whatever they could to keep themselves distinct from others, with the other religions suppressed as lowly as possible. Each believed this was God's will for his chosen people, as each group believed itself to be.

In the midst of this sad history emerged religious literature composed by medieval Jews who interpreted their faith, gave expression to their deepest feelings, composed their prayers, and disclosed their plans and expectations for their future on the basis

[11] S.W. Baron, *A Social and Religious History of the Jews* (in 6 vols.; New York, 1957), vol. IV, 133-34.
[12] Graetz, *History*, 50-51, 65, 66-67.
[13] Margolis and Marx, *A History*, 498.
[14] Baron, *Social and Religious History*, V, 27.
[15] Baron, *Social and Religious History*, IV, 138.

of their religious beliefs. The redemption literature that emerged was closely related to the fifth-columnist nature of the Jewish life in the Middle Ages. If Christians, instead of Jews, had been the minority, they might have written similar literature, but rather than speculate on the "might have been" history, we will next consider the status of Jews in the Middle Ages in the history that was.

Jewish power and wealth. — Jews were some of the earliest people to abandon agriculture as an occupation and become involved in international trade. There were several reasons for this: 1) Some rabbis considered farming the lowest form of occupation, meant only for men with strong backs and weak minds. 2) Land was easily taxed and immovable. Since Jews owed their primary loyalty to the promised land, they did not tie their allegiance too tightly to other land. 3) In times of persecution, land could easily be confiscated, leaving the Jews penniless. 4) Farming ceased to be a lucrative occupation in comparison with other businesses.[16] As tenants in other lands, Jews continued to be upper class citizens even though the attitude toward them varied from time to time and from country to country. This both enabled them and forced them to migrate from one land to another according to the national reception. There were more Jews in Asia throughout the Middle Ages than in Europe, with the exception of Spain, where Jews thrived for many years.[17] Moslems, by and large, allowed Jews more freedom than Christians did. They taxed both Christians and Jews discriminatively, but not oppressively. Jews were entrusted by Moslems with the collection of poll taxes from Christians as well as Jews and held posts of honor in the court.[18] Solomon Al-Muallem of Seville was Ali's court physician,[19] and others gained distinction in science and poetry.[20] During the reigns of Charlemagne and his son Louis (A.D. 742-840), a Jew was one of Charlemagne's ambassadors. Certain Jewish merchants were granted special protection, and a special imperial officer in Lyons saw to it that Jewish privileges found no resistance. In Lyons the market day was changed from the Jewish sabbath on Saturday to the Christian sabbath on Sunday because Jews would not trade on their sabbath.[21] Jews were allowed to employ Christian workmen and import Christian slaves. It was customary for Jews to circumcize all their slaves within one year and require servants to work

---

[16] Baron, *Social and Religious History*, IV, 151.

[17] Graetz, *History*, 383.

[18] Graetz, *History*, 312.

[19] Graetz, *History*, 324.

[20] *Ibid.*, 312.

[21] Margolis and Marx, *A History*, 349.

on Sunday, but at the same time Christian clergymen were forbidden to baptize the slaves of Jews to enable them to regain their freedom. Jews farmed the taxes even over Christians in this Christian country.[22] In some situations Jews were treated on equal terms with the nobles and clergy of Christians. The same sum was fixed as a compensation for the murder of a Jew, a nobleman, and a priest. Graetz shows his pro-Jewish bias in appraising this situation as "equality between Jews and Christians before the law."[23] In these conditions Jews were equal only with *the most privileged* Christians of the nation. The dukes of Austria committed the financial administration of the duchy to the hands of the Jews. Solomon, a Jew, was the master of the mint for Leopold I (A.D. 1177-1194). Leopold II (A.D. 1198-1230) had another Jew for a banker.[24] In Granada Jews were more highly favored than Arabs. Graetz called this preferred status one in which Jews enjoyed "so complete an equality."[25] After the death of King Habus of Granada, a Jew named Samuel was appointed first assistant to Habus's successor, Badis (Oct., 1037). This was a higher appointment than the title indicates, because the pleasure-loving Badis paid little attention to the government, and Samuel really became acting king of Granada.[26] He was succeeded in that position by his son, Joseph. In a small country of Himyara in southern Arabia, a converted Jew, Yussuf Dhu-Nowas, in the sixth century actually became king. Jews erroneously claimed that he was a descendant of David's line. In the tenth century the Jews in the Chafton Mountains lived under the leadership of their own king.[27] When a Jew was appointed *wezīr* in Egypt, a contemporary poet wrote:

The Jews of our times reached the goal of their desire and came to rule. Theirs is the dignity, theirs is the money! Councillors of the state and princes are made of them. O People of Egypt! I give you advice: Become Jews, for Heaven has become Jewish.[28]

Prosperity and problems. — Jewish wealth did not guarantee

[22] Graetz, *History*, 161.
[23] Graetz, *History*, 292. Unfortunately, Graetz did not use footnotes, so it is not possible today to check his sources of information, so his declarations should be accepted only with some reservation.
[24] Margolis and Marx, *A History*, 376.
[25] Graetz, *History*, 261.
[26] Graetz, *History*, 258.
[27] Graetz, *History*, 220-21.
[28] J. Mann, *The Jews in Egypt and in Palestine under the Fatimid Caliphs* (New York, 1970), I, 17.

security. It aroused resentment and hatred of the taxed Christians and exploited lower classes. Jews had to secure themselves from the violence of the mobs by buying protection from the rulers. This was a tenuous situation. If the rulers were strong, they did not need the Jewish support, and they ruled Jews with a tight fist. If they were weak, they needed it and were willing to negotiate, but they were unable to hold back the mobs, anyway.[29] The lower class mobs were frequently led and encouraged by small businessmen or low ranking clergymen who had borrowed more money from Jewish money lenders than they could afford to pay back together with high interest rates.[30] Jews tried to come to terms with the church, as well, and they sometimes did, but the common people assumed that the church leaders or public officials who defended the Jews were doing so because they received bribes and not because it was just for them to do so.[31] Some Jews sought protection by becoming Christians and marrying Christians, but they continued to belong to the upper class and continued their same extortionistic money lending and tax collecting practices, so they were resented just as much as they had been as Jews, which indicates one of the real serious causes of friction between Christians and Jews. It was not just the religious affiliation but also the oppression that the Christians resented most.[32] When Samuel's son, Joseph, succeeded his father as acting king of Granada, he behaved so arrogantly to his Christian subordinates and was so conspicuously nepotistic that he promoted Jews into the highest positions of the state. The envy which non-Jews held toward him and his Jewish relatives and friends quickly turned to violent anger.[33] In England, King Henry III provided Jews with the desired protection but raised taxes against Jews so high that the Jews raised their interest rates accordingly, thus passing on the cost to the consumer. This, of course, outraged the Christian mobs, so the vicious circle continued.[34] When a Jew killed a monk in England (A.D. 1147) a bloody slaughter of Jews followed, but members of the mob were not satisfied until they had forced the guards to give them the records of Jewish loans kept in the church's custody, which they promptly burned in a bonfire.[35] With the Peasants'

[29] Baron, Social and Religious History, VI, 141.
[30] William of Newbury, ed. Howlett i.312, 317. J. Jacobs, The Jews of Angevin England, "Documents and Records," (London, 1893), 118, 130.
[31] Baron, Social and Religious History, IV, 142.
[32] Baron, Social and Religious History, IV, 121; Margolis and Marx, A History, 458.
[33] Graetz, History, 275.
[34] Graetz, History, 571.
[35] Baron, Social and Religious History, IV, 126.

Crusade, mobs went wild. They could not be bribed and tempered. In many different places at the same time mobs massacred many Jews and burned houses and synagogues. This was not done under the direction of the church, but even against the threat of excommunication imposed by numerous clergymen,[36] further indicating the non-theological basis for Jewish-Christian friction. There were also religious motivations. Christians reasoned that they should not go to distant Palestine to kill the enemies of Christ without also killing those enemies near at hand.[37] Suspicions were so high that Christians blamed Jews for the Black Death that plagued Europe, thinking that Jews poisoned wells and rivers which supplied the drinking water. Some believed there was a universal Jewish plot to kill all Christians in this way. From this distance, this seems a ridiculous assumption, since Jews also used water from wells and rivers and also died of the Black Death, but little was known about disease in those days. All peoples were superstitious. Jews taught that the Lord had sent plagues upon the Egyptians, changing water to blood, *only for the Egyptians,* and they anticipated miracles like this to happen in the last days to destroy Israel's enemies by magic. Christians feared Jewish power and ability, and they would not have known how much of this anticipation was wishful thinking and how much was really possible.[38] Pope Eugenius III took advantage of these feelings by issuing a bull announcing that all those who joined the Crusades were absolved from payment of interest on debts owed to Jews.[39] The hostility surrounding Jews and Christians was not only from the one side. The Jew, Solomon bar Simson, gloated over the downfall of crusading bands in the Balkans and Asia Minor:

The enemies [i.e. Christians] have nonetheless not yet given up their evil designs, and every day start out on another expedition to Jerusalem. But the Lord has delivered them like sheep to slaughter, and set them aside for extermination. Mayest thou "render unto our neighbors sevenfold into their bosom," and inflict upon them thy retribution commensurate with their misdeeds. Give them sorrow to their hearts, place thy curse upon them, "pursue them in anger and destroy them under the heavens of the Lord," for "the Lord hath a day of vengeance, a year of recompense for the controversy of Zion." At the same time may "Israel be saved by

---

[36] Baron, *Social and Religious History,* IV, 101.
[37] William of Newbury, i.317, Jacobs, *The Jews of Angevin England,* 130.
[38] Margolis and Marx, *A History,* 404.
[39] Graetz, *History,* 349.

the Lord with an everlasting salvation. Ye shall not be ashamed nor
confounded" for ever and ever more.[40]

In ways like these Jews and Christians expressed their hatred
toward one another. They killed, oppressed, and tried to destroy
one another so as to secure their own position of divine privilege.

Jewish military acts. — During the Middle Ages Jews met most
of their problems with money, because that was what they had,
and that was what was needed to provide them security, but it was
not their only resource. In the East, where they were less involved
in international business, free Jews lived in the Chafton Mountains
in large numbers under the rule of a Jewish king who felt strong
enough militarily to join battle with the Persian army.[41] They used
weapons to defend themselves against their enemies and to make
guerilla raids in the valley for booty.[42] In Himyara there was a
standing Jewish army. During the Crusades, when Jews discovered
that they could not settle their differences with the mobs by bribes,
some organized in armed units to fight the Crusaders.[43] During the
sixth century Jews joined cause with the Samaritans at the chariot
race in Caesarea and massacred many Christians, destroying their
churches at the same time.[44] Theophanes said Samaritans, together
with Jews, offered to furnish 50,000 troops to Persia if Persia
would refuse a peace treaty with Justinian, but prepare to fight
him instead. This was probably in relationship to Chosroe's campaign of A.D. 540.[45] When the Persians captured Palestine in the
seventh century they received support from Jews under the leadership of a certain very wealthy Benjamin who organized troops
from all over Palestine. They are said to have provided 26,000
Jews for the conflict that killed 90,000 Christians when the Persians stormed and captured Jerusalem, July, 614.[46] Jews also
formed a fifth column to admit Ṭāriq ibn Ziyād and his Moslem
troops into Spain, enabling them to cross over into Europe from
North Africa (Apr. 27, 711), and they assisted the Moslems in

[40] Baron, *Social and Religious History*, IV, 143.
[41] A. Asher, *The Itinerary of Rabbi Benjamin of Tudela* (London, 1840), II, 132-135; see
also D.M. Dunlop, "The Khazars," *The World History of the Jewish People*, ed. C. Roth
(Israel, c 1966), 11, 325-56.
[42] Graetz, *History*, 17.
[43] Baron, *Social and Religious History*, IV, 102-104; Margolis and Marx, *A History*, 366.
[44] Graetz, *History*, 17.
[45] Baron, *Social and Religious History*, III, 57. See also Targ. Lam 4:22.
[46] Graetz, *History*, III, 19-20; E. Gibbon, *The Decline and Fall of the Roman Empire*
(Chicago, c1954), 124.

capturing important towns in Spain.[47] In the twelfth century, while Saladin was gaining strength against the Christians, a Jew who said he was the expected Messiah organized tens of thousands of Jewish troops in Persia for the purpose of overthrowing the Christians, and possibly the Moslems, and gaining control of Jerusalem by military force. Jews apparently controlled the roads in pre-Crusade Europe and could either guarantee or impede safe passage to travelers.[48] This may have made it difficult for Christian pilgrimages to the holy land and provided further irritation to Christians who later came through with armed forces and killed Jews in large numbers as they went. The military activities that took place in the Middle Ages under the motivation of the Jews, Christians, and Moslems were mostly holy wars led by people who believed they were doing God's will in destroying other religious people whom they believed to be God's enemies. All groups used the same zeal and whatever forces were available to them in their attempts to destroy their enemies and establish themselves as the chosen people ruling a holy empire. Serious prophets appeared throughout this period who interpreted the major international crises in which Jews, Christians, and Moslems were involved in terms of their calculations of the events destined to take place before the end of the foreign rule and the establishment of the Jews to power, ruling from Jerusalem under the leadership of a Davidic messiah. There was a close relationship between the messiahs who appeared and the literature related to redemption.

Messianic movements. — The sons of David were enough of a threat to the Romans after the fall of Jerusalem that some were brought to Domitian. They were asked about the Messiah and his kingdom. When they said the messianic kingdom was heavenly and would happen at the end of the age, they were released (*HE* IIIxxx.1-4). If Domitian had known that the age whose end they meant was the Roman age and the heavenly kingdom would have its capital at Jerusalem, he might not have let them go so easily. It was only a few years later (A.D. 132-35) until Romans fought another bitter war against the Jews under the leadership of Bar Cochba who was endorsed as the Messiah by the prominent Rabbi

[47] F.C. Borgos, "Christian Spain," *The World History of the Jewish People*, XI, 357-58. It was not a new experience for one group of covenanters to form a fifth column against another. The Jews invited Tiglath Pileser to plunder Northern Israel; John Hyrcanus' supporters invited Pompey to enter Jerusalem. Other acts of sabotage were associated with Moses, Cyrus, Esther, Judith, and Constantine. Even the legendary factors of these personages show the type of heroism that was popular.

[48] I.A. Angus, "Control of Roads by Jews in Pre-Crusade Europe," *JQR*, 48 (1957-58), 93-98.

Akiba (Ber 23b-24a). After this fatal destruction many rabbis tried to discourage Jews from immediate expectations of future messiahs for two reasons: 1) They probably deduced that two failures at war with Rome indicated that this was not the right time for Jewish deliverance, and 2) they did not want to aggravate the Romans again with further threats of war which would bring about the anticipated reprisals. They were never successful, however, in suppressing the Jewish messianic hopes (TAZ 1:19).

Christian expectations. — Christians continued to look forward to Christ's return, and Jews continued to anticipate a messiah who would destroy Rome. At the time of Origen, a certain Judas thought the seventy weeks in the Book of Daniel would reach their climax in the tenth year of the reign of Severus (A.D. 193-211). He believed the time of the antichrist was already near, and Rome would soon be defeated by the second coming of Christ (*HE* VI.vi-vii). During the days of Hippolytus (2nd-3d century), a bishop in Pontus said the end of the age would take place that very year. Members of his diocese left their land untilled and sold their cattle to get ready for the event (Hippolytus, *In Dan* 4:18). In the third century a prophetess from Cappadocia started a large multitude on a trip to Jerusalem, expecting Christ to return (Cyprian, *Epistle* 75:10).[49] The pestilence in the middle of the third century in Egypt was interpreted in terms of the earlier plagues of Egypt before the exodus (*HE* VII.xxi). Three prophets announced that the paraclete was soon to come to the village of Pepuza in Phrygia. Their message caused so much excitement that marriages were dissolved and a very ascetic discipline was undertaken.[50] Hippolytus calculated that the sixth millennium would be the turning point that marked the end. This was to come, according to him and several other Christian leaders, about A.D. 500.[51] Cyril of Jerusalem, in the fourth century, said the birth pangs of the Messiah had already begun.[52] Many Christians interpreted Constantine's victory in terms of a new exodus and compared Constantine himself to Moses. They thought Jesus had been the moving force behind this

---

[49]Abbe Duchesne, *The Early History of the Christian Church* (in 3 vol.; London c1957) I, 197.

[50]Duchesne, *Early History*, 197.

[51]Fragments from *Commentaries on Dan* 2. For support of the Christian reckoning by which they held the ministry of Christ to be at the 5,000 or 5,500th year, see A.H. Silver, *A History of Messianic Speculation in Israel* (Boston, c 1957), 6, 16-19. For Jews this was also a period when eras changed. According to Ibn Daud the period of the Amoraim ended and the period of the Saboraim began at A.D. 500. (A. Ibn Daud, "The Succession of the Saboraim," *The Book of Tradition*, tr. and ed. G.D. Cohen [Philadelphia, 1967], V.33).

[52]Cyril of Jerusalem, "Catechesis IX. Illuminandorum," *MPG* 33, 869-916.

whole divine event which may have meant that they thought this
was the equivalent to the second coming (*HE* IX. ix, 1, 3-10; X.i. 5-
6; ii, 1). Although some Jewish Christians still looked toward
Jerusalem for the second coming(Jerome, *In Esaiam*60:1-2 [*MPL* 24,
c587]), most Christians thought the Christian age had begun.
During the eleventh century, however, there arose new apocalyptic movements in Christianity. There were several factors to
stimulate these: 1) Jerusalem was in the hands of Moslems; 2) this
was the end of the millennium predicted in Rev 20; 3) there were
similar movements and hopes going on at the same time in Judaism
and Islam; and 4) like other religions of the period, Christians were
aroused by a shower of meteorites (April, 1095) and other
astrological signs.[53] William of Tripoli argued that the Jews had
had their day and were gone; the Moslems would soon also be
destroyed, but Christ would soon return and kill the antichrist,
and Christianity would endure forever.[54] Moslems also had
messianic expectations at that time, but most messianic movements during the Middle Ages came out of Judaism.

Jewish hopes. — Zunz listed more than seventy-five different
messianic movements from the second to the twentieth century.[55]
One of the earliest of these movements was in the fifth century.
Since Israelites spent four hundred years in captivity in Egypt, it
seemed to contemporary Jews that the four hundred years that
began with the fall of Jerusalem (A.D. 68 as they reckoned) would
have as its latest possible date A.D. 468. This was further confirmed by the tradition that the age would not last more than eighty-
five jubilees. Through *gematria* some reasoned that this was also
supported by Job 38:11: *Up to here you shall come, but no further.*
Here (פה), equals eighty-five, according to numerical value,
meaning eighty-five jubilees is as far as the exile can last.[56] At about
that time a certain pretender in Crete promised Jews that he would
open the Mediterranean Sea for them so that they could cross over
to the promised land on dry ground. Many Jews believed, and at
his direction, jumped off a cliff into the sea and were drowned.[57] In
A.D. 640 a Jew from Pallugta on the Euphrates said he was the
Messiah. He collected four hundred followers who burned three
Christian churches and killed the superintendent of the district
before they were stopped by troops, and their leader was

[53] S. Runciman, *The History of the Crusades* (Cambridge, c1951), I, 115.
[54] P.A. Throop, *Criticism of the Crusade* (Amsterdam, 1940), 134-35.
[55] L.Zunz, *Gesammelten Schriften* III (Berlin, 1875-76), 224-31.
[56] Baron, *Social and Religious History,* IV, 167.
[57] W.D. Wallis, *Messiahs: Their Role in Civilization* (Washington, D.C., 1945), 27.

crucified.[58] Near the turn of the century the Persian Jew Abū 'Īsā al-Iṣfahānī led a messianic movement of some 10,000 Jews and provoked the anger of the caliph. When Mansur (A.D. 754-75) came to the throne Abu Isa fled northward with his followers. His forces were defeated by the Moslems and Abu Isa was killed.[59] A Christian announced that he was the Messiah and gathered a large Jewish following for the imminent return to Zion involving a political revolt. He was soon killed by Jews after he was turned over to them by Omar II, and his following was dispersed (ca. A.D. 720)[60] When the eighty-fifth jubilee cycle passed (A.D. 468) without a successful messianic movement, Jews pinned their hopes on the 256th nineteen year lunar cycle, beginning A.D. 1085-86. This was also near the millennium of years following the fall of Jerusalem. These hopes were also discouraged by the First Crusade (A.D. 1096). Solomon bar Simson complained, "We had expected [the 256th cycle] to bring salvation and comfort in accordance with the prophecy of Jeremiah [31:6], but which turned to grief and sorrow."[61] When the Moslems first began their movement, Jews looked to them to run interference for the Jews in driving out the Christians, but they soon considered them the enemy. When the Crusades began, Jews considered Moslems and Christians to be the forces of Gog and Magog. They expected one to destroy the other before Jews took general command of the area.[62] During the first three Crusades there were at least eight Jewish messianic movements from all over Europe and the East; Byzantium, Khazaria, Mesopotamia, Palestine, Morocco, Yemen, Spain, and France. Pious Jews had promised Moslems that their messiah would appear before Islam had lasted 500 years. When that time approached (A.D. 1107) Jews did not wait for a messiah to appear but selected a pious and virtuous teacher from their midst, Ibn Aryeh, and appointed him to be their expected redeemer.[63] In A.D. 892 Saadia predicted a time that is now unknown for the Messiah.[64] Maimonides predicted A.D. 1216, and Rashi opted for

[58] Wallis, Messiahs. 27.

[59] Wallis, Messiahs. 27.

[60] Wallis, Messiahs. 27; A.Sharf, "The Jews of Byzantium," World History of the Jewish People. 11. 56.

[61] Baron, Social and Religious History. V, 199.

[62] See "That Day," from I. Ginsberg (ed.), Ginzē Schechter (New York, 1928), I, 310-312. See the table of contents for its translation in this collection.

[63] Baron, Social and Religious History. V, 200-01.

[64] H. Malter, "Saadia Gaon's Messianic Computation," Journal of Jewish Lore and Philosophy. I (1919), 45-59.

1290.[65] Ḥiyyah calculated five dates ranging from A.D. 1136 to 1448. Near the middle of the twelfth century David Alroy declared himself to be the Messiah and summoned Jews from all over the world to come to Persia to support him in his military movement to storm Jerusalem. He gathered tens of thousands of Jewish troops before his movement was stopped.

Messiahs did not stop at the end of the thirteenth century, but this survey stops at that point. The sixth millennium of Jewish reckoning began at A.D. 1240. Since Jewish eschatologists considered a day to be a thousand years to the Lord; the Lord worked in creation six days before he rested; and the promised "rest" was understood to mean acquisition of the land, the sixth millennium would be the millennium or "day" of the Messiah. During this millennium the Messiah would appear, introduce a new age with Israel in charge before the day of rest which would amount to a millennium of Jewish rule. Because of this calendrical interpretation of sabbatical eschatology, there were just as many messianic movements after the thirteenth century as before. Today, some modern Israelis are actively at work, interpreting modern events in terms of prophetic expectations and their own calculations of the messianic age and the age to come.[66]

Messianic life and literature. — Redemption literature is a type of fifth-columnist literature, composed by a group of people who acted secretly in ways contrary to the approval of the government then in power. Therefore it was necessarily written in a kind of code which only members of the column could understand. The code was the OT and the history of Israel and its hopes. This knowledge was woven midrashically and apocalyptically into various literary media and was very prominent throughout the Middle Ages. Sarachek said,

How variously, through the aptitudes of the scholars, did this faith assert itself? In Saadia, throughout the labyrinthine paths of theology; in Rashi, through pietism; in Maimonides, through rational conviction and ethical insight; in Gabirol, through the art and genius of poetry. In anguished supplication and lilting lyric he sounded the familiar melodies in the symphony of the Messianic drama.[67]

---

[65] J. Sarachek, *The Doctrine of the Messiah in Medieval Jewish Literature* (New York, c1968), 59.

[66] R.H. Eisenberg, *Birth Pangs of the Messiah in our Time* (Jerusalem, 1970) and *Let us Research and Return* (Jerusalem, 1973); A.I. Klein, *The Book of the Prophets of Truth*, additions by J.A. Wolf (Israel, 1960); H. Schveli, *The Book of Calculations of the Redemption* (Jerusalem, 1974); and S. Shilo, *The War of the Russian Magog in Israel: The Year 1973* (Jerusalem, 1973). All in Hebrew.

[67] Sarachek, *The Doctrine*, 67.

It took expression in dogmatic theology, sermons, letters, poetry, and apocalyptic prophecy. It was by no means "fringe literature." It occupied the attention of the best scholars and religious leaders of the day. It was sung at feast days and included in daily prayers. It was related to contemporary situations within the Jewish community, from which it originated and to which it spoke. This is why it is necessary to understand the history and beliefs of the people to which it belongs in order to understand its meaning.

Familiarity with this literature in relationship to the life of its authors and readers, however, will provide biblical scholars a clue for understanding the Jewish and Christian literature that preceded it in time in relationship to people with similar goals and expectations, as well as methods of literary expression. This is particularly true of apocalyptic literature and midrashic literature which occurs in the OT, NT, and intertestamental literature. Brief notes will accompany the translations to help clarify concepts and terms for the reader for whom this literature provides a new venture in reading. Some of the following definitions may also help those unfamiliar with this type of literature to understand it more easily and completely so as to appreciate it more fully.

Definitions

Messiahs. — Medieval Jews expected two messiahs, one to precede the other. The word messiah means anointed one, usually referring to the one anointed to be king of Israel or the one anointed to be the high priest of Israel. Unless specifically indicated as the high priest, the Messiah generally was considered one of the two military and political messiahs. Jews expected history to repeat itself. The first king of the twelve tribes was King Saul, from the tribe of Benjamin, which was initially related closely to the Northern Kingdom called Israel, Ephraim, Samaria, Joseph, or the ten tribes. After Saul was killed, David became the great king who ruled both north and south Israel. This had been possible because Saul had first run interference, weakened the Philistines, and begun the administration of the United Kingdom. Therefore Jews believed that someone would arise from the northern tribes, lead a strong military force, overthrow the Romans, and rule for a short time before being killed by the Romans, just as Saul had been killed by his arch enemies, the Philistines. After the death of the Messiah of Ephraim, the Messiah of David would appear and lead the Jews to military victory and triumphant rule, just as David had done after the death of Saul.

The Messiah of the line of David was also called Yinon, Nino, the shoot, David, Jesse, the son of David, the son of Jesse, and other titles that made sense by association.

Proper names.— Many proper names used in medieval Jewish literature have symbollic significance whose meaning is necessary for an understanding of the message. The following are listed in alphabetical order:

1.   Adbiel and Mibsam—sons of Ishmael. Since Moslems claim to be descendants of Ishmael, these names are used to mean contemporary Moslems (Gen 25:13).

2.   Araboth—The area in the lower Jordan Valley and south of the Dead Sea. This is part of the wilderness area through which Jews were expected to come when they reentered the land in the last days, as Jesus had done earlier (Mt 19:1;20:29; 21:1), following the typology of the first wilderness experience. In some contexts araboth means "heaven."

3.   Armilos—The personification of Roman Christians. He is described in monstrous terms as an antichrist who would kill the Messiah of Ephraim and be killed by the Messiah of David. The earliest datable reference to Armilos occurs in the works of Saadia Gaon. Armilos was mentioned, either earlier or later, in Targ. PsJ Isa 11:4.

4.   Azza and Azazel—Azazel, at least, and probably Azza by association, were fallen angels (Enoch 8:1-3; 9:6; 10:4, 8; 13:1; 69:2). All sin was ascribed to Azazel (10:8); he and his army were to be thrown into the abyss (Enoch 54:5).

5.   Dishan and Dishon—Royalty of the children of Seir in the land of Edom. Since Edom was identified with Rome, Dishan and Dishon represent the Romans or Christians (Gen 36:21).

6.   Edom—Descendants of Esau who aided the Babylonians in taking Jerusalem before the Babylonian captivity. After this they were bitterly hated by the Jews (Ps 137; Obadiah). Because of a similar feeling content towards the Romans, the Romans and Christians were called Edom or Esau.

7.   Eitan—The Ezrahite, son of Zerah, son of Judah. A Levite musician (I Chron 6:42) noted for wisdom (I Kgs 4:31); author of Ps 89.

8.   Er and Onan—Sons of Judah by his Canaanite wife. Therefore they represent the Jews (Gen 38:3-4).

9.   Ephraim—Son of Joseph who was believed to have inherited Samaria as his possession. Therefore Ephraim represented the Samaritans, or Ephraim was the Messiah of Joseph or Ephraim, a forerunner of the Messiah of David.

10. Gileadite—Elijah, the forerunner of the Messiah, who was from Gilead. He was also called the Tishbite (SS 4:2; 6:5).

11. Hafzi-bah—the mother of Nehemiah, son of Hoshiel, the Messiah of Ephraim.

12. Hagar—Sarah's maid who gave birth to Ishmael from Abraham. Since Ishmael was held to be the ancestor of the Arabs or Moslems, the Moslems were also called the son of Hagar or son of the maid.

13. Heiman—the Ezrahite, son of Joel, son of Shemuel. One of the Levitical singers (I Chron 6:33); author of Ps 88.

14. Ishmael—Abraham's son through Hagar, the maid of Sarah. Symbolically, Ishmael represents the Moslems who claimed to be descendants of Ishmael.

15. Jabez—One of the descendants of Judah who prayed for the extension of his boundaries, and his prayer was answered (I Chron 4:9-10).

16. Kedar—One of the sons of Ishmael. Therefore he symbolized the Moslems.

17. Kenites—A tribe in southern Palestine, mentioned in Num 24:21-22 as the motivation for Balaam to continue his parable. He predicted their fate of captivity. In later exegesis, they represent the Christians who were overcome by the Moslems.

18. Korah—A Levite who led an insurrection against Moses in the wilderness. The ground opened up and consumed the group (Num 16:1-35). In the resurrection, however, they are destined to be raised and reunited with the rest of Israel.

19. Kasil and Kemah—Stars that were objects of worship (Amos 5:8).

20. Lebanon—The country north of Galilee. Symbolically, it represents the temple at Jerusalem where incense or *labonah* was offered.

21. Menahem son of Amiel—The expected Messiah son of David.

22. Mishma, Dumah, and Massa—Sons of Ishmael. Therefore they represent the Moslems (Gen 25:14).

23. Meshech and Tubal—Territories in Gog, the land ruled by Magog (Ezek 38:2-3). Multitudes of uncircumcised from these areas caused terror in the promised land (land of life), so the Lord will destroy them utterly (Ezek 32:26). In the Middle Ages these were identified with Christians and/or the Moslems.

24. Muzzah and Shamman—Sons of Esau. Therefore they represent the Romans or Roman Christians (Gen 36:13).

25.   Nebioth—the Nabateans, an Arab tribe from the area mostly south of the Dead Sea.

26.   Nehemiah son of Hoshiel—the name given to the person expected to be the Messiah of Joseph who was expected to suffer in behalf of the Jews and destroy their enemies, thus preparing the way for the Messiah son of David.

27.   Oholibamah—The daughter of a Hivite who was the wife of Esau. Therefore Oholibamah symbolized Edom, a name used to mean Rome or the Christians (Gen 36:2).

28.   Oholibah—Symbolized Jerusalem or the Jews, often in contrast to Oholibamah, the Christians, or Oholah, the Samaritans (Ezek 23:4).

29.   Rakkah as Rimmon—Rimmon is a location near Gibeah (Jdgs 20:45-47), and Rakkah is probably Tiberias in Galilee (Mg 6a). The Messiah was to come from Rakkah. See "Book of Zerubbabel" BL 3:8.

30.   Responsa—The written replies of famous rabbis to religious questions asked by laymen or congregations. They were later circulated widely as systematic theological doctrine or catechetical materials. Some of Paul's letters belong to this tradition.

31.   Seir—A city in Edom named after one of Esau's sons. Therefore used to symbolize Rome or the Christians.

32.   Shekinah —From the Hebrew שכן "to dwell." Originally this represented the tent of meeting where the presence of the Lord dwelled on earth and was made visible through the smoke and the fire. This became a euphemism for the Lord.

33.   The Shittim Valley—In biblical times this was a valley in Moab (Num 25:1; Micah 6:5; Jonah 4:18). It seems to have been associated with Abel-Shittim or "the Shittim meadow." The name Shittim means acacia trees, so there was evidently a valley where these grew. In the Middle Ages, Jews gave this valley a theological significance. They believed (correctly or not) that this was near Jericho and that it was united by water channels to the Kidron Brook. This would be Wadi Qumran. They may have considered the whole Jordan Valley the Shittim Valley. The dead were supposed to be thrown up from the Dead Sea on to the shore in this valley. This seems somewhat related to the eschatological expectations of Ezek 47:1-12.

47.   Another dimension may have been that this was the last valley in Moab before entering the promised land. This was Israel's contact with the wilderness. Here the party of Korah and the wilderness generation would be restored before the land was

restored. People were to gather here before the restoration, just as the Israelites gathered before the crossing of the Jordan.

34.   Ten tribes—Since there was no official return from the Assyrian captivity as there had been from the Babylonian captivity, and since there was a belief that the promised land should include all twelve tribes of Israel, there was some concern for these people. It was not imagined that they had perished from the earth, because Jews confronted them in the diaspora quite frequently. They were evidently on something of a par with the Jews in similar situations, holding similar offices, etc. (Graetz, *History*, 341). Maimonides said, "They have been found to be much inferior to the heathens." (Baron, *A Social and Religious History*, V, 172). The Jews learned that there was a large number of independent Jews in Khazaria, and there were reports that the tribes of Dan, Naphtali, Gad, and Asher lived farther east as well as in Africa (Margolis and Marx, *A History*, 278). During the sixth century Samaritans united with the Jews to offer Persia 50,000 troops to fight the Christians. This knowledge plus a lot of imagination and faith convinced Jews that the hidden Samaritans would return and run interference for them, doing most of the military work before the reestablishing of the United Kingdom.

35.   Zerah and Nahath—Descendants of Esau. Therefore they symbolize Romans or Christians.

Significant words.—The following words that are not proper names are symbolic to medieval Jewish literature.

1.   Bondage—A term used to describe Jewish existence in the diaspora, whatever the conditions of Jews in relationship to freedom and prosperity, if they were not free to return to the promised land under the rulership of their own king, a son of David. The term is not limited to those who are in prison, but it has a religious symbolism to sabbatical eschatology.

2.   Captive—A Jew in the diaspora, whatever his condition of wealth and prominence, who cannot return to the promised land under Jewish rule. He is therefore symbolically "in bondage."

3.   Cherubim—Heavenly beings that are usually related to the altar, either in heaven or at Jerusalem. In appearance, they have human heads, bodies like lions, wings like birds, etc.

4.   Comfort—The special attention God gives the Jews when he restores them to their promised land under Jewish rule (Isa 40:1).

5.   Dog—A Jewish term for a Gentile.

6.   Dove—The Jewish people (Ps 74:19).

7.   Footstool—Jerusalem temple (I Chron 28:2; Ps 99:5; 132:7; Mt 5:35; Makkoth 24b).

8. Foreigner—Another term for Gentile.

9. Gazelle—In Arabic poetry, the lover or sweetheart. To Jewish poets of Arabic descent it symbolized Jerusalem.

10. Gematria—A method of exegesis which assumed that the scripture was coded and could only be properly understood if the important words were evaluated according to their numerical value, since each letter of the Hebrew alphabet had a numerical equivalent. If two terms or words had the same numerical value, they were assumed to have a predestined relationship to each other in eschatological understanding.

11. Goat—The Hebrew word for male goat is שׂעיר (sair). The proper name *Seir* (שׂעיר) refers to a descendant of Esau and a location in Edom. Since both words are similar in sound and spelled alike, the word for male goat was used to symbolize the Christians who were held to be the spiritual descendants of Esau. It may also have had some overtones related to the scapegoat to be destroyed on the Day of Atonement, but that is not necessary.

12. Iniquities—The charges made in the treasury of merits for sins committed.

13. Ibex—A term used by Spanish poets for a lover. Jewish Spanish poets used it to refer to Jerusalem, their "true love."

14. Hasid—Generally used to refer to a pious man or a saint.

15. Horn—Symbolically used to describe a general, king, or messiah, who would rescue Jews and defend them by killing the Gentiles in battle.

16. Inherit—To gain possession, either by donation from ancestors or by some other means, such as military conquest.

17. Maid—Hagar, the maid of Sarah who gave birth to Ishmael. Therefore it was used symbolically to refer to the descendants of Ishmael, the Moslems.

18. Lion—Sometimes used to symbolize Judah. At other times it means prince or ruler who will defend Jews in battle.

19. Perfect one—Abraham (Jub 23:10).

20. Perfect ones—the patriarchs.

21. Promised land—the United Kingdom, the land "promised" to the seed of Abraham.

22. Stranger—Gentile.

The Translation

A translation always requires a compromise involving a choice among the various meanings which any word holds in one language. Sometimes the translator must choose whether to communicate the literary style of the original author or the meaning he intended, since both cannot be carried over into another language. Poetry is more difficult to translate than prose, because a one syllable word in one language may have its equivalent in another language with a two or three syllable word, and synonyms in different languages do not have the same value in rhyme. Sometimes the word has no exact equivalent in another language and must be translated periphrastically. All of this breaks the meter and loses the rhyme. Puns and wordplays lose their force in many translations because the same relationship does not exist between the translations of the words involved. Some of the literature translated here is extremely difficult to render into another language. Originally, this was beautiful literature, written in Hebrew that rhymes and is in regular meter, although in Arabic meter rather than the meter of the Psalms. Some of this poetry further tests the translator because it includes many allusions to scriptural passages whose content and exact quotation the reader is expected to recognize and understand without seeing it entirely. Thus two words of a line of poetry fit beautifully into the meter and rhyme of the poem but make no sense by themselves until they are recognized as part of a longer quotation from scripture, the whole of which is necessary to the meaning of the line. The translation is made for people who do not normally recognize such allusive quotations, so footnotes and additions to the quotation must be made to alert the reader to the implications intended. This, of course, breaks the poetry. In situations such as these, the translator has to choose which of the possibilities he wishes most to communicate. If he is translating poetry to be sung, he must consider the meter to be of great importance. Then he may neglect the full meaning for the full meter.

In this translation, choices have generally been made in favor of meaning at the expense of style. This means many "wooden" expressions appear in the English text where a more beautiful translation might have been possible if the full meaning of the Hebrew had been sacrificed to some extent. This means that one line of Hebrew has been translated by one line of English, but the lines in English are frequently longer and do not rhyme or have consistent meter. This choice has been made for the benefit of scholars who want to understand as fully as possible the force and form of the Hebrew translated. Where possible an attempt has been made to translate a Hebrew subject by an English subject, a Hebrew verb by an English verb, etc., so that anyone who checks the English with the original can see how this translation was derived from this Hebrew original. Little attempt has been made to "improve" the style of the original author. A tediously repetitious original usually has been translated into equally repetitious English, with a few exceptions: 1) The historic present of the author has been regularly changed to make the tenses coherent in context. 2) The *waw* (ו) which is frequently used in Hebrew as a conjunction, meaning "and," or "but" has been omitted entirely many times in English, or its part in a compound sentence has been restructured into an English participial phrase. 3) Sometimes synonyms have been chosen for a Hebrew term used excessively to avoid the tedium required of a consistent translation.

Words with more than one meaning. — Some Hebrew words can hold different meanings. For example, the Hebrew ארץ can mean "earth," the entire inhabited world, or "land," the particular land that God has chosen for his special people, Palestine. Sometimes the context shows clearly that ארץ means "earth" in contrast to heaven, and in others it is just as clearly a term meaning the land of Canaan. But there are many other instances in which the context could support either meaning. At such times translators who believe Jews were very universalistic in their outlook render the Hebrew by the English "earth," and those who think Jews were nationalistic and Palestine-centered render these terms by "land." This translation follows the second course, and others may disagree with the translation on occasion.

Another term, frequently used in Hebrew is עולם which can have a temporal meaning, "age," or a spacial meaning, "world" or "universe." Because there are idioms that employ this term whose translation has been widely used, and uncritically translated by a spacial meaning, the translations here may seem surprising. For instance, עולם הזה and עולם הבא are normally translated "this world" and "the world to come," distinguishing between earth and heaven or between this universe in which human beings now live and some unknown universe. In disagreement with that translation, the same idiom is here regularly rendered "this age" and "the age to come," meaning the messianic age or the following age of "rest" when Israel is in political control of the world in distinction from the current age when Jews are scattered in the diaspora, holding citizenship in other countries and giving allegiance to other political powers.[66] Both ages take place here, on this earth, but are distinguished by the position of the Jews in the

[66] Dr. Lehrman, Dr. and Mrs. Lapide all accept the spacial translation and have resisted my translations of עולם

administration. Whenever the fortunes of the Jews changed, a new
age began, here on earth.[69] Sometimes an age was thought to be
fifty years, or a jubilee. This is motivated by sabbatical
eschatology which anticipated the release of diaspora Jews to
return to Palestine from their "captivity" to claim the promised
land as their "original possession" (see Mekilta, *Amelek* 2:186-88).
Expressions like "from age to age" have a meaning similar to "from
generation to generation," rather than "from world to world"
When one age ended, another began, just as one day follows
another and one year follows another. Rabbis said the age of Esau-
Edom-Rome had to end before the age of Jacob-Israel-the Jews
could begin (IV Ezra 6:7-10). Ages were thought to grow old and
become ripe, just like human beings or fruit. They then passed
away and came to an end, without interfering with the existence of
the inhabited world. Sometimes notes with accompanying explanations indicate why this expression was translated "age" rather
than "world."

Another related idiom, רבונו של עולם, normally rendered
"Master of the world" or "Master of the universe," is here consistently translated "Master of the age," meaning that God is the
ruler in the messianic age or the age of "rest" which follows as
distinct from this age where he does not rule, but politics are
governed by Gentiles, in rabbinic opinion.[70] God can only be king
and rule the world when his chosen people are in political control
of the promised land and the temple functions at Jerusalem. Many
Jews today believe that the Lord has always ruled the universe and
always will, so they express their faith by the expression they
translate, "Master of the world," but medieval Jews were not
governed by modern theology.[71] If עולם were to mean "world,"
then the related expression רבונו העולמים, should be translated "Master of the worlds" or "universes" to be consistent,[72] but
here this is translated, "Master the ages," meaning all the temporal
ages in their proper sequence.

To be sure, Jews believed God created this world, but he first
created day and night, which involved time. Especially in

[70] *Consequences,* 61-62.
[71] See E.J. Wiesenberg, "The Liturgical Term melekh Ha-'olam," *JJS* 15 (1964), 1-56
and "Gleanings of the Liturgical Term *Melekh Ha'olam,*" *JJS* 17 (1966), 47-72. J.
Heinemann, "Once Again *Melekh Ha'olam,*" *JJS* 15 (1964), 149-54, objected to Wiesenberg's suggestion that the term be given a temporal force.
[72] Although Wiesenberg argued for the temporal value of עולם he rendered
מרי לכול עולמים,"Lord of all the worlds" in GA 20:12-13.

apocalyptic thought-forms, the predestined order of the ages was very important.

IV Ezra said:

With a measure he has measured the times;
by number he numbered the times;
he will neither move nor stir
until the predicted measure is fulfilled (4:37).

Psalms of Solomon 18:12-14 professed:

He has established the lights in their courses
for determining the seasons from day to day,
and they do not deviate from the path which he commanded
for them.

In the fear of God their path [is taken] each day,
from the day in which God created them until the age [to come], and they have not deviated since the day he created them, from generations of old they have not left their course if God did not command them through his servants.[73]

This translation is the result of an attempt to translate Hebrew thought-form and message in such a way that English thinking and speaking people can understand it, whether or not they agree with it. Very little attempt has been made to improve the content or style of the original author. For example, in perfect consistency with their concept of "ages," medieval Jews frequently used the expression עתיד לבוא, which is nearly always rendered "destined to come," even though it seems stylistically redundant and inferior in English to various expressions, such as "will be," "to come," and "in the future," but such translations would not give the impact of predestined events which the medieval Jew understood and was basic to his theology.

Many other expressions, such as these, will be observed in reading, and notes will sometimes explain their meaning further, but the general approach and purpose will be consistent with these examples.

Some mechanics of translation. — In the Hebrew, quotations from scripture were frequently abbreviated, assuming from a couple of words that the reader would understand the whole passage intended. Since that is not the case with the average Christian or Jew today, quotations are completed in brackets. Another problem deals with versification of the manuscript. Wherever

[73] *To the Hebrews* (Garden City, 1972), 6. See also IV Ezra 6:19-20; 9:2; 11:39; 12:9, 21; 13:18; 14:5, 10-12; II Bar 13:5-7; 19:5; 27:1-15; 29:8; 30:3; 39:5; 48:19; 56:2; 59:8, 11; 69:4; 76:5.

possible, versification numbers are carried over into the translation. Sometimes this is not completely possible, because adjec-
tives, for example, which should precede the noun in English,
follow it in Hebrew. If the line breaks after the noun in Hebrew,
the adjective of the next line is placed in the preceding line, *but it is
Italicized* to show that it belongs to the next line.

HISTORY AND DOCTRINE

Introduction to Saadia Gaon

Saadia ben Joseph al Fayyumi was born in Upper Egypt (A.D.
892). In 928 he was invited to become Gaon (head of the academy)
at Sura in Babylon. His conflict with the exilarch there caused his
replacement in 930, after which he spent seven productive years in
writing at Baghdad. He was reinstated to his office of gaon five
years before his death (A.D. 942). He was active in literary polemics against the Karaites and a proposed change of calendar.
These were just some of the ways in which he was very influential
in shaping the orthodoxy and unity of Judaism of the future. He
was the first great Jewish writer since Philo, and, like Philo, he
helped his people adapt and interpret their traditional faith in
terms of their contemporary culture. He wrote widely on matters
of exegesis, the Hebrew language, Jewish law, philosophy, doctrine, and religious polemics.[1]

BOOK OF CONVICTIONS AND BELIEFS

Treatise VIII

Deliverance

Saadia Gaon[2]

Our God (May he be magnified and exalted) has informed us
through his prophets that he would allow us, the congregation of
the children of Israel, to escape from this situation in which we are
given, and that he would gather our scattered [fragments] from the
East of the land and from the West of it, and bring us to his holy
estate and make us dwell in it. Then we will be his treasure and his
inheritance, according to his saying, *Thus says the Lord of armies,
"Behold I will save my people from the land of the East and from
the land of the setting sun, and I will bring them, and they shall
dwell in the midst of Jerusalem"* (Zech 8:7-8).

[1] See W. Bacher, "Saadia b. Joseph," *JE*. 578-86.
[2] Text from ספר הנבחר באמונות ובדעות לרבנו סעדיה בן יוסף פיומי תרגם
לעברית באר והתין יוסף דויד קאפה (Jerusalem, 1970), 237-60. RPL

His prophets have expanded on this subject to the extent that they have written many books about it. This information has not reached us from the late prophets only, but [even] from the emissary[3] [himself], the master Moses, our teacher. We partake of the promise from the beginning, already in the Torah, *The Lord your God will restore your captivity [and have mercy upon you, and he will turn and gather you from all the peoples where the Lord your God has scattered you. If your outcasts are at the end of heaven, from there the Lord your God will gather you and take you. The Lord your God will bring you to the land which your fathers have conquered, and he will conquer it and make you more prosperous and numerous than our fathers]* (Dt 30:3-5). [4] Moreover, signs and wonders have confirmed [this promise] for us, and we accept it.

I have begun to study this matter and this topic by way of research, but there is nothing in it that requires an exact analysis. All of it is straight forward, except one thing. I will mention it when I reach the middle of this essay.

But the principle of salvation is necessary on the basis of many premises. One of them is the signs and wonders of Moses who first spoke of it, the signs which were performed for the prophet Isaiah and other prophets, in addition, who proclaimed it, of whose (238) apostolicity there can be no doubt, according to his saying, *He confirms the word of his servant; he fulfills the counsel of his messengers* (Isa 44:26).

Another of them [the premises] is that he is just and cannot act perversely. Already he has brought against this nation great and extended tribulations. There is no doubt that we are partly punished and partly tested by them, but everyone of them [has] a limit and an end. It is not possible that they will be without limit. When it is finished, it is necessary that he put an end to the punishment of some and a limitation for others, just as he has said,

---

[3] An emissary (שליח) is an agent, ambassador, or a messenger sent with a commission, who has the power of attorney to act in behalf of the one who sent him. He speaks with the authority of the one who sent him, so, therefore, a man's agent is like the man himself (Ber 5:5; LamR 1:18-19; §53; SSR 1:2 §3). The emissary in rabbinic literature held the same position as an apostle (ἀπόστολος) in the NT (Mt 10:40-42; Jn 13:20; 14:9, 28; I Cor 5:1-5). See further *To The Hebrews* (Garden City, 1972), 7.

[4] Captivity for Israel was used metaphorically to refer to the conditions of the Jews whenever they lived in the diaspora with Palestine under non-Jewish rule, whatever their economic or social condition. Jews were "captives" and "slaves" only in the sense that they were not free to return to Palestine under the rule of the Son of David. See *To The Hebrews*, 69-70.

For her iniquity is paid off, because she has received from the Lord's hand double for all her sins (40:2).[5]

[The third] of them [premises] is that he is faithful to his promise, his words enduring and his commandment, eternal, as he said, *The grass dries up; the flower fades, but the word of our God will stand for the age* (Isa 40:8).

[The fourth] of them [premises] is that we can deduce these promises from his first promise when we were in Egypt, where he promised us only two things: He would judge our oppressors for us, and he would give us great wealth. This is his statement: *Also the nation whom they will serve, I will judge, and after that they will go out with great wealth* (Gen 15:14). Already our eyes have seen that which he has done for us: dividing the sea, the manna, the quails, the assembly at Mount Sinai, the turning back of the sun, and other such things [as these]. It is all the more so since he has promised us great and generous things of goodness, wealth, exaltation, strength. He will grant us double for the affliction and subjection that has happened to us, as he said, *For your shame which was double, and the reproach, they rejoiced. Therefore, [for] their portion [in their land, they will inherit double—joy of the age will be theirs]* (Isa 61:7).

That which has happened to us is compared to the twinkling of an eye [for] its swiftness, and the reward which he will give us because of it is widened mercy, just as it is said, *For a short instant I have forsaken you, but with great mercy (239) I will gather you together* (Isa 54:7).

It transpires, then, that because of these tests and the analogy to that which has happened in the past, he is destined to do for us doubly doubled above that which he has promised us, such that we will not be able to measure it quickly, but to sum it up, as it is said, *He will do good to you and multiply you more than [he prospered and multiplied] your fathers* (Dt 30:5).

For this reason he repeatedly mentions the exodus from Egypt in many places in the Torah so as to remind us of that which we have seen. If anything is left of that which he promised us in the deliverance of Egypt which he did not say specifically in this deliverance, it is already included in his general statement: *As in the days of your departure from Egypt I will show him marvelous things* (Mic 7:15). Therefore you will find us expecting him and watching, not doubting, not worrying, not becoming impatient,

---

[5] This depends on a "treasury of merits" concept of divine justice, and also an understanding of the rules for sabbatical release explained in the introduction.

but increasing in courage and steadfastness, as he said, *Be strong, and let your hearts be courageous, all of you who wait for the Lord* (Ps 31:25).

Whoever sees us in this situation will be surprised at us or consider us to be fools, because he was not tested in that which we have been tested, and he has not believed what we have believed. He is like someone who has not seen wheat sown, and when he sees the scattering into cracks of the ground so that it might sprout, he will consider [the sower] to be a fool. In the end it will become clear to him at the time of harvesting that he [the observer] is the fool, when [the harvester] takes for every measure [sown] twenty or thirty measures. Thus the scripture makes an analogy for us: *They that sow in tears will reap in joy* (Ps 126:5).

Or, it is like someone who has not seen a child being reared, who mocks at the one whom he sees rearing the child and being held down by all his necessities. He says, "What does this man expect?" But when he grows and learns science and wisdom and becomes a king and leads armies, that man will know that he only mocked himself. With what kind of an analogy does [the scripture] make when we watch the male child? (240) It says, *Before she travailed, she gave birth; before pain came to her, she gave birth to a boy* (Isa 66:7).

2

One might say further, "One before whom the measurement of the heavens is like the measurement of a span,[6] more or less, how can it be difficult for him to announce prophecy from it? One before whom breadth of the sea is like the hollow of the hand [in size], how can it be difficult for him to gather our scattered remnants from it? One before whom the measurement of the dust of the earth is something that is measureable, why should he not be able to bring us from its extremities? Why would it not be easy for him before whom its [the earth's] mountains are something that can be weighed, to build his holy mountain? Therefore he says in the opening of these comforting passages, *Who measures water with the palm of his hand, and who marked off the heavens with a span, [enclosed] in a measure the dust of the earth, weighed the mountains with a scale, the hills with a balance* (Isa 40:12)? One before whom all the nations are like a drop from a bucket or like a speck of dust on a balance, could he not subdue them before him?

---

[6] A span is the distance from the tip of the thumb to the tip of the little finger when stretched so as to be as far from each other as possible.

As he says, *Behold the nations are considered as a drop from a bucket and like dust of a balance* (Isa 40:15). One who shakes the earth of them just as we take the edges of a writing tablet and shake it, [why should he find this difficult]? As he says, *To seize the corners of the earth, and the wicked will be shaken off from it* (Job 38:13).

If I had said [only] that he created everything from nothing, it would be enough for me to learn from this [the certainty that God can deliver Israel], but I specified these matters because he specified them. It is not possible for our hearts to consider at all [the possibility] that the situation in which we find ourselves is not known to him, or that he will not act justly or deal mercifully, just as he has reprimanded us, *Why do you say, Jacob, and speak, Israel, "My ways are hidden from the Lord, and my case is passed over by my God"* (Isa 40:27)? It is not [right to think] that he is not able to save and to fulfill our requests, as he says, *Behold the hand of the Lord is not shortened [to prevent him] from saving, and his ears are not deaf [to prevent him] from hearing* (Isa 59:1). It is [further] not [true] that he has rejected us and cast us off, but (241) as he has said, *For the Lord your God is a merciful God; he will neither fail you nor destroy you. [He will not forget the covenant which he swore to your fathers]* (Dt 4:31).

Therefore (May God have mercy upon you), we believe that he has permitted our enslavement two times. One of them is the time of repentance, and the second is the time of the end. Whichever of them comes first, we will become worthy of redemption. If we do repentance, he will not look to the end,[7] but it will be just as it is said in the Torah, *And it will happen when all these things come upon you, [the blessing and the curse which I have set before you, then you will remember among all the nations where the Lord your God has pushed you,] and return to the Lord your God, [you and your children, and obey his voice in all that I command you this day, with all your heart and soul]; then the Lord your God will restore your fortunes, [have compassion upon you, and gather you again from all the peoples where the Lord your God has scattered you. If your outcasts are at the end of heaven, from there the Lord your God will gather you and take you. The Lord your God will bring you to the land which your fathers have*

---

[7] The "end" is the end of the "prison" sentence, after the "captive" has served his term completely with no pardon or shortened sentence for good behavior or repentance. Practically and politically, this meant the end of the diaspora "captivity" and the end of the Gentile rule in the world. At the end Jews were expected to return to Palestine and rule the world from Jerusalem.

*conquered, and he will conquer it and make you more prosperous
and numerous than your fathers. The Lord your God will circumcise your hearts and the hearts of your seed so that you will love
the Lord your God with all your heart and with all your soul, so
that you may live. The Lord your God will give all these curses to
your enemies and opponents who pursue you. Then you will
return and pay attention to the voice of the Lord and do all his
commandments which I command you today. The Lord your God
will prosper you through all the work of your hands, the produce
of your womb, the produce of your livestock, the produce of your
land, for the Lord will again enjoy making you prosper, just as he
made your fathers prosper. If you pay attention to the voice of the
Lord your God, observing his commandments and his statutes
which are written in this book of the Torah, if you turn to the Lord
your God with all your heart and with all your soul]* (Dt 30:1-10).

If, however, we do not [adequately repent], we will remain [in
captivity] until the time of the end. If so, there will be for some of
us punishments and for others of us, trials, as the matter is well-
known, with the coming of every general catastrophe, [each] at
one of the times, such as famine, sword, and pestilence. For part of
the human race these will be punishments and for others, trials.
Even in the flood, it is inconceivable that there were no young
people and small children being tested.[8] They will receive their
reward. Just as there can be no doubt for us that there were among
our fathers in Egypt, many righteous men, and they withstood the
trial until the end had been fulfilled.[9] Therefore, let no man say, "If
there had been among you a righteous man, you would have been
redeemed,[10] for our lords and crowns, Moses, Aaron, and Miriam
had already been in slavery more than eighty years before the end
had been fulfilled (paid off). There were also many righteous persons like them.

3

It is proper for me to mention the time of the end, and I say that
the Lord (May he be magnified and exalted), already showed
his prophet Daniel three angels: one above the waters of the Tigris

[8] Young people (בנים) and small children (עטים) were those not yet twenty years of
age and therefore not legally responsible for adult decisions. See further *Consequences*,
181-84.

[9] The end referred to here was the end of the "captivity" in Egypt before the exodus.

[10]The discussion of redemption is here properly couched in economic terms, in which the
righteous man was considered to be comparable to a large contribution given to pay off a
fine. See introduction for details.

and two standing on the shore, asking the one who was above the water when the deliverance would be. This is his statement: *I, Daniel, looked and behold there were two others standing, one* (242) *on the one bank of the river here, and one on the other bank of the river, there* (Dan 12:5). Then the angel standing above the water imposed an oath upon himself concerning the predetermined end, even though [Daniel] did not request him to swear. Daniel said, *I heard the man dressed in linen who was above the waters of the Tigris, and he raised his right hand and his left hand to heaven and swore by the life of the age that it was for a time, two times, and half [a time]* (Dan 12:7). The two angels heard from him, *A time, two times, and half [a time],*[11] and they were satisfied with that, because they understood its interpretation. But Daniel did not know the interpretation, *A time, two times, and half [a time],* so he asked the angel standing above the water, saying, *I heard, but I did not understand; [then I said, "O my lord, what will be the latter end of these things]"* (Dan 12:8).

The angel volunteered by first telling him the reason he had kept the answer secret before he interpreted it, saying, "Indeed, I kept it secret so that the general public and the ignorant people would not become disturbed, because they do not desire, and their apprehensions are not in accord with the apprehensions of the wise. [The latter] desire the reward of the age to come and life eternal, but [the former] desire something that will quickly come into existence according to possession and glory of the world. Only the wise, therefore, understand, as it is said, *Go, Daniel, for the words are kept secret and sealed until the time of the end. Many will be purified, made white, and refined [but the wicked will act wickedly; and none of the wicked will understand; but the wise will understand]* (Dan 12:9-10).

Then he [the angel] explained to him [Daniel], that it would be *a thousand, three hundred, thirty-five days* (Dan 12:12), just as he said, *Blessed is he who waits until the completion of a thousand, three hundred, thirty-five [days]* (Dan 12:12). The word *days* is a cycle of a year, according to the statement, *Days will be his redemption* (Lev 25:29). [The passage], *Until a complete year is fulfilled for him* (Lev 25:30), supports it.

We observe that every end time which the Lord gives to a certain kingdom, he gives only in years, not days. There are times when he interprets the years, according to his statement, *It will happen after seventy years, the Lord will visit Tyre* (Isa 23:17),

---

[11] Meaning "a year, two years, and half a year"—thus three and a half years.

and here is his statement, *After forty years I will gather the Egyptians* (Ezek 29:13). There are times, however, when he uses the expression of the cycle, "years," but he calls them *days*, just as he said to our lord Ezekiel, the priest (upon whom be peace), *I have allowed for you the years of their iniquity for the number* (243) *three hundred and ninety days* (Ezek 4:5). An examination of the word "years" and the word *days* tells us that *days* [in this passage] are "years," and this applies [also] to the passage [in Daniel].

Daniel understood how the interpretation, *A time, two times, and half [a time]*, became *One thousand, three hundred, thirty-five years*, and he was silent. But we (May the Lord be gracious to you) must try to understand the topic, *A time, two times, and half [a time]*, and we have examined [it] carefully. We discover that it fits together if we assume that it was his intention when he said, *times*, [to mean] the time of the kingdom of Israel.[12] If so, then the end will be about one and a half times the years of their kingdom. It is commonly agreed that undoubtedly all the times of the kingdom [total] eight hundred, ninety years, no more, no less. There were four hundred, eighty before the construction of the house, four hundred, ten building the temple, and half their [totals], four hundred, forty-five. The sum total is one thousand, three hundred, thirty-five, no more, no less.

His statement is, *From the time the continual offering is taken away and the allowance of the abominating sacrilege, a thousand, two hundred, ninety days* (Dan 12:11)—the event which happened with the second house at the beginning of its construction. This would be after the time this subject was spoken in Daniel [by] forty-five years.

His statement is, *Until two thousand, three hundred evenings and mornings, then the sanctuary will be made right* (Dan 8:14). It is necessary to subtract one half from it [this number], because it divides the days and makes them nights and days. One half is one thousand, one hundred, fifty years, and this time will be (244) one hundred, eighty-five [years] after the time which was spoken to Daniel, so as to complete the end of the three times in the same final year.

4

I will say further concerning the place of doubt, because there are three [different] times of this end which are specified for this

---

[12] Just as Daniel allegorized the seventy years which Jeremiah prophesied to mean seventy weeks of years (Dan 9:2, 24), of which the last half-week of years is three and a half years before the end, so Saadia allegorized still further to mean that instead of only three and a half years, the expression alluded to the entire time of the kingdom of Israel, i.e., 890 years.

enslavement of ours. Here we see that the Lord has left a place for doubt also in the first two enslavements, so that we may not reach the conclusion that there is no doubt evident, but [that] it is this end only which is not clear. But when we see the two preceding ends,[13] of whose truth we have had proof, when compared to this, doubt vanishes from our minds.

I will explain this by saying that the place of doubt in the enslavement of Egypt is the time of four hundred years when the seed of Abraham were strangers, bowed down, and enslaved, as he said, *You must surely know that your seed will be a stranger in a land that is not theirs, and they will serve them* [the owners]; *and they* [the owners] *will afflict them four hundred years* (Gen 15:13). That is from the birth of Isaac. This period of four hundred, thirty years, [is one] in which the thirty years when Abraham was a stranger are included. The departure of Abraham from Haran to the land of Israel is spelled out clearly; his departure from Cutha to Haran is not spelled out clearly. The thirty years must be for the journeying of Abraham, as he says, *The settlement of the sons of Israel when they lived in Egypt was thirty years and four hundred years* (Ex 12:40). But how Abraham was called the sons of Israel, and how Haran and the land of Israel were called Egypt, there are many explanations which have no place for mention here.

The entire time of their settlement in Egypt was, nevertheless, two hundred, ten years, and no man is able to think that they settled [in Egypt] four hundred years, because the number of years of the lives of Kehath, Amram, and Moses prevent him from this, but this is not the place for its explanation. It is evident, [however] that there are three [different] times: four hundred years, four hundred, thirty years, and two hundred, ten years.

For the enslavement in Babylon there are two [different] periods. One of them is fifty-two years. This is his statement: (245) *When seventy years have been completed for Babylon, I will visit you* (Jer 29:10). The second [period] is seventy years. His statement is, *To complete the destruction of Jerusalem, seventy years* (Dan 9:2). Between the beginning of the Babylonian rule and the destruction of Jerusalem, there were eighteen years, as he said, *In the seventh [day] of the fifth month was the nineteenth year of King Nebuchadnezzar, [king of Babylon, Nebuzaradan, the captain of the bodyguard, a servant of the king of Babylon, came to*

---

[13] The end of the captivity in Egypt and the end of the captivity in Babylon. It is clear that Saadia anticipated the same kind of end to the Roman-Arabian captivity, to be followed by the restoration of the promised land.

Jerusalem. He burned the house of the Lord, and the king's house and all the houses of Jerusalem] (II Kgs 25:8-9). So there was a period of fifty-two years [from then] until the time when Cyrus became king, and he gave permission to them to build the house, and they were building it that year. They stopped [construction] for seventeen years until seventy years had elapsed, as he said, *Then they discontinued work on the house of God which is in Jerusalem; and it was discontinued until the second year of the reign of Darius, king of Persia* (Ezra 4:24).

Just as the three different periods, four hundred, four hundred, thirty, and two hundred, ten did not jeopardize the first end, so also the two different periods, fifty-two and seventy [years] did not jeopardize the second end. Thus three different periods, one thousand, one hundred, fifty, one thousand, two hundred, ninety, and one thousand, three hundred, thirty-five will not jeopardize the third end, because the Wise One has favored his nation with wisdom so that they can find out everything in it.[14]

5

Since I have already interpreted and explained these ends, I will now say that we already know that if our repentance is not complete, we will continue [in exile] until he finalizes the end. If he should finalize the end and we would not have repented, it is possible that salvation would take place while we are sinners. When the time has extended, and we had not repented, he would restore us without repentance, and this would be with the appearance of the redeemer. But the tradition transmitted by the prophets is that hardships and disasters will come upon us, at whose hands we will choose to repent and [then] deserve deliverance. Here is a saying of one of our earlier [teachers]: (246) "If Israelites do pennance, they will be redeemed, but if not, the holy One blessed be He will raise up a king for them whose decrees will be more severe than Haman. Then they will repent and be redeemed" (San 97b).

They tell us further that the cause of this will be the appearance of a man from the seed of Joseph on a mountain of Galilee. He will gather to himself men who are left from the nation. His face will be [set] toward the house of the sanctuary after the Romans will

---

[14] Like others, Saadia assumed that the Bible contained all the truth in the world. God also gave his chosen people enough intelligence to find out the needed information from that given in the Tanak. Therefore the task of scholarship was to learn which statements in the scripture could be applied to which corresponding events in history, so that all history might be understood as the fulfillment of prophecy.

already have seized it, and he will dwell in it for a certain time. After this, a man named Armilos[15] will fight against him. He [Armilos] will fight with them, subdue the city, massacre, take captives, and destroy. The man from the seed of Joseph will be included among the slain.

A great hardship will come against the nation at that time, the most difficult of all [the afflictions] will be the break-down of their relationships with all [other] kingdoms, until [finally the afflictions] will drive them to the wilderness where they will be hungry and afflicted. Because of the wrath that will pass over them, many of them will leave the religion, but the purified ones who are left will stay. Then the prophet Elijah will be revealed to them, and redemption will come.[16]

After I had heard these words, I examined the scripture and found in it a place for all of their points. To begin with, [the claim] that Romans will take the house of the sanctuary in the time of deliverance [is supported by the passage] which says, *Saviors will go up against Mount Zion to judge Mount Esau* (Obad 21). [Also the claim] that one of the sons of Rachel will be appointed over the war with whom [is fulfilled] as it is said, *Therefore, hear the counsel of the Lord which he has counselled against Edom, and his plans which he prepared against the inhabitants of Yemen if the youngest of the flock does not drag them* (Jer 49:20). [The point is valid] that a few, not many, from the nation will be gathered to him, as his statement [confirms], *I will take you, one from a city and two from a family, and bring you to Zion* (Jer 3:14). [The promise] that the conqueror will overpower (247) them, take them captive, and destroy them [is borne out], as he said, *Behold a day is coming for the Lord, and he will divide your booty in your midst* (Zech 14:1). [The text] continues, *I will gather all the nations to Jerusalem for war; [and the city will be taken, the houses plundered, the women raped, half the city will go into exile, but the rest of the people will not be cut off from the city* (Zech 14:2). [The prophecy] that the man who will stand at the head will be

---

[15] This is the earliest datable recorded use of the term, Armilos, which evidently is a Hebraized form of "Romulus," with the prosthetic *alef* added to dissimulate the consonants differently. Armilos personified Rome and the Christian church. He was considered the son of satan and the antichrist.

[16] Elijah would only appear to a pure people. Therefore there were many Jewish and Christian monastic groups who tried to keep an area as pure as the temple for the Shekinah to dwell. Jews at Passover made special efforts to remove every kind of defilement from the house, because they expected Elijah to appear on Passover. Since the Lord could save with a few, just as well as with many, it was not necessary that the group be large. It had to be perfect or righteous.

among the slain, and that they will weep and mourn for him [is supported by the scripture], in which it is said, *They will look at me whom they have stabbed, and they will mourn for him as mourning for an only son. [On that day the mourning in Jerusalem will be as great as the mourning for Hadadrimmon in the plain of Megiddo]* (Zech 12:10-11). [The point] that great hardships would come against the nation at that time [is also supported] as he said, *There will be a time of hardship such as has never been* (Dan 12:1). [The claim] that hatred will develop between them and many of the nations until they drive them into many wilderness areas [is justified by scripture] as he said, *I will bring you to the wilderness of the peoples, [and I will judge you there, face to face]* (Ezek 20:35). There they will hunger, thirst, and be afflicted, just as it happened to the first ones, as he said after that, *Just as I judged your fathers in the wilderness of the land of Egypt, so I will judge you* (Ezek 20:36). [The claim] that they will be purified and refined like silver and like gold until he knows how [great is] their expectation and how [great is] their faith [is supported by scripture], as he said, *I will make you pass under the staff, and I will bring you into the bond of the covenant* (Ezek 20:37). [Another point is] that these events will cause those whose faith is weak to leave their religion, and when they say, "This is what we were hoping, but this is what came upon us," he spoke against them in the following [verse], *I will purge some of you who rebel and transgress against me* (Ezek 20:38). And [finally, the point is justified by the scripture] that to those who are left the prophet Elijah will be revealed, as he says, *Behold I am sending you the prophet Elijah [before the day of the Lord, that great and terrible [day], comes, and he will turn the heart of the fathers to the children and the heart of the children to the fathers]* (Mal 3:23-24).

Now it is evident that these basic points are all interpreted in the scripture, and it further provides for us the tradition of their outline and order, one [point] after the other as they were formulated. May the One be praised who favored us by giving us advance knowledge of these hardships so that they will not come upon us suddenly and cause us to despair. With reference to their occurrence, he said further, *From the corners of the earth we have heard songs, "Glory to the righteous." [But I say, "I pine away, I pine away. Woe is me! For the treacherous deal treacherously, the treacherous deal very treacherously. Terror, the pit, and the snare are upon you, O inhabitant of the land"]* (Isa 24:16-17).

6

I will say one thing about the two positions, that is, if we do not
repent, then the misfortunes of the Messiah son of Joseph will take
place.[17] If we repent, however, and cancel them, the Messiah son
of David will be revealed to us (248) suddenly. If already the
Messiah son of Joseph has preceded him, he will be like an
emissary before him; he will lead the nation; and he will prepare
the way, as he said, *Behold I am sending my messenger, and he
will prepare the way before me* (Mal 3:1), as if he were cleansing
the perpetrators of major transgressions and those who commit
minor offenses within the nation with fire, as he said further on,
For he is like a refiner's fire and like laundry soap (Mal 3:2).

But if [the Messiah son of Joseph] does not come, the Messiah
son of David will come to us suddenly, as he said, *Suddenly the
Lord whom you seek will come to his temple* (Mal 3:1).[18] He will
lead men with him until he reaches the house of the sanctuary, and
if it is in the hand of Armilos, he will kill him and take it from his
hand. This is that which he said, *I will wreak my vengeance upon
Edom by the hand of my people, the Israelites* (Ezek 25:14), but if
it were in the hand of someone else, also this man would be from
Edom.

If the son of Joseph will not come, that which will strengthen
their hearts, bind up their wounds, and comfort their souls will
come to them at the hands of the son of David, as he said, *The
Spirit of the Lord God is upon me, because the Lord has anointed
me to proclaim good news to the afflicted; he has sent me to bind
up the broken hearted, and to announce to the captives release* [of
jubilee], *[to open the prison for prisoners], to proclaim the year of
the Lord's favor* (Isa 61:1-2).[19] [The prophet Isaiah] introduces here
[various] kinds of reward of honor, strength, and splendor, as that
which he said later, *To appoint for the mourners for Zion, so as to
give them beauty instead of ashes* (Isa 61:3), and they will build

[17] This is the earliest datable reference to the Messiah son of Joseph as a forerunner for the
Messiah son of David, but it is based typologically on Saul of Kish who ran interference for
David.

[18] Note that Saadia felt no theological difficulty in calling the Messiah, "the Lord." His
only objection to calling Jesus "the Lord" would have been that he did not accept Jesus as
the Messiah.

[19] The year of the Lord's favor would be the national jubilee, when the Lord would
release the "captives" from their "bondage" in the diaspora and give them back the
promised land, which had been held in payment of the debt incurred until jubilee (Lev 25:8-
10). This would take place at the appointed time, regardless of the number of sins accumulated, because they had worked off their "debt" at half wages, i.e., they had paid
"double for all their sins" (Isa 40:2; 61:7).

up the land and inhabit it, as he said, *And build up the ruins of the age* (Isa 61:4).

Then Gog and Magog will hear the events pertaining to the son of David—the high quality of his people and his land, the abundance of their wealth, and their confidence without walls, doors, locks, or anything like that, he will want to subdue them, as it is said in the passage on Gog, *And they will say, "I will go up to a land of unwalled villages; I will come to a quiet people, those who live in confidence, all dwelling without walls, locks, or doors"* (Ezek 38:11). Then he will gather with him men from many peoples, and they will pass through lands until they come to them, as he said, *You will come from your place from the extreme regions of the North, [you and many peoples with you]* (Ezek 38:15). He will separate the peoples who come with him into two groups; the first is composed of those known to be lost, . and the second, men who were capable when they entered into religion.

Against those [destined] for destruction, he said, *I will gather all the Gentiles and bring them down into the Valley of Jehoshaphat* (Joel 4:2). He also said, *Announce* (249) *this among the nations, "Sanctify war!*[20] *arouse the mighty men; [let all the men of war come forward. Let them come up!] Beat your ploughshares into swords, your pruning hooks to spears. Let the weak man say, "I am a warrior!" Act! Come! all the nations round about. Let them be gathered there! Bring down your mighty men, O Lord. Let the nations be aroused and come up to the Valley of Jehoshaphat, [because there I will sit to judge all the nations round about.] Put in the sickle for the harvest is ripe. [Come, descend! for the olive press is full. Strike the wine presses, for their evil is great.] Mobs, mobs in the Valley of Decision* (Joel 4:9-14).[21]

For those who have been capacitated,[22] however, are the ones of whom it is said, *For then I will turn to the peoples a pure language,*[23] *so that all of them may call in the name of the Lord* (Zeph 3:9).

---

[20] Since the Lord was a Man of War and the Lord of Armies, fighting in behalf ot his chosen people was considered a holy enterprise, blessed and sanctified by the priests, with soldiers under certain ascetic purity rules (Dt 23:9-14; 1QM 7:3, 4-5, 9).

[21] The battle between Israel and the Gentiles was understood as the necessary activity of the judgment day, when the wicked would be judged adversely and therefore lose the battle. The righteous Israelites would be judged "not guilty," and therefore be vindicated by the destruction of their enemies in war.

[22] I.e., declared "not guilty" by God.

[23] A "pure language" was one free from Gentile influence, therefore Hebrew.

Three[24] kinds of plagues will fall upon the heretics in that day: 1) Some will perish from that which will come upon it, of fire, brimstone, and hail, as he said, *I will cause to rain upon them torrents of rain, hail, fire, and brimstone* (Ezek 38:22). Part will perish by the sword, each man against his neighbor, as he said, *"And I will call upon him for all my mountains, a sword," said the Lord God. "The sword of each man will be against his brother,"* (Ezek 38:21). 2) For part, [each man's] flesh will rot and his bones decay, as he said, *This will be the plague which the Lord will inflict [on all the peoples who fought in war against Jerusalem]: [Each man's] flesh will rot while he is standing on his feet* (Zech 14:12). [This condition will continue] until whenever a man extends his hand to the hand of his friend to hold on to him, [his friends' flesh] will come off into his hands, as he said, *It will happen on that day that there will be a great tumult of the Lord among them, and each man will take hold of his neighbor, and his hand will rise up over the hand of his neighbor* (Zech 14:13). 3) The rest will bear signs of what has happened to them, like an eye gouged out, [a broken nose], or an amputated finger. These will go to the ends of the world and report what they have seen, as he said, *I will place among them a sign, and I will send some of them [as] refugees to the nations, Tarshish, [Put, Lud, who made the bow, Tubal, and Javan, who draw the bow]* (Isa 66:19).

Also those who are purified will form four groups:[25] 1) Some will serve the Israelites in their dwellings. These are the [most] respected [of them], as he said, *Kings will be your foster fathers [and their queens, your nursing mothers]* (Isa 49:23). 2) Part of them will function as servants in the cities and villages. Of them it is said, *And the house of Israel will possess them in the Lord's land as male and female slaves; they will take captive those who were their captors, and rule over those who oppressed them* (Isa 14:2). 3) Part of them will work in vineyards and fields, as he said, *Strangers will stand and feed your flocks; foreigners will be your plowmen and vinedressers* (Isa 61:5). 4) The rest will return to their land where they will be subject to her [Israel], as he said, *And it will happen that everyone (250) who is left of all the Gentiles who come against Jerusalem will come up each year to worship the king, the Lord [of armies, and to keep the feast of booths]* (Zech 14:16). Every nation which does not celebrate the feast, no rain

[24] Some later texts read "four," dividing no. 1 into two kinds of plagues. See also Rabbi Hai Gaon.

[25] Of the Gentiles. Those not justified would have been already destroyed, either by war or the plagues. See also II Bar 72:4-6.

will fall upon them [its people], as he said, *It will happen that who- ever does not go up from the families of the earth to Jerusalem to worship the king, the Lord of armies, there will be no rain upon them* (Zech 14:17). Then the Gentiles will see that it is extremely important that they approach the Messiah, which is that they bring someone [a Jew] from their midst, [each man] from his nation, as a gift, as he said, *The peoples will take them and bring them to their place* (Isa 14:2). He said [further], *They will bring all your brothers from all the nations, a gift to the Lord* (Isa 66:20).[26]

Every nation will do this according to its ability. Those who are rich will bring Israelites on horses, mules, carts, and carriages, the most dignified manner, as he said, *They will bring all your brothers from all the nations a gift to the Lord, upon horses, in chariots, in litters, upon mules, and upon carriages* (Isa 66:20). The poor among them [the Gentiles] will carry them [the Israelites] upon their shoulders and their children in their bosoms, as he said, *Thus says the Lord God, behold I will raise my hand to the Gen- tiles, and I will raise my ensign to the peoples, and they will bring your sons in [their] laps [and your daughters will be carried on their shoulders]* (Isa 49:22). Whoever is in [the islands] of the sea, they will transport by ship, accompanied by silver and gold, as he said, *For the islands will wait for me, and ships of Tarshish [first, to bring your sons from afar, their silver and gold with them]* (Isa 60:9). If he is in the land of Ethiopia, they [the Gentiles] will bring him in boats of bulrushes until he reaches Egypt, because there are in the cataracts of the Nile, mountains protruding from the water. It is impossible for vessels of wood to navigate in it without being wrecked, but the boats of bulrushes, covered with pitch, are not broken [by them], as he said, *O land of whirring wings which is beyond the rivers of Ethiopia, which sends ambassadors by sea and in vessels of bulrushes upon the water* (Isa 18:1-2). The ex- pression, "whirring wings" (*kenephim*) [describes a region] whose corners (*kenaphot*) are covered and hidden from human beings, as he said at the end of the passage, *In that time gifts will be brought to the Lord [of armies from a people tall and smooth, from a people feared near and far]* (Isa 18:7). There it is said, *From beyond the rivers of Ethiopia, my suppliants, the daughter of my dispersed ones, will bring* (251) *a gift* (Zech 3:10).

[26] This explanation is also given in Saadia's commentary, f. 39 and 43. See B. Cohen, "Quotations from Saadia's Arabic Commentary on the Bible from two Manuscripts of Abraham ben Solomon," *Saadia Anniversary Volume* (New York, 1943), 135, 137. There were Jewish Christians, whom Jerome called *semi-Judaei*, who had similar expectations for the literal fulfillment of Isa 61 (Jerome, *In Esaiam*. XVII.1x, 1-3; 11, 15-28).

Whoever of the Israelites is left in the wilderness, and there are there none of the Gentiles who will bring them, the Lord will bring him as quickly as if a cloud should lift [him] and carry [him], as he said, *Who are these that fly as a cloud, and as the doves to their cotes* (Isa 60:8), or as if the winds had carried him, as he said, *I will say to the north [wind], "give up," and to the south [wind], "Do not hold back. Bring my sons from a distance, my daughters from the ends of the earth"* (Isa 43:6).

When those who are alive are gathered together with [others] who are alive, as I have described, then there will be the resurrection of the dead, as I have explained earlier. The son of Joseph will be at their head and in front of them, because he is the righteous servant who endured the trial, and the Lord will greatly reward him. Then the Lord (May he be exalted and magnified) will renew his sanctuary, just as it has been described for us, *For the Lord will build Zion. It will appear in his glory* (Ps 102:17). The plan and the temple will be just as Ezekiel has interpreted, *In the twenty-fifth year of our exile* (Ezek 40:1). In it there will be pearls and precious stones, just as Isaiah said, *I will make your battlements of rubies and your gates of carbuncles* (Isa 54:12). He will build up all the land until there is no place of ruin or desolation left in it, as he said, *The parched ground will become a pool, and the thirsty ground springs of water* (Isa 35:7). Then the light of the Shekinah will be revealed, rising up over the house of the sanctuary, until all [other] lights will be dark or shaded in relationship to it, as I have already explained in my second treatise that it will be brighter than any light, as he said, *Arise, shine! for your light has come, and the glory of the Lord has risen upon you; for behold darkness will cover the earth and gloom, the Gentiles, but upon you the Lord will arise,*[27] [and his glory will appear upon you] (Isa 60:1-2). [It will be so bright] that all who do not know the way to the sanctuary can walk to that light whose shining is drawn from heaven to earth, as he said, *Nations will walk to its light, the kings to the brightness of your rising* (Isa 60:3).[28]

Then prophecy will increase in our nation, and even our children and our slaves will prophesy, as he said, *It will happen after this, I will pour out my spirit on all flesh, and your sons and your daughters will prophesy; [your old men will dream dreams,*

---

[27] Rise in the sense of the sun's rising and shining.

[28] At the temple, where a fire would burn continually to cook and consume the sacrifices as well as to provide a pillar of fire and cloud, joining heaven to earth, there would be such a large fire that it would light up the whole city at night and could be seen from a great distance. See further *To The Hebrews* 157-62.

and your young men will see visions]. Also upon your male and female slaves [in those days, I will pour out my spirit] (Joel 3:1-2). [This will continue] until if a man walks to a land (252) among the rest of the lands, and he says, "I am one of the believers," they will say to him, "Tell us what happened yesterday and will happen tomorrow" in things that are sealed to them. When he tells them, they will be sure that he is from the nation [of the Israelites], as he said, *Their seed will be known among the Gentiles, and their offspring in the midst of the peoples* (Isa 61:9).

The believers will continue in this position all the days of the age;[29] they will not change their position, as he said, *Israel will be saved by the Lord, a salvation of the ages. You will not be embarrassed nor made to appear foolish until ages unlimited* (Isa 45:17). It appears to me that he only said this expression, *until ages unlimited,* in this, of all places, to verify for us the truths of redemption with all that is the strongest in the language and to dismiss anyone who says that it will be transient or come to an end.

He has informed us that the people will choose obedience and not rebellion as the matter is interpreted in the passage, *And the Lord your God will circumcise your heart* (Dt 30:6), and with the passage, *I will give you a new heart and a new spirit [I will put within you. I will remove the heart of stone from your flesh, and I will give you a heart of flesh]* (Ezek 36:26). This will be their choice for many reasons: 1) They will see the light of the Shekinah and prophecy released upon them. 2) They will enjoy sovereignty and well-being with no hand against them, and no afflictors oppressing them. 3) And all the rest of their surrounding interests will prosper.

He informed us that pestilence, illnesses, and plagues will all disappear and also weakness and worry, but there will be for them an age which is all joy and happiness, until they will appear as if their heaven and earth had been renewed for them, as I have interpreted in the passage, *For behold I am creating a new heaven and a new earth: [the first will not be remembered and will not come to mind], but they will rejoice and be glad endlessly [that which I am creating. For behold I am creating Jerusalem. Rejoice and be glad with her!] I will rejoice in Jerusalem, and I will be glad with my people. The voice of weeping and crying will no more be heard in it* (Isa 65:17-19).[30]

[29] I.e., the messanic age or the age of sabbath rest to follow.

[30] Both in the expectation of II Isaiah and of Saadia, the central factor of the new creation was the creation of a new city, Jerusalem.

What a glorious generation! All will be joy and gladness, all obedience and service,[31] all loving kindness and exclusiveness. About it he says, *Whose sons are like plants [full grown in their youth]...whose garners are full, providing every kind of store...whose oxen are laden with no breach and no breaking out* (Ps 144:12-14).

7

Now I will give another of these interpretations against that which I have learned, that men from those who call themselves Jews imagine that these promises and comforts were all [fulfilled] during the period of the second house.[32] They have already passed and nothing whatever is left of them [to be fulfilled]. But he annuls that which they conjecture [as] a basis upon which they build their arguments. All these encouraging things which we see belonging to redemption, as he said, *The sun will not go down any more [nor the moon withdraw itself]* (Isa 60:20), and *It will not be uprooted or overthrown again for the age* (Jer 31:40). All this will be given if the people are obedient to the Lord. They say that this is just like that which Moses, our leader, said to Israel, *So that your days and the days of your children may increase* (Dt 11:21). When they sinned, their rule was cancelled and their kingdom ceased. Thus some of these promises took place with the second temple and were finished, and others did not take place because the people sinned.

I took (May the Lord show you favor) the basis of the words of these men that it is conditional, and I brought it to the task of exactness and found it invalid from several points of view: 1) One, that the promises of our leader Moses (upon whom be peace) explained them to be conditional, because he said, *If you really keep all this commandment which I command you [loving the Lord your God, walking in all his ways, and cleaving to him, then the Lord will drive out all these nations before you, and you will dispossess*

---

[31] Obedience and service to God, not to the Gentiles. It is clear that Saadia believed firmly that all Gentiles were destined to serve Jews. The generation that would be all joy and gladness would have little to do except offer prescribed sacrifices which Gentiles would supply.

[32] These arguments are based on the supposition that all of the promises made in scripture will be fulfilled in the days of the Messiah. Rabbi Yohanan said, "Every prophet prophesied only for the days of the Messiah" (Ber 34b). The Jews who had no further messianic expectations believed that all the promises given in the Torah were fulfilled by the restoration of the temple and the return from Babylon to the promised land. Like Saadia, they believed all promises not yet fulfilled would have to be fulfilled. No promise of God would fail. The disagreement was the extent to which prophecy had already been fulfilled.

nations greater and mightier than you] (Dt 11:22-23). *If you really pay attention to his voice and do all that which I say, I will be an enemy to your enemies* (Ex 23:22), and he says, *And it will happen because you pay attention* (Dt 28:1) and all such as this. But there is nothing at all conditional about these consolations, but rather they are definite and absolute promises.

Furthermore, our leader Moses (upon whom be peace) was not satisfied that it be given to his people under the condition, "if keeping," "if hearing," and leaving the opposite open for their comprehension that they learn from this, that if they do not adhere to [the conditions], he will not fulfill [the promises]. Just the opposite is the case. He explained to them that if they did not fulfill [the demands], the word would be reversed against them, as he said, *And it will be that if you completely forget the Lord your God [and go after other gods and serve them and worship them, I sternly warn you this day that you will surely perish] like the nations which the Lord destroyed before you, thus you will perish* (Dt 8:19-20). He also said, *When you beget children and grandchildren [and have grown old in the land, if you act corruptly by making a graven image in the form of anything, and thus do what is evil in the sight of the Lord your God, so as to make him angry], I call heaven and earth to testify against you this day [that you will soon utterly perish from the land which you are going over the Jordan to possess; you will not live long upon it, but will be utterly destroyed]* (Dt 4:25-26). He said further, *If your heart turns away and you do not pay attention [but are drawn away to worship other gods and serve them, I declare to you this day that you will perish]* (Dt 30:17-18), and all [passages] like these. But the consolations—these he did not give with any [conditions] at all, much less did he say the opposite, [namely, that which would happen in case Israel failed to meet the conditions].

Another [premise] is that he made (254) the way of these promises like the way of the flood in the days of Noah (upon whom be peace), that even if men sinned to the limit of their sinfulness, "I will not bring a flood against them, because I have already sworn that it will not happen again, but there will be other punishments. Thus I have sworn that I will not turn away your kingdom." His statement is, *For this which I have sworn is like the water of Noah to me, [May the following unmentioned curses come upon me] if the waters of Noah pass over the earth. Thus I have sworn not to be angry with you nor rebuke you* (Isa 54:9). Even if the people were to sin, he would punish them in whatever way he wishes, but not with the abolition of their kingdom.[33]

Another [premise] is that he has announced that the people will choose obedience to him and not rebellion, as we have previously explained. He [God] knows everything just as it will happen, just as we said earlier. If so, then it is impossible that there would be there any iniquity or sin which would not be known to him. When there would be no sin—therefore no condition was given, and further if there had been there a condition, it would not have injured them. So much the less if there were no conditions.

Moreover, since in the Torah he has already taken an apparent oath against this, and therefore it is impossible that it should not be just as we have explained. He swore and said, *For I raise my hand to heaven and say, "As I live for the age, [may the following unmentioned curses come upon me] if I whet the lightning of my sword, and my hand takes hold on judgment, I will take vengeance on my adversaries, and I will pay back those who hate me]. I will make my arrows drunk with blood, [and my sword will consume flesh with the blood of the slain and the captives, from the long haired heads of the enemy]. Shout for joy, O nations, [of] his people, [for he avenges the blood of his servants, and he takes vengeance on his adversaries, and makes atonement for the land of his people]"* (Dt 32:40-43). This explanation brings to nothing all that which they imagined or that which they constructed in the matter of conditions and provisions.

8

Since I have already uprooted the basis of their defense, I will reply to them with fifteen answers. Of these, five are proofs from the scripture, five are insights from tradition, and five of them are logical deductions.

Of the five [arguments] which are from scripture, the first is that these consolations require that all Israelites gather together to the house of the sanctuary, and that not one of them will be left in exile, as he said, *And I will bring them to their ground, and I will not leave any of them there* [in Babylon] (Ezek 39:28), but only forty-two *thousand, three hundred, sixty* of them returned at the time of the second temple, (255) as he said, *All were like one congregation, forty-two[34] thousand, three hundred, sixty* (Neh 7:66).

---

[33] Some rabbis disagreed. They held that the acquisition of the land was a conditional promise, dependent upon Jewish behavior (Mekilta, *Amelek* 4:132-43).

[34] Text says, "Two myriads of thousands," an evident scribal error that disagrees with the preceding clause, the Masoretic text, and the LXX.

The second [argument] is that they will be gathered from the islands of the sea, just as he said, *From Elath, Shinar, Hamath, and the islands of the sea* (Isa 11:11). In the first exile [Jews] did not go to one of the islands, much less return from there.

The third [argument] is that the Gentiles will build the wall of the house of the sanctuary, as he said, *The sons of the stranger will build your walls, and kings will minister to you* (Isa 60:10). It is not enough that they did not build for us any part of the second temple, but [instead] they were hindering us. We were continually at war concurrently with construction, just as that which he said, *They were building the wall. Those who carried burdens were packed in such a way that each one worked with one hand and with the other held his weapon. Each of the builders had his sword fastened at his side while he was building* (Neh 4:11-12).

The fourth [promise] is that the gates of the city would be open day and night, while [people] entered and left securely, as he said, *Your gates will be open continually, day and night.[They will not be closed]* (Isa 60:11). But we find in the second temple they closed them before sunset and they did not open them until the heat of the day, as he said, *And he said to them, "Do not open the gates of Jerusalem until the heat of the sun"* (Neh 7:3).

The fifth [promise] is that there would not be left one nation that was not under Israel's rule, just as that which he said, *For the nation and the kingdom which does not serve you will perish* (Isa 60:12). But there is no doubt that they and their lands were subject to kings at the time of the second temple, just as that which he said, *See, we are slaves today, and the land which you gave to our fathers, to enjoy its fruits and its good gifts. See we are slaves* (Neh 9:36). These constitute the five [proofs] which are from scripture.

[These are] the five [evidences] which are from tradition: The first is that the people were to light fires from the wood which had been the weapons of Gog for seven years, as he said, *The residents of the cities of Israel will go out and make fire from weapons and burn [them], shields, bucklers, bows, arrows [handpikes, and spears, and they will make fires of them for seven years]* (Ezek 39:9).

The second [assurance] is that the Egyptian Nile will run dry in one place and the Euphrates in seven places for people to travel [over] them, as it is said, *The Lord will pronounce* cherem *upon the tongue of the sea of Egypt. He will wave his hand over the river [with a scorching wind, and strike it into seven channels so that men may cross on dry land]. There will be a highway from Assyria for the remnant of his people which is left* (Isa 11:15-16).

The third [proof] is that the Mount of Olives will split into two from the east and the west until it is divided, (256) and half of it will be from the north corner and half from the south corner. Between them there will be a large valley, as he said, *The Mount of Olives will be divided into halves from the east to the west [so that there will be a very great valley. Half of the mountain will move northward, and the other part, southward]* (Zech 14:4).

The fourth [proof] is that the building of the house of the sanctuary would be according to the pattern of the house (Ezek 43:11) from beginning to end.

The fifth [proof] is that a spring of water will pour out from the house of the sanctuary and expand and continue until it becomes a great river which no one would be able to cross, as it is said, *And behold water will issue forth from under the threshold of the house eastward [(for the temple faced east), and the water will flow down from below the south end of the threshold of the temple, south of the altar]...And he will measure a thousand...and it will be a river that I cannot pass through, [for the water will rise; it will be deep enough to swim in, a river that could not be passed through]* (Ezek 47:1, 5). On the two banks of that river there will be some of every kind of fruit tree, [bearing] its fruit continually, and its leaves will not wither. From it [there will be] food and healing, just as he said, *Alongside the river, there will grow on its banks on either side, [all kinds of trees for food. Their leaves will not wither, and their fruit will not fail, but they will bear fresh fruit every month, because the water for them will flow from the sanctuary. Their fruit will be for food, and their leaves for healing* (Ezek 47:12).

We have not heard that any of these five [promises] has taken place [during the time of the second temple], but what we have heard shows that none of them happened at all.[35]

These are the five [insights gained] from obvious deduction: The first is the belief of all creatures and their [confession of] the Oneness of the Lord, as that which he has said, *The Lord will become king over all the land* (Zech 14:9). Now we see them in their error and heresy.

The second is the exemption of everyone of the believers from paying taxes, and [giving] gifts of money and food to anyone except him, as he said, *The Lord has sworn by his right hand and*

[35] Therefore the promises must apply to the *next* generation.

his strong arm," [May the following unmentioned curses come upon me] *if I give your grain again [as] food for your enemies"* (Isa 62:8). Here we see the entire nation [of Israel] paying taxes and being obedient and subject to any nation under whose hand it is.[36]

The third [promise] is the end of war from among human beings so that one will not lift up sword against the other, as he said, *They will beat their swords to ploughshares and their spears to pruninghooks; [nation will not lift up sword against nation]* (Isa 2:4). But we see them worse than they ever were in war and murder! If someone offers this explanation, saying that they were not fighting against religion, he should note that they are contending and overpowering one another because of their religions more than they [ever] were.

The fourth [insight] is that the animals will make peace with one another, so that the wolf and the sheep will eat [together], and the lion will eat (257) straw, and the young child will play with serpents and vipers, as he said, *The wolf will dwell with the sheep; the bull and the bear will eat [together]. They will not hurt nor destroy* (Isa 11:6-9). Now we see them with their natural [impulses] and damages. Nothing at all has been changed in them. If someone offers the explanation that this is also a parable, saying that it is only intended to mean that the wicked men of the human race will be enabled to be at peace with the meritorious, even this is not true, but the opposite is the case. There is more plundering, abusing, and overpowering the weak now [than ever before].

The fifth [promise] is that he will inhabit the cities of Sodom and restore them to the places where they were, as he said, *I will return their captivity, the captivity of Sodom and her daughters* (Ezek 16:53), and he said, *The sisters of Sodom and her daughters will return to their former [condition]* (Ezek 16:55).

Already the Torah said that its waters were sweet and they used to water the ground from it abundantly, as he said, *Lot raised his eyes and saw all the plain of the Jordan that it was well watered* (Gen 13:10). It also says, [that the region of Sodom was] like *the garden of the Lord* (Gen 13:10), as the scripture said, *A river went out from Eden to water the garden* (Gen 2:10). It said it was *like*

---

[36] The relationship of taxation to redemption has been a serious issue with Jews. They first considered themselves free from the Syrians when the taxation was removed in the time of Simon (142-135 B.C. *Ant.* XII.7 [213-214]). They rebelled when Archaelaus was deposed and Romans took up their own taxes (*B.J.* II.124). Jews continued to rebel until after the temple was destroyed in A.D. 70. The question of whether a Jew should pay taxes to Caesar or not was a religious issue (Mt 22:15-22). Jesus agreed with Peter that foreigners should pay the taxes and the sons be exempt (Mt 17:26).

the land of Egypt (Gen 13:10), as he said, It is not like the land of Egypt from which you left where you sowed your seed, and you watered [it] with your foot, like a vegetable garden (Dt 11:10). But look! The city is destroyed, a repository of salt. Its salt and bitterness killed it, just as that which happened (when Lot's wife became a pillar of salt). These present states of affairs provide irrefutable arguments that these comforting passages have not yet been realized.[37]

9

All that which we have said in response to these [who claim that the messages of comfort in the scripture applied only to the second temple] also provide an answer against the Christians, omitting only that which we mentioned on the subject of the second temple. They [the Christians] do not imagine that the promises began [their fulfillment] at that time. They stipulate the date for them one hundred, thirty-five years before the destruction of the second temple (258).

Especially to these, i.e., the Christians [I will give] another answer, which is that mentioned by the prophet (upon whom be peace) in the passage "seventy weeks" (Dan 9:24). The interpretation [accepted] among us is that they [mean] four hundred, ninety [years], of which forty-nine are from the beginning of the exile of the people until the beginning of the building of the second house, as he said, Know and understand, from the going out of the word to return and rebuild Jerusalem until the messianic prince, seven weeks [of years] (Dan 9:25). Four hundred, thirty-four of them continue [during] the existence of the house, including [periods of] disuse, cessation [of services], and prevention of construction, as he said, After sixty-two weeks [of years], you will return and rebuild, extensive and diligently, but in difficult times (Dan 9:25). This is that which we mentioned in the passage, Then you discontinued work on the house of God (Ezra 4:24).[38] The last week—part of it will [be marked by] peaceful conditions between the nation and some of the kings, and the other part [will be marked by] violation [of treaties] and war with all of them, as he said, He will make a firm covenant with the many for one week, and for half a week [of years he will cause sacrifice and offering to cease (Dan 9:27). He will make the land desolate and destroy

---

[37] Therefore, they will all be fulfilled in the future.

[38] Reference may be to some other treatise in this volume of doctrines, but it is not in any part of this treatise.

many of its men, as he said, *Upon the wing of detestable things that make desolate until the extermination and that which was determined is poured over the one who makes desolate* (Dan 9:27).

Now this period which is of seventy weeks [of years] includes prosperity and righteousness and [also] cessation of the kingdom, the priesthood, and prophecy, according to that which he said in the introduction, *To complete [penance for] the transgression, to finish [payment for] sin, to atone the iniquity, and to introduce righteousness of the ages, to seal the vision and prophet, and to anoint the holy of holies* (Dan 9:24).[39] This is like a man who says, "I spent fifty days [altogether] including both good and evil—marriage, illness, and business." After that he expatiates. He announced that at their end he would put a stop to every anointed priest. He would not be found, according to that which is said, *After sixty-two weeks [of years], the anointed one will be cut off and be no more* (Dan 9:26). There is no intention in this message of any *definite* man (259) himself, but the intention is every anointed priest, as he said in the Torah, *If the anointed priest* (Lev 4:3); *and the anointed priest will bring* (Lev 4:16); and *The anointed priest in his place* (Lev 6:15), and all such [passages].

The high priest will be cut off from the nation after this time, as the Lord (May he be exalted and glorified) has informed us. These [Christians] say that [the reference], *The Messiah will be cut off and be no more* (Dan 9:26) is intended to apply to one specific man. This is unacceptable from many points of view. One, because the word "anointed" (Messiah) is not especially for one particular man, but it is said of every priest and king. Furthermore, the word "will be cut off," if it refers to murder is only said about one who is murdered because he is guilty [of a crime punishable by death], as he said, *Everyone who eats it will be cut off* (Lev 17:14). Also this event is [associated] with the destruction of the sanctuary as that which sanctions him, *The people of the prince who is coming will destroy the city and the sanctuary, but his end will be with a flood* (Dan 9:26).

More convincing than all this is [that from the time of the report which told this to Daniel until the time which they imagine is only

---

[39] In the treasury of merits theology, sins, transgressions, and iniquities had to be balanced with corresponding virtues before the books could be balanced and the promise made to Abraham be fulfilled. There were different ways of saying this. Three ways were here placed in parallel position:
1. The penance for the transgression had to be completed.
2. The payment of counter balancing merits for sin had to be made.
3. The iniquities had to be atoned so that there was no deficit.

two hundred, eighty-five years, whereas all the [number pro-
phesied] are four hundred and ninety [years]. Of this number,
seventy are before the construction of the second house and four
hundred, twenty [while] it was in use. I have found people [Chris-
tians] who had no counsel [to refute these objections] but to add a
date. They imagine that the Persian kingdom existed over the land
of Israel about three hundred years before the Greek kingdom, and
that the number of their kings at this time was seventeen. I answer
them with the scripture from the Book of Daniel that it is not
possible that there were between the Babylonian kingdom and the
Greek kingdom more than four kings from the kings of Persia over
the land of Israel. According to that which the angel said to Daniel
(upon whom be peace, *Now I, in the first year of Darius the Mede,
stood up to strengthen and fortify him. I tell you the truth. Still
three Persian kings (260) will arise, and the fourth will be exceed-
ingly more wealthy than all [the rest of them], and according to his
strength in his wealth, he will stir up everything [against] the
Greek kingdom* (Dan 11:1-2). This argument, then, has solved [the
problem] from all its sides.

These refutations [may be used] against them [the Christians],
apart from that which there is against them on the subject of rejec-
tion of the Torah, and in addition to what [may be presented]
against them on the subject of the Oneness [of God], and in addition to other things which are not suitable for this book.

SUMMARY

This discussion on the doctrine of redemption was an integral
part of Saadia's book on basic beliefs and convictions. This was
accepted systematic theology of his day. The following are some
of the central assumptions and convictions reflected in this essay:

1. All knowledge necessary for faith and guidance is contained
in the scripture. That which is not in the scripture is not in the
world.

2. There have already been two redemptions in the history of
Israel: 1) the exodus from Egypt and the conquest of Canaan, and
2) the exodus from Babylon and the restoration of the temple and
the holy city, Jerusalem. The next redemption at the hands of the
Messiah will be similar in kind but more glorious and extensive
than the previous ones have been.

3. All promises that have not already been fulfilled will be

fulfilled in the days of the Messiah, when God redeems the Jews from the Romans. These promises have not been explicitly fulfilled by the restoration after the Babylonian captivity. Therefore we can still expect their fulfillment.

4. It is proper to search the scripture to find the needed text and its true meaning through allegory to apply to the doctrine of redemption.

5. The Jews are God's chosen people and are destined to rule the world. The Gentiles are all enemies of God and are destined to be destroyed in the war of Gog and Magog, put to death by the promised plague, or be enslaved to the Jews after God redeems Israel.

6. The treasury of merits theology and sabbatical eschatology belong together as basic to Saadia's doctrine of redemption.

7. Saadia concluded that redemption would take place at the end of 1335 years, but he did not say when this period had its beginning. Therefore scholars, medieval and modern, have conjectured dates ranging from A.D. 964 to 1403 as the times when redemption was believed to have begun. He evidently did not calculate from A.D. 70, as would seem obvious, because his commentary on Dan 12:11 indicates that the verse refers to an event which took place during an earlier period of the second temple, forty-five years after the first prophecy, but he gave no hint of the nature of the event.[1] Redemption involved the messianic birth pangs, the suffering and hardship associated with the wars of Gog and Magog, the appearance of a Messiah son of Joseph, who had suffered for the sins of Israel and would lead troops to Jerusalem, and finally be killed by Armilos, whom the Messiah son of David would later kill. The blessed state that would follow would take place on this earth, with its center at Jerusalem. The difference between life before then and life after redemption would be the status of Jews in the world in comparison with the status of Gentiles. Assumptions of Saadia Gaon and his basic teachings were similar to those views proclaimed earlier by some anonymous preacher to some unknown congregation. These are now preserved in *Pesikta Rabbati*.

---

[1] See further H. Malter, "Saadia Gaon's Messianic Computation," *Journal of Jewish Lore and Philosophy*, I (1919), 45-59.

MESSIANIC SERMONS

Mourners for Zion[1]

Piska 34

(158a)   *Rejoice greatly, daughter of Zion; shout, daughter of*
Jerusalem!
behold, your king comes to you [righteous and redeemed;
he is afflicted and riding upon a donkey,
a colt the foal of a donkey] (Zech 9:9).

This is that which was said by Isaiah through the Holy Spirit,
*Their seed will be known among the nations, their offspring in the
midst of the Gentiles* (Isa 61:9). With respect to whom did Isaiah
say this verse? He only spoke it with respect to the mourners for
Zion, because the holy One blessed be He is destined to give them
victory over their enemies, as it is said, *Their seed will be known
among the nations* (Isa 61:9). Do not read, *their seed* (זרעם), but
their arm (זרועם). Who will stand up for them with an *arm*?
(158b) The holy One blessed be He will stand up for them with an
arm, as it is said, *Lord show favor to us; we have waited for you;
be their* arm *in the mornings, even our salvation in the time of
trouble* (Isa 33:2). *In the mornings* refers to those who rise up early
every single *morning* to seek his mercy. *Our salvation in the time
of trouble.* These are the mourners who covet salvation evening,
morning, and noon. Oppression has been great for the Israelites
who are despised and a mockery. When they see those [anti-
Jewish] decrees of another year when the Messiah is revealed in
their midst, coming one after the other, with no let up, they will
understand at once and say, "In our days there has not been
anything like this. Perhaps the Messiah will arrive."

These are the [anti-Jewish] decrees from which they will
understand: In Nisan, on the eve of the seventh Sabbath [of
years],[2] a west wind will go out, and snow will come down from
heaven and hit the seed [that was sown]. After this, misfortunes
will occur every single month, doubling [their force each time].
Then [Israelites] will understand and say, "Surely this [marks the
birth pangs of] the king Messiah!" Even so, their views will not be
made up until the seventh [year]. They will be sentenced until their
faces are black as a pot's rim. How will they be sentenced? With

[1] Text from M. Friedmann (ed.), *Pesikta Rabbati* (Wien, 1880), 34-37. RPL
[2] Jubilee.

famine. The hearts of Israelites will only be broken through famine. Then the righteous ones of the generation will remove their tefillin, lay them on the ground, and say to him, "Master of the age, we have not acted properly all these years. Like sheep, we have gone astray." The holy One blessed be He will say to them, "It is forgiven." Then he will kiss them and place a crown upon them. The one who has merit [of the Torah] will be saved by the Torah, but what will support the one who has no merit of the Torah? You will learn that everyone who believes from the first year will have his reward doubled over and over again.

All who see them will acknowledge them (Isa 61:9). These are the mourners for Zion. The holy One blessed be He will appoint angels of destruction over his world. They will continue destroying all the days of redemption. The mourners for Zion will enter and leave with them. It is like a man who enters the house of his friend and then leaves without being harmed. [When the Israelites] see them, they will sit and say, "We laughed at them without cause; we scorned their words without cause." Rabbi bar Ḥanina said, (159a) "The merit of these [mourners for Zion] nurtured them, but our imagination followed them [improperly]. Concerning that hour Isaiah said, *Gentiles will see your righteousness* (Isa 62:2). These are the Gentiles who see the righteousness of the mourners for Zion. *And all the kings, your glory* (Isa 62:2). These are *kings. Your glory.* These are resourceful *kings* who see your *glory.* Therefore it is said, *Their seed will be known among the nations* (Isa 61:9).

Another interpretation: *Rejoice greatly, daughter of Zion; [shout, daughter of Jerusalem]; behold your king comes* (Zech 9:9). This one who is called *king* is destined to rule over the first generations and the last generations. The holy One blessed be He will proclaim to all the righteous men of every generation, saying, "Righteous men of the world, even though the words of the Torah are necessary for me, because you have waited for my Torah and not for my kingdom, there is an oath [on record] before me that I, myself, will testify in favor of everyone who waits for my kingdom, as it is said, *"Therefore, wait for me,"* says the Lord, *"for the day when I rise up to testify"* (Zeph 3:8). That is for the mourners who agonised with me over the destruction of my house and the desolation of my temple. Now I will testify in their favor, as it is said. *A contrite and a humble spirit* (Isa 57:15). Do not read *contrite* (את דכא) but *he made me contrite* (אתי דכא). These are the mourners for Zion who humbled their spirits, heard their

abuse, and remained silent, not defending their own goodness.[3]

Another interpretation: *For the day when I rise up to testify*
(Zeph 3:8). On *the day when I rise up to testify* for the Messiah,
whose scale of merit balances that of my household.[4] All these
attributes were before me, but you would not wait for me. They
will say to him, "Master of the age, you gave us a heart of stone,
and it led us astray. If Azza and Azazel, whose bodies were fire
when they fell to earth, sinned, would it not be all the more so for
us?"[5] He told them, "The mourners merit him, because they
praised him, and they rejected their own desires." In the hour all
the righteous ones of the world are destined to weep. (159b) They
will say to him, "Master of the age, they succeeded in the design,
but we did not succeed." In that hour, the holy One blessed be He
will say to them, "Do not weep, my holy ones, my noble ones; I
have already heard your prayer. Lest you forfeit the reward for
your Torah [study], all the reward [for your Torah study] will be
doubled, as it is said, *Therefore the Lord will wait to show mercy
to you. Therefore he will exceed in being merciful to you, for the
Lord is a God of justice. Happy are all they who wait for him.
People who dwell in Zion and Jerusalem will not weep. He will
pardon you [in response] to the voice of your outcry. When he
hears, he will answer you* (Isa 30:18-19). The merciful One is he
who gives you reward of the Torah. He will show favor to you
who eat [in] the days of the Messiah. *When he hears, he will
answer you* is for the age to come, and all those good things which
I will do for you are in virtue of the Messiah, who has been hidden
all these years.

Rabbi Yannai said in the name of Rab, "The holy Only blessed
be He will make everyone who watches for salvation lie down in
the Garden of Eden, as it is said, *I will feed my flock, and I will
make them to lie down* (Ezek 34:15).

Righteous and redeemed is he (Zech 9:9). This is the Messiah,
who vindicates his judgment over Israel, who laughed at him when

---

[3] Their acceptance of unfair abuse added sins to the demerit of their enemies and merits to
Israel's treasury of merits. See Mt 5:38-48; Rom 12:14-21.

[4] This is similar to Christian theology that claims Jesus' merit was enough to cover all the
sins of Christians. Paul, however, added his own sufferings to the treasury of merits to
complete that which was lacking in Christ's afflictions (Col 1:24). The Messiah of Joseph
was expected to suffer enough in seven years to cancel the sins of all Israel. The pronoun
"my" refers to God.

[5] Azazel was one of the fallen angels, and Azza may have been, too (Enoch 8:1-3; 9:6;
10:4-8; 13:1; 69:2). All sin was ascribed to Azazel (10:8); he and his army were to be
thrown into the abyss (54:5).

he sat in prison. He will be called *righteous.*[6] Why is he called *redeemed*, except that he vindicates judgment over them, saying to them, "You are all my sons, are you not?" Because you will all be saved by the mercies of the holy One blessed be He.

Afflicted and riding upon a donkey (Zech 9:9). This is the Messiah. Why is he called *afflicted*? Because he was *afflicted* all those years in prison when the transgressors of Israel laughed at him.[6] *Riding upon a donkey*, because the wicked have no merit of their own, [so] they continue to mention the [merits of the] fathers. By the merit of the Messiah, the holy One blessed be He shields them, makes them walk on a right path, and redeems them, as it is said, *They will come with weeping, and with supplications I will lead them. I will make them walk to the rivers of water in a right path, in which they will not stumble, because I have been a Father to Israel, and Ephraim is my first born son* (Jer 31:9).

Why does the scripture say, *He?* This is for the days of the Messiah, *he* is for the age to come, and none will come with him. His enemies *will clothe him with shame* (Ps 132:18). These are those who are divided because of him. *Upon him his crown will shine* (Ps 132:18). *Upon him* and *upon* those who exalt him.

Messianic Promises

Piska 35

(160a)   *"Sing and rejoice, daughter of Zion; for behold I am coming, and I will dwell in your midst," says the Lord* (Zech 2:14).

This is what was said through the Holy Spirit by Solomon, *If it is a wall, a turret of silver is built upon it. If it is a door, we will enclose it with cedar boards* (SS 8:9). With respect to whom did Solomon say this passage? He said it only with respect to the congregation of Israel. When the second temple was built, the Shekinah did not dwell in it, because the holy One blessed be He said, "If all Israelites come to the land, [the Shekinah] will dwell in it; if they do not, they can only employ a *bat qol*," as it is said, *Many of the priests and Levites and heads of the fathers' houses, the old men who had seen the first temple with their own eyes on its foundations, wept with a [loud voice, when this house was before their eyes]* (Ezra 3:12), saying, *Who among you who are left, who have seen this temple in its original glory? How do you see it today? Is it not small in your eyes*(Hag 2:3)?

---

[6] At which time he was suffering to cancel the sins and iniquities which Israel had accumulated.

Why half weeping and half rejoicing? The old men who had seen in glory this temple in which the Shekinah dwelled, and they saw the second temple in which the Shekinah did not dwell, were weeping. But their sons, who had not seen the glory of the first temple, saw the construction of the second temple, and they were glad. Therefore it is said, *Many of the priests and Levites and heads of fathers' houses [...wept...] and many with a shout of joy raised up their voice* (Ezra 3:12).

Rabbi Isaac said, "Why did not the Shekinah dwell in the second temple, which the exiled [Israelites] built? Because it was built by Cyrus, king of Persia, who was from the seed of Japhet,[7] and the Shekinah would not dwell in the works of the hands of Japhet. But the first house which the sons of Israel, the sons of Shem,[8] built the Shekinah dwelled in it, as it is said, *God will beautify the belongings of Japhet, but he will dwell in the tents of Shem* (Gen 9:27)."

Concerning the congregation of Israel, Solomon praised and said, *Who can find a woman of valor? Her price is far above rubies* (Prov 31:10). This scripture passage speaks only with reference to the Israelites. When they were exiled from their land, the ministering angels were saying to the holy One blessed be He, "Master of the age, when the Israelites were dwelling in their land, they held fast to idols, how much more so now that you have exiled them among the Gentiles!" What did the holy One blessed be He answer? "I am confident concerning my children that they will not abandon me and hold fast to idols, but will commit themselves to me every single hour. It is not enough that they commit themselves to me, but they will bring others near, under my wings.[9] If you wish, come and look at Egypt. Ten plagues only I brought against them, and they were unable to stand them, so they perished and became extinct, as he said, *They are extinct; they are quenched like a wick* (Isa 43:17). I brought only a few hardships against the kingdom of Babylon, and they were unable to stand them but rather were extinguished and left the world, as it is said, *Behold the land of the Chaldeans, this people no longer exists; the Assyrians established it for a wilderness; they raised siege towers; they stirred up its palaces. He made it a ruin* (Isa 23:13). But even though I bring hardships and tribulations against the Israelites in

---

[7] Japhet was one of the sons of Noah from which the Greeks were said to have descended (Gen 9:18-19). From his line descended Magog.

[8] Shem was one of the sons of Noah from which all the Semites from the eastern border of Egypt to Babylon descended (Gen 9:18-19).

[9] I.e., they will make proselytes.

the world, they are not repelled from me, but they remain for the age and for ages."

She will achieve good for him all the days of his life (Prov 31:12). *The holy One blessed be He* said to (160b) the ministering angels, "Come and I will tell you the righteousness of my children whom I burdened with many troubles in the world. I brought tribulations upon them in the world in every generation and in every hour. They did not kick against them when they called themselves, "wicked," and they called me "righteous" to my face. They say, in this expression, "But we have sinned; we have committed iniquity; we have acted wickedly; we have transgressed; we have rebelled; we have revolted; we have turned away from your commandments and ordinances, and it has been valueless to us. But you are righteous over all that comes upon us, for you act in truth, and we have acted wickedly. Therefore Solomon was praising the congregation of Israel [when he said], *Who can find a woman of valor* (Prov 31:10)? Therefore it is said, *If it is a wall* (SS 8:9).

Another interpretation: *Sing and rejoice* (Zech 2:14). Come and see what is written above about the subject, *"And I will be to her," says the Lord, "a wall of fire around, and I will be the glory in her midst"* (Zech 2:9). What is the *And I*, except thus said the holy One blessed be He, *"I and* all my household will make for Jerusalem a *wall* in the time to come, and I will command angels to guard her, as it is said, *I have appointed guards over your walls, Jerusalem"* (Isa 62:6). After the fire surrounds her, who will be able to enter into her midst? In the future, however, righteous men will walk in fire, just as a man who walks in the sun on a cold day, and it is enjoyable to him. If you are surprised at this word, come and see Ḥananiah, Mishael, and Azariah (Dan 2:19). At the time when Nebuchadnezzar threw them in the midst of the fiery furnace, they were walking like a man who walks in the sun on a cold day, and it is enjoyable to him, as it is said, *He answered and said, "I see four men loose, walking in the midst of the fire, and no harm has come to them. The appearance of the fourth is like a son of God"* (Dan 3:25). The text does not say, "The first," but *the fourth*. This is Gabriel, who was walking behind them as a disciple waiting on his teacher. This is to teach you that the righteous are greater than the ministering angels.

Another interpretation: *And the appearance of the fourth*. When Nebuchadnezzar saw Gabriel, he recognized him and said, "This is the one I saw in the war of Sennacherib, at the time when he burned them." Rabbi Eliezer the great said, "In the hour when Nebuchadnezzar saw Gabriel, all his limbs trembled, and he said, "This is the angel whom I saw in the war of Sennacherib, when he seemed like a small nozzle of fire, and he burned all his camp!" Therefore, it is said, *A wall of fire around* (Zech 2:9).

Is it not true that the dwelling place of the holy One blessed be He is only in heaven? [Look at the text] where it is said, *Above the heavens is his glory* (Ps 113:4). Then what is *I will be the glory in her midst* (Zech 2:9)? Rabbi Joshua ben Levi said, "To inform all the inhabitants of the world, the praise of the Israelites. Because of them the holy One blessed be He brings the Shekinah down from the highest heaven, and makes it dwell on earth. Thus it is said, *"And I will be to her,"* says the Lord, *"a wall of fire around, and I will be the glory in her midst"* (Zech 2:9). (161a) Another interpretation: *Sing and rejoice* (Zech 2:14)...*and many nations will join themselves to the Lord* (Zech 2:14-15). Rabbi Hanina bar Papa said that the scripture speaks only with respect to that hour when the holy One blessed be He will judge all the Gentiles in the future. At that time, the holy One blessed be He will bring all the proselytes who were converted [to Judaism] in the world and judge all the Gentiles before them. He will say to them, "Why did you leave me to serve idols who have no true reality?" They will say to him, "Master of the age, if we had come to your door, you would not have received us." He will say, "The proselytes who were converted [to Judaism] from your midst will testify against you." At once the holy One blessed be He will bring all the proselytes who were converted [to Judaism], and they will judge them and say to them, "Why did you abandon him to serve idols who have no true reality? Jethro--was he not a priest of idolatry? When he came to the door of the holy One blessed be He, he received him. Were we not idol worshippers? When we came to the door of the holy One blessed be He, he received us." At once all the wicked ones will be ashamed because of the reply of the proselytes. Then he will pass judgment, and they will depart from the world, as it is said, *At once they are both stupid and foolish; the instruction of vanities is wood* (Jer 10:8). Therefore it is said, *Sing and rejoice* (Zech 2:14).

Another interpretation: *Sing and rejoice* (Zech 2:14). When will this promise be fulfilled? At the time when the holy One blessed be He redeems Israel. Three days before the Messiah comes, Elijah will come and stand on the mountains of Israel, weep and mourn for them, and say, "Mountains of Israel, when will you stop being waste, dry, and desolate?" His voice will be heard from one end of the world to the other. After that he will say to them, "Peace has come into the world, as it is said, *Behold, upon the mountains are the feet of the one who proclaims good news of peace* (Nahum 2:1; Isa 52:7). When the wicked hear, they will all be glad and say, one to another, "Peace has come to us." On the second day, he will come and stand on the mountains of Israel and say, "Good has come into the world, as it is said, *Proclaiming good news of good* (Isa 52:7). On the third day, he will come and say, "Salvation has come into the world, as it is said, *Proclaiming salvation* (Isa 52:7). When he sees the wicked that they are saying thus and so, he will *say to Zion, "Your God has become king"* (Isa 52:7). This teaches that to Zion and her children salvation comes, but not to the wicked. In that hour the holy One blessed be He will show his glory and his kingdom to all those who come into the world. He will redeem Israelites and appear at their head, as it is said, *The breaker has gone up before them; they have broken out and passed the gate. They went through it. Their king passed by before them, with the Lord at their head* (Micah 2:13).

Messianic Sufferings

Piska 36

(161a) *Arise, shine, for your light has come, and the glory of the Lord has risen upon you,*
For, behold, darkness will cover the earth,
and deep darkness, the Gentiles;
but upon you the Lord will rise, and his glory will be seen upon you (Isa 60:1-2).

This is that which was said through the Holy Spirit by David, king of Israel, *For with you is the fountain of life, and in your light shall we see light* (Ps 36:10). With respect to whom did David say this verse? It was only said with respect to the congregation of Israel, which said to the holy One blessed be He, "Master of the age, because of the Torah which you have given me, which is called the *fountain of life* (Ps 36:10), I am destined to enjoy myself in your light in the future."

What is meant by *In your light we see light?* What is the *light* whcih the congregation of Israel expects? This is the *light* of the Messiah, as it is said, *And God saw the light that it was good* (Gen 1:4). This teaches that the holy One blessed be He watched for the Messiah (161b) in his works before the world was created, and then hid the Messiah under his throne of glory [to wait] for his generation.[10]

[10] I.e, the appointed time.

Satan said to the holy One blessed be He, "Master of the age, for whom is the light which is hidden under the throne of glory?" He said, "For the one who is destined to turn you back and make you look foolish with an embarrassed appearance." He said, "Master of the age, show him to me." [God] said to him, "Come and see him." When [Satan] saw him, he trembled and fell on his face and said, "Surely this is the Messiah who is destined to make me, and all the Gentile princes in Gehinnom, fall, as it is said, *Death is swallowed up forever,* and *The Lord will wipe away the tear from all the faces* (Isa 25:8). In that hour the nations will rage. They will say to him, "Master of the age, who is this, into whose hands we will fall? What is his name? What is his nature? The holy One blessed be He will say to them, "He is the Messiah. His name is Ephraim, my righteous Messiah. He will raise his stature and that stature of his generation. He will enlighten the eyes of the Israelites, and he will save his people. No nation or tongue will be able to stand against him, as it is said, *The enemy will not beguile him, and the son of perversity will not afflict him* (Ps 89:23). All his enemies and adversaries will flee, as it is said, *I will beat down his adversaries before him* (Ps 89:24). Even the rivers will stop flowing into the sea, as it is said, *I will set his hand on the sea, his right hand on the rivers* (Ps 89:26).

The holy One blessed be He will begin [to talk] with him [about] the condition. He will say, "These which have been hidden are those near you. Their iniquities are destined to humble you with a yoke of iron. They will make you like this calf, whose eyes have grown dim. They will choke your spirit with a yoke. By the iniquities of these, your tongue is destined to cleave to the roof of your mouth. Do you want this?" The Messiah will say to the holy One blessed be He, "Perhaps that hardship will last many years?" The holy One blessed be He will say, "By your life and the life of my head, [I swear] that I have decreed one week [of years] upon you, but if your soul is sad, I will drive them out at once." [The Messiah] said to him, "Master of the ages, with the joy of my soul and the gladness of my heart, I will take [these sufferings] so that no Israelite may perish; but not only that those who are alive will be saved in my days, but also those who are hidden in the dust; and not only that the dead of my days may be saved, but also those dead who died from the days of the first Adam until now; and not these only but also that the abortions may be saved in my days; and not only that these be saved in my days, but all those that came to your mind to create, that were not created.

Under these terms, I want [to do this]. Under these term, I will take [these sufferings]."[11]

At that time the holy One blessed be He will appoint four beasts which will carry the Messiah's throne of glory. Then his enemies and the princes of the kingdoms will say. "Come, let us bring charges against the generation of the Messiah, so that they may not be created for the age." The holy One blessed be He will say, "How can you bring charges against that generation which is treasured and pleasant and with which I am happy, in which I take delight, which I support, and which I desire, as it is said, *Behold my servant, whom I support, my chosen one whom my soul desires; I have put my spirit upon him, [he will bring justice to the Gentiles]* (Isa 42:1)?[12] How, then, can you bring charges against it [the Messiah's generation]? Behold I will destroy (162a) all of you kindlers of fire from fires of sparks! But I will not destroy one soul [of the Messiah's generation]." Therefore it is said, *"For with you is the fountain of life, and in your light shall we see light"* (Ps 36:10).

They say that during the week [of years] in which the son of David comes, they will bring iron beams and lay them on his neck until his stature is bowed low. He will cry aloud and weep, and his voice will reach heaven. He will say to [God], "Master of the age, how great is my strength? How strong is my spirit? How much breath [do I have]? How long will my members last? Am I not flesh and blood?"[13] Concerning that hour, David used to weep and say, *My strength is dried up like a potsherd* (Ps 22:16). At that time, the holy One blessed be He will say to him, "Ephraim, my righteous Messiah, you accepted [these punishments] upon yourself already since the six days of creation. Now let your pain be like my pain. From the day when wicked Nebuchadnezzar went up and destroyed my house, burned my temple, took my children exile among the nations of the world, by your life and by the life of my head, [I swear] I have not entered [my temple to sit on] my throne.[14] If you do not believe, look at the dew which has fallen on my head, as it is said, *My head is filled with dew, my locks with drops of the night* (SS 5:2).

[11] This agreement is based on the treasury of merits theology. The Messiah was required to suffer enough to pay off all the sins of Israel. See introduction for details.

[12] Meaning that he will wreak vengeance on the Gentiles as they deserve.

[13] In many places the term, "flesh and blood," refers to the Gentiles. Here, however, that is not true. The Messiah is "flesh and blood," i.e., human.

[14] This means the Lord was not king when there was no temple and no son of David on the throne. This concurs with the conclusions of other rabbis. See Sifrē *Debarim* 32:10; Yalkut I. 408 to *Vayakhel*.

At that time [the Messiah] said, "Master of the age, now my mind is settled. It is enough for a servant that he be like his master." Rabbi Levi said, "At the time when the holy One blessed be He says to the congregation of Israel, *Arise, shine, for your light has come* (Isa 60:1), it will say to him, 'Master of the age, stand at our head.' Then the holy One blessed be He will say to it, 'My daughter, you have spoken properly, as it is said, *My beloved spoke and said to me, "Arise, my love, my beauty, and come away"* (SS 2:10). "For the oppression of the afflicted, for the sighing of the poor, now I will arise," and the Lord'" (Ps 12:6).

Another interpretation: Why is the congregation of Israel in this world compared to a cripple? Because he is not able to come and go, and the Gentiles mock them and say to them every day, "Where is your God? Why does he not deliver you?" It will say, "I have a day which is appointed for my king to reveal himself because of me. He will seize me and stand me on my feet, as it is said, *For the oppression of the afflicted, for the sighing of the poor, now I will arise*, says the Lord, *I will establish for him the deliverance for which he longs* (Ps 12:6). My beloved will answer and say to me, '*Arise, my love, my beauty, and come away*'" (SS 2:10).

Rabbi Isaac said, "In the year in which the king Messiah is revealed, all the kings of the Gentiles will be provoked with one another. The king of Persia will be provoked with the king of Arabia. The king of Arabia will go to Edom and take counsel from them [the Edomites]. The king of Persia will return and destroy the whole world. All the Gentiles will be disturbed and frightened. They will fall on their faces and pangs will seize them like the pangs of a woman giving birth. Israelites will be disturbed and frightened, and they will say, 'Where shall we go? Where shall we come?' [God] will say to them, 'My children, do not be afraid. All that I have done, I have done only because of you. Of what are you afraid? Do not be afraid. The time of your redemption has arrived. This latter redemption will not be like the former redemption, because the former redemption was oppressive for you, and subservience to the kingdoms that followed it. But [in] the latter redemption, you will have no oppression, and subservience to the kingdoms will not follow it.'"

Our rabbis have taught: In the hour when the king Messiah is revealed, he will come and stand on the roof of the house of the sanctuary. He will announce to the Israelites and say to them, "Afflicted ones, the time for your redemption has arrived. (162b) If you do not believe, look at my light which shines upon you, as it is said, *Arise, shine, for your light has come, and the glory of the Lord has shone upon you* (Isa 60:1). Only upon you it *shines*, but not upon the Gentiles, as it is said, *For behold, darkness will cover the earth, and deep darkness, the Gentiles; but upon you the Lord will shine, and his glory will be seen upon you* (Isa 60:2).

At that time the holy One blessed be He will make the *light* of the king Messiah and of the Israelites *shine*. All the Gentiles will be in *darkness* and gloom. They will all walk to the light of the Messiah and of the Israelites, as it is said, *Nations will walk to your light, and kings to the brightness of your shining* (Isa 60:3). They will come and lick the dust from under the feet of the king Messiah, as it is said, [("The inhabitants of] the isles will entreat him and *lick the dust of his feet"* (Isa 49:23). They will all come and fall on their faces before the Messiah and before the Israelites and say to them, "Let us be slaves to you and to the Israelites." Every single Israelite will have two thousand, eight hundred slaves, as it is said, *It will be in that day that ten men will take hold, from all the languages of the nations; they will take hold of the shirt tail of a Jew, saying, "Let us go with you, for we have heard that God is with you"* (Zech 8:23).

Vindication
Piska 37

(162b)   *Rejoicing, I will rejoice in the Lord; my soul will delight*
                                        in my God;
          for he has clothed me with garments of salvation;
                        he has covered me with a robe of
                        righteousness,
          As a bridegroom adorns himself with ornaments, and as his
                        bride puts on her jewels (Isa 61:10).

This is what was said through the Holy Spirit by Jeremiah, *Then will the virgin rejoice in the dance, and young men and old men together; I will change their mourning to joy, and I will comfort them and make them rejoice from their sorrow* (Jer 31:13). With respect to whom did Jeremiah say this passage? He only spoke with respect to the days of the Messiah, when the holy One blessed be He will abundantly provide great benefits for the Israelites, as it is said, *How great is your goodness, which you have stored up for those who fear you! You have performed for those who take refuge in you before the sons of men* (Ps 31:20). This teaches that the fathers of the world will arise at Nisan and say to him,

"Ephraim, our righteous Messiah, even though we are your fathers, you are greater than we are, because you suffered for the iniquities of our children. Seven measures passed over you so that they would not pass over the first ones nor the last ones. You were a laughing stock and a derision among the Gentiles because of the Israelites. You dwelled in darkness and gloom, and your eyes did not see light. Your skin cleaved to your bones, and your body was dry as wood. Your eyes grew dim from fasting, and your strength was as dry as a potsherd. All of these [punishments] were because of the iniquities of our children. You wanted our children to enjoy some of this goodness which the holy One blessed be He would provide abundantly for Israelites. Perhaps it is because of the distress which you suffered extremely (163a) that they fettered you in prison, [and] your mind is not at rest from them." He said to them, "Fathers of the world, all that I have done, I did only for you, your sons, your glory, and the glory of your children, that they might enjoy some of this goodness which the holy One blessed be He will provide abundantly for the Israelites." The fathers of the world will say to him, "Ephraim, our righteous Messiah, let your mind be at rest, because you have put the mind of your Creator and our minds at rest."

Shimon ben Pazzi said, "Then the holy One blessed be He will raise the Messiah to the heaven of heavens, and he will spread upon him the splendor of his glory before the Gentiles and before the wicked Persians. [God] will say to him, 'Ephraim, our righteous Messiah, be the judge of these and do with them whatever your soul desires. If [God's] mercies had not been extremely powerful in your behalf, they would already have destroyed you from the world in an instant, as it is said, *Is not Ephraim a dear son to me? Is he not a pleasant child? For whenever I speak of him I earnestly remember still. Therefore my heart longs for him. Mercifully, I will have mercy on him,' says the Lord* (Jer 31:20). Why does it say, *Mercifully I will have mercy on him* (Jer 31:20), [using the word *mercy*] two times? *Mercifully* is for the time when he will be in prison, when every single day the Gentiles will gnash their teeth, wink their eyes, shake their heads, and open wide their lips, as it is said, *All who see me mock me; they [shoot out] the lip; they shake the head* (Ps 22:8). *My strength is dry as a potsherd; my tongue cleaves to my throat; and you lay me in the dust of death* (Ps 22:16). They roar against me like lions, as it is said, *They open their mouths against me like a tearing, roaring lion. I am poured out like water, and all my bones are out of joint;*

my heart has become like wax. It is melted within me (Ps 22:14-15).They roar over him like *lions,* and try to swallow him, as it is said, *All our enemies have opened their mouths against us. Terror and the pit have come against us, desolation and destruction"* (Lam 3:46-47).

I will have mercy on him (Jer 31:20) is for the time when he will go out of prison, because not one kingdom, not two kingdoms, and not three kingdoms will come against him, but a hundred and forty kingdoms will surround him. Then the holy One blessed be He will say to him, "Ephraim, my righteous Messiah, do not be afraid of them, because all of these will die with the breath of your lips, as it is said, *With the breath of his lips he will kill the wicked* (Isa 11:4). At once the holy One blessed be He will make for the Messiah seven canopies of precious stones and pearls, and from the midst of every single canopy will flow four rivers; one of wine, one of honey, one of milk, and one of pure balsam. Then the holy One blessed be He will embrace him before the righteous ones, and bring him into the canopy. All the righteous ones will see him, and all the pious ones, the holy ones, and all the mighty men of the Torah of every generation will see him.

The holy One blessed be He will say to the righteous ones: "Righteous ones of the world, Ephraim, my righteous Messiah, has still not received [payment] for half his hardship. I have still one measure which I will give him, which no eye from the world has seen, as it is said, *Eye has not seen, O God, besides you, [what] he will do to those who wait for him"* (Isa 64:3). At that time the holy One blessed be He will call the north wind and the south wind and he will say to them, "Come, honor, and lay down before Ephraim, my righteous Messiah, all kinds of spices from the Garden of Eden, as it is said, *Awake, North wind; come, South [wind], blow upon my Garden; let its spices flow. Let my beloved come to his garden and eat his pleasant fruits "* (SS 4:16). Therefore it is said, *Then will the virgin rejoice in the dance, [the young men and old men together; I will change their mourning to joy, and I will comfort them and make them rejoice from their sorrow"]* (Jer 31:13).

Another interpretation: *Rejoicing, I will rejoice* (Isa 61:10). *Rejoicing* in the days of the Messiah; *I will rejoice* with the downfall of wicked Rome. *My soul will delight in my God* (Isa 61:10). This is the war of Gog and Magog.

Another interpretation: *Rejoicing, I will rejoice in the Lord* (Isa 61:10). *Rejoicing* is for deliverance from the judgment of Gehinnom. *I will rejoice* in the evil impulse when it is uprooted from the

midst of Israel. *My soul will delight in my God* (Isa 61:10) when
our iniquities are forgiven.

(163b) Another interpretation: *Rejoicing, I will rejoice in the Lord;
my soul will delight in my God* (Isa 61:10). *Rejoicing* when the
angel of death is swallowed from their midst. *I will rejoice* for the
days of the Messiah. *My soul will delight in my God* for the age to
come which has no end.

For he has clothed me with garments of salvation (Isa 60:10).
The holy One blessed be He will wear seven garments from the
day when the world was created until he rejects wicked Edom.
When he created the world he wore glory and majesty, as it is said,
You are clothed with glory and majesty (Ps 104:1). When he was
revealed to us on the sea, he wore pride, as it is said, *The Lord is
king; he is wearing pride* (Ps 93:1). When he gave the Torah to his
people he was wearing strength, as it is said, *The Lord will give
strength to his people* (Ps 29:11). When he was released from the
Chaldeans, he wore vengeance, as it is said, *He put on garments of
vengeance* (Isa 59:17). When he forgives the iniquities of the
Israelites, he will wear a white garment, as it is said, *His garment
was white as snow* (Dan 7:9). When the Messiah is revealed, he
will wear a garment of righteousness, as it is said, *He will wear
righteousness as a coat of mail* (Isa 59:17). He will wear a red garment, as it is said, *Why are your garments red* (Isa 63:2)? This is
vengeance of Edom. In that hour the ministering angels will say to
the holy One blessed be He, "Master of the age, the attractive
garment which you are wearing is more becoming to you than all
the previous garments which you wore, as it is said, *This one is
glorious in his apparel* (Isa 63:1).

(164a) *As a bridegroom adorns himself with ornaments* (Isa 61:10).
This teaches that the holy One blessed be He will put on Ephraim,
our righteous Messiah, a garment whose splendor will shine from
one end of the world to the other, and Israelites will make use of
his light. They will say, "Blessed is the hour when he was created.
Blessed is the womb from which he came (see Lk 11:27). Blessed is
the generation whose eyes see him; Blessed is the eye that waited
for him, whose lips open [to pronounce] blessing and peace, whose
speech quiets the spirit, whose heart meditates confidence and
tranquility. Blessed is the eye which merits him, whose tongue
speaks pardon and forgiveness for the Israelites, whose prayer is a
sweet savor [to the Lord], whose supplication is pure and holy.
Blessed are his fathers who merited goodness of the [messianic]
age, but who are hidden forever."

And as a bride puts on her jewels (Isa 61:10). Why is the congregation of Israel compared to a bride? To tell that just as a bride is received only with her jewels, so also the adversaries of [the Israelites] can only be put to shame by their [the Israelites'] merit.[15]

Another interpretation: *And as a bride puts on her jewels* (Isa 61:10). Just as a *bride* is laden with favor before all who see her, so also the congregation of Israel at the time when she came up from Babylon at the end of the sabbatical year was laden with favor before all the kingdoms. If your soul should say, just as this *bride*, when the days of her joy are completed, returns to her occupation, so also the congregation of Israel will have enslavement after her redemption; the scripture says, *[And the ransomed of the Lord will return] and come to Zion with singing, with joy of the age upon their heads* (Isa 35:10; 51:11).

Summary

The author of these sermons looked forward to redemption as the time when the social structure on this earth would be reversed. Those who now were happy would then suffer and those who were now suffering would then be happy. The time of redemption depended on the amount of suffering Jews were willing to accept at this time. The more they suffered the better. Like Christians, Jews should walk the second mile, turn the other cheek (Mt 5:38-40), bless their persecutors (Rom 12:14-20), and in other ways suffer in the flesh (I Pet 4:1). The best example of this is the mourners for Zion, whose virtue would later be rewarded. The Messiah of Ephraim also had suffered immensely in prison for the sins of Israel, and he would enter Jerusalem afflicted, and riding on a donkey. When, according to the treasury of merits, there had been enough suffering, then the Lord would redeem the Jews, overthrow the Gentile kings, introduce the Messiah, rebuild Jerusalem, establish a sanctuary where the Shekinah could dwell, provide Jews with high status and numerous slaves. At the same time the Gentiles would be made to suffer.

The author believed, as other rabbis, that the Lord was not king when Israel was not free from foreign domination. Even the

---

[15] I.e., the merit of Israel will outweigh the Gentiles in the treasury of merits. Then the Lord will "foreclose" the Gentiles because of the comparative deficiency. Paul said, "If your enemy is hungry, feed him; if he is thirsty, give him [something] to drink; for by so doing you will heap burning coals upon his head (Prov 25:21-22). Do not be overcome by evil, but overcome evil with good" (Rom 12:20-21; see also *Consequences*, 31-41).

second temple was not approved because of Gentile influence. Therefore, there was no place for the Shekinah, no throne for the Lord, and the Lord was not king. When the Lord redeemed Israel, he would again become king and his Shekinah would dwell in Jerusalem. Like Saadia, he believed that the Messiah son of Ephraim must precede the Messiah son of David, and like Saadia, he believed the Messiah son of Ephraim must suffer meritoriously for Israel. This author, however, emphasized the suffering role primarily because he was convinced in the merit of vicarious suffering. Although he believed there was a heaven and a Gehinnom, the Garden of Eden and redemption would take place for Jews here on earth, centered around Jerusalem.

Introduction to Maimonides

Moses ben Maimon, philosopher, talmudist, astronomer, and physician, was born in Cordova, Spain (A.D. 1135) and died in Cairo, Egypt (A.D. 1204). At Cairo he became the personal physician to Saladin's vizier who bestowed many distinctions upon him. He was a giant among the Jewish scientists and philosophers of his day, and he produced the most satisfactory results in his efforts to combine philosophy with religion. To this day he is admired as the protagonist of Judaism. His extensive scholarly works reflect his keen analytical ability, his high purpose, and his comprehensive academic achievement. Jews from all over Europe and the East turned to him for advice and direction. The letter to Yemen, part of which is here translated, was written in A.D. 1172 to Jacob ben Nathanael, chief of the talmudical academy in Yemen. It reflects the widespread and intense belief in the immediate arrival of the Messiah. In the untranslated portion of the letter, Maimonides dealt with personal matters and religious counsel on practical problems, such as the polemics necessary to refute the Moslems and the Christians. He was very practical and prudent in his counsel, but he also believed the Messiah would come during his own lifetime. This letter also indicates the social, political, economic, and military implications of this doctrine of redemption that were closely related to the political leadership of the Messiah in restoring the Jews to a position of international leadership from their ancient capital of Jerusalem. The recipients of this letter were not odd people with peculiar beliefs, but they were typical of twelfth century Judaism, both in the East and in the West.[1]

EPISTLE TO YEMEN

III

Calculating the End

Maimonides[2]

Now you mentioned the topic of ends and the views of our rabbi Saadia. This is what is necessary for you to know about them.

---

[1] See further I. Broydé, "Moses Ben Maimon," *JE*. 73-82.
[2] Text from J. Kafih, אגר. ת, רבי מושה בן מימון (Jerusalem, 1972). RPL

Note first that you must realize that no man will ever be able to know the precise time of the end. Just as Daniel explained and saw that the matters are closed and sealed (Dan 12:9). Of course, there are many hypotheses which some scholars directed toward this, and what they imagine they have achieved [the accurate date]. Already [the scripture] told us in advance about it. It is said, *Many will wander to and fro, and knowledge will increase* (Dan 12:4), that is, there will be many views. Already the Lord has explained through his prophets that many men would calculate the end times for the Messiah, but they have proved false, and they were not fulfilled. We warned against doubting because of this. He said, "Do not let the fallaciousness of their calculating lead you astray, but everything which adds to the delay should add to the hope for him." He said, *He hastens to the end. He will not lie. If he seems slow, wait for him, for he will surely come and will not be late* (Hab 2:3).[3]

Be sure that even the end whose time the Lord explained, such as the exile of Egypt, was not known exactly. He said, *They will serve them [the Egyptians]; and they [the Egyptians] will afflict them for four hundred years* (Gen 15:13). There was difficulty about it. [Some] men then calculated that this meant four hundred years from the time the servitude began, which was seventy years after Jacob went down into Egypt. [Other] men thought that it was the time when the word took place, the event *between the pieces* (Gen 15:17). When four hundred years had been completed after the event *between the pieces,* some Israelites left Egypt, thirty years before Moses arose. They thought the exile had already completed [its predestined duration].[4] They were destroyed. The Egyptians killed them and made the servitude more severe. Thus the scholars (May they be remembered for good) who know the history of our nation, inform us. Concerning those who imagined the redemption had failed, David (upon whom be peace) said, *The sons of Ephraim, my archers; those who shoot the bow, turned back in the day of battle* (Ps 78:9).

The correct time was four hundred years from the time when Isaac, the seed of Abraham, was born, as [the Lord] (May he be

---

[3] The subject seems to be the Messiah, though grammatically it is possible that the subject is predestined time, and the pronouns should be rendered "it."

[4] Here Maimonides compared the exodus from Egypt to the exodus from the "fourth kingdom" without any essential change in eschatology. He assumed that the people in Egypt calculated times just as the Jews of his time were doing. The redemption sought by Jews of Maimonides' day was precisely the one gained in the exodus from Egypt and the entrance into the promised land.

exalted) said, *Your seed will be a stranger in a land not theirs. They will serve them [the Egyptians] and they [the Egyptians] will afflict them for four hundred years* (Gen 15:13). In the midst of their existence as strangers, they will dominate them, subjugate them, and afflict them. This is the way he interprets the passage, the four hundred years are years of being strangers, not of being slaves. This was not made clear until he sent the great prophet [Moses] and [now] it is [certain that] from the day Isaac was born until the Israelites left Egypt, exactly four hundred years elapsed. If this was the case with the time whose duration was defined, how much the more so with the time which is extended that frightened and worried the prophets. They dragged and extended [their prediction] until the prophet said by way of question, *Is it for the age that you will be angry with us? Will you draw out your wrath from generation to generation* (Ps 85:6)? Also Isaiah, in his description of the long extension, said, *They will surely be gathered together, a prisoner over his pit. They will lock the prison, but after many days, they will be visited* (Isa 24:22).

Already Daniel has explained to us the strong depth of this end time and its impossibility of being known (Dan 12:9). Therefore the scholars (May they be remembered for good) warned against calculating the times and pin-pointing the time when the Messiah would come, because they caused the masses to stumble, and they led them astray when that time arrived, and he failed to come. Their saying was, "May the minds of those who calculate the times blow up!" (San 97b: "May their breath expire!"), because they are a stumbling block to people, and therefore [the rabbis] cursed them. May the Lord prove their explanation false and destroy their counsels!

We find excuses for our rabbi Saadia. It is necessary to say this, for that which has come to my hands is as follows: even though he knew that the Torah warned against this, because the men of his generation multiplied views and misconceptions among themselves. It was likely that the religion of the Lord would disappear, if he (May he be remembered for good) had not disclosed from it [the Torah] that which was hidden, according to that which had already been [disclosed] and strengthened that which had been weak. He calculated, published, and edited both by speech and pen. He tried with complete earnestness to captivate the masses of the people by calculating the times so as to encourage their hope for truth. He (May he be remembered for good), all his work was for the name of Heaven (Pirke Aboth 2:6).

We should not condemn him for his mistaken [calculations of] the times which he made, for the basis of the matter is that which I have described to you.

But what is this which I see that you incline toward [a belief in] astrology, the connections that exist, [and] that which is destined to happen?[5] Dismiss everything of this [nature] from your imagination, just as you launder your soiled clothes from their dirt, because these are things which have no approval in the circles of the accomplished scholars, even if they are not learned in Torah, how much the more so those who are learned in the Torah, is their futility clear and obvious in learned discussions of truth, but this is not the place to mention [them] here.

You should know that when our leader Moses (upon whom be peace) arose, the astrologers had already agreed on the basis of astrology that the nation [of Israel] would not succeed; there would be no escape from its position [of servitude] for the age. At that time, when they imagined [they had reached] the depth of humiliation, good fortune came to it, and there arose in it a choice human species and redemption.[6] [It happened at] that very time when the star gazers agreed that the air of the land of Egypt would be wholesome, vegetation would grow, and human beings would be especially fortunate, the plagues began. Isaiah said in his description of these conditions, *Where then are your wise men? Let them tell you and make known what the Lord of armies had counselled Egypt* (Isa 19:12).

Thus the kingdom of the wicked Nebuchadnezzar: at the time when his wisemen and seers agreed with the star-gazers and everyone who claimed that he had advance knowledge in this matter that this was the beginning of their prosperity, and that their rule would continue, then the kingdom was destroyed, and it perished, just as the Lord had promised. Isaiah said further, mocking them about this [and] deriding them because they claimed ability to predict future events, and [the divided] kingdom itself which imagined that it had scholars who were able to use their wisdom. He said, *Let them arise now and deliver you,*

[5] This further reference to astrology and prophecy shows how influential that movement was during the Middle Ages.

[6] The chosen people, the Israelites, who left Egypt to establish the nation on the promised land. The exodus and the conquest of Canaan was called redemption, just as the reestablishment of the Davidic kingdom under the rule of the son of David, ruling from Jerusalem, was called the anticipated redemption. Both are nationalistic, military, and political. There is no indication at all that Maimonides knew anything about a spiritualized redemption, kingdom of God, or eschatology such as those views proposed by nineteenth and twentieth century European and American eschatologists.

those who divide the heavens, gaze at the stars, [who at the new moons predict what will happen to you] (Isa 47:13).

This is the way the matter will be for the days of the Messiah (May he be revealed quickly), because when the Gentiles imagine that the nation [of Israel] will not have a kingdom for the age, no self-rule, and no exaltation from its present position, and all the star-gazers, magicians, and soothsayers. At that time the Lord will prove their imaginations and erroneous opinions false, and he will reveal the Messiah. Isaiah said, in his interpretation of this topic, *Who frustrates the omens of liars, and makes fools of diviners; who turns wise men back and makes their knowledge foolish; who establishes the word to his servant and fulfills the counsel of his messengers, who says to Jerusalem, "She shall be inhabited," and of the cities of Judah, "You shall be rebuilt"* (Isa 44:25-26). This is the correct view which every Israelite should hold, but do not turn to the words of someone who says there is a connection [between this and] the small or large [stars].

I notice that you say there is but little science in your land, and there you are cut off from scholarship. You have given as the reason the connection to the earthly trigon. Be assured that this situation is not unique to your land, but it exists today in all Israel, that is the shortage of scholars and the weakness of science (See JGit 1:5). The real reason, therefore, is that which [the Lord] (May he be exalted) threatened through Isaiah, and he said, *Therefore, behold I will again amaze this people [with something] wonderful and marvelous: the wisdom of their wise shall perish, and the discernment of their scholars shall be hidden* (Isa 29:14).

There is no [celestial] reason [for this], not from the earthly trigon and not from the fiery trigon. This is proved by Solomon, king of Israel, of whom the scripture testified, *He was the wisest of all men* (I Kgs 5:11). He existed only in the midst of the earthly trigon. The same was true of Abraham, our father, (upon whom be peace), who was the pillar of the age (Tanḥuma Ex 19; ExR 2:13). He it was who discovered the primal cause of the ages and appointed a single foundation for all men. Also Isaac and Jacob, all three of whom carried the throne of glory in their hearts when they achieved it in truth, just as he said, "The fathers are the chariots" (GenR 82:7). These three fathers were also in the midst of the earthly trigon.

All this becomes clear, with that which was already known, because there is a small meeting of Saturn and Jupiter (שבת וצדק). When they are gathered together a second time, there will be approximately twenty changes of the sun [i.e., years], and they will not cease meeting in this trigon itself, for twelve meetings. There will be a duration in the connection in the first trigon, one for every two hundred, forty years. After this, it will pass over from their connection to another trigon. This one is called the medial conjunction, the conjunction that transfers the misfortune (ההוה) every two hundred, forty years. It takes place according to this order: when these two stars meet in a constellation with an appointed degree, this is the degree which will continue until there are gathered in the strong degree every nine hundred, sixty years. This is the enormous conjunction [which happens] every thousand years, less forty years. That is the meeting of Saturn and Jupiter in the first minute of Aries until they are joined a second time.

When you review the last reckoning, all that I have said will make sense to you. Thus Abraham, Isaac, and Jacob existed in the earthly trigon, and so also David and his son, Solomon. I have only explained this to you so as to remove this confusion from you, so that you will not suppose that there is in the trigon any cause for this [situation].

You say that men have calculated the coming conjunction, and have found that all seven stars will come together in one fortune (constellation of the Zodiac). The report is not correct no matter who told you this. There are no discoveries of a meeting of the seven [stars] at all, not in the next conjunction nor in the fifty conjunctions after that! This is not at all possible, even in ten thousand years [according to the views held] among those really well-versed in the movements of the stars. These words [you have heard] are only words of someone who knows nothing about calculations. According to your description of his intelligence, when he said there will be a flood of air and dust, it is proper for you to know that these words and [others] like them are vain and false words. Do not accept in your midst the view that [words] are true when they are found written in a book, because a liar lies with his pen just as he lies with his tongue, and this [method of communication] will not prevent him from [doing] it. Those who hold the view that written words are [inevitably] true are simple ignoramuses, but the veracity [of the statement] is only shown in another manner. Remember that just as the blind man gives over his guidance to one who can see to lead him, because he knows that he has no eyes to show him the right path; and just as one who is no expert in healing transfers his guidance to a physician to direct him because he does not know the things that damage and the things that help, and he gladly accepts from him all that he says; thus it is proper for the majority of scholars to hand over their leadership to farsighted seers who can really see, and be satisfied with this which they teach them which individual view is correct and which one is incorrect. Next to the prophets are the scholars who study night and day concerning the views, methods, and opinions so that they might discern the correct ones from the incorrect.

After this introduction, listen to me, because all that you have heard or found written from these words and those like them are all words which have no truth in them, but they are arrogant, foolish, false, or their goal is to destroy the Torah and raze its walls. Here you see the impudence in saying [there will be] a flood of air and a flood of dust.[7] Thus, they will say, a flood of fire! All of this is to delude and deceive so as to show that even the flood [of Noah] was only a torrent of water. It was not from the Lord to punish the inhabitants of the earth concerning their destruction, just as [the Lord] explained in the book [that directs us from error]. According to this [misguided] way, however, Sodom and its rivers were not changed because of [the people's] unbelief and wickedness, as he explained and said, *[I will go down and see whether they have done altogether] according to their cry which has come to me; [and if not, I will know]* (Gen 18:21). Thus every single work which is done by the Lord in the world will be something forced by [planetary] conjunctions, [according to these people]!

This is the introduction which they want to advance so as to raze the foundations of the Torah, so as to become heretics, walking in their strivings and animal lusts like animals and ostriches. Concerning these views, [the Lord] (May he be exalted) warned in his book and informed us saying, "If you rebel, then I will bring plagues upon you, punishing you for your deeds: If you are of the opinion that the sicknesses among you are something which happened accidently, and it is not caused by your rebellion, then I will double it." This is what he said in "Admonition"; *If you walk contrary* (קרי) *to me, then I will also walk contrary* (בקרי) *to you, and I will strike you, even I, seven times for all your sins* (Lev 26:23-24). קרי (contrary) means "an accident" "something that happens." He said, *If you make my punishment an event that happens by chance, I will increase [the punishment] upon you, making that accident seven times for your sins* (Lev 26:23-24)!

---

[7] See the table of contents for a translation of the astrological prophecy mentioned here.

You can see from all that I have told you up to this point that it is clear that the subject of the Messiah does not depend upon astrological insights in any manner or means. Already one of the learned men from our midst here in Spain predicted the end through astrology. He predicted that the Messiah would be revealed in a certain year. There is not one of our scholars or *ḥasidim* who has not belittled his views, reproached him for what he did, and they have rebuked him very severely, but ensuing events have treated him more severely and punitively than anything which we did. The time when he said the Messiah would be revealed, the rebel of the region of Maghreb went out and issued an [anti-Jewish] order for the conversion [from Judaism] that reached you. He has only brought the severity of the exile upon us, but a drowning man grasps at straws.[6]

Therefore brothers, *fortify yourselves, be strong, and let your hearts be courageous, all you that wait for the Lord* (Ps 31:25). Let each encourage the other, implant this conviction concerning the Messiah (May he be speedily revealed) deeply in your hearts. *Strengthen the weak hands and make firm the knocking knees* (Isa 35:3). Be assured that the Lord has already announced to us through Isaiah, the national herald of good news, that the exile would be extended strongly upon us and that many would imagine from it that the Lord had abandoned us and withheld his mighty works from us (May this never be). Therefore he has promised under oath that he would not abandon us and he would not relinquish us. He said, *Zion will say, "The Lord has forsaken me; the Lord has forgotten me"* (Isa 49:14). But he has replied, saying, *Can a woman forget her sucking child that she should not show pity on the son of her womb [These may forget, but I will not forget you]* (Isa 49:15). Through the first emissary [Moses], the Lord has announced this, saying, *For the Lord your God is a merciful God. He will not fail you nor destroy you [nor forget the covenant of your fathers which he swore to them]* (Dt 4:31); and he said, *The Lord your God will return your captivity [and have mercy on you. He will return and gather you from all the peoples where the Lord your God has scattered you]* (Dt 30:3).

My brothers, this is the greatest of all foundations of the Israelite doctrine (San 10:1), that is necessary for a man to arise from the seed of Solomon, son of David. He will take over our

---

[6] It is evident that Maimonides knew something about astrology, even though he denied its validity.

leadership. He will gather our dispersed and our exiles. He will disclose the true religion; he will destroy everyone who sets himself against him, just as the Lord promised in the Torah, saying, *I see him, but not now; I behold him, but not near. [A star will step forth from Jacob; a scepter will arise in Israel. He will beat down the corners of Moab, and break down all the sons of Seth]. Edom will become a possession* (Num 24:17-18), because the time of his revelation will be a very great and difficult time for the nation, as he said, *There will be none remaining, shut up or left at large* (Dt 32:36). Then the Lord will disclose him, and he will do that which he promised concerning him. The prophet in his vision told of the difficulty of the time of his revelation, *Who can endure the time of his coming* (Mal 3:2)? This is the correct doctrine of that which is bound to happen.

But concerning his time, already it was explained in all the words of Daniel, Isaiah, and from all that the scholars have mentioned that he will arise only when the kingdom of Edom and Arabia are expanded in the world, just as the situation is today.[9] Of this there can be no doubt or question. [In] the last [part] of Daniel, the one whom he describes is the Ishmaelite kingdom and the rise to power of a certain one [Mohammed], and shortly after the arrival of the Messiah [will take place]. Thus Isaiah explained that the proof of the advent of the Messiah was the appearance of the crazy person [Mohammed]. He said, *Rider on a donkey, a rider on a camel, two men riding on horses. [Pay attention. Pay very close attention]* (Isa 21:7). The *rider on a donkey* is the Messiah, as he said, *Humble and riding on a donkey* (Zech 9:9). He will only come in the wake of the rise [to power] of one *riding on a camel*—that is, the Arabian kingdom. He said, *two men riding on horses*. This refers to two nations, Edom and Ishmael. Thus is given an explanation which allows no doubt from the vision of the statue (Dan 2) and the vision of the beasts (Dan 7), mentioned in Daniel. These words are seen from the literal reading of the scripture.

But the precise time truly no one knows; but I have in my possession a marvelous tradition which I received from my father, who received it from his father's grandfather's grandfather, going back to the beginning of our exile from Jerusalem. It is just as the prophet promised and said, *The exiles from Jerusalem who are in Spain* (Obad 20). This [tradition] is that there is among the passages of the prophecy of Balaam, a passage in which there is an

---

[9] By "Edom" Maimonides meant Rome. By "Arabia" he meant Islam.

allusion to the return of prophecy to Israel, following the passage, according to which it is already said in the Torah passages, which, even if that which is intended in them is a definite topic, they contain a hint of a different topic. Such as when Jacob said, *Go down from there* (Gen 42:2), according to which we lived in Egypt for the number רדו, *go down*, two hundred, ten years [according to gematria] (GenR 71:2). Also our leader Moses said, *When you beget children and grandchildren, you shall have grown old in the land* (Dt 4:25). We remained in the land of Israel from the day we entered until the exile of King Jehoichin, the number ונושנתם *(You shall have grown old)*, [which is] eight hundred, forty years [in gematria]. Many [passages] like this could be cited.

Through this prediction we received, he, that is Balaam, said, *In time he will say with reference to Jacob and Israel, "What has God accomplished"* (Num 23:23)? There is in [this passage] a secret [message], from which time is to be counted from the six days of creation until that time, and prophecy will return to Israel. The prophets said to them, *What has God accomplished* (Num 23:23)? This message was [given] in the thirty-eighth year after the exodus from Egypt. There elapsed from the beginning date until the day two thousand, four hundred, eighty five years, for the symbol ב'ת'י'מ'ח' [=2,448 years. ב'י'ת'י'פ'ה' =2,485 years] means redemptions. According to this deduction and this interpretation, prophecy will return to Israel in the year four thousand, nine hundred, seventy years from creation (A.D. 1210).[10] There is no doubt that the return of prophecy must precede the Messiah, as he said, *And it will happen after this, I will pour out [my spirit on all flesh, and your sons and your daughters will prophesy. Your old men will dream dreams, and your young men will see visions. Also [on] your male and female servants in those days I will pour out my spirit. I will perform wonders in heaven and on earth, blood, fire, and vaporous smoke. The sun will be changed to darkness and the moon, into blood before that great and terrible day of the Lord comes]* (Joel 3:1-4). This time is more correct, as it is said to us. We have said that it is correct after we [already] warned [you] about it and said that you should keep this from becoming public,

---

[10] The date of A.D. 1210 was not a very distant date from the time of this correspondence (A.D. 1168). Add 38 to 2,448 and the total is 2476, the central point between the redemptions. Doubled is 4952 and not 4970, as Maimonides holds. See also AZ 9a. This precise specification of a date for redemption is surprising after Maimonides had already apologized for Saadia and condemned astrologers and others for being precise about their calculations. This shows the wide-spread intensity of eschatological expectations at that time, the longing for redemption, and the demand for specific dates for expected events. These expectations were not limited to the fringe areas of Judaism.

so that it will not seem belated in human eyes. You see we have told it to you, and God knows the truth.

Now your statement that this time is that of which Jeremiah spoke, *It is a time of hardship for Jacob, but he will be saved from it* (Jer 30:7), is not so. Nevertheless, there is a definite hint in this [passage] to the war of Gog and Magog, and it will take place some time after the revelation of the Messiah. The sign of the Giron Gate, however, and all others like it,[11] are very weak [suggestions]. Some of them are related to scholars, but they are not [really] theirs. Some of them are allusions and riddles and therefore do not turn to anything dealing with this subject.

III
False Messiahs

That which you said about this man in the city of Yemen who claims that he is the Messiah, I am not surprised about him nor about those who follow him, because he is undoubtedly a fool. He is not guilty for being ill, nor should he be upset because of his sicknesses, if he has not caused them. Those who follow him do so because of their difficult position, and their foolishness on the subject of the Messiah [is understandable]. They imagine his exalted degree, and they think that he will arise just as Ibn Mahdi, whom they have seen. But I am surprised about your report. You, who, as a son of the Torah, who have already learned some of the saying of the scholars, [thinking] perhaps he is [the] true Messiah![12] Do you know, my brother, that the Messiah will be a very great prophet, greater than all the prophets since our leader Moses? Do you not know that one who lays claim to prophecy, if false in his claim, is guilty [of a crime punishable by] death, because he has dared to damage this great position, just as a [person] was killed for prophesying in the name of idolatry. [The Lord] (May he be exalted) said, *But the prophet who speaks contemptuously in my name a word which I have not commanded him to speak, [or that will speak in the name of other gods, that prophet shall die]* (Dt 18:20). What proof has he brought to you of his lies [more than] specifying for himself the mere claim that he is the Messiah?

How surprising are your comments about him, that he is known for his asceticism and he is not very learned! Does this indicate that he is the Messiah? He has brought you to this [erroneous

[11] A. Jellinek, *Bet ha-Midrasch* (Jerusalem, 1967) II, 79.

[12] The learned recipient of the letter with the highest post of administration in Judaism in Yemen apparently believed the person described was the real Messiah. Since this was true of him, how much the more so for the average or "normal" Jew of that time.

judgment] because you have not paid attention to the [high] level [of status] the Messiah holds, how his appearance will come about, when it will be, and especially, his identifying marks.

Regarding his level [of status], it is the highest and most eminent rank among the prophets next to our leader Moses, and the Lord has distinguished him with things in which our leader Moses was not distinguished (San 73b). In describing him, he said, *His delight shall be in the fear of the Lord* (Isa 11:3), *the spirit of the Lord shall rest upon him* (Isa 11:2), *And righteousness shall be the girdle of his loins* (Isa 11:5). [The Lord] (May he be exalted) will call him six names: He said, *For a child is born to us; a son is given to us. The government will be upon his shoulder, and he will be called 1) Wonderful, 2) Counseller, 3) Mighty God, 4) Eternal Father, 5) Prince of Peace* (Isa 9:5). It is not possible to be so eulogistic in describing him as that which [the Lord] (May he be exalted) had said, *You are my 6) son; today I have begotten you* (Ps 2:7). This is to let us know that the degree of his exaltation is above all human beings.

We teach of every prophet that he be definitely wise and that the Lord has made him a prophet, because in general among us [it is held that] prophecy is only given to the wise, the mighty, and the rich (Shab 92a; Ned 38a). They explain that "mighty" is one who conquers his [evil] impulse (Pirke Aboth 4:1); a "rich man" is rich in knowledge (Ned 41a). Whenever a man claims that he is a prophet but is not a marvel in wisdom, he is not to be trusted. All the more so if an *'am haaretz*[13] claims that he is the Messiah. From the proof that [the man is question] is an *'am haaretz* is that which you described of his ordering people to give all their possessions to charity. They did not pay attention to him, and they were right, but he was in error, because he took issue with the judgment [of the scripture and rabbis] which is that it is not proper in our teachings that a man should give all his wealth to charity, but rather only a part. [The Lord] (May he be exalted) said, *If a man really devotes some of all which is his* (Lev 27:28), and those [rabbis] who receive the traditional commentary, say *Some of all that is his* (Lev 27:28), but not all *that is his* (Arakin 28a; Arubin 8:13). They

---

[13] The *'am haaretz* was the Canaanite who lived in the land before the Israelites conquered it. He was considered the pagan, Gentile, and other unkind libels. When Nehemiah returned to Jerusalem to rebuild the walls, he considered the Jews who had not gone to Babylon but continued in the land to be the "people of the land" (עַם הָאָרֶץ), and treated them just as disrespectfully as the early Israelites treated the Canaanites. Since that time, the *'am haaretz* was considered to be the Jew who was not so well enlightened as the scholarly Jews who came from Babylon. These were the rural people, the Palestinian Jews, the ignoramuses. The title was intended to be insulting.

have said that the desired boundary for them is one fifth (Arakin 28a; Ket 50a, 67a). There is no doubt that his stupidity which led him to claim that he was the Messiah is that which directs him to command people to make themselves penniless of all their wealth and give it to the poor. Then they will suffer reversal and be poor while the poor become rich. Then they are obligated, according to stipulation, to return their wealth to them again. This will happen. The possessions between the poor will revolve endlessly, and this is definitely stupidity.

Now, on the topic of the way the Messiah will arise and when he will arise: He will arise in the land of Israel, contrary to what you might expect, and in it [Israel] you should wait his disclosure, as he said, *Suddenly he will come to his temple* (Mal 3:1). Concerning the way he will arise, no one knows anything about that until he appears. It is not [true] that he is the Messiah when it is said about him that he is so and so, son of so and so, from the father's lineage of so and so, but rather a man will arise who is not known before his revelation, and signs and wonders are performed at his hand.[14] They are the proof of the veracity of his claims and the legitimacy of his family tree. [The Lord] (May he be exalted) said, when he described this position, *Behold a man whose name is "Shoot," and he will shoot up from his lowly origin* (Zech 6:12). Also Isaiah said when he described his revelation without knowing him, his father, his mother, his father's lineage, family, or his relatives, he said, *And he will grow up like a sapling, and as a root out of dry ground* (Isa 53:2). After his disclosure in the land of Israel and the gathering of the dispersed of Israel to Jerusalem and the rest of the cities of the land, then the word will be spread from the East and the West until it reaches you at Yemen, and those east of you in India, as [the Lord] (May he be exalted) said through Isaiah, *that send emissaries by the sea, [even in vessels of papyrus upon the waters, go, swift messengers, to a nation that has been pulled and plucked to a people that suffered terribly from their beginning onward]* (Isa 18:2). The word will not be changed so as to begin at the ends [of the earth] and the word spread to the land of Israel.

But the inclusiveness of his eminence as he is described by all the prophets from Moses to Malachi, you can gather them from all twenty-four [books of the Tanak], but the special [messages] in them about him, when he is revealed, the Lord will cause the

---

[14] Even though Maimonides here said that the Messiah would come from unknown stock, he earlier insisted that the Messiah descend from Solomon's line.

kingdom of the earth to tremble at the report. Their governments will become weak; they will discontinue their resistance against him, not in war and not in rebellion; that is to say, they will not dispute with him nor contradict him, but they will tremble from his marvelous deeds which will be revealed, and they will keep absolute silence. Isaiah said in his description of the reaction to him of all the kings, *All the kings will close their mouths because of him* (Isa 52:15). He will destroy whoever wants to destroy him in his visitation and by his speech. None will escape; none will get away from him. This is his statement: *He will strike the land with the staff of his mouth* (Isa 11:4). Disturbances and wars go out from the east of the land to the west. This will not be at the beginning of his disclosure only, but after the war of Gog, as Ezekiel has explained (Ezek 39:7-14). I do not see that there is in this man who has been disclosed in your midst any of these [signs].

You know that Jesus the Nazorean (May his bones be crushed) with all the numerous things which the Christians relate to him that he did, when he restored the dead to life, as they have imagined and from those miracles which they fabricate, until, even if we would accept them according to their claim, they would still not succeed with their arguments with us in their claim that Jesus is the Messiah, for we have against them in the scripture nearly a thousand proofs that they are not sound, even according to their own claims. [A man] will not magnify himself to this [exalted] degree unless he wants to make himself the object of derision.

In summary, regarding this man: If he had been saying this with malice and depreciation, in my opinion, he would have been guilty [of a crime punishable by] death, but that which seems more reasonable, and it is possible that it is the correct [judgment], is that he is already unbalanced, and his mind is confused. I advise you with counsel that is good both for you and for him, that he be fettered several days until it becomes public knowledge among all the Gentiles that he is demented. Then circulate the message and publicize it widely among all people. After that, you may free him, and with this you may deliver his soul at the outset, because when the Gentiles hear of him after this position [in jail], the claim will cause them to mock him and refer to him as a madman, which he is. Then you will deliver yourselves from damage by the Gentiles. If you allow the matter [to continue] until he is well-known among the Gentiles, you will destroy him and possibly bring punishments upon yourselves.[15]

[15] Messiahs normally instigated insurrectionist movements which prompted the Gentile

Remember, my brothers, that the Lord has hurled us, because of the multitude of our iniquities, into this Ishmaelite nation which has treated us very cruelly and devised means to injure and hate us, just as [the Lord] (May he be exalted) assured us, *Our enemies will be our judges* (Dt 32:31), and no nation has stood over Israelites more oppressively than it has, and none who has distinguished [itself] in our subjection, humiliation, and our hatred than they have, until the plundered king of Israel, when he foresaw, through the Holy Spirit, all the hardships which would pass over Israel, cried out, lamented, and called for help in respect of no nation except the kingdom of Ishmael. He said, *Woe to me, that I live with Mishech that I dwell with the tents of Kedar* (Ps 120:5).[16] Observe that they have distinguished Kedar from the rest of the children of Ishmael, for the crazy man, according to their public reports, is only from the sons of Kedar, according to his published genealogy. Also Daniel described our oppression and humiliation until we are made, "like dust for threshing" in the kingdom of Ishmael (May it be subdued speedily). He said, *And some of the army and some of the stars will fall to the ground and be trampled upon* (Dan 8:10). But concerning even our existence, we have endured their subjugation, their lies, and their falsehoods, which a man can hardly bear, and we have become like that which the prophet said, *I will be like a deaf man who cannot hear and like a dumb man that does not open his mouth* (Ps 38:14). It is just as our scholars (May they be remembered for good) have directed us that we should bear the lies and falsehoods of the Ishmaelites with attentiveness and silence. They tied the suggestion concerning this to the names of his [Ishmael's] sons, *Mishma, Dumah, and Massa* (Gen 25:14), "Listen, be silent, and endure" (Targ. Jon. Gen 25:14). We have accustomed ourselves, both small and great, to endure their oppression, just as Isaiah commanded, saying, *I gave my back to the smiters, and my cheeks to those who pluck out hair* (Isa 50:6). But with all this we do not escape the force of these oppressions and their continuous assaults, but all that which we have endured and extended ourselves to be at peace with them,

---

governments to suppress them as quickly as possible as a normal police protection for Gentile citizens. Maimonides wanted to stop this particular Messianic movement without any Gentile intervention with military forces. True believers of such messianic movements, however, depended on God's military power and miracles to strengthen their own forces, under the leadership of the Messiah, to overthrow the stronger Gentile military power. Maimonides favored this insurrection at the right time, A.D. 1210.

[16] Kedar, a descendant of Ishmael, is another name for Arabia, which is also called Ishmael, and here refers to the Moslems.

they [still] stir up conflicts and wars, just as David described to us, *I am all peace, but when I speak they are for war* (Ps 120:7). All the more so if we should disturb the peace and lay claim before them of a kingdom with delusion and vanity, with which we would be giving ourselves over to destruction.

"Appendix"[17]	"Text"
Here I will describe to you briefly, stories that have happened since the establishment of the Ishmaelite kingdom, so that you may receive instruction from them.	It is necessary for you to know that at the beginning of the days of Islam,
One of them [the stories] originated from the East beyond Isfahan.[18] A great number of Jews [was organized], hundreds of thousands, and with them was a man who claimed that he was the Messiah, and they wore armor and drew swords. They killed everyone whom they met.[19] According to the story which	a man arose from the other side of the river, and he claimed that he was the Messiah. He went out at the head of ten thousand Israelites,

is known to me, they reached as far as Baghdad. This was the beginning of the Umayyad rule (Omar I, A.D. 634-44). The king said to all the Jews who were under his rule, "Bring out your wise men to [meet] these men, [to see] if their claim is valid, and he is the one whom you expect. If that is clear, we will make [a covenant] of peace with you, according to your terms. But if their claims are

[17] J. Kafih, רבי משה בן מימון, אגרות (Jerusalem, 1972), lists this as an appendix, questioning its authenticity. The relationship between the "appendix" and the "text" is a parallel one, in any case. The "appendix" is either an expansion of the "text" or the "text" is a summary of the "appendix." The two are not contradictory, and both reflect events believed to have happened.

[18] A city in ancient Persia and modern Iran.

[19] Although Maimonides claimed just before that the Jews wanted "to be at peace with them, [but] they still stir up conflict and wars," it is apparent here that these messianic movements were not activities led by Jews who were passive victims of oppression. They wanted peace only *after* they had defeated the Gentiles in war and could rule them peacefully from that position.

false, I will join battle with them. Several scholars went out to them and said to them, "We are men from the other side of the river." Then they said [further] to them, "Who motivated you to go out?" They said to them, "This man whom we recognize as a *hasid,* a man of eminence.

Appendix	Text
He is one of the sons of David, and	
	and he performed a miracle
he was with us when he was a	There was in our midst a
leper. We know this, and we	leper who admitted that
agree that he is well and whole,	he was healed.
and this is one of the signs of	

the Messiah. They imagined or explained, saying, "With the Messiah, [applies the verse], *Stricken, smitten of God, and a leper* (Isa 53:4). [This means] that he will be a leper" (San 98b).

	But he was not successful [in his military expedition], and Israelites remained in the land of Isfahan after that

Then [the scholars] explained that this was not correct and that he did not have even some of the signs of the Messiah, much less all of them. They said to them [further], "Our brothers, until this [provocation] you were near to your land, and the possibility for you to return [was imminent], but if you attack the land, you will perish, and you will destroy the words of Moses, for your people think that the Messiah has already appeared and was defeated (San 98b). You do not have a prophet with you, and there is no sign in your hands. They heard their words. Then King so-and-so brought out to them thousands of dinars by way of hospitality, so that they might leave the land. When they had gone far from him and returned to their place, he desired the Jews, and he collected from them all that he had given, and he placed on them a distinguishing symbol which everyone should write on his garment: "Cursed!" He had to hang a patch in front and a patch behind him, and all the congregation of Khorisan and Isfahan have continued in severe exile until this day. This we have learned by word of mouth.

Appendix	Text
	in severe exile, and great oppressions came upon them because of him.

Appendix	*Text*
One of which we are certain	Also one arose from the West, from Fez,

and whose veracity we know
because of its proximity in time,

| happened fifty years ago or | about forty-five years before |

less. A *hasid* came, an eminent
person, a scholar from among the scholars of Israel, known by the
name of Moses Dari. He came from the city of Dara to Spain to
study under our rabbi Joseph Halevi (May he be remembered for
good) Ibn Migash, whose report reached you. After that he came
to the capital of the land of Maghreb (i.e., Morocco), called Fez.
People gathered to him because of his *hasidism*, virtue, and
scholarship. He said to them, "The time of the Messiah is near. Already the Lord has informed me of this in a dream." He did not
claim (May the Lord live!) just

as this fool [of which you
wrote] did, that he was

the Messiah, but	who
he said [the Lord] announced	claimed that he was the herald of
him that the Messiah	good news,

would appear

But men followed him and
believed his words. My father (May he remember the righteous for
blessing) turned people away from him and warned them against
following him, but only a few listened to my father. The majority,
in fact almost all, followed Rabbi Moses (May he remember the
righteous for blessing). The finality of his word he promised future
events, and all were fulfilled. He would say, "I was informed yesterday that this and this [will happen]," and it would take place
exactly as he said, until [one time] he told them that on that Friday
there would be a very great rain [storm], and it would happen that
blood would come down. This would be the sign when he said, *I
will provide portents in heaven and on earth, blood and fire [and
columns of smoke]* (Joel 3:3). This happened in the month of
Marheshvan, and the great and powerful rain came down that Friday, and the water was pouring down a viscuous red as if it were
mixed with [red] clay. This was the portent of his for which all
people [who were Jewish] believed that he was undoubtedly a
great prophet. This was not prohibited by the Torah, for as I have
told you concerning prophecy, that it will return before the
Messiah comes, and when his words were verified among

Appendix	*Text*
the majority of people,	
he said to them	
that the Messiah was coming	and that the Messiah would be
that year, on the evening of	revealed that year,

Passover. He ordered people
to sell their belongings, and they should borrow in obligation from
the Gentiles [with a promise] to
pay each dinar back with ten,
and that the commandments of the Torah would be fulfilled on the
festival of Passover (Kelim 12:7), because they would not see them
again. So they did this, and
when Passover arrived,

and nothing at all happened,	but his words were not fulfilled. Because of him, severe hardships passed over the Israelites. One of those who saw all these things told me about them.

the [Jewish] people were very
heavily burdened, because
many of them had squandered their possessions for very trifling
amounts, and their debts made the people fall down [from the
weight]. Also the matter was widely publicized among the Gentiles
by their neighbors and servants. If any was found, he was killed,
and there was no place for him in Moslem territory after that.
[Rabbi Moses Dari] went out to the land of Israel and died there
(May he be remembered for good). He (May the Lord live!) already had promised at the time of his departure [future events]
according to all that which happened in the land of Maghreb,
both small and great.

My father (May the righ-
teous be remembered for blessing) told me

about fifteen or twenty years,	About twelve years
approximately, before	before
the event (ca. A.D. 1102-07),	this,
important scholars arose in	another arose in
the city of Cordova, a city	Spain, in the city of Cordova,
in Spain, and they were well-	
informed in the movements of	

planets. They agreed that the Messiah would come that year. After
that they made an interrogation of a dream night after night,

Appendix   *Text*
and it was verified to them   and he claimed that he was
that the Messiah was to be one   the Messiah.
of the men of the land. They set
their eyes on an important *hasid,* called Arieh, who was teaching
people. They produced signs and told stories just as Dari did until
it reached the attention of all men. When the chiefs of our congregation and their men who were learned in the matter were congregated in the synagogue, they brought this man called ben Arieh,
and they flogged him with many [stripes]; they required him [to
pay] a fine, and they dismissed him on the condition that he keep
still about this, but he allowed those who claimed him to claim it,
and he did not warn them. He taught them according to that
which is an offense requiring punishment. They also
punished all the men who were   There was almost a complete
joined to him,   destruction [of the Jews there]
                                    by the enemies of the Israelites
                                    because of him.

and they only escaped from the
Gentiles with great difficulty.[20]

   About forty years before   Before
the event of ben Arieh in   him,
Spain, a man arose in France,   a man arose in France,
in the large city of Linon,[21]
which was more than tens of
thousands of Jewish families,
and he claimed that he was   and he claimed that he was
the Messiah. There was a   the Messiah. He performed
miracle of his among them   signs according to his words,
when he used to go out every
moonlight night. He went up to the tops of tall trees in the forest
and fluttered in the air and descended from tree to tree as if he
were flying. This is that which was said with [respect to] the Messiah, *With the clouds of heaven there came one like a son of man
[and he came to the Ancient of Days, and he was presented before
him. To him was given the dominion and glory and a kingdom]*
(Dan 7:13-14).[22]

   [20] It was the Jewish leaders, who, like Maimonides, tried to repress some messianic movements before they broke out into military rebellion involving much bloodshed.
   [21] Probably Lyon.
   [22] The verse was probably applied originally to Judas the Maccabee (See *To the Hebrews,*
38-48). A messiah who came similarly was not to be distinguished only by skills in aerial
locomotion, but in his successful attempt to gain leadership over the kingdom on the
promised land.

Appendix	*Text*
Many testified to them and followed him. The French realized it and killed many of them and plundered them, and he was also included [among those] murdered. Some of them imagine that he is hidden until this day.	but the French killed him and murdered with him the congregation of Israelites.

Conclusions

These are the words which the prophets already testified in advance and informed us that which I have told you, that when the days of the Messiah draw near, pretenders and impersonators will increase, but their words will not be fulfilled. They and many with them will perish, according to that which Solomon (upon whom be peace) understood through the Holy Spirit that this nation when it is snared in exile would agitate them to insurrection at a time that was not designated.[23] They would be destroyed in this [attempt], and hardships would overtake them. He warned [them] against this and put them under oath concerning it by way of a parable. He said, *I put you under oath, daughters of Jerusalem, [by the gazelles and by the hinds of the field, that you do not arouse or stir up love, until it please]* (SS 2:7; 8:4). Now, our beloved brothers, take this oath, and do not stir up love until it please (Ket 111a).

May the Creator of the world with a measure of mercy (Ḥag 12a; GenR 12:15; 21:9; Mid Ps 75a) remember us and you to gather the exiles of his inheritance and his company (Dt 32:9), so that we may see the Lord's favor and visit his temple (Ps 27:4). May he bring us out from the valley of the shadows of death in which he has made us dwell and turn away the darkness from our eyes and the gloom from our hearts. May he fulfill in our days and in your days [the verse]: *The people who walk in darkness have seen a great light* (Isa 9:1). May he cause darkness to fall, in his anger and in his wrath, on all those who rise up against us, and enlighten our darkness, just as he has promised us, *For behold,*

[23] Maimonides did not try to curb messianic beliefs or insurrectionist movements generally. The two went together, and he believed that Israel would be restored only by a messianic insurrectionist movement, but he wanted to restrain those movements which he did not think would succeed.

darkness will cover the earth and deep darkness, the Gentiles, but upon you the Lord will rise (Isa 60:2).

May peace be upon you, our friend and beloved one, master of wisdom, increasing understanding. Upon all our brothers, the students, all the people of the land, peace, peace like light and great peace until there be no moon (Ps 77:7). Amen. Selah.

Now that which I want from you is that you send a copy of this book to every single congregation in the cities and villages, so as to strengthen their faith and establish their footsteps, that you read it before the congregation, and the [select] individuals, so that you may be among the righteous ones of *the many* (Dan 12:2). After you have added to it definite warnings against the evil of making it public to the Gentiles. Then will happen that which the Lord will prosper from it. I have written it and I am very much afraid of this, but I have seen that the justice of "the many" was adequate to bear the danger concerning it. It is further [reassuring to know] that I have sent it to a man like you and the secret of the Lord and those who fear him (Ps 25:14). Those who fill the places of the prophets already have promised us, saying, "There will be no punishment for a virtuous mission" (Pes 8a-b). There is no greater virtue than this. Peace to all Israelites.

Summary

Signs of the times. — This letter was prompted by a letter from the leader of the Jewish congregations in Yemen at a time when Jews were being forced to give up their religion and become converts, either to Christianity of Islam. Under such difficult times, some became converts and others looked for signs that the Messiah would appear and lead them in a revolution against the current ruling powers. Maimonides agreed that these hardships were "birth pangs of the Messiah," the hardships that were predicted by the prophets to take place before the end of the current evil era. Maimonides expected the Messiah in due time, but he was quick to correct any notion that the messianic movements that were taking place then were the fulfillment of prophecy. Far from being the prophet like Moses, which Deuteronomy foretold, Mohammed was a crazy man, in Maimonides' judgment.

Calculating the end. — There were many who accepted Saadia's prediction of the date for the end of the Roman and Arabic ages and the beginning of the Messianic age, but the time he predicted had evidently passed, because Maimonides apologized for Saadia's mistake. Medieval and modern scholars have not agreed on the date predicted by Saadia, because it is not known when his beginning period of calculation was, but there seems to have been an understood and agreed upon time which Maimonides and his readers both understood to have been the year Saadia predicted. Had there been any uncertainty, Maimonides would not have found it necessary to admit that Saadia was mistaken in giving an exact date. Although Maimonides said no one could know the exact date, he predicted that the end would take place A.D. 1210. This means that messianic expectations and calculations were so prominent then that even cautious defenders of the faith, like Maimonides, were eschatologically oriented. Like Saadia, Maimonides based his theology on scripture and traditional interpretation. The end was compared in kind to the end of the "captivity" in Egypt and the conquest of Canaan, and Maimonides said there were those who miscalculated the end of that "captivity" as well.

Astrology and prophecy. — The group was also favorably impressed with an astrological prophecy, part of which is still extant, a translation of which is included in this collection. Maimonides said it was invalid, but in his refutation, he discloses his own familiarity with astrology. Since astrology professed to predict the future, medieval Jews who were very much interested in the future, were naturally attracted by it, but Maimonides declared that it had no validity for predicting the Messiah. From prophecy, however, it was certain that the messianic age would follow the Moslem age immediately. He understood that the end of that age was not far away.

False messiahs. — The number and nature of those associations with messianic movements indicate that the crusaders were not the only religious militarists who were trying to gain control of Jerusalem near the millennium after the fall of Jerusalem and just before the beginning of the sixth millennium, according to Jewish reckoning. The millennium that should follow A.D. 1240 was the millennium before the millennium of the sabbath. When a day in the sight of the Lord is a thousand years, A.D. 1240 would begin *Erev Shabbat,* when the Messiah would be expected to appear and overthrow Gog and Magog before the thousand years of "rest." Very shortly before the turn of the millennium, Maimonides predicted the appearance of the Messiah, but he warned against following false messiahs who appeared before that time. Whenever the Messiah came, there would be the war with Gog and Magog during which time the Messiah would overthrow the Moslems and the Christians so that the Jews could reign supreme. This would involve a tremendously well led and conducted war which might be sabotaged by precocious leaders who led rebellions prematurely. Small military movements would be overthrown and the Jews associated with them, killed or severely punished for treason and national sabotage. Maimonides wanted to prevent that. In dealing with the messianic pretender in Yemen, Maimonides was eager to get the movement interpreted at once to the Gentiles as the act of a lunatic who had no Jewish following, before it got out of hand. Actually, this false messiah had the considered support of such prominent scholars and leaders as the president of all the Jewish congregations of Yemen.

Maimonides gave the qualifications of a true Messiah and the events associated with his appearance, which included the war of Gog and Magog and the submission by treaty or force of all Gentile kings to his rule. Messiahs who came before the time of Maimonides predicted or failed to move in exactly the way Maimonides understood to be prophesied were considered false.

Among the pretending messiahs was one from Isfahan who led a Jewish army of thousands of troops, killing everyone they met on their way to Jerusalem. This was one of the Jewish equivalents of a crusade, although it anticipated the Christian movements by many years. Some Jews of that time believed the Messiah had already come and had been defeated in war.

The "end" of the "captivity" was expected to be so much like the exodus from Egypt and the succeeding conquest of Palestine that Mar Moses Dari instructed Jews to borrow all the money they could from Gentiles, just as the Hebrews had done earlier in Egypt, at fantastic interest rates, because before the year was up, the Messiah would appear, lead them to Jerusalem, introduce the messianic age, and they would not be required to pay back the borrowed money.

The expected miracles, military movements, and prophetic powers all effectively attracted Jews to follow many types of messiahs, so fervently they believed the end was near. The military movements of the crusaders fit in well with their millennial expectations, representing Gog and Magog who would be defeated in the Valley of Decision. Like the Christians of the same time, the Jews believed it was God's will for them to evict the "heathen" from the promised land and rule it themselves. That was the religious, but nonetheless political and military, expectation associated with the messianism in the twelfth century. The counsel given by Maimonides in this letter sheds a great deal of light on the eschatological beliefs of Jews during the crusades. The following letters show how other Jews responded to the actual movement of the Crusaders.

THE TEN TRIBES AND
THE VALLEY OF DECISION

Author Unknown[1]

(1) ...Go]d to Zion, according to the word of G[od, and now there will be gathered to you] (2) many [na]tions who say, "You blaspheme!" May our eyes see Zion, (3) but they do not know the designs of the Lord (Micah 4:11-12), and still *the threshing floor* (Micah 4:12) is not filled.[2] (4) But, be assured, our brothers, blessed of the Lord, that in this year has been fulfilled (5) the promise of our God. The Eastern Europeans have come in countless numbers[3] --(6) thousands of thousands, with their women and all their wealth. (7) Our God has gathered to *the threshing floor*[4] Gentiles, and Jews asked of them (8) and said to them, "Why have you left your houses and your places, (9) and departed?" The important and great ones *among them* answered and said, (10) "The mountains of darkness were close to us, but now they are bathed in great light." (11) We saw a nation and tents without number,[5] and *we* could not (12) understand their language. One man came out from their midst (13) and told us, "Go your way. Take note, we have come."[6] (14)...concerning this we have been pursued, but we arrived (15) and say, "Truly, our God has fulfilled his promise.

---

[1] Jacob Mann, "Messianic Movements in the Days of the First Crusade," התקופה 23 (1925), 253-59. Cf. II Bar 77:17-19; II Esdras 13:39-50. RPL

[2] "Threshing floor" is here used metaphorically to mean "battle field," where human beings will be trampled as wheat is trampled to beat out the wheat from the straw and chaff.

[3] Crusaders, whom the author has mistakenly identified with the lost tribes of North Israel.

[4] The predestined threshing floor is the Valley of Decision, at the border of Jerusalem, where Gog and Magog are prophesied to gather for defeat, just before the Davidic kingdom is restored to the Jews.

[5] Apparently understood as a fulfillment of Isa 49:9: *Saying to the prisoners, "Come forth," to those who are in darkness, "Appear." They shall feed along the ways, on all bare heights shall be their pasture.* These people who were coming from Europe appearing from mountains of *darkness* into a great light. They had left their houses and places (line 8) to pasture *on all bare heights.*

[6] I.e., "Don't stand in our way. We are coming through!"

Those who were exiled (16) in darkness are the other [ten] tribes.[7] When (17) the Eastern Europeans have all gone to the land of Israel, and *the threshing floor* will have been filled, (18) then our God will say, *Arise and thresh, daughter of Zion* (Micah 4:13)! (19) All the congregations have been aroused and turned to the Lord with fasting (20) and almsgiving among the places of Khazaria. They went, as they said, (21) seventeen congregations, to the wilderness of the Gentiles (Ezek 20:35), but we do not (22) know whether they met the tribes or not,[8] nor if (23) from the land of France, where they sent a messenger with letters (24) in Greek (Constantinople). Still we are not enlightened, from that which was written. (25) It was written to you and also in Greek in a place [called] Abydos (26) which is near Constantinople. Small congregations have arisen, (27) according to the words of Daniel, the pleasant man, sons of apostates of Israel. (28) They said, "Elijah has been revealed to us, according to that which is written, *and sons of apostates* (Dan 11:14).[9] (29) We did not receive them--- neither we nor the congregation of (30) Constantinople, but we banned them, and we outlawed them, (31) but it was told before your honor,[10] that which happened in Salonica (32) in the holy congregation. Crowds of Jews and uncircumcised ones came (33) and the governmental authorities, and they tell that Elijah was revealed in an appearance, and not in a dream [only], (34) concerning the men involved, and [there were] many signs and wonders.[11] (35) This was announced both by the uncircumcised

---

[7] When the Jews involved in this narrative saw the great masses of people, they assumed that prophecy was being fulfilled. So high were their messianic expectations they thought nothing else could take place. The ten tribes were traditionally expected to return under the leadership of a messiah son of Joseph to defeat the Romans at Jerusalem. It did not occur to them that these troops would be the Romans (Christians) themselves.

[8] Convinced that they were nearing the end of their exile when they would be restored to the promised land from all the nations, they acted accordingly. In the chapter where Ezekiel promised that they would be returned, he also said he would send them out to the wilderness areas among the nations. When the Jews heard of the armies marching toward Palestine, they went out to the wilderness areas where judgment was to take place and the covenant renewed before entering the land. These Jews expected to join forces with the "ten tribes" and return to Palestine with them. At the time of this writing, the author did not know what happened to these seventeen congregations.

[9] Apparently the author and his congregation doubted that these seventeen congregations acted correctly. Elijah had not come, so these may be the rebellious Jews whom Daniel predicted would try to force God's hand and would be destined for failure. There were different ways to interpret signs.

[10] Meaning, "You have heard."

[11] Which were promised to take place before the Messiah introduced the messianic age and led the troops in gaining control of the promised land.

and the Jews, and it was disclosed (36) to Rabbi Eliezer, the son of Rabbi Judah, the son of Rabbi (37) Eliezer the great,[12] and, as the foreigners say, he gave (38) him a staff,[13] but with clear miracles which happened in Salonica, (39) the uncircumcised testified in good faith. The Jews stopped (40) all work.[14] Also our Rabbi Tobias[15] sent a disciple (41) with an open letter to Constantinople to announce the news to them. (42) A Jew was there from our place, and he had a scholarly inclination.[16] (43) He saw the writing which Rabbi Tobias sent, and written it it, (44) "Signs and wonders happened in our places, and also Elijah was revealed (45) to us." This Jew of Lugaz, the uncircu[mcised], testifies--(46) His name is Michael Niemec--[17] who saw the writing of our rabbi Tobias (47) with his own eyes that a certain Michael son of Rabbi Aaron, the חבר,[18] who was in Salonika (48) where he was blind in both eyes. His eyes were opened, and he [now] sees with both eyes. (49) Also Rabbi Nissim[19] knows him, and this Michael acted extemporaneously. (50) He did not take a digest of the letter, which if he had brought for us, we would (51) send to you that you might believe this matter. Moreover, it was evident (52) to us that the head of the [rabbinic] school, Rab Abiathar, the priest,[20] (53) wrote the explicit letter from Tripoli to the congregation of Constantinople. (54) There were present four men who saw the documents when they were in the hands of Lugaz, (55) the uncircumcised, and also they did not bother to bring us the epistle, (56) because they were illiterate. Now we hope that we will receive a message (57) from Rabbi Tobias and from the holy congregation, for we are amazed (58) at the great miracle which happened in Salonika, where the *uncircumcised* hated (59) the Jews inexorably,

[12] Perhaps the nephew of Rabbi Tobias, author of לקח טוב.

[13] Like the one used by Moses and Aaron in Egypt to perform miracles. Traditionally, Hafzi-bah, the mother of the Messiah of Joseph, was to bring forth a staff with which miracles would be performed in the last days.

[14] So that they would be prepared to leave at once for the promised land when the Messiah appeared. Early Christians behaved the same way (II Thes 3:6-10).

[15] Prominent Jewish leader and scholar of the end of the eleventh and the beginning of the twelfth centuries. He was the author of לקח טוב. He also was deeply involved in the messianic activity of that time.

[16] Literally, "had the odor of scholarship." Probably meant he could read and write and was more learned than most people of that time.

[17] So Mann, "Messianic Movements," fn. 8. Text reads יי נמטש.

[18] A חבר was a layman, who, after the temple was no longer in service, kept his own home as free from defilement as the temple and himself as free from defilement as a priest, so that there would be a holy place for the Shekinah to return.

[19] Rabbi Nissim ben Nahorai was one of the leaders of the congregation of Postat at the end of the eleventh century. See Mann, "Messianic Movements," 259, fn. 1.

[20] Known as the gaon of Palestine from A.D. 1083 on.

as *Rabbi Nissim* knows, (60) so if the miracle and great wonder had not happened, and the news of it reached (61) the king, there would not be left a remnant or fugitive of "the enemies of Israel."[21] (62) But now they dwell in great security with no poll tax or land tax,[22] but [on the contrary], (63) sit [wearing] their prayer shawls, unemployed,[23] (64) and we do not know what to expect. (65) We are afraid lest the matter be disclosed to the Gentiles and they kill us,[24] (66) but now the government itself and the bishop (67) all say [that] Jews should not live in Salonika. (68) "Sell your possessions," [they say], "and the king Caesar (69) will help them.[25] No man will be able to touch them, and you still (70) do not go, even though we have clearly learned *your* Messiah stepped forth." (71) Praise God, we are not afraid, and praise (72) God also we have returned to the Lord [in] repentance, with fasting and almsgiving. (73) Many [of us] fast every day, but others, on Mondays and Thursdays, (74) receiving flagellations[26] and confessing their sins with their iniquities. Before (75) we heard the report of Salonika, *Jews and also uncircumcised* were seeing (76) visions, and we would not know (77) any of the [events] around Salonika, and we did not believe their words, (78) but [instead] rebuked them until a Jewish priest saw (79) in his dream, before it was reported, that all the Roman congregations (80) would gather together in Salonika and from there go forth, but we rebuked him [also]."[27] (81) We said that they were the enemies of Israel, and how, until Tobias came (82) from Thebes and brought a document [saying] that signs and wonders had taken place (83) in Salonika and that other congregations were gathering there. Then, behold, (84) Tobias will come there, and he will tell you all that he has

---

[21] Code name for Israelites.

[22] Which Moslems almost universally required of all non-Moslems. Jews here were evidently privileged.

[23] Waiting for the end time and the appearance of the Messiah.

[24] This was apparently a very large and carefully organized movement, including the leadership of the most prominent scholars of that time and area. They were prepared to lead or join a military movement to recover Jerusalem. If their enemies learned of this movement, of course, they would crush it before it became successful.

[25] Jews there were *persona non grata*.

[26] Self-inflicted whippings to counterbalance the sins still held against Israel in the treasury for which punishment had not yet been received. A traditional aspect of Jewish and Christian asceticism.

[27] Although they rebuked him, just to be on the safe side, the author reflects a keen interest and desire for still stronger evidence that he could believe, namely a written report of miracles from Rabbi Tobias.

heard and seen,[28] (85) and the outcome of the dream which the Jewish priest saw. Now, our brother, if (86) God favors you, if you have a report or good news (87) which we know, and which our master, the head of *the school* has heard and knows, (88) you also [will] have heard and known, and you might do us (89) the favor of writing to us that which you know and have heard. (side 2, line 90) Do not be at all afraid, even if the king hears it.[29] (91) We are not afraid. If a document comes from your honor, (92) all our congregations will be strengthened in repentance. May God pay you (93) a good reward,[30] and may you merit seeing *the beauty of the Lord and visiting (94) in his temple* (Ps 27:4). (95) I, Menahem,[31] want to go to the promised land this year (96) so that I might see the East European [Crusader] troops that will go over as a multitude, (97) but I do not know where they will spread out. May God guard you (98) and us. Amen.

Summary

The author of this letter was reporting to the recipient many of the international activities that were taking place and interpreted by many as signs that God was about to restore the Jews to the promised land and begin the battle against the Gentiles there. The author was seriously considering the validity of each claim and accompanying action. Many Jews thought the Crusaders were members of the ten tribes who were on their way to Jerusalem to evict the Moslems so that the Jews could then rule. They went out to meet them to join forces and make the military victory more certain. The author had not learned at the time of the letter that the Crusaders were not comrades in arms, but another group of covenanters who also thought that they alone were the chosen people, destined to rule the world from Jerusalem. This meant that they were not going to fight with the Moslems and then give the victory over to the Jews, but they were planning to rule themselves.

---

[28] The purpose of the letter is apparent here. Since the author has received no direct word from Rabbi Tobias, he has written to someone who will see him in person very soon. This person, then, can send a letter to the writer soon to clear up all the reports that are circulating. He wanted to be cautious, but he did not want to suppress valid messianic reports just because he lacked information.

[29] Providing encouragement needed to continue to take part in a dangerous subversive movement that could lead to death if discovered.

[30] A prayer for benefits for the favor asked and the risks taken.

[31] The unknown author of the letter. Since the letter was preserved by Rabbi Nissim, the letter was originally written to him or some of his acquaintances.

Since Jews were intent on being the rulers, Jews and Christians fought throughout the Crusades, contesting for control of Jerusalem after the Moslems were defeated. They went to meet the Crusaders in the same frame of mind as that with which the Jews of Babylon much earlier went to meet Cyrus and negotiate terms of participation. At the time of Cyrus the author of Second Isaiah promised that Gentiles would do the fighting, and after the victory, finance the restoration of the promised land and the return of Jews from all over the world. The author of this letter was very much interested in the judgment of Rab Tobias concerning all of these things. In לקח טוב, Rab Tobias later told some of the events that happened in A.D. 1096, the time of this Crusade, which indicates that the Crusaders' response to the Jewish desires was negative. His comment on Leviticus is as follows:

"*He who brings you from the land of Egypt to be [your God]* (Lev 11:45). So that thus I have brought you *from the land of Egypt* that you may transfer yourselves to sanctify my Name, *to be your God* against your will, I am the Lord. I am the Lord [who is] trustworthy to pay wages. Our scholars (May they be remembered for good) wrote of an event with Pappos and Walulinos, his brother, when Tyrainos killed them in Laodicia, he said to them, 'If you are from the people of Daniel, Hanniah, Mishael, and Azariah, let your God come and deliver you from my hand, etc.' I will write down as a memorial the event which the saints of the Most High did, the congregation of Genatzia, when they gave themselves, their wives, their sons, and their daughters over on one day on the eve of the festival of Shevuoth when they were slaughtered as one man so as to sanctify the name of the God of Israel in the year 4,856 (A.D. 1096) of the creation of the world (103) when they provided a memorial of the inhabitants of the land, to go up to inherit dwellings on high. For them and for those like them, in place of the blood of the righteous ones, I, the Lord, am faithful, to pay good reward."[32]

Rab Tobias also commented: "So that they might see the unity of the righteous ones who were killed for the sanctification of your name were repenting against their will and giving praise to your great Name, just as it happened in our days with the German congregation in the year 4,856 (A.D. 1096) when the sons of Sair [Edomites = Christians] set their hands to go up against the pleasant

---

[32] Rab Tobias ben Rabbi Eliezer, מדרש לקח טוב ויקרא (Wilna, 1884), אמור, p. 123 (62a).

land, and they put their hands against the congregations, and they [the congregations] were slaughtered for the sanctification of your Name, with no exception."[33]

The same Tobias who was involved with the congregations who went out to meet the Crusaders is the one who wrote later about the deaths of these righteous ones. It is possible that the Crusaders slaughtered them, and they are the ones who were credited with being given against their will for the sanctification of the Name. Whether or not this is true, it is clear that there were deep, messianic feelings related to international movements. Both Jews and Christians were prepared to fight military battles to gain control of the promised land. These were some of the tragic consequences of millennial eschatology.

THE PRIESTLY HERALD OF GOOD NEWS

Author Unknown[34]

7. ...and Obadiah, the proselyte, arose from Damascus and went (8) to Dan, which is in the land of Israel, and Israelites [came], (9) men who are few and humble, and they worked wi[th] the proselyte Obadiah. (10) [In those] days, in the month of Elul, a priest from the sons of (11) Israel came, one of the Bible scholars whose name was Solomon (12) on his way to Dan, and he said to Obad[iah], the proselyte, and to the Je[ws] (13) who were in Dan, that in another two and a half months God would gather (14) his people the Israelites, from all the lands (15) to [Jeru]salem, the holy city. The proselyte Obadiah said (16) to Solomon, "How [do you] know this, Sir?" (17) Solomon said, "I am the man whom Israelites (18) are seeking," Then the proselyte Obadiah answered and said, "Look, I have heard that you are from the seed of Aaron the priest, and today (19) nineteen years [have elapsed] since I entered the covenant (20) of the God of Israel, and I have not heard that Israelites (21) are seeking sal[va]tion through [someone from the tribe of] Levi, but rather (22) through the prophet Elijah and the messianic [k]ing from the seed of (23) David, king of Israel. But now...(25) concerning your words. Then Solomon said...(26) "I eat no bread; I drink no water." Then *the proselyte Obadiah* said (27) to him, "What do you eat and drink?" (28) Solomon said,

---

[33] Buber's introduction to מדרש לקח טוב ויקרא, 24 (12b)-25 (13a).
[34] Hebrew text from Mann, "Messianic Movements," 260-61. RPL

"Pomegranates, figs, Almond[s], (29) nuts, Sycamine [figs], dates, and apples which [come] (30) from various trees, and I drink milk." Then *Obadiah* said to him (31) that he was a proselyte. Solomon was happy with him and said (32) to him. "Do not g[o] to Egy[pt] because from now until (33) two and a half months, we and all Israelite *men of the diaspora* will be (34) [ga]thered in Jerusalem." *The proselyte* Obadiah said (35) to Solomon, "I will go to Egypt and return (36) with our brothers, the Israelites who are in Egypt to (37) Jerusalem." Solomon was silent. Then Solomon went to (38) Tyre, and after the proselyte Obadiah went to Tyre and he came [back].

Summary

According to a colophon belonging to another document attributed to Obadiah, he became a proselyte in 4,862 of creation (A.D. 1102). At the time of the experience described here, he had seen a proselyte for nineteen years. This would have been about A.D. 1121. Mann[35] noted the active messianic movements in Mohammedanism at that time. At about the same time there was a certain Rabbi Moses Dari who made many predictions that came true. When he prophesied the very time when the Messiah would appear, however, he was mistaken. Many Jews had borrowed extensive amounts of money at 1000% interest, thinking the Messiah would come, they would all move to the promised land and never have to pay it back. Much suffering was caused by his prediction, according to Maimonides, and he was expelled to Palestine.

Like him, the Levite Solomon, said all Jews would go to Palestine for the final battle with the Gentiles. Obadiah was somewhat skeptical but willing to cooperate. There is no further report on the activity which Solomon stimulated, but in Persia arose another messianic expectation involving both father and son that proved to be disappointing.

THE HOPE THAT FAILED
Author Unknown[36]

(1)   ...in the days of the end time, and his n[ame] was Alafdel. *In those days...arose sons of* (2) *apostates of the people, and they were eager to make the vision stand,* (3) *but they stumbled* (Dan

[35] Mann, "Messianic Movements," 341-42.
[36] Hebrew text from Mann, "Messianic Movements," 336-37. RPL

11:14) in their words.³⁷ In the mou[ntains] which are in the land of
Kazaria,³⁸ (4) a Jew arose whose name was Solomon ben Duji, and
the name of his son (5) was Menahem,³⁹ and with them was a man
of glib speech, and his name was Ephraim ben (6) Azariah, the
Jerusalemite, who was well-known in ben Sahlon, and they wrote
(7) letters to all the [Jews both n]ear and far (8) in all the lands
which surrounded them and (9)...their letters [were sent] a very
great distance. (10) In all places where, on the face of the land,
(11) Jews are foun[d a]mong the people who, (12) under the whole
heaven, their re[port] reache[ed and] they *all* said (13) that the
time had come when Go[d] would gath[er] (14) his people Israel
from all the lands to Jerusal[em], (15) the holy city, and that
Solomon ben [D]uji was Elij[ah], and his son, (16) the Messiah. It
happened when all the J[ews] heard, (17) who were in all the lands
the words of their wri[tings]; they were *very* glad, (18) and they
waited for days and month[s], but [they did not] he[ar] nor see
(19) anything, and many of the Jews...(side 2, 20) Many indulged
in fasts and prayers and almsgiving, for they were waiting (21) the
salvation of God as he said through (22) his servants, the prophets.
When they failed to see anything, *their hearts* were broken (23)
within them, very much, and the Jews were ashamed (24) before
all the Gentiles, for all the Gentiles and uncircumcised heard (25)
the reports which came to all the Jews and all of them were (26)
laughing and mocking the Jews and saying, (27) "Look, the Jews
planned to fly, but they have n[o win]gs⁴⁰ (28) to fly to their land."
They continued to rene[w and] to teach and (29) to curse the Jews,
and the Gentiles were saying that everything (30) Jewish was false
and vain.⁴¹ In *those* days (31) in the city whose name was
Barakubah, which was a day's journey (32) from the city of
Adina,⁴² one of the Jews arose there, (33) a well-known man in
Ben Shadad, who was wise in his own eyes. (34) He made up
his mind to report a *vision*, but *he stumbled* (Dan 11:14) and told
many lies. (35) The king of Adina sent and took him and (36) the

---

³⁷ They were mistaken.
³⁸ A city in Persia.
³⁹ Perhaps the same leader who was otherwise known as David Alroy. His resistance
movement became so strong, and his designs so well-known that the king of Persia
threatened to kill all the Jews in his kingdom if he were not restrained. After he ignored all
warnings, a Caliph bribed David's father-in-law to kill him secretly.
⁴⁰ There is a report of the same, or a similar, event in relation to Alroy when many people
gathered to be carried on the wings of angels to Jerusalem, one night. They waited all night,
but the angels never came.
⁴¹ This is the end of the report on Menaham, Ephraim, and Solomon. The rest of the
report deals with another personality, Ben Shadad.
⁴² A city in Babylon.

Jews who were with him and put them in *his* [the king's] prison.
(37) Then Ben Shadad and the Jews who were with him (38) in
prison, and Ben Shadad prayed to...

Summary

These are cursory comments about a very prominent
personality, David Alroy, in all probability. His father, Solomon,
began a messianic movement which his son continued. The
movement gathered so many Jews together in a plan to overthrow
the king of Persia and recapture Jerusalem that the king arranged
to have him killed. One of the stories about Alroy is that he told
the Jews the angels would come on a certain night and carry them
to Jerusalem, as the scripture promised. This did not happen, but it
did not stop the movement until he was killed.

The fragment about Ben Shadad is too small to be very
informative. It does not claim that he was supposed to be a
messiah, but the fact that he and his followers were thrown into
prison implies that. The document breaks off with Ben Shadad
praying in prison. The continuing narrative may have told of his
release from prison, just as Peter (Acts 12:1-11), Paul, Silas (Acts
16:19-36), and Alroy were supposed to have been, but that is only
a conjecture.

JERUSALEM AND THE MESSIAH
Author Unknown[43]

Holy One of Israel, build Jerusalem![44]
Send us a redeemer, the proclaimer of good news.[45]
Pity the one unpitied, O holy One, dwelling in the heavens.
Say to Zion, "Arise!" and *turn the hearts of the sons to
                                        the fathers* (Mal 3:24).
Send *[out] your light and your truth* (Ps 43:3), the Levites
                                        with your song,
the priests for your [liturgical] service, with sacrifices and offerings,
Who can express your praise? For there is no end of praise.
Please deliver us from the oppressor, and let us worship you as
                                        in the years of old.

[43]"Song for the Sabbath Day," **סדר עבודת ישראל,** ed. Rabbi I. ben A.J. Dove
(Jerusalem 1937), xx. RPL

[44]Ariel, the name given to Jerusalem by the Romans after the Bar Cochba war.

[45]The redeemer was normally expected to be the son of David, and the proclaimer of
good news was to be his forerunner, Elijah (Mal 3:1). Here one figure seems to be expected
to fill both roles. This might be Melchizedek. See *To The Hebrews*, 119.

From distortions and distractions, turn every heart away.
Accept and beautify all deeds which they do before you sincerely.
Sons of the perfect ones[46] seek refuge in you; strengthen them
                                before they eyes of all.
Place honor and a crown on the head of your Messiah, and exalt
                                his throne for [his] session.

Summary

This is an impatient request that God act in behalf of the Jews.
The worshipper wanted the Messiah crowned, Jerusalem rebuilt,
worship restored to the temple, and the status of the Jews
enhanced before all the world.

THE ISHMAELITE SAVIOR
Author Unknown[47]

The year of favor[48] (?) to be redeemed without cost (Isa 52:3) from Edom,
    When they were avenged, vengeance from Edom by the Egyptians.
    Also this is the year, nine hundred, forty-five (A.D. 1185).
    At its end there will be those who pour out the blood of Edom.
    The distinguished one will wreak vengeance against Edom,
    the affliction of a people escaping from a wild ass (Gen 16:12)
                                and Edom.

Summary

This poet expected the Moslems to avenge the Christians at the
end of the very year in which he was writing (A.D. 1185). Once
this was done, he expected the Jews to escape from the Moslems as
well as the Christians. First, however, the Christians had to be
weakened by the Moslem forces. This would happen in the year
1185.

Mann has correctly noted the relationship between this poem
and the historical events of the time. In A.D. 1187 Saladin
defeated the Romans at the Horns of the Hittim, near Tiberias.
The author may have known of Saladin's preparations as well as

---

[46] The patriarchs, Abraham, Isaac, and Jacob.

[47] This is a fragment found in the Geniza of Egypt. The Hebrew text is from J. Mann,
Texts and Studies (New York, 1972) RPL

[48] The text reads שנת רצון אֶחָת, with אֶחָת pointed.

the troops gathering to David Alroy in resistance to the Crusaders.[49] The next document shows the character of the Messiah, according to Maimonides.

THE MEASURE OF THE MESSIAH
Maimonides[50]

I.   The Messianic king is destined to arise and to restore the kingdom of David 1) as it was (Kid 66a) 2) in the first kingdom, to build the sanctuary (Zeb 45a), and to gather the exiles of Israel. They will restore all the customary laws in his days as they were formerly. 4) They will offer sacrifices and observe sabbath year releases and jubilee (Sifra Lev 25:10), 5) according to all the commandments prescribed in the Torah. Everyone who does not believe in him, who does not wait for his advent, not only the rest of the prophets alone does he deny, but the [very] Torah [itself] and Moses our teacher.

You can see that the Torah testifies concerning him, as it is said, *The Lord your God will restore your captivity and have mercy upon you. Again he will gather you [from all the peoples where the the Lord your God has scattered you]. If you have been evicted to the ends of heaven, [from there the Lord your God will gather you, and from there he will bring you]. The Lord [your] God will bring you [into the land which your fathers possessed, that you may possess it]* (Dt 30:3-5). 7) These are the words which are explained in the Torah. They include all the words which have been said through all the prophets, even in the passage on Balaam as it said, and there he prophesied of the two messiahs, the first messiah who is David who saved Israel from the hand of her oppressors, and the last messiah who will arise from his descendants, who will deliver Israel [at the last]. There he said, *I see him, but not now* (Num 24:17). This is David. 8) *I behold him, but not near* (Num 24:17). This is the messianic king. *A star stepped forth from Jacob* (Num 24:17). This is David. *A staff will arise from Israel* (Num 24:17). This is the messianic king. *He beat down the corners of Moab* (Num 24:17). This is David, 9) and thus he says, *He struck Moab and measured them with a [measuring] line* (II Sam 8:2). *He will shatter all the sons of Sheth* (Num 24:17). This is the messianic king, of whom it is

[49]See Mann, *Texts and Studies* II, 458.

[50]The text is from Maimonides, ‏"ספר סופתים משנה תורה ",הלכות המלכים"‏, ed. M.D. Rabinowitz (Jerusalem, 1962) XIV, *perek* 11, I-IV, 1-46 (412-17). SMI.

said, *He shall rule from sea to sea [and from the river to the ends of the land]* (Zech 9:10; Ps 72:8). *Edom will become an acquisition* (Num 24:18). This is David, as it is said, *Edom will become servants for David* (II Sam 8:14). 11a) *[Seir] will become an acquisition* (Num 24:18). This is the messianic king, as it is said, *Saviors will go up into Mount Zion [to rule Mount Esau, and the kingdom will be the Lord's]* (Obad 21). 12)

II.   Even in the cities of refuge, he says, *If the Lord your God enlarges your border...then you shall add three other cities [to these three]* (Dt 19:8-9). From the age, this promise has not been fulfilled (Num 35:14; Josh 20:2). 13) The Lord does not command in vain, 14) but with the words of the prophets no evidence is necessary, because all the books [of the prophets] are full of this promise. 15)

III.   Do not entertain the opinion that the messianic king is required to perform signs and wonders (Dt 13:2), 16) renew things in the age, or raise the dead 17) and other things such as these 17a). That is not so, because, note that Rabbi Akiba was the great scholar of the mishnaic scholars, and he used to support[51] 18) ben Kozibah the king (BK 77b). He used to say of him that he was the messianic king (JTaanit 4:5). 20) He and all the scholars of his generation imagined that he was the messianic king until he was killed in his iniquities 21) When he was killed, it became known to them that he was not [the Messiah], and scholars had not asked of him a sign or a wonder (LamR 2:2; San 93b; Ber 34b). 22) The important words among these are that this Torah, its statutes and traditional laws are for the age, and for ages of ages. 23) [Believers] must not add to them or remove [any] of them. 24)

IV.   If a king from the house of David should arise and study 24) in the Torah and engage himself in the commandments as David his father, according to the written and oral Torah, and make all Israelites to walk in it and to hold to it firmly, 26) and should he fight the wars of the Lord, 27) then this would prove that he was the Messiah. If he were to act and succeed, 29) build the sanctuary in its place, gather the exiles of Israel, then this man would surely be the Messiah. He will direct the whole world to worship the Lord together, as it is said, *Then I will change the Gentiles to [speak] a clear language, to call upon the name of the Lord, and to serve him [with] one shoulder* (Zeph 3:9). 32)

51Literally, "raise his weapons."

If 33) he does not succeed this much, or is killed, it is certain that he is not the one whom the Torah promised. He is like all the kings who were perfect and approved when they died, but the holy one blessed be He raised him only to test many with him, as it is said, *[Some] of the teachers will stumble, so as to test them, purify them, and make them white until the time of the end, for it is still for the appointed time* (Dan 11:35).

Even about Jesus the Nazorean, 34) who imagined that he was the Messiah, but was killed at the hands of the court, 35) Daniel already prophesied, as it is said, *The sons of the apostates of your people will be tempted to initiate the vision,* 36) *but they will stumble* (Dan 11:14). Is there a greater stumbling block than this of which all the prophets spoke? That the Messiah would redeem the Israelites, deliver them, gather their exiles, 37) and strengthen their virtues [was expected]. But he [Jesus] caused the Israelites to perish by the sword, scatter their remnants, humble them, change their Torah, and lead much of the world astray to worship a god other than the Lord.

But the thoughts of the Creator of the world are [so strong that] there is not strength enough in man to overtake them, for his ways are not like our ways, and our thoughts are not his thoughts (Isa 55:8-9). 38) All these words of Jesus, the Nazorean, and of this 39) Ishmaelite who arose after him, are only [destined] to make the way 40) straight for the messianic king and to prepare all the world to serve the Lord together as it is said, *For then* 41) *I will change the Gentiles to [speak] a clear language, to call upon the name of the Lord, and to serve him [with] one shoulder* (Zeph 3:9).

How is that? Already the world is completely filled with the words of the Messiah 42), the Torah, and the commandments, and these words have been spread into distant islands and among many people with uncircumcised hearts, and they negotiate with these words and with the commandments of the Torah. Some say, "These commandments were true [at one time], but they have already been annuled in this time. 43) They are not valid for generations."

Others say, "There are secret matters in them, and they should not be understood according to their literal meaning. 44) The Messiah has already come, 45) and he has revealed their secrets. But when the messianic king truly arises, he will succeed, exalt, and be magnified. 46) They [the Christians] will all repent at once and realize that their fathers have inherited falsehood, and that their prophets and their fathers have led them astray."

Summary

This analysis of the role of the Messiah is very similar to the description that is given in Maimonides' *Epistle to Yemen*. The difference is that the letter dealt with specific emphasis related to the pseudo-messiah who had arisen in Yemen. This essay is more thorough and objective. Maimonides' source of authority is the scripture. The expected Messiah would be a human being, a successful king of David's line. He was directly compared to David himself and to other pretenders, like Bar Cochba. He would rule the entire world from Jerusalem, and all the peoples of the world would have to learn Hebrew. Jesus and Mohammed were both false messiahs, but they extended the teaching of the Torah and Jewish customs to prepare the world to accept the true Jewish Messiah, when he comes. Therefore they both fit into God's plan for the messianic age.

Another famous scholar to analyze the doctrine of messianism and redemption was the Rabbi Hai Gaon.

THE TOPIC OF SALVATION

Hai Gaon[52]

Since you have asked to have explained to you how the salvation will be, from beginning to end, as well as the resurrection of the dead and the new heaven, if I were to explain every single point in detail, time would not permit, but I will [instead] speak generally about every point, and say:[53]

The beginning of salvation [is that] for which the scholars have given a sign saying, "The week [of years] when the son of David comes, etc." (San 98a). In that week Edom will rule over Israel, no less than nine months nor more than three years, because Israelites will take the kingdom only from the hand of Edom,[54] as it is said, *And Edom will become a possession* (Num 24:18), *and he will go*

---

[52]Follows the text (A) of E. Ashkenazi, Taam Zakenim, תשובת שאלה ובנו האי גאון זה צריך לאמור על ענין הישועה (Frankfort a.M., 1854), 59a-61a, except when the reading was difficult. On those occasions, variants were accepted from R.A. ben R. Azriel, ספר ארוגת הבוסם, ed. E.E. Urbach (Jerusalem, 1939) I, 256-262 (B). These are indicated by § §. Omissions following B are noted by a footnote. Substitutions are noted by both. SML

[53]Omitted with B is, "In the years that remain before the end are eight years." Eight does not make sense with the "week" that follows. Ibn Shemuel, מדרשי גאולה (Jerusalem, 1968), altered the text to read, "seven."

[54]As elsewhere in rabbinic literature, "Edom" means Rome. The understanding of the scripture here is that God promised that Israel would overthrow Rome, and not Ishmael, the Moslem Arabs, which was the other possibility.

down from Jacob [and he will destroy the remnant of the city]
(Num 24:18-19), after the Edomites have taken the kingdom from
the hand of the Assyrians,[55] as it is said, *And the ships from the
land of the Kittim* (Num 24:24),[56] after the Assyrians have taken
the kingdom from the hand [A = "side"] of the Kenites, which is
the government of the Ishmaelites,[57] as it is said, *Nevertheless, the
Kenites will be burned* (Num 24:22). Therefore when we see that
Edom has ruled the land of Israel, we believe that our salvation
has begun, as it is said, *Saviors will go up [to Mount Zion to rule
Mount Esau, and the kingdom will be the Lord's]* (Obad 21).

In that time a man from the sons of Joseph will arise,[58] and he
will be called the Messiah of the Lord, and many men in Upper
Galilee will gather themselves to him, and he will be their king.
Also other men will collect themselves to him, two or three from
one city and four or five from another city. Concerning that hour,
he said, *And I will take you, one from a city and two from a
family* (Jer 3:14), but most Israelites will remain in their exile, for it
will not be made clear to them that the end has come.

Then the Messiah son of Joseph with the men collected to him
will go up from Galilee to Jerusalem. He will kill the procurator of
the king of Edom and the people who are with him. Concerning
that hour he says, *And I will wreak my vengeance against Edom
through my people Israel* (Ezek 25:14), and he will dwell in
Jerusalem several days.

When all the peoples will hear that a king has arisen for the
children of Israel in Jerusalem, they will arise against them in the
rest of the lands, and they will drive them out and tell them, "Until
now you have been with us in [good] faith, since you did not have
a king or prince, but now that you have a king, you may not dwell
in our land!"[59] Many Israelites will go out to the wilderness areas
which are near their countries. Concerning that hour, he says,
And I will bring you to the wilderness of the peoples (Ezed 20:35).
They will dwell there in tents, and many of them will lack bread

---

[55]Or, possibly the Syrians, as in the War Scroll and the Habakkuk Commentary.

[56]As in the Habakkuk Commentary, the Kittim are the Romans.

[57]The Ishmaelites are the Arabs or Moslems. These are also from the territory formerly
held by the Kenites, so they were called Kenites. Rabbi Hai Gaon also expected Israel to
destroy the Moslems.

[58]Omitted in agreement with B are the words בדברא בלבד. Ibn Shmuel altered the text
to read במדבר אלוהים.

[59]The question raised here was one of double loyalty. So long as Jews had no other
government to which to owe allegiance, they were welcome in other lands. When they had
their own government, other governments suspected that they would exist in their lands as
saboteurs.

and water. Concerning that hour, he says, *Again I will make you dwell in tents* (Hos 12:10). They will suffer according to their deeds. Concerning that hour, he says, *And I will make you pass over under the staff, and I will bring you into the established covenant* (Ezek 20:37). Many will leave the covenant of Israel, because they will detest their lives. Concerning them, he says, *I will make you pass over* (Ezek 20:37), *and I will select from you the rebels and those who transgress against me. [I will bring them out of the land where they sojourn, but they will not enter the land of Israel]* (Ezek 20:38).[60]

It will happen that the Messiah son of Joseph and all the people who are with him will dwell in Jerusalem, and Armilos[61] will hear their report. Then he will come and perform magic and enticements to lead many of them astray. Then he will go up and engage in battle against Jerusalem, and he will conquer the Messiah son of Joseph and his people. He will kill some of them, take some of them captive, and divide their booty. Concerning that hour, he says, *And I will gather all the Gentiles to Jerusalem for war* (Zech 14:2). Even the Messiah son of Joseph will be killed, and there will be great suffering for Israel. Concerning that hour, he says, *And they will look at me whom they stabbed. They will mourn for him, as one mourns for an only child and weep bitterly over him, as one weeps over a first-born.] On that day the mourning will be as great [in Jerusalem as the mourning for Hadadrimmon in the plain of Megiddo]* (Zech 12:10-11).

Why will permission be given to Armilos to murder the Messiah son of Joseph? So as to break the heart of the dissidents in Israel, who have no faith. They will say, "This is the man in whom we have hoped; he has already come and been killed,"[62] but no salvation will be left for them [the Israelites] any more. They will leave the covenant of Israel and cling to the Gentiles, and they [the Gentiles] will murder them. Concerning them, he says, *They will kill all the sinners of my people with the sword* (Amos 9:10). Those who are left will stay in Jerusalem. They will be tested and purified. Even these who go out to the wilderness areas will be tested, examined, and of those, about two parts will vanish and about a third will be left. Concerning them, he says, *"It will hap-*

---

[60]Using the text, *I will make you pass over under the staff* (Ezek 20:37), which referred to admission into the covenant, Rab Hai omitted the last of the text and used it to refer to those who pass over or leave the covenant. These are not the covenanters but the apostates.

[61]A figure personifying Rome or Christianity.

[62]Compare the comment of some of Jesus' followers after the crucifixion: *But we hoped that he was the one to redeem Israel* (Lk 24:21).

pen in all the land," says the Lord, "two thirds [of those] in it will be cut off, and the third will be left, [and I will bring the third into fire and I will test them as silver is tested"] (Zech 13:8-9). All the birth pangs of the Messiah will pass over them in that hour, which are described in many places from the scripture and from words of our sages. After this, they will cry out and the holy One blessed be He will hear their cry, as it is said, *He will call on my name, and I will answer him* (Zech 13:9).

In that time Elijah will be revealed from the wilderness to those who are in the wilderness places, and he will restore their hearts, as it is said, *He will turn the hearts of the fathers [to their children and the hearts of the children to their fathers, lest I come and smite the land with a curse]* (Mal 3:24). Also the Messiah son of David will be revealed to those who are left in the land of Patros, for already the Messiah son of Joseph will have subdued the people before him, as it is written, *Behold, I am sending my messenger, and he will prepare the way before him [and suddenly he will come to his temple, the Lord whom you are seeking]* (Mal 3:1). Then the Israelites who are in the wilderness places will follow Elijah until in Judah the Israelites who are in the land of Israel will meet with the Messiah son of David. Concerning them he says, *In those days the house of Judah and the house of Israel will go [and they will come together from the land of the north upon the land which I provided for their fathers]* (Jer 3:18).

Most of those who are murdered will be in the midst of the land for forty days, because when the Messiah son of Joseph is murdered, his corpse will be discarded for forty days, but nothing unclean will touch it until the Messiah son of David comes and revives him by the word of the Lord. This will be the beginning of the signs which will take place, and it is the resurrection of the dead which he will revive.

Then the Messiah son of David, Elijah, and the Israelites who come from the wilderness areas to Jerusalem will dwell in tranquil security for many days. They will build houses and pland vineyards and they will succeed in cattle and business, until Gog hears of them, as it is written, *I will say, "I will go up against an undefended land; I will come [against] a quiet people, dwelling in confidence"* (Ezek 38:11). And the land of Gog and Magog are in the land of Edom, for thus it is said about him, *The chief prince of Meshek and Tubal* (Ezek 38:2). He will bring the peoples from all the areas around him and from Edom, as it is said, *The parts of the north and all its flanks [of soldiers], many peoples* (Ezek 38:6).

Even many peoples from every single city and every single state through which he passes will gather under the wings of the Shekinah the good men of the Gentiles. Then all of them will come to join battle, and they will fight against Jerusalem with the Messiah, son of David, Elijah, and the men in her. Concerning that hour, he says, *Behold I am setting Jerusalem [as] a cup of reeling* (Zech 12:2), and[63] *[You, son of man, prophesy against Gog and say, "Thus says the Lord God, 'Behold, I am against you, Gog, chief of Meshek and Tubal. I will turn you around, drive you ahead, and bring you up from the regions of the North, and I will bring you against the mountains of Israel. I will strike your bow from your left hand, and I will make your arrows fall from your right hand. You will fall upon the mountains of Israel, you and all your hordes and the peoples who are with you. I will give [your corpses] to the ravenous birds of every kind and to the beasts of the field for food. You will fall ypon the surface of the field, because I have spoken,' says the Lord. 'I will send a fire into Magog and all those who dwell securely in the coastlands, and they will know that I am the Lord, and I will make my holy name known in the midst of my people Israel. I will not let my holy Name be profaned again, and the nations will know that I am the Lord, the holy One of Israel.[64] Look, it is coming and it will take place,' says the Lord God. 'That is the day of which I have spoken. Those who dwell in the cities of Israel will go out and burn and make fires of weapons, shields, bucklers, bows and arrows, clubs, and spears, and they will make fires with them for seven years'"]* (Ezek 39:1-9). In that hour, *there will be a great earthquake in the land of Israel* (Ezek 38:19). Even *the Lord will go out and fight against those Gentiles* (Zech 14:3) with four kinds of punishments: Some of them will perish by fire and brimstone and missiles for a catapult, which are meteor stones. Concerning them, he says, *Torrential rains and meteorites, fire, and brimstone* (Ezek 38:22). Some of them will perish, one with the sword of the other, as it is said, *I will call upon him to all the mountains, a sword. [The sword of a man will be against his brother]* (Ezek 38:21). Some of their flesh will rot, limb by limb. Concerning them he says, *This will be the Plague* (Zech 14:12). Then each man will seize the hand of his neighbor to lean upon him, and his hand will fall off, as it is said, *And each man will seize the hand of his neighbor, [and his*

---

[63]Rab Hai adds "and everything which is said in the passage on Gog." For this, Ezek 39:1-9 has been substituted.

[64]Literally, "I will not profane my holy Name again." The author assumed that the Lord's Name would not be profaned if he himself had not initiated the action.

hand will rise up over the hand of his neighbor] (Zech 14:13). On some of them there will fall a blemish of blindness or a broken arm or leg or slashed nose and ear, and they will flee and go to distant states, and they will tell what their eyes have seen, as it is said, §*I will place on them*§[65] *a sign, and I will send some of them away [as] refugees [to the nations, to Tarshish, Put, and Lud, who draw the bow, to Tubal and Javan, to the coastlands afar off, that have not heard my fame or seen my glory; and they shall declare my glory among the nations]* (Isa 66:19).[66]

In that hour all the Gentiles will consider and say, "What gift [does a man] offer to this king? Are not all silver, garments, and weapons unimportant to him? But the sons of his people and his council [will say], "We will bring him a gift, as it is said, *And they will bring all your brothers from all the nations [as] a gift to the Lord* (Isa 66:20). Every nation will offer [to bring] them [each in the style] according to its wealth, some of them with horses, with horsemen, covered wagons, with mules, and with carriages, and some of them will carry them on their shoulders, as it is said, *And they will bring your sons in [their] laps* (Isa 49:22). Some of them in boats of Tarshich, as it is said, *And boats of Tarshish at the first to bring your sons from afar* (Isa 60:9). Some of them in papyrus vessels, as it is said, *Who sends messengers in the sea, in papyrus vessels on the surface of the water* (Isa 18:2). *From beyond the rivers of Ethiopia [my supplicants, the daughter of my dispersed ones, will bring my offering]* (Zeph 3:10). This is because there are no wooden boats able to go there because of stones and rocks which are concealed in the water. The rest of the Israelites which are in wilderness areas where there are no peoples there to bring them, our God will carry them as with his wind, as it is said with the north wind, *Saying to the north [wind], "Give!" and to the south [wind], "Do not hold back"* (Isa 43:6); and just as they are carried on the cloudlets and on the cloud, as it is said, *Who are these flying like a cloud* (Isa 60:8)? And when these exiles come, he will separate for them the sea of Egypt in one place and the river [Euphrates][67] in seven fords. Concerning that hour, he says, *I will open up rivers on bare hills, [and springs in the midst of the valleys; I will make the wilderness a pool of water, and the dry land springs of water]. [the myrtle, and the olive tree in the wilderness]* (Isa 41:18-19) to provide cover for them, but there will

[65]A is incoherent, וסתי מקום. B is used here, which is considered with the scripture passage quoted.
[66]See also Saadia Gaon, "Deliverance."
[67]See also Saadia, "Deliverance," part 6.

not be left one Israelite alive in any place. All will come to
Jerusalem, as it is said, *I will not leave any of them there alive
anymore. Only the dead will be left* (Ezek 39:28).[68]

Then he will blast with a great trumpet,[69] as it is said, *In that day
a great trumpet will be sounded* (Isa 27:13). Some say that Zerbu-
babel will blow this trumpet. But why will there be a great earthquake? So that when the bones that have been trampled on in the
land will arise and whoever is built into buildings and whoever is
burned in the bricks, and whoever is buried under the debris,[70] and
bone will approach bone, just as it is written in the chapter on the
valley (Ezek 37). Then the holy One blessed be He will stretch ten-
dons on them, cover them with flesh, and wrap skin over them,
but there will be no breath in them. After that the holy One
blessed be He will bring down the dew of life from heaven which
contains the light of breathing life, as it is written, *Your dead will
live; my corpses will arise; [they will jump up and sing, those who
dwell in the dust because of the dew of lights in your dew]* (Isa
26:19). They will realize that they were alive and that they had
been dead, and after that they are revived, as it is written, *And
you will know that I am the Lord when I have opened your graves
and when I have raised you from your graves, my people* (Ezek
37:13).

Everyone who has a deformity will arise at first with his deformity. If he is old, he will come in his old age and leanness of his
flesh, so that people will not say, "These are other creatures." After that the holy One blessed be He will heal them, as it is said,
*Then the eyes of the blind will be opened [and the ears of the deaf
will be unstopped; then the lame man will leap like a hart]* (Isa
35:5-6). Then *your youth will be renewed like an eagle* (Ps 103:5).
[We shall raise up against him] seven shepherds and eight princes
(Micah 5:5), and they are: Adam, Seth, Methuselah, Abraham,
Jacob, Moses, and David; and the *eight princes* are Jesse, Saul,
Samuel, Amos, Zephaniah, Hezekiah, Elijah, and the Messiah. For
whom is this the resurrection of the dead? For everyone who has
been righteous among the Israelites from the very beginning, and
also for the one who has sinned and done penance. But the one

[68]Heavily dependent upon Saadia, "Deliverance," part 6.

[69]The jubilee trumpet announcing that the period of "slavery" was over and the land
would be restored to the "original owners."

[70]Notice the literalness with which Rab Hai understood the resurrection. Since bodies
would have decayed and been assimilated accidently into all sorts of new forms, he
assumed some miracle would be required to reunite the various parts from their present
position.

whose iniquities exceed his merits and has not done penance will not arise in the days of the Messiah, as it is said, *Many of those who sleep in the dust of the ground will wake up, [some to life for the age, and others to disgrace, to reproach for the age]* (Dan 12:2). Therefore our sages have taught us. "He became ill and stretched out to die. They were saying to him, 'Confess! because this is the way of all those who die.' But if he does not know how to confess, they tell him, 'Say, "I have sinned; I have committed iniquity; and I have transgressed. May my death atone for all my iniquities."'" This is so that every Israelite may merit resurrection of the dead. Therefore, the dead whom the holy One blessed be He is destined to revive will not return again to their dust, as it is said, *These for life of the age* (Dan 12:2), and he says, *He will be called "holy," everyone who is written for life in Jerusalem* (Isa 4:3). Then Israelites will be surprised and will say, "From where have all these suddenly come? as it is said, *And she will say in her heart, "Who has given birth to these for me"* (Isa 49:21)? Even the Gentiles will be surprised, as it is said, *Who has heard anything like this? Who has seen anything like this* (Isa 66:8).

After those who have died and who are alive have been gathered, the temple will be revealed to us, and its plan in its position, according to the vision which Ezekiel, son of Buzi, the prophet-priest, saw. There are some who say it will come down from heaven onto its place, as it is said, *Jerusalem, which is built like a city whose fellowship in united to her* (Ps 122:3).

Then all the Israelites will be prophets, as it is said, *And it will happen after this, I will pour out my spirit on all flesh, [and your sons and your daughters will prophesy. Your old men shall dream dreams, and your young men shall see visions]* (Joel 3:1). [Even] the male and female slaves of Israel [will be included], as it is said, *Also on the male slaves and upon the female slaves [in those days, I will pour out my spirit]* (Joel 3:2). The Gentiles who are left will be converted, as it is said, *Because then I will change for the peoples a clear tongue [to call upon the name of the Lord, all of them]* (Zeph 3:9).[1] *And they will say, "Let us go up to the mountain of the Lord, to the house of the God of Jacob, and he will teach us of his ways, and we will walk in his paths. For from Zion the law will go out, and the word of the Lord, from Jerusalem* (Isa 2:3). When they come before the messianic king, he will command

---

[1] Rab Hai assumed that only Jews would be allowed to speak Hebrew (the clear tongue). Since the scripture promised that the Gentiles would all speak Hebrew, this meant they would all become proselytes.

their swords and wars to perish, as it is said, *They will beat their swords to plow shares, [and their spears into pruning hooks; nation shall not lift up sword against nation, neither shall they learn war any more]* (Isa 2:4).[72]

Then Sodom and Gomorrah will dwell in their cities and the entire valley, lest there be any flaw in the land of Israel in the transformation that takes place in its midst, as it is written, *Your sister, Sodom, and her daughters will return to their ancient position* (Ezek 16:55). Also every evil beast will perish from the land, as it is said, *And the wolf will dwell with the sheep, [and the leopard shall lie down with the kid, and the calf and the lion and the fatling together, and a little child will lead them. The cow and the bear shall feed; their young shall lie down together; and the lion shall eat straw like the ox. The suckling child will play over the hole of the asp, and the weaned child shall put his hand on the adder's den]. They will not hurt, and they will not destroy in all my holy mountain* (Isa 11:6-9).

The people whom the messianic king will find will live long lives, and they will die,[73] as it is said, *They will not build and another dwell; they will not plant and another eat, [for as the days of the tree are the days of my people]* (Isa 65:22). A young lad or a youth will not die, as it is said, *There will be no longer an infant of days [who dies] nor an old man who will not complete his days, for a lad will die at the age of one hundred, [and the sinner, a hundred years old, will be cursed]* (Isa 65:20). He will uproot death from the age,[74] as it is written, *Death is swallowed up in victory* (Isa 25:8). The dead in the days of the Messiah will live for life in the age to come[75] by the merit of the perfectly righteous. A man, a hundred years of age, will not die a certain death, but thus it will

[72]Peace would come when the Gentiles were forced to submit to Jewish domination. At that time Gentiles would be forbidden to have arms, so they could not rebel. That would guarantee peace.

[73]This means the days of the Messiah will take place on earth, and it is not a condition of deathless existence.

[74]That is not from the "world" or from "eternity," as עולם is frequently translated, but from the age to come.

[75]This distinguishes the days of the Messiah from the age to come. The days of the Messiah here precede the age to come. The days of the Messiah are those whereby the Messiah comes and overthrows all of the Gentiles and reestablishes Israelite rule from Jerusalem. The age to come is the age of peace and prosperity that follows. Both take place here on earth (See M. Waxman, גלות וגאולה בספרות ישראל [New York, 1952], 215, 221-22). Notice that Rab Hai thought Jews would gain admission into life in the age to come by the merit of the perfectly righteous. Christians, who consider Jesus the perfectly righteous, pray that "by the merits and death of thy Son Jesus Christ, and through faith in his blood, we and thy whole Church may obtain forgiveness of our sins" and so receive life in the age to come. *Ritual of the Methodist Church* (Nashville, c1964), 27.

be in the time of salvation: Whoever dies at the age of one hundred will be like one who now dies at the age of twenty, and even if there is a man a hundred years old; if he sins against a man and curses him, it will not cause him to suffer, because he will not appear in their eyes to suffer, since he will be young like a twenty year old man to us.

In those times, when the temple and Jerusalem are revealed, the Shekinah will come down from heaven and be established as a pillar of fire from the earth and [will reach] up to heaven, as it is said, *And the Lord will create on the dwelling of Mount Zion [over every institution and over its assemblies a cloud and smoke by day and the shining of a flaming fire by night]* (Isa 4:5). Everyone who beseeches (Heaven) [parenthesis in text] to come to Jerusalem will see from his [own] country that pillar of fire, and he will walk in its light until he reaches Jerusalem, as it is said, *And the Gentiles will walk to your light* (Isa 60:3), because that light will be greater than the light of the sun and the moon which makes the two of them pale, as it is said, *The moon will be ashamed, and the sun will be embarrassed, because the Lord of armies will rule on Mount Zion and in Jerusalem* (Isa 24:23).

In that hour they will see the heaven and the earth as if they had been renewed and as if [the] heaven and earth of enslavement has passed away and were changed, and a new heaven and earth were brought in their place,[76] as it is said, *For behold I am creating a new heaven and a new earth* (Isa 65:17). Also they will see Jerusalem and Israel as if they were new, and as if Israel and Jerusalem of enslavement had been changed and passed away, and as if others were brought in their place, [an Israel and a Jerusalem] of joy and gladness, as it is said, *For behold, I am creating Jerusalem a delight and her people, gladness* (Isa 65:18).

They will dwell in their kingdom until the end of the age. There are some who say until the completion of seven thousand years from the days of creation (A.D. 3240). There are [some who say] many thousands [of years] with no known limit. After this heaven and earth will come to an end, as it is said, *For heaven will vanish like smoke; [the earth will wear out like a garment, and they who*

---

[76]The real change here is not a new heaven and a new earth in essence, but a change of character of the present heaven and earth. This is brought about by a change of control. In the present age, the Gentiles rule and the Jews are more or less subservient. In the age to come, Israel is destined to rule, and the Gentiles are destined to be slaves (Isa 61). This difference is enough from a Jewish point of view that it is "as if heaven and earth of enslavement had passed away and were changed, and a new heaven and earth were brought in their place." Compare Rab Hai's expectations to those of the NT seer (Rev 21).

*dwell in it will die like gnats; but my salvation will be for the age,
and my righteousness will have no successor]* (Isa 51:6).

The dead will live and see the salvation, and they will go out by
themselves to the world-to-come, as it is said, *My salvation will be
for the age, and my righteousness [will not be taken away]* (Isa
51:6). In that hour the holy One blessed be He will create another
heaven and earth, apart from these, and the righteous will dwell
among them for an age and for ages of ages, as it is said, *For just as
the new heaven and the new earth which I am making will stand
before me continually, thus will your seed and your name stand*
(Isa 66:22).

> May the Lord look from heaven in your favor;
> may he listen from on high to your supplications;
> may he turn to you with his mercy.
>
> May he leave it[77] with you to bring you out of your servitude;
> may he build the sanctuary and complete the temple in your
>   lifetimes,
> and build his house in your days.
>
> May he bring near the end of your redemption,
> accelerate quickly the coming of your Messiah,
> and gather your dispersed ones from among your enemies.
> May the Lord of mercy speak to bring that time and that period
>   near!
> May this be [his] will. Amen!

Summary

In dealing with the topic of salvation, Rab Hai Gaon was
heavily dependent upon the earlier work of Saadia Gaon in some
parts of his essay. Like Saadia, Hai considered the scripture as the
only authority for determining the nature of the coming salvation.
He was familiar with the tradition that the Messiah from North
Israel should precede the Messiah from Judah. He was also familiar
with Armilos and the death and resurrection of the Messiah of
Joseph.

Through his essay, Rab Hai interpreted salvation as the
deliverance of Jews from the diaspora to a position of world control from Jerusalem. This transformation would take place in a real
war with Gog and Magog, which was another name for the op-

---

[77]His mercy.

posing Gentiles. The battle would be fought at the edge of Jerusalem, and the enemy would be defeated by the force of arms, aided by physical ailments and natural disaster with which the Lord would afflict the Gentiles so as to give victory to the Jews. The Gentiles would be the ones who transported the Jews back to Jerusalem where they could rule the Gentiles. An earthquake would dislodge all decayed and disintegrated parts of Jewish corpses from the buildings, bricks, or debris into which they had been assimilated. Once broken loose from their surroundings, these parts would reunite into corpses which would then be revived to take part in the age to come, which would be the age following the victorious war against the Gentiles. This restoration of the Davidic kingdom, with rule extending over all the Gentiles, would be such a glorious age it was figuratively described as a new heaven and a new earth.

This salvation which Rab Hai anticipated was restorative and utopian in nature. It involved the restoration of the Jewish rule from Jerusalem, but it was to be more extensive than the rule of David or the Hasmoneans. This all was understood, however, in very practical, political, and military terms.

THE ORIGIN OF ARMILOS

Saadia Gaon[78]

Our sages (May they be remembered for good) have said (8) that in the last days a king, whose name is Armilos, will rule in Edom. He will go out from Rome, (9) and he will rule the entire world. He will have six fingers on each hand, and he will go as far as Jerusalem, and he will rule over her for nine months. (71:1) During his days there will be great hardship for the Israelites. He will want to lead the Israelites astray, following his lies, but they will not want to do his will. Therefore, they will go out to wilderness places, just as our fathers went out into the wilderness, and they will gather the tribes.(2) The Messiah son of Joseph ben Hoshiel will come forth. He will take men from Israel with him, and he will make war with the wicked Armilos, but he will not prevail over him, since Armilos will be stronger than he and will kill the Messiah son of Joseph. All Israelites will mourn for him, families [by] families (Zech 12:12-14). After this, the Messiah son of David

[78]Text from B.M. Lewin, אוצר הגאונים: מסכת יומא וסוכה (Jerusalem, 1934), 70-72 (*daf* 193). This and the reference in Saadia's "Convictions and Beliefs" are the earliest references to Armilos in datable documents. SML.

will arise, whose name is Menahem ben Amiel, but the Israelites will not believe him until he revives the Messiah son of Joseph before them. Then Elijah (May he be remembered for good) and Michael will appear before them in that hour. The reason Armilos came forth [is to fulfill the prophecy], as it is said, *and the house of Jacob*[79] *will become a fire, [and the house of Joseph,*[80] *a flame, and the house of Esau*[81] *will be stubble. They will burn them and consume them, and there will be no survivor of the house of Esau. The Lord has spoken]* (Obad 18).

When we said that in his days there will be hardship for them [the Israelites], as it is said, (4) *He will hope to change the times and the law, and they will be given into his hand for a time, two times, and half a time* (Dan 7:25). It is well-known that this Armilos came forth from a stone which is in Rome, (5) as it is said, (6) *For behold the stone which I have set before Joshua* (Zech 3:9). When we said that he will rule for nine months, [we have proof from scripture] as it is said, *Therefore he will give them until the time [is completed] for a pregnant woman to give birth* (Micah 5:2). When we said that he would drive out the Israelites, and they would go to the wilderness areas and he will lead them like blind men in a way which they have never known, [the scriptural proof is], as it is said, (8) *I will lead the blind in a way [that they do not know]* (Isa 42:16). At that time they will seek mercy before the Lord that the Shekinah might dwell with them and walk with them in those wilderness areas. In that connection, Solomon has said, (9) *Come, my beloved, let us go out into the field*[82] (SS 7:12). Why will they go out into the wilderness places? As it is said, (10) *I will bring you to the wilderness of the Gentiles* (Ezek 20:35), and it is written, (11) *Behold I will allure her and bring her [to] the wilderness* (Hos 2:16). They will be hungry and thirsty, and our sages (May they be remembered for good) said that this grief, which is mentioned, will come upon them for forty-five days: Tebeth and half of Shebat. Many will go astray after the wicked one. They will say, "Woe to us! Is this the one for whom we have waited expectantly for many years and many times?" The righteous ones among them will be going from pillar to post of Israelites to speak to their hearts and to strengthen them in the unity of the Name. The sages (May they be remembered for good) have said that they would be hungry and thirsty, as it is said, (12)

[79]Here, apparently, the Jews.
[80]The Samaritans from North Israel.
[81]The Edomites; i.e., the Romans and Christians.
[82]Apparently an invitation by the Shekinah to the Israelites, "the beloved."

Just as I have judged your fathers (Ezek 20:36). This is hunger, as it is said, *to kill all this congregation with famine* (Ex 16:3), and the thirst, as it is said, (14) *And the people there will be thirsty for water* (Ex 17:3). How [can you prove] that they will go astray? As it is said, (15) *I will purge out the rebels and those who transgress against me from among you* (Ezek 20:38). There will be proselytes, but they will not enter the land, as it is said, (16) *Strengthen the weak hands* (Isa 35:3).[63]

Therefore [Solomon] said, *Let us arise early [to go] to the vineyards* (SS 7:13). He urged, *There I will give you my love* (SS 7:13). *Going out* (SS 7:13)--these are the two messiahs, the son of Joseph[64] and the son of David.[65] And he urged, *The love apples give forth fragrance* (SS 7:14). [This is] the gathering of the Israelites with the tribes. Therefore he said, *The new with the old* (SS 7:14), and the righteous and the wise men among them will see, as it is said,[66] *[Over our doors are all choice fruits ...which I have laid up for you, my beloved]* (SS 7:14).

Introduction to Abraham bar Ḥiyya

Abraham bar Ḥiyya (A.D. 1065-1136) was a rabbi in Barcelona, Spain and also an astronomer and philosopher. He was the first European rabbi to produce an eschatological work, and he strongly influenced Nahmonides and Abravanel. Whereas most other Jewish scholars dealt with the date when the end was expected to come along with other theological considerations related to redemption and ethics, Abraham bar Ḥiyya took all the ethical, biblical, and political dimensions for granted. He then concentrated on one point: *When* would the desired end come? How long did Jews have to endure the diaspora? To reach this decision, he used Daniel, the prophets, and the Torah together with his knowledge of astrology. He noted that the coming grand conjunction of Saturn and Jupiter which happened every 2859 years promised the transformation of the cosmos and humanity. From his peculiar use of choice biblical passages, Ḥiyya came not to just one date, but several: 1230, 1448, 1358, 1403, 1349, and 1335.

[63]It is not readily apparent how this text proves that the proselytes should not enter the land. Perhaps they are the "weak hands" to be strengthened, but not admitted. Ibn Shmuel (מדרשי גאולה, *loc. cit.*) thought the text was misplaced, so he rearranged it after "...in the unity of the Name" (11).

[64] The Samaritan Messiah.

[65]The Judean Messiah.

[66]The text breaks here. The following quotation is conjectured from the scriptural context of the discussion.

Since the next grand conjunction was to take place in A.D. 1464, all of these dates are close enough to be considered. Ḥiyya also distinguished between the time of the end and the time of the resurrection, which would happen later. Rabbi bar Ḥiyya compiled his extensive conclusions and methods in a book, *The Scroll of the Revealer*. Excerpts from that book have been translated and are reported here. These will introduce the reader to the author's logic and show the extensive effort medieval Jews made to relate their theological beliefs to their calendrical expectations and plans.

Introduction to *The Scroll of the Revealer*

One of the most thorough and impressive works on Jewish eschatology during the Crusades is the extensive book (155 pages) of Rabbi bar Ḥiyya, מגלת המגלה (Berlin, 1924). The book not only shows the extensive research done by Rabbi Ḥiyya, but it reflects the vast concentration that was being done in his day. This is only one of the many works available at that time, and this one has survived intact.

The book is written in five chapters, which are called "gates." Rabbi Ḥiyya leads the reader from one gate to the other as if he were going from the outer fence into the inner sanctum and had to pass through each portal on the way. At the end of each chapter he closes one gate to open another. The first gate introduces the work done by Gentiles on this subject. This he did not consider to be vital. It only reflected disagreement and inadequacy of evidence without the Torah, the prophets, and the writings. The fifth gate deals with astrology as it had been applied by Jewish scholars to the topic of the end of days of the exile. This does not contradict any biblical evidence, but it is of limited value, since God will create a new heaven as well as a new earth in the end of days. Therefore the current movements of the stars are of relative unimportance. The central part of the book analyzes the Bible from many points of view, from Genesis through Daniel, showing the different ways by which scholars can use biblical materials to calculate the very days of the end. There are always two dates apparent, one is for the redemption and the second follows with the resurrection of the dead. Also the three chapters reach similar dates. There is a lot of imaginative and inventive use of material and forced logic, but the enthusiasm and concentration that has been applied to the subject is obvious throughout.

Excerpts have been selected and translated to introduce the

reader to much of the author's logic and his most important conclusion without making him overly weary with tedious detail.

THE SCROLL OF THE REVEALER

Gate Two

After we have related the opinions of the Gentile scholars and of their disputes in the days of old, and we have seen from their words that all of them were weary and that they were feeble, and their strength had become so weak in the attempt to reach the end of the matter and to arrive at its fundamental meaning [that] they have restored wisdom to its foundation, and they have commanded [us] to search for its true meaning from other sources, as it is written, *God understands the way, and he knows its place* (Job 28:23). It is clear to us that there is no [definite] interpretation on this subject except that to be found in the Torah, the holy writings, and the words of our sages (May they be remembered for good) who have received [it] directly from the Holy Spirit. It is because we found that the scripture permits us to search out this matter, as it is said, *Remember the days of the age; consider the years of generation after generation* (Dt 32:7). [This] enables us to *consider* the number of *the years* and the *generations* to repeat and to *remember the days of the age* and their characteristics, as it is written, *Ask, now, of the former days* (ראשונים) *which were before you, since the day when God created man upon the earth* (Dt 4:32). We see from this that we are commanded to *ask* and to inquire concerning the character of *the days since* their *beginning* (מראשיתם).To these scriptures we cling tightly in our hands, and they have fortified our hearts to study deeply *the days of the age* and investigate their characteristics, how many there are. Though the logical conclusion would be that this research would prove good for Israel, the matter is strengthened in our hands even more, since we have found a hint for it in the Torah.

At the beginning of our comments we say that if we came across two verses, one giving one figure for *the days of the age* or the end time when salvation will come, and the second verse gives another number, this matter should not hinder us, but we will be happy and satisfied if we discover [that] they are equalled to the teaching of our sages (May they be remembered for blessing), the pillars of the age, who offered two interpretations on one subject, both derived from scripture passages. When dealing with this subject, they said how many were the days of the Messiah: Rabbi Eliezer said, "A thousand years, as it is said, [for a thousand years in your sight are] as yesterday (Ps 90:4)." Rabbi Joshua said, "Two thousand years, for it is said, [Make us glad] as many days as you have afflicted us, [and as many years as we have seen evil] (Ps 90:15). To the holy One blessed be He, two days and [another] day are a thousand years (Ps 90:4)." Rabbi Berakhiah said, "Six hundred years, as it is said, As the days of a tree shall be the days of my people (Isa 65:22), and we learned that a tree can last for six hundred years." Rabbi Jose said, "Sixty years, as it is said, As long as the moon, generation of generations (Ps 72:5). A generation is twenty years; generations are forty years. [This totals] sixty years." Rabbi Akiba said, "A hundred years" (San 99a).

Here you see one subject being interpreted many [different] ways. Thus they said, "A day of the holy One blessed be He is a thousand years." Rabbi Abbihu said, "Seven thousand, as the days of the bridegroom, for it is said, For as a young man exposes a virgin (Isa 62:5). How many are the days of a bridegroom? Seven days, as it is said, Complete this week (Gen 29:27)" (San 99a).

Hence you must not be surprised if we come across a change in the number of days which we examine, but should two passages agree [in calculation, it is more convincing], and all the more so when three, which refer to this same subject, and they all give one number, it fortifies our belief all the more on this theme.[87]

We are now going to see about the research concerning their end; it has been said that the holy One blessed be He gave the Torah to Israel at the end of the twentieth generation. The fourth [day of a thousand years] is not completed before the twenty-eighth generation draws to its end. If you ascribe to every single day seven generations ($4 \times 7 = 28$), you will be counting for the fourth day [of creation], eight generations from the giving of the Torah until the end of the twenty-eighth generation. There will [then] be for [every] eight generations one thousand years, less twenty years (20 years equals one generation). You will thus find that from the giving of the Torah until the sealing of the vision, there are a thousand years, because the Torah was given in the year one thousand, four hundred, forty-eight (1312 B.C.), and the vision was sealed in the year three thousand, four hundred, forty-eight (312 B.C.). Concerning this, they say, A day of the holy One

[87]This excerpt introduces the reader to the logic by which the scripture study should be approached. Omitting many pages of argument, the conclusions of "gate two" are included in the next excerpt which begins with page 44. SML

blessed be He *is a thousand years* (Ps 90:4), because there is no day of the holy One blessed be He more than the rest of the days except when he displays his glory over his works. Should you say that [since] *all* the days are [days] of the Lord, why do you call the fourth day [of creation] *only* "the day of the holy One blessed be He"? Hence is it said to you: Behold all the mountains are mountains of the Lord, but only Horeb is called the mountain of God. All the staffs are his, but only the staff of Moses is called the staff of God (Ex 4:20). All the clouds are his creations, but only the cloud which was over the tent was called the cloud of the Lord (Num 10:34). Similarly, you may say that all the days of creation are creations of the holy One blessed be He, but only the fourth day is called the day of the holy One blessed be He, in which at its beginning the Torah was given to Israel, and at its end prophecy was removed from the age. Hence one can say that the *baraitha*[66] began to count the thousands [of years] of the Torah from the time when the pronouncement began to speak to human beings until the time when prophecy ceased from the age. It was [therefore] proper that this time be called the time of the Torah. You can cite proof for this from the scripures, where it is said, *I was near Him [as] a master craftsman, and I was every day a delight, rejoicing before him at all times* (Prov 8:30).

You might say [that] *rejoicing* here refers only to the establishment of the Torah and of prophecy being heard by human beings, because it says at the end [of the passage]: *delighting in the sons of men* (Prov 8:31). Thus the Torah says, *The Lord created me [at the] beginning of his way* (Prov 8:22). *Before the creation of all created things, before the earth appeared, when there were no depths or fountains, before the mountains and the hills [existed] [I was brought forth; before he had made the land and the other countries, the first of the dust of the earth. When he established the heavens, there was I when he made a circle on the face of the deep. With his finger [he made] the heavens above; with strength, the springs of the deep. When he set his conditions for the sea, the water did not pass over his command. When he marked off the foundations of the land, I was near him as a craftsman]* (Prov 8:24-30). *I was near him as a craftsman* (אמון), as a man who increases his love and supports it until he gave me to the sons of men. The days when I was *delighting in the sons of men* were two days, as it is written, *I was a delight, day, day, (everyday)*.

---

[66]A *baraitha* is a literary unit in the Aramaic Talmud which is written in Hebrew and begins with the words, "Our sages have taught." Here AZ 9a.

He said, *day, day,* and he did not say, "two days,"[89] because one of them was the prophecy with no Torah, namely from the days of the flood until the giving of the Torah and the second day was prophecy with the Torah, that is from the giving of the Torah until the sealing of the vision. Thus he says, *Rejoicing before him at all times* (Prov 8:30). *Rejoicing in his habitable earth* (Prov 8:31) and *delighting in the sons of men* (Prov 8:31). *Rejoicing in his habitable earth* (Prov 8:31), namely, when the prophecy was in the land with no Torah but *delighting in the sons of men* (Prov 8:31). For every time the Torah and prophecy are handed over into their hands before the Lord, I rejoice and am glad *at all times* (Prov 8:30). It was not necessary with a craftsman who was before the Lord, before the age was created,[90] to mention days, because they [days] provide a reason for time. The Torah was given precedence over all creatures before the Lord as well as over that which is above the natural order, as we have explained above.

Here is a broad hint for you that the thousands [of years] of the Torah are two days [of creation]. This interpretation of this passage [of scripture] (Prov 8:30) does not refute the interpretation which we offered above at the beginning of the gate.[91] It does not refute it, but both are *correct to him who understands, and upright to those who find knowledge* (Prov 8:9). It is said that just as the Torah was hidden before the Lord for two days, namely the first and the second [days], thus the Torah and prophecy were revealed to the sons of the age in two days which were the third and fourth [days of creation]. We now possess a strong confirmation and a good [argument, showing] how many are the thousands [of years] of the Torah.

Now we come to examine the two thousand [years] of the Messiah to ascertain [how many they actually are]. You may suggest only two hypotheses regarding them, since they have no third, in my opinion. They produce two "ends of time" which come to us, one of which we can grasp. We have a tradition that the Messiah was born on the day the first house was destroyed, in the year three thousand, three hundred, thirty-eight (422 B.C.). This calculation which we have may be regarded as a genuine one, for it is the opinion of all believers, or you might say that it refers

[89]The expression, "Day, day" in Hebrew means "daily," but it is given special significance here to suit the needs of the research student.

[90]Important to semitic thought is the belief that the Lord created time as well as material. From the eschatological point of view, his creation and organization of days, months, jubilees, and ages are more important than the universe.

[91]Meaning the beginning of chapter or "gate" two.

to the calculation of the hope of the Messiah and the expectation of his advent, which originates from that opinion. From the two we can properly estimate this time, for according to the opinion of our rabbis (May they be remembered for blessing) was [that it took place] at the end of the fourth day, which leaves of the days of the age two thousand, six hundred, sixty-two [years] for the three days which are left $(7-2-2=3)$. Part of one of the days is eight hundred eighty-seven years and a third is near eight hundred, ninety years which are between the giving of the Torah and the destruction of the house. If you allow two thousand [for the days of] the Messiah, a thousand, seven hundred, eighty are double the days which are between the giving [of the Torah] and the destruction [of the temple].

If you begin to count from the destruction [of the temple], two days will be completed in the year five thousand, one hundred, eighteen years (A.D. 1358). Concerning this year Daniel spoke, *From the time of the removal of the continual offering and the sacrilege that causes appalment is set up, a thousand, two hundred, ninety days* (Dan 12:11). If you count them from the second destruction [of the temple] which was in the year three thousand, eight hundred, twenty-eight, you will be able to calculate five thousand, one hundred, eighteen [5,118 (A.D. 1358) minus 3,828 (A.D. 68) = 1,290], and the *baraitha*[92] will confirm the opinion given above concerning the calculation. If you count the thousands of [years of] the Messiah from the sealing of the vision in which the thousands of [years of] the Torah were completed, you will be adding to the years of the thousands of the Messiah another three thousand, four hundred, forty-eight [years] (312 B.C.), you will arrive at five thousand, two hundred, twenty-eight years (A.D. 1468), which is near to the final end time which we discovered above. There are only twenty years between them [the two resultant calculations], just as there are between the two calculations with the sealing of the vision, because the opinion of the calculation of the days and the generations were the number of the day of the fourth thousand years, minus twenty. The sealing of the vision was in the year three thousand, four hundred, twenty-eight (332 B.C.). The opinion of our sages is that these are two thousand complete years, and that the sealing of the vision was in the year three thousand, four hundred, forty-eight (312 B.C.)[93]

[92]See note 88.

[93]The sealing of the book with the visions (Dan 12:4) was to have taken place about three years before the dedication of the temple under the leadership of the Hasmoneans in the seventh decade of the second century B.C.--not the fourth century.

If you count the thousands of [years of] the Messiah according to the opinion of their calculation, you will complete [the total] in the year five thousand, two hundred, eight (A.D. 1448), according to the number of the final end time, no less and no more. This is according to the first hypothesis. The second hypothesis is [that] when the thousands of [years of] the Torah are completed in the year three thousand, four hundred, forty-eight (312 B.C.) or four hundred, twenty-eight (332 B.C.) and there remain for the age two thousand, five hundred, seventy-two [years] for three days [until A.D. 2240], there will be the years of the days of the anticipation of the Messiah, one thousand, seven hundred, fourteen [years], and you will complete [that number] in the year five thousand, one hundred, sixty-three (A.D. 1403).[94] Concerning this year Daniel said, *Blessed is he who waits and arrives at the days, one thousand, three hundred, thirty-five* (Dan 12:12). If you count them from the destruction [of the second temple] you will reach the calculation of the year five thousand, one hundred, sixty-three (A.D. 1403) [68 + 1335 = 1403]. This is the interpretation of the *baraitha,* according to the cryptic hint it contains and which appears in the tractate *Avodah Zarah* 9a from the words of our sages (May they be remembered for blessing.) This *baraitha* is according to the literal interpretation of the text, and it is fundamentally true. We support it, for we believe that the interpretation which they have given was revealed to them, but that they did not wish to disclose it, so that the end time would not be so far away [and therefore] difficult in the eyes of those of little faith who were in the majority at that time. Now, however, since the end time is not so distant, there is no sin in its revelation. When these two end times are perceived, both of them will be confirmed by proof and made strong by the Torah, the prophets, and the writings,[95] as well as the sayings of our sages (May they be remembered for blessing). Our hearts incline toward this calculation, and our mind is made up about it, for we know that both hypotheses are true. We have said that perhaps the first end time will be for the advent of the redeemer [bringing] the salvation of God, and that the second end time refers to the resurrection of the dead.

---

[94]Seven millennia are calculated as the length of time to be substituted for the seven days of creation. At the end of the sixth millennium, or *'erev Shabbat,* the millennia of "rest" is to begin. Since four days have been completed, there must still be three more days with which to reckon.

[95]The entire Bible: The Pentateuch, the prophets, the Psalms, wisdom literature, and the five scrolls, called the Tanak.

It has been made clear to us, and we have accepted [the belief] that the resurrection of the dead will come after the redeemer.[96]

Gate Three

If you ask: Since the Gentiles comprise seventy-two nations, according to the Gentile scholars, and according to the number seventy-two elders whom Moses gathered for Israel, together with Eldad and Medad who were left in camp, whereas here he lists only seventy nations, "What happened to the remaining two nations?" [Then I] answer you that one nation [is composed of] the sons of Moses, our teacher, to whom the holy One blessed be He promised that his sons would be *a great nation*, as it is written, *I will make you a great nation* (Ex 32:10).[97] For the number of his sons in the days of the Messiah will be like the number of a nation even greater than [all] the seventy-two nations. The second nation is the sons of Levi, who were not counted among the Israelites. In the days of the Messiah, they will be as the number of one nation. Thus you find that their number by which they were counted for service of the tent in the wilderness of Sinai was eight thousand, five hundred, eighty (Num 4:48). If you multiply this number seventy times, [the result] will be six hundred thousand, six hundred [$8,580 \times 70 = 600,600$]. You will [then] find that the servants of the service of the tent from the Levites constituted the seventieth part of Israel. Israel constituted about one seventieth of the Gentiles. Just as the holy One blessed be He chose Israel for himself from all the nations to be exclusively the heir of the world which [is comprised of] seventy nations or about seventy [times as many], thus he chose from among the Israelites for his service the Levites who constitute about one seventieth of Israel. After seventy generations from the exodus from Egypt until the Messiah will be completed, the number of generations of Israelites who will arise from their graves will correspond to the number of the seventy nations who are in the world, and the Levites will correspond in number to one nation among them, and the sons of Moses will correspond in number to another nation. All of them will comprise seventy-two nations, and they will fill every settlement and will possess the dwellings of all the Gentiles.

[96]The conclusion of "Gate Two" on page 47; the next excerpt begins in the last part of the third gate, page 77.

[97]To force two more nations into the picture, Rabbi Hiyya treated the children of Moses, which was an expression used to mean all the Hebrew people, and the Levites, who were part of the Hebrews, as it they were separate nations.

Concerning them, he says, *The earth will be full of the knowledge of the Lord as the waters cover the sea* (Isa 11:9).

We find that the scripture excludes the number of Levites counted from one month old and above while [Israel was] in the wilderness of Sinai [the number being] three hundred males. It does not include them in the number of Levites given under all the first born of the Israelites, because the number of families of the Levites in the wilderness of Sinai, if you include them [those one month old and older] amount to twenty-two thousand, three hundred (Num 3:22, 28, 34). The scripture gives them a total of twenty-two thousand only (Num 3:39) and excludes from them the three hundred over and above the first born of the Levites. This number is about one part in seventy of all the number of the Levites ($300 \times 70 = 21{,}000$ or *about* 22,000). Just as the Lord separated the Levites from the midst of the sons of Israel and did not include their number with the number of the Israelites because they were given to him in place of all the first born of the Israelites, thus he separated the first born of the Levites from the midst of the Levites and did not include their number with the number of the Levites. Just as he separated the Levites, about one part in seventy of the people of Israel, so were the first born of the Levites about one part in seventy of the Levites. We find that the number of Levites from the age one month and older, together with their first born, were about one part in twenty-seven of the Israelites (22,273). There are twenty-seven more Levites than first born of the Israelites, subtracting from the number of the first born of the Levites [22,300 Levites minus 22,273 first born Israelites equals 27]. This number is equal to the twenty-seven kingdoms that drank the cup of wine of wrath from the hand of Jeremiah (Jer 25:15-28), all of whom will *stagger and be crazed because of the sword which I will send among them* (Jer 25:16). The Israelites will take over their kingdoms and occupy their dwellings. You will find that the number of first born of the Israelites above the number of the Levites is two hundred, seventy-three [22,273 − 22,000 = 273), and you will find in this number a broad hint concerning the time of the exile and the time of the deliverance and redemption, because the holy One blessed be He commanded [the Israelites] to redeem these *over and above* [first born] and said, *The redemption of the two hundred, seventy-three first born Israelites over and above the Levites* (Num 3:46) and said, *You shall take five, five*[98]

---

[98]This is similar to the logic applied to the expression "Day, day." See note 89. This logic is possible on the basis that there is nothing superfluous in the Bible.

shekels per head (Num 3:47). This repetition of *five* is significant since only one *five* would have been adequate, as he said to Israel in the chapter on the shekels: *A beka a head [a half a shekel, by the shekel of the sanctuary]* (Ex 38:26). Hence he could have said but once here, *five shekels per head*, but because he repeated, *five, five*, we interpret the first *[five]* to hint at the time of settling the land from the exodus from Egypt until the exile of Titus, and we interpret the second *[five]* concerning the exile from the destruction of the second house until the resurrection of the dead.

The complete redemption was *five shekels* every time of which will be according to the number of those *over and above* [273 × 5 = 1365]. Because of this hint, the shekels which they [paid] to atone for each soul was half a shekel, as it is written, *Everyone who passes the census, half a shekel according to the shekel of the sanctuary* (Ex 30:13). He separates one tenth of the silver of the redemption of *those over and above* the first born to make known that the time of the kingdom and the exile will be according to the number of those *over and above* the first born of the Israelites, ten times. The shekels were *a half a shekel* (Ex 38:26). Just as the money was divided into two halves, [thus also the time was divided] a half [for the time of] the kingdom and a half [for the time of the exile.] If you multiply the number of those *over and above* (273) by five, corresponding to the first *five* (Num 3:47), [the total] will be one thousand, three hundred, sixty-five, corresponding to the money of the redemption (Num 3:50). If you add this number to the [date of] the exodus from Egypt, you have three thousand, eight hundred, thirteen years (A.D. 53). The exile [instigated by] the wicked Titus was in the year three thousand, eight hundred, twenty-eight (A.D. 68), which is fifteen years more than this number. If you add to the [date of] the exile of Titus the number of those *over and above* (273) times five, corresponding to the second *five* (Num 3:47), which is likewise a thousand, three hundred, sixty-five years, you have five thousand, one hundred, ninety-three years (A.D. 1433). We [then] discover from the Torah that the resurrection of the dead will be in the year five thousand, two hundred, eight (A.D. 1448). Between it [1448] and this calculation [1433] there are fifteen years, just as there were between them [the two figures, A.D. 53 and 68] at the time of the exile. You find that the reckoning of those *over and above* is less than the number arrived at by fifteen years in the exile and fifteen years in the redemption, the two of which combined are thirty years. Thus we find that the addition in the habitation of the

Israelites in Egypt, between the hint [given to Abraham at the covenant] *between the parts* (Gen 15:17) is thirty years. [At the covenant] *between the parts*, he says, *They [the Israelites] will serve them [the Egyptians] and they [the Egyptians] will afflict them [the Israelites] for four hundred years* (Gen 12:40). Also here is a hint of the time of the kingdom and the exile and when the time expired, he added fifteen years to each one of them [the halves], and two of them total thirty years. Concerning this hint, the scriptures repeat *five* (Num 3:47), one for the redemption [from] Egypt and the second for the redemption of the exile which will be the redemption of the age with the salvation of God. Because of this, the scriptures call the money by two names: first *redemption money* (כסף הפדיום) , as it is written, *Moses took the redemption money* (כסף הפדיום) (Num 3:49), that is to say, *the redemption money* for the exodus from Egypt which was past and which was by the hand of Moses, as it is written in the passage, *Moses took the redemption money:* but at the end [of the passage] it says, *redemption money* (כסף הפדוים). *Moses gave the redemption money* (כסף הפדוים) *to Aaron and his sons* (Num 3:51). That is to say, when there will be a *redemption* (מדוים) in the days of the future redeemer with Elijah as the messenger[99] who is from the seed of Aaron (BM 114a-b).

You are able to interpret from the number of those *over and above* are two hundred, seventy-three (רגע) . According to the number two hundred seventy-three (רגע) a cycle which will pass from the creation of the age until the time of redemption, for the resurrection of the dead will be for the calculation cubed of the cycle of two hundred, seventy-four, which is five thousand, two hundred, six (A.D. 1446). From this he said, *over and above* (Num 3:46), that is to say, those cycles which are *over and above* the cycle of redemption. Your sign concerning this midrash is *For his anger is but for a moment; a lifetime is in his favor* (Ps 30:6). The scripture says, "If you have to wait for *his anger* and bear the yoke of the exile until the two hundred, seventy-three cycle [is over], let it not seem harsh in your eyes, for *a lifetime is in his favor.*[100] From *his favor* you have only a sixty-eight [year] cycle, because that is the numerical value of the word *lifetime* [חייפ =8+10+10+40=68]. Sixty-eight cycle[s] total one

---

[99]As an apostle (שליח) or agent appointed with the authority of the one who sent him (Ber 5:5).

[100]The contrast is between the two times: 1) his anger and 2) his favor. One is the exile and the second is the redemption. It is not clear just how these "cycles" are calculated. רגע means "instant," and it equals 273 in *gematria.*

thousand, two hundred, ninety-two [68×19=1,292. But why 19?], corresponding to the years of the sixth day, which is the generation of Yered (or domination) which is the period of the exile. If you count from the destruction of the second house, sixty-eight cycle[s], and you add them to the years of the exile, you will have five thousand, one hundred, twenty-years (A.D. 1340) in which will be revealed the signs of redemption [3,828 + 1292 = 5,120 which = A.D. 1340] and the restoration of the kingdom to its former condition and for his great salvation. The interpretation of *a lifetime in his favor* will be just as it was *in his favor* before the sixty-eight cycle[s] which spell *lifetime* numerically. Thus you will be *in his favor* at their conclusion, as it is written, *In the evening, weeping lasts the night, but in the morning there is joy* (Ps 30:6). If they dwell in darkness *in the evening* at their beginning, at their conclusion, they will have light.

We come now to explain the sign which he gave us in the forty years which our fathers spent in the wilderness, and we will bring proof for it from another place. It is said, "If you calculate the generations from Adam until Moses our teacher, the [number] will be twenty-six generations. Add to them the sixty-nine succeeding generations (forty years for each generation) from the exodus from Egypt until the generation of the Messiah son of David."

We find that scripture counts from the seed of David in the books of Chronicles (I Chron 3:10-24), from Solomon until Anani (I Chron 3:24) there are sixty-two men with their names. If you add to their number, the name of the generations from Adam until David, you will find that from Adam until Anani there were ninety-five generations. Now it will appear clearly to you that the scriptures in Chronicles [propose] to count for you all those generations only to give you a hint concerning the redemption that is coming at the end of those generations. This calculation is as follows: From Adam until Abraham, there are twenty generations and from Abraham until David, thirteen generations.[101] This means that from Adam until David there were thirty-three generations, and you have left sixty-two generations until the time of the redemption [33 + 62 = 95]. You will find that in Chronicles the census of the sons of David and his grandsons [totals] sixty-two men who are mentioned there between sons and brothers so as to complete sixty-two generations. These are: from Solomon until

---

[101]Mt 1:17 counted fourteen generations between Abraham and David, but he may have forced that number to synchronize with his needs.

Josiah, sixteen generations, namely: Solomon, Rehoboam, Abijah, Asa, Jehoshaphat, Joram, Ahaziah, Joash, Amaziah, Azariah, Jotham, Ahaz, Hezekiah, Manasseh, Amon, and Josiah. This totals seventeen. Josiah had four sons: Yoḥanan, Jehoiakim, Zedekiah, and Shallum. They are numbered among four generations,[102] because the four kings from the sons of Josiah were mentioned among the kings of Judah. The first was Jehoahaz, as it is written, *The people of the land took Jehoahaz the son of Josiah and anointed him, and made him king in his father's stead* (II Kgs 23:30). This is Yoḥanan who was reckoned first here. The second was Jehoiakim, as it is written, *Thus said the Lord to Jehoiakim the son of Josiah, king of Judah* (Jer 22:18). The third was Shallum, as it is written, *For thus said the Lord with respect to Shallum the son of Josiah, the king of Judah, who was king in place of his father Josiah* (Jer 22:11). The fourth was Zedekiah, as it is written, *King Zedekiah the son of Josiah became king in place of Coniah the son of Jehoiakim* (Jer 37:1). The kingdom of everyone of them was mentioned explicitly by name. Because of this they were reckoned in four generations. This totals twenty generations. The sons of Jehoiakim, Jeconia and Zedekiah, are two. This [brings the total up to] twenty-two generations. This Zedekiah was not Zedekiah son of Josiah, but Zedekiah son of Jehoiakim whose kingdom was mentioned in the book of Chronicles, at the end of the kingdom of Jehoiakim, as it is written, *He made his brother Zedekiah king* (II Chron 36:10). Because we found Jeconia and Zedekiah the sons of Jehoiakim are reckoned among the kings, they were considered legitimate to be included with the others [in order to bring up the total] of twenty-two generations.

The generations from Adam to Zedekiah son of Jehoiakim were fifty-five. Forty generations are left, and they counted in Chronicles in this order: Asir, Ahealtiel, Malkiram, Padiah, Shenazer, Jekomiah, Hoshmiah, Nedabiah, Zerubbabel, Shemeiah, Mashulam, Ḥananaih, Shulumit, Ḥashubah, Ohel, Berakiah, Ḥesadiah, Yoshab, Ḥesed, Pelatiah, Yeshiah, Raphiah, Arnon, Obadiah, Shekaniah, Shemiah, Ḥamush, Yigael, Beriah, Neariah, Shaphat, Elioenai, Hezekiah, Azriḳam, Hoduyahu, Elishib, Paliah, Aḳob, Yoḥanan, Daliah, Anani. Here you have from Adam until Anani ninety-five generations. Every place where brothers were mentioned, he mentioned their number explicitly so that you would count every one of them as a

---

[102]Because he needs four generations to suit his calculations, even though they all belong to one generation.

generation by itself. When he says, *The sons of Shemaiah...are six; the sons of Neariah...are three; and the sons of Elioenai...are seven* (I Chron 3:22-24), [these] complete the ninety-five generations until Anani. Our sages (May they be remembered for blessing) have told us that Anani is the name of the Messiah (*Tanḥuma, parashat Toledoth*). With these words they open our hearts and motivate us to search the number of the end time from these generations, because there is a hint in their numbers.

You may find a hint of this in the blessing with which Jacob blessed Judah, as it is written, *Judah, your brothers will praise you; your hand will be on the neck of your enemies; your father's sons will bow down before you* (Gen 49:8). You will find in this verse a hint of David king of Israel who is the eleventh generation of the sons of Judah and David before whom all the tribes of Israel prostrated themselves. We do not find that the brothers of Judah prostrated themselves before Judah as this verse infers, but eleven of his sons, according to the eleven words in this verse,[103] *The sons of* his *father bowing down before* him (Gen 49:8). That is the eleven of your sons, corresponding to the number of words of this verse. This hint is repeated in the verse which follows with twelve [units of words].[104] *Judah is a lion's whelp; from the prey, my son, you have gone up. He stooped; he crouched like a lion, and as a lioness. Who dares to stir him up* (Gen 49:9). In this verse are twelve words, corresponding to the number of generations from our father Jacob until David. Thus he says here, *My son*, that is to say, this king who is the twelfth [in the succession of generations] is *mine* among the sons. How is it that *from the prey, my son, you have gone up*? [because it has] eleven letters,[105] and he was the eleventh of the sons of Judah son of Jacob. He will succeed to the kingdom and be rescued *from the prey* of Saul, who was seeking to kill him.

In the third verse, he says, *The scepter will not depart from Judah, nor the staff from between his feet, until Shiloh comes, and to him will be the obedience of the Gentiles* (Gen 49:10). He reveals the hint, interpreting it as meaning that there is no rulership except in his tribe alone. *The staff (tribe) will not depart from between his feet* [means] his rulership will not be given to another tribe until Shiloh comes--until Shiloh is destroyed. The [correct]

---

[103]Not really "words," but units of letters, including prefixes, suffixes, etc.: יהודה אתה
יודוך אחיך ידך בערף איביך ישתחוו לך בני אביך.

[104]See note 103.

[105] מטרף בני עלית.

interpretation of *comes* (יבא) is "will be destroyed" or "will be hidden," as [we gather from] the command, *You shall go to your fathers* (Gen 15:15).[106] After the destruction of *Shiloh; to him will be the obedience of the Gentiles*. The Israelites enter to make David [their] king. We discover that the kingdom of David at Hebron was fourteen years after the destruction of *Shiloh*, and that the number of words in this verse is fourteen.[107] The destruction of *Shiloh* took place the year that Eli died, and in that year Samuel was appointed as prophet. He continued for eleven years until the kingdom of Saul. Saul was king for twenty years.[108] After Saul died, David became king (Seder OlamR *perek* 13). It is [thus] evident that from the destruction of *Shiloh* until the kingdom of David there were fourteen years, according to the number of the words in the verse, *The scepter will not depart...*(Gen 49:10). You will further discover that David became king over Israel at the age of thirty-seven, as it is written, *David was thirty years old when he began to reign, and he was king for forty years over Hebron. He ruled over Judah seven years and six months; and in Jerusalem he reigned over all Israel and Judah for thirty-three years* (II Sam 5:4-5). When he became king over Israel, he was thirty-seven years of age, and the number [of words in] these three verses from *Judah, your brothers will praise you* (Gen 49:8) until *the obedience of the Gentiles* (Gen 49:10) comprises thirty-seven, corresponding to the age of David when he became king over Israel. That is to say, at the time when *the Gentiles were obedient to him*, he was thirty-seven years of age. All these scripture verses hint at the kingdom of David.

I am astonished at the sages and scholars who say *until Shiloh comes* (Gen 49:10) is a hint at the Messiah son of David (GenR 98:8). How was it possible for our father Jacob to provide a hint to his sons of the coming redemption after this long exile without first giving them a hint at the outset of the marvelous redemption and glorious kingdom that would come to them first through our teacher Moses and finally through King David? But it is right and proper that our father Jacob should have first provided information to Judah in two verses, after which came a hint of the Messiah. You will find that there are eighteen words in the verse, *Tying his colt to the vine and his donkey's colt to the choice vine, he washes his garments in wine, his vestments in the blood of*

---

[106]Meaning, "You will die" or "You will be destroyed."

[107]לא יסור שבט מיהודה ומחקק מבין רגליו עד כי יבא שילה ולו יקהת עמים = 14 "words" or units of words.

[108]According to Acts 13:21, Saul reigned for forty years.

grapes (Gen 49:11) and the verse, *His eyes will be red with wine, and his teeth whiter than milk* (Gen 49:12), thus corresponding to the number of kings from the sons of David and his descendants from Solomon until Jeconiah son of Jehoiakim. Each word hints at every one of those kings. You will observe that the verse, *his eyes will be red with wine* (Gen 49:12), hints at the Messiah, because he says to the one whose *eyes will be red* and this provides a reason for the color *red* which is like blood. That is to say, the first kingdom which will be like the *eyes* which are in the head and in which there will be wars and blood[shed], as it is written, *He washes his garments in wine, his vestments in the blood of grapes* (Gen 49:11). [This] hints at David who was the first of the kings of whom the scripture said, *You shall not build a house to my name, because you have shed much blood upon the earth before me* (I Chron 22:8). Because of this, it is said at the beginning of the last verse, *eyes will be red.* This is the first kingdom of David, and at its end he says, *His teeth will be whiter than milk.* This refers to the second kingdom of which it is said, *David my servant will be their prince for the age* (Ezek 37:25).[109] This second kingdom will be *whiter than milk.* You will find in these scripture passages a hint of the first kingdom and of the redemption coming at the end. Who knows whether or not there is in all the names of the generations and kings a hint concerning wise matters [whose secret] we are [now] unable to solve.

You see [proof of their relationship] from all the reasons by which the subject of salvation and the resurrection of the dead were mentioned explicitly in the Torah and the rest of the holy writings. You can produce all this calculation from the chapter, *If you walk in my statutes* (Lev 26:3), from *Then the land will enjoy its Sabbaths* (Lev 26:34), and from *I will chastise you myself seven-fold for your sins* (Lev 26:28). But I have not wanted to expatiate, because it is interpreted in many books composed of this subject,[110] and the reasons and proofs which I would have advanvanced are sufficiently [well presented] in them to be convincing. It will not be too hard for you to see many expositions pointing to five thousand, one hundred, eighteen and five thousand, two hundred, eight (A.D. 1358 and 1448).

[This] time may seem distant in your eyes, and this may not satisfy you, but have confidence in your Creator and wait for his salvation every day, because he is able to hasten it. You may be

---

[109]The messianic or governmental age when Israel was ruled by her own king.

[110]This calls attention to the extensive interest and work done on this subject at that time.

absolutely sure that the redemption and kingdom will precede the resurrection of the dead, and the signs of the redemption will precede the redemption. With all these times you cannot provide a briefer time before many writings which give to every subject of those periods being changed when they were not equal just as you have seen in the gates that have passed.

May the holy One blessed be He hasten for his people the Israelites goodness and salvation at every time and at the end of everything, may he fulfill his goodness. May he revive our dead ones and fulfill for us his good promise which he promised us, as it is written, *The Lord your God will restore your fortunes, be merciful to you, return and gather you from all the Gentiles where the Lord your God scattered you* (Dt 30:3). It is [further] written, *If your outcasts are in the limits of heaven, from there the Lord your God will gather you and from there he will take you* (Dt 30:4). It is [also] written, *The Lord your God will bring you into the land which your fathers acquired, and you will possess it, and he will make you more prosperous and numerous than your fathers* (Dt 30:5). All the evidence which has passed has been appropriate to make us stop, but because I have seen numerous people who speak about the end time bring evidence from the Book of Daniel, and they see that the end time is explained in it more than in the rest of the accepted books, I saw fit to close this gate and open the gate which comes after it with an examination of the end time from the Book of Daniel with the help of God and his salvation.[1]

After they [the scholars] arrived at [the secret] concerning this total, they provide for it two explicit periods according to the number of years. They informed us of the beginning of the period from which to begin as well as its end, as it is written, *From the time when the continual offering will be removed and the setting up of the sacrilege which causes appalment, a thousand, two hundred, ninety [years]* (Dan 12:11). *The time when the continual offering will be removed* is the beginning of the destruction of the second house of which Gabriel said to Daniel at the time of his prayer, *and for half a week he will cause the sacrifice and the offering to cease* (Dan 9:27). The cessation of *the sacrifice and the offering* (Dan 9:27) is the removal of *the continual offering* (Dan 12:11). This is the time from which we begin to count these days. Its end is *the setting up of the sacrilege which causes appalment* (Dan 12:11). This is the annihilation of the wicked kingdom and

---

[1]"The conclusion of "Gate Three" on page 83. The next excerpt from "Gate Four" begins on page 107.

the destruction of *the abomination* of the house which defiles the sanctuary. With its abominations, it will be *the sacrilege which causes appalment*, because it defiles the sanctuary with its abominations, as it is written, *On the wings of the sacrilege which causes appalment* (Dan 9:27) because of the abominations of the wicked kingdom *spreading a wing* (Dan 9:27) over the house. It will be, because of this, the age of *appalment* (Dan 9:27).

Finally, there will be a sacrilege *which causes appalment*, as it is written, *Until the decreed end is poured out on the desolator* (Dan 9:27), i.e., the age will be desolated in the beginning because of the abominations of the kingdom. *Spreading a wing* (Dan 9:27) over the house and at the time when *the decreed destruction* (Isa 10:22) will come over the Gentiles, it will be *a sacrilege which causes appalment* (Dan 12:11). Concerning it he said here, for *the setting up of the sacrilege which causes appalment*. You will find that the topic which was told at first to Daniel closed and hidden, but at the end of the prophecy it was explained to him clearly and revealed. If you begin to count *a thousand, two hundred, ninety* (Dan 12:11) years *from the time when the continual offering will be removed* (Dan 12:11), [you will learn] that it is in the year three thousand, eight hundred, twenty-eight (A.D. 68). It will [then] complete for you the calculation in the year five thousand, one hundred, eighteen [3,828+1,290=5,118 or A.D. 1358]. It is the time of *the destruction* of the Gentiles and the advent of the redeemer in this precise [time].

Now you can divide these days into *two times and a half* (Dan 12:7). If you calculate this way and say that the first *time* was completed at the beginning of the Ishmaelite kingdom, a time when its troops conquered the land of Israel from the hand of Edom. That is the year four thousand, three hundred, eighty-eight years of the age (A.D. 628) which is five hundred, sixty years after the destruction of the house [68+560=628]. These are the days of the first *time*.

The end of the second *time* will be at the occasion when Edom conquered the land from the hand of Ishmael in the year four thousand, eight hundred, fifty-nine (A.D. 1099). From the time Ishmael overpowered him [Edom] until this year are four hundred, seventy-two years [1099−628=471 plus],[112] and these are years of the second *time*. The years of [these] *two times* are one thousand, thirty-two years, and it is apparent that *half a time* is one fourth as

---

[112]With all the careful calculating required for a study like this, also occasional approximations are necessary to come out "right."

many years a two times, that is two hundred, fifty-eight [258×4=1032] years. *Two times and half a time* are one thousand, two hundred, ninety years [258×5=1290]. This is the calculation according to him who divides these days into *two times and half a time*. The verse which follows it says, *Blessed is he who waits and comes to the days, one thousand, three hundred, thirty-five* (Dan 12:12). Between it [1,335 days] and this verse [1,290 days] are forty-five years[=days]. [This] refers to the wars of Gog and the rest of the wars that will follow at the beginning of the days of the Messiah which will last for forty-five years. The scripture praises him who *comes to* the end of these wars. The one who ponders this verse from a different angle does not calculate the second *time* from the occasion when Edom conquered the land from the hand of Ishmael,[113] because we cannot find [any] mention of the end of the second *time* [which] is immediately preceding this subject. He mentions it, however, four verses later, as it is written, *Those who violate the covenant, he will seduce with flattery, but the people that knows its God will hold firm and act* (Dan 11:32). It is [also] written, *Those who teach the people will make the many understand, but they will stumble with the sword, in flame, in captivity, and in plunder [for many] days* (Dan 11:33). Also the scripture [says], *When they stumble, they will receive a little help, and many will join themselves to them with flattery* (Dan 11:34), and the scripture [continues], *Some of those who teach will stumble to test them, purify them, and make them white* (Dan 11:35). At the end of this verse, it says, *Until the time of the end for it is yet for the time appointed* (Dan 11:35). Because of this you may set one measure for *two times* which is five hundred, sixty years. There will be a period of *two times* from the destruction of the house until the end of the second *time*, one thousand, one hundred, twenty years. The end of the second *time* will be the year four thousand, nine hundred, forty-eight of the age (A.D. 1208). In it the wicked kingdom of Edom will prevail over the land, and it will be joined to the kingdoms, as it is said, it will be joined to *the time of the end* (Dan 11:35). *The king will do as he wishes* (Dan 11:36). [The period] between this year and the year in which Edom captured the land from the hand of Ishmael is about ninety years [1208−90=1118 and not 1099!]. Concerning these years, the verses mentioned above come to teach you that the kingdom of the

---

[113]Rabbi Hiyya tried to relate Daniel to facts of the Middle ages. Moslems began at A.D. 628. Therefore the period between 68 and 628 was the first *time*. Crusaders overpowered the Moslems, beginning at A.D. 1099, which was the second *time*.

wicked Edom will be afflicting the Israelites with all its power on the land all these years in which the time of the second *time* will be completed. *The time of the end* which is *half a time* will begin and there will be left one hundred, seventy, of *the one thousand, two hundred, ninety* years (Dan 12:11) which are given in this verse. It is the beginning of *the time of the end* (Dan 11:35) which comes after the second of the *two times*. During these days, there will be revealed signs of redemption, and it [redemption] will be known to all who pace the earth. At their conclusion, Michael will arise, as it is written, *At that time Michael the great prince will arise* (Dan 12:1). When he arises, great tribulations will begin at the beginning of the days of the end, as it is written, *It will be a time of tribulation such as has never been since there was a nation until that time* (Dan 12:1). At the end [of that verse], it says, *In that time your people will escape, all who are found written in the book* (Dan 12:1). Concerning this escape, he says, *Blessed is he who waits and comes to the days, a thousand, three hundred, thirty-five* (Dan 12:12), because this is forty-five years after *the time of the end* (Dan 11:35).

He praises this time and says, *Blessed is he who comes to* it of those who *wait* for him, because at that time the holy One blessed be He will fulfill for his people all the good things which he is destined, in his mercy, to give them. With this he seals the book and says, *Go to the end, and you will rest and arise to your lot at the end of days* (Dan 12:13). With this he explained to him the resurrection of the dead, and he announced the time and promised that he would *arise* and ascend from his grave. When he had sealed the chapter of the events at the end of the prophecy, at the conclusion of the third time with the mention of the resurrection of the dead, as it is written, *Many of those who sleep in the dust of the ground will awake* (Dan 12:2). Likewise he sealed the chapter of the days of the end with the mention of the resurrection of the dead to Daniel, as it is written, *You, go to the end, and you will rest and you will arise to your lot* (Dan 12:13), that is to say, "*Go to* your *end*, and fill your days which are decreed to you."

There are those who say, *Go to the end* (Dan 12:13). *Go to the end* of the seventy years after the destruction of the house, because this is *the end* [of your way and the time] in which you stand, i.e. if your *end* is completed at the end of seventy years, and the construction of the second house is not yet completed, [then] you will not see the completion of its construction. You will learn from this that Daniel died in the second year of Darius, because this is the end of the calculation of the seventy years of the first exile, and *to the end* refers to the end of the calculations of *the end*. He says, *Go to the end and you shall rest* (Dan 12:13). Read into this verse the death of Daniel, the *rest* in which he trusted which is the resurrection of the dead.

We find that the dead of human beings are divided into five categories and that the scripture calls every division by a separate name. The first part deals with the dead of the wicked Gentiles who have no wisdom, fear, and no Torah, neither do they recognize the sanctification of the Lord. These dead are like the dead of livestock and wild beasts, whose souls perish together with the destruction of their bodies. They have no merit, no obligation, and no punishment for the age to come. [This] death which is difficult in the eyes of all the sages, the scripture calls them "empty headed," because when the soul dies together with the body, then that man is blotted out from this age and the age to come. Like the generation of the flood, of whom it says, *He blotted out every living thing that was on the face of the earth* (Gen 7:23). It is [also] written, *They were blotted out from the earth* (Gen 7:23). *I will blot out the man whom I have created* (Gen 6:7). This is what it says about the man who walks after the hardness of his heart and the presumptiousness of his desires: *The Lord will blot out his name from under the heavens* (Dt 29:19). The second division of the dead are those who go down to Gehinnom and the pit of destruction, from which they will not come up until ages after ages. These are the wicked Gentiles who are wise but do not fear Heaven. [They] do not [have] the Torah or merit for having kept the commandments. In the same category are the Jewish idolators who died in their apostasy without repentance. This death is called destruction, as it is written, *I will destroy that soul* (Lev 23:30); *I will cut him off from the midst of his people* (Lev 20:3). *Thus may all your enemies be destroyed, O Lord* (Jdgs 5:31). The third division comprises the dead who have virtue but who have incurred guilt in that they have not been atoned. They are deserving both punishment as well as reward. They will be punished at first according to their transgressions until they have been atoned, but at the end they will merit the Garden of Eden. This death is called "cutting off," and you can say that all those who deserve *karet* ("cutting off")[114] and die will be punished for their iniquity in the age to come, for death does not atone for their iniquity. This is the

---

[114]For a more extensive study of the relationship between "cutting off" and unpardonable sins, see *Consequences*, 306-13.

difference between death at the hands of Heaven and "cutting off," for death at the hands of Heaven atones for their iniquity, as it is written, *They shall bear their sin; they shall die childless* (Lev 20:20). They will die because of their sin, but their souls will not be punished. In the case of "cutting off" it says, *That soul shall be cut off from his people* (Gen 17:14), because the soul will be punished for that iniquity. It will not partake of the custom popular among his people [who believe that] when they die, that event atones for their iniquity, as it is written: *[May the following unexpressed curses come upon me] if this iniquity is forgiven for you until you die* (Isa 22:14). The fourth category is that of the death of the righteous who walk at once into the Garden of Eden without any punishment. This death is called "going," as it is written, *You shall go to your fathers in peace* (Gen 15:15). Sometimes it is called "gathering," as it is written, *Also you shall be gathered to your people* (Num 27:13); *I am gathered to my people* (Gen 49:29). If the holy One blessed be He promises the righteous with the resurrection of the dead, he calls their death a "rest," as it is written, *His rest shall be glorious* (Isa 11:10). Just as he said to Daniel in this [passage], *Go to the end, and you will rest* (Dan 12:13). The fifth category is the one that excels them all. These are the ones who walk into the Garden of Eden while still alive, and they do not taste death. This division of called "taking," as it is written with [respect to] Enoch, *He was not, because God took him* (Gen 8:24) and [also] with Elijah (May he be remembered for blessing), *If you see me when I am taken from you* (II Kgs 2:10). These are the five classes into which death will be divided according to the scholars who carry on research on this subject, based on the Torah. In his writing, Daniel was assured of life in the age to come and in his resurrection from the dead, as it is written, *You, go to the end, and you will find rest, and you shall arise to your lot* (Dan 12:13). *Go to* your *end* in this age. *You shall find rest* for the age to come. *You shall arise to your lot* is for the resurrection of the dead. Because he said to him, *to your lot*, we see that those who arise during the resurrection of the dead do not all arise at once, but each generation stands according to its *lot*. All the dead of Israel who are in every city will arise from their graves in their *lot*, and they will fill the places of their dwellings after the destruction of the Gentiles and the annihilation of all the governments. There will not be left of the wicked Gentiles a single man, but the Israelites will arise and inherit the dwellings of the Gentiles. Because of this, the holy One blessed be He scattered the Israelites among the Gentiles in all the dwellings of the earth, so that when they arise from their graves in the future they will be the residents of the place in all the dwellings of the earth, and you will call all the lands of the world the land of Israel. Then the land of Israel will expand its borders to a great extent until it will fill all the world. He said, *to the end of days* (Dan 12:13) to give him a sign of the resurrection of the dead that it will be at *the end* of the years of *two times and a half* (Dan 12:7). *The end* which the angel who raised his right hand and his left to heaven gave him. It was like saying, *You will rest* in your death, and *you will arise in your lot* in the fulfillment of *the end* which the man of the *right hand* or the one who raised his *right hand* gave to you. This is the interpretation of *the end of the days (the right hand)*, in my opinion. Our rabbi Saadia (May he be remembered for blessing) did not share this opinion of *the end of days*, for in his commentary on the Book of Daniel the word הימין here was not like ימין "right hand," the opposite of "the left hand," but it was like הימים "the days." The *nun* in ימין stands in the place of *mem* in ימים. The same is true of חטין (Ezek 4:9), בחיין (Job 24:22), [and] צדנין (I Kgs 11:33), as well as your ways to blot out מלכין (Prov 31:3), for all of which the *nun* is [given] in place of *mem*. This is the opinion of our rabbi Saadia Gaon; but as for me, when I found a way to explain ימין as it is, without any change or alteration, it was right to my eyes to explain it as ימין *right hand*, which is the opposite of *left*. I do not wish to dispute on this matter with our rabbi Saadia, but I say that there is not a great deal of difference in the two interpretations, and I do not refute his opinion altogether. I seal the fourth gate. May it be the will of the Lord to grant us merit for speaking correctly and to lead us in the right way.[115]

Nor will you find with reference to the scholars of this belief [astrology], these two years: They are the year five thousand, two hundred, eight (A.D. 1448) and the year five thousand, two hundred, twenty-eight (A.D. 1468). They are always likely to introduce great innovations into the world. There are proofs of the accuracy of both opinions for the year to be counted first for the firm union. We are not able to decide between these two opinions nor to choose which one to support, because each one of them [the astrologists] gives [good] reasons for his position.

We find a hint from the verse for it, just as you see from the research which we have conducted in the preceding "gates,"

---

[115]This is the conclusion of the "fourth gate," page 110. The final excerpt includes the very end of the entire book, pages 154-55.

namely that these two different [years] are eligible for the resurrection of the dead which is the most fearful, great, firm, and wonderful of all signs which [happened] before it. Because of this, I have not [considered it] right to interpret all the differences of these [celestial] unions [in] one word from the words of the scholars of astrology when they calculate that there will be renewals in the world in these unions, because all their words and experiments cease in this place, because the scripture arouses us, and the holy One blessed be He has promised us in that time there will be a removal of the powers of all the stars, and he will give to all the army of heaven and the creatures of the land different forces. He will renew new signs which have not been in the world before. There will be a decree of the stars and their dominions, separated in that time from the activity of this age.

We have seen written in the Book of Daniel the order of the custom of all the kingdoms from the construction of the second temple until the time of the redemption and with his coming to the time of the salvation and redemption, he announces the end and its time. He will not interpret another word of the subject, and he will not announce the custom of great good things which come after it. Whether it is because these subjects were explained in the rest of the books of the prophets or whether it is because we are not permitted to explain them according to the holy One blessed be He, seeing in that time the new creation from the six days of creation because they stand before him, but they are hidden so that he can show them and bring them out through the activity of the days of the Messiah.

Because of this, we will seal this gate with this and come to request mercy before the Lord of mercies, so as to hasten for us his announcements of good things and that he may hasten to redeem us, gather our exiles, fulfill for us his good word which he has promised us through his prophets and his seers, as it is written, *"For as the new heavens and the new earth which I will make stand before me," says the Lord, "so shall your descendants and your name stand"* (Isa 66:22), and it is written, *I will put my words in your mouth, and I will hide you in the shadow of my hand, stretching out the heavens, and establishing the earth, and saying to Zion, "You are my people"* (Isa 51:16). It is written, *You know that I am in the midst of Israel, and I am the Lord your God. There is no other, and my people will not be ashamed for the age* (Joel 2:27), and it is written, *But they will rejoice and be glad until [ages untold] until that which I am*

*creating, for, behold, I am creating Jerusalem, a rejoicing, and
her people, a joy* (Isa 65:18).
    Completed is the composition of the scroll
        which reveals the secret of the redemption.
            Praise to the One who dwells above!
    May it be the will of Heaven to direct us in the true way to make
our hearts keep, do, and fulfill his holy Torah. Monday, the first
of the month of Nisan (A.M. 4946 = A.D. 1186).

Summary

Rabbi Abraham Bar Hiyya ha-Nasi was a celebrated Jewish
mathematician, astronomer, and philosopher of the twelfth century who turned his energies to eschatology during the Crusades in
order to stablilze the faith of his people. In 1136 he was mentioned
in writing together with the ascription given for the dead: "May he
remember the righteous for blessing." This implies that he was
dead by that date. Baer thought he wrote his book on eschatology
about A.D. 1129.[116] The date A.D. 1186 at the conclusion of the
book must refer to the date at which some scribe finished copying
this scroll.
    Rabbi Abraham believed that the Crusades were themselves the
wars that were to come at the end of days, and he used his
mathematical skill to be more precise about the time the Messiah
would come. The 1290 days referred to in Dan 12:11 are taken to
be the years after the destruction of the temple in A.D. 68. Add
1290 to 72 and you have the number A.D. 1358. This he considered to be the date when the redeemer would appear and the
Gentiles would be destroyed. From other bases, such as adding the
two thousand years of the Messiah to the date when the vision was
sealed (either 312 or 332 B.C.) the date would be 1448 or 1468. The
days of the Messiah would precede the resurrection of the dead, so
it is possible that one date can apply to the appearance of the
Messiah and the other for the resurrection. The days of the
Messiah would last until the end of the sixth millennium (A.D.
2240) when the age of peace would be introduced. Rabbi Abraham
had a complete theory about the dead on the resurrection. The
wicked Gentiles would be finally destroyed as well as apostate
Jews who had not repented. For others, there would be periods
of punishment prior to admission into the Garden of Eden.

[116]I. Baer, "רבי אברהם בר חייא הנשיא", אנציקלופדיה העברית I, 301. See
also G. Schwartz, "Abraham bar Hiyya ha-Nasi," *JE* I, 108-09.

After the resurrection all the homes of the Gentiles would be in the possession of Jews who would then rule the whole world from Jerusalem.

Introduction to Naḥmanides

The Spanish theologian, Moses Ben Naḥman (A.D. 1194-1270), succeeded Maimonides in the time but not in opinion. Naḥmanides respected Maimonides very highly, but spent most of his academic life opposing the liberal views of Maimonides. He was a philosopher who was attracted by the school of Jewish mysticism known as the cabbala and was strongly influenced by Ḥiyya's application of astrology to the interpretation of prophecy and the coming of the Messiah. He was selected as the scholar to represent Judaism in the famous debate with the Christian, Pablo Christiani. Reports of this debate are all tendentious and apologetic.[117] His success or failure is not so important for this study as the recognition of his status in Judaism of his day. He also wrote a commentary of the Bible that was widely used. Most important for this examination is *Book of Redemption* which tells his eschatological views. These do not agree with those of Saadia Gaon, Judah Halevy, or Maimonides, but they reflect an important theologian's views during the Middle Ages. He agreed with the earlier scholars in believing the arrival of the Messiah and the return of the Jews of Palestine under the rule of the Messiah to be the most central point of Jewish faith. His careful study and his dependence upon Ḥiyya will be evident in the translation that follows.

THE BOOK OF REDEMPTION

The Fourth Gate

Rabbi Moses Ben Rabbi Naḥman

I

We know that the good and correct end time can be explained from the Torah of Moses our teacher (upon whom be peace). By this I mean the end of the repentance and worship. But with the subject in which we are [now engaged] is that end time which is

[117]The text is taken from I.M. Aaronson, ‏ספר הגאולה לרבינו משה בן רבי נחמן‎ (Jerusalem, c1959), 59-71, including only the final chapter or "gate" of his thesis.

distant and separated from us because of our sins until a spirit from above uncovers us. But the end of days and the time are hinted at in five places in this book [Daniel]. Of them, as he said in his first vision: *He will wear out the saints of the Most Hight, and he will think to change the times and the law, and they will be given into his hand for a time, two times, and half a time* (Dan 7:25). Daniel did not understand, however, because he said, *My thoughts greatly alarmed me, [and my complexion changed], but I kept the matter in my mind* (Dan 7:28). In this end time, at the end of the book, in the last vision, after which it was said to him, *In that time Michael the great prince who stands over the sons of your people will arise, and there will be a time of trouble such as had never been from the beginning of the nation until that time, and at that time your people will [just barely] escape, all who are found written in the book* (Dan 12:1), and at the end of the subject, it is written, *Then he said to the man clothed in linen who was above the waters of the stream, "How long will it be until the end of the wonders"* (Dan 12:6). The answer is this: *For a time, two times, and half a time, and when the shattering of the power of the holy people is completed, all these things will be accomplished* (Dan 12:7). This tallies with the first number, for the words מועד and עדן are synonymous, the only difference being that one is in Hebrew and the other is in Aramaic. Also with respect to this he said, *I heard, but I did not understand* (Dan 12:8).

In the second vision, when he saw *the little horn* (Dan 8:9) that removed *the continual offering* (Dan 8:11) from *the general of the army* (Dan 8:11), it is asked there, *How long will be the vision of the continual offering and the sacrilege that causes appalment, the forteiture of the sanctuary and the army to be trampled under foot* (Dan 8:13)? The answer is this: *Until two thousand, three hundred evening and morning [sacrifices] and the sanctuary will be restored properly* (Dan 8:14). At the end of the book [it says], *From the time that the continual offering is removed and the setting up of the sacrilege that causes appalment will be one thousand, two hundred, and ninety days* (Dan 12:11), but there is still another calculation: *Blessed is he who waits and comes to the one thousand, three hundred, and thirty-five days* (Dan 12:12).

Note that the scholar Rabbi Abraham[118] (May he be remembered for blessing) says that these days are the real days, and he searched [in] foreign books in order to explain that this was the custom *from the time the continual offering is removed* (Dan

---

[118]Evidently Rabbi Abraham Bar Ḥiyya, ha-Nasi, author of "The Scroll of the Revealer."

12:11) until the second destruction. *Blessed is he who waits and comes* (Dan 12:12) he interprets in this way: [The Israelites] will thus remain in hardship at the end with the coming of the redeemer. These are very harsh words, because we do not find in the writings, *days*. They came to fulfill "months," mentioned privately, although they are "a year and two years." Further, what is the relevance of the destruction of the second house now that he speaks about the *end of the wonders* (Dan 12:6), and there is already singled out for him a vision by itself, as I have explained? What is the reason for saying, *Blessed is he who waits and comes to the one thousand, three hundred, thirty-five days* (Dan 12:12)? Woe to the one who *comes to* them, because they are days of hardship. Had there been a beginning for this number, we would say, *Blessed is he who waits and comes to* the completion of this number, but since there is no hint in the book for the beginning of this number, hence their end is not mentioned. This being so, it is not relevant to say, *Blessed is he who waits and comes to the one thousand, three hundred, thirty-five days* (Dan 12:12), except when he actually comes to them: Thus he interprets: *two thousand, three hundred evening and morning [sacrifices]* (Dan 8:4) because they are the days that will continue in hardship with Titus. The difficulty concerning this [explanation] will then arise, as we have said [above]. It will be even more difficult than this, for concerning this it is said in that vision, *For the vision is for the end time* (Dan 8:17). Thus *the continual offering was removed, and the place of his sanctuary was overthrown* (Dan 8:11) can only mean the destruction [of the temple] (See Dan 9:24). *The sanctuary will be restored properly* (יצדק) (Dan 8:14) can only mean *righteousness* (צדק) of the ages [or *restored properly* for the ages] (Dan 9:24). *[The anointing of] the holy of holies* (Dan 9:24) refers to the Messiah (the anointed one), for thus it is written. There are many scholars of the past generations who have studied these end times, but they have failed miserably. There was one of them whose errors became public because of the time for which he was hoping, whereas some of them, whose words bear witness against them because the promise they foretold was not realized. The scholar mentioned decreed that Daniel did not know the end time, just as [Daniel] also admitted at a later time, *I heard, but I did not understand* (Dan 12:8, 10). He explained, *but those who teach understand* (Dan 12:10); that means with the coming of the redeemer, but not now.

You should not be surprised about these things, because true scholars--I mean scholars of the Mishnah and the Talumd (May they be remembered for blessing(--have made mistakes in their calculations, as they said, "The sages taught: Rabbi Nathan says, 'This verse pierces and goes down to the abyss, *For the vision is yet for the appointed time. It will speak, at the end, and not lie. [If it is late, wait for it, for it will surely come, and it will not delay]* (Hab 2:3). Not as our rabbis when they interpreted [the verse], *Until a time, two times, and half a time* (Dan 7:25), and not as Rabbi Simlai, who used to interpret, *Yet once [more], it is a short time, [and I will shake the heavens and the earth]* (Hag 2:6; San 97b). Indeed, I think that their errors were according to God's will in concealing the end time, as it says, *Many will run to and fro and knowledge will increase* (Dan 12:4), not because the end time is deeply hidden in this book. The reason for the concealment of the beginning was that the exile was extended and so the end time was made more distant, as it says, *But seal up the vision, for it pertains to many days [from now]* (Dan 8:26; 12:4). Now we in this generation are lowly of stature and ability and limited in knowledge and insight, and our souls have so much to endure of the exile and hardships that our heart has become like dead flesh which can no longer feel the knife. So how can we rise to the heights to open our mouth and speak of the number of the end time and know and produce·the secret which is hidden in this sealed book in which the great scholars go astray? Except that we are nearer to the truth, having the advantage of living after much time has passed, so that we are nearer to the end in time. Perhaps the decree which was made to conceal it has been annulled because the reason for its annulment is the one pertaining *to many days,* because it says, *Many will run to and fro, and knowledge will increase* (Dan 12:4). This is the hint provided that we are permitted to examine *(run to and fro)* the end time in this book so that we may *increase* in *knowledge* through it. From the expression, *Those who teach will understand* (Dan 12:10), we learn that when the end time comes near, *Those who teach will understand* (Dan 12:10) these mysteries.

Before we open our mouth to speak on the subject of the end time, we wish to apoligize for that which the scholars (May they be remembered for blessing) have said: "May those who calculate the end times expire!" I think that the intention was as we have already said, that some of them [the scholars] (May they be remembered for blessing) knew that the end time would extend long after them, for they said to Rabbi Akiba, "Grass will grow up over your cheeks, and still the son of David will not have come"

(JTaanit 4:5). They simply did not wish that the matter should be revealed to the multitude lest their hopes become weakened from it. Now they have removed from us these prohibitions concerning calculations on the end of days [of the Roman rule]. Indeed others of our persuasion have already composed books on this theme. It will not be a default to the people when we also voice our opinion on this subject. Perhaps they will have an addition of goodness and comfort when our words agree with [their] opinion and are nearer, with God's help, to wisdom in this age. You see there are reasons for the words of our sages (May they be remembered for blessing): "May the bones of those who calculate the end times be crushed, because they used to say, 'Since the end time had come', but again [the Messiah] did not come, he will never come-- but wait for him, as it is said, *If he is late, wait for him, [for he will surely come]* (Hab 2:3; San 97b).'" The intention in [saying] this was that they knew some of the men of their generation who had decided that the end time was near to that time, but they increased the stumbling blocks in the way between bringing it near and removing it far away. Hence it was a delay for the *'amĕ ha-areṣ* in the matter. It was necessary, therefore, to conceal it from the human vision and to continue watching for its implementation. Now that which we have said [above] will not be damaged by its removal. It is not for this reason, because *our words with respect to the end time are words of doubt and possibility,* and we have no word appropriate for making a firm decree of truth and to make a decisive statement about it that is certain. We are no prophets who can reveal the secrets of God (May he be blessed), but we hope for the time to come, and [then] *we will believe the matter completely.* From the establishment of the words and seasons in our interpretation, we can perhaps say that it will be according to our words, but blessed is the one who knows the truth.

II

Be sure that God will help you and disclose to you everything that is sealed, because our opinion [regarding the end time] agrees partly with the views at the end of the Book of Daniel as well as with those who preceeded us, because it is the calculation of the end time of the redemption and the time of *the removal of the continual offering* (Dan 8:11). That is the time of the destruction when the house was completely removed. It was not for a half a week that he destroyed the *sacrifice and offering* (Dan 9:27), for then it was not removed. The *days* which are written here are [to be counted] "years." Parallel to this is *For a full year* (ימים) *it will be his right of redemption* (Lev 25:29). They employed the expression, *days,* in reference to the sealing of the vision: *From the time of the removal of the continual offering* (Dan 12:11) with the destruction of the house until *the setting up of the sacrilege* which removes *that which causes appalment* (Dan 12:11), he will destroy from the world *a thousand, two hundred, ninety* years (Dan 12:11), because then the Messiah son of Ephraim will reveal himself, whom we accept in this context, and he will give *the sacrilege which causes appalment* (Dan 12:11). It is said of him in the cabbala,[119] in *Pirke Hekhaloth,* that he will walk for forty years, and he will gather [troops] from the outcasts and will wage wars. He will die in the battle of Gog, until the Messiah son of David reveals himself and conquers them and gathers us together completely and purifies us. Then we will escape, according to all that is written in all the books of the prophets. This period will last five years, and these are forty-five days which are added in which *he who waits and comes to the one thousand, three hundred, thirty-five days* (Dan 12:12). According to the view of the Talmud, which interprets from *the setting up of the sacrilege which causes appalment* (Dan 8:13) that an image was set up in the temple. The verse will be laconic, that is to say, *From the time of the removal of the continual offering* (Dan 12:11) and when we put in its place *The sacrilege which causes appalment* (Dan 12:11), *until the end of the wonders* (Dan 12:6), concerning which you ask, they will be *a thousand, two hundred, ninety days* (Dan 12:11). Rabbi Abraham (May he be remembered for blessing) replied, "If they are years, [then] how can a man wait a thousand years and witness its arrival? It is written, *The days of our years are seventy years* (Ps 90:10), but there is no sense to this question, for it is possible that the verse refers to the people, namely *blessed* is the generation that *waits* and *comes to* the days of the redemption. It is also possible that with the time, *a thousand, two hundred, ninety* (Dan 12:11) it says, *Blessed is he who waits* from that generation and *comes to* [the final] *forty-five days* [required for waiting] for the complete redemption. Then all the land will be tranquil and quiet. Now there are two verses properly paired to apply to the days of the redemption, and in our opinion, they hint that everyone *who waits* will *come to* (Dan 12:12) that time, because our souls trust in

---

[119]Jewish mystical literature of the Middle Ages and later. Part of Pirkē Hekhaloth is translated here in the Book of Zerubbabel.

the Name [of God]. Even those who died in the exile will awake and witness the redemption in the days of the redemption.

III

Notice that the scholars of the Mishnah testify in the interpretation that Rome will seize the kingdom from [the men of] the second house when they conquer the Greeks, two hundred, six years before the destruction (A.D. 136). If you add this number to *a thousand, three hundred, thirty-five* (Dan 12:12), [then] that is the end time of our complete redemption (A.D. 1199). We have existed under the hand of Rome and Shekhaniah who sold us to them, one thousand, five hundred, forty years. For the year *one thousand, three hundred, thirty-five,* in which there will be our complete redemption. *Blessed is he who waits and comes to it* (Dan 12:12).

Observe that the first exile of our people was decreed between the parts (Gen 15:17) that until their return to the land, four hundred forty years [would transpire], as it is written, *They [the Hebrews] will serve them, and they [the Egyptians] will afflict them [the Hebrews] for four hundred years* (Gen 15:13). These were days of affliction and exile at the hand of others, *but the fourth generation will return here* (Gen 15:16). This is the end time for their return to the land, and there in that honored position, namely *between the parts* (Gen 15:17), it was hinted to our patriarch [Abraham] (upon whom be peace) the servitude of the four kingdoms, as the scholars (May they be remembered for blessing) explain in the Talmud.[120] When you make *one time* (עדן) [equal to] four hundred, forty years, and the second *two times* (עדנין) of eight hundred, eighty [years], and *a half a time* (עדן) of two hundred, twenty [years] (Dan 7:25), the total comes to one thousand, five hundred, forty years [440+880+220=1540]. Therefore it is said to Daniel that from the time the fourth beast prevails, we will be given into his hand for *a time, two times, and half a time* (Dan 7:25) which are three appointed times of the first exile and a half an appointed time, and they are, as we have explained, one thousand, five hundred, forty [years]. In this vision, he did not speak of the time of the removal of the continual offering, but only of the rule of this beast, just as it is clear from the scriptures. Thus in the last vision, when he was speaking of the king of the north and of his end, he gave as [this time], *a time* (מועד) , *two times, and half [a time]* (Dan 12:7). I know that it was well-known to Daniel, how many days [constitute] the מועד

and the עד, because he understood the secret which we have explained. Yet he did not understand the end time, because he did not know when that kingdom would begin. I speak with a "perhaps," because in his part the numbers bear a particular name. He did not say "three times (מועדים) and a half." This is to hint to us that we were fit to have been redeemed at the first *time* or at the end of the three, but God was watching for our repentance to him and to reveal his goodness to us, but because we conducted ourselves according to our custom, he gave us time and justified decision to leave us to the completion of the end time, for this was appropriate for those like us today. This was the opinion of the scholars (May they be remembered for blessing) that many end times were decreed at the beginning for our future redemption, and you may discern this from some of their words [as well]. Some of them (May they be remembered for blessing) believed in the redemption, that it would be in their own days, that they would almost see the shooting forth of the horn for the Israelites.

IV

[The next topic of discussion will be] the vision of *the evening and morning [sacrifices]* (Dan 8:14) which told in the second vision that it would be *two thousand, three hundred evening and morning* [sacrifices] (Dan 8:14), because then *the sanctuary* would *be restored properly* (Dan 8:14). Read at the beginning of the kingdom of Israel to refer to the days of the first messiah, David [the king] (upon whom be peace), the *morning*, and at the end of the exile, the *evening*. He said, *For the anointing of the holy of holies* (Dan 9:24). The words, *He will restore properly* (יצדק) means that he will *restore* the sanctuary to its *proper position* (צדקו) He explains: For a *holy one* asked a certain person who was *speaking* so that he would pay attention to Daniel, *How long is the vision* (Dan 8:13) concerning *the continual offering* (Dan 8:13) which he would return after *it was removed* (Dan 12:11) at the hands of *the little horn* (Dan 8:9) which was mentioned. He is the king of Rome. *How long* is *the sacrilege that causes appalment setting up* (Dan 8:13)? For [the sanctuary] is *appaling* to me, [because it contains] "an image." *How long for the sanctuary and the army of heaven and the stars to be trampled underfoot* (Dan 8:10-13)? Just as it is written, *Trample them* (Dan 8:10). The words, *How long*, we used in the sense of "How long shall we wait for the vision of the *continual offering* which is *given over* [for] the appaling *transgression*? And how long will the sanctuary and *the army be be trampled under foot* (Dan 8:13)? It is possible that the word does not belong here or in its parallel: *How long will it be until the end of the wonders* (Dan 12:6). He does not ask, "How many days will the destruction last?" but only "When will the Just One return, and when will the sanctuary be returned to its former might? This is the answer: *Until the evening of two thousand, three hundred* years (Dan 8:14), he will visit the holy kingdom. That is the vision. Then he will restore the *sanctuary properly* (Dan 8:14). The crown will return to its primitive splendor. The subject matter of this answer is this: It is about the one who first builds the house of the continual offering, and that is David our king (upon whom be peace). For he prepared everything, and it is called by his name, as our sages (May they be remembered for blessing) have interpreted, *Look to your own house David* (I Kgs 12:16). He is the one who gave the appaling *transgression* (Dan 8:13), for *he destroyed every male in Edom* (I Kgs 11:16), and until the Messiah arises in his place from his sons, he will be in this number. This is according to the prophecy of Balaam and in accordance of the interpretation of the scholars of Israel (May they be remembered for blessing) when he spoke of these two Messiahs, the father and the son,[121] that God will hasten his redemption so that we may see them quickly, in our days. When you probe this number, you must take [into consideration] the forty years when David (upon whom be peace) was king (I Kgs 2:11), with four hundred, ten [years] for the time of the first house and four hundred, ninety [years] for the time of the exile and the second house. You may add their total to one thousand, three hundred, thirty-five [40+410+490=940; 940+1335=2275] which are from the destruction until the Messiah son of David and you will discover that the total is two thousand, two hundred, seventy-five. [The total is] deficient by twenty-five from the number of the scripture, because it says until *two thousand, three hundred* (Dan 8:14) [2,300−2,275=25] took place until the end of the calculation. But when he said, *until evening* (Dan 8:14), he tells us that although it was near to the end of the number, he would not widen its end time. It seems to me more likely that this number is from the time when the *star will step forth* (Num 24:17) until *a scepter shall arise* (Num 24:17). By this I mean, from the day the first messiah was born until the time the second messiah will be born is the time of the exile for our community.

If you reckon the seventy years of the life of our lord David, for he was thirty years old when he began to rule, until the numbers

---

[121]Meaning David, the king, and the Messiah son of David.

mentioned, [that is] until the time of *one thousand, three hundred, thirty-five [years]* (Dan 12:12) after the destruction of the second house, then this redeemer Nino will come,[122] as we mentioned above. There will then be exactly *two thousand, three hundred* (Dan 8:14). But even this Daniel did not understand, as it is written, *I was astonished at the vision, and I did not understand* (Dan 8:27), because he did not know the beginning of the number and that which is called *morning* (Dan 8:14). At the end of the book, when it was explained to him that [the starting point is] from the day of the destruction [of the second temple] until the advent of this redeemer, namely, the Messiah son of David is *a thousand, three hundred, thirty-five [years]* (Dan 12:12). Then he understood all the visions, because he added from his own knowledge before the destruction twenty-six years until the completion of *a time* (עדן) , *two times, and half a time* (עדן) (Dan 7:25) which is *a time* (מועד) , *two times, and half [a time]* (Dan 12:7) from the kingdom of that beast which is well-known, because he [Daniel] already knew the secret of the times (מועדים) , only he did not understand the beginning of the periods in the first place. Thus he now added to the time of the destruction, years, *until* the completion *of two thousand, three hundred* (Dan 8:14), and he found that the calculation came out to the beginning of the chosen kingdom. When the angel said whenever he was asked, *Go, [Daniel], because the words are sealed* (Dan 12:9), it was so that the words should not be understood. After this, he said, *From the time the continual offering is removed* (Dan 12:11) and *Blessed is he who waits and comes* (Dan 12:12), just as if he had spoken about something else and not about the answer to his questions. He solved for him all his doubts so that even the first visions were not seen in vain.

V

Everyone, however, adds an explanation to the other, just as you can see in the subject of the kingdoms; for in the beginning he did not know [anything] about them except that there would be four. In the second [vision] they added to him the explanation that they [the kingdoms] were the Medes and the Greeks (Dan 8:20-21). Also with the secret beast which had no known form at the beginning, appears now in the second vision that it is the small horn which is Greece (Dan 8:9),[123] and in which he was told the

[122]Nino is one of the many names for the expected Messiah.
[123]Not just Greece, but the Greek king, Antiochus IV, Epiphanes.

end of days, [but] he did not understand it. In the third vision, however, the whole subject of the kingdoms was explained to him. Also their end times which were hidden tell how everything was explained to him in this vision in its totality. About this he wrote, *The word was revealed to Daniel* (Dan 10:1), that is to say, it was not like the first vision from which he did not understand the end time, because this was the beginning of the section, and that which came after this: *In those days, I Daniel, [was mourning for three weeks]* (Dan 10:2). On the twenty-fourth day of the first month, he returned to explain when it happened and how this vision came to him, from which the word was revealed to Daniel. Behold now everything that was hidden was told to him, and the matter was concluded with the expression, "days." All this in order that it should be a subject concealed from human beings, but he promised that those who are wise would understand when the time drew near.

Now I will support my thesis with some supporting words for which favor will be found by the mind for logic is in their midst. It is that which I calculated, the years of the existence of Israel in the land. I saw that they are equaled by the number from which they will be exiled from it in conformity with their teaching of "measure for measure." Observe that they existed in the land for four hundred, forty years before the construction of the house of the sanctuary and four hundred, ten years while it was standing. They were visited [with favor] and they went up at the permission of Cyrus, nineteen years before the construction of the second house. It was standing for four hundred, twenty years. This totals *one thousand, two hundred, ninety* (Dan 12:11) [440 + 410 + 19 + 420 = 1289 or ca. 1290], corresponding to the number which Daniel said in the exile. For the year ninety, in which there will be redemption they will return to the land, just as they were exiled from it in the year four hundred twenty-two after the construction of the second temple. Notice that the existence of the land and the exile from it are both equal in number, no less and no more (It is not proper for me to introduce the years of Babylon into this, because it is well-known that from the beginning they were punished and exiled from it according to the number of years of the sabbatical year releases. In the second exile from the days of the second house there was punishment against them, because they repented for their sin in that they ate the same food as their enemies. The truth is, moreover, that in the days of Babylon, no man had enough food, for the land was waste, and no one plowed nor harvested, as it is written, *All the days that it lay desolate to fulfill seventy years* (II Chron 36:21). They said, "for fifty-two years no bird was seen in the land of Israel, etc." [Shab 145b]. These are the days of Babylon). The secret of this topic from the words of our sages (May they be remembered for blessing) which they interpreted from scriptures is revealed. They (May they be remembered for blessing) said, *Your land, foreigners devour it in your presence* (Isa 1:7; Intro. LamR).

Moreover it is said that corresponding to *the forty years* (Ps 95:10) of the wilderness, they add the forty-five mentioned above in the text, *he who waits and comes* (Dan 12:12). For forty of them, are for the wars of the first Messiah, as we have explained from the words of the cabbala. He rises up for us in the place of our teacher Moses for the redemption. The five years are to purify the land and to divide it among our tribes, as they did for many days in the time of Joshua. This is a suitable and attractive support [for my thesis].

I have still [another] sign that is good, beautiful, reliable, acceptable, and one which I have calculated from the [Hebrew] letters in *gematria: And they will afflict them for four hundred [years]*.[124] [The numerical value of these Hebrew letters] total one thousand, two hundred, ninety-three years. You may substract the *waw* (ו=6) and you have approximately the number of the exile, if you [also] add half a week, as it is said, *For half a week he will cause the sacrifice and offering to cease* (Dan 9:27), for this is the time of real affliction, one thousand, two hundred, ninety-three [1293 − 6 = 1287 + 3½ = 1290½]. *From the time of the* complete *removal of the continual offering* (Dan 12:11), just as I interpreted, and the time, *And they will afflict them for four hundred [years]* is one thousand, two hundred, ninety-three (Gen 15:13).

This is because God made a covenant with Abraham to do good to him and his descendants, and he informed him that the subject of the exile is an extra gift and said to him, *Be convinced [that your descendants will be sojourners in a land that is not theirs. They will be slaves there and will be oppressed for four hundred years]* (Gen 15:13). [Thus] the first exile was told to him, whose calculation was specific, whereas the others were hinted at, just as our sages (May they be remembered for blessing) interpret the

---

[124]Gen 15:13: וענו אתם ארבע מאות is evaluated numerically as follows: 6 + 70 + 50 + 6 + 1 + 400 + 40 + 1 + 200 + 2 + 70 + 40 + 1 + 6 + 400 = 1,293. The word, "years" (שנה) would upset the calculation by adding another 355 years.

verse, *Behold a dread and deep darkness fell upon him* (Gen 15:12). In this the number of the end time is hinted at, thus agreeing with the subject, but the hint which we assigned at the beginning of our discussion from the passage, *When you beget children* (Dt 4:25) is from the verse, *When you are in tribulation, and all these things come upon you in the end of days, [then] you will return to the Lord your God [and obey his voice]* (Dt 4:30), for if you count *You, and all these things come upon you in the end of days,*[125] you arrive at the total, according to the reckoning of *gematria* of one thousand, two hundred, ninety one from the second destruction [of the temple] [68 + 1291 = A.D. 1359]. [This] is hinted at in the chapter (Dan 12:11) until the coming of the first redeemer, the Messiah son of Joseph, for in that year which is added in the calculation, will be fulfilled in us, *Then you shall return to the Lord your God and pay attention to his voice* (Dt 4:30). This is the beginning of our true redemption. As soon as we return and pay attention to the voice of God (may his name be blessed and exalted), he will hasten our redemption and say, "Enough sufferings!" because he alone is the God of loving kindness and mercy. Before his will there is neither end time, appointed season, nor days. May he direct us in the path of his service that we may see the light shining in his Torah, and in his great loving kindness we will behold a wonder and a sign when the end time of the wonders are brought near. Amen.

Summary

Rabbi Moses Ben Rabbi Naḥman (Naḥmanides or Ramban) composed his thesis according to the same structure as that of Rabbi Abraham. He was influenced by Rabbi Abraham and imitated his structure or else both followed a form that was popular in their day. Naḥmanides also reached conclusions very near to those of Rabbi Abraham, although he found a different basis for supporting the figure 1,290 as a touch stone. From the fall of Jerusalem, he calculated 1,290½ or 1,293, which do not deviate far from the number given in Daniel. He was less dogmatic than Rabbi Abraham, acknowledging that he was dealing in probabilities and that he had no prophetic insight from God on this matter. Like Rabbi Abraham, he felt a need to justify this kind of

[125]Dt 4:30: ‎1291-לך ומצאוך כל הדברים האלה באחרית הימים. To get this number it was necessary to break one word from another clause. Without the "You" (‎לך) the count would have been 50 short.

research. Why should he in his day arrive at conclusions that were unknown to the great sages that preceded him? He concluded that the earlier scholars may actually have known these conclusions but withheld them from the people because they were so distant. In his time, however, when they were much nearer to the end, such reticence was no longer justifiable. Nahmanides did not go into so much detail about the consequences destined for various kinds of dead when the judgment day came, the earthly advantages of the Jews in the days of the Messiah, and the disastrous results directed to the Gentiles. He probably understood most of these, but he did not emphasize them as explicitly as did Rabbi Abraham.

Summary of Doctrine

The medieval Jewish doctrine of redemption was interpreted by such great scholars as Saadia Gaon, Hai Gaon, Maimonides, and Nahmanides. It was expressed in sermons, letters, responsa, and calculations. The expectations were consistent: Messiahs, judgment, battles of Gog and Magog, reversal of world status, construction of the temple at Jerusalem, world rule, and ages of peace. These expectations were implemented by messianic movements in medieval history, as the next section will show.

PROPHETIC MOVEMENTS

THE MESSIAH BAR COCHBA

Rabbi Shimon Ben Yohai taught: Akiba, my master, was interpreting, *A star* (כוכב) *stepped forth from Jacob* (Num 24:17):
Cozbah (כוזבא) *stepped forth from Jacob.* When Rabbi Akiba
saw Cozbah, he said, "He is the messianic king!" Rabbi Yohanan
ben Torta said to him, "Akiba, grass will grow up in your cheeks,
and still the son of David will not come" (JTaanit IV.68d).

THE BAR COCHBAH REVOLT

Eusebius[1]

The rebellion of the Jews, of course, again progressed in intensity and extent. After military assistance had been sent to him from
the king, treating their insanity unsparingly, Rufus, governor of
Judaea, went out at once against myriads of men, children, and
women. Carefully observing the law of war, he reduced their
country to slavery. At that time, a man named Bar Cochebas,
which means "Star" (Βαρχωχεβας ὄνομα, ὅ δὴ ἀστέρα
δηλοῖ) was their military leader. On the one hand, he was a
murderous man and an insurrectionist, but on the other hand, he
even held the affectionate designation [of Son of a Star] as [if he
were] a light come down from heaven. As if [he were a leader]
over slaves, he spoke marvels, enlightening those who had been
badly treated. When the war had reached its peak, during the
eighteenth year of the rule [of Hadrian] [Jewish forces were concentrated at] Beitar (Βηϑϑηρα) , a certain very strong citadel
situated not very far from Jerusalem. During the time that they
were hemmed in from the outside, the revolutionaries were
reduced by means of famine and thirst to the final destruction even
of the one who had caused the madness to them, after he had paid
the deserved penalty in full.

All the nation was shut off from that [leader] and from the area
around Jerusalem by a legal decree and orders from Hadrian who
further commanded [them] not to go up so as to see the patriarchal
base, even from a distance. Ariston, the citizen of Pella, tells the
story. Thus the city was bereft of the nation of Jews. A complete
ruin of those ancient inhabitants, a race of Gentiles had come and
were settled, and the Roman city which afterwards took the place

[1] Eusebius, *HE.* IV.vi.1-4.

[of Jerusalem] was named Aelia in honor of the conqueror, Aelios Hadrian.

Summary

The revolt led by Bar Cochba lasted from A.D. 132-35 and was a very fierce struggle for a people who had been completely suppressed just sixty years earlier. During that time Bar Cochba minted coins and negotiated business as a ruler. He was considered a messiah by the great Rabbi Akiba, and some of his letters have been discovered in a cave at Murabaat. The religious nature of this war became so well-known that it motivated Marcion to lead a movement distinguishing Christianity from Judaism because of Judaism's belief in a God of war. Bar Cochba's messianic movement became widely known, but there were other messiahs who were just as devoted to their task whose names are nearly forgotten. One leader at Crete called himself Moses.

THE REDEEMER AT CRETE

Socrates[2]

At this time [of Theodosius the younger (A.D. 412-54)] some of the Jews in Crete became Christians because of the following tragedy: A certain Jew deceptively pretended to be Moses, and he said he was sent from heaven so that he might remove the Jews who lived on the island, (64) leading them through the sea, for he said that he himself had saved Israel long ago through the Red Sea. For a whole year he went about every city on the island, and he persuaded the Jews who dwelled in them to believe, to give up all their money, and to leave their possessions, for he promised to lead them through the dry sea to the promised land. Now since they had been nourished on such hopes as these, on the one hand they neglected all work, and on the other hand, they despised also those things they already had acquired. They left [them] to anyone who happened to take them.

Then, on the day which the Jewish deceiver indicated, he himself would lead, and all they would follow together with their wives and small children. Then he led them to a certain cliff, overlooking the sea. Giving the sign, he commanded and they hurled themselves down against it [the sea]. The first ones did this. They

[2] Socrates, *Ecclesiastical History*. VII.xxxviii. 63-64; MPG. LXVII, 825-28.

approached the cliff and died at once—some were torn to bits by the cliffs, and others drowned in the water. Even more would have been destroyed if God had not foreknown. Christian merchants and fisherman happened to be near. These, drawing up the drowning people, saved [them]. Then, aware of the madness of suffering so wretchedly, they warned the others against throwing themselves down, reminding them of the destruction of the first ones who had hurled themselves down. Those who then knew the folly, blamed the questionableness of their religion, but the false Moses hurried to get away, and they were unable to find him.

THE END OF THE FOURTH BEAST[3]

2. Justus said, "The Most High God knows that I speak the truth, and I do not lie, that in Sykamine after Maurikius the king died (A.D. 602), we were standing beneath the house of the Lord and the leader of the Jews among us explained:

Why are we Jews rejoicing that King Maurikius has died, and Fakus has become king through blood? We have to see the actual reduction of the Roman Empire. If the fourth palace, that is Romania, is diminished and broken to pieces just as Daniel said, really it is nothing else than the ten fingers, the ten horns of the fourth beast, and further, the little horn which changes all knowledge of God, and at once the end of the world (ἡ συντέλεια τοῦ κόσμου) and the resurrection of the dead [takes place]. If this happens, we will have been misled in not accepting the coming Messiah, for before the crushing and division of the fourth beast and the ten horns, the Messiah of the root of Jesse will come in the name of the Lord, the Lord God.

The Sykamine Jews who were standing sneered..."

Summary

This report shows the influence a political change might have on Jewish religious movements. It also shows that some Jews laughed at other Jews' enthusiasm.

THE "NOT-SO-SERENE" MESSIAH[4]

At that time the Jews were beguiled, just as they had been at the time of Theodosius the Younger by a certain Jew who took on a

[3] Greek text from N. Bonwetsch, *Doctrina Iakobi Nuper Baptizati* (Berlin, 1910), 63.
[4] Translated from a fragment included in some texts of *Espana Sagrada*, Trat. 27, Apend. 2, 53: *Espana Sagrada. Theatro. Geographico-Historico de la Iglesia de España*, VIII. Also "The Responsum of Rabbi Natronai Gaon," שערי צדק, V.2-6, 1.

name that completely misrepresented his character, Serene, and covered them with a cloud of error. He called himself the Messiah and announced that they would be flown to the promised land. He commanded them to give away all their possessions so that they would return empty handed. When this came to the attention of Ambiza, he added all they had abandoned to the [state] treasury. He [Ambiza] called in Serenus and asked him if he thought he was the Messiah of God...

THE SYRIAN MESSIAH[5]

In those days (A.D. 723), the Jews who lived in Spain were rebelling, because the report came to them that in Syria a certain Zonoria, Ramaj, appeared who said of himself that he was the promised Messiah for whom they were watching. All the Jews who were in Spain and France went to Syria, abandoning their possessions. Embieza, the Amir, seized all their goods, their houses and possessions, for the benefit of the state.

Summary

Jews in the Middle Ages expected the prophecy of Isaiah to be fulfilled literally. Therefore Jews were to be returned to Jerusalem "flying like a cloud" (Isa 60:8). There are reports of this same event taking place in relationship to Alroy in the twelfth century, and it probably occurred on occasions that are no longer recorded. It may also have had a legendary character attributed to messiahs after they were believed to be false. Nonetheless, some Israelis interpret the return of Russian Jews to Israel by plane at the expense of the United States as the fulfillment of Isa 60. Serene was a native of Syria at the beginning of the eighth century. When interrogated by the Moslem leader, Serene said he had only done what he did to mock the Jews, so he was turned over to the Jews for punishment.[6] Another Syrian messiah was called Seor.

THE MESSIAH SEOR[7]

At that time (A.D. 619), a Syrian, whose name was Seor, said of himself that he was the Messiah, but when he was seized by the government, he said, "I have become a laughing stock among the Jews."

[5] A.Z. Aescoly, התנועות המשיחיות בישראל (Jerusalem, 1956), 131.

[6] See further M. Seligsohn, "Serene," *JE*, XI, 202.

[7] Aescoly, *Messianic Movements*, 131.

THE GREAT HOMECOMING[6]

To the great and noble people of the Jews,
from the priests and leaders in Galilee, Greeting:
Be informed that the time of our exile of our people is completed
and finished. The day of the gathering of our tribes has arrived
(הגיע). Look, the kings of the Romans have commanded that our
city, Jerusalem, be returned to us. Please, hurry and come to Jerusalem to the feast of Sukkoth, for our kingdom will arise in Jerusalem.

ABU ISSA[9]

The Issenes are associated with the name of Abu Issa Isaac Ben
Jacob the Isfahanite, who is also called Ofid of God (servant of
God). He was at the time of Elmantzar and the beginning of his
revelation was in the time of the last Omiad kings, Marwan Ben
Muhammed Elhamar. Those of the Jews who followed him
constitute a large mob. They used to say that he had shown signs
and wonders, and they believed that, at the time when they would
go into battle over him, he would make a line around his men with
a myrtle branch, and he would say to them: "Stand in the midst of
this circle and the sword of the enemy will not overtake you."
When his enemies approached the circle, they would withdraw,
for they would be afraid because of his amulet or because of the
charm which he was using.

Then Abu Issa alone on his horse drew a boundary line and he
fought with the Moslems and struck them a mighty blow. He went
to the sons of Moses Ben Amram who crossed over to the wilderness areas to tell them the word of the Lord. They say that after
they had attacked the men of Elmantzar at Ragaes [Persia], he and
his men were killed.

Nevertheless, Abu Issa really said that he was the prophet and
apostle of the expected Messiah, and he believed that there were
five messianic apostles who had preceded him, one after the other,
and he also believed that God had spoken to him and cast [the lot]
upon him to redeem the Israelites from the hands of the wicked
peoples and the insolent kings. He further believed that he was the
Messiah who had been chosen among the sons of man and that he

---

[6] Aescoly, *Messianic Movements*, 90.
[9] Aescoly, *Messianic Movements*, 123-24.

would ascend in stature above the degree of the prophets who had preceded him. He had arisen to the degree of the shepherd, and he thought that the shepherd was also the Messiah.

In his book he rejected all the sacrifices, and he prohibited the food from anything that came from life—either poultry or livestock. He commanded against the ten prayers and remembered also all their times and reached out from the Jewish way with many great commandments written in the Torah.

Summary

The messiahs and their related activities and results included here range all the way from the second century with Bar Cochba to the thirteenth century. Bar Cochba led the bloody war against Rome that lasted from A.D. 132-35. This movement was endorsed by Rabbi Akiba, one of the respected rabbis of the time, as a divinely ordained messianic movement. The Messiah at Crete in the fifth century was reported in Christian histories because of the Christian converts obtained because of the pseudo-Moses's failure. In the seventh century leading Jews understood that the current Roman regime was the last to exist before Jews took over international rule. A little later a Syrian messiah was suppressed as were others a century later. Galilean leaders were certain that the end of the captivity had come and their new government was to begin that very year (whenever that was). This was based on information they had received from the Roman government, which apparently did not materialize. During the Omiad rule Abu Issa led a movement that gained a great deal of recognition, because he had made some basic changes in religious practices, but most of all because he promised to deliver the Jews from their enemies in battle by the use of magic, such as that employed earlier by Moses and Aaron. One of the most prominent was the Persian Jew, David Alroy, who received recognition from Jews all over the then known world. The extent of his military activity and influence is not fully known, but he was a contemporary of Saladin, and some Jews believed that Saladin would be the forerunner of the Messiah David Alroy, whom they supported with money and with personal services as volunteers. These movements reflect the serious political and military nature of Jewish eschatology, part of which was being expressed at the same time Christians reflected their corresponding eschatology by their expansion under Constantine and the Crusades at the end of their first millennium.

DAVID ALROY

Virga's Text (V)[10]

About seven years before the decree about which we spoke above, Israelites experienced severe hardships at the hands of a scoundrel who made himself a messiah. He angered the king and princes very much against the Jews, because they [the king and princes] said that they [the Jews] were seeking a downfall of their [the king's and princes'] kingdom in their [the Jews'] seeking a messiah. That cursed one was called by the name of David el-David, from the city of Amdaiah. There was a large congregation in the area—about a thousand homes filled with wealthy, important, and successful [Jews]. That congregation was the first of the congregations that lived around the Sambation River.[11] There were more than a hundred congregations [in the area]. It is situated at the beginning of the land of Media. They speak the language of the Targum (Aramaic). From there to the city of Gilan [is a distance requiring] a fifty days' walk. They are under the dominion of the king of Persia, to whom they have paid taxes every year for the last fifteen years of more than one gold piece [each]. That man David el-David studied at the school of the chief of the exile, Ḥasdai by name, and before [another] great man, the dean of the academy in the city of Baghdad. He became a very great scholar in the Talmud, all secular studies, books of magic, sorcery, and witchcraft. The man David el-David, because of his strength and arrogance, rebelled against the king. He gathered the Jews who lived in the Ḥaphton Mountains and incited them to go out to fight against all the Gentiles. He displayed signs before them, and they did not know what the source of his power was. Some used to say it was through sorcery and contrivances, whereas others said that his great power was from the Lord. Those who associated with him used to call him "Messiah," and they praised and exalted him.

Mann's Text (M)[12]	*Rabbi Binyamin's Text (RB)*[13]
In the year of the fifth	

[10] S. Ibn Virga, ‏ספר שבטי יהודה‎ (Jerusalem, 1947), 74-76. SML

[11] The Sambation River was a mythological river thought to be somewhere between the West and the far East. Jews expected the twelve tribes to appear suddenly sometime from beyond this river to rescue the Jews from the diaspora.

[12] J. Mann, "Documents Inedits," *REJ.* 4 (1882), 188-89, Bodleian Library Op. add. 8-36. Catalog no. 2425.

[13] E. Halevi (ed.), ‏ספר מסעות רבי בנימן מטודלה‎ (Frankfort a.M., 1904), 72-75 (26:279-495).

M

millennium, nine hundred, twenty-three, (A.D. 1163),

there arose a man whose name was Alroy from the city of Amdaiah. He studied [before] the head of the diaspora, Rabbi Ḥasdai, and before Eli, dean of 430) the academy, and before the Gaon Jacob from the province of Baghdad. He became proficient in the Torah of Moses, *halakah*, Talmud, all secular scholarship, the Arabic language and its literature, and in books of magic and sorcery. He decided firmly to rebel against the king of Persia and to gather Jews together

to fight against the Gentiles and to seize Jerusalem.

He used to give the Jews signs through false miracles and tell them that the Lord had sent him to subdue Jerusalem.

Some of the Jews believed him and called him the Messiah.

RB

Twelve years ago, there arose a man whose name was Alroy from the city of Amdaiah. He studied before the head of the diaspora, [Rabbi] Ḥasdai, and before Eli, dean of the academy, [and before] the Gaon Jacob in the province of Baghdad. He became proficient in the Torah of Moses, *halakah*, Talmud, all secular scholarship, the Arabic language and its literature, and in the books of magic and sorcery. He decided firmly to rebel against the king of Persia and to gather the Jews who were dwelling in the mountains of Ḥaphton to fight against all the Gentiles and to seize Jerusalem.

He used to give the Jews signs through false miracles and tell them that the Lord had sent him to subdue Jerusalem and to bring them out from under the yoke of the Gentiles.

Some of the Jews believed him and called him "our Messiah."

V

When the king of Persia heard the activities of the man, and how successful he was and [how] people were drawing near, and congregating [to him], he became very much afraid. He sent an emissary to him [David], [commanding] that he come to him under great security so that he [Alroy] might display his signs [before the king]. If they were [true] signs, [the king] would know that [Alroy] was really a messiah, and [the king] would understand that God had made [Alroy] king, and [the king] would confess him, and bow down before him, and serve him, because it was God's will that had made him king. David el-David came to the king without any dread or fear. The king asked him, "Is it true that you are the Messiah?" David el-David replied, "I am a messiah, and the Lord has sent me to redeem the people, the Israelites." The king answered, "I will place you in prison, and if you can release yourself from there, I will then know that you are a messiah, but if not, your punishment for your folly will be imprisonment for the age.[14] I will not kill you [just] because you are an idiot.

M	RB
When the king of Persia heard of his plans and how he had been successful in gathering and congregating the people, he was afraid. [Then] he sent an emissary to him, [commanding] that he come to him in the hope that [the king] might see [Alroy's] signs and his deeds. If there were [genuine] signs, then [the king] would know that [Alroy] was the real Messiah, and [then the king] would know that [Alroy] was [really] from the Lord. He came to him with no fear and dread,	The king of Persia heard this report [and] he sent [for Alroy] to come and to speak with him.
and the king said to him, "Are you the king of the Jews?" [Alroy] said, "I am, because the Lord has sent me to redeem his people, the sons of Israel."	He came to him with no fear, and discussed things with him. [The king of Persia] said to him, "Are you the king of the Jews?" [Alroy] said, "I am."

[14] An idiom patterned after the expression עבד עולם, "slave for an age." This is the slave who, at the end of his service term for his creditor, chooses to continue his dependent relationship until jubilee. The prisoner for the age would probably stay in prison for the length of time the king ruled or until the next jubilee. Neither slaves nor prisoners for the age were expected to survive their masters.

M	RB
The king	At once the king became angry and
commanded [the guard] to seize him and put him in prison.	commanded [the guard] to
	put him in prison where prisoners of the king were bound until the day of their death, in the city of Dustan which is along the river Gozen, which is a large river.

V

After David el-David had been apprehended, the king sent to invite all his princes and advisers, and he asked them [for their advice concerning] what he should do with the Jews who were committing crimes and rebelling against his kingdom. While they were engaged in council, they heard how David el-David had released himself from prison and had gone a long distance away. They did not know which way he went.

When the king heard [this], he sent horsemen and officers after him to seize him. The horsemen went and returned to the king and said to him, "Near the river we heard his voice, but [since] we could not see him physically, how could we seize him?" The king thought it was perhaps a deception and that through a bribe they [the emissaries] had released him. They said that they could not apprehend him. Then he mounted a horse and ran after [David]—[the king], his servants, and princes. They went near the river, but they did not see him. They called him, and he answered them, "You idiots! Look, I am going where I please. If you are capable, chase me!" He spread out his scarf on the river Gozen and crossed the river. The king, and also his servants, saw how he crossed. Then the king said, "No one can do anything like this except one whom [the gods] have made king—I mean to say, the king of the age. It must be from there [heaven] that they have made this man king, and we must offer praise." His servants and princes said to him, "We have seen things done with sorcery which appears *only* [being deceptive] to the eye." The king then commanded that they bring a rowing boat and cross the river, and many horsemen galloped after him, but they did not overtake him, because he traveled a ten day journey that day.

M

After three days,
the king was speaking with
his generals and servants concerning the Jews.
Then he looked, and behold
David was coming to meet him,
because he had liberated himself from prison without
permission from anyone
[to do so].
When the king saw him,
he was frightened, and
he said to
him, "Who has brought you
here?" [Alroy]
said to him, "My wisdom
has stood me in good stead,
because I am not afraid of you."

At once the king cried out
with a loud voice and said,
"Seize him!" His generals and
servants said to him,

"We do not see him, but [we]
only [heard] the sound of his
voice." The king immediately
marvelled
at [Alroy's] sagacity.
[Alroy] answered and said to
the king, "Look, I am leaving."
He left, and the king and his
servants followed him

until they came alongside
the river. Then [Alroy]
took his scarf, spread it out
upon the water and crossed
over on the top of it. The king's
servants saw him crossing on
the water on his scarf.

RB

At the end of 483) three days
the king sat down to speak with
his generals and servants concerning the Jew who had rebelled
against the king. Just then
David who
had released him-
self from prison without
permission from anyone, came.

When the king saw him,

he said to
him, "Who has brought you
here? who released you?" [Alroy]
answered, "My intelligence. 484)
You bound me,
but I am not afraid of you
or of all your servants."
At once the king cried out,
saying
"Seize him!"
His servants answered him and
said,
"We do not see him, but we
only heard the sound of his
voice." At once the king feared
his own sanity.

[Alroy] answered and said to
the king, "Look, I am leaving."
He left, and the king
followed him, and all the generals
and servants of the king followed
their king until they came to the
shore of the river. Then [Alroy]
took his scarf, spread it out
upon the water, and crossed
over on the top of his scarf.

M	RB
They pursued him hotly in small fishing boats, but they could not overtake him. They said that there was no magician in the world like this man. That day he took a walk of ten days with the aid of the tetragrammaton, and he told the Jews that which had happened to him. They were all astonished at his wisdom.	They pursued him hotly in small fishing boats, but they could not overtake him. They said that there was no magician in the world like this man. That day he took a walk of ten days with the aid of the tetragrammaton, and he told the Jews that which had happened to him. They were all astonished at his wisdom.

V

When the king saw that he could not succeed this way, he took another way. He sent emmissaries to the chiefs of the exile [commanding] that they seize that man and bring him to [the king]. If they did not, he would kill them all, young and old together, and he would afflict tortures on all the heads of the exiles and burn them afterward, one by one. He also sent a letter to Amir Al Modain, who lived in Baghdad that he should apply the greatest diligence to this case, and he also [commanded] the heads of the exile [to act in this matter].

M	RB
After this [the king]	After this the king of Persia
sent to Elmainim, to the Caliph who was in Baghdad the lord of the Ishmaelites, to [ask him to] speak with the head of the diaspora and the deans of the academies to prevent David from doing such things as these. "For if not," he said, "I will kill all the Jews that are found in all the cities of his [sic.] kingdom by the sword, and there will be hardship in all the cities of Persia."	sent to Amir, 485) to the officiating Caliph who was in Baghdad, the lord of the Ishmaelites, to [ask him to] speak with the head of the diaspora and the deans of the academies to prevent David Alroy from doing such things as these. "For if not," he said, "I will kill all the Jews that are found in my entire kingdom." Then there was a great tribulation in all the congregations in the land of Persia,

V

The heads of the exiles were then assembled, and they sent emissaries to David el-David that he turn away from his rebellious activities. Then it would go well with him and with the whole community of Israel who were in severe danger. Should he not withdraw, there would be a ban of the age decreed upon him, both in this age and in the eternal age. They also sent a letter to Zakai, the president who was in the land of Assyria and to Rabbi Joseph Bakhran Alfalah, the seer who was there, asking them also to write in their own names. For it was a time of trouble for Jacob, one in which it was necessary for the deliverance of the many mercies of Heaven. They all sent letters to David el-David to warn him strongly to turn away from his evil way. He received all the letters, read them, but scorned and laughed at them, paying no attention [to them], and he did not tremble because of them.

M	RB
The Jews sent a written message to the president of the diaspora and to the deans of the academies in the land of Baghdad, saying	and they sent 486) letters to the chief of the exile and to the deans of the academies 487) who were in Baghdad,
"Why should all the Jews	"Why should both we and the congregations who are in the kingdom die before your eyes?
die before your eyes? Restrain this man that he might not be the cause of innocent blood shed in the midst of Israel."	Restrain this man, and do not shed innocent blood."
They then	Then the chief of the diaspora and the deans of the
wrote a letter to David, saying, "The time of redemption has not yet arrived, because not by human strength will salvation come, for salvation belongs to the Lord.	academies wrote to him: 488) "Be informed that the time of redemption has not yet arrived.
	We have not seen our signs. Lest *a fire* 489) mount with the wind, we say that
We tell you that you should restrain yourself from doing such things as	you should restrain yourself from doing again such things as

these, but if you do not, then
you will be an outcast in
all Israel."

Such were the letters sent to
him

in order to make him discontinue his doings. When he received these letters, he read
them, scorned and laughed,
and kept still. He paid no attention to them at all.

these, but if you do not,
you will be excommunicated from
all Israel."

At once they sent [it] to him.
Likewise Zakai, the president
who was in the land of Syria,
and Rabbi Joseph, the seer of
the place Borahan, the district
there,
[all] sent letters to
Alroy. The president and the seer
wrote additional letters to him
to arouse him and warn him, but
he did not accept [the advice] nor
turn away from his evil way.

V

The merciful God put it in the heart of a king, a Turkish king
whose name was Zaid el-Din, who was a subject of the Persian
king. He was a very good friend of the Jews, and he knew the
father-in-law of David el-David. [Zaid el-Din] said to [the father-in-law], "You know [the problem facing] your people, how they
are in dire straits with the Persian king. You are obliged, therefore,
to save yourself and your people. The Jews will give you ten
thousand pieces of gold, and I will guarantee that you will
[receive] them. From me you shall let them know whether you will
kill that sinner who has placed many innocent lives in danger [or
not]. You will also receive a reward from God for the deliverance
of your innocent people.

M

The merciful God put it
in the mind of Zain el-Din, king
of the Turks, one of the
subjects of the king of Persia.

RB

A king arose whose
name was Zain el-Din, king
of the Turks. 492) He was a
servant of the king of Persia,

M	RB
He was a friend of the Jews and knew David's father-in-law. [Zain el-Din] said to [the father-in-law], "You know your people, how they are in severe oppression with the king of Persia. Therefore it is your duty to save your people. The Jews will give you ten thousand gold pieces, and I will be surety for them. You may demand them from my hands."	and sent to David Alroy's father-in-law, and gave him a bribe of ten thousand gold pieces to murder David Alroy secretly.

V

The man, determined to execute the task of the deliverance of his people, [was urged on also by] his love for money. He invited David el-David that night to a drinking party at which [the father-in-law] made him completely drunk. Toward midnight, when he was certain that [David] was dead drunk, [the father-in-law] seized him and cut off his head and brought it to the king Zaid el-Din.

When the king saw the head, he said, "May his blood be upon your head." The king Zaid el-Din sent the head to the Persian king with trustworthy witnesses that [would assure him that] he was the Messiah about whom he had asked. Then the anger of the king was alleviated from David el-David, but he asked for vengeance from every place to be taken against the Jews who continued [following] after him [David]. [The king] asked all communities to submit to him all those who continued [following] that accursed man. They answered that since they did not know them [the followers], where could they search for them? Then the king commanded [them] to apprehend them. From their prisons, they negotiated means of appeasing the king [which they were successful in doing] with a lot of money, a hundred talents of gold.

M	RB
	He did this: He went to his house when [Alroy] was
That night he [the father-	

M

in-law] invited David to a
drinking party and made him
completely drunk. At mid-
night, when he was certain
that [David] was drunk
and asleep,
[the father-in-law] seized him
and cut off his head which he
had brought by Zain el-Din [to
the king], and the land was
quiet.

RB

sleeping, and

he killed him in his bed, and
[thus]
were his conspiracies and
schemes annulled.

The wrath of the king of
Persia did not turn away from
the Jews who were in the mountains and who were 493) in his
land. When they realized this, they sent to the chief of the diaspora
to come with their help to the king of Persia. 494) They came with
good words and words of appeasement, and they both appeased
[the king] and were [themselves] appeased. They gave [the king]
about a hundred talents of gold, and the land was quiet after this,
and his anger 495) subsided.

Summary

The report of David Alroy is recorded here in three different
texts which are somewhat variant. They agree that he arose in
Amadiah, Persia, claimed messiahship, and attracted such a
following that he threatened the king of Persia. He was a brilliant
scholar in all subjects, including sorcery. When called by the king
to account for his activities, he was imprisoned. He released himself from prison, was invisibly present, walked on water, traveled
ten times as fast as it was humanly possible to do. When the king
was unable to capture and suppress him, he required the Jews of
the country to do so. This was done by paying David's father-in-
law to kill him in his sleep. Jews in Persia were required to pay still
more to appease the king's anger even after this, and there were
followers who continued to be suppressed after the death of
David. The Jewish practice of using money to satisfy the king and
gain security for themselves was employed many times during the
Middle Ages.

There are many similarities in these narratives about the
Messiah Alroy and the Messiah Jesus and his followers. Some of
these are probably legendary. Like Jesus, he was tried before a civil

leader and asked if he were the king of the Jews (Jn 18:33). Like Jesus, Alroy performed miracles, and people were astounded at his wisdom (Mk 2:12; Lk 2:47). Like Peter (Acts 12:6-11), Paul, and Silas (Acts 16:25-40), Alroy escaped from prison marvelously. Like Jesus, Alroy was expected to be the redeemer of Israel (Lk 24:21). There is another ending to the Alroy story which may or may not be legendary.

POSTSCRIPTS ON THE MESSIAH[15]

Maimonides wrote that the sultan asked him [David] if he was the Messiah. He said, "Yes." The king asked him, "What sign [can you give me for proof]?" He replied that if they would cut off his head, he would return to life. Then the king commanded [that it be done], and they cut off his head, and he died. They [then] said that this happened so that he would not die after severe tortures. Some of the simple people expect that he will return and live, but the idiot has not yet come.

I found, according to Maimonides, that he said in the beginning of the Ishmaelite kingdom, there arose a man from beyond the river who said he was the Messiah. The Israelites were in great danger [because of him]. As a result, ten thousand Israelites abandoned their faith. His miracle was that they had a leper, and he awoke [from a sleep] well. Finally he fell, and the Israelites were left in the same exile and hatred.

Similarly a man from the West in the city of Fez said that he was the Messiah, and many distresses were renewed for the Israelites. Ten years before this, a messiah arose in the city of Cordova, and there was almost an annihilation of the remnant of Israel. Also in France a man arose and many communities were killed because of him. Also in the time of Rabbi Solomon Ben Abraham Avnet, a messiah arose, as it is written in his "Responsa."

Thirty-two

In the Persian kingdom, at a different time, a Jew arose and made himself a messiah. He was very successful and gathered to himself many Israelites. When the king heard about all his acts of power and that it was his [the Jew's] intention to go to war with him [the king of Persia], he sent and gathered the Jews who were in his land and told them that if they did not successfully remove that man [the Jew] from him [the king], they would know surely that

[15] Virga, ‏ספר שבטי יהודה‎ , 76-77.

he would cause an evil sword to pass through all of them and destroy them, children and women [as well as men] all in one day.

Then all the people of Israel assembled together and went to that man, fell before him to the ground, supplicated before him intensely, cried out and wept so that he would turn away from his path. Why should he place himself and all the afflicted ones of his people in danger? The king had already sworn to destroy them with the sword. How could he endure [to see] the destruction of all the [Jewish] communities in Persia? David el-David answered, "What can the king of Persia do? Is he not afraid of me and my sword?" They asked him, "What miracle [have you to show] that you are the Messiah?" He answered that because he was successful no other sign was needed of a messiah. They replied, "Many have done this, but have not succeeded!" Then he sent them away in fierce anger.

On the second day, they returned to him with fasting and with their little children in front of them so that they might move him to pity. Then he said, "For the sake of these little children, I will do this: If the Persian king will give me the expenses I laid out in the preparation for this war [against others than the Persians], I will return to my place and will not harm him." The Jews said to him, "How will a noble king like the king of Persia stoop to give back the expenses laid out by a Jew?" The cursed, false Messiah replied, "If you return [to me] a second time, [then] even if he gives me all the provisions and half of his kingdom [besides], I will not be reconciled."

When the Jews saw the evil of his heart, and that no amount of real argument would help, they went away, bitter and weeping before the king and said, "Our lord, king, no authority wielded by the crown of the kingdom, no law and reason seem adequate to remove the idiocy of this one who has been made an idiot by it. We have seen that man. With regard to this matter, he is a definite fool. He would not pay attention to us and to all that we told him, namely that he had placed our lives in great danger, although we are innocent. Therefore we are puzzled. How can our lord pay attention to the words of this idiot? Because if he [the king] would leave him [alone], he [the false Messiah] will cause his own downfall, as we have found with all the words of falsehood. Liars fall, since they have no feet [on which to stand]. It is like a tree that falls when it has no roots. The words we spoke to this man were enough to break the heart of stone, but he abides by his folly, and even told us that if our lord would give him all the expenses he had incurred in order to make this war, he would return to his land. Is not all this enough to testify what a notorious fool he is?

The king replied, "Why do you call him a fool because of this? If he has become impoverished as a result of his preparations for war which were very expensive because of his assurance of victory in war, and he returned on his way [causing me no harm, the suggestion seems good]. Therefore hurry and return to that man and say to him that I respond favorably to that which he asks, and that he may send a man with his ledger book in full confidence and faith, and I will pay him at once in good currency. This is the way it was done.

Summary

Virga reported another ending to the David Alroy biography. This conclusion was that David volunteered to have his head cut off, claiming the ability to come to life again. The king had him killed and that was the end. This was a story supposedly told by Maimonides. Virga also summarized other messianic activities Maimonides told in his letter to Yemen.

Still a third ending to the Alroy story is that he bargained with the king of Persia to leave his country if the king reimbursed him for his military costs, implying that he had been engaged in military activity. The king was willing to do so, and the Messiah left Persia. This is not an impossible story. The plan of extorting financial support to sustain troops against the threat of attack is as old as Saul's successor to the United Kingdom. David's main purpose was to conquer Jerusalem, but he also threatened to overthrow Persia. The king of Persia, like the Moslems, might have welcomed his cooperation with Saladin against the Crusaders, so long as he did not turn his forces against him. The story of the historical David Alroy has not yet been told, but there are some reasons to believe that he led powerful Jewish forces at the time of Saladin and was well prepared to overthrow Jerusalem. He obviously attracted attention from Jews all over the then civilized world. The next account of his activity is composed as if it were an epistle from an enthusiastic pro-Alroy, messianic Egyptian Jew, the son of the great Maimonides. Although it is probably pseudepigraphical, it accurately reflects messianic expectations and zeal of the time.

THE MESSIAH AT IFSAHAN[16]

To the honor of our brothers and friends of the holy congregations, the holy people, the children of Eitan, the offspring of the
perfect man,[17] who dwell in the western communities, my brothers
and friends of the congregation of Fez. I am your younger brother,
Moses, son of Maimonides (May he be remembered for blessing). I
have written for your honor that you may announce the good
news from the one who dwells in the heavens and has made us rejoice in the advent of Yinon.[18] May he comfort us with the comfort
of Zion. I announce to you, friends and brothers, that I have heard
good reports from merchants who came from Babylon to Egypt
and to Jerusalem. They said that there was a king of the Jews who
had been living there [who] came forth and appeared and who is
now in Ifsahan. Everyone who comes with merchandise has said
this. Also those who come from Acre and Damascus and other
cities also said [that this was true]. Although I, Moses, heard [all
this], I did not pay attention to [these] matters, because I said to
myself, "Perhaps they are mocking us, making fun of us, and reproaching us." I was distressed inwardly because of this matter
and because of their reproach and blasphemy, but then I saw that
everyone who came said the same as the others. When the reports
came, one after the other, I [then] became suspicious and said,
"Maybe it is true [after all]."

I was pondering these things until two prominent, rich merchants from Damascus appeared. They were traveling with
merchandise to Babylon, and they had been to Mecca where the
grave of the prophet Mohammed is.[19] After this they came to
Egypt. When they saw me, they turned and greeted me. I returned
their greeting and said to them, "Please sit down with me, for I
wish to talk with you."[20] They sat down alongside me, [and] I
asked of their well being, how their business was, as well as the
well being of our brothers, the communities of Babylon and those
in distant places. After this, I said to them, "You are my friends

---

[16] Hebrew text is from A. Neubauer, "Documents Inedits," *REJ*, 4 (1882), 174-77.

[17] Eitan was a psalmist (Ps 88:1; 89:1), probably a Levite. The perfect man is Abraham.

[18] One of the names for the Messiah.

[19] The abbreviation is המש׳ which probably is for הפעל משובשת, "work of confusion or error," but it clearly means Mohammed.

[20] Literally, "I will take a journey in words," a picturesque way of saying that he would
like to discuss their travels with them.

and companions, with all [my] heart and soul. I will now ask you [something], and you must tell me [the truth]. Do not deceive me." They said, "We will not lie, but we will tell you the truth [about] whatever you ask." I [then] said to them, "What about the report I have heard from you [Arab merchants]? Is it true or not?" Those Ishmaelite merchants [then] said to me, "That which you have heard is, indeed, true, for when we were in Babylon in an inn, according to the custom of merchants, we were sitting at the door of the inn, chatting with each other.[21] A Jew passed by, and two reckless and worthless scoffers seized him. They were mocking the Jew and reproaching him. We were being entertained by these pranks and with the Jew until two merchants of *Sheba and Seba* (Ps 72:10) came out and said to those worthless men, "You are fools and ignoramuses! Do you not fear God, and have you no embarrassment for human beings? Look whom you are reproaching and reviling. Already the holy One blessed be He has raised his prestige and his fortune. Their Messiah, for whom they have waited, has come forward, and he is now in Ifsahan! All the Gentiles are going up to him as well as two prominent families, the sons of Kedar and Nebaioth, who have attached themselves to him and believe in him."[22] Those Ishmaelites told me further, "If you do not believe what we have said, there are two of the most wealthy Jews of Babylon [who] will come and tell you, and [then] you will believe.

I waited four days for those Jews, and they came. I sat with them and asked them, "How about the report which I have heard from the Ishmaelites? Were they telling the truth or were they mocking us?" Those Jews said, "The Lord has seen our affliction, and he will redeem us, just as he redeemed our fathers." They said that they were in Babylon, and they saw Jews who had come with merchandise and they said that it was true. A man had arisen in Ifsahan, and his name was Abisaid Ben Daudi, who said he was the general of the Messiah's army, and that he would appear in another seven years. An assembly of Israelites and some Gentiles [as numerous] as the sand of the sea, joined themselves to him, including Nebaioth and Kedar. When he saw that all those families joined them, he told them that still it was not the end. He hid himself for seven years, and the Jews told me that the seven years would be over this year and that more had joined themselves to him than those who gathered to him at first. The Jews said to me that Jews who had heard from other Jews told them that they saw

---

[21] Literally, "traveling in words."
[22] The sons of Kedar are the Arabs, and the sons of Nebaioth are the Nabateans.

that when he arose to ask for something or for prayer, a pillar of cloud appeared over his head, reaching heaven. After this, Jews and some of the elders of Nebaioth and Kedar said to him, "Our Lord, our king, the Messiah of the Lord, we live here in quietness, a large and prosperous congregation, we are countless, but our brothers, the Israelites are living in exile. How long will this be for us? Command us, and we will go out to our brothers who are among the Gentiles and subject to the [Roman] government." He said to them, "Please do not [do so], my brothers, because the time of the end has not yet arrived, and I was only sent because the cry of the daughter of my people from distant lands has been heard, and their cry has reached the throne of the One who dwells in the heavens until I came. I was sent to give a promise to the saddened hearts of the Israelites so that they might bear [with patience] the burden of the years that remain for them among the Gentiles, and I was prevented from revealing the end time, but it is near.

When I, your brother Moses, heard this from the mouth of the Jews, then my soul was at rest, and I was happy. That night, *sleep* fled *from my eyes* (Gen 31:40). I arose and was studying in the *gemara*[23] when I found eighteen rules which the sages of the age said [could not be answered] *until* [the Messiah] *comes and teaches righteousness* (Hos 10:12).[24] I arose and put [the questions] in writing, to the best of my humble knowledge in verse and in words suitable to come before that man [the Messiah]. Then I called my brother David and spoke to him and promised him that I would make him great and illustrious. I gave him two hundred Egyptian dinars as well as the letter with the questions, and I sent him to Ifsahan. I also gave him a letter that the officers of the king should honor him when he calls on them.

He left for Ifsahan and was delayed there for ten days. Then he returned to me after a year and a half. If it were not that I do not wish to prolong my message, I would have written to you everything which my brother told me, but I have written only that which is most important to you.

My brother David saw him. They [the followers at Ifsahan] were taking oaths in his name, saying, "By the life of our king, the Messiah of the Lord." My brother David brought me four letters. In one of them, he [the Messiah] interpreted for me fifteen of the eighteen questions, but he said three would not be told to me.

[23] The talmudic commentary on the Mishnah.
[24] Or *until he* [the teacher of righteousness] *comes and teaches righteousness* or *until* [the Messiah] *as well as the teacher of righteousness comes:* עד יבוא ויורה צדק.

I, Moses your brother, before [this] had been studying in those *halakhot*, and I had clarified some of them, but I was not able [to interpret] the rest. When they came to the hand of this man [the Messiah], he interpreted them well, as was proper, line by line. I [then] said to myself, "If he had interpreted the three that are left, I would have said that he had not [acted] correctly, because our teachers have left them sealed up *until the teacher of righteousness comes* (Hos 10:12)."[25] When he did not interpret them, I said, "Of course! He has [acted] on [the basis of] truth," so he said, "They were not told to me, and I cannot interpret them *until he* [the teacher of righteousness] *comes and teaches righteousness* (ויורה צדק)" (Hos 10:12). When the congregation of Ifsahan said to me in the letter which they sent me in reply by the hand of my brother, they said, "Many families have joined themselves to us, also [the families of] the Nebaioth and Kedar." I rejoiced and said, "This is what the prophet (upon whom be peace) said, *All the flock of Kedar* [father of the Arabs] *will be gathered to you; the rams of Nebaioth* [the Nabateans] *will serve you. [They will come up with acceptance on my altar, and I will glorify my glorious house]* (Isa 60:7). He [the Messiah] sent, in his letter with my brother David, "For three more years I will not go forth from the cave, because my time has not arrived to go out until the end of the time. [This will be] on the fourteenth of Marheshwan, when my luck will be good."

I will tell you further the story of what happened there to the king in the south of Egypt from the sons of the Turks and the sons of Japhet.[26] He believed in the religion of the prophet Mohammed,[27] and the name of his city is Aden. Under his authority were twelve thousand Israelites. They had one judge whose name was Rabbi Menaham. He was a great man in Israel, a scholar and a god fearing man. The king sent for them and said, "Let the enemies of Israel [i.e., the Israelites][28] renounce their faith or die!" Rabbi

---

[25] This additional information used in interpreting Hos 10:12 makes the first alternative translation in footnote 24 most likely. The "teacher of righteousness" (מורה צדק) was a priestly office associated with the Messiah son of David, possibly the high priest who should accompany the royal Messiah. See further "The Priestly Teacher of Righteousness," *RQ* 6 (1969), 553-58. The man to whom the letter was sent was the royal Messiah, but the priestly Messiah had not been identified yet. Since the subject in Hosea was not clear, the Messiah might have identified himself as the subject. The author of this letter praised him for not making that identification.

[26] The Greeks.

[27] See footnote 19.

[28] It was customary among Jews not to mention the term "Jews" or "Israelites" in a bad light, lest the reference itself become an omen to make it come true, therefore, they used the term "enemies of Israel" as those upon whom the affliction should come.

Menahem answered the king, "My lord, give us time—seven days." When Rabbi Menaham with the elders of the congregation left, they were weeping before the princes and the governor, and they made a compromise with him. They gave him fourteen talents of silver, and he allowed them to continue in the religion of Israel. The following year [the king] said to them, "Give me fourteen more talents of silver, or the enemies of Israel [i.e., the Israelites] must renounce their religion or die." They sold all that they had, and there was not left for themselves anything on which to live, and they gave it [the money] to them. Many of them fled, and the rest of them, the poor of the land, were forcibly converted from the religion of Israel. He destroyed synagogues and schools.

Rabbi Menahem fled and escaped with a sack on his loins to the top of the mountain in the kingdom of another king. Soon after, fifteen or eighteen months, that king heard this report,[29] and trembling seized him [the king]. His courage sagged, and he was frightened. He had no strength to stand. He sent letters to Rabbi Menahem until he found him. He promised him great well being. He came to him and said, "I myself know that I have sinned in that act, but now, send and gather all your brothers and build synagogues and schools." The king gave them back twenty-five talents of gold and gave them silver and gold to build synagogues as they had been before. So they did this, and he appointed from them about four thousand men. Also those who were left heard the report,[29] and the elders of the congregation came and said to Rabbi Menahem, "How long will this snare be for us? Let us go to Ifsahan." Rabbi Menahem said to them, "No, my brothers, because it is not the season of the time of the end." When they were about to depart from him with words, he said, "Do not thrust yourself [out, without careful thought]. Give me some of the money of the congregation, and I will go. If the report is true, I will send for you." Rabbi Menahem and fifteen of the prominent men of the congregation walked for fifteen months. Twelve of them and Rabbi Menahem reached Ifsahan, but three of them died of thirst, for the way was long, and they were walking through the wilderness. When they entered the city and came before the man [the Messiah], Rabbi Menahem went out and wrote to the rest of the congregation and said to them, "The word and the report are true, and he is, in my opinion, like our leader Moses (upon whom be peace)." The congregation, whoever was able to walk, left secretly.

[29] Apparently the report that the Messiah in Ifsahan was organizing a threatening military movement that caused the king to make a truce with the Jews.

When I, Moses son of Maimonides, was sitting later after I had received this report, a scribe of the king came to tell me what the king had said to me: "Stand over the treasury and weigh the gold and send [it] to me." For the king was engaged in war, and the king was Saladin. The scribe of the king who brought the letter of the king said to me that the king had said to you in a loud voice, "I know that these uncircumcised people, who are coming from the ends of the lands, the kings of the East and the kings of the West have come to fight with me over Jerusalem and the house of the sanctuary." Saladin said, "The holy One blessed be He will put a spirit of confusion in them until they will die by my sword, by famine, and by pestilence. Also it is not for me to rule over the kingdom of God,[30] because I know that the king [of the Jews] will come now and take the lands from my hands and from their hands, but thus has it been my good fortune that the king of the Jews will take [them] from my hand peacefully and not with war. Perhaps I will find favor in his eyes.

I wrote this letter thus. I saw all these things in the writings of the Gaon Rabbi Moses who sent to the West and to the congregation of Fez, but when I copied these words from the Arabic language to the holy language and when I came to Rome, I told it to the respected Rab Leon (May he be believed). He was very happy about them, and he ordered me to write all the things for him.

Summary

The previous accounts of David Alroy, in their present form, were written by anti-Alroy forces after the event. They included the legendary, miraculous elements, but they were very careful to show that Alroy was a scoundrel, a false prophet, and an enemy of the Jews. It is certain that that was not the entire Jewish feeling about the matter or he would not have had such a large following as he did. These authors were trying to assure Persian authorities that Jews were themselves a very patriotic, non-rebellious people. This reflects the same kind of apologetic motif to the Persians that the Acts of the Apostles presents to the Romans.

The information about David reflected in this letter, however, is from a different point of view. All things are directed to provide confidence in David's reliability. The son of Maimonides is the esteemed person supposedly writing the letter. He was reluctant,

---

[30] Clearly the promised land. For further defense of the thesis that the kingdom of God meant the promised land see *Consequences*, 1-90.

and resistant to all temptations to believe in such a messiah, but he finally received such firm evidence from such reputable sources that he checked out the data himself and bore testimony to the validity of David as a messiah. Even the Gentiles were flocking to this Messiah urging him to begin his movement. Quite different from other reports, however, he was unwilling to act until the time was exactly right. His scholarship in such matters was impeccable. Also the well-known Rabbi Menahem reluctantly checked the rumors and was convinced that this was the new Moses and wrote back to his congregation to come to follow Alroy. The new Messiah drew so much fame that the great Saladin initiated negotiations with the Jews for terms of peace with him. The time was right and international conditions were such that a treaty or alliance between Alroy and Saladin is a reasonable possibility. This letter was apparently written while the messianic movement was still flourishing. It would make no sense as a later forgery.

It is not certain that all of these reports (of Abisaid Ben Daudi, David el-David, and David Alroy) are about the same person, but it seems unlikely that there would be two leaders in the same country at the same time leading so many Jewish troops as this.[31]

The next report is not about Alroy, but it shows some of the messianic excitement that went on in Baghdad just forty years earlier (A.D. 1120). Jews were being persecuted; bribes were paid; Elijah was seen in a dream; and Moslems were fearful for the security of their government. Goitein learned that Moslems reported a very similar situation at the very same time, confirming the historicity of the event.[32] The text is not complete.

MESSIANIC TROUBLES

1)...to liberate them after they were punished, and they were (2) in this hardship for a number of years, and (3) the source of these misfortunes *was* (2) an *evil* (4) man called Ibn Abu Shuja (5) (May he be cursed! and may the name of the wicked ones perish!) (6) They were holding over them [the obligation] to pay a thousand dinars (7) until they removed the sign of disgrace [i.e., the distinctive badge] of the women and annuled (8) the decree with the help of God (May he be exalted), and now there is no (9) one wearing it except middle and upper class [Jews], either (10) stranger or local resident, and some time elapsed from then (11)

---

[31] See further E. Ashtor-Strauss, "Saladin and the Jews," *HUCA*, 27 (1956), 305-26.
[32] Hebrew text from S.D. Goitein, "A Report on Messianic Troubles in Baghdad in 1120-21," *JQR*, 43 (1952-53), 57-76.

until this year that has [just] passed (12) which was the year 1431 of the Seleucid Era (A.D. 1119) (13) when a young woman appeared, known as the daughter (14) of Joseph, son of the physician, and they are people (15) whose deeds are good before God (May he be exalted). (14a:1) It was noticed that the maiden walked in the ways of her father—in continually (2) fasting, praying, and giving to charity. They proposed (3) a match for her, but she refused and said, (4) "I will not turn aside from my way, because marriage (5) will distract me in these matters; but (6) our master Daniel (May the Lord guard him), (7) son of our master, president of the academy (May the righteous be remembered for blessing) took charge of arranging this *match* (6) and married her off, (8) and she remained with her husband a few months (9) until the month of Elul. There had already passed from the month (10) twenty-five days, when she descended one Thursday (11) and announced that she had seen in a dream (12) our lord Elijah (upon whom be peace; may he be remembered for blessing), and he (13) said to her, "Go down to these people (14) and tell them in my name, that God (May he be exalted) has already (15) brought near the salvation. It will not be left until [large portion missing] (15b: 2) that the sultan knew and he became angry (3) at this man when *his tax* (4) was stopped, (4) and he sought a pretext to make things difficult for them, (5) but he did not have the power to accomplish it. (6) When this information reached (7) the sultan, it was evil in the eyes of the sultan, and he said, (8) "Let the Jews be congregated! They are saying, 'Look, (9) our kingdom is revealed, and there will not be left after the appearance (10) of our kingdom, a [single] kingdom.'"[33] The caliph became *very* angry (11) at this and wrote (12) at once to the *chief* (13) Kadi, (13) Ibn Damghani (14) after the command to seize the Jews (15) and to concentrate them in the mint. (16a:1) He appointed the couriers [to take charge of them] (2) and threatened to murder them, and he mentioned (3) in a letter which he sent to (4) the Kadi, "This people—*its end* has come, (5) and I am compelled (6) to take any revenge on them in this time of mine (7) unless a prophet is revealed to them, or they follow (8) the rules of the Gentiles [i.e., Moslems]. Do not defend them before me, (9) O Kadi, or before all the Gentiles [i.e., Moslems]." Then *the Kadi* (10) wrote (10) to him, "As far as I

---

[33] Goitein, "Messianic Troubles," 66, astutely observed: "When the Seljuq Sultan proclaimed that the Jews, after the establishment of their kingdom, would not leave a single other realm in existence, he certainly was not quoting any actual utterance of a Jewish leader; but the true Messianic idea was, of course, that every knee should bow before God and His representative on earth."

know, (11) my lord Caliph, God will continue (12) his kingdom. This people—(16b:1). No one has ever harmed it (2) and succeeded. And as for what you have said, 'This people—(3) its end has come,' rather, this people—(4) their time continues with God (May he be blessed)." (A single line survives of a solitary leaf). That is all I have to say, and yours is the grandeur[?]. (17a: two lines are written on the blank side of another document. 1) (when he went) to the house of the exilarch they found (2) in his house and with him [?] and one hundred [?] of his disciples. (17b: 1) ...the ashes, and they (2) continued, bent in prayer and fasting, and they (3) cried out to God (May he be praised) (4) to deliver the Israelites. At that time he knocked at the door, and they went out (5) to him, and when he saw him, our master, that he (6) was already freed, he prostrated himself on the ground to (7) God (May he be praised) weeping—he and everyone (8) who was with him. And he raised his hands to (9) heaven in thanksgiving to God for your [*sic.*] liberation—(10) also because our liberation is near, if God wills. (11) He asked about him, about the dream—what it was, (12) and who helped him. He said to him, "Who commanded you (13) to ask me about this?" He said to him, (14) "The caliph," so he told him about this, (18a: 1) how it was. Then Abu Sahl Ibn Kammuna came (2) to the caliph, and he narrated [?].. (3) to him the dream, precisely. *The caliph* (4) derided [it], (4) laughed, and said, "Indeed, how light (5) headed are the Jews, if they rely on (6) the opinion of a woman. Tomorrow I will burn (7) the woman, and I will permit the taking of the lives of the Jews, and *the conversation* (8) took place (8) after it had turned dark, and after the *wezirs* (9) had retired (9) when he had *this* (10) evil notion (10) and not an hour passed until (11) our lord Elijah was revealed (upon whom be peace, and may the remembrance-of the righteous be for a blessing), and in his hand (12) was a pillar of fire, and he stood over (13) the head of the caliph, and when he saw him, (14) he looked with fright, and he was struck mute from great fear. (Broken text: 1,2,3,4). (5) which was brought to the wezirs and to the heads of the families (6) through a bribe, so that *the Gentiles* [i.e., Moslems] (7) would not know (7) that the tax had been removed from them, (8) and they attacked them for they believed (9) that if juzya is taken from the Jews, *this* (10) would be (10) good for them, but if it were relaxed (11) it would bring upon them punishment (or penalty). Peace!

Summary

This report is too broken to deduce all of the events that were initially described. This text now shows no messiah leading troops but instead some of the peripheral events related to a messianic movement. On the one side is shown the reaction of a Jewish community with a pious woman who saw Elijah in a dream. On the other side is seen the caliph and his reaction to the threat involved. He correctly understood that a successful messianic movement would involve the destruction of his kingdom. He wanted to kill those involved before the movement got out of hand, but he was restrained by the Kadi and finally an appearance of Elijah to him. The story ends with Jewish taxes removed. The next report comes from France with the appearance of a prophet who said the Messiah would be revealed in the year A.D. 1233.

THE PROPHET OF REDEMPTION[34]

1) Thus said the Lord: "Keep the law, *and practice justice, for my coming salvation is near*" (Isa 56:1). (2) The respected, exalted and noble...Alexandria. May their Rock guard them and be (3) their help. Help will come from the Lord (Ps 121:1-2). (4) generous, perfect, in great abundance, blessed... (5) That which it is necessary to inform you [is that] the Lord will guard you. [It is a letter which has been received from] Marsailles, [France] from Rabbi Joseph Ben Rabbi Abraham... (7) This which they have heard is a story of an event which would never cross one's mind...(8)...letters...to Tunis one letter, and the other...(9) letter which reached is in Arabic [*...strengthen the weak hands]* (10) *and fortify the feeble knees* (Isa 35:3). *Behold I am send[ing to you the prophet Elijah]* (Mal 3:23). (11) *The redeemed of the Lord will return* (Isa 51:11) *and it will be in the last days, the mountain of the house of the Lord will be established at the head of the mountains, and it will be raised above the hills. The Gentiles will flow toward it, and many nations will go and say, "Come, (13) let us go to the mountain of the Lord"* (Isa 2:2-3). Our eyes will see; [our hearts] will re[joice; and our souls delight in his true salvation]. (14) Thus the Lord raise your superiority. A letter has reached us from [...and it is said that] (15) letters have arrived from France from ...(15) Ma[n]asseh, of Saintes, [France], that a prophet had arisen among them [...]. (17) His prophecy and piety which he called the land concerning..., and (18) his word has fulfilled; and he said, in the

[34] Text from W. Asaph, ‏"תעודות חדשות על גרים ועל תנועה משיחית"‎ ‏ציון‎, 5 (1940), 112-24. Also Aescoly, *Messianic Movements*, 188.

year A.D. 1226 will begin...(19) a great gathering, and our lord Elijah (May he be remembered for blessing)...(20), and that in the year A.D. 1233 the Messiah son of David will come...(21) and the kingdom will return to the daughter of Jerusalem. *Israelites...*will see. (22) He said further: In this year...will come. (23) He and his brothers crossed over to the land of Israel. He will return [with]... (24) signs and wonders if the Lord is willing. This prophet...(25) in the station of the Lord and in the class of all men...(26) in the midst of the cloud they will hear a voice speaking to [the prophet...] (27) at his hand is a word from the Tetragrammaton which will cause his comparison...(28) with the distinguished sage, the great and pi[ous teachers]. (29) For three days with their nights will he remain in constant prayer and supplica[tion...]. (3) Rabbi Elazar from Wurmeiza asked this also...(31) It is true, and there is no deceit in his mouth. After this, behold if...(32) Whenever they tested him, they found him speaking the truth. After this, behold he explain[ed passages] (33) in the Talmud of which they had never heard, and he revealed [secrets of the Torah, the prophets] and the hagiographa of which they had never heard. This is (the content of the letter which was written) (35) in the holy language. This letter is equal to the text out from [the scripture...] and this is the copy of the letter which was sent to Kaba[s...] the great, and for the construction of the altar in Jerusalem. Amen. Eternity. Selah. and Sha[lom].

DISTURBANCE IN PRAGUE[35]

In the year 1235 [the Jews] were forced to evacuate the city [Prague] and to disperse themselves over its provinces because they were preparing to raise an army and were displaying letters containing announcements that their messiah had come.

CHRISTIAN AND JEWISH EXPECTANCY[36]

Many of the Jews began to rejoice, and they imagined that they would see their Messiah coming and that their redemption would be drawing near in that very year, for it was the year 1241 when the [plan of] the Lord was to be realized. When suspicions were aroused that they were intending to stir up trouble against the Christians, they lost their favor in the eyes of many [people], but they were protected by the ruling emperor.

[35] Aescoly, *Messianic Movements,* 190.
[36] Aescoly, *Messianic Movements,* 191.

Summary of Prophetic Movements

The prophetic and messianic movements narrated in this section took place from the second through the thirteenth centuries. They occurred in Judah, Galilee, Syria, Persia, France, and Czechoslovakia. They involved dreams, prophecies, calculations, bribes, negotiations, recruiting troops, leading military movements, performing miracles, and making plans to return and repossess the promised land. The messiahs expected and realized were not divine beings but human leaders who expected to direct armed forces, overthrow all of the Gentiles, and rule the world from Jerusalem. None of these prophecies was fulfilled; none of the messianic movements succeeded; but the theology continued and so did the expectation of redemption and the appearance of messiahs. The theology behind these movements was nurtured by prayers and hymns. These will be shown in the next division.

POETRY AND PRAYER:
THE VOICE OF AN EXILED PEOPLE

An Introduction to Judah Halevy

One of the best loved of all Jewish poets is the Spanish physician, Judah Halevy (A.D. 1080-1141). He was also a philosopher (i.e., theologian) whose treatise, *The Kuzari*, is still studied widely by Jewish theologians. It is basically an apologetic treatise answering questions to refute Christians, Moslems, and Karaites. Nonetheless, he was best known for his poetry. His poetry rhymed in Hebrew and balanced according to Arabic meter. Halevy was so steeply versed in the Bible that his poetry includes allusions to biblical personalities, events, or ideas in nearly every line. Some of these are treated midrashically in poetry. Without recognizing these allusions, some of his poetry makes no sense, and it is difficult to translate into English. He was passionately devoted to the promised land, the suppression of the Gentiles, and the establishment of the Messiah on the throne in Jerusalem. He believed the Moslems would be abolished in A.D. 1130. Halevy's final years were spent in Palestine where he traveled and urged many others to migrate in anticipation of the messianic age.

A DOVE ON A ROOF

Judah Halevy[1]

My dove,[2] through dark streets she wanders.
She goes to seek the one she loves.

[Lord], heal her! She gives her voice to weeping,
for her affliction is as great as her infidelity.
She has counted a thousand [years],[3] and he has not removed
        her yoke.
The [once] great people sits like a woman who has lost
        her child (Lam 1:1).
In prison,[4] she calculates end time after end time.

---

[1] H. Shirman, השירה העברית בספרד ובפרובאנס II, 474. RPL
[2] The Jewish people.
[3] Since the fall of Jerusalem in A.D. 70.
[4] Meaning in the exile. All Jews not permitted to return to the promised land free from foreign rule were considered to be captives or prisoners, no matter what their status, freedom, or wealth in exile.

I imagined myself wandering [in] a wilderness.
I was [like] *a bird on a roof alone* (Ps 102:7).
I wept, [and] because of my weeping, I was convulsed.
My tear has not dried from my cheeks;
it is poured out over your city[5] that is desolate.

Heart, broken by anxieties, be comforted.
It is time to be comforted, in memory of times past.
Who, fighting the divine statutes, has prevailed?[6]
My hope for you is not deceived;
it continues, and your covenant is not false.

WAITING FOR CONSOLATION
Author Unknown[7]

Has the mercy of God forgotten the remnant of Jerusalem's
fugitives?
Has he gathered his mercies in anger,[8] rejected his sanctuary
and threshold?
Has he not remembered the footstool[9] for his feet, in his wrath?

His mercies are customary, but where are his marvelous deeds
and loving kindness
of which he told us when he rewarded them according to his
mercies?
I will say in the multitude of my sorrows, "Fall, please, into
the hand of the Lord,[10]
for great are his mercies. Let us wait and be consoled to his
word,
for the lovingkindness of the Lord has not destroyed us,
for his mercies are not exhausted."

[5] Jerusalem. Palestine is also called the Lord's land in IV Ezra 9:8; 12:34.
[6] They just miscalculated the term of their imprisonment. The statute is fair and unerring; the covenant is not false; but Jews misunderstood when the end of their captivity had been reached.
[7] D. de Sola Pool, *Book of Prayer* (New York, 1947), from Hebrew text, 79. RPL
[8] He has kept his mercies to himself, not extending them to his people.
[9] The temple. See I Chron 28:2; Ps 99:5; 132:7; Lam 2:1; Mt 5:35; II Esdras 6:4; Makkoth 24b.
[10] In spite of the way the Lord has neglected his people, it pays to wait until he shows mercy on his people again rather than to accept any alternative.

ISRAEL AND ITS ENEMIES
Judah Halevy[11]

From of old you were the residence of my love; my love
          camped where you camped.
The reproaches of my enemies were sweet to me because of
          your name.
He permitted them. They oppressed that which you oppressed.
My enemies learned your wrath, and I accepted it with love,
for they pursued the victims whom you struck.[12]
From the day you despised me, I despised myself;[13]
for I will not honor what you have despised,
until the anger passes, and you send again redemption
to your inheritance, whom you redeemed.

GOD AND HIS CHILDREN
Author Unknown[14]

ע) *The tribe* of Judah, oppressed and troubled [while] the lion
          roars in the forest.

ח) *Hoping* for your redemption, fathers and sons are afflicted
          and poor.

ע) *Stand in the breach* (Ps 106:23); lest we be scorned. Why,
          Lord, do you stand afar off?

י) Your *dove*[15] has reached the gates of death. [You who] sit
          [over] the cherubim, appear!

ה) *Grant* us help from the oppressor. Is the arm of the Lord too
          short (Isa 50:2)?[16]

ח) *Renew* our days in the old exile. Awake! Why do you sleep?

ז) *Remember* your children in a land not theirs. Let no stranger
          come near them.

ק) *The end* you have set, reveal to the solitary one.[17] Let Mount
          Zion rejoice,

---

[11] Shirman, *The Hebrew Hymn*, II, 467. RPL

[12] The enemies only pursued the victims whom God had chosen to afflict.

[13] Halevy respected the Lord's judgment. The Jews would not be afflicted if the Lord did not despise them. Since the Lord despised them, they must be despicable. Therefore Halevy despised himself. He would not disagree with God.

[14] From Hebrew text of Pool, *Book of Prayer*, 398. The unknown author seems to have been Shemaiah Hazaki, judging from the acrostic. RPL

[15] The Jews.

[16] A rhetorical question.

[17] Let the Jews know exactly when they will be restored to the land.

י)   the daughters of *Judah* be glad!
May our cry go up to the highest heaven! to the King [who] sits on
the throne of mercies.

REDEMPTION AND COMFORT
Author Unknown[18]

Lord, act for the sake of your name! Erect the temple of your place
in which to *make* your flock *rest.*[19] O Lord, in the light of your
face (Num 6:26),
deliver me from fear; lead me to my destiny.
O Lord, hear my voice. Give help and support to those in haste.
Please help those who are left behind, O Lord, Creator of
mountains.
Redeem your people from violent men, your flock from the hands
of shearers.
O Lord, Maker of lightning, draw the end of comfort near.[20]
Pity the unpitied nation, *O Lord, Man of war* (Ex 15:3).
Dwell as of old in our tents continually, O God, our Creator.
The Lord, our King, is our savior.

Introduction to Abulafia

Tadros Ben Judah Abulafia (A.D. 1240-1298) was an early
cabbalist. He was born in Aragon and spent most of his life wandering. He once set out to convert Pope Nicholas III. The pope
heard about it and had a stake prepared with orders to have him
burned when he arrived. Before he got to the pope, however, the
pope died. Later Abulafia claimed that he was the Messiah. He
wrote several books which concentrated on *gematria.*

LOVE SONGS
Tadros Ben Judah Abulafia[22]

A. Daughter of Arabia
A fire from my heart, and from my eyes, floods.

---

[18] I. Ben A.J. Dove (ed.) סדר עבודת ישראל (Jerusalem, 1937), 316. RPL
[19] Jerusalem. See Ps 23:2, 5.
[20] Comfort for covenanters will come when the dispersion is ended, and they are allowed
to return to the promised land.
[21] See further P. Bloch, "Abulafia," *JE,* I, 141-42.
[22] Shirman, *The Hebrew Hymn,* IV, 428-31. RPL

Hell is in my heart, but my eyes are like seas.[23]
My tears are white, but they are red as blood.
A fire was sent wandering within me; it has mixed my tears with
        blood.
Refined in the crucible of pain, and with my heat [kindled], are
        extinguished within me.

Those who heard the singular strength of my love
yesterday asked me who my ibex is.
I answered them, "A daughter of Arabia is my beloved,
but her cheek is half Edom (Gen 25:30) and half Aramean (Gen
        28:5).[24]
[At] its shining, it shames the great bear, Pleades, and [outshines]
        the stars from the heights.[25]

I slept and the beautiful and innocent one said,
"Is the lover asleep?" I answered her, "Terrible
is the life of love! There is no rest for me in slumber,
but I have slept and slumbered. Perhaps my dream will catch you,
and I will tremble in fear (Job 6:10) of your leaving, in my
        lying down and rising up" (Dt 6:7).

My heart burns, and there is no helper or support.
I will say, "How in the fire of your gathering and anger
will you burn my heart, when it was your footstool of old?"
You will answer, "What do you care if I burn my footstool?"[26]
Sing, my heart, and be glad when I burn it in my anger.

Come, and if in a dream a gazelle[27] of loves
comes willingly, if only with pleasant words
your utterance, even a little (Ezek 16:47), will quench the inner
        fire.
Visit me, even in a dream; give me your grace, even if only
        "shalom!"[28]
for your words, though few, will quench the thirst of the longing
        one.

---

[23] The fires of hell have not been enough to dry them.
[24] The Hebrew for Edom also means "red," and that for Aramean also means "White."
[25] The word for heights also means "Rome."
[26] Jerusalem. I Chron 28:2; Ps 99:5; 132:7; Lam 2:1; Mt 5:35; II Esd. 6:4.
[27] Gazelle represents the lover in Arabic poetry.
[28] So hungry is he for love, he would relish even a casual greeting.

B. Daughter of Canaan

I will be glad with my cup,[29] and I will rejoice. I will *go down* and
come *to my garden* (SS 6:2).
I will hear the song of a dove and the voice of a swallow, for then
my tongue will sing.

Words of my love will speak clearly, in spite of envy and anger.
With the graceful ibex[30] I will sing, her cheeks like *a full moon*
(SS 7:3).
Music in a garden I will arouse. I will open my lips in the midst of
the garden,
like a swallow and a swift[31] over a flower, I will sing, and they
will answer me.

I will sprinkle ashav[32] on my right, and the fragrance goes up on
my left.
I smell myrrh of cinnamon; I eat boiled and roasted [meat].
I press my lips, and I drink my wine, and I arouse my flute.
I kiss her and drink until I have quenched my thirst.

My opponents say [it is] so that I will rebel against my love, and
betray [her].
"How is it with you, man? Will you act and do as a daughter of
Canaan likes?"
I reply and answer, "If her love is like a yoke,
it is a yoke of love, true, a flower for my forehead, a chain for my
neck."

If you hinder my desire like a miser, I will scatter my tears freely.
I will show my wounds, and perhaps she will have pity in seeing
my wounds.
Her pleasure in me has ceased, and I am sick. I am so lean that to
my friends
I am hardly visible. The observer looks, but he does not see me.

Ibex, please return to me; heal my pain with a kiss.
She answers, "I am afraid, lest my enemy see you."
I say, "If in my sickness I cease, and my body is no longer with me,
if [anyone] really looks at me, because of my leanness, he will not
see me.

[29] My lot, my fate, that which I am required to accept.
[30] In Arabic poetry, the ibex is the feminine sweetheart. Here it represents Jerusalem.
[31] A bird very much like a swallow.
[32] Evidently a kind of perfume.

SABBATH AND REDEMPTION
Author Unknown[33]

To enjoy [the Sabbath] like the age to come,[34] the day of Sabbath
    rest;
all who enjoy themselves in it merit great joy;
from pre-messianic tribulations they will be delivered into well
    being;
our redemption will shoot forth, *and pain and sighing will pass
    away* (Isa 51:11).

SIN AND THE SANCTUARY
Author Unknown[35]

Our Guilt is greater than that of any people, our embarrassment,
    than that of any generation.
Joy has been exiled from us; we are heartsick in our sins.
Our desire is destroyed; our glory is disarrayed.
The dwelling place of the house of our sanctuary was destroyed
    because of our iniquities;[36] our palace has become a
    desolation.
The beauty of our land[37] is for strangers;[38] our strength for
    foreigners;
but still we have not turned away from our errors.
How can we shamelessly and with stiff necks say before you,
    O Lord, our God
and the God of our fathers, that we are righteous, and we have not
    sinned,
we who have truly sinned?

Introduction to Amittai Ben Shephatiah

Little is known about Amittai Ben Shephatiah except for his

---

[33] Dove, *Worship Manual,* 200-201. RPL

[34] The age of peace following the great war with Gog and Magog.

[35] Dove, *Worship Manual,* 326. RPL

[36] Like the Hebrew who could not repay his debt to his fellow Hebrew and was required either to forfeit his land until jubilee or work at half wages until the sabbath year, when Israel's debt of sin became more than she could repay, she was removed from the land and treated like a slave until the sabbath or jubilee year.

[37] Jerusalem and the temple.

[38] The Crusaders.

liturgical poems. He was an Italian poet at the beginning of the tenth century.[39]

ISRAEL DELIVERED BY THE LORD
Amittai Ben Shephatiah[40]

א) *Israel* is delivered a salvation of the ages by the Lord.
Even today they will be saved before you, [O you who] dwell on high,
for you are the Master of forgiveness and the Lord of mercies!

ש) Your *gates* they knock,[41] like poor and humble [people],
Attend the outpourings of their hearts, O Lord who dwells concealed,[42]
for you are the Master of forgiveness and the Lord of mercies!

פ) *Terrified* are they from all their hardships, mockers, and revilers.
Please do not forsake them, O Lord, God of their fathers,
for you are the Master of forgiveness and the Lord of mercies!

ט) May your *kindnesses* succor them on the day of testing.
From the midst of distress, provide them redemption and freedom,
for you are the Master of forgiveness and the Lord of mercies!

י) *They will be saved* before the eyes of all, the wicked men will not rule them.
May you destroy Seir and his father-in-law,[43] and let *deliverers go up* to *Zion* (Obad 21).
for you are the Master of forgiveness and the Lord of mercies!

ה) *Pay attention*, O Lord, to the voice of their supplication.
Let their prayers ascend to the heavenly place of your dwelling,
for you are the Master of forgiveness and the Lord of mercies!

[39] R. Gottheil, "Amittai Ben Shephatiah," *JE*, I, 521.
[40] J. Shirman (ed.), *Anthologie der Hebraischen Dichtung im Italien* (Berlin, 1934), 1. RPL
[41] They knock at the Lord's door, asking admittance.
[42] Out of sight and reach for human beings.
[43] Seir symbolizes Christians; his father-in-law, Ishmael, symbolizes Moslems (Gen 28:9).

Introduction to Abraham Ibn Ezra

Abraham Ibn Ezra (A.D. 1092-1167) was a good Bible scholar and poet, although he was not so systematic as Saadia Gaon in his theological presentation. Neither was he so passionate and nationalistic as Judah Halevy or Gabirol. He was less emotional than either. His writings consist principally of his commentaries and his poetry.[44] His strong messianic beliefs are shown in short interpretations of scripture or short poems. He was personally an adventurous person who traveled widely and held diverse interests. He inspired and influenced Maimonides. Many of his poems are preserved in Jewish Prayer Books.

TRUE LOVE

Abraham Ibn Ezra[45]

On her ascension with *perfumed myrrh* (SS 3:6), her fragrance
   will rise,
leaning with perfect peace *upon the beloved* (SS 8:5) like an ibex.

Quietly the buck[46] drew her in the days of youth, and she[47] rushed
   to him
like thirsty people running to the water of a river. He laid her
   bare.[48]
The days he bound her to him stormed her heart, and she said,
"Will the beloved declare his desire?"[49] I will accept his word.
He will be more pleasant than honey in time of peace, and remedy,
   in illness."

She is the first of all delicate ones; with pride he loves her.
She is tender in the shadow of his wings, until the beloved moves
and rejects her. She watches the ways when he will bring her back.
At night she watches *Kasil and Kimah* (Amos 5:8).[50] She stands

---

[44] His commentaries are recorded alongside the OT text in מקראות גדולות (New York, c1951).

[45] Shirman, *The Hebrew Hymn*, II, 622. RPL

[46] The Lord.

[47] Israel.

[48] Exposed her to himself.

[49] Will he make a covenant, propose marriage?

[50] She consults astrology which was very popular in the Middle Ages. See the works of Rabbis Ḥiyya and Naḥmonides.

and asks for him.
If the *time is delayed* (Jdgs 5:28), she will be still and wait.[51]

What will you fear, and [why will] your heart be timid, lovely
    friend?
I will sanctify my Name and *allot* (Zech 2:16) the sanctuary. I will
    send a messenger,[52] and
a redeemer will come to redeem you, because I will *allot*
    (Zech 2:16) you. If the enemy
reviles both of us, he will bring about the end. She will say,
"This God is true! Blessed is the people he chose for an
    inheritance!"

MY DISGRACE

Amittai Ben Shephatiah[53]

א) *How,* more than all the
        nations   have I been lowered to the [very]
                              depths,

and from the day I was
        given   is there no help and recoveries?
ב) *Why* are all the neighbors,[54] from the midst of their destruc-
                              tions rebuilt?

and I, how many years,   lament over two destructions?[55]
ג) *Confusion* of all daughters   in gladness and with music,
and the daughters of Judah
and Israel who are
        gloomy,   always in mourning and lamen-
                              tation!

ד) *Those who know* me
        insult [me]:   "What's the matter with you,
                              poor and wretched
                              beings?

for from of old [you were
        treated as]

[51] The time for the end of her exile and prison sentence. Israel is pictured as a lover who is
impatient for her mate to return.
[52] Elijah (Mal 3:1).
[53] H. Brody and M. Wiener, *Anthologia Hebraica* (Leipzig, 1923), 47. Part of an acrostic
poem. RPL
[54] Gentiles.
[55] Of the temple, 586 B.C. and A.D. 70.

important sons,   but now [you appear] as empty vessels and dogs!

נ)   *Visions* of the end of the captivity!   How long [will you act] with such stupidity?

Do you not know for sure   that your hope is vain and folly?"

ד)   When I hear *this* in bitterness of soul I will cry out and announce,   my eyes surely weep.

"How long, O Lord, have I cried for help, but you did not listen" (Hab 1:2)?

ע)   *Holy,* Dweller of Araboth[56]   may our prayers be acceptable.

You who have shown us many hardships,   show us, please, good comforts!

Introduction to Levi Ibn Altabban

Levi Ben Jacob Ibn Altabban was a Spanish grammarian and poet. Judah Halevy, his younger contemporary, called him the "King of Song." This early twelfth century poet wrote many liturgical poems. He is best known for his penitential and melancholy hymns.[57]

PROMISE AND PROBLEMS
Levi Ibn Altabban[58]

The Lord:
Oppressed, for the duration of the exile, [she] lost her children, *afflicted* cruelly (Isa 53:4), *frightened and defiled* (Zeph 3:1).
To the temple I will restore your sanctuary for dominion.
I will *repair* your *breach* (Isa 58:12). I will provide your wound a remedy. I will accept you and *love you willingly* (Hos 14:5).

Israel:
Until salvation [comes], will I be waiting?
I, deprived of shade and sukkah,[59]

[56] Heaven.
[57] H.G. Enelow, "Altabban, Levi B. Jacob Ibn," *JE,* I, 464.
[58] Shirman, *The Hebrew Hymn,* II, 335.
[59] Any type of shelter. May reflect the flimsy shelters made for Sukkoth.

like a straying sheep, like a *lamb (rahel)*[60] *weeping* (Jer 31:15)?
My *harvest is past* (Jer 8:20); the time of [grape] picking (בצירי)
      is over.
My *pain* (צירי) (I Sam 4:19; Isa 21:3) is increased; and my
      messenger (צירי)[61] has not come.

The Lord:
Beloved, put on beautiful garments.
Don a crown for glory and a covering,
for still you will remove the shame; wages
you will receive; *Zerah and Nahath* (Gen 36:13) will soon be
      broken;[62]
you will be happy rather than forsaken.

Israel:
My times have passed with pain and tumult.
My iniquities have *covered* my *face* with *shame* (Jer 51:51).
Of all my sons I am left deprived.
I will labor in vain. If you do not compensate
in your grace and mercy, *where can I go* (Gen 37:30)?

The Lord:
I will surely raise up the destroyed sanctuary,
and I will raise up your horn[63] in the city of the great king.
To the poor devastated one my salvation will come near.
I will destroy the wicked ones, the evil seed,
but love will cover all transgressions (Prov 10:12).

SUPPLICATION
Levi Ibn Altabban[64]

O Lord, why are you like a man confused,
like a mighty man unable to save (Jer 14:9)?
On us your name is called (Jer 14:9), *One who strengthens in*
      time of trouble (Ps 9:10),
One who speaks in righteousness, mighty to save!

---

[60] Notice the play on words: lamb (רחל) and Rachel (רחל) weeping for her children.
[61] Elijah (Mal 3:1).
[62] Sons of Esau, symbols of the current Romans or Christians.
[63] The Messiah.
[64] Shirman, *The Hebrew Hymn,* II, 337.

Together we *lie in torment* (Isa 50:11), and the enemy has planned,
    considering that you are not a savior.
Tested in exile twice, your people from fire and water
    cry aloud, but there is no savior.
Thousands have oppressed them. There they are, trembling from
    destruction, but you
are a God who hides himself, the God of Israel, a Redeemer!
Enemies vilify them in their captivity: *Where is the One who*
    brings them up from the sea (Isa 63:11)
and is their savior?
Arise and meet them and see! Repay the insulter and arrogant one,
if *the hand* of the Lord is not *too short* to save (Isa 50:2).
Break the bow of mighty men, and let every mighty oppressor
    know that you will save a poor people.
In its anger, my eye sheds tears. *How long, O Lord, will I cry out*
    and you will not pay attention?
I cry to you, "Violence!" but you do not save (Hab 1:2).

A REGISTERED COMPLAINT

Judah Halevy[65]

A dove you have *borne on the wings of eagles* (Ex 19:4).
Its nest is in your bosom, in the innermost rooms.[66]
Why did you leave her to roam in the forests
with *nets spread out* (Isa 19:8) on every side?
Strangers incite her with other gods,
but *in secret she weeps* (Jer 13:17) for the Lord of her youth.
Dishan and Dishon[67] flatter her (Gen 36:21).
She raises her eye to her *first husband* (Hos 2:9).
Why did *you abandon my soul to Sheol* (Ps 16:10)?
I know there is no one but you to redeem (Ruth 4:4).

Will the locks of the flawless one be forever uncovered (Isa 47:2),
booty (בזה) and loot (שמה) to *Mizzah* (מזה) *and*
    Shammah (שמה) (Gen 36:13)?[68]
The son of the maid (Gen 21:10)[69] clothed me with terror,

---

[65] Shirman, *The Hebrew Hymn*, II, 472-74. RPL
[66] The holy of holies in the temple. In *Hekhalot Rabbati*, the innermost palace in the Garden of Eden is called "The Bird's Nest."
[67] Sons of Esau. Here it means Rome and the Christians.
[68] Children of Esau. Here it symbolizes Rome and the Christians.
[69] The maid is Hagar and the son is Ishmael. Here it refers to Arabs or Moslems.

for *with a high hand* (Ex 14:8) *he shot the bow* (Jer 4:29;
        Gen 21:20).
My tent *('oholi)* is a high place *(bamah)* for Oholibamah
        (Gen 36:2).[70]
Oholibah (Ezek 23:4),[71] how will you still hope, and how long?
There is no miracle, no sign, no vision, or appearance.
If you ask to see *when will be the end of the wonders* (Dan 12:6),
prophecies answer, *You have asked too hard a question*
        (II Kgs 2:10).

Delicate daughters, exiled from cities,
from restful beds and *quiet resting places* (Isa 32:18),
dispersed among (בינות) *an ignorant* (לא בינות) *people*
        (Isa 27:11),
with mocking lips and foreign *speech* (Isa 28:11).
Yet they kept the faith; among them they were nurtured,
but to pictorial idols they *refused to submit* (Ex 10:3).
Why, at a *distance, stands* the One who dwells in the skies
        (Ps 10:1)?
My subduer[72] crushes, and my Beloved[73] is far away
and for the end of days we shall keep on asking (I Sam 20:6;
        Neh 13:6).

The banner of brotherhood is removed from me;
A proud foot is upon me, a yoke, and a chain;
and I, chastened by *cruel punishment* (Jer 30:14),
exiled, imprisoned, angry, and rejected,
with no *prince*, no *commander* (Nahum 3:17), *no king and no
        officer* (Hos 3:4).
An oppressor turns to me, and the Rock turns away.
He destroyed, in his wrath, "the Place" of his *footsteps* (Dt 2:5).[74]
He burned, in his anger, his door post and threshold.
A fire kindled, in his anger, and burned down to Sheol (Dt 32:22).

Will the Lord reject for ages (Ps 77:8)?
Is there no *end to* my *appointed time of* my *vision* (Dan 8:18-20)?
Arise, O Lord, and let my enemies *be scattered* (Num 10:35)!
Return to my dwelling, to the innermost temple!

---

[70] Oholibamah was Esau's wife, so this refers also to Christians or Romans.
[71] Jerusalem. Here it means the Jews. Ezek 23:4.
[72] The Gentiles.
[73] The Lord.
[74] The Place is a name given for the temple which was also called his footstool.

Reveal to my eyes your glory as from Sinai!
Pay back my *[taunting]* *neighbors* (Ps 79:12); avenge my sorrows.
Descend with the dew of salvation for one who is *fearful and afraid* (Jdgs 7:3).
Bring down from his throne the rebellious son of the maid,[75]
quickly, lest I go *down* to *Sheol in my sorrow* (Gen 42:38).

DANGEROUS LOVE
Judah Halevy[76]

The graceful ibex (Prov 5:19)[77] has gone from her residence.
Her Lover is angry; why does she laugh?
She laughs at the daughter of Edom[78] and the daughter of Arabia[79]
who are asking to love a Friend she loves.
Yes, they are savage, and how can they compare
to *an ibex,* leaning on her buck.[80]
Where is prophecy? Where is a lamp, an ark of the covenant, a clinging Shekhinah?
No, my enemies, *do not* quench *love* (SS 2:7; 3:5).
If you quench her, she kisses fire.

Introduction to Solomon Ibn Gabirol

Solomon Ibn Gabirol (d. 1070) is considered the first outstanding poet of redemption. His personality shines through all of his poetry. He has been highly praised as a philosopher, sometimes called "the Jewish Plato." His philosophical system reflects no Jewish influence, but his poems disclose him as a zealous, Jewish nationalist who longed for the redemption of Israel and the return of the Jews to the promised land. He has sometimes been compared to a song bird, but his poems are mostly lamentations and complaints. He seemed to be an incurable pessimist who bitterly complained about his fortune in general, so it was normal for him to transfer his bitterness to his poems. He thought God was unfair to leave the Jewish people, his own chosen ones, to be so

---

[75] Ishmael. Here it means the Moslems.
[76] Shirman, *The Hebrew Hymn,* II, 466. RPL
[77] Jerusalem.
[78] The Romans or Christians.
[79] The Arabs or Moslems.
[80] The Lord.

miserable in the diaspora as they were at the time and refuse to vindicate them before the Gentiles. He wove his poetry around traditional prophecies and promises which he thought God was slow in fulfilling. Nonetheless, he believed that sooner or later God would reward the Jews for their suffering and fulfill his promise. He wrote just at the millennium after the fall of Jerusalem. He was convinced that the time was up; the end must be at hand; how could God wait any longer? Ibn Ezra reported in his commentary on Dan 11:31 that Gabirol calculated the end on the basis of *gematria* and astrology, trying to make deliverance contingent upon the great conjunction of Saturn and Jupiter (A.D. 1464).[61]

GOD AND ISRAEL
Solomon Ibn Gabirol[62]

The Lord:
ש) *Childless one* (Isa 49:21), consumed one,[63] why do you weep?
Has your heart despaired of waiting?[64]

Israel:
Your appointed end is late, and my darkness extends.

The Lord:
Be hopeful, afflicted one, a little longer,
for I will *send my messenger to prepare* my *way* (Mal 3:1).
Over Mount Zion I will *pour out my king* (Ps 2:6).
The herald *will surely come* (Hab 2:3) to prepare *your way* (Ps 77:20).
Say to Zion, *The Lord is King* (Ps 97:1)!
Look your king will yet *come to you* (Zech 9:9).

Israel:
ל) *In vain,* my God, how long can I wait?
How long will you continue the exile of the bulwark,
while the sons of Rachel (רחל) are shorn like a lamb (רחל) (Isa 53:7)?
And I, nonetheless, *continually wait* (Ps 71:14).

[61] See מקראות גדולות X, 77b.
[62] From the Hebrew text of I. Zangwill, *Selected Religious Poems of Solomon Ibn Gabirol* (Philadelphia, 1923), 22-24.
[63] Israel.
[64] Waiting for the end of the exile and Gentile domination of the world.

The Lord:
> Be hopeful, afflicted one, for a redeemer and a forgiving one,
> for I will not abhore you for the age.
> Just a little while [longer], and you will be mine, and I, yours.

Israel:
> נ) *When will the turtle dove* draw near and arrive (SS 2:12)?
> Closed and sealed [secrets] when will you explain?[85]
> When will you destroy the palace of strangers?

The Lord:
> Be hopeful, afflicted one, *for a shelter and a hiding place*
>   (Isa 4:6),
> for you still have a healer and an ample provider,
> and Caphtor will be still as on the day of the *Island of*
>   *Caphtor* (Jer 47:4),[86]
> and the discarded flower will bloom in splendor on your fore-
>   head.
> ה) *My multitude* long ago was destroyed all at once.[87]
> From Nof[88] and Babylonia soon we were sought.
> I am still like *a speckled bird of prey* (Jer 12:9).
> Four kingdoms are gathered over me.[89]
> It has eaten my flesh and is still not sated.
> Be hopeful, my afflicted one, for the Rock who has sworn
> that the lover wo left *will surely come* [back] (Hab 2:3).

THE DELAYED HOMECOMING

Solomon Ibn Gabirol[90]

> ע) [Those] *plundered* and wandering, you will gather to Zion.
> [Those] sold without price[91] you will return to *a resting place*
>   (Ps 23:2).
> Restore the service [of priests] who wear embroidered
>   garments.

---

[85] Secrets about the time when the Gentile rule will come to an end and the sovereign authority of the world be given to the Jews (Dan 12:4).

[86] The battle when the Lord was destined to destroy the Philistines.

[87] In Noah's flood.

[88] A city in Egypt.

[89] The Gentiles (Dan 2:36-40; 7:3-12, 17-18; 8:3-14, 20-21).

[90] From the Hebrew text of Zangwill, *Selected Religious Poems,* 20-21.

[91] For "slaves."

Nourish the report of the family of *Jabez* (I Chron 4:9-10)[92]
to praise and sing to your name, O Most High.

ל) Hurry! Raise *a banner to* the Gentiles (Isa 49:22).
Conquer pain, and *gird up his loins* (I Kgs 18:46).[93]
Gather my crowds, and collect *my dispersed* (Zeph 3:10).
Renew redemption like Tanis and Hanis.[94]
Clothing the righteous one with righteousness, like a coat of mail.

מ) *My enemy speaks* to me *insultingly* (Prov 18:23),
seeking to destroy the expectation of my faith.
He contests me to my face, "How long will you wait?"
I answer him that the Lord will not reject [me] for the age.
He is a fortress for the humble, a fortress for the poor.

ה) *Restore the divorcee* (Lev 21:7)[95] to the *acquired* heritage
(Dt 2:5).[96]
Visit the critically ill, punished by the oppressor.
Consumption in every mouth abandoned and destroyed.
Renew the righteousness of the three patriarchs,[97]
and subdue the aliens like a scorching desert storm (Isa 25:5)!

THE DUOLOGUE

Solomon Ibn Gabirol[98]

The Lord:
ש) *Captive* daughter of Zion, tested in the furnace of affliction,
ש) *The oath* of your fathers I swore for my sake.
ש) I have heard *your cry* (Jer 8:19); it has reached my dwelling.
ש) I *have heard* (Lam 3:56), for I am merciful.

Israel:
ש) *I am bowed* very low (Isa 51:14), for my hand has no
strength.

---

[92] Jabez was one of the sons of Judah who prayed, "O that you would bless me and enlarge my border, and that your right hand might be with me, and that you would keep me from harm so that it might not hurt me" (I Chron 4:1,10). Gabirol wanted the Lord to implement this prayer for the Jews.

[93] I.e., the loins of Elijah for his arrival.

[94] Cities in Egypt.

[95] Israel who has been rejected from her "husband's" house into the exile (Isa 54:6-8).

[96] The promised land.

[97] Abraham, Isaac, and Jacob upon whose merits later Jews could depend.

[98] Zangwill, *Selected Religious Poems.* 28-29. RPL

ש) Your good *Name* and forgiveness is requested by every
  petitioner.

ש) *Return, for I have no redeemer but you* (Ruth 4:4).

ש) *Return,* O Lord, [to] *myriads of thousands* (Gen 24:60) of
  Israelites.

The Lord:

ל) *To whom,* therefore, *have I sold you* (Isa 50:1)? A man of
  your conflict will come.

ל) *To whom a divorce document* (Isa 50:1)? I will defend your
  case.

ל) *Like* a tower of fire, I will be around you.

ל) *Why* do you weep, and why does your heart break?

Israel:

ל) *Why do I cry out, "Violence!" and you do not* answer
  (Hab 1:2)?

ל) *To* demolish and destroy, the crowd says.

ל) *To* strangers we are sold, *Er* and *Onan* together
  (Gen 38:3-4),[99]

ל) *as* male and female slaves, and there was no buyer.

The Lord:

מ) *Who* are you that you fear an insulting man?

מ) *I will send my messenger* (Mal 3:1), as [you learn from] the
  writing of the seer.

מ) *Scattering* Israelites [I will stop, and] I will gather from here
  and there.

מ) This will be a sign—*Tomorrow.*

Israel:

מ) You have set *an appointed time* for me to gather my
  chieftains.

מ) I have seen no *miracle* to erect my sanctuary.

מ) No one has come *announcing,* "Peace!" to my holy place.

מ) *Why* has the son of Jesse not come?

The Lord:

נ) *Look, I have sworn by myself* (Isa 45:23) to gather my
  conquered ones.

נ) *Will the kings* (Isa 60:3) not then *bring* you *gifts* (Isa 18:7)?

---

[99] The first two sons of Judah.

ה) *Look,* I have set my saints [as] a witness to the Gentiles.

ה) *Look,* I have seen the son of Jesse.

POSTPONEMENT AND PATIENCE
Abraham Ibn Ezra[100]

If *my enemies speak evil to me* (Ps 41:6), I will say, "My foot is
     slipping."

The God of Abraham is my [God]; *the fear of Isaac was mine*
     (Gen 31:42).

I was studying in the books of the prophets (Dan 9:2) the words of
     Isaiah in his composition

were read before me that *the salvation to come is near* (Isa 56:1).

Yes, generations pass and go, but the people of God will stand in
     its *pain* (Lam 1:12).

A thousand years of *marvel* (Dan 12:6)[101] will pass. With deep
     anguish

he says, *If you will redeem, redeem; if you will not redeem, tell me*
     (Ruth 4:4).

You saw, Ezekiel, visions, and to me you raised parables.

Did you seek to see my word and ask the angels.

When will the end of these wonders be (Dan 12:6)? For the year of
     redemption has not come.

You replied to me through prophecies, "What is in the hand of
     teachers (Dan 12:3)

to do?" *The Lord hid* [it] from me and did not tell me (II Kgs 4:27).

Who will allow me to form an alliance with Daniel, a man of
     precious things,

who knows the interpretation of a matter and understands
     parables and riddles?

I will implore him with a broken heart, and I will ask him about
the end, to see if it has passed and if his prophecies are for the
     future.

Men of understanding will tell me (Job 34:34), *What is this that
     you ask? It is mysterious* (Jdgs 13:18).

---

[100]Shirman, *The Hebrew Hymn,* II, 617-18. RPL

[101]Since the fall of Jerusalem. This was written shortly after the first millennium following
A.D. 70.

My scholars and learned ones are benumbed, and no one knows
what.
From much weeping my eyes are darkened, for the time of my redemption is hidden.[102]
I will search in the Torah of the Lord; I will find my desire there,
for God will return my exiled multitudes, even if they are pushed
to the ends of the earth
This is my comfort. Therefore, *I will speak, and it will relieve me*
(Job 32:20).

HELP!

Joseph Ibn Abitur[103]

א) Whom have you abandoned forever? for is our abandonment
forever?

ב) *With* whom are you angry forever? for will you be angry with
us forever?

ג) *Exile* to whom have you decreed without redemption? Will
there be a second exile for us?

ד) *Generation* after generation, whom have you enslaved? Shall
I keep silent from seeking freedom?

ה) *Is* there not deliverance from every snare? For every hardship
have I seen an end?

ו) *Then* why is my exile so long, ever wider and increasing more
and more?

ז) *Remembering* his mercy for all those far from him, will he refuse mercy on his clinging ones?

ח) Showing *favor* and pity on strangers, will he refuse to show
favor to his children of his womb?

. . .

ק) *Arise* and see that our enemies have multiplied, and we are not
able to raise our eyes.

ר) *He who sees* his sons killed before his eyes, how can he be so
harsh? How can he restrain himself?

ש) *Shadai,* You are our Father! How are we considered orphans?

ת) *Are you able* to see us in distress when it is possible for you to
relieve us?

[102] Kept secret.
[103] H. Brody and K. Albrecht, *The New Hebrew School of Poets* (London, 1906), 14-15.

JOB IN EXILE

Abraham Ibn Ezra[104]

If my strength were the strength of stones (Job 6:12); if my heart
were iron;
I could carry the yoke of the maid,[105] and *the sons of my mother
[who] are enraged over me* (SS 1:6).
As I remembered the by-gone days, I enjoy my lot in the world.
The glory of God in the house of ages was all that was left to me.
Ah, how will I find comforts, for my precious one has turned
away.
How can a tent[106] restore my spirit [when] *an Arabian lives
there*[107] (Isa 13:20)?
Ah, for a scattered sheep; behold it is a prey for a lion!

My *days go down* (Jdgs 19:11), but my *misery goes up*
(Gen 2:6)![108] Light is turned from me
to hostile darkness, and I am finished; *God* does not *pursue me*
(Job 19:22).
I am searched out until *the sound of a falling leaf* really *persecutes*
me (Lev 26:36).
I go from destruction to destruction, for snares surround me.
I have stumbled until every *stone in the field* opposes me (Job 5:23).

I am filled with eternal shame; I have no pleasures.
All my ill-wishers rejoice and have their vengeance,
for my flesh is consumed, but the *bones* remain (Job 19:20).
I pour out my soul with my spirit; I pray to my father.
Perhaps he will turn to my heart and bring the *redeemer*
(Job 19:25).[109]

[104] Shirman, *The Hebrew Hymn*, II, 620. RPL
[105] The maid is Hagar, whose children are the Ishmaelites or Moslems. *If* his strength were
as he suggests, *then* he could bear this "slavery," but as it is, he cannot.
[106] The temple.
[107] The Arabs or Moslems have control of the temple area in Jerusalem. The Oracle
against Babylon said it would be so desolate that not even an Arab could live there. Out of
context, Abraham Ibn Ezra applied the verse ironically to Jerusalem where Arabians
actually did live, although he thought they should not.
[108] As misery increases, the days of life left decrease.
[109] This verse seems strongly influenced by Job 19:19-26. Like Job, Ibn Ezra complained
that his friends were against him. He expected to see God, even after he would be deprived
of his flesh and skin. He expected a redeemer. Scholars have disputed the translation of Job
19:26, which the RSV renders: "And after my skin has been destroyed, then from (or
without) my flesh, I shall see God." Since Job's problem was a skin disease that was

EXPRESSED FEELING
Amittai Ben Shephatiah[110]

Lord, Lord, God, merciful and gracious,
of long patience, great loving kindness, and truth,
who keeps loving kindness for thousands,
who bears[111] iniquity, transgression, and sin, and cleanses...
Forgive our iniquities and our sins, and cling to us!

א)　*I will remember,* God, and I will speak
　　　when I see every *city [firmly] built on its tel* (Jer 30:18),[112]
　　　but the city of God humbled to lowest Sheol.
　　　In spite of this, we belong to the Lord, and our eyes are
　　　　　[directed] to the Lord!

מ)　*Measure* of mercy, roll over us,
　　　submit our supplications before your Creator,
　　　and request mercy and favor for your people,[113]
　　　for every heart is faint, and every head is sick!

ת)　*I have consolidated* my tent pegs upon the thirteen tenets,[114]
　　　and within gates of tears, for they are not joined.
　　　Therefore, I have poured out my heart before him whò tests
　　　　the hearts.
　　　I have confidence in these and in the merits of the three
　　　　patriarchs.

---

consuming his skin and flesh, it makes good sense literally to follow the imagery to
understand that after his flesh had been consumed by disease, even then, in that condition,
he would see God. Ibn Ezra understood it that way, saying, "After the flesh is consumed the
bones remain."

[110] H. Brody and M. Wiener, השירה העברית מבחר (Jerusalem, 1934), 48. RPL

[111] That is, God endures or tolerates carrying the sins people load upon him for a long
time without becoming irritated. He is long suffering.

[112] This is a satire on Jer 30:18: "Thus says the Lord: Behold, I will restore the fortunes of
the tents of Jacob, and have compassion on his dwellings; the city shall be rebuilt upon its
tel, and the palace shall stand where it used to be." The poet complained that all the other
cities of the world were sitting firmly built on their tels or mounds, but not Zion, as
Jeremiah had promised. Instead it was humbled to the lowest Sheol.

[113] Mercy here is personified and addressed as an intermediary that should receive
requests from Jews and present them before God at the opportune time. This is the same as
praying to angels to intercede for the supplicant to God.

[114] Seemingly, the thirteen tenets of Maimonides' creed or possibly the *middoth* of R.
Ishmael. Amittai lived before Maimonides. If these were the same tenets, Maimonides
appropriated them rather than originating them.

May it be your will, you who hear the voice of weeping,
that you place our tears in your leather bag,[115]
and deliver us from all fierce decrees,
for our eyes are turned to you alone!

A DIALOGUE ON REDEMPTION
Author Unknown[116]

Zion:
My God, hasten my redeemer; let your servant enlighten me,
the one who proclaims good news (Isa 52:7), my God, the prophet
Elijah.

The Lord:
How beautiful (SS 1:10; 6:4; Isa 52:7) *upon the mountains*
(Isa 52:7)
are the messengers of the Creator of the mountains and *the feet
of those who proclaim good news* (Isa 52:7), saying, *Return!
Return!* (SS 7:1).

Zion:
My God, hasten my redeemer; let your servant enlighten me,...

The Lord:
My beloved, *as a short* (SS 3:4) instant, every sickness, every
plague
I will afflict on your enemies. *The day of vengeance is in my
heart.* (Isa 63:4).

Zion:
My God, hasten my redeemer; let your servant enlighten me,...

The Lord:
Your king will come to you (Zech 9:9); *you are all beautiful* (SS
4:7) and *my beloved* (SS 4:7; 6:4) is before you, the Gileadite (SS
4:1; 6:5), the Tishbite.

Zion:
My God, hasten my redeemer; let your servant enlighten me,...

[115] As in the bag of a shepherd. Just as God was to preserve the merits of the patriarchs, he was expected to give special credit in the treasury of merits for all these tears.
[116] Dove, *Worship Manual*, 316.

The Lord:
The lips (SS 4:11) of young doves *distil nectar* (SS 4:11),
for the time of clemency for her has come, for Zion, the inheritance of *The Pleasant Land* (SS 2:9; Dan 11:41).

Zion:
My God, hasten my redeemer; let your servant enlighten me,...

OUT OF THE DEPTHS

Benjamin Ben Zeraḥ[117]

I will speak out and find relief (Job 32:20), for my spirit urged,
for the bitterness of my soul and the weight of my bondage
among all the nations and languages, I alone am oppressed,
walking from day to day backwards and not forwards.
You have passed the verdict over me saying, *To generation after*
         generation (Ps 77:9).
Without the overflowing mercies to bring me to freedom
you have pushed me away as if with both hands
and not as one who pushes away with the left hand while drawing
         near with the right [one].
I have been humbled in Babylon; I was brought low in Media;
I sank deep in Greece, and now by the hand of malicious
         evildoers.[118]
If my strength were the strength of stones and my flesh [as tough
         as] brass (Job 6:12),
[would I be able] to stand and bear all these hardships?
This destruction and desolation has been mine for many years—
a thousand,[119] and yet [I am] bereaved and forsaken,
fettered and in prison, *plowed up like a field* (Micah 3:12),
disgraced like a thief, *head lowered* (Esther 6:12) like a mourner.
My sanctuaries are defiled, and my saints profaned;
my incense offerings are desecrated and soiled.
The clutching of my sins, the binding of my transgressions,
and the *iniquity of my pursuers* (Ps 49:6) have brought [all this]
         upon me.
Great Might! Do you not realize
that I am afflicted doubly? For each seah [of sin there are] two
         seahs [of punishment]?[120]

[117] H. Brody and M. Wiener, *Choice Hebrew Hymns.* 212-15. RPL Eleventh century.
[118] The fourth and worst of the beasts. Here it means Rome.
[119] A millennium since the fall of Jerusalem in A.D. 70.
[120] Normal rates for repayment of debts by labor. See introduction.

They oppress me and crush me, all who come and go.
Every mouth has devoured me until my strength is gone.
Hurry, hasten to the groaning of your children,
those who sign and moan (Ezek 9:4) and are miserable!
I am weary of bearing (Isa 1:14) the exile and captivity
from the trampling of the feet of an *ungodly nation* and *no people*
    (Dt 32:21).
They say, "Where is your king and the Rock of your strength?
Let him roll up his sleeves (Isa 52:10) and defend you!"
You have counted the times of redemption, and they are
    exhausted.[121]
Hope of deliverance has ceased and gone.
My morale is trodden into the ground
when I hear their vilification and the extent of their invective.
Your decisions are just, and your judgments are fair.
I vindicate all that has come upon me.
Rise up, O God, and fight my cause!
Make public my judgment and verdict!
See my desolation and the desolation of your temple,
if not for my sake, act for your own sake!
The oath to the parents and their covenants
do not annul, for you are a trustworthy God.
Remember their love, and revive their seed
before they perish from their subduers.
They are your children, your pleasant plant (Isa 17:10).
Grant your tender mercies to their remnants.

I will keep still and restrain myself,[122] but my heart will grieve
    within me.
When I see those bowing down to Bel and praying to one dead,[123]
    causing me grief,
I will guard my mouth with a muzzle (Ps 39:2) *and my pain is
    agonized* (Ps 39:3).
My bowels, my bowels, I am pained at my very heart.

The hand that suppresses overpowers me greatly,

[121] After A.D. 70, the first end time would have been the first jubilee (ca. A.D. 119), then 70 years, like the period spent in Babylon (A.D. 140); then 420 years, like those spent in Egypt (A.D. 490). The turn of the millennium (A.D. 240) would have marked a time of expectation, and there were others, but the final date would have been a full millennium after A.D. 70. When this passed without redemption, many Jews thought God would never restore his people to the promised land. All their end times had passed and failed.
[122] Note the contrast between this line and the first line of the poem.
[123] Possibly Jesus.

domineering in anger and wrath, crushing and plundering.
My afflictors crush me, and I am discarded like a trampled corpse.
I will crouch over my bed every night; I will make my couch flow
     with tears.

You have moulded me as clay (Job 10:9); I am like a street for
     those who tread on me.
My back is smitten, *and my cheeks are torn* (Isa 50:6) by the hand
     of my evil-doers.
I look to the right and to the left, but my path is not smooth,
and I, *My feet have almost slipped* (Ps 73:2).

This I will reply to my heart while my innermost being is troubled:
Idol worshippers have continued their course, and their reputation
     is not impaired.
I [on the contrary] have been changed and emptied from vessel to
     vessel, and my glory has been vilified.
Behold, I am bitterly longing for peace.

I have sunk to the depth, pushed by a strong hand, and I am
     languishing with illness.
The city is forsaken [by its] inhabitants; the palace is abandoned,
     and the town is destroyed.
A bear will confront me and seize me in the wilderness.
We have come into fire and water, but you will bring us out for
     sustenance.

My strength has stumbled in my iniquity, and my breath has
     shortened.
At the time the goat[124] dominates, and *the singing* has stopped
     (SS 2:12).
I called out to *him who has brought me forth from the womb*
     (Ps 22:9), *from distress, and he answered me*
     (Ps 118:5).
In all their affliction he is afflicted (Isa 63:9).

How much, now, have misdeeds multiplied and increased the guilt
to be hidden in my bosom (Job 31:33), to be covered in my breast.
My inheritance is ablaze and put to pillage.

---

[124] The consonants used to spell "goat" and Seir are the same. Ben Zeraḥ has intentionally
confused the two. Mount Seir is in Edom. Therefore Seir represents Rome or the Christians.
The time of the goat is the time Christians dominate.

Cities are laid waste where no one dwells; and the land is a total
destruction.

The male goat[125] and his father-in-law[126] scatter me and *make* me a
desert (Isa 5:6).
One attacks the other, and this to destroy me.
How long will you keep still and gaze at sin and wickedness
and not have mercy on Jerusalem and the cities of Judah with
whom you are angry?

They *have opened* their *mouth* (Ps 119:131) to swallow, and their
throat is open like a grave (Ps 5:9)
to rob from every side and devour from every direction.
I have cried out from the pain of my heart, when I saw how late
the rescue was,
and I say, "Who will give me respite?"

My heart is impatient, and my soul is full of yearning
from the burdens of aliens and the servitude to my oppressors.
Fight my opponents, O Lord, and those who embitter my soul
do not turn toward obduration!

I have sought you. Come to my rescue, O Lofty and Hidden One!
Let your ears be attentive from the dwelling place of the hall.[127]
In you, forever reposes my hope and my trust; please do not reject
me in shame.
Let Israel wait for the Lord, from now and to the age.

MIRACLES AND REDEMPTION[128]

May he who performed miracles for our fathers, redeeming
them from bondage and freedom, redeem us soon.[129] May he
restore our dispersed ones from the four corners of the earth. May
the first month of...on the day of...be a good omen for us.
All Israelites are brothers. Let us say, "Amen." May the holy One

[125] Slightly mispronounced to mean Seir, meaning Christians.
[126] Ishmael (Gen 28:9), meaning the Moslems.
[127] The temple.
[128] Pool, *Book of Prayer*, 214. RPL
[129] The miracles referred to are the ones performed in Egypt prior to the redemption which meant the deliverance from Egypt to the promised land. The expected redemption was also from bondage to the Gentiles to freedom on the promised land.

blessed be He renew it[130] for us and for all his people, the Israelites, for life, peace, joy, gladness, salvation, and comfort. Let us say, "Amen."

GOOD NEWS AND REDEMPTION[131]

May it be the will of the God of heaven that we may hear and receive good news, good news of redemption and comfort from the four corners of all the earth. Say, "Amen."

EXILES AND JERUSALEM[132]

May your God extend his arm to gather your scattered ones. May he hasten the time when it will be proclaimed, "Go out from your bondage." May he send the angel of his covenant to restore your hearts. Prepare his way, and the crooked will become straight, and he will gather you into his city.

REDEMPTION AND RULE[133]

Blessed be the name of the Lord of the age. Blessed be your rule and your residence. May you be pleased with your people Israel for the age. Manifest the redemption by your right hand for your people in the house of your sanctuary. Make us enjoy the salvation of your light, and receive your prayers with mercy. May it be your will to extend our days in prosperity. May I be an officer in the midst of righteousness. Have mercy upon me, and protect me and all my family and your people, the Israelites. You nourish and provide for all. You are the ruler over all. You reign over kings, and the kingdom is yours alone.[134] I am the servant of the holy One blessed be He who bows before him, and before the glory of his Torah at all times. I do not put my trust in man nor put reliance in any Son of God,[135] but in the God of heaven, for he

---

[130] The month involved, but its overtones are for the kingdom. See *Consequences*, 136-43.

[131] Pool, *Book of Prayer*, 214. RPL

[132] Dove, *Worship Manual*, 244. RPL

[133] Dove, *Worship Manual*, 205. RPL

[134] But it only exists when a Davidic king rules from Jerusalem.

[135] Possibly an anti-Christian allusion.

is the true God; his Torah is true; and his prophets are true. He abundantly provides goodness and truth. In him I put my trust, and to his glorious holy name I offer praise. May it be your will to open my heart through the Torah and fulfill the requests of my heart and the heart of all your people, the Israelites, for salvation, life, and peace.

HANUKKAH DELIVERANCE[136]

I will mention your mercy in song and in happiness, because you delivered your people from hardship to well being; you have avenged our vengeance by your faithful priests.[137] The Greeks sought to annul the Torah of our God. Your hand has delivered us from hardship and oppression.[138] Therefore, there has been appointed for us eight days of dedication to give thanks, to glorify, and to praise the mighty deeds of our God. Let us merit the consecration of the altar in our days. Please let your loving kindness be for my comfort in your bountiful grace. Provide me with my apportioned bread.[139] With all my strength I will praise your oneness. Everyday I will bless you, our compassionate Savior. Let our eyes see the salvation of your people. Helper of the down trodden, you are God. Hasten to redeem us, coming to Zion [as] a redeemer, quickly, in our days.

SABBATH REST AND THE AGE TO COME[140]

You have rested and appointed it a day of rest and enjoyment for your people the Israelites for their generations. Thus, O Lord, our God, make us and all your people the house of Israel deserve to rest in a rest for which there is no end and a purpose for the age to come which is all good and long,[141] and which will place your blessing upon us. Amen.

[136]Dove, *Worship Manual*, 205. RPL
[137]The Hasmoneans.
[138]Through the Maccabean rebellion.
[139]Compare with the Lord's Prayer (Mt 6:11).
[140]Dove, *Worship Manual*, 177. RPL
[141]Just as the restoration of the promised land was reckoned in terms of sabbatical eschatology, so the acquisition of the land was considered the promised rest. There is no expectation here of everlasting rest, but only of long life. See further Jos 21:43-45; Heb 3:7-4:11; *To the Hebrews*, 68-74. This is part of a longer prayer.

GOD'S WRATH AND REMNANT[142]

Save us, O Lord, our God, and gather us from the nations to praise your holy Name, to be praised in your praise (Ps 106:47)...O Lord, in your grace, let your anger and your wrath please turn away from your city, Jerusalem your holy mountain, for in our sins and in the iniquities of our fathers, Jerusalem and your people [are exhibited] as a reproach to all our surroundings. Now, our God, hear the prayer of your servant and his requests, and look with favor on your desolate temple, for the sake of the Lord...Gather our dispersed ones from the four corners of the earth. Let all the Gentiles recognize and know that you are the Lord, our God. Now, O Lord, *you are our Father; we are the clay, and you are the Potter. All of us are the work of your hand* (Isa 64:8). Save us for the sake of your Name, our Rock, our King, and our Redeemer. O Lord, pity your people, and do not give your inheritance up for reproach.

REPENTANCE AND SALVATION[143]

12) Our Father, our King, restore us to complete repentance before you.
19) Our Father, our King, inscribe us in the book of good life.[144]
22) Our Father, our King, inscribe us in the book of redemption and salvation.[144]
24) Our Father, our King, shoot forth salvation for us soon.
26) Our Father, our King, raise the horn of your Messiah.[145]
38) Our Father, our King, avenge in our presence the poured-out blood of your servants.
40) Our Father, our King, act, for your sake, and save us.

REDEMPTION AND RETURN[146]

Instruct us, O Lord, our God, to know your ways. Circumcise our hearts to fear you.[147] Forgive us so that we may be redeemed.

[142]Dove, *Worship Manual*, 112-13. Part of a long prayer. RPL
[143]Dove, *Worship Manual*, 110-11. Parts of a long prayer. RPL
[144]Membership role of those destined to live on the promised land in the future.
[145]Equip the Messiah for the war with the Gentiles necessary to recover the land.
[146]Dove, *Worship Manual*, 108.   RPL
[147]Dt 10:16; Jer 4:4. Just as circumcision distinguished the body of Jewish males from Gentile males, so the heart obedient to the Lord was distinguished from the Gentile heart.

Remove us from pain. Fatten us in the pastures of your land.[148] Gather our scattered ones from the four corners of the earth. Let those who you know are erring be judged, and let your hand wave over the wicked.[149] But let the righteous rejoice in the building of your city and in the construction of your temple and in the shooting forth of a horn belonging to your servant David and in the lighting of a candle for your Messiah, the son of Jesse. Answer before we call. Blessed are you, O Lord, hearing prayer.

SALVATION AND LIFE IN JERUSALEM[150]

Our God and the God of our fathers, may our remembrance, our pledge, the remembrance of our fathers, the remembrance of your servant, the son of David, the Messiah, the remembrance of your holy city, Jerusalem, and the remembrance of all your people, the house of Israel arise, come, arrive, be seen, desired, heard, visited, and remembered before you for escape, goodness, favor, kindness, mercy, life, and peace on this feast of [Unleavened Bread, Shavuoth, Succoth].

Remember us, O Lord, our God, on it for goodness; visit us on it for blessing; deliver us on it for life;[151] and with a promise of salvation and mercy, spare and favor us; have mercy upon us; and deliver us. For our eyes [are turned] toward you, for you are God, a King [who is] gracious and merciful.

RESTORATION AND JUBILEE[152]

Sound the great trumpet (Isa 27:13), [declaring] our freedom; *raise a flag* (Isa 13:2) to gather our exiles; gather us together from the four corners of the earth. Blessed are you, O Lord, our God, gathering the refugees of your people, the Israelites.

Restore our judges as at first, and our counsellors as in the beginning.

---

[148]The promised land.

[149]The way Moses raised his hand and wand over the enemies so that they perished in the battle against the Israelites (Ex 17:9-13).

[150]Dove, *Worship Manual*, 99, 263, 302, 387-88, 348, 411. RPL

[151]I.e., give us back the promised land, and let us live there. See *Consequences*, 120-31.

[152]Dove, *Worship Manual*, 92-93. RPL

Turn away from us grief and sighing.
Rule over us in loving kindness and mercy, you alone, O
    Lord,
and vindicate us in judgment.
Blessed are you, O Lord, King, loving righteousness and
    justice.

ELECTION AND SALVATION[153]

Bring us for peace from the four corners of the earth; and lead us
upright to our land, for you are a God accomplishing salvation,
you have chosen us from every people and language, and you
brought us near for your great Name.

COMFORT FOR JERUSALEM
Judah Halevy[154]

א)   Let your heart take courage and wait your appointed season.
      Why do you calculate the end time and become alarmed"

ה)   Strengthen yourself; speak and *compose a poem* (Jdgs 5:12,
      for *Oholibah* (Ezek 23:4) is your name, and in you is my
         tent.[155]

ו)   Mock the word of scorners, even if they roar
      against you. Slowly lead your flock.

ז)   Your beloved will answer you; he is the one to answer you.
      He is *the balm for* the *pain* (Jer 51:8), and he is the grief.

ה)   Perform your loving kindness well in your hope of your
      redeemer.
      Do not tremble (Dt 20:3). Behold, the splendor of my work!
      Say to those who boast of king and general,
      "My king is the holy One of Jacob, the Rock of my redeemer!"

Introduction to Mordecai Ben Shabbethai

Rabbi Mordecai Ben Shabbethai is known mostly for his
liturgical poetry. He lived from about A.D. 1140 to about 1240

[153]Dove, *Worship Manual*, 80-81. RPL
[154]H. Brody, *Diwan des Abu-l-Hasan Jehuda ha-Levi* (England, 1971), II, 248. RPL
[155]This is a play on words: *Oholi* means "my tent." *bah* means "in it."

as a citizen either of Greece or Italy. His penitential prayers are his best loved poetry.[156]

THE MYSTERY
Mordecai Ben Shabbethai[157]

My soul has dwelled too long in the tents of Kedar and the
    Ishmaelites.[158]
My day goes down (Jdgs 19:11)[159] and turns; my light darkens,
    and the shadows flee.
The end of the exile is unknown; my *vision is sealed* (Dan 12:4);
    the Lord has hidden [it]
from me. He has not told me (II Kgs 4:27).

I asked my prophets and my seers who prophesy because of me,
"Do you know *when the wondrous end will be* (Dan 12:6) in
    which he set to redeem me?"
They answer me, *Why do you ask this? It is mysterious* (Jdgs
    13:18), and they do not tell me.
It is a mystery to me; *it is a mystery* to me; woe to me!

DREAMS
Judah Halevy[160]

You dozed, slept, and arose frightened.
What is the dream you dreamed (Gen 37:10)?
Perhaps your dream showed you your enemy,
that he was poor and humbled, and you were exalted?
Tell the son of Hagar: "Add to the hand of pride
from the son of your lady whom you angered!"
I have seen low estate and desolation in the dream.
Perhaps when I arise, thus already you have laid waste,
and [in] the year *tetatz* (חתץ =A.D. 1130) all your pride will be
    broken (*tutatz*- חותץ).[161]

---

[156]J.Z. Lauterbach, "Mordecai B. Shabbethai," *JE*, IX, 15.
[157]Brody and Wiener, *Choice Hebrew Hymns*, 275. Stanzas 7 and 8 of 15 stanzas.   RPL
[158]Ishmaelites or sons of Kedar are Moslems.
[159]The day passes.
[160]Brody, *Diwan*, II [86], 302.   RPL
[161]In *gematria*, חתץ =890. A.D. 240+890=A.D. 1130, the day Moslems will be crushed.

You will be ashamed and embarrassed from [that which] you
    schemed.
Is that you who are called *a mouth speaking great things*
    (Dan 7:8, 20)?
You who fought in the sanctuary of my dwelling?
You who are now *miry clay with feet of iron* (Dan 2:43)?[162]
You who have come to the end—will you be exalted?
Perhaps God will strike you with a stone (Ps 91:12) which wipes
out the image and will pay you back that which you advanced
    (Dan 2:34-35)!

Summary of The Voice of an Exiled People

Objectively, life for the Jews in the Middle Ages was not very
bad, if they could have been happy in the diaspora. There they
were upper class people who were the envy of the Christians and
Moslems. Had their religion not required them to be dissatisfied in
the diaspora and interpreted this existence as prison, captivity,
and poverty, there might have been few problems. They believed,
however, that they were destined to rule all the world in which
they lived. Against this lofty goal, their lives seemed miserable.
They considered the rulers of the governments in which they lived
as unjust usurpers and enemies, so it was difficult to maintain
good relationships with them. The longings and complaints
expressed in this section of poems and prayers show their
subjective understanding of their condition. The next section will
show their messianic expectations for deliverance and redemption.

---

[162]Halevy's dream comes in the form of scripture he wanted fulfilled, namely the end of
the fourth kingdom which had to totter before the saints of the Most High could reign
supreme. The statue with the feet of pottery and iron was the fourth and weakest. It was led
by Antiochus IV, the mouth speaking great things. This would happen, he believed, in the
year A.D. 1130.

MESSIANIC EXPECTATIONS

ZION AND THE MESSIAH
Solomon Ibn Gabirol[1]

Peace to you my beloved, the white and the crimson.
Peace to you from Rakkah as Rimmon.[2]
Run to meet your sister; go, please, to save her.
Break out with the son of Jesse [against] Rabbah[3] of the
    Ammonites.
What's wrong with you, [my] beauty? Stir yourself, [my] love,
and let your voice ring like a dress with a sound of bells.
The time for which you long, love, I will hasten to bring now.
I will descend upon you *like the dew of Hermon* (Ps 133:3).
Let God restore his temple on his dwelling.
Nobody seeks my peace, and my enemy devises evil.
Like a deaf adder (Ps 58:4),
an enemy pierces my liver, and now I am wretched.
A man of violence my lover has sent to his *garden* (SS 4:12, 16).
Zion, why do you weep, for *look! my king comes* (Zech 9:9).
God will swiftly lighten my darkness for his own sake,
will send the root of Jesse, and he will build my sanctuary.
Peoples *will bring gifts* (Isa 18:7) to build it.
He will redeem Israel from Ammon[4] and from Ishmael.[5]
Those who wait for the redeemer, his trustworthy one.

THE MESSIAHS OF JOSEPH AND DAVID
Author Unknown[6]

God has completed [this gift][7]
[for Noah, Shem, Abraham, Isaac, and][7] Israel,

[1]David De Sola Pool, *Prayers for the Festivals* (New York, 1947), 121-22. RPL
[2]Rimmon is a location near Gibeah (Jdgs 20:45-47) and Rakkah is probably Tiberias in Galilee (Meg 6a). See "Book of Zerubbabel" BL 3:8.
[3]Rabbah here means the Christians, probably on the basis of Ezek 25 where both the Edomites and the Ammonites come under condemnation for the same behavior at the time Jerusalem fell. Since Edom continued to be the epitomy of Evil to Jews since then and since Christians and Romans were equated with Edomites, Gabirol felt free to apply the name Ammon to the Christians as well. Rabbah was the capital city of Ammon.
[4]The Christians.
[5]The Moslems.
[6]Hebrew text from I. Levi, "L'Apocalypse de Zorobabel et le Roi de Parse Siroes," *REJ*, 71 (1920), 61-63.
[7]Following Ibn Shmuel, *Redemption*, 108, who filled in the lacunae to the best of his ability.

for Judah, Moses [and Aaron, priest of God],[7]
and that which sprouted [in the tent of witness of God]...[7]

[And I asked him to speak to me][7] in the name of God,
and he said [to me: "Listen to me, and I will tell you the word of
     God:][7]
In the Fifth year [M]enahem son of Am[iel] [will come],[7]
and he will say, 'I [am the M]essiah, son of Joseph, son of Israel!'
He will shake [the ends of] the earth with the word of God.[8]
[With him][9] will be myriads of [Eph]raimites, called of God
[and also][10] thousands of [men from] Manasseh whom God has
     chosen,[11]
and all Israel will go up to Jerusalem and be gathered to him,
and he will offer a sacrifice, and it will be pleasing to God.
All Israel will be united to their tribes.
Then Armilos[12] will come and stab Menahem son of Amiel,
but the Messiah will come and revive him by the word of God,
and all Israel [will say][13] to him,
'Who will give salvation to Israel from Zion?'
He will say to all Israel,
'I am the Messiah, son of David, son of Judah, son of Israel;
I am the one whom God has raised up;
I am called "redeemer." Jacob will rejoice;
[and Israel will be glad]; and all the Gentiles
will be as if they were not..."'

THE COMFORT OF MENAHEM

Eleazar Kallir[14]

א) *I will be comforted*   From where to be comforted?
               You will comfort mourners.
א) *Then* with seven shepherds

[7]Following Ibn Shmuel, *Redemption,* 108, who filled in the lacunae to the best of his
ability.
[8]The text has the abbreviation for "he says to him" (איי׳ל) which I have translated as if it
were the word "God," rather than an abbreviation.
[9]Accepting Ibn Shmuel's correction, exchanging ועמו for והם
[10]Accepting Ibn Shmuel's correction of וגם for והם
[11]Levi filled in the lacunas of this line and the one preceding with the aid of *Pirke de Rabbi
Eliezer,* chapter 10, page 19.
[12]A variant text reads Harmilos (הרמילוס)
[13]Following Ibn Shmuel's correction, exchanging יאמרו for יאמינו
[14]מחזור מנהג רומא קמחא דאבישונא (Bologna, 1540), II, 196a-196b. I. Davidson,
אוצר השירה והפיוט (New York, 1924), I, 308 [6785] ascribes it to Kallir.

            (Micah 5:5),   brothers and friends,
            to provide pleasant comforts.

ב) *With seven*[15] *and eight*[16]   you will see *[from Amana]*
                                    (SS 4:8),
            eight princes (Micah 5:4)

ב) *with* them. How will I be
            comforted?   but I will not be comforted
            until Menahem comes.

ג) My *undeveloped form*, the
            coming distress   will distress him very much,
            for he cut his bed short.

ג) *Exile* will not consume him; he was treacherous, and he
                                      ate,[17]
            but how will the temple be comforted?

ד) It *is silent* and discouraged.   He will clap his hand to hand,
            for his head is bowed.

ד) *Sanctuary*, how will it be
            comforted?   I will not be comforted,
            until Menahem comes,

ה) *He waits* three hundred   Methusaleh to see
            the coming opposition,

ה) *united* in days   with a righteous and perfect
                                      man[18]
            to perfect the generations.[19]

ו) *And* from the spirit he will
            not judge.   Fearful, he will keep still.
            How will the footstool[20] be comforted?

ו) *But* how will he comfort me? I will not be comforted
            until Menahem comes.

ז) Melchizedek *plans*   forever righteousness,
            justice, and righteousness.[21]

ז) He brings out *a gift* and
            set in order   the table. He acts valiantly,[22]

[15]Micah 5:4: Seven shepherds are Adam, Seth, Methuselah, Abraham, Jacob, Moses, and David, according to Rab Hai Gaon, "The Subject of Salvation."

[16]Micah 5:4: Eight princes are Jesse, Saul, Samuel, Amos, Zephaniah, Hezekiah, Elijah, and the Messiah, according to Rab Hai Gaon, "The Subject of Salvation."

[17]Esau ate the meal he bought from Jacob with his birthright (Gen 25:29-34).

[18]Abraham.

[19]Probably through his merits in the treasury of merits.

[20]The temple (I Chron 28:2; Ps 99:5; 132:7; Isa 66:1; Lam 2:1; II Esdras 6:4; Makkoth 24b; Mt 5:35).

[21]The word "Melchizedek" means "king of righteousness."

[22]Melchizedek brought out bread and wine to serve Abraham, and he blessed Abraham (Gen 14:18-20).

pronouncing a benediction.

ח) This *month* he will fulfill
   the priestly law.   He is a priest to God,
   testing the hearts.[23]

ח) *Hannah,* how will he be comforted?   I will not be comforted
   until Menahem comes.

ט) He will stir up *goodness* and
   justice.   He will stir up from the east
   and pray for the city.[24]

ט) *The provision* of my host   thirteen months
   the covenant of Ezraḥi (Ps 89:1-3).

י) *He will fear the name*
   (Gen 22:12).   He will appear and call.[25]
   The mountain will return and consider.[26]

י) My *grief,* how will it be
   comforted?   I will not be comforted
   until Menahem comes.

כ) *When* the sun set, he slept.   Take from the stones of
                                          the hall
   twelve [steps of a] *ladder* (Gen 28:12).

כ) *Like* a vision, *going up*
   and coming down   leaves of nard,
   the fear of those *going down* (oppressors) (Gen
   28:12).

ל) *For* salvation he hopes,   finality and hope
   in the name of God is expected.

ל) *Lebanon,*[27] how will it be
   comforted?   It will not be comforted
   until Menahem comes.

מ) *He says,* "Send, please;   be gracious and forgive, please;
   and if I have no grace, please

[23]God was expected to set up his throne for judgment and open the books on New Year's Day and postpone his final verdict until the Day of Atonement, allowing the intervening days for repentance. At this time he would test the hearts of the covenanters. Kallir may have known of a tradition, now familiar from 11Q Melch. that Melchizedek was to come at the end of days, at the last jubilee, and proclaim release for the captives, and atonement for their sins. This would be the appointed time of favor of Melchizedek, fulfilling Isa 52:7 and 61:1-2. It is "this month" about which Kallir spoke.

[24]Abraham praying for Sodom (Gen 18:23-32).

[25]The angel at Mount Moriah, calling to Abraham (Gen 22:11-12).

[26]Mount Moria.

[27]Rabbis called the temple "Lebanon," since it was the place where Frankincense *(Labona)* was offered.

נ) *decrease* the wrath   from me, a wall
   to see the comfort."

ס) *At last* a man from Bethlehem, with *a shoot* (Isa 11:1), a re-
    deemer to comfort,
   from its roots as a stitch to be comforted.

ס) *They nurture* me with raisin
   cake   bread for my man,
   the trunk of Jesse.

ע) His *city,* a prisoner,   to whistle good news,
   the feet of one proclaiming good news (Isa 52:7).

ע) His *people,* then he will
   comfort.   The merciful One will say
   through Menahem,

פ) *"Turn* the powers   of gifts and libations,
   eight princes" (Micah 5:4).

פ) A choice and good *blossom,* the son of Kish,[28] proclaiming
    good news
   to comfort the good mountain,[29]

צ) *crying out* with Mizpah[30] like a firm one prepared,
   a watcher of the vision of salvation but still not
    appointed.

צ) *Zion* will be comforted. She will arise [and] receive
    mercy at the hands of
    Menahem.
   At once they will arise from the land.

ק) The *end* of the day of hiding,[31] the trampling to tread
   with the shepherds of Amos (Amos 1:1).

[28]The Messiah of Ephraim or Joseph was to come from Saul's kingdom or North Israel. Jews, from the time of the Babylonian captivity, dreamed of a reunification of North Israel to Judah, of course, under Judah's rule. Here the dream is for the people of Ephraim or Manassah (both from North Israel or Samaria) to run interference for the Jews by initiating the first conflict with the Romans. Afterwards the main Messiah son of David from Judah would be victorious and would rule from Jerusalem, with the Messiah of Ephraim as a subordinate officer. Jewish literature of the Middle Ages preserves many instances of the assumption of the Messiah of Joseph preceding the Messiah of David, but Kallir identified the Messiah of Ephraim with Saul of Gibeah. This is a further basis for determining the future by the past. That which was is that which will be. Just as Saul ran interference for David, so the son of Kish (Saul) would run interference for the son of David in the end of days.

[29]Zion.

[30]Samuel cried out at Mizpah to the Lord to save the Israelites gathered there from the Philistines who were about to attack. Then the Lord thundered against the Philistines, threw them into confusion, and the Israelites defeated them in battle (I Sam 7:5-11).

[31]Traditionally, the Messiah of David was believed to be in hiding and to have been so from the time of creation, the time of David, or at least from the fall of Jerusalem (A.D. 70). At the appointed time he would come out of hiding and lead the Israelites against Rome. Before that time he would not be recognized, even if seen.

ק) *A voice* among the shepherds,   "Draw near and advance;
     turn east."

ו) *A song*, alas, the fear   Zephaniah saw,
     Rejoice and shout! (Zeph 3:14).

ר) You will surely have *mercy*.   Zion will be comforted
     through Menahem.

ש) *"Return, return* (SS 7:1);   Pay us to restore
     the shoot and the Tishbite.[32]

ש) His *name* is Abiad,   the seven appointed,
     prepared and established

ת) to request *comforts*,   *the cup of salvation* (Ps 116:13),
     to lay down *four craftsmen* (Zech 2:3).

ת) *Return* [and] receive money.   Zion will be comforted
     through Menahem [the comforter].

JERUSALEM AND THE REDEEMER
Author Unknown[33]

Holy One of Israel, build Jerusalem![34]
Send us a redeemer, the proclaimer of good news.[35]
Pity the unpitied one, O holy One dwelling in the heavens.
Say to Zion, "Arise, and *turn the hearts of the sons to the fathers*"
     (Mal 3:24).

Send [out] your light and your truth (Ps 43:3),[36] the Levites with
     your song,
the priests for your service of liturgy, with sacrifice and offerings.
Who can express your praise? About you there is no adequate
     praise.
Please deliver us from the oppressor, and let us worship you as in
     the years of old.

From distortions and distractions, turn every heart away.

[32]The "shoot" is the Messiah (Zech 3:8; 6:12), and Elijah is the Tishbite (Mal 3:1).

[33]Dove, *Worship Manual*, xx. RPL

[34]The text reads "Ariel.".

[35]As in the Melchizedek Scroll (11 Q Melch.), the Messiah in this poem was expected to announce the good news that the kingdom was to be restored and also to "redeem" the Israelites by driving out the Gentiles. In other literature, Elijah announced the good news, and the Davidic Messiah was to bring it about. Not all expectations were in agreement on details, but they all involved the restoration of the land.

[36]Light and truth were supposed to originate from Jerusalem, in Jewish judgment: *From Zion shall go forth the law, and the word of the Lord, from Jerusalem* (Micah 4:2).

Accept and beautify all the deeds which they do before you
          sincerely.
Sons of the perfect ones[37] seek refuge in you. Strengthen them
          before the eyes of all.
Place honor and a crown on the head of your Messiah, and exalt
          his throne for [his] session.

JERUSALEM AND THE HORN OF SALVATION

Author Unknown[38]

Return to your city, Jerusalem, in mercy;
dwell in its midst, as you have promised;
construct her [as] a building for the age, soon, in our days;
and establish the throne of David in her midst, quickly.
Blessed are you, O Lord, Builder of Jerusalem.

Send forth *the shoot*, David, your servant, quickly (Zech 3:8;
          6:12).
Raise his *horn* in your *salvation* (Ps 18:3; Lk 1:69),[39]
for we have hoped for your salvation all the day.
Blessed are you, O Lord, sending forth *the horn of salvation*
          (Ps 18:3).

THE HIDDEN MESSIAH

Solomon Ibn Gabirol[40]

Lying on golden beds in my palace,
when, Lord, will you prepare for the red-haired one?[41]
Why, dear gazelle,[42] do you sleep, as the dawn
ascends like a flag on the top of Tabor and Hermon?

---

[37]The patriarchs: Abraham, Isaac, and Jacob.
[38]Dove, *Worship Manual*, 96-97, 302. RPL
[39]This seems to reflect "The Magnificat" (Lk 1:69) more than any OT passage. The "horn" was used metaphorically for a ram's horn, used to attack opponents and defend the herd. In Jewish literature a horn sometimes referred to weapons, but more often to a military leader or king who used weapons (Dan 7:7-8). Here the horn of salvation is the shoot (Zech 3:8; 6:12) of David, the Messiah, who would overthrow the Gentiles and provide salvation for the Jews on the promised land.
[40]Zangwill, *Selected Religious Poems*, 6. RPL
[41]David.
[42]The Messiah.

From the wild asses (Gen 16:2),[43] he turns and reaches out to the
graceful doe.[44]
Here I am like you, and also you are like me.
He who comes into my palace will find my treasure—
juice, pomegranite, myrrh, and cinnamon.

JOY AND THE MESSIAH
Author Unknown[45]

The Messiah, son of David, our justice,
hasten quickly for our redemption.
Please spread your peace over us;
establish your holy sanctuary for us
Daily our help is in you;
Make us happy [with] the joy of the ages.

THE MESSIAH AND LIFE IN THE AGE TO COME[46]

Blessed be our God who has created us for his glory, separated
us from erring ones, given us the true Torah, and planted in our
midst for the life of the age. May he open our hearts by means of
his Torah and place his love and his fear in our hearts to do his will
and to serve him wholeheartedly. We strive in vain and labor in
confusion. May it be your will, O Lord, our God, and the God of
our fathers, that we may keep your statutes in this world and may
merit life and inherit prosperity and blessing for the years of the
days of the Messiah and for the life in the age to come.[47]

[43]Ishmael. Here it refers to his descendants, the Moslems.
[44]Jerusalem.
[45]Dove, *Worship Manual*, xviii. RPL
[46]Dove, *Worship Manual*, 128-29. RPL
[47]Sometimes the days of the Messiah were considered coterminous with the age to come.
More often, however, the days of the Messiah were considered those in which the Messiah
appeared and through a period of tribulation and military conflict, overthrew the Gentiles
and established a period of "rest" from Israel's enemies, while the Messiah would rule from
Jerusalem. This period of "rest" and world dominion was "the age to come." In this prayer,
the Jews who were worshipping hoped only to live to a ripe old age of prosperity on the
land, through the messianic age into the next age, the age to come, not forever.

THE MESSIAH AND LIFE IN THE AGE TO COME[48]

There is no one apart from you, our King, for life in the age to come, none but you to redeem us in the days of the Messiah.

GOOD NEWS OF THE MESSIAH[49]

Make us happy, O Lord, our God, with your servant the prophet Elijah and with the kingdom of the house of David, your Messiah. Let him come quickly to gladden our hearts. On his throne, let no stranger sit, and let no others inherit his glory anymore, for you have sworn to him by your holy name that his light would not be quenched for ages on end. Blessed are you, O Lord, shield of David.

THE REDEEMER AND LOVINGKINDNESS[50]

Blessed are you, Our God and the God of our fathers, the God of Abraham, Isaac, and Jacob, the God [who is] great, mighty, and fearful, God most high, rewarding with good lovingkindness, Creator of everything, remembering the lovingkindness of the patriarchs, and bringing a redeemer to their offspring for the sake of his name, with love. A king, helper, savior, and shield. Blessed are you, Lord, shield of Abraham.

GLORY AND THE MESSIAH[51]

Give glory, O Lord, to your people, praise to those who fear you, hope to those who seek you, answer for those who wait for you; joy for your land, gladness for your city, a flourishing horn to your servant David, a clear light to the son of Jesse, your Messiah, quickly, in our days.

---

[48]Dove, *Worship Manual*, 211. RPL
[49]Dove, *Worship Manual*, 211. RPL
[50]Pool, *Prayers for the Festivals*, 285. RPL
[51]S. Singer, *The Daily Prayer Book* (London, 1944), 405. RPL

THE TEMPLE AND THE MESSIAH[52]

Our King and our God, the God of all flesh, make your Name unique in your world; build your city; establish your temple; complete your temple;[53] draw the end near, the coming of your Messiah; redeem your people; make your congregation happy.[54] Act for the sake of your Name; act for the sake of the angels on high; act for the sake of your right hand; act for the sake of your righteousness; act for your sake, if not for ours, so that your beloved may be delivered. May your right hand deliver us, and answer me.

Summary of Messianic Expectations

Jewish eschatology was unified. Jews were dissatisfied with the diaspora and wanted to be restored to the promised land. This could not be done without a messiah. Therefore complaints about life in captivity were mingled with messianic expectations and vice versa. The ultimate goal was gaining control of the promised land and from there exercising control over all the Gentiles. The center of this governmental dominance was Jerusalem, and many poems and prayers were directed to Jerusalem and the temple there. The most beautiful of these was Judah Halevy's "Longing for Zion."

[52]Dove, *Worship Manual*, 104. RPL

[53]This implies that the temple was still under construction, sometime between its beginning in 20 B.C. and its destruction in A.D. 70.

[54]These requests are overlapping. If God made the congregation happy, he would rebuild the city, draw the end near, reveal the Messiah, etc.

THE HOLY CITY

LONGING FOR ZION

Judah Halevy[1]

Zion, will you not ask for the peace[2] of your captives[3]
who demand[4] your peace and who are the remnant of your flocks?
From *the West, the East, the North, and the* South (Gen 28:14),
        Peace!
far and near, greet *from every side* (I Kgs 5:4) of you.
Peace for *the captive of desire* (Zech 9:12), flowing tears *like dew
of Hermon* (Ps 133:3),[5] longing to let them fall upon your
        mountains.
To weep for your affliction, I am a jackal; when I dream of
the return of your captivity, I am a harp for your songs.
My heart will throb loudly for Bethel[6] and Peniel,[7]
for Maḥannaim,[8] the meeting places of your pure ones.
There the Shekinah[9] dwells for you, and your Creator
opens your gates[10] before the gates of heaven,
and the glory[11] of the Lord alone will be your light (Isa 60:19-20).
        There will be no
sun, moon, and stars [as] your lights (Isa 60:19).

[1]Shirman, *The Hebrew Hymn* II, 485-89. RPL

[2]Greet them, "*Šhalom!*" This greeting includes a prayer: "May all your indebtedness to the treasury of merits be cancelled." See *Consequences,* 234-37.

[3]"Captives" are all Jews in the diaspora who are not free to return to the promised land, free from foreign rule, regardless of personal liberty, wealth, social status, or political prestige and influence. See *To The Hebrews,* 69-70.

[4]Not just a greeting, but an insistence that God pardon Zion.

[5]Hermon is the tallest mountain in the Golan Heights, northeast of the Sea of Galilee.

[6]The place where Jacob saw a vision of angels going up and down on a ladder to heaven, reminding him that the place where he was lying, namely the promised land, was holy ground. This was during his flight from Esau. (Gen 28:12-19).

[7]On his return to confront Esau before entering the promised land, Jacob wrestled all night at the Jabbok river and received the name "Israel." (Gen 32:24-31).

[8]The place where the army of angels met Jacob after his successful separation from the forces of Laban in his return from "captivity" to the promised land (Gen 32:1-3, 31). All three locations are centered around Jacob, Esau, the promised land, the inheritance, and angelic guidance.

[9]The visible representation of God's real presence on earth. It was seen in the column of smoke that joined earth to heaven and provided a channel through which God could descend to earth. It burned continually at the temple. See *To The Hebrews,* 157-163.

[10]Probably the Golden Gate that provided the entrance to the temple area from the Mount of Olives, the place where the Messiah was expected to appear; or Halevy may have thought of the column of smoke as a gate to heaven, like Jacob's ladder.

[11]The "pillar" of fire by night from the fire on the altar provided lots of light for the surrounding area. Without electricity, this light far overpowered the small lamps and torches used elsewhere in Jerusalem. This was known as the glory of God.

I will choose for my soul to be poured out in the place where
the spirit of God is poured out over your chosen ones.[12]
You are a royal house; you are *the throne of the Lord* (I Chron 29:23).
How can slaves[13] sit on the thrones of your mighty ones?
Who will permit me (Ps 55:8) to wander in the places where
God was revealed (Gen 35:7) to your seers and your messengers?
Who will make me wings so I may wander far off?
I would cast the broken pieces of my heart among your broken pieces!
I will fall on my face on your land; I *will be greatly pleased with
          her stones;*
I will love your *dust* (Ps 102:15).
Also when I stand at *the graves of my fathers* (Neh 2:3, 5).
I will be amazed at Hebron over your *renowned grave*
          (Gen 23:6, 19).[14]
I would go through your forest and your vineyard. I would
          stand on
your Gilead and be astonished at your Mount Abarim,
Mount Abarim (Dt 32:49, 50), *Mount Hor* (Dt 32:50), where there
          are
two *great lights* (Ps 136:6-7), your luminaries and your teachers.[15]
The life of souls, the air of your land, and from *the myrrh of
          freedom* (Ex 30:23),
the grains of your dust (SS 3:6), *the dripping of honeycomb*
          (Ps 19:11), your rivers!
It would please my soul   *to walk naked and barefoot* (Isa 20:2-3)
          over
the desolate ruins where your holiest dwellings were:[16]
in the place of the ark, which was hidden (Jer 3:16; Yoma 50b;
          52b-53b; 70b), in the place of your cherubim,
who dwelled in your innermost rooms![17]
I would cut off and throw away my hair,[18] and I would curse
the time your saints were defiled in an unclean land.
How can it please me to eat and drink, when I see

[12]The chosen people. The sentence seems to paraphrase Ps 84:10.
[13]Gentiles, destined to be slaves for Jews (Isa 61:5-10), according to Jewish understand-ing.
[14]The cave of Machpelah, where Sarah was buried.
[15]The "great lights" are the sun and the moon, but here used metaphorically, perhaps, to refer to Moses and Aaron. Aaron was buried on Mount Hor in the Wilderness of Zin (Dt 32:50-51).
[16]Where Jews are forbidden to walk for fear of stepping on the land covering the temple, ark, and other vessels. This is considered sacrilege.
[17]The holy and the holy of holies, where only priests were allowed.
[18]His "Nazirite's crown" (Num 6:5-8).

dogs[19] *dragging* your *young lions*[20] (Jer 15:3; Ezek 38:13)?
Or how can *the light* of day be *sweet to my eyes* (Eccles 11:7)
            while still
I see in the ravens' beaks[21] the corpses of your heroes?
The cup of sorrow, hold it! Let up a little, for already
my loins are filled (Ps 38:8), and my soul, *from* your *bitterness*
            (Job 9:18).
When I remember *Oholah*[22] (Ezek 23:4), I drink your wrath;
then I remember *Oholibah*[23] (Ezek 23:4), I will find your *old wine*
            (Ps 75:8).
Zion, perfectly beautiful! *You bind* love and grace [around your
            neck] (Prov 6:21) from of old.
With you are bound the souls of your *haberim.*[24]
They rejoice at your tranquility, suffer
at your desolation, and weep over your wounds;
those who, from the pit of captivity, long for you and pray
each in his place (Zeph 2:11) toward your gates.
The flocks of your multitude, who went into exile and were
            scattered
from mountain to *hill* (Jer 50:6), and they have not forgotten your
            fold (Jer 50:5).
Those who hold fast to your skirts and strengthen themselves
go up and take hold of the branches of your *palm trees* (SS 7:9).
Will Shinar and Parthia[25] compare with you in greatness?

Can they compare their vain practices to your *Thummim and
            Urim* (Neh 7:65)?
To whom will they compare your messiahs and to whom, your
            prophets?
And to whom, your Levites and your princes?
He will change *and sweep away the splendor* of all *idol-
            worshipping* kingdoms (Isa 2:18).
Your *strength is for the age, for generation after generation,* your
            crown (Prov 27:24).

[19]Gentiles.

[20]Princes.

[21]Gentiles thought of as scavangers.

[22]Samaria, which Halevy despised, since it represented the anti-Judaic capital of North
Israel.

[23]Jerusalem, which Halevy loved.

[24]*Haberim* were the Jews who tried to keep priestly purity in the diaspora when the
temple was not standing, so that there would be a place for the Lord to dwell. They treated
their hearths as altars and their homes as the temple in matters of purity.

[25]Shinar symbolizes the cultural achievements of Baghdad, the Moslem center, and
Parthia symbolized the achievements of Byzantine Christianity.

Your God *has longed for* you *as a habitation* (Ps 132:13). *Blessed
is the man whom
he chooses. He will be brought near and will dwell* in *your courts*
(Ps 65:5).
Blessed is he who waits, arrives (Dan 12:12), and sees the rising of
your light. Your dawns will break upon him
to see the prosperity of your chosen ones and to exult with
joy (Ps 106:5) in your return to your past youth.[26]

My heart is in the East, but I am at the end of the West.
How can I taste that which I eat, and how can it please me?
How can I pay my vows and obligations while still
Zion is in the snare of Edom, and I am [tied] with an Arabian
       fetter?
I would gladly abandon all the benefits of Spain, just as
I value highly the privilege of seeing the dust of the destroyed
       sanctuary!

Beautiful view! (Ps 48:3) joy of the world! city of the great king!
My soul longs for (Ps 84:3) you from the corners of the West.
My deep *affection is kindled* (Gen 43:30) when I remember times
       past
your glory which went into exile, and your dwelling which was
       destroyed.
Who will permit me on the wings of eagles [to fly] (Ps 55:7) until
I irrigate with my tears (Isa 16:9) your dust and let them mingle?
I have demanded you, and even if your king is not in you, and
       even if in the place
of the balm of Gilead (Jer 8:22) there is a serpent, a snake, and
       also a scorpion,
I will desire your stones and kiss them.
The taste of your clods will please me more than honey.

Introduction to Solomon Ben Isaac Gerundi

Gerundi was a Hebrew poet and relative of Moses Naḥmanides.
He lived in Gerona, Catalonia in the second half of the thirteenth
century. See further A. Brody, "Gerondi, Moses B. Solomon
D'Escola," *Jewish Encyclopedia* V, 638.

---

[26]Before Jerusalem and the temple had been destroyed.
[27]Shirman, *The Hebrew Hymn,* III, 326-28. RPL

JERUSALEM IN LAMENTATION
Solomon Ben Isaac Gerundi[27]

You are drunk, but not from wine (Isa 51:21). Throw out your
timbrels!
Shave [your head]; cut [your hair] (Micah 1:16); and bow your
head!
Raise a lamentation *upon the bare heights* (Isa 41:18), and wander
in every direction.
Cry aloud before the Lord for the destruction of your thresholds;
for the life of your infants, raise your hands to him!

How has the oppressor and enemy come against Zion, the city of
dominion?
How did the foot of the impudent[28] step on the holy ground?
When they entered, they found priests, guardians of the order.
They stood at their watches; and they did not leave their tasks[29]
until their blood was poured out like the waters of the flood.
The uncircumcised and defiled people entered *beyond the curtain*
(Num 18:7),[30]
the place where the high priest is afraid to walk.[31]
He destroyed your *planks* (Ezek 41:16) and *the lattice-worked
windows* (I Kgs 6:4).

The voice of wailing of the daughter of Zion is heard from a
distance.
Cry aloud, *Heshbon* (Jer 48:34);[32] weep bitterly, *Mephaath*
(Jer 48:21);[33]
"Ah, for I *have drunk the cup and drained the dregs* (Isa 51:17).
Lions have devoured me, *sharp teeth* (Job 41:22) of a grinder.
Daughter of Babylon,[34] *who is to be destroyed* (Ps 137:8); wicked
daughter of Edom" (Lam 4:21).

---

[27]Shirman, *The Hebrew Hymn* III, 326-28. RPL
[28]The Roman soldiers who captured Jerusalem in A.D. 70 and destroyed the temple.
[29]See also Josephus *BJ.* VI [277-300].
[30]The curtain that separated the holy from the holy of holies.
[31]For fear of being consumed by the fire the way the sons of Aaron had been (Lev 10:1-2;
Yoma 5:1; Lk 1:21-22).
[32]Because of the destruction that was destined to come upon her.
[33]Because of the destruction that was destined to come upon her and all Ammon.
[34]Here meaning the Romans in parallel with the following clause bearing the expression
"daughter of Edom."

How do you complain, Zion, when your sin is known?
Because of the multitude of your iniquities, he exiled your
    ignorant people.
Because you disobeyed your watchmen[35] and listened to the voice
    of your idols.

Do not rejoice, my enemy, about the crushing of my horn.
For I have fallen; I will rise, and the Lord will help me!
Behold my God who scattered me will gather me.
My Rock who sold me will redeem me from you,
for the cup which passed to me will pass to you.
Then, *in the clefts* of your rocks, I will *smash your* little ones *to
    pieces* (Ps 137:9).

THE HOUSE OF GOD
Judah Halevy[36]

I will come to you with my eyes toward your residence,
with my heart leaning on you, drawing it to your will.
A stranger and a sojourner in *your tent* (Lev 25:35) to find favor
    in your eyes,
I have brought it to you and presented it before you.
You have pursued me hotly (Gen 31:36), and I pursue hotly after
    you.
So that I might be near you, I have moved far from my relatives.
I go out at your heels, swift, and do not restrain myself.
Those who forsake you were outraged against me, but I held fast
    to you.
I take refuge in the shadow of your dwelling, to glisten *in the light
    of your face* (Ps 89:16).

One day on the ground of God *is better than a thousand* on alien
    ground (Ps 84:11).
More treasured are the ruins *of the Mount of God* (Ezek 43:15)
    than the palace of any prince.
For in these I will be redeemed, and in this I will serve a merciless
    one.
You only I ask, and without you I receive no help.
[There is] strength in your right arm and protection for those who
    believe in you.

[35]The prophets.
[36]Shirman, *The Hebrew Hymn* II, 490-91. RPL

My soul *is like a drought* (כחרב) *in the hot wilderness* (בצי ון)
    (Isa 25:5), [longing] for the dew of Horeb (חרב) and
        Zion (ציון).
My secret, the secret of the Most High, is to travel to Lebanon and
    Sirion (Dt 3:9).
My eyes, like the eyes of a poor man, [long] to see *the Valley of
    Vision* (Isa 22:1).
My face [is turned] to Hebion,[37] the place of the tablets of
    revelation,
bundles hidden in your ark *around your table* (Ps 128:3)

calling for light and turning away darkness before morning.
Enough of the profanation of your Name in the mouth of one who
    speaks lies!
The Name by which we are praised we are wounded and stabbed.
You will sell *something precious* to *a despised one* (Jer 15:19),
        the precious sons of Zion;
for the sons are yours, and the flock is yours.

MY DREAM

Judah Halevy[38]

My God, *Your dwellings are lovely* (Ps 84:1)!
Your nearness in vision *is not in riddles* (Num 12:8).
My dream brought me *to the sanctuary of God* (Ps 73:17).[39]
I performed his precious ministry:[40]
the burnt-offering, the meal-offering, and the drink-offering
    (Num 29:16).
Round about is a column of heavy smoke.
I was pleased when I heard the singing of the Levites
in their assembly for the order of the services.
I rose up, O God, and I was still with you (Ps 139:18).[41]
I gave thanks, and it was pleasant to praise you.

---

[37]Traditionally, the place where the ark is hidden.
[38]From the Hebrew text of N. Salaman, *Selected Poems of Jehudah Halevi* (Philadelphia, 1924), 9. RPL
[39]In his dream, he was transported to the temple area in Jerusalem.
[40]In his dream, he functioned as a priest before the altar.
[41]He awakened from his dream. He was not really in Jerusalem, but he was still with God, so he gave thanks for the pleasant dream.

JERUSALEM
Judah Elharizi[42]

Heyman, the Ezrahite (Ps 88:1) said:
I traveled from the land of *Nof* (Isa 19:13)[43] to *the beautiful Nof* (Ps 48:3).[44]
The time made me wander; *it circled and turned* (Isa 22:18).
I said to my friend,
"You have *lain* long enough *among the sheep folds* (Jdgs 5:16),
sitting between *the oven and the stoves* (Lev 11:35)![45]
I will bring you up from the affliction of Egypt (Ex 3:17)
to see the goodness of Jerusalem.
I will set my *striving* (Hab 1:9) to the Lord's mountain,[46]
the city which the Lord chose (Dt 12:5),
where of old the just and virtuous dwelled,
seeing the face of the king, those who sat first in the kingdom (Est 1:14).
When I came to her borders, and I saw her palaces,
I kissed her ruins, and *embraced her dust* (Ps 102:15).
I said, *"How good are your tents,*
Mount Zion, *and your dwellings* (Num 24:5).
How pleasant are your lands and your residences!
I will [willingly] die, now that I have seen your face."
Then I *raised* my *parable, and said:*

My soul has emigrated from Spain to Zion.[47]
From *the depths* (Ps 69:3) it has ascended to the clouds.
She rejoiced (Zech 9:9) greatly the day she saw the Mountain of God.
It was the day for which she had always longed.
How much the *hasidim* longed to see [it] but were not permitted (Mt 13:16-17; Heb 11:39-40).
But she is sinful. How did she merit [this privilege]?
The Rock *made* her body *strong* (Isa 58:11) in Zion.

[42]Shirman, *The Hebrew Hymn* III, 170-75. RPL d. A.D. 1235.
[43]Nof is a city in Egypt.
[44]Nof also means "view," and here it refers to the beautiful view of Jerusalem.
[45]This is an allusion to those who did not come out at once to help Barak and Deborah fight the Philistines at the time of crisis. The oven and stoves may symbolize the Christians and the Moslems among whom Jews were living in the Diaspora.
[46]Jerusalem.
[47]Elharizi was evidently alluding to Nof, Egypt, metaphorically in the second line to refer to the exile and captivity generally. Here he speaks of Spain.

After she had weakened, her vigor had vanished and her eyes had
        grown dim
in the far West, she was considered dead
until she revived in the city of the Lord, in Zion.
Zion, which many governments have honored,
but no human eye has seen [anything] like her splendor.
I do not know if the heavens bent down before her,
or if she ascended beyond the heavens.[46]
The city in which the Shekinah dwells
and whose glory is revealed to the eyes of men, [and]
whose spirit falls upon children,
answers before they call for prophecy.
The eye which has not seen the brightness of her form
does not lack darkness, but has not seen light.
She is beautiful, even if she is left stripped naked of splendor.[49]
Without ornaments *the graceful ibex* (Prov 5:19) is [still] lovely!
Has not the eye with the heat of my heart for its sighing
drawn from the falling water of tears?
Where is the Shekinah of God, and where is his brilliance?
At noon, how has the precious sun waned?
The height of incense (SS 4:6),[50] how she has fallen to the depths
after she had risen above the exalted peaks!
Her council left the treasured dwellings,
because she did not obey the decree of the Rock, her Creator.
She abandoned *the companion of her youth* (Jer 3:4), but
she loved somebody else and roved after him.
A jealous spirit passed over him.[51] (Num 5:14).
He made her *drink the bitter, cursed waters of an adulteress*
        (Num 5:24).
She became a curse in the midst of her people (Num 5:28),
until *her thigh fell* quickly, *and her womb swelled* (Num 5:22).[52]
She hopes to be purified with the waters of exile.

[46]Some high mountains are usually in the clouds, with their peaks out of sight. On cloudy days, lower hills are covered with clouds as well. Sometimes Mount Tabor, for instance, is surrounded by clouds. At such times, ancient men believed that the God of Heavens "lowered" the heavens so that he could be personally present on the mountain top. This is the importance of clouds in theophanies, such as Sinai, The Mount of Transfiguration, and the appearance of the one like a son of man coming with the clouds before the Ancient of Days. See further *To The Hebrews*, 157-62.

[49]Cities were often personified as women, and when destroyed, as if a woman had been stripped of her clothing and left embarrassed (Ps 137:7; Lam 4:21-22; Nah 3:5-7).

[50]This refers to Jerusalem. Rabbis interpreted all the references to "Lebanon" in Deuteronomy to mean Jerusalem, the place where *labonah* (incense) was offered.

[51]He suspected his wife of adultery.

[52]When tested for her faithfulness, she had an abortion, testifying to her guilt.

Until now she has not become pure; she is still not clean.
It has now been one thousand, one hundred,
forty-eight [years] that she has been exiled from her home.[53]
She is separated from the midst of her residence in Zion.
Until now, Zion has been expiating for her sabbatical years
          (Lev 26:34).
She is awaiting the time of favor, but her eyes, from waiting,
have grown dim, and her soul is consumed from yearning.
She weeps when she sees a congregation of strangers[54] which
goes up to the house of God, but she cannot go up.
The arm of God is not *shortened* [that he cannot] save her (Isa 50:2)
and gather his people again, restoring the favored ones to the house.
The Rock will still restore her to the bridal carriage, and again
she will return to freshness[55] after she has become worn out!
When I had completed arranging the fruit of my waiting,
the grace of my standard prayer (Job 41:4),
before my King,
I stood up from bowing on my knees to run to and fro in the city.
The fire of sighing burns my ribs,
and the scathing grief burns the ribs,
and my eyes flounder in tears.
I will lift up my eyes (Ps 121:1), and I will see the place of the sanc-
          tuary and the court,
from where our iniquities removed the pure lamp,[56]
and a foreign fire has burned in its place.
While I was still walking with my soul longing,
and tears dropping
like a river rushing,
I saw across from me a man from among the citizens of the city,
          who said to me,
"I think that you are from the outer edge of the exile
and from foreign lands."
I said, "Yes, indeed, and now I wish to ask something of you."
He said, "Here I am.
Ask, and I will answer!"
I said to him, "When did the Jews come to this city?"

---

[53]1,148 + 68 A.D. = 1216. The date has been calculated from the destruction of Jerusalem, which many Jews date at A.D. 68.

[54]Moslems who had been in charge of the temple area since the Battle of Ḥittim A.D. 1187.

[55]To marital enjoyment.

[56]The fire burning in the temple, signifying the real presence (the Shekinah).

He said, "From the day the Ishmaelites[57] captured it,
Israelites inhabited it."
I said, "Then why do they not [still] inhabit it, when it is in the
hands of the uncircumcised?"
He said, "Because they have said that we killed their God,[58]
and we have disgraced them. If they find us in its [the city's]
                        midst, then
they would devour us alive.[59]
If we made sacrifices that were abominable to them, would they
                        not stone us?"
I said, "Then why did you come to this place?"
He said, "Because God is jealous for his Name,
and he might pity his people," and he said [further],
"It is not good that the sons of Esau are heirs of my holy temple
while the sons of Jacob are separated,[60]
lest the Gentiles say with zeal,
God has abandoned his first born son in hatred
and exalted the son of the divorced woman[61] above the [son of the]
                        married woman,[62]
and he cannot prefer the son of the beloved over the son of the
                        hated woman.'
Then God will stir the spirit of the king of the Ishmaelites, in the
year four thousand, nine hundred, fifty of creation (A.D. 1190).[63]
The spirit of counsel and might will rest upon him (Isa 11:2).
He and all of his troops will go up from Egypt
and besiege Jerusalem.
Jehovah will give it into his hand, and he will command a voice[64]
                        to pass through every city,
to everyone, great and small,
saying, *Speak to the heart of Jerusalem* (Isa 40:2),

[57]The Ishmaelites (Moslems) captured Jerusalem from the Christians in A.D. 636. While
they were in control, they permitted Jews to live in Jerusalem. When the Crusaders
recaptured Jerusalem, they denied Jews this privilege.
[58]This is a reference to the crucifixion. The Christians are the ones called "the uncircumcised."
[59]These two Jews were illegally present in Jerusalem.
[60]I.e., exiled from their city.
[61]Hagar, the maid of Sarah, whom Abraham divorced after Isaac was born. Her son,
Ishmael, represented the Moslems in Jewish thought.
[62]Sarah, Abraham's true wife and the mother of all Jews.
[63]This is just fifty years before the sixth millennium, or the beginning of the last jubilee
before the new millennium. It is not exactly the date when Saladin overthrew the Crusaders
in A.D. 1187 at the Battle of Hittim, but it is close enough to satisfy a sabbatical eschatologist.
[64]A town crier making this announcement.

so that everyone who wants from the Ephraimites may come to
    her,[65]
who is left from Assyria and Egypt (Isa 11:11),
those who *have been expelled to the ends of heaven* (Neh 1:9).
Let them be gathered to her from every corner
and camp within her borders.
Now we are dwelling in the shadow of relished tranquility,
if it does not become interrupted and broken,
for we are afraid of the wickedness of the deeds committed in her
and violence and evilness which is in her[66] midst,
of the fire of hatred and division,
which burns in her,
dividing the hearts of those who dwell in her.
For they are all chiefs,
extremely cruel,
and each man seeks evil for his neighbor.
Fathers hate their first born sons,
and sons, their parents.
The sons gather wood (Jer 7:18),
and the fathers want to start the fire.
All the works of their hearts are dual;
they do not act in the name of heaven;
everyday they increase conflicts and divisions;[67]
and all hearts are divided
until I call the name of the city, *the rock of discord* (I Sam 23:28).
The chiefs which are set over them
are as *thorns in their eyes* (Num 33:55; Josh 23:13).
One chief prepares to damage the other and the other is against him,
and everyone is like *thorns to the side* of his fellow (Num 33:55).
There are, further, among them inciters, enticers,
and dividers among brothers.
This one spreads out his net
and sets his bow with strength (Gen 49:24).
This makes the wood pile higher and kindles the fire.
Therefore we send up our prayers to God

[65]Ephraimites were Samaritans whom medieval Jews expected to come from all over the diaspora and join forces with the Jews by first running interference for Jews and later giving over the power to the Jews.

[66]Jerusalem.

[67]Sectarian divisions existed during the Crusades among Christians, just as there have been traditional divisions among Christians, Jews, and Moslems. This is a natural product of the doctrine of election, in addition to the normal economic, social, and personal reasons for divisions.

to destroy the thorns from our midst,[68]
and [ask that] we may see his salvation eye to eye,
and that *he will just turn away from us this death* (Ex 10:17).
Then *he raised his parable* (Num 24:3), and said:
"A fire of dissension burns day and night
among us, and divides loving hearts.
If the few just and perfect do not quench it,[69]
the wrath of God will be kindled among us.
For every illness a man will find a remedy, but
jealousy will break the neck until [it goes down] to Sheol.
God will bear all the iniquities, and even
will manifest patience, but he will not bear division."
The narrator said, "And when he had finished his narration,
I asked his name,"
He laughed at my musing
and said, "Do you not recognize your friend, Ḥeber, the Kenite?"
My heart rejoiced at having found him,
and I was bound in the bonds of his fellowship.
I took delight in his company
all the days of my stay in his land.

Summary

This poem was written when messianic hopes were high. The Battle of Ḥittim (A.D. 1187) had been fought, and Jews were given more access to Jerusalem than they had had under the Crusaders, but there were still Crusaders in the country until the fatal battle of Acre (A.D. 1291). The author apparently wrote this poem in the year A.D. 1216—1,148 years after the fall of Jerusalem. He spoke of Saladin's activity as if he were still predicting it, but this is clearly post eventum. Just as II Isaiah applied the name Messiah to Cyrus of Persia who was about to deliver the Jews from Babylon (Isa 45:1), so Elharizi attributed the messianic prophecy of Isa 11:11 to Saladin. He was not alone in attaching messianic expectations to Saladin. This was true of the small fragment "The Ishmaelite Messiah," the pseudepigraphical letter from Moses Maimonides about the Messiah at Ifsahan, and some of the accounts of David

[68]Destroy the Christians in military conflict, overthrowing the Crusaders, just as the Crusaders had overthrown the Moslems. There were military, messianic movements during the Crusades which attempted to do exactly that.
[69]The merits of the just and righteous will cancel debits in the register and thereby reduce God's wrath.

Alroy imply a relationship to Saladin's activity. Elharizi also calculated his sabbaths so as to make Saladin's victory at the Battle of
Hittim to coincide with a jubilee year in relationship to the sixth
millennium (A.D. 1240), even though Saladin's victory happened
three years earlier.

There are some allusions that are not clear. The Ishmaelites
drove the Christians from a ruling position in Jerusalem twice:
once in A.D. 636 and again after the Battle of Hittim in A.D. 1187.
To which of these did he refer when he said the Jews had come to
the city "from the day the Ishmaelites captured it"? On both occasions Jews were permitted to occupy Jerusalem, but the discussion
was carried on as if the Crusaders were still in charge of Jerusalem
and would kill the two Jews if they knew they were there. This
may refer to the early Crusader period when Crusaders had recaptured Jerusalem, or it may mean that Christians still had some
control of Jerusalem until the great Battle of Acre (A.D. 1291). It is
made still more difficult to follow by the apparent identification of
the sons of Esau (Christians) with the Ishmaelites (Moslems) at one
point. This document deserves more careful study in relationship
to other documents related to Saladin and Alroy.

Messianic expectations and disappointments were expressed in
poetry during the Middle Ages, but also in prayer. Some of the
following prayers breathe the hopes and demands of Jews during
this period.

HANUKKAH PRAYER
Author Unknown[70]

For the miracles, deliverance, mighty deeds, saving acts, and the
wars which you have waged for our fathers in those days and in
this time,[71] [we are grateful]: In the days of Mattathias, son of
Yohanan, the Hasmonean high priest,[72] and his sons as when the
wicked Greek kingdom stood over your people Israel, to make
them forget your Torah and to make them transgress the statutes

[70]Dove, *Worship Manual*, 100-101. RPL

[71]"Those days," meaning the times of the fathers, Joshua, the judges, David, and other
biblical heroes. "This time" may mean the time of the Hasmonean heroes.

[72]The Hasmoneans were levitical priests, descended through Joarib, but not from the line
of Zadok (GenR 97; 99:2). Therefore they had to justify their positions as high priests by an
appeal to the "order of Melchizedek" (Ps 110:4; I Macc 14:27). Some Jews considered their
leadership "iniquity in the holy of holies" (Assump. Mos 6:1; see also *Ant.* XII.372-76). The
pro-Hasmonean author of this prayer, however, attributed high priestly descent to these
respected heroes. See *To The Hebrews*, 94-97.

of your will; you, in your great mercy, stood up for them in the time of their distress; you pleaded their case; you judged their dispute; you wreaked their vengeance; you delivered mighty men through weak men; wicked men through righteous men; scoundrels through those who practice your Torah. You have made for yourself a great and holy name in your age,[73] and for your people Israel, you have brought about a great salvation and deliverance as on this day.[75]

AMRAM'S KADDISH
Author Unknown[76]

May his great Name be magnified and sanctified in the world which he created according to his will. May his kingdom rule in your lifetimes and in your days, and in the lifetimes of the whole house of Israel, quickly and in the near future. Amen.

May his great Name be blessed for the age, and for ages of ages may he be blessed. Amen.

May his holy Name blessed be He be praised, honored, magnified, exalted, glorified, extolled, and lauded more than all blessing, hymn, praise, and comfort that can be said in the world. Say, "Amen."

May the prayers and supplications of the whole house of Israel be accepted before their Father in heaven. Say, "Amen."

May there be great peace from Heaven, life, abundance, salvation, comfort, and deliverance for all Israelites. Say, "Amen."

May he who makes peace in his heavens make peace for all Israelites.

May his great Name be magnified and sanctified in the age he is destined to renew. [May he] raise the dead, rebuild the city of Jerusalem, build the temple, root out foreign worship in his land, and introduce holy worship of Heaven in its place.

May the holy One blessed be He rule his kingdom and his glory

[73]God's age was the age when God was king. This was evident when Jews were in control of the promised land and had a Davidic king on the throne. The author of this prayer thought the Hasmoneans filled the requirements as well as a Davidic king might. For him, the age to come had come.

[74]As in most cases of the OT, salvation meant deliverance from the enemy through a military victory.

[75]"As this day" presumes a condition of freedom not known in Judaic Palestine after Herod the Great. This suggests that this prayer was written after the Hasmonean victory, ca. 140 B.C. and before Herod, ca. 38 B.C.

[76]D. De Sola Pool, *The Kaddish* (Jerusalem, 1964), xii. RPL

in your lifetimes and in your days, and in the days of the whole
house of Israel, quickly and in the near future. Amen.

THE TEMPLE AND SACRIFICE
Author Unknown[77]

Our God, and the God of our fathers, because we have sinned,
we were exiled from our land.[78] We were removed from our
ground, so we are not able to go up and appear and prostrate ourselves before you in the house of your choice, in your glorious
habitation, in the great and holy house over which your name has
been called, because of the hand which was sent against your sanctuary.[79] May it be your will, Lord our God and the God of our
fathers, merciful King, that you return and have mercy upon us
and upon your sanctuary, in your great mercy.[80] Rebuild it
quickly, and enhance its glory. Our Father, our King, our God,
reveal the glory of your kingdom upon us quickly.[81] Appear and
be elevated over us before the eyes of every living being. Bring
near our dispersed ones from among the Gentiles and our scattered
ones gather from the ends of the earth, and bring us, O Lord our
God, to your city Zion with joy and your holy city Jerusalem with
happiness of the age.[82] Please, our God, there let us perform before
you our obligatory sacrifices continually as prescribed and additional ones according to our custom.[83] The additional offering for
the festival day of this holy assembly, let us perform and offer before you with love, according to the commandment of your pleasure, as you wrote in your Torah through your servant, Moses.

GOD'S PRESENCE AND THE TEMPLE
Author Unknown[84]

Our God and the God of our Fathers, merciful King, good and

[77]Pool, *Prayers for the Festivals*, 289. RPL
[78]This is the logic of sabbatical eschatology.
[79]The hand of the Romans, A.D. 66-72.
[80]Mercy was understood in very practical terms as the following sentence indicates:
"Rebuild it [the sanctuary] quickly."
[81]God would become king and the glory of his kingdom revealed when Jerusalem and the
temple were restored and free from foreign rule.
[82]The "age" mentioned is probably the messianic age when the diaspora Jews were
promised a return to Jerusalem to restore it (Jer 42:12).
[83]This would involve the restoration of the temple.
[84]Dove, *Worship Manual*, 344. RPL

benefactor, we request [that you] return to us in your abundant
mercy, because of our fathers who did your will;[85] build your
temple as at the beginning, and establish it in its appointed place.[86]
Show it to us constructed, and make us happy with its reconstruction; return your Presence into its midst; return the priests to their
[ritualistic] tasks, the Levites to their cantillation and songs, and
the Israelites to their dwellings.[87] There we will go up and appear
and prostrate ourselves before you and eat there from the
sacrifices and Passover offerings whose blood has touched the wall
of your altar to please you. May the words of my mouth and the
meditations of my heart be acceptable to you, O Lord, my Rock
and my Redeemer. Amen.

PASSOVER SACRIFICE AND THE TEMPLE
Author Unknown[88]

Master of the age, you have commanded us to sacrifice the Passover offering in its appointed time, the fourteenth day of the first
month, and that there should be priests in their service roles,
Levites at their platforms, and Israelites in their positions, reciting
the *hallel*.[89] But now, because of our iniquities, the house of the
sanctuary is destroyed, and the Passover offering fails to be given.
We have no priest in his position, no Levite at his platform, and no
Israelite in his place, but [instead] we offer our oral prayers.
Therefore, may it be your will, O Lord our God and the God of
our fathers, that the utterance of our lips may be counted to you as
if we had sacrificed the Passover offering at its appointed time,
and we had stood in position and the Levites had chanted and had
praised and given thanks to the Lord. But [as for you], rebuild
your sanctuary at its place, and we will go up and offer to you the
Passover sacrifice just as you wrote for us in your Torah by the
hand of your servant Moses.

NEW MOONS, SACRIFICE, AND THE TEMPLE
Author Unknown[90]

You have given the first of the months to your people, a time of

[85]This is an appeal that God draw on the merits of the fathers in the treasury of merits to
cancel the deficit in the time of the worshipper.

[86]Jerusalem.

[87]When the priests were legitimate and functioning properly in a reconstructed temple at
Jerusalem, it was believed that this would guarantee the presence of God in their midst.

[88]Dove, *Worship Manual*, 343. RPL

[89]Ps 118.

[90]Dove, *Worship Manual*, 333-34. RPL

atonement for all their generations. When they used to offer before you conciliatory offerings and goats for sin-offerings to atone for them. May there be a memorial for all of them and salvation of their souls from the hands of the enemy.[91] Build a new altar in Zion! Then we will offer whole burnt first-of-the-month offerings on it, and we will offer male goats on it for expiation. We will all rejoice in the service of the house of the sanctuary and with the songs of your servant David, which are heard in your city, and which are said before your altar. Bring them the love of the age,[92] and the covenant of the fathers remember for the sons. Bring us to your city, Zion, with joy, to the house of your sanctuary, Jerusalem, with happiness of the age.[93] There we will bring before you the required offerings continually, in order and number, according to their specifications. This supplementary sacrifice of the first of the month we will perform and offer before you with love according to the commandment of your desire, just as you have written in your Torah through your servant Moses.

OFFERINGS AND THE TEMPLE
Author Unknown[94]

Let the merciful One restore the service of the house of the sanctuary in its place.[95] May it be your will, O Lord our God and the God of our fathers, that the house of the sanctuary be built quickly, in our days, and place our portion in your Torah. There let us worship you in fear as in the days of the age[96] and in the years of old.[97] Pledge to the Lord a grain offering of Judah and Jerusalem as in the days of the age and as in the years of old.[98]

---

[91]Not the devil or some other abstract concept, but the nationalistic and political enemy that prevented Jews from returning and reestablishing the kingdom.

[92]Probably the messianic age or the following age to come or "sabbath rest." Love is closely related to keeping covenant. See *Consequences.*

[93]These are all interrelated requests, expected to take place at the same time.

[94]Dove, *Worship Manual,* in many places with some variations. RPL

[95]Dove, *Worship Manual,* 363.

[96]The "days of the age" may be parallel with "years of old," or they may be intended as similar in content but at the opposite ends of time. The "years of old" would be the good old days of the Davidic kingdom, and the "days of the age" would be the days of the messianic age in the future. In either event, it is a temporal and not a spacial concept, such as "world."

[97]Dove, *Worship Manual,* 104, 190, 221, 242, 265, 303, 336, 350, 357, 363, 390, 422, 431.

[98]Dove, *Worship Manual,* 104, 190, 221, 242, 265, 303, 336, 350, 357, 390, 431.

THE TEMPLE OF LIFE
Author Unknown[99]

May it be your will, our Father who is in heaven, to erect the temple of our life and restore his presence in our midst, quickly, in our days.

THE TEMPLE OF LIFE
Author Unknown[100]

Because we and our fathers have sinned before you, our city has been destroyed, the house of our sanctuary is laid waste, our heart's desire is exiled, and the glory was taken from the temple of our life.[101]

BLESSING OVER FOOD
Author Unknown[102]

For the produce of the field, for the treasured, good, and ample land which you desired and gave us an inheritance to our fathers to eat from its fruit and to be filled by its goodness [we are thankful]. Have mercy, O Lord our God, upon your people Israel, your city Jerusalem, your glorious dwelling place Zion, your altar, and your temple. Build the holy city Jerusalem quickly, in our days; bring us up to its midst; and make us happy in its construction. May we eat of its fruit and be filled by its goodness and bless you for it in holiness and purity.[103]

AFTER EATING FIGS, POMEGRANITES, GRAPES, OLIVES, OR DATES
Author Unknown[104]

Blessed are you, O Lord our God, King of the age, for the tree

[99]Dove, *Worship Manual,* 124. RPL
[100]Dove, *Worship Manual,* 238. RPL
[101]For the meaning of "life" in biblical thought, see *Consequences,* 110-149.
[102]Singer, *Daily Prayer Book,* 432-33. RPL
[103]More important to the Jew at mealtime than daily food was the reconstruction of the Davidic kingdom and temple worship.
[104]Pool, *Book of Prayer,* 445. RPL

and the fruit of the tree, for the produce of the field, for good, wide, and precious land, which you willed to give our fathers as an inheritance. Our Lord God, have mercy upon us and upon your people the Israelites, upon your city Jerusalem, and on the dwelling place of your glory Mount Zion. Build the holy city Jerusalem quickly, in our days.[105] Bring us up to its midst, for you are good, and you do good to everything. Blessed are you, O Lord, for the land and for its fruit.

BLESSING OVER FOOD
Author Unknown[106]

Blessed are you, O Lord, for the land and for food. Have mercy, O Lord our God, on Israel your people, on your city Jerusalem, and on the kingdom of the house of David, your Messiah. May the glory of the house be enlarged quickly.

Comfort us doubly (Isa 40:9). Blessed are you, O Lord, building Jerusalem in his mercy. Amen. Blessed are you, O Lord our God, King of the age, the King who is good and does good to all. He has done good; he does good; he will do good. He has rewarded us; he does reward us; he will reward us until [the age], [with] grace, kindness, and mercy. May he make us merit the days of the Messiah. He who makes peace in his heavens, may he make peace upon us and upon all Israelites.

JERUSALEM AND SACRIFICE
Author Unknown[107]

May our prayers be as pleasant to you as whole burnt offering and *Korban*. O Merciful One, in your great mercy, restore your presence[108] to Zion in mercy. There we will serve you with fear as in the days of old and as in years gone by.

---

[105]Produce raised in the promised land reminded the worshipper that the Davidic kingdom was in the hands of the Gentiles, so they prayed that the kingdom would come so that they might eat the fruit in Palestine.

[106]Dove, *Worship Manual*, 562. Part of a long prayer. RPL

[107]Dove, *Worship Manual*, 358. RPL

[108]When the proper priests were properly functioning in a reconstructed temple at Jerusalem, it was believed that this would guarantee the presence of God in their midst.

PRAYER AND WORSHIP AT ZION
Author Unknown[119]

Be pleased, O Lord our God, with your people, the Israelites, and with their prayers. Restore the service to the sanctuary of your house; the fires of Israel and their prayers receive willingly with love; may the service of Israelites, your people, be continually for [your] pleasure. May our eyes see your return to Zion with mercy. Blessed are you, O Lord, who returns his presence to Zion.

GOD'S KINGSHIP IN ZION
Author Unknown[110]

May you become king, O Lord, you alone, over all your works on Mount Zion, the dwelling place of your glory, and in Jerusalem your holy city, as it is written in your holy words, *The Lord will be king for the age; your God, O Zion, for generation after generation. Halleluyah!* (Ps 145:10).

ZION AND THE SHEKINAH
Author Unknown[111]

You, in your great mercies, take delight in us and desire us. May our eyes see your return to Zion in mercies. Blessed are you, O Lord, who restores his Shekinah to Zion.

PRAYER AND PROMISES
Author Unknown[112]

Return in mercy to your city Jerusalem, and dwell in her midst as you have promised. Rebuild her soon, in our days, [as] a building of the age. Establish quickly the throne of David in her midst. Blessed are you, O Lord, Builder of Jerusalem.

[109]Dove, *Worship Manual.* 389, 405, 413, 426, 343.
[110]Dove, *Worship Manual.* 396, 411, 424, 433. RPL
[111]Pool, *Book of Prayer,* 66, 277, 323. RPL
[112]Singer, *Daily Prayer Book.* 117. RPL

ZION AND GOD'S RULE
Author Unknown[113]

Appear from your place and rule over us, our King, for we are waiting for you. When will you rule in Zion? Dwell [there] quickly in our days for the age and until [ages of ages]. Be magnified and sanctified in the midst of Jerusalem, your city, for generation after generation, for eternity of eternities.[114] May our eyes see your kingdom[115] according to the word that was spoken in the songs of your might through your righteous Messiah David.

BEFORE RETIRING AT NIGHT
Author Unknown[116]

May our eyes see, our hearts rejoice, and our souls be glad at your salvation, when it is said in truth to Zion, *Your God has become King* (Ps 97:1).[117] The Lord is King; the Lord has been King; the Lord will be King; the Lord will be King for the age and until [ages of ages], for yours is the kingdom.[118] You will rule in glory for ages until [ages], for we have no king but you.

FASTING AND SACRIFICE
Author Unknown[119]

Master of the ages[120] it is revealed and known to you at the time when the house of your sanctuary was standing, a man [who]

---

[113]Singer, *Daily Prayer Book*, 327. RPL

[114]This is one of the few occasions, referring to future time, that the word "eternity" (נצח) was used. The term was known and could have been used more if that had been the intended meaning.

[115]God's kingdom was something human eyes could see, and it would be inaugurated whenever God ruled over Zion.

[116]Singer, *Daily Prayer Book*, 441. RPL

[117]It can only be truly said that God is king when there is a messianic king on the throne of David from Jerusalem.

[118]This seems to refer to the Davidic kingdom, centered in Zion.

[119]Dove, *Worship Manual*. 105. RPL

[120]The expression "Master of the age" is rendered by some, "Master of the world," or "Master of the universe." When the term is plural (עולמים) it can only be rendered "Master of the ages" and be fair to the number. If so, then the singular should be rendered accordingly, "Master of the age."

sinned offered a sacrifice [to you]. But only the fat and blood [of the animals] are sacrificed, and you, in your great mercy, atoned.

Now I sit in fasting and diminution of my [own] fat and my [own] blood. May it be your will that my fat and blood which is diminished today may be as if I had sacrificed it to you on the altar and pardon me.

ZION IN EXILE

Author Unknown[121]

Have mercy, O Lord our God, upon us your people Israel, Jerusalem your city, Zion your glorious dwelling, the mourning, destroyed, and desolate city which was given into the hands of foreigners, and trampled by tyrants. The legions have devoured her, and the idol-worshippers have inherited her, but you have given her to your people Israel; you gave her as in inheritance to the seed of Jacob. Arouse her as an inheritance to the seed of Jacob. Arouse her, O Lord our God, from the dust. Wake her up from the land of her ailment. Reach out over her like a river of peace, like a river gushing over the glory of the Gentiles, for with fire you have burned her and with fire you are destined to rebuild her; as it says, *"I will be to her,"* says the Lord, *"a wall of fire around about, and I will be for glory within her"* (Zech 2:5). Blessed are you, O Lord, Builder of Jerusalem.

Summary of The Holy City

Central to Israel's eschatological expectations was the city of Jerusalem and its temple. The nation, its government, its religion, and its future hopes were all centered around this one location. The boundaries of the promised land changed. The early boundaries reached as far as the northern hills of Galilee. David's and Solomon's kingdom extended as far as the northern boundaries of modern Lebanon. By New Testament times Jews looked forward to conquering Rome and ruling all the territory around the Mediterranean. In the Middle Ages Jews hoped to overthrow the Christians and the Moslems and rule all the territory then governed by both, from England to India, but all of this was to center

---

[121]From the Worship Manual (מחזור) of the Roman Congregation (Bologna, 1540) I, p. 16b (187a). RPL

around Jerusalem. When Jews were not even permitted to live in Jerusalem, they prayed for its restoration and wrote hymns glorifying the city and its temple. The question that kept arising was when. When would God redeem his people and restore his nation, city, and temple to his people? These hopes were closely tied to the day of judgment, the Day of Atonement, New Year's Day, the resurrection of the dead, the day of vengeance. This would be the day the tide would turn, Gentiles would be suppressed, and Jews would be exalted. There were many hymns and prayers that concentrated on this theme. It was an instinctive point of their eschatology.

THE DAY OF VINDICATION

THE TIME OF REDEMPTION
Judah Halevy[1]

Jerusalem, *make your oppressors drink the cup* of your bitterness
(Isa 51:22-23)!
The time has come for your enjoyment, and God to return to your
rooms.[2]
Hear your festal crowd! Peace from all sides![3]
Celebrate, O Judah your feasts! Fulfill your vows (Nah 1:15).

Reassure the timid heart, *and strengthen the knocking knees*
(Isa 35:3),
for still four flags (Num 2)[4] will come up to [the] three feasts:[5]
1) *the wretched Jews* (Neh 3:34), 2) those who are ill with love for
you,
3) your mourners, and 4) your sad ones *who love [even] your dust*
(Ps 102:14).

Those who have laid burdens on me say that my protector has
turned from me.
I know that my *redeemer is strong* (Prov 23:11), and he will act
wonderfully
as of old, as on the day when he added my flag *for six hundred
thousand foot soldiers* (Ex 12:37).

Thus your dispersed he will gather. *He will strengthen the bars of
your gates* (Ps 147:13).
Impoverished prince![6] Why under the hands of the oppressor and
afflictor, [are you]
wandering and reeling on the surface of the earth,
and the daughter of Edom[7] *is lying in the bosom*
(Micah 7:5).[8]
He weeps, *and the son of the Egyptian mother[9] mocks him* (Gen 21:9).

[1]Shirman, *The Hebrew Hymn*, 470. RPL
[2]The holy of holies in the temple.
[3]"Peace," meaning "paid up!" More collateral than needed to remove the indebtedness of
sin to the treasury of merits.
[4]Each of the tribes was stationed under a flag or standard for the division of the land.
[5]New Year's Day, Sukkoth, and Passover.
[6]The Messiah of Joseph, believed to be hidden and suffering to pay off Israel's sins.
[7]Christians.
[8]In Jerusalem, the temple site.
[9]Moslems. Sons of Hagar, the Egyptian.

All this is to *purify your dross* (Isa 1:25) and restore you to your
youth.

Look! The sin is pardoned; the Lord desires [once more] his people.
For *the impatient,* long suffering *soul* (Num 21:4) will be found a
solace and a remedy.
A spirit from on high will go out to all your people, to the
[farthest] borders,
to *revive your murdered ones* (Ezek 37:9) and to *free your captives*
(Zech 9:11)!

THE DAY OF VISITATION
Judah Halevy[10]

Who will restore me the days of youth?
I call to God, and he will answer me.

Earlier times are pleasing to my soul.
Dressed in purple and embroidered decorations,[11]
I went out to my husband in the dance of maidens
(Jdgs 21:20-24).
My beloved saw me and desired me.
He bound me [by his] love and enticed me.

Days of fulfillment reached me.
The voice of the turtle in the *land was heard in my*
ears (SS 2:12).
I was then in my oppression at the hands of my
tormentors.
I slept, and my beloved supports me,
and for times of love he prepared me.

My beloved spread out the wings of his kindness
over me. He put bracelets on my arm.
He[12] crushed my overseers, cut off his[13] refugees
(Obad 14).
The day the wicked hoped to destroy me,
his right hand seized me to support me.

[10]Shirman, *The Hebrew Hymn* II, 484. RPL
[11]Apparel worn by priests.
[12]Change of subjects. The "He" here is not "my beloved," but the sons of Edom.
[13]The Lord's refugees, namely the Jews.

Distinguished from a myriad, he sanctified those he
    elected.
From the wilderness he came with his troops.
On the day he bestowed on those who fear him the
    law he loves,[14]
his Torah and statutes he taught me.
Even against kings he honored me.

Today, for my iniquity, my soul dries up.
From the rooms of my residence I am separated
until my Lord comes with a new covenant.
Again he will send an ambassador of good news,
    and he will visit me.
He will change darkness to light in my behalf.

MESSIANIC BIRTH PANGS

Levi Ibn Altabban[15]

My heart trembles within me, fearing the day *of extermination*
    (Ezek 7:24).
Dreads fall upon me, and my soul is very anxious.
I have feared lest my feet might be trapped in sin.
Pangs seized me like the pangs of a woman giving birth.

The light of our eyes has darkened, *a land of trouble and anguish*
    (Isa 8:22).
How can we lift up our forehead if we have no righteousness?
Our sins have been a pitfall and a stumbling block for us.
Therefore, you have punished us and placed us in hard-pressed
    exile.
With our strength impaired, *you brought us into the net* (Ps 66:11).

Our evil intention, if disclosed? Protect us with your mystery![16]
For the *heat of* mighty *wars* (Isa 30:32) with Edom, whose hand is
    lifted
to bring from them *a lion, an adder, and a flying serpent* (Isa 30:6).

---

[14]Giving the Torah at Mount Sinai.
[15]Shirman, *The Hebrew Hymn* II, 334. RPL
[16]This statement is shrouded with mystery to the modern reader. Maybe the author fears Jewish subversive activity will be discovered and prays that there will be no "leaks" of information to the Gentiles, but this is a guess.

Like a stream of water gushing *until it surrounds* the soul
  (Jonah 2:6)—
oppressing, hurrying, hissing, and making work hard.

He is near to all those who call upon him and repent in anguish.
Redeem your people who are left like a tree stripped of its leaves.
Enemies from every side like locusts are gathered.
As a father has mercy for his sons, have mercy on its [Israel's].
  infants!
As an eagle stirs up its nest, he hovers over his nestlings (Dt 32:11),
and restores to his tents the captives.[17] Have mercy upon her who
  lost her children and is abandoned.

Take notice, for other lords are dominating us,
and they search until *all faces pale* (Joel 2:6).
Please humble the scorpions, the thorns, and the thistles,[18]
and bring near the vision: *The child plays over the hole of an asp,
and the weaned child over the den of an adder will reach his hand*
  (Isa 11:8).

PREPARE FOR REDEMPTION
Author Unknown[19]

Come, my love, to meet the bride. Let us welcome the Sabbath,
keep and remember with one utterance, God especially
  commanded us.[20]
The Lord is one, and his Name is one, for distinction, splendor,
  and praise.
Come, let us go to meet the Sabbath, for it is the fount of blessing.
It was poured out at first from of old, the last in deed, first in plan.
The temple of the king, the city of the kingdom, arise, leave from
  the midst of ruin.
You have dwelled long enough in the valley of weeping; he will
  surely have pity on you.
Shake yourself from the dust; arise (Isa 52:2)! Put on garments of
  splendor, my people!

[17]The Jews to their dwellings in Palestine.
[18]All Gentile forces.
[19]Pool, *Prayers for the Festivals*, 16. RPL
[20]The *Shema'*: Hear, O Israel, the Lord our God is one Lord; and you shall love the Lord
your God with all your heart, with all your soul, and with all your might (Dt 6:4).

Through the Bethlehemite, son of Jesse, redemption draws near to
   my soul.
Awake! Awake! for your light has come (Isa 60:1); arise and glow!
Awake! Awake! Tell the song. The *glory* of the Lord *is revealed
   upon you* (Isa 60:2).
Do not be ashamed; do not be embarrassed; why do you prostrate
   yourself? Why do you moan?
The afflicted of my people take refuge in you, *a city shall be built
   on its tel* (Jer 30:18).
Your plunderers will be plundered; all your devourers will be
   removed.
Your God will rejoice over you, like the joy of a bridegroom over
   his bride.
You will go forth right and left, but you will fear the Lord.
Next to you is Parzi's son.[21] Let us rejoice and be glad.

THE DAY OF SALVATION
Author Unknown[22]

Truly, your savior has come; *the voice of my beloved, behold it
   has come* (SS 2:8).
He has come with many troops to stand on the Mount of Olives.[23]
On arrival, he will blow a trumpet;[24] under him *the mountain will
   split* (Zech 14:4).
He will beat and blossom and shine, and *half the mountain will
   break off from the east* (Zech 14:4).
He will raise the voice of his speech; he will command all the saints
   with him.
To all mankind a *bat qol*[25] will be heard in the world.
The overburdened seed of his mercy was born like a child from the
   womb of his mother.
The one in travail, who is this? *Who has heard anything like this*
   (Isa 66:8)?
The pure one made all this. *Who has seen such things as these*
   (Isa 66:8)?

[21]The Messiah.
[22]Dove, *Worship Manual*, 380-81. RPL
[23]Following Zech 14, the Messiah was expected to appear on the Mount of Olives and
prepare his encounter with the Gentiles before reestablishing the kingdom.
[24]The trumpet announcing the jubilee year when captives were to be set free and the land
restored to its original owners (Joel 2:1; Isa 27:13; Lev 25:8-10).
[25]A divine message to human beings.

Salvation and a time of unification. *Who can create the land in a
single day* (Isa 66:8)?
A mighty height and depth [...] *if a nation is born at one time*
(Isa 66:8).[26]
At the time the Illuminator redeems his people, *at evening, there
will be light* (Zech 14:7).
Saviors will ascend on Mount Zion (Obad 21) for Zion, the
woman in travail, will bear (Isa 54:1-3; 60:4).

It will be heard in all your borders; *expand your encampment*
(Isa 54:2).
Set your dwellings as far as Damascus. Receive your sons and
daughters.
Rejoice you lily in Sharon! for sleepers in Hebron have arisen.[27]
Turn to me and be saved. *Today, if you hear my voice* (Ps 95:7).
A man will shoot forth whose name is "Shoot" (Zech 6:12). He is
David himself.
Rise up, like sleepers in the dust! Jump up, dwellers in the dust,
and sing for joy!
The foremost nation, in crowning its king, enhances his
deliverances.
The name of wicked ones he destines for destruction; the one who
performs kindness to his Messiah David.
Grant deliverances to the people of the age,[28] for David and his
seed, until the age.

LONGING FOR THE DAY
Judah Halevy[29]

O Lord, how long will you hide the vision of your comfort?[30]
How long will you refuse to silence the noise of your opponent?
How long will you make a cloud of your anger dwell over me?
How long will you be angry with the prayer of your people (Ps 80:5)?

[26][...] implies that this might be a minced oath: ["May the following unmentioned curses come upon me], if a nation is born at one time." This would mean, of course, that it does not happen. Here, however, the unexpected could happen miraculously, and the one time on which it could occur would be the Day of Atonement, when Israel's sins might be forgiven, so the kingdom could be restored. See further *Consequences*, 222-37.

[27]The three patriarchs buried there.

[28]The messianic age when the deliverance would take place.

[29]Shirman, *The Hebrew Hymn* II, 477. RPL

[30]Comfort is the term to describe the relief felt by Jews when God would restore his promised land (Isa 40:1).

My thoughts have despaired of seeing your face,
for my times are delayed and all the times to come.
A bitter voice tingles my tongue to you, God of the armies,
how long until the end of the wonders (Dan 12:6),
concealed in your storehouses and sealed with your seal?

The son whose dwelling you appointed above the stars of glory,
how has his star [31] fallen and his lights become obscure!
From the midst of the dwelling, [gazing through] his window, he
          longs for your house, and he groans!
When, O my Rock, will I come and appear before God (Ps 42:3)
to stand guard in your halls and to gaze upon your splendors?

How shall I conceal my poverty after I have been exiled?
The kingdom of Agag has been raised and my kingdom,
          humbled.[32]
Seir displays valor and overpowers the son of my maid.[33]
When, O my Rock, will I also labor for my house (Gen 30:30),
the house, a doorstep for my feet and held firm in your altitudes?

My *Guard will not slumber* (Ps 121:4), and I will *not* let him
          sleep (Ps 121:4).
Surely in my great sin, *like a bereaved bear, I will encounter him*
          (Hos 13:8).
When will my head be raised? When will there be an acceptable
          time for me to seek him?
When, O my Rock, will I rise and once again beseech him
in your jealousy for your Name, for your city, and for your
          people?

WHILE THE ARK TRAVELS

Author Unknown[34]

I will open my lips, and I will respond with a song.

[31]The term "star" was used for the Messiah (Num 24:17). Bar Cochba was the son of a star.

[32]The Israelites vowed to destroy the Amelekites at the earliest opportunity. Saul finally completed this genocide, saving only Agag, the king, for the victory procession (I Sam 15:1-33). Here the "kingdom of Agag" is the Christian church or Rome, both of which were destined to be completely destroyed as the Amelekites were. Halevy complained that in his time, the "Amelekites" seemed to prosper.

[33]Seir, the mountain of Edom, represents the Edomites or Christians. The Ishmaelites or Moslems are descendants of Hagar, Sarah's maid. In Halevy's time, the Crusaders were overpowering the Moslems.

[34]From the worship manual (מחזור) for the congregation at Rome I, 105a. RPL

I will sing to the God of life *while the ark travels* (Num 10:35).
I will call God the praised One. At the time of our salvation, he is
        willing.
A redeemer comes to Zion; then we shall call out loudly:
"Open the land of salvation! Fulfill the prayer of the poor.
Israel is delivered; *the tongue of the dumb will sing* (Isa 35:6).
Restore our captives, O God of life, our Redeemer."
We will fulfill our vows, and Aaron will atone.[35]
Let your enemies be scattered (Num 10:35), O God, *let those who
        love you sing* (Jdgs 5:31).
The day you fight your battle, they will return to [their] strength.
We shall be redeemed; ours is the God of gods.
A fortress and troops he will overpower and prevail.
My strength will be God. Sorrow and grief will flee.
Let us sing, as the scripture says, *And it happened
when the ark traveled [that Moses said, "Rise up, O Lord, and let
your enemies be scattered; let them that hate you flee before you"]*
        (Num 10:35).

THE DELAYED DAY OF REDEMPTION

Rabbi Moshe Ben Nahman[36]

Raised on the throne of fire, burning with the wind,
held fast to you with hooks are creatures and powers.
He is not carried, but he carries all of those who trust in your name.
Both for evil and the truthful, you are a God of forgiveness.
Angels and illustrious ones are counted at your command.
Whether they go down or up[37] they are your orders.
From fear of you they tremble, and at your word they are
        restored.
How much the more so feeble men, formed of clay!
What is their worth in the day you arise for *judgment* (Ps 149:7).

You have shown that kingship is becoming to you.
It is not diminished or defective, but equal with respect to all
        peoples,
but it applies especially to us, and we are required [to fulfill] your
        commandments.

---

[35]For all Jews.
[36]Shirman, *The Hebrew Hymn* III, 320-21. RPL
[37]Angels on the ladder in Jacob's vision (Gen 28:12).

You have an arm of salvation, and we have an expectant soul.
Please do not defer the yearning, *for my days are few* (Ps 39:6).

O, you who are seated on high, over all the tallest heights
        (Ps 113:5-6),
and stoop low to consider *the protection for a gourd* (Jonah 4:10),
hope in you is not deceived, and you do not shame the poor.
My soul   waits for you, expecting the day of redemption—
the day we will be satisfied on Mount Zion, *happy in your
        presence* (Ps 16:11).

IN THOSE DAYS AND IN THAT TIME

Eleazar Kallir[38]

In those days and in that time,
        in the first month, the month of Nisan,
א)   *in fact* in its fourteenth day, Menaḥem son of Amiel will come
ב)   *in* the Valley of Arabel. His goodness will shoot forth,
        dressed in his colorful *garments of vengeance* (Isa 59:17).
In those days and in that time,
        in the second month, the month of Iyyar,
ג)   *things hidden* by those who store things for sabbatical years
        will be revealed.
The council of Korah will go up before the eyes of all the
        tribes.[39]
ד)   *The banners* of Asaf will be decorated from the *Araboth* of
        Moab to the Shittim Valley.[40]
In those days and in that time,
        in the third month, the month of Sivan,
ה)   *those* who died in the wilderness will arise, and a great
        earthquake will attack the walls,[41]
ו)   *and* on the mountain tops there will be an abundance of grain,

---

[38]From the worship manual (מחזור) for the congregation at Rome, I, 196b-197a.

[39]Traditionally, the council of Korah was to be raised in the last days and reunited with the rest of Israel in the Valley of Shittim.

[40]Perhaps the broad valley (the Arabah), extending from Jericho to the hills of Moab, including the whole Jordan Valley in between. It probably reaches to Wadi Qumran, so that it could have direct contact with the Valley of Jehoshaphat, across from the temple site. See W.R. Farmer, "The Geography of Ezekiel's River of Life," *BA* 19 (1956), 17-22. Also see the Book of Zerubbabel.

[41]According to Hai Gaon, "The Subject of Salvation," an earthquake was required in the last days to loosen decayed and disintegrated parts of corpses that had since been made into bricks, buildings, and mortar. After the earthquake these parts would all reassemble as Ezekiel prophesied.

and the agitation of the land, and the secret of the mystery
will be told.
In those days and in that time,
in the fourth month, the month of Tammuz

ז) *wrath* and transgression will be found everywhere, and a king
will go out apart from heaven.

ח) *power* and Satan will say to him, "Go forth!" Freedom and
salvation will be found for the remnants.
In those days and in that time,
in the fifth month, the month of Ab,

ט) *purity* will wear *garments of his vengeance* (Isa 59:17), and
the *Mount of Olives will be split open* from his anger
(Zech 14:4).

י) The Messiah *will come forth* in his greatness[42] *like the rising of
the sun in its might* (Jdgs 5:31).
In those days and in that time,
in the sixth month, the month of Elul,

כ) *Success*, Ben Shealtiel will proclaim,[43] and Michael and
Gabriel will come down[44]

ל) *to* prepare the military vengeance of God, and not one enemy
of Israel will be left.
In those days and in that time,
in the seventh month, the month of Tishri,

מ) *confusion* and turmoil in every nation [will be]

נ) *terrible* when he takes for himself a nation from the midst of
a nation.[45]
They will say, *Come, let us destroy them from being a nation*
(Ps 83:5),

נ) despising a *person*,[46] abominating a nation.
In those days and in that time,
in the eighth month, the month of Marḥeshvan,

ס) there will be a *storm* in the first exile, and in it a rose will go
out to the wilderness,

---

[42]Military greatness, comparable to that employed by Deborah and Barak in defeating
the Philistines.

[43]Zerubbabel was the son of Shealtiel. He was the king believed to have been kept in
heaven until the time of the end of the diaspora, when he would be revealed as the Messiah
son of David, who would restore Israel.

[44]The guardian and military angels of Israel.

[45]The Jews organized within the nations of the diaspora a fifth columnist group that
caused anxieties to various governments.

[46]Probably the Messiah of Joseph, who, as the suffering servant, was *despised and
rejected of men* (Isa 53:3).

y) *ten* thousand will be revealed with support,[47] and the last will not be like the first.

> In those days and in that time,
> in the ninth month, the month of Kislev,

פ) *suddenly* a sword will fall from heaven, and blood of the uncircumcised will flow like rivers of water,

צ) *fresh* from three to nine it will roar like [cascading] water, and the dead will rise and live after two days.[48]

> In those days and in that time,
> in the tenth month, the month of Tebeth,

ק) The daily watchmen will *cry*,[49] "Woe to us for the day has passed!"

ר) There will be *hunger* for forty-five days, and there he will be praised: "Blessed be the Lord everyday!"

> In those days and in that time,
> in the eleventh month, the month of Shevat,

ש) there will be a *paralysis* with ninety [thousand] and a hundred thousand wearing armor

ש) *which* with a fourth does battle with the rib,[50] the thousand and there, *One pursues a thousand* (Dt 32:30).

> In those days and in that time,
> in the twelfth month, the month of Adar,

ת) there will be *constantly* three men in its construction, Tishbi, Menahem, and also Nehemiah.[51]

ת) *Beauty* serves it appointment with them, and there every soul will praise the Lord!

As it is written, *Every soul will praise the Lord* (Ps 150:6), Halleluyah! and it is said, *I will guard this city to deliver it for my sake and for the sake of my servant David* (II Kgs 19:34), and it is said, *For the Lord will comfort Zion. He will comfort all its ruins* (Isa 51:3).[52]

---

[47]Military support, such as the movements Maimonides described.

[48]Hos 6:2: *After two days he will revive us; on the third day, he will raise us up, that we may live before him.*

[49]The one who watches the calendars and calculates the times to predict the end time. See also Ezek 33:7.

[50]Possibly Sampson (Jdgs 15:15-17).

[51]Elijah the Tishbite, Manahem, Messiah of David, and Nehemiah, Messiah of Ephraim.

[52]This last collection of scriptural quotations is not part of the poem.

THAT DAY
Author Unknown[53]

Side 1:

That day, when the Messiah son of David will come
to a people (2) who has been hard pressed,
these signs will appear (3) in the world[54] and will be brought out:
earth and heaven will vanish; (4)
the sun and moon will eclipse;[55]
the sun[56] and those who dwell on the land (5) will be silenced.[57]
The king from the West[58] with the king from the East[59]
will beat each other to dust,
but [the king] from the West will rule,
his troops (7) will be strengthened in the land.
From the land of Yaqtan (Gen 10:26—west) will come forth a king,
    (8)
and they will strengthen his camps in the land.
All those who dwell on the land (9) will be beaten down
    (Lam Rabbati 1:22),
and the heavens over the land (Mdr. Ps 17:14) will produce dust,[60]
    (10)
and the winds will blow in the land.
Gog and Magog, (11) each will strike the other,[61]

[53]Possibly Kallir. See Ibn Shmuel, *Redemption,* 155-57. The text is translated from the Hebrew L. Ginsberg (ed.). שעכטער ׳ גנזי (New York, 1928) I, 310-12. RPL
   This poem is based on Amos 8:9: *"And it will happen in that day,"* said the Lord God, *"and the sun will go down at noon, and I will make the land [on] a bright day dark."*
   [54]This may refer to the natural phenomena predicted in the astrological prophecy here called "Days of Tribulation."
   [55]One of the major signs predicted in the astrological prophecy, scheduled to take place A.D. 1186, just a year before Saladin's famous victory over the Crusaders at the Horns of the Hittim.
   [56]This word seems unrelated to the sentence. Ginsberg is probably correct in thinking that it is a scribal error and should be omitted.
   [57]Those who dwell on the land (יושב הארץ) are the people who live in the land who are not citizens. In this case, they are the Christians and Moslems. From a Jewish point of view, they are the ones who live on the land who should not be there.
   [58]The Crusaders. It is not certain whether any particular Crusade is intended here. This may be a general description, after the event, of the way the events developed. The Crusaders came from the West.
   [59]From the East were the Moslems, the defenders at first, but after many battles, the Crusaders took control of the promised land and ruled it from Jerusalem. The following line of beating each other to dust may not refer to any one battle, but the consequence of many battles.
   [60]This seems like a reference to the prophecy that was partially fulfilled in A.D. 1186.
   [61]Shortly after the famous eclipse prophesied, there was a crucial battle fought at the Horns of the Ḥittim, near the northern shore of the Sea of Galilee. The opposing forces,

and panic will kindle in the heart of the nations.
The transgression of all Israelites will be removed.[62]
Side 2:
They will no longer be removed from the house of prayer.[63]
Blessings and consolations will be showered upon them,
and *they will be inscribed* in the book (3) of life.
Then the kings from the land (4) of Edom will be finished,[64]
those who dwell in Antioch will rebel (5) but make peace.
Mauzia (Syria) the Samaria will be comforted, (6)
and Acre and Galilee will receive mercy.[65]
The Edomites and the Ishmaelites (7) will fight in the Valley of
          Acre[66]
until the horses sink (8) in blood and whinny [in panic].
Gaza and her daughters will be stoned (9),
and Ascalon and Ashdod will be confounded.
Then Israel (10) will go out from the city and advance.[67]

---

here called Gog and Magog, were the Crusaders, on the one hand, and the Moslem forces led by Saladin on the other. The Crusaders were soundly defeated, after which the Moslems recovered Jerusalem. There were Jewish messianic movements at the same time, and there may have been correspondence between Alroy and Saladin, providing Jewish support for Saladin.

[62]The defeat of the Crusaders was a sign to the Jews that the final battle of Gog and Magog, here seen as forces opposed to each other, was being fought. The predicted defeat of these Gentile forces would be followed by the restoration of the land of Palestine to the Jews. This would happen only after Israel's sins had been removed, and there were no sins against Israel in the treasury of merits. The succession of events assured the author that this was the case.

[63]When the Moslems regained control of Jerusalem Jews were given permission to settle in Jerusalem. The Crusaders had "removed them from the house of prayer." See E. Ashtor-Strauss, "Saladin and the Jews," *HUCA* 27 (1956), 305-26.

[64]Crusaders were on their way out. It was just a matter of time until they would be completely driven from the land.

[65]Crusaders would be forced to evacuate all these places.

[66]This may refer to the famous siege of Acre, which began April 5, 1291. Moslems successfully drove every Christian from the city. They attacked Acre with more than 66,000 horse and 160,000 foot soldiers. Acre held 40,000 inhabitants, of whom 800 were knights and 14,000 were infantry. A current description of the battle on May 18 was: "They [the Moslems] came on foot, in numbers past counting: first those who bore great high shields, and after the throwers of 'Greek fire,' then dart throwers and those who shot feathered arrows, so thickly that it was as if rain was falling from the sky." The Saracens began to undermine the tower, shoring up their tunnels with props. The Christians surrendered, and the Saracens entered in such large numbers that the tower collapsed, killing thousands of Turks and Christians together. Two thousand mounted Turks were crushed outside the tower when it fell upon them. This was such a strategic battle, with so much blood shed, that the description given of the battle in the Valley of Acre may be a description of the author's understanding of the battle. See further M. Benvenisti, *The Crusaders in the Holy Land* (Jerusalem, c1970), 90-93.

[67]Either from Acre or Jerusalem. The following describes the author's opinion of the events that would follow for the Jews. These were the normal expectations associated with the days of the Messiah. They do not describe events that took place, but the ones expected.

For forty-five[68] (11) days they will not taste grain.
Their Messiah will be revealed (12), and they will be comforted.
The secret mystery of their king they will enjoy, (13)
and they will sing praise to their king!
But none of the wicked (14) will be acquitted in judgment.

Summary

This seems to be a poem written after the famous Battle of Acre in A.D. 1291, summarizing the entire experience of the Crusades in Palestine. The beginning attacks of the Crusaders, their victory and rule from Jerusalem, the prophesied natural phenomena predicted by the astrological prophecy, the Battle of the Horns of the Hittim, July 5, 1187, and the final Battle of Acre. The author of this poem understood these all to be signs of events leading up to the appearance of the Messiah. Moslems and Christians were Gog and Magog. Both had fought so hard that they had both been weakened. This was the appropriate time for the Messiah to appear and lead the Jews in battle against the remnants of the Moslems left after the Christians had already been evacuated. This would be the day when Jews regained control of the promised land. These were the beginning of the days of the Messiah to be followed by the age to come, when Jews would rule from Jerusalem.

THE BOOK OF THE SIGN
Abraham Abulafia[69]

א) The mouth of Yadod I have sanctified/ from of old, from the day I knew his name/ until this day, and still/ I will be sanctified by his name, and at/the mouth of his holiness I will truly live.

ב) *In* his name I have sworn of old/ for by him I will swear in the/ oath of the kingdom of the Mes/siah, the Lord who changes in my name stubble for chaff.

ג) *Geradlia* Ben Shabaldelia/ he called me Yahani[70] in my name/ which is renewed, which is sanctified/ in his name which is renewed and which/ is sanctified in the mouth of the scholar.

[68]This forty-five day period of fasting before the disclosure of the Messiah is reflected in many medieval documents.
[69]A.Z. Aescoly, *Messianic Movements*, 198-207. SML
[70]*Yah ani* means "I am Jehovah."

ז) *I stabbed* with my sword the heart / of those who denied him, with the spear of my tongue / which was his name and with which / I killed those who denied him, and I / killed his enemies with righteous judgment.

ה) *I turned* the evil ways / to right ways with the power of / the name which is honored and / revered, who looks down / upon those who recognize him on earth.

ו) *And* I will prophecy in his name / both in four and three letters[71] / when I am in the house[72] / toward the south, the upper [chamber in] in the small wall near Joseph.[73]

ז) I have surely *remembered* the name / of Yadod Eldino[74] / distinct in my name and [stored] specially in my heart, / and I divided into two parts the four [letters].

ח) *Half* of *his name* was Viat, / and [the other] half of his name / was Viatua, these [letters were] from this and these from the other, / and all of it is inscribed on a banner.

ט) *Tayib*[75] were the letters / of half of one name / and Tayib were the letters of the other half of the name, and in them is an instrument victorious against Satan.

י) This *Yav* Bizbi killed / Legato. / Tilo came from Gato. / Gitalo is the king of demons, / the father of sorcery.

כ) *Everyone* who rules in Rome and its council / his strength will grow faint, / and weak / will be his might from the time of the giving / of the Torah and afterwards and there is not a ruler among his tribes.

ל) The demons came *to kill* / and the satyrs were killed / and were given for slaughter in that one day / both large and small / at the hands of a young and tender king.

מ) *Meribo*[76] died in Rome / [killed] in his rebellion by the strength of the name / of the God who lives and endures, for Ya/dod fought against him both on / dry land and through Yas-pi.[77]

נ) *Against* Yadod and against / his Messiah will it be for you as a sign, a wonder, and a trustworthy witness that / we have conquered with the aid of the name Viat.

ע) *Rejoice* and be glad / you who instruct my people, for / Yadod

---

[71]The Tetragrammaton (יהוה) and Yadod (ידד).

[72]The temple on Mount Zion.

[73]The North wall of the holy of holies toward Samaria or "Joseph."

[74]"His judge is God."

[75]"Good" in Arabic.

[76]מריבן seems to be a proper name with some mystical significance.

[77]Context suggests that this is a code name for the Reed Sea.

dwells in our midst / and my heart is within me today / on account of this it rejoices and is glad.

 y) *The eye* sees, and the heart is happy / the ear hears, and all / the body dances, and the foot / is provoked to anger[78] because every man / dances in circles.

פ) *The mouth* speaks in its own tongue, / and the heart answers from its dwelling. / The heart whispers at his will, / and the mind receives its idea. / His ear and his eye understand his imagination.

צ) A trustworthy *messenger* is this / [which] Yadod sent to you / who dwell in the Island of Sicily / to rescue you [from] abominable peace offerings.

ק) *The end* of the appalment[79] has arrived / as well as the destruction of those who worship the sun / and the moon.[80] Behold he comes, for / Yadod tests and proves / by his name the heart of every worshipper.

ר) The men of *the island really see* / the sight of the help / of my God who goes out / from Micenia to the south and the west / to shed blood and kill Gentiles.

ש) *There* Yadod of armies / is arranging the weapons / for his battle line, / and he is putting in order the arrangement of his troops so that he may wreak vengeance upon his enemy.[81]

ת) *The sign* is brought forth by Yadod / from the sparks of his flame and from / the chamber of his anger and the fire / which flames he draws out / from its sheath and departs.[82]

The enemy has half the name of the / name which comes from one root. In the first of the month / his work will be revealed with / its existence covered at the end [of the month]. He made a covenant in his name / to sanctify to him in the eyes of all / living beings, and before the sun / and the moon until / it is known in the land.

II

Therefore thus / said Yadod, the God of Is/rael: Have no fear of / the enemy, for *I and He* /will fight against him to deliver / you from his hand. / Let not your heart be weak / in the sanctification

---

[78]Stamping feet to the beat of the music.

[79]Reference to the appalment or the "abomination of desolations" that defiled the temple with the entrance of Antiochus Epiphanes. Three years later (a time, two times, and half a time), Judas cleansed the temple. This is the point in religious progress about which the author spoke here. The temple was just about to be cleansed and the land restored.

[80]The astrologists who were numerous in the thirteenth century.

[81]In the author's time the enemies were the Christians and the Moslems.

[82]The sign of the *tau,* which looks like an X or a cross. See Ezek 9:4.

of the name of the One who wreaks / vengeance on behalf of his covenant. / Set your hearts, O men, / how to know / Yadod, the God of Israel / in his name, and arouse yourselves / through him to be wise in his truth. / The life of every living being who speaks / is he, and he revives / the dead and saves / the living with the dew of his favor / and with generous rain.[63] Who has told from the first / to the sons of Israel that they will be redeemed in the name of Yadod? / Was it not Moses, the son of Am/ram, the son of Kehat, / the son of Levi, the son / of Jacob, the son of Isaac, the son of / Abraham, when he recalled in his book the name, "I will / be what I will be" and said to them, *I will be has sent me to you* (Ex 3:14). Yadod the God of arm/ies of Israel, have mercy on your holy people. Ga/ther them to the city of *your* sanctuary[64] / for the sake of your name. So as to sanctify / his name in the eyes of those that see him / and so as to mention in holiness and in purity, / I will write him explicitly. See the name which is great, / mighty, and revered, / both in four [letters][65] and in three [letters][66] as it is engraved on the mountain, / I am Yadod his God.

III

The coming day is the day / of judgment, and the day / of memorial it will be called. / A time of judgment / has arrived, and the period of the / end has been fully completed. The heavens will become [part of] the earth, / and the earth will be [part of] he/aven, because of the God of / judgment. Yadod / is his name, and his law is the law of truth. / His judgment is fair.

IV

The days of hope / and the mark of desire / have met / the days of joy / and the line of reproof / are separated. The pointed hands / and the measured palm have been expanded / for the north touches / the south, and the south / meets his north.

V

...Yadod, the God of heaven / has heard the cry of the sons of Jacob, / and he sent one proclaiming good news to his

[63]In Jewish thought resurrection was closely related to rain and dew.
[64]Jerusalem.
[65]Jehovah(יהוה).
[66]Yadod(ידד).

people, and Zech/ariah is his name. Behold the people who are humble, whom / every nation has plundered, and all people / held in contempt.[67] Behold this day will be for them a day of good tidings.[68] Zechariah who will proclaim the good news will ride on a thick cloud, / but the cloud will be a cloud of dew, and the dew will be fine / [and] light, although the cloud is [also] very heavy. / Behold his chariot will be one of fire, and his horses / horses of the spirit, and his attendants will be Hayyot,[69] belching forth flames, and the cloud / will surround the mountain of mountains[90] a/round, and the spirit announcing the good news will shake the whole earth as they hover around. Judg/ments and words will renew his heart / within him, and with a writing of fire he will / write them with a flaming pen. Fearful / and dreadful will be the power of the pen, and the ink, blood. / Its name is within it, and drops of its dew / will irrigate land, irri/gating the dry ground. The dry land will be drained / of its moisture, and the bow and the arrows / will sharpen the Torah until / the windows of the firmament are cleft / with the arrows of his arrows. The wind of his arrows / will hover over the hearts, burning / the kidneys and scattering all the winds, and there will be no healing for the bodies. The strong wind / which will prevent the heart from harm, proclaiming the good news, will breathe the breath of life into the nostrils of every / living being. The upper spirit *will be* the spirit of *the living* God. / He will stir up / the heart of every one who is wise [enough] to hear the voice of Yadod and to teach [people] his truth / [so that] they will cleave to him and swear by his na/me. The one proclaiming good news will be brought. / He will not come [by himself] because twelve [people or things] will prevent him from coming, / but Yadod has arranged [the way] to deal with all this, / having learned from war how to destroy / all his enemies before him, before his appearance. / The Lord said to Zechariah, the one proclaiming good news, "Raise *your* voice / with the pen of your tongue, and write with / three of your fingers the words / of this book. God has become / a help to his people. Then Zechariah wrote / all that which the Lord commanded him / to write. / He will surely come quickly, and after / relating and narrating the words of the God of / life to the Jews [who have been circumcised] in the flesh but uncircumcised in the heart (Jer 9:25; Ezek 44:7), but the poor *to whom* / he was sent, and for whom he was revealed, /

[67]The Jews.

[68]Good news that the land will soon be restored to the Jews (Isa 61:1).

[69]Heavenly Sphinx-like beasts that are present at the altar in the temple (Ezek 1:13-14).

[90]Mount Zion.

did not set their hearts on the form of his coming. / They began to say about him and about his God / words about which it is not possible / to speak. They [therefore] commanded Yadod to speak / to the Gentiles, both of uncircumcised heart and flesh / in his name. He did so and spoke to them, / and they believed in the good news of Yadod. But they did not return to Yadod, because they trusted / in their swords and their bows. Then did Yadod har/den them / to destroy them,[91] but he had compassion upon the Israelites, / his people. He selected for himself a time and an occasion for the day / of good news and the name of Yadod is "My Strength" (see Ex 15:2). It will happen on that day that *Yadod* will search / with joy and gladness / and with seven candles (Zech 4:2) and with the brightness of a five [fold fire] all the tops of the / mountains. He will find among the lions and the bears, a scattered sheep / without a shepherd. / Yet the lion did not devour it / nor the bear consume, but Yadod / will surely find the crest of the mountain, / since its name is Mount Nafal. / Upon it will dwell the shepherd of his flock for twenty / years, until the time of anger is past / and the wrath in which *the new shepherd* sleeps / will be appeased. At that time, Yadod *the God of Israel* will arouse / the heart of the shepherd, and he will awake from his sleep, and he will awaken the hearts / of those who sleep in the dust, and the dead will revive, / and the flock[92] will come to their pastures.[93] / They will never be scattered again, and the shepherd[94] / will break the fangs of the lions, / and he will set the teeth of the bears on edge. He will tie / shackles around their necks so that they cannot / injure, and they will not be able / to destroy [anyone] / without the rebuke of the Lord Yadod / the God of Abraham who told Yadod the shepherd how to break the teeth of the / lions who have not left of those who wor/shipped idols a living soul. For the young lions have been trained to prey on people, for if / they do not consume enough of their prey, they will / die. Now, after *Yadod* has agreed / to restore those who rejected him, / the lion and the lamb will pasture together (Isa 11:6). Now you who are wise hearted scholars, / seek Yadod with your hearts both day / and night, and seek his truth, / and cleave to him. / Remember his name, for his name is an engraved memorial, and the spirit of Yadod speaks, / and with it is made / the covenant of / the salvation of the ages. / It is hidden from all Gentile scholars of /

[91]As he did Pharaoh years before.
[92]The Jews of the diaspora.
[93]Palestine, the promised land.
[94]The Messiah (see Ps 2:9; Pss. Sol 18).

the land, and it reveals the nakedness of the sorcery which is / in their thought. Now, you, of Yadod / his exclusive ones, and his inheritance, the Israelites, after / he has separated you alone from them to be / his seclusive portion, and the unity of his name / he has put over the three of you. Why do you deal treacherously and make your spirit flee / from you, since you have been assigned to be the garland and the glory / and the praise: the priest, the Levite, and the Israel/ite are three true witnesses of the spirit / against the three degrees of measure, the chiefs of the three ag/es. You will live with the three of them / the life of the spirit, as the life of the sun and the moon / and the stars. Therefore, lift up your eyes / to the heavens and look with the eyes of / your heart to the heaven of heavens and see / the battle-line of the God of life, here / are arranged in orderly fashion the Torah of Yadod, / so that all who acknowledge him, who call upon the name of Yadod, / and who seek his wisdom / from those who instruct will be called holy / in the sanctity of the name of his God.

VI

In the year five thou/sand and forty-five / (A.D. 1285),[95] in the third month / by the reckoning of the moon, in the *tenth* month / by the reckoning of the sun, in the *fifth* ye/ar of the cycle[96] / in the month of Kislev. On the sixth day / which was the first of the month, according to the reckoning / which is calculated from the years of the creation of A/dam, Yadod aroused the spirit / of Zechariah to teach and to multiply / the books of his prophecies and to complete / half the book. For among his books / he wrote one book which is half / of the book, in order to hint at the [one] half of the name and at the name and [then] at the [other] half of the name. When the first day / will be completed, then the one name will [also] be completed. On the same day, *Zechariah the shepherd* will begin / to write mir/acles of wisdom and wise thoughts by means of the let/ters of the Torah. / From these letters Zechariah will explain the distinct name / and will expand the Tetragrammaton / and will unify the special name [of God]. He will place it [his name] in the mouth of[97] his disciples and teach it to those who follow him until he reveals his secrets and has *made known* his end times. / He teaches his ways to all / those of a wise

---

[95]The year five thousand in Jewish reckoning is A.D. 1240.
[96]Jubilee cycle. A.D. 1280 was evidently a jubilee year.
[97]So that it can again be pronounced without fear.

heart until they have said of it, "Enough!" / It is sufficient for all those who know him, / and all his friends will rejoice in him. / This will be to them the first and the *last* jo/y. He is engraved in their heart, and their spirit is the spirit of the God of life......Then Yadod will send to his people a physician to heal the wound of their blow, when he makes / known to his scholars his name. The scholars / of Israel were ill and were smitten with every / sickness and plague which was not even writ/ten in the book of the Torah of Moses,[98] the / man of God among the curses.

Then Yadod said to Zechariah, / "Be well! Go, and I will send you to / a nation of a smitten heart, to heal *its* illness. / The balm of my name and my memory *(zechari yah)* / take with you." Yadod gave the gi/ft of grace and a portion of loving kindness to Zechariah and he went to the lands of / the Gentiles where Israelites were scattered, / and he began to speak, and with that which he began / he concluded, because he called upon the name of Yadod / the God of the age from the beginning to / the end in a straight line, not deviating / to the right or to the left. Only some of the scholars of Israel wanted to hear from his mouth the wisdom of the name / and his sublime halakhot. *Yadod* appeared / to the healthy ones of them, / and they also requested [him] to heal the sick / souls at the mouth of Zechariah, / those who denied / the wisdom from on high and those / who were smitten with mortal plagues, and spoke / haughty words against Yadod and / his Messiah and against all those who had been made well / and against all those that were associated with them and who knew / the severity of their illnesses / and who had flocked to the physicians until the hearts of *those who were associated* melted / and their spirits grew weak from pursuing / after those who know the name, but they were prevented. Concerning this and similar things / the anger of Yadod was kindled against / those who denied his name, and he sent them / a preacher, and his words were as reproach and disgrace in their eyes. They made him flee from city to city and from place to place / until his arrival in the city of Mastema[99] in the land of Comatina, and there he dwells / against his wish for many days. It will happen / in those days that Yadod will say to / Zechariah, "Write for yourself *this* book / the part dividing the thoughts / of the scholars of Israel who boasted. That is why I did not desire this generation / which says, 'Why

[98]The plagues written in the Torah are four: 1) wild beasts, 2) sword, 3) pestilence, and 4) famine (Lev 26:22-26; see also Ezek 5:12, 17, *et passim*).

[99]Satan. The city of Mastema is probably Rome.

should we consider the name of Yadod, and what hope is there for us in him? / ...Is not / the calculation from the books of the counting of *silver* good [enough] for us / and of the gifts of gold? For in them we are able / to help ourselves and all those who love us. / Has this Yadod not promised us wealth and glory and possessions of / wealth for the multitude, and the inheritance of fields / and inheritance of vineyards?" ...This day Yadod has loved us / because he has given us much and excellent wealth. / What shall we offer him in religious service, and with what shall we sacrifice / to him except with money? These foolish... / ...when against whom I have vowed / to do for them, and I have been willing to do good / to them. It was for the sake of my name that I have done [this] to them. They have received from the *first way* / in my name, but the second they did / not want.

I, Zechariah, when I heard / this from Yadod, and I wrote that / which he commanded me, and I revealed through this name of his. / Wonders of wonders Yadod informed us / in his great, mighty, and fearful Name. / He revealed to us the ways of his secrets and the secrets of / his calculations... / ...Therefore you who love / the day which sanctions the truth of the resurrection, open / the eye of your hearts and see the time of its coming. / For already the time of the end has arrived to / arouse and awaken those who sleep in the / dust from the slumber which envelopes darkness / and from foolish dozing / ...and the end time of salvation and the day / of the redemption has come. Yet there is no one who / will pay attention today to this phenomenon. / There is no salvation except in the name of Ya/dod, and his redemption is not for the one who / does not seek him through his name. Therefore I, Zechariah, who destroys the building [also] builds up destruction. / I have written this small book in the name / of my small Lord so as to reveal in it the secret of the great Yadod ... / ...But whoever does not arouse / from his sleep and whose soul is not awakened / will sleep the sleep of the age, and he will not revive./...

At that time *Yadod* said / to Zechariah who loves his name / ..."Zechariah, my friend, pay attention in my / name, for through it you will cleave to me. / Please do not reveal its secrets / except through his writings."... / ...When I, *Zechariah Ben Maali of Alumiel the son of Yadod*, heard / the one who mentioned / the name Yadod... / I fell on my face to the ground. / My heart saw and rejoiced. *Yadod* raised me up / ... / ...and he showed / me the form of his name, engraved in / my heart. I looked and saw in it *my* im/age and my likeness wandering in two / ways, in the appearance, in the form of two letters of the names of God. One image, one form / I saw, and I thought I would distinguish / between them, but I saw they were tied / the two of them, one to the other...

...Then Yadod said to me when I saw / his explicit and special / name in blood / my heart was divided between blood for ink and ink for blood. Yadod said to me, / "Look, your soul is blood, there, / and there is ink, / and there is your spirit, / and here is your father and your mother, / pining for this my name and memorial *(Zechari Yah)."*

VII

My God showed me a new vision in the name / renewed by the spirit which renewed itself on the *fourth* day / of the seventh month, which is / the first moon at the beginning of the eight/eenth year of my visions. *I was* seeing in a vision, / and behold a man came from the West / with a very large army and the number of the mighty men / of his camp was twenty-two thousand men.

The splendor of that man and the glory and might of his heart caused all the earth to quake, and it made the hearts of the men of valor convulse. With him were mighty men / armed [with spears and swords] and countless cavalry and infantry, apart from / his mighty men. On his forehead was a sign[100] sealed in blood and ink at the two corners. / The form of the sign was like the form of a staff cast down / between them, and the sign was very mysterious. / The color of the blood was black, and it had changed to red. / The color of the ink was red, but / it had become black. The color of the decisive sign between / the two appearances was a white... / ...it rotated at his command, / and a whole military troop journeyed on. When I saw / his face in a vision, I trembled and my heart recoiled... / ...Speech fled from my spirit. It came to pass that when the man beheld / the strength of my fear and trembling / he opened his mouth and spoke, and he [also] opened my mouth / to speak, and I answered him according to his word. As I spoke I strengthened myself and was transformed into a *different* man. / I opened my eyes; I looked; and behold / the appearance of a slandering eye welling forth from / the sign on his forehead. The sign on his forehead *the man called* / the poison of death, / but I called it the elixir of life, for I changed it from death to life. The man saw

---

[100]Like those who wore the sign of the cross or the *tau* on their foreheads (Ezek 9:4).

the transformation which I had effected / to the glory of the God of Israel, and he rejoiced with me / very much and blessed me [with] a blessing of the age. He opened / his mouth to me and said in a loud voice, / "Blessed be the righteous shoot, and blessed / be his parents and teachers, and blessed be the people who come / with him, and blessed be the men who obey him. / Blessed be Yadod, the God / the God of Israel, his God who had blessed him [with] a blessing of the age [as] his blessing, for from [this blessing] all / will exist, grace and loving kindness surround it, and righteousness / and justice are within it. Arrows of mercy its bow / shoots forth, and from shedding the blood of the heart its sword restrains. / O mighty man, your heart is a flower planted in Eden, a blossom / that has shot forth from the heaven of heavens, because my war / is victorious, and the resemblance of my forehead, their character, the color / you have changed, and *you have stood upright* in all my vicissitudes and thoughts. / You have raised ink and by my ink have you been exalted. / You have hallowed the sign and by a sign and wonder / you have been exalted. / You have hallowed the sign and by a sign and wonder / you have been sanctified by the great and holy name, which has thus been called / .../...This name which is revered and respected will be your help and the sign / on the forehead will proclaim you.../...and he will extend to you the golden scepter / ...to make you live the life of the age. / This will be for you as a sign on the day when I wage war / with the inhabitants of the land, whom I will reveal to your ears / and you will see with your [own] eyes and understand in your heart the sign / which is explicitly hidden and sealed in my forehead... / ...The Rock of Israel judges character and judges measure for measure / so that those who dwell on high will return to dwell below [on the] earth. The nether regions will then become the heights of heaven. / The horn of the kingdom and the shofar of the government / will blast Baal Peor and will make the sound heard / from age to age, from boundary to / boundary... / ...to wreak vengeance from those who had shed innocent blood and behaved immorally... / ...[They will be called in] Torah and mitzwot, wearing / garments of revenge, and they will shoot arrows of judgment / into their hearts... / ...[I will announce] *good* tidings / to mention the names.

When I heard the blessing from the mouth of *this* man / who came to fight the wars of the Lord Yadod, the God of armies /.../ I bowed down and prostrated myself before him, and gave / praise to Yadod, the God who sent him / ... / ...The mighty reports of his hands / ... / ...made the heart of every strong man tremble and melted the strength of every / mighty man, and all the kings of the land and the mighty men / of the camps returned from their disaster empty-handed, / and after they had been estranged from their hopes, and every single one of them escaped with him and also caused *his servants* to flee / from fear of him. At that time, I placed my soul in my hands, I, Berakhiyaho[101] Ben Shluwiel, a servant / of Yadod, the God of Israel, and I made supplication / before him that he should inform me what will be the final outcome of our people after *these* wars. / I raised my eyes, and behold / three mighty men were pursuing one another.[102] / One ran after the other, *about* the distance / of a bow-shot apart from each other. *Each man* said / to his fellow, "Run and fight / against me!" I saw, and behold the *first* one ran / towards the second, and *the second* fled [from him]. As he fled, he shot after him / a sharp arrow. The arrow fell at his feet / ...It touched his foot, and clung to him. / The man began to cry *very* loudly / with a bitter [voice]: "O Yadod, God of my fathers, [help], for / the arrow which / *struck me* will slay me [for it is filled] with poison / which was in it!" While he was still speaking, his foot / swelled up like a goat skin bottle filled with air / ... / until it swelled up his limbs and the parts [of his body] like yeast. When I heard the sound of his cry / my mercy was stirred toward him, and I ran and came near / to him. I whispered in his ear, and his pain vanished / from all his body, because of my whispering. When / the first mighty man who had struck him / in the foot with his arrow saw that he was healed from his pain / through my whispering, he ran towards him with his spear, struck him on his navel, / and drove it into his belly. / His bowels fell to the ground. He fell / there, and he died. When the third one saw that / the first one killed the second, he ran after / the first with his sword drawn in his hand, and struck him / once, twice, and a third time, until / [he had given him] ten blows, and from the tenth he died.

I approached the smiter, greeted him, / and said to him, "May Yadod be with you, mighty man / of valor!" Now, O Lord, tell *me*, please, / the solutions of this war / which I have seen in the vision." Then he showed me an old man of great age[103] / sitting on

[101]Means "my blessing is Jehovah." Aescoly, p. 210, fn. 33, says Berakhiyaho means "Abraham," and Shluwiel means "Samuel."

[102]Judging from the military conflicts of the author's day, these three men may have represented the Christians, the Moslems, and the Jews—the last were the final victors.

[103]Such as the Ancient of Days who gave the kingdom to be one like the son of man and the saints of the Most High, namely Judah and the Jews of the Maccabean times. See Dan 7:13-14, 22. Also *To The Hebrews*. 38-51.

the throne of judgment. His clothes were blue and purple. He said, "Go, ask / that man who is sitting in the mountain of judgment, / and he will tell you and inform you what / these wars are and what will be their sequel, / for he is one of the sons of your people. I went up to / the mountain of judgment, and I approached the old man, / and I bowed down and prostrated myself and fell on my face / ... / ..., and he said to me, "My son, may your arrival be in peace; peace, / peace to you and to all who love you, because from the war you were delivered and all my wars / will be victorious for you. / Now, be sure and understand that *many* days / and years I have hoped for you here until your arrival. / Now I will tell you the solution of the / wars which you saw: The three / men who were pursuing one another, are the three kings who will arise from the three / corners of the earth, possessors of three conflicting philosophies. / They will line up for war, one with the other... / ...The third whom you saw / striking the first who was victorious over / the second... / is the king of the East[104] who / conquered the South who killed the North[105] / through the name of Yadod who struck the tenth / blow / continually, according to our measure... / ...He is not from among the sons of our people, only Yadod / sent him to fight for us against all our enemies. / Of the three kings, there are three / names of might, like the names of their generals / on high. The name of the one is Kadriel;[106] / the second is Magdiel;[107] and the name of the third / is Elpiel.[108] The name of the mighty man whom you saw / in the vision at the beginning is Toriel.[109] My name? I am Yahoel[110] who agreed to speak with you years ago, because he called your name: "You are Israel." / Royel,[111] the seer, the son of Makroel,[112] / is still living, for from the place of life you were decreed / if you choose, and you will live with the living. / ...Look! The fifth mighty man is my Messiah, / who will rule after the wars of the days of the four / kingdoms.[113] This is the solution which is revealed to all... / ...Now, you, my son Royel, thus Yadod the God of Israel has said

[104]The Moslem King.
[105]Byzantine and Roman Christians.
[106]My Potter is God.
[107]My blessing is God.
[108]My myriad is God.
[109]My Torah is God.
[110]Jehovah is God.
[111]My seer is God.
[112]My source is God.
[113]The four Gentile kingdoms that rule Palestine before the reestablishment of the Davidic kingdom (Dan 7:3-8).

to you, 'Write down all that which you saw in a book / and call the name of the book, "The Sign," and it will be / as a sign to all who see it, to know that Yadod / has spoken well concerning his people Israel, and already / he has agreed to save them. Then send the book / to Spain, and do not be afraid of anyone, and do not / be ashamed of human beings.../''' I acted according to all that *the old man* commanded me / and behold I have sent him to you today / for a deliverer to say, "Yadod be with you / when you return to him in this forty-eighth year (A.D. 1288) with a perfect heart."

Summary

This Cabbalistic "Book of the Sign" is clearly an eschatological prophecy, although its terminology is such that it is difficult, if not impossible, for the twentieth century Christian to understand all of the implications. Some general observations note the messianic emphasis with Zechariah as the Messiah of David who was suffering in hiding until the proper time to be revealed. The wars that are identified both with the four kingdoms of Daniel before the rule of the saints of the Most High and also the two men who were killed in combat, leaving only the one devoted to Yadod as a survivor. These probably were intended to be the wars of Christians and Moslems prior to the Battle of Acre (A.D. 1291). The Moslems were expected to finish off the Christians; Jews would kill the Moslems; and they would be left alone to rule, just as the saints of the Most High after the defeat of the four pagan kingdoms reported in the Book of Daniel. The distinguishing "sign" was painted on the foreheads. It both signified life and death. Its sign among pagans meant destruction where, like in the Book of Revelation, the sign of the "beast" promised security. But from a religious point of view, it indicated those who were among the elect who alone had life and would be redeemed and raised in the judgment.

Summary of The Day of Vindication

These poems and prophecies that anticipated the day of vindication wanted that day to come soon, and some of them specified the very year on which they expected it to occur. They also indicated what they expected to happen on that day. At that time the Battle of Gog and Magog would be fought; the political enemies would be destroyed; the son of David would succeed the son of Ephraim; Jews would all be redeemed and established in the Garden of Eden. This was all redemption literature. It showed the same basic theology as seen in other poetry, prayers, responsa, and historical accounts of prophetic movements. Those who say redemption literature is "fringe literature" point to the Talmud and Midrashim as the "normative Judaism" which is free from these eccentric influences. The next investigation will be into this very literature which is not so free from redemptive themes and nationalistic expectations as some would lead us to believe.

REDEMPTION IN THE TALMUD
AND MIDRASH

WHEN THE SON OF DAVID COMES

Rabbi Naḥman said to Rabbi Isaac, "Have you heard when *Bar Nafle* will come?" "Who is *Bar Nafle*?" he asked. [Rabbi Naḥman] said, "The Messiah." [Rabbi Isaac] said, "Do you call the Messiah *Bar Nafle* (בר נפלי)?" He answered, "Precisely. As it is written, *In that day I will raise up* (San 97a] *David's tent which is rickety* (הנופלת) (Amos 9:11). [Rabbi Naḥman said to him] "This is what Rabbi Jonathan said, 'The generation in which the son of David will come is one in which the scholars are few, and the eyes of the rest [of the people will fail with grief and longing. There will be much trouble and severe [anti-Jewish] decrees will be renewed, the second [hardship] will follow quickly after the first one.'"[1]

The teaching of the sages comes [to our aid]: The week [of years] in which the son of David comes: In the first year, this verse will be fulfilled: *I will provide rain in one city, and I will not provide rain on the other* (Amos 4:7). The second [year], the arrows of famine will be sent out. In the third [year], there will be a great famine. Men, women, and children, *hasidim,* and men of [miraculous] deeds will die, and the Torah will be forgotten by students. In the fourth [year] there will be satiety and no satiety. During the fifth [year], there will be a great abundance. [People] will eat, drink and be merry, and the Torah will return to its students. In the sixth [year], there will be voices; in the seventh [year], wars. At the close of the seventh [year], the son of David will come. Rabbi Joseph said, "Many weeks [of years][2] have been thus, but he has not come." Rabbi Abaye said, "Were there in the sixth [year] voices and in the seventh [year], wars? And were they further in their [prescribed sequence?"[3]

In which your enemies reproached, O Lord, when they reproached the footsteps of your Messiah (Ps 89:52). It has been taught: Rabbi Judah said, "The generation in which the son of David will come, the house of assembly will be for harlots; Galilee will be destroyed; Golan[4] will be desolate; men of the border [region] will wander around from city to city [as fugitives], and they will not be pitied.[5] Wisdom of scholars will be despised; those who fear sin will be rejected; the face of that generation will be

[1]These are the "birth pangs" of the Messiah. SML
[2]Literally, "sevenths." The context requires that "sevenths" be understood as "sevenths of a jubilee" or a week of years. Many such weeks, like the one described had come and gone.
[3]And not voices in the seventh and wars in the sixth.
[4]Ancient Gabalena. "Harlot" is a Jewish code name for Gentile.
[5]People will not show them hospitality by inviting them to stay in their homes. Cf. SSR II.13, 4.

like the face of a dog;[6] and truth will fail, as it is said, *Truth will fail, [and he who turns away from evil will be plundered]* (Isa 59:15). What is meant by, *Truth will fail* נעדרת (Isa 59:15)? The sayings of the school of Rab teaches, "It will be made into flocks (עדרים, עדרים) and vanish." What is meant by, *He who turns away from evil will be plundered* (Isa 59:15)? The sayings of the school of Rab Shila: "Everyone *who turns away from evil will be plundered* by the multitude." Raba said, "I formerly believed that there was no truth in the age.[7] [Then] a certain one of the rabbis, whose name is Rab Ṭabuth (others say Rabbi Ṭabiyomi was his name), who if he were given all the treasures of the age would not change his word, said to me, "One time I came to a place whose name was Kushta (truth), and no one changed his word, and no one died from there before his time. I married one of the women from there, and I had three sons from her. One day he was sitting in his house, and [his wife] was combing her hair. A neighbor lady came knocking at the door. He thought it would not be proper [to say that his wife was combing her hair], he said to her, "She is not here." His two sons died. Men of that place came to him, and they said to him, "Why was this?" He told them this event which happened. They said to him, "Please leave this place, and do not incite death against it because of you."

It has been taught: Rabbi Nahorai said, "The generation in which the son of David comes, young men will insult elders. Old men will stand up [in deference] to young men. Daughters will rise up against their mothers, and daughters-in-law against mothers-in-law. The face of that generation will be like the face of a dog, and a son will not be bashful in the presence of his father.[8]

It has been taught: Rabbi Nehemiah said, "The generation in which the son of David comes, impudence will increase; honor will be abased; the vine will produce its fruit, but wine will be expensive;[9] all the kingdom will be converted to heresy; and there will be no one to rebuke them. [This] supports Rabbi Isaac because Rabbi Isaac said, "The son of David will not come until all the

---

[6] In Jewish and Christian expression, the word "dog" was used derisively to mean "Gentile" (see *Consequences*, 184-89). This may mean that the generation in which the son of David comes will be one of strong Gentile appearance, like Palestine before the Maccabean rebellion.

[7] This age, before the Messiah comes.

[8] The generation will be strongly influenced by Gentile views and teachings, and children, who pick up Gentile ways, will not show the proper respect to their fathers or their fathers' tradition. Cf SSR II.15, 4.

[9] There will be so much heavy drinking.

kingdom is converted to heresy." Raba said, "What is the verse, *It is all turned white; he is clean* (Lev 13:13)?"[10]

Our rabbis taught: *"For the Lord will judge his people [and repent because of his servants] when he sees that their power is gone, and there is none shut up or left* (Dt 32:36). The son of David will not come until informers multiply." Another interpretation: Until the scholars diminish in number. Another interpretation: Until the last *perutah* is gone from the purse. Another explanation: Until they have given up hope of redemption, as it is said, *There is none shut up or left* (Dt 32:36). [It will be] forsaken, as it were, without supporter or helper for the Israelites, just as Rabbi Zera, when he found [one of] the rabbis busy with it [calculating the times of the end], would say to him, "Please, I beg of you, do not extend it, for it has been taught: Three things come unannounced, and these are they: The Messiah, [something] found, and a scorpion."

Rabbi Kattina said, "Six thousand years the world will exist, and one [thousand years] it will be desolate, as it is said, *The Lord alone will be exalted on that day* (Isa 2:11)."[11] Abaye said, "Two [thousand years] it will be desolate, as it is said, *He will revive us after two days. On the third day, he will raise us up, and we will live before him"* (Hos 6:2; Ps 90:4).

It has been taught in accordance with Rabbi Kattina: "Just as the seventh [year] is dormant for one year in seven years, thus the age[12] is dormant a thousand years in seven thousand years, as it is said, *The Lord alone will be exalted on that day* (Isa 2:11), and it says [also], *A psalm, a song for the Sabbath day* (Ps 92:1), when it is all Sabbath, and it says, *For a thousand years in your eyes are as yesterday, for it will pass"* (Ps 90:4).

[The Tanna] Debe Eliyahu teaches, "The world exists six, thousand years. Two thousand [years] were desolation; two thousand [years] of Torah; [and] two thousand years are the days

---

[10]A reference to leprosy. A leper was judged unclean because he had skin of two different colors. Colors of skin were not to be mixed, they thought, any more than grain in the field, beasts under one yoke, or threads in one garment. Once a person's body was completely covered with some skin disease, his skin then would all be of one color. He was clean, even though more seriously diseased than before. By analogy, when a generation became completely bad, it was "clean" and ready for the Messiah.

[11]The desolate world cannot be exalted.

[12]To follow the imagery of a year being dormant, the comparative element (עולם) should also be temporal and rendered "age," rather than "world," but that which is dormant *during* the seventh year is the field, and therefore *during* the age, the world will be dormant.

of the Messiah; (San 97b) but in our iniquities, which are many, some of them, which have passed, have been lost."[13]

Elijah said to Rab Judah, the brother of Rab Sulla, the *ḥasid*, "The [duration] of the age is no less than eighty-five jubilees, and in the last jubilee, the son of David will come (ca A.D. 490). [Rab Judah] said to him [Elijah], "At its beginning or at its end?" [Elijah] said to him, "I do not know." [Rab Judah asked further], "Will it be completed or will it not be completed?" [Elijah] said to him, "I do not know." Rabbi Ashi said, "Until then, do not expect him; from then on, expect him."

Rab Ḥanan Bar Taḥlifa sent [the following message] to Rab Joseph, "I met a man in whose hand was a scroll, written in Assyrian [alphabet] but in Hebrew language. I said to him, 'Where did you get this?' He said to me, 'I was employed by the Roman army, and I found it among the archives of Rome.'[14] In it was written, 'After four thousand, two hundred, ninety years of the creation of the world (A.D. 530), the world will be left [desolate].[15] Some of them [the years that follow] will be [marked by] wars with sea monsters; some of them will be [marked by] wars of Gog and Magog; and the rest will be the days of the Messiah.[16] The holy One blessed be He will not renew his world until after seven thousand years.'"[17] Rab Aha, the son of Raba, said, "'After five thousand years,' was the statement."

It has been taught: Rabbi Nathan said, "This verse pierces and goes down to the abyss:[19] *For the vision is still for an appointed time. It will speak, at the end, and not lie. If he is late, wait for him, for he will surely come, and he will not be late* (Hab 2:3). Not as our rabbis when they interpreted [the verse], *Until a time, two times, and half a time* (Dan 7:25); and not as Rabbi Simlai, who used to interpret, *You feed them the bread of tears and make them drink in tears a third time* (Ps 80:6); and not as Rabbi Akiba, who used to interpret, *Yet once [more]; it is a short time, and I will shake the heavens and the earth* (Hag 2:6), but the first kingdom[20]

[13]According to tradition, Abraham was fifty-two years old when the third millennium began. The fourth millennium ended one hundred, seventy-two years after the destruction of the temple (ca. A.D. 240 . So Soncino, *loc. cit.*). This means the Tanna was speaking near the end of the second two thousand year period. Like most calculators, he expected the days of the Messiah to follow shortly.

[14]So he obviously purloined it.

[15]Literally, "Orphaned."

[16]After the Gentiles are defeated, and the Messiah is enthroned.

[17]Ca. A.D. 3240.

[18]A.D. 1240—a much more likely prediction, since it was much nearer.

[19]To the very heart of the matter.

[20]The kingdom of David and Solomon.

[lasted] seventy years; the second,[21] fifty-two [years]; and the kingdom of Ben Kozibah,[22] two years and a half."

What is meant by [the verse], *it will speak at the end, and it will not lie* (Hab 2:3)? Rabbi Samuel Bar Naḥmani said that Rabbi Jonathan said, "May the bones of those who calculate the end times be crushed!" For they used to say, "Since he reached the end [appointed], and again he did not come, he will not come; but wait for him, as it is said, *If he is late, wait for him* (Hab 2:3)." Perhaps you will say, 'We are waiting, but he is not waiting.' The scripture says, *Therefore the Lord will wait to show favor to you. Therefore he will be exalted so as to be merciful to you* (Isa 30:18). Since we are waiting, he is waiting. Who is hindering [his coming]? The measure of justice impedes [him], and since the measure of justice impedes, why do we wait?[23] To receive the reward [that comes from waiting], as it is said, *Blessed is everyone who waits for him* (Isa 30:18).[24]

Abaye said, "[There must be in] the world no less than thirty-six righteous men, approved before the Shekinah in every generation, as it is said, *Blessed is everyone who waits for him* (Isa 30:18). In *gematria* ‏לו‎ ('for him') equals thirty-six." But was it not the saying of Raba, "The row of those who stand before the holy One blessed be He are eighteen thousand, as it is said, *Approximately eighteen thousand*" (Ezek 48:35)? There is no difficulty. One [refers to] those who see through clear glass,[25] and the other [number refers to] those who see through a glass that is not clear.[26] Who are all these souls? The saying of Hezekiah is that Rabbi Jeremiah said in the name of Rabbi Shimon Ben Yoḥai, "I saw the sons of the Most High, and they are few. If there are a thousand, my son and I are among them; if there are a hundred, my son and I are among them; if there are two, my son and I are they." There is no difficulty. One [refers to] those who enter with restrictions and the other [the thirty-six refers to] those who enter without restrictions.

Rab said, "All the [calculated] ends have passed, so the matter

---

[21]The Hasmonean kingdom.

[22]A.D. 132-35. All three periods were considered "days of the Messiah," because Israel was established under her own king.

[23]Since nothing either Jews or God can do about it. It all hangs in the balance of the scale of justice. Jews can add to the treasury, but they cannot by-pass it.

[24]Rewards in the treasury of merits.

[25]Speaking in terms of very strict righteousness, therefore the thirty-six.

[26]The eighteen thousand.

depends only on repentance and good works,"[27] but Samuel said, "It is enough for the mourner that they endure his mourning."[28] According to the Tannaite, Rabbi Eliezer said, "If the Israelites do repentance, they will be redeemed, but if they do not do repentance, they will not be redeemed." Rabbi Joshua said, "If they do not do repentance, they will not be redeemed, but the holy One blessed be He will raise up against them a king whose [anti-Jewish] decrees will be as harsh as Haman's. Then the Israelites will do repentance, and he will restore them to the right [way]." Another *baraitha* teaches: Rabbi Eliezer said, "If Israelites do repentance, they will be redeemed, as it is said, *Return, repentant children. I will heal your backslidings*" (Jer 3:22). Rabbi Joshua said to him, "Is it not already said, *You have been sold for nothing and not for money. You will be redeemed without cost* (Isa 52:3). *You were sold* to idolatry. *You will be redeemed without money*—without repentance and good works." Rabbi Eliezer said to Rabbi Joshua, "Has it not already been said, *Return to me, and I will return to you* (Mal 3:7)? Rabbi Joshua said to him, "Has it not already been said, *For I will be master over you, and I will take you, one from a city and two from a family, and I will bring you [to] Zion* (Jer 3:14)?[29] Rabbi Eliezer said to him, "Has it not already been said, *In returning and rest you will be saved*" (Isa 30:15)? Rabbi Joshua said to Rabbi Eliezer, "Has it not been already said, *Thus said the Lord, the Redeemer of Israel and his Holy One, "To the one whom a soul despises and to the one whom a nation abhors, to a servant of rulers.* (San 98a). *Kings will see and arise. Princes will arise and prostrate themselves"* (Isa 49:7)?[30] Rabbi Eliezer said to him, "Has it not already been said, *'If you return, O Israel,' said the Lord, 'return to me'"* (Jer 4:1)? Rabbi Joshua said to him, "Has it not already been said, *I heard the man dressed in linen who was on the water of the river, and he raised his right and his left hands to heaven and took an oath by the life of the age that it would be for a time, two times, and half a time. When the one who shatters the power of the holy people has finished, all these things will be completed"* (Dan 12:7)?[31] Then Rabbi Eliezer was silent.

Rabbi Abba said, "You have no [sign of the] end more obvious

[27]On the basis of sabbatical justice, they should have been released before then. The term had evidently been extended because of additional sin. This, then, must be balanced by corresponding repentance and good works.

[28]The diaspora Jew is described here as the mourner. While mourning, how can he be expected also to be doing good works?

[29]Without any special conditions of additional repentance and good deeds.

[30]While still abhorred. Without repentance and good deeds about which to boast.

[31]Without repentance and good works.

than this, as it is said, *You, O mountains of Israel, will produce branches, and you will yield your fruit for my people, the Israelites, [for they are ready to come]"* (Ezek 36:8). Rabbi (Eliezer) said, "Even [more obvious] than this, as it is said, *For before those days there will be no salary for a man and none for a beast, both in going out and coming in, there will be no peace from affliction* (Zech 8:10). What is the meaning of [the passage], *Both in going out and coming in, there will be no peace from affliction"* (Zech 8:10)? Rab said, "Even the disciples of the wise men of whom peace is written, *Great peace is there for those who love your Torah* (Ps 119:165), *there will be no peace from affliction"* (Zech 8:10). Samuel said, "Until all the measures are equal."[32]

Rabbi Ḥanina said, "The son of David will not come until a fish is sought for a sick person, and it cannot be found, as it is said, *Then I will make their water deep and their rivers to run like oil* (Ezek 32:14), and it is written, *In that day I will make a horn shoot forth from the house of Israel"* (Ezek 39:21).

Rabbi Ḥama Ben Ḥanina said, "The son of David will not come until the despicable (הזולה) kingdom[33] ceases from [ruling] Israel, as it is said, *I will cut off the despicable ones (הזלזלים) with pruning hooks* (Isa 18:5), and it is written after it, *In that day gifts will be brought to the Lord of armies of a people that is stretched and bald"* (Isa 18:7).

Zeiri said that Rabbi Ḥanina said, 'The son of David will not come until the arrogant men have ceased in Israel, as it is said, *Because then I will turn away from your midst those who rejoice in your pride* (Zeph 3:11), and it is written, *I will leave in your midst a poor and humble people, and they will take refuge in the name of the Lord'* (Zeph 3:12).

Rabbi Simlai said in the name of Rabbi Eliezer, son of Shimon, "The son of David will not come until all the judges and officers are gone from Israel, as it is said, *And I will turn my hand back against you, and I will smelt away your dross with lie [and remove all your alloy], and I will restore your judges"* (Isa 1:25-26).[34]

Ulla said, "Jerusalem will be redeemed only by righteousness, as it is said, *Zion will be redeemed in judgment and her returnees, in righteousness"* (Isa 1:27).

Rab Papa said, "When the arrogant cease [from Israel], the magi[35] will cease [from Persia]; when judges cease [from Israel],

---

[32]Until there have been accumulated enough suffering to balance the sinfulness.
[33]Rome.
[34]Which will be necessary, because no judges will be left then.
[35]May here refer to Persians in general.

the high ranking officers [of Persia] (ירפת׳זרג) will cease. When the haughty cease to exist, the magi cease to exist, as it is written, *I will smelt away your haughty ones and remove all your alloy* (Isa 1:25). When the judges cease to exist [in Israel], the high ranking officers [in Persia] will cease, of which it is written, *The Lord will take away your judgments; he has cast out your enemy"* (Zeph 3:15).

Rabbi Yohanan said, "When you see a generation which is continually diminishing, wait for him [the Messiah], as it is written, *This afflicted people you will save* (II Sam 22:28). Rabbi Yohanan said, "When you see a generation on which many hardships have come like a river, wait for him [the Messiah], as it is said, *When the oppressor, like a river, comes, the spirit of the Lord will raise a standard against him* (Isa 59:19); and [the following text] supports it, *A redeemer will come to Zion* (Isa 59:20).

Rabbi Yohanan said, "The son of David will come only in a generation which is all meritorious or all sinful. In a generation which is all meritorious, of which it is written, *Your people are all righteous; they will inherit the land for the age* (Isa 60:21). In the generation which is all sinful, of which it is written, *He saw that there was no man, and he was astonished because there was no intercessor* (Isa 59:16), and it is written, *For my sake I will act"* (Isa 48:11).

Rabbi Alexandri said, "Rabbi Joshua Ben Levi interjected, 'It is written, *In its time* (Isa 60:22), and it is written, *I will hasten it;* [if] they are meritorious, *I will hasten it;*[36] [if] they are not meritorious, *in its time.'"* Rabbi Alexandri said, "Rabbi Joshua Ben Levi interjected: 'It is written, *One will come with the clouds of heaven like a son of man* (Dan 7:13), and it is written, *Afflicted and riding upon a donkey* (Zech 9:9). [If] they are meritorious, *with the clouds of heaven;* [if] they are not meritorious, *afflicted and riding upon a donkey'"* The king Shapur said to Samuel, "You have said the Messiah will come on a donkey. I will send him a white horse of mine." He [Samuel] said to him, "Do you have a white dappled horse?"[37]

Rabbi Joshua Ben Levi found Elijah when he was standing at the

---

[36]Shorten the sentence for good behavior.

[37]It is not clear why Samuel asked for a white dappled horse, but the offer seems to have been a plan to weaken Rome. If the Jews were to start a military rebellion against Rome, Persia would be willing to strengthen the movement by providing supplies. This means that the Persian king understood the Messiah to have been closely associated in Jewish minds with military resistance. That is why countries found it necessary to suppress these messianic movements that threatened to overthrow foreign powers from within.

entrance of Rabbi Shimon Ben Yoḥai's cave. [Rabbi Joshua] said to him, "Will I be in the age to come?" [Elijah] said to him, "If the Lord wills." Rabbi Joshua Ben Levi said, "I saw two, and I heard the voice of a third." [Rabbi Joshua] said to him, "When will the Messiah come?" He said to him, "Go, ask him about it. He is sitting there at the gate of the city." [Rabbi Joshua asked], "What are his signs?" [Elijah replied], "He is sitting among the poor who are afflicted with leprosy, and they untie all [their bandages] and tie them [again] at one time, but he unwraps one and binds one [again]. He said, "It may be that I will be wanted, and I must not hinder." [Rabbi Joshua] went out to meet him. He said to him, "Peace be upon you, Master and Teacher." [The Messiah] said to him, "Peace be upon you, son of Levi." [Rabbi Joshua] said to him, "When will you come, Sir?" [The Messiah] said to him, "Today." [Rabbi Joshua] went to Elijah. He said to him, "What did he tell you?" [Rabbi Joshua] said to him, "Peace be upon you, son of Levi." [Elijah] said to him, "He assured you and your father [a portion] for the age to come." [Rabbi Joshua] said to him, "He lied to me by saying that he would come today, but he has not come." [Elijah] said to him, "This is what he said to you, *Today, if you hear my voice* (Ps 95:7).

The disciples of Rabbi Jose Ben Ḳisma asked him, "When will the son of David come?" He said, "I am afraid that perhaps you will seek a sign from me." They said to him, "We will not seek a sign from you." He said to them, "When this gate falls and is rebuilt and falls and is rebuilt and falls [a third time],[38] there will not be enough [time] to rebuild it [again] before the son of David comes." They said to him, "Our Rabbi, give us a sign." He said to them, "Did you not say this to me, that you would not seek a sign from me?" They said to him, "Even so, [we want one]." He said to them, "If so, let the water of the cave of Panias change to blood,'" and it was changed to blood. When he was dying, he said to them, "Put my coffin deep, [San 98b] because there is not a single palm tree in Babylon to which a Persian horse will not be tied, and you will not have a coffin in the land of Israel in which a Median horse will not eat straw."[39]

Rab said, "The son of David will not come until the [Roman] government is stretched out over Israel for nine months, as it is said, *Therefore, he will give them up until the time of a woman's*

[38]See "The Secrets of Rabbi Shimon Ben Yoḥai, Horowitz text, 190-91: "When you see that the western Gairun which is in Damascus has fallen, the kingdom of the Easterners will have fallen.'"
[39]See also SSR 8:9 §3.

pregnancy is completed. Then the rest of his brothers will return to the sons of Israel" (Micah 5:2).

Ulla said, "Let him [the Messiah] come, but let me not see him." Thus also said Rabbah, "Let him come, but let me not see him." Rab Joseph said, "Let him come, and may I be meritorious so that I might sit in the shadow of his donkey's saddle. Abaye said to Rabbah, "What is your reason [for not wanting to see him]?" Perhaps it is because of the birth pangs of the Messiah?[40] It has been taught, "The disciples of Rabbi Eliezer asked him, 'What should a man do so as to be saved from the birth pangs of the Messiah?' [Rabbi Eliezer answered], 'Let him work in the Torah and [make] the contributions to the *hasidim.'*[41] He said [to Rabbi Eliezer], 'Perhaps sin will be the cause [of the Messiah's delay so that he will not see him].'[42] In the words of Rab Jacob Bar Idi, Rab Jacob Bar Idi interjected, "It is written, *Behold, I am with you, and I will guard you wherever you go* (Gen 28:15), and it is [also] written, *And Jacob was afraid and deeply troubled"* (Gen 32:8). He was afraid perhaps sin might be the cause [of God's promise being annuled], as it is taught, *Until your people cross over, O Lord* (Ex 15:16). This is the first advent [into Palestine]. *Until this people whom you purchased cross over* (Ex 15:16), this is the second advent.[43] Say, "From then on Israelites were qualified [for God] to perform a miracle for them at the second advent, just as at the first advent, but sin misled them.'"

Thus [also] Rabbi Yoḥanan said, "Let him come, but let me not see him."[44] Resh Laḳish said to him, "What is the reason? Unless perhaps because of the scripture, *Just as a man flees before a lion, and a bear meets him, [He comes into his house], leans his hand against the wall, and a snake bites him* (Amos 5:19). Come and I will show you an illustration of it in this world. When a man goes out to the field, and a bailiff meets him,[45] it is as if a lion had met

[40]The birth pangs of the Messiah involved the bloody war necessary to overthrow the Romans, the Moslems, or both, before Israel could rule the territory then controlled by both.

[41]Repentance and good deeds might win the merit of a miracle which would "hasten the end," reduce the sentence, and perhaps establish the Messiah on his throne with a minimum of birth pangs.

[42]Since birth pangs accompany the advent of the Messiah, sin would add to the sentence and postpone the coming of the Messiah. If the Messiah did not come in their lifetimes, they would be spared the preceding birth pangs.

[43]The first advent was the crossing of the Jordan and acquisition of the land by Joshua; the second would be the reestablishment of the land by the conquest led by the Messiah.

[44]And have to suffer the birth pangs that accompany his advent.

[45]To serve him some kind of notice, such as a notice that his mortgage was overdue, and the field would be taken as payment.

him. He enters the city, and a tax collector meets him, it is as if a bear had confronted him. He enters his house and finds that his sons and daughters had overtaken with famine. It is as if a snake had bitten him, but [his reason for not wanting to see the Messiah] is because of the scripture, *Ask, now, and see if a male bears a child. Why have I seen every man's* (גבר) *hand on his loins like a pregnant woman giving birth and all faces turned pale* (Jer 30:6)? Raba Bar Isaac said that Rab said, "Who understands his strength (גבורה)?" What is the meaning of [the verse], *And all their forces turned pale* (Jer 30:6)? Rabbi Yoḥanan said, "It is the family above and the family below. When the holy One blessed be He says, 'These [Gentiles] are the work of my hands, and these [Israelites] are the work of my hands. How can I destroy these [Gentiles] because of these [Israelites]?'" Rab Papa said, "The saying is, 'The ox [the Israelites] runs and falls; a horse [the Gentiles] is put in its stable.'"[46]

Rab Giddal said Rab said, "Israelites are destined to eat [during] the years of the Messiah." Rab Joseph said, "It is obvious. Who else would eat for them? Will Ḥilek and Bilek eat for them?"[47] This was in opposition to the interpretation of Rabbi Hillel, who said, "There will be no Messiah for the Israelites, because they have already consumed him in the days of Hezekiah."

Rab said, "The World was only created for David." Samuel said, "For Moses." Rabbi Yoḥanan said, "For the Messiah." What is his name? Rabbi Shila's school said, "Shiloh will be his name, because it is said, *Until Shiloh comes* (Gen 49:10). The school of Rabbi Janni said, "His name is Yinon,[48] for it is said, *His name will be for the age before the sun, Yinon is his name*" (Ps 72:17). The school of Rabbi Ḥanina said, "His name will be Ḥanina (favor), as it is said, *Where I will not give you favor*" (Jer 16:13). Some say, "His name will be Menaḥem ben Hezekiah, for it is said, *Because Menaḥem, restoring my soul, is far from me*" (Lam 1:16). Our Rabbis say, "Hiorah (leper) Debi Rabbi is his name, as it is said, *Therefore he has borne our sicknesses and carried our sorrows, but we considered him a leper, struck by God, and afflicted*" (Isa 53:4).

Rab Naḥman said, "If he is alive, he is [someone] like me, as it is written, *His noble one shall be from him, and his ruler will go out from his midst*" (Jer 30:21). Rab said, "If he were among the living,

[46]The Gentiles are in Palestine (stable) because the Jews (ox) stumbled. Once the stable is occupied it is difficult to regain possession of it.
[47]Probably indefinite names like Tom, Dick, and Harry.
[48]One of the accepted names for the Messiah.

he would be like our sainted rabbi. If he were from the dead, he would be like the most excellent man, Daniel. Rab Judah said Rab said, "The holy One blessed be He is destined to raise up for them another David, as it is said, *They will serve the Lord their God and David, their king, whom I will raise up for them* (Jer 30:9). 'I raised up' is not said, but *I will raise up.*" Rab Papa said to Abaye, "But it is written, *And David, my servant, will be a prince for them for the age* (Ezek 37:25), like Caesar or a viceroy."[49]

Rabbi Simlai explained: "What is the meaning of the scripture, *Woe to [you] who long for the day of the Lord. Why is this day of the Lord [important] for you? It is darkness and not light* (Amos 5:18). This can be compared to a rooster and a bat who were waiting for the light. The rooster said to the bat, 'I look forward to the light because it is light for me, but you, what is the light for you?'" [San 99a] A certain heretic said to Rabbi Abbahu, "When will the Messiah come?" [Rabbi Abbahu] said to him, "When darkness covers these men!"[50] [The heretic] said, "You escape to curse me!" [Rabbi Abbahu] read, "It is written, *For darkness covers the earth, and gloom, the Gentiles, but the Lord will rise up over you and his glory will appear upon you*" (Isa 60:2).

It has been taught: "Rabbi Eliezer said, 'The days of the Messiah [will last] forty years, as it is said, *For forty years I will take hold of the generation*'" (Ps 95:10). Rabbi Eliezer Ben Azariah said, "Seventy years, as it is said, *And it will happen on that day that Tyre will be forgotten for seventy years, according to the days of one king*" (Isa 23:15). "Who is this special king?" He said, "This is the Messiah." Rabbi said, "Three generations, as it is said, *They will fear you with the sun and before the moon, a generation and two generations*" (Ps 72:5).

Rabbi Hillel said, "There will be no Messiah for the Israelites, because they already consumed him in the days of Hezekiah." Rab Joseph said, "May the Lord forgive Rabbi Hillel. When did Hezekiah [rule]? During the first temple. But if Zechariah was prophesying during the second temple, saying, *Rejoice greatly, daughter of Zion; shout, daughter of Jerusalem, for your king will come to you, a righteous man and a savior. He is afflicted and riding on a donkey, on a colt, the foal of a donkey* (Zech 9:9), [the prophecy could not apply to the earlier Hezekiah]."

Another [*baraitha*] taught: Rabbi Eliezer said, "The days of the Messiah are forty years. Here it is written, *He will afflict you, and*

---

[49]Obviously a political figure.
[50]These Gentiles and heretics.

make you happy, and he will feed you [with manna] (Dt 8:3), but that [other] passage is written, Make us glad according to the days you have afflicted us" (Ps 90:15). Rabbi Dosa said: "Four hundred years, as it is written, They [the Israelites] served them, and they [the Egyptians] afflicted them [the Israelites] four hundred years" (Gen 15:13), and the scripture concludes, Make us happy according to the days you have afflicted us" (Ps 90:15). Rabbi said, "Three hundred, sixty-five years, according to the number of the days [of the rotation] of the sun, as it is said, For a day of vengeance is in my heart, but a year of redemption has come" (Isa 63:4; see also Num 14:34). What does [the expression], For a day of vengeance is in my heart, mean? Rabbi Yohanan said, "I have revealed [it] to my heart; to my limbs, I have not revealed [it]." Rabbi Shimon Ben Lakish said, "I have revealed it to my heart; to the ministering angels I have not revealed [it]." Abimi, the son of Rabbi Abbahu, taught, "The days of the Messiah [will last] for Israel seven thousand years, as it is said, A bridegroom, rejoicing over a bride, [thus] the Lord your God will rejoice over you" (Ps 9:4). Rab Judah said Samuel said, "The days of the Messiah will endure like [a period of time, extending] from the day the world was created until now, as it is said, Like the days of heaven over the earth" (Dt 11:21). Rab Nahman Bar Isaac said, "Like the [period of time extending] from the days of Noah until now, as it is said, For this is to me the waters of Noah by which I have sworn" (Isa 54:9). Rabbi Hiyya Bar Abba said Rabbi Yohanan said, "All the prophets prophesied only for the days of the Messiah, but for the age to come, Eye has not seen, O God, except you [that which God] will do for those who wait for him" (Isa 64:4), and he differed with Samuel, because Samuel said, "There is no difference between this age and the days of the Messiah except the subjection to [foreign] governments only." Rabbi Hiyya Bar Abba said Rabbi Yohanan said, "All the prophets prophesied only for the repentant sinners, but as for the completely righteous, Eye has not seen, O God, except you (Isa 64:4); and he differed with Rabbi Abbahu, because Rabbi Abbahu said (that Rabbi Yohanan said), "The place where repentant sinners stand, there the completely righteous cannot stand, as it is said, Peace, peace to the one who is far off and to the one who is near (Isa 57:19). At first the one who is far off; then the one who is near. What does far off mean? Far away from the root. What does near mean? Near the root, and now Rabbi Yohanan said, To the one who is far off—Who is far off from sin. Who is near—who is near to sin and has been removed from it."

Rabbi Ḥiyya Bar Abba said Rabbi Yoḥanan said, "All the prophets prophesied only for the one who marries his daughter to a disciple of the wise, one who engages in business for a disciple of the wise, and one who benefits a disciple of the wise with his possessions; but of the disciples of the wise, themselves, *Eye has not seen, O God, except you* (Isa 64:4). What does *Eye has not seen* mean? Rabbi Joshua Ben Levi said, "This is wine that has been kept with its grapes since the six days of creation." Resh Laḳish said, "This Eden, no eye has seen from the age. Perhaps you will say, 'Where did Adam live?' 'In the garden,' and if you say, 'The garden is Eden,' the scripture teaches, *A river went out from Eden to water the garden*" (Gen 2:10).[51]

Summary

The extent to which prominent rabbis considered, discussed, and debated the subject of the Messiah's arrival shows that this was a very important part of their doctrine. Even those who suggested that he would never come did so in the context of sabbatical calculations that had failed, and they continued to exhort, "But wait for him." They gave some strained interpretations to numerous scriptural texts that they brought to bear on the subject. The roles of repentance and good deeds were set over against the sheer requirements of sabbatical justice: the captive should be returned on the sabbatical year, even if the debt had not been completely paid. The roles of sin and punishment, virtue and reward were considered within the context of the treasury of merits. These rabbis did not go into detail about the various personages involved, such as the Messiah of Joseph, his mother, Hafzi-bah, Armilos, and others. The center of interest was David's son, the time of his advent, the nature and extent of birth pangs related to the wars of Gog and Magog, his name, his relation to the resurrection, and the days of the Messiah. They compared the days of the Messiah to the government of Rome and expected that the Messianic reign would be over a similar territorial government. The difference would be the status of Jews in that kingdom in relationship to the Gentiles. The days of the Messiah would make the Gentiles subject to the Jews rather than vice versa. This is not all that the rabbis had to say on the subject, but this much was organized into one major topic because of its importance.

[51]Since the river went from Eden to the garden, the garden was not in Eden. This dissertation is from Sanhedrin 96b-99a.

BARGAINING WITH TIME

[For the famine has been] in the midst of the land (Gen 45:6). Rabbi Hananiah said, "After four hundred [years have elapsed] since the destruction of the temple, if a man says to you, 'Take a field worth a thousand dinars for one dinar,' do not take [it], in expectation." Another Tanna [said], "Four thousand, two hundred, thirty-one years from creation of the age, if a man says to you, 'Take for yourself a field worth a thousand dinars for one dinar, do not take [it]." What is the difference between them? Three years of expectation more [for the Tanna] (Avodah Zarah 9b).

Summary

This is the earliest reference to a date by the calendar now followed by most Jews, from the creation of the world. Four hundred years is probably based either on the years spent in Egypt or ten times the number of years spent in the wilderness. 400+68=468, based on the date Rabbi Hananiah had in mind with A.D. 68 considered the date for the destruction of Jerusalem. A.M. 4231=A.D. 471. This is three years later than A.D. 468. The practical considerations that were taken into account show the seriousness with which rabbis took their calculations.

THEOLOGY AND LITURGY

Rabbi Aha said, "Why did they put the redeemer of Israel into the seventh benediction?[52] It is to teach you that Israel will only be redeemed on the seventh."[53] Rabbi Jonah, in the name of Rabbi Aha, [said], "*A Song of Ascents, When the Lord Restores the Captivity to Zion* (Ps 126:1), is the seventh song. This is to inform you that Israel will only be redeemed on the seventh." Rabbi Hiyya Bar Abba said, "Why did they establish a healer of the invalids in the eighth benediction? It corresponds to circumcision, which is on the eighth [day], because my covenant was life for him."[54] Rabbi Alexandri said, "Why did they establish the blessing of years as the ninth benediction? To correspond to, *The voice of the Lord breaks*

[52]Of the Eighteen Benedictions. See Singer, *Authorized Daily Prayer Book,* 44-54. This discussion is translated from JBerachot II (17a). SML

[53]The seventh year, jubilee year, millennium, etc.

[54]With circumcision, the child enters the covenant and becomes "alive." See *Consequences,* 110-149.

the cedars (Ps 29:5), because he is destined to *break* all the lords of gates." Rabbi Levi, in the name of Rabbi Aha Bar Ḥanina [said], "Why did they find it suitable to bring into proximity, 'The Blessing of the Years' and 'The Gatherer of the Exiles of Israel'? Because of *And you, mountains of Israel...will bear fruit for my people Israel* (Ezek 36:8). Why? Because the exiles are gathering and drawing near, and the judgment will make the tyrants subject and the righteous happy. It teaches that he will include the heretics and the wicked ones in the subjection of the tyrants. But the proselytes and elders [he will include] with the promise of the righteous. [He will include] David in the blessing for "The Builder of Jerusalem," after the Israelites return *To seek the Lord their God and David their king*" (Hos 3:5). The rabbis said, "That messianic king: if he is not someone living, his name is David; if he is not someone timid, his name is David." Rabbi Tanḥuma said, "Where do you find the proof? *And he bestows his grace to his Messiah, to David*" (Ps 18:50). Rabbi Jehoshua Ben Levi said, *Shoot* is his name." Rabbi Judan Ben Rabbi Ayyabo said, "'Menaḥem' is his name." Ḥanina Ben Rabbi Abbahu said, "There is no contradiction between these opinions. According to these opinions, he is both *Shoot* and he is also 'Menaḥem.'"

Summary

In their analysis of the reasons why the Eighteen Benedictions were organized in the very way they now are, the rabbis looked for reasons based on important theological doctrines: Redemption, restoration of the captives, circumcision and life, fruitfulness of the restored land in the future, subjection of tyrants and heretics, reconstruction of Jerusalem, and the establishment of the Messiah as king of Israel. The centrality of redemption in this discussion is obvious.

ZION[55]

At the time when the holy One blessed be He sought to destroy the house of the sanctuary, he said, "When I am in its midst, the Gentiles will not touch it, but I will close my eyes from it, and I will swear that I will not cleanse it[56] until the time of the end, then

[55]Introduction to LamR 24 (6d).
[56]The temple was defiled even before it was destroyed.

the enemies will come and destroy it." At once the holy One blessed be He swore by his right hand and returned it behind him, for thus it is written, *He returned his right hand behind him before the enemy* (Lam 2:3). At that time the enemies entered the temple and burned it.[57] After it had been burned, the holy One blessed be He said, "Again I have no residence in the land. I will take my Shekhinah from it, and I will go up to my first habitation,[58] for thus is it written, *I will go and return to my place until they have become guilty and see my face"* (Hos 5:15). Then the holy One blessed be He wept and said, "Woe to me! What have I done? I have made my Shekhinah dwell below for the sake of Israel, but now that they have sinned, I have returned to my first place. Heaven forbid that I become a laughing stock for the Gentiles and an object of scorn to human beings!" Then Mettatron came, fell on his face, and said to him, "Master of the age, I am weeping, but you must not weep." He said to him, "If you do not permit me to weep now, I will enter the place where you are not permitted to enter,[59] and [there I will] weep, as it is said, *If you will not hear it, my soul will weep in secret because of pride"* (Jer 13:17).

The holy One blessed be He said to the ministering angels, "Come, and let us go together to see my house, what the enemies have done to it." At once the holy One blessed be He and the ministering angels went with Jeremiah before him [the holy One blessed be He]. When the holy One blessed be He saw the house of the sanctuary, he said, "Certainly this is my house, and this is my resting place into which the enemies have come and done as they pleasèd." The holy One blessed be He wept and said, "Woe to me, because of my house! My sons, where are you? My priests, where are you? My lovers, where are you? What can I do with you? I warned you, and you did not return in repentance." The holy One blessed be He said to Jeremiah, "Today I am like a man who had an only son, who made him a canopy, but he died in the midst of his canopy."

ZION[60]

All the prayers of humanity[61] are only for the earth: "Lord, may

[57]Titus in A.D. 70.

[58]In heaven. He condescended to make his presence dwell at Zion when the temple was standing.

[59]The holy of holies in heaven.

[60]GenR 13:2 (32b). SML

[61]The word rendered "humanity"(ברי ות)usually refers to all humanity. Here it seems to mean only the Gentiles in contrast to the Jews.

the land serve; Lord, may the land succeed." All the prayers of the Israelites are only for the house of the sanctuary: "Lord, may the house of the sanctuary be rebuilt; Lord, may the house of the sanc- tuary be rebuilt."

ZION[62]

Why are they [the Israelites] compared to the stars, but not to the sun and the moon? Abraham is compared to the sun, Isaac to the moon, and Jacob, to the stars, as it is said, *The moon will be confounded, and the sun will be ashamed, for the Lord of armies will rule on Mount Zion and in Jerusalem, and across from his elders [he will display] his glory* (Isa 24:23).

ZION[63]

From your temple over Jerusalem, kings will bring your gifts (Ps 68:8). Is not *from the temple to Jerusalem* an easy thing?[64] But just as the *gifts* are established *from the temple* to Jerusalem, thus processions with *gifts* are destined to be established *from the temple* for the messianic king.[65] This is what is written, *All kings will prostrate themselves before him* (Ps 72:11). Rabbi Cohen, the brother of Rabbi Ḥiyyah Bar Abba, said, "Just as the Shekinah is established *from the temple* to *Jerusalem,* thus the Shekinah will fill the world *from* one end of the world to the other, as it is written, *And his glory will fill all the land. Amen. Amen.* (Ps 72:19).

MESSIAH[66]

He said, "All the gifts which our father Jacob gave Esau, the Gentiles are destined to return to the messianic king in the future. What is the proof? *The kings of Tarshish and the Isles will return a gift* (Ps 72:10). It is not written here, 'They will bring,' but *They will return.*"

[62]NumR 2:13 (6c). SML
[63]EstherR 1:4 (3b). SML
[64]To carry such a short distance as from the temple to Jerusalem.
[65]Just as David had stores of wealth in the temple (*BJ* 1 [61]).
[66]GenR 78:12 (149d). SML

MESSIAH[67]

The Lord said, *Like the land of Hadrach* (Zech 9:1). What is *Hadrach*? Rabbi Judah and Rabbi Nehemiah [explained it thus]: Rabbi Judah said, "It is a place called *Hadrach.*" Rabbi Jose Ben Durmaskit said, "By the [temple] service, [I swear] that I am from Damascus, and there is a place whose name is *Hadrach.*" Rabbi Nehemiah said, "This is the Messiah, who is *Had* (sharp) and *rach* (soft). Sharp to the Gentiles and soft to the Israelites." Another explanation of *Hadrach*: This is the messianic king who is destined to guide *(hadrik)* all those who enter the age in repentance before the holy One blessed be He. *And Damascus will be his resting place* (Zech 9:1). Is *Damascus his resting place*? Is there any *resting place* other than the house of the sanctuary? As it is said, "This is my *resting place* from now on" (Ps 132:14). He said, "Jerusalem is destined to be expanded on all sides until it reaches the gates of *Damascus,* and the exiled will come and *rest* under it," to fulfill that which is said, *Damascus is his resting place* (Zech 9:1)—as far as *Damascus is his resting place.*"

MESSIAH[68]

My beloved answered and said to me (SS 2:10). *He answered* through Elijah. *And said to me,* through the messianic king. What did he say *to me?* "Arouse yourself, my beautiful friend, and leave." Rabbi Azariah said, *For behold the winter* (הסתו) *has passed* (SS 2:11). This is the kingdom of Cutheans[69] which seduces (שמסיתה) the world and leads it astray with its falsehood. The scripture testifies, *For if your brother, your mother's son...*[70] *[entices you* (יסיתך) *secretly, saying, 'Let us go and serve other Gods'...you shall not yield to him or listen to him]* (Dt 13:7, 9). *The rain has left and has gone* (SS 2:11). This is the subjection [of Israel].[71] *The flowers* (הנצנים) *appear in the land* (SS 2:12). The conquerors (הנצוחות) *appear in the land.* Who are they? Rabbi Berekiah, in the name of Rabbi Isaac, [said], *"The Lord showed me four craftsmen"* (Zech 2:3). These are they: Elijah, the messianic

---

[67]SSR 7:5 §3 (37a). SML
[68]SSR 3:13 §4 (17c). SML
[69]Here, evidently, the Christians, whose kingdom was Rome. Normally Samaritans.
[70]Esau, Rebecca's son. He was the father of the hated Edomites. Because Jews hated Romans as much as Edomites, they were also called Edomites. Here Christians are the "brothers" who were enticing the Jews to leave their faith.
[71]Israel's exile would be gone like a rain that is over, and she could return to her land.

king, Melchizedek, and the military Messiah.[72] *The time of singing* (זמיר)*has come* (SS 2:12). *The time of* the Israelites *has come* for redemption. *The time of* the uncircumcision *has come* to be cut off (להזמר).[73] *The time of* the kingdom of the Cutheans[74] *has come* to be destroyed. *The time of* the kingdom of heaven[75] *has come* that it may be revealed as it is said, *And the Lord will become king over all the land* (Ps 47:7). *The voice of the turtle dove is heard in our land* (SS 2:12). Who is this? This is *the voice* of the messianic king. He says, *How beautiful upon the mountains are the feet of the one who proclaims good news* (Isa 52:7).

MESSIAH[76]

These are *the four craftsmen* (Zech 2:3). David comes and interprets: *Gilead is mine* (Ps 60:7). This is Elijah who is one of the inhabitants of *Gilead. Manasseh is mine* (Ps 60:7). This is the Messiah who will arise from the sons of *Manasseh,* as it is said, *Before Ephraim and Benjamin, Mannasseh.*[77] *[Stir up your might and come to save us]* (Ps 80:3). *Ephraim is the fortress of my head.* This is the military Messiah, who will come from Ephraim, as it is said, *His first born bull, splendor is his* (Dt 33:17). *Judah is my scepter* (מחוקקי) (Ps 60:7). This is the great redeemer who will come from the sons of the sons of David.

ISRAEL'S FUTURE[78]

People will serve you (Gen 27:29). The seventy nations. *And nations* (לאמים) *will prostrate themselves before you* (Gen 27:29). These are the Ishmaelites,[79] the sons of Keturah, of whom

---

[72]Suk 52a, in parallel, has the Messiah son of Joseph, who was expected to lead the war against the Romans.

[73]Either that the uncircumcised will all be destroyed, or that their foreskin will be cut off, and they will become proselytes to Judaism.

[74]The Christians, whose kingdom was Rome.

[75]The Davidic kingdom. See *Consequences,* 42-90.

[76]NumR 14:1. SML

[77]Literally, "Ephraim, Benjamin, and Manasseh," but the sense of the passage requires dislocating the conjunction, so that Manasseh can have precedence and prominence over Ephraim and Benjamin.

[78]GenR 66:4 (131b-c). SML

[79]Moslems, who claim to be descendants of Ishmael. Dedan was one of Ishmael's sons. One of Dedan's children was called לאמים (Leumim), which is the same word used to mean "for the nations," or Gentiles.

it is written, *[The sons of Dedan were] Assurim, Letushim, and Leumim* (Gen 25:3). *Be lord over your brothers* (Gen 27:29). This is Esau and his chiefs.[60]

ISRAEL'S FUTURE[61]

I bought for myself male and female slaves (Eccles 2:6). These are the Gentiles, as it is said, *And also upon my male and female slaves, in those days, I will pour out my spirit* (Joel 3:2). In the future they will be *slaves* to the Israelites, as it is written in Isaiah, *Strangers will stand and feed your flocks, [and foreigners will be your plowmen and winedressers]* (Isa 61:5).

ISRAEL'S FUTURE[62]

Just as this vine is more lowly than all the trees, and it rules among all the trees, thus Israelites appear as if they were humble in this age, but for the future they are destined to inherit from one end of the world to the other. Just as this vine, one branch reaches out from it [the trunk] and subdues many trees, thus the Israelites, one righteous man reaches out from them and rules from one end of the world to the other. The scripture shows: *And Joseph was ruler over all the land* (Gen 42:6).[63] *The Lord was with Joshua, [and his report was in all the land]*[64] (Josh 6:27). *The name of David went out into all the lands* (I Chron 14:17), *and Solomon was ruler among all the kingdoms* (I Kgs 5:1). *For Mordecai was great in the king's house, [and his fame went forth throughout all the provinces]* (Est 9:4)....Just as this vine, everyone who drinks from it, his face shines, and everyone who does not drink from it, his teeth are blunted, thus Israelites, everyone who comes and is yoked to them, finally it will be that he receives what is his from under their hands.[65] Just as this vine, in the beginning it is trampled

---

[60]Esau was identified with Rome and the Christians. Since Christians and Moslems, or the Romans and the Arabs, were the primary enemies of the Jews, they were considered the Gentiles who were destined to be slaves to the Jews. They were together also identified with all Gentiles and the seventy nations.

[61]EcclesR 2:8 §1 (7c). SML

[62]LevR 36:2 (52c-d). SML

[63]In context, this refers to the land of Egypt, but is here used to mean the world. The Hebrew for "world" (ארץ) is the same as that for "land."

[64]In context, the land of Palestine. Here it is taken to mean the world.

[65]This is intended to show that it is beneficial to become yoked to the Jews, but the

with the foot, and after that goes up to the table of kings, thus Israelites appear as if they are rejected in this age, as it is written, *I was a derision to all my people, and their song*[66] *all the day long* (Lam 3:14). But in the future, *The Lord will place you on high* (Dt 28:1), as it is written, *Kings will be your foster fathers and their queens, your nursing mothers* (Isa 49:23). Just as this vine climbs over every single departure,[67] thus the Israelites are scribes over all the kingdoms.

ISRAEL'S FUTURE[88]

And [a remnant] will be left in Zion (Isa 4:3). It is written, *And it will happen when Jerusalem is conquered* (Jer 38:28). He said to them, "Even that will not be hardship but happiness, because on that very day, Menahem (the comforter) will be born and on that day, Israelites will receive a settlement for their iniquities, for Rabbi Samuel Bar Nahman said, 'Israelites will receive full settlement for their iniquities on the day the house of the sanctuary was destroyed, as it is said, *Your iniquity has been completed, daughter of Zion.*[89] *He will not exile you any more'"* (Lam 4:22).

DAYS OF REDEMPTION[90]

[The interpretation of] Rabbi Judan and Rabbi Hunia: Rabbi Hunia, in the name of Rabbi Eliezer, the son of Jose the Galilean and Rabbi Hunia in the name of Rabbi Eliezer Ben Jacob, said, "*The voice of my beloved! Look, he is coming* (SS 2:8)! This is the messianic king. At the time he says to the Israelites, *In this month you will be redeemed* (Ex 12:2), they will say to him, 'How can we be redeemed? Has not the holy One blessed be He already sworn that he will make us subject to the seventy nations?' He will give

---

picture here given is clearly one of subservience. Those who become yoked to the Jews will be provided for the way a master provided for his slaves. The slave receives whatever comes from his master's hands, and no more. This is a necessary deduction of a theology whose adherents presume that all other peoples must be their servants.

[66]The implication is that it is a taunting song.

[67]The word "departure" is inadequate to render the word מעס and still give the idea of something like a goal or end which is exceeded.

[88]NumR 13:5 (52d).

[89]Suffering has paid for sins. No more debits in the heavenly record.

[90]SSR 2:8 §2 (16c). SML

two answers in reply: 1) He will say to them, 'If one of you goes into exile to the Barbarians and one from you goes into exile to Samatria, it is as if you had all gone into exile. Is it not only that this sovereign kingdom[91] levies troops from all over the world, from every single nation? One Cuthean[92] or one Barbarian comes and subjects you, it is as if you had been subject to all the nations and as if you had been subject to the seventy nations.' and 2) 'In this month you will be redeemed,'[93] as it is said, *This month is the first of the months for you"* (Ex 12:2).

DAYS OF REDEMPTION[94]

Another explanation: *My beloved is like a gazelle* (SS 2:9)....Just as a *gazelle* appears and returns and is hidden, is seen, and returns, and is hidden, thus the first redeemer [Moses] appeared and was hidden,[95] returned, and appeared.[96] How long was he hidden from them? Rabbi Tanḥuma said, "Three months." This is what was written: *They met Moses and Aaron* (Ex 5:20). Judah, son of Rabbi, said "Intermittently. Thus the last redeemer will be revealed from them; he will return, and he will be hidden from them.[97] How long will he be hidden from them? Forty-five days. This is what is written: *From the time of the removal of the continual offering and the giving of the abominating sacrilege, a thousand, two hundred, ninety-two days* (Dan 12:11), and it is written, *Blessed is he who waits and reaches a thousand, three hundred, thirty-five days* (Dan 12:12) [1335 − 1290 = 45]. What are these additional [days]? Rabbi Yoḥanan Ben Ḳaṣartah said in the name of Rabbi Jonah, "These are the forty-five days when he will be hidden from them, and those are the days Israelites will pluck salt wort and roots of broom bushes and eat [them]. This is what is written, *They will pluck salt wort, leaves of shrubs, and the roots of broom bushes for their sustenance* (Job 30:3). Where will he

[91]Rome.

[92]Christian.

[93]The second point is that it has been promised, and a promise transcends all other bases for judgment.

[94]SSR 2:9 §3 (17a). See also NumR (NASO) 11:2. Conclusion from RuthR 5:6 (9d). SML

[95]When he fled from Egypt after he had killed an Egyptian (Ex 2:11-15).

[96]When he reappeared with Aaron, after his experience with the burning bush, when he and Aaron demanded release of the Hebrews from Egypt (Ex 3:1-11:10).

[97]Traditionally, the Messiah son of David was supposed to have been hidden ever since his birth when the temple was burned, or even since the beginning of creation; but he was hidden. In hiding he suffered and was rejected by Israel.

lead them? Some say [to] the wilderness of Judah. Some say [to] the wilderness of Sihon and Og. Those who say, [to] the wilderness of Judah [argue]: 'This is what is written: *Again I will make you dwell in tents as in the days of the feast [Sukkoth]'* (Hos 12:10). Those who say the wilderness of Sihon and Og [argue]: 'It is written, *Behold I will allure her and lead her to the wilderness [and speak tenderly to her, and I will give her her vineyards from there]'"* (Hos 2:16-17).[98]

Everyone who believes in him, obeys him, and waits will live, and whoever does not believe him will go to the Gentiles, and they will ultimately kill him. Rabbi Isaac Bar Marion said, "Finally, at the end of forty-five days, the holy One blessed be He will be revealed to them, and he will bring them down manna upon them, and *There is nothing new under the sun"* (Eccles 1:9).

DAYS OF REDEMPTION[99]

The voice of my beloved. Look! he is coming (SS 2:8). Rabbi Judah, Rabbi Nehemiah, and the sages [discussed it as follows]: Rabbi Judah said, *The voice of my beloved. Look! he is coming* refers to Moses. At the time when he came and saw the Israelites, *In this month you will be redeemed* (Ex 12:2) They said to him, 'Our teacher, Moses, how can we *be redeemed?* Has not the holy One blessed be He said to Abraham, *They will serve them, and they will afflict them for four hundred years* (Gen 15:13)? Still we have only completed two hundred, ten years.' He said to them, 'Since he desires your redemption, he pays no attention to your calculations, but he *leaps over the mountains, [bounding over hills]* (SS 2:8). *The mountains and hills* here mean only "end times" and "intercalations."[100] He *leaps* over the calculations, over the "end times" and "intercalations," and in this month you are to be redeemed, as it is said, *This month is for you the first of the month"* (Ex 12:2).

Summary

These passages from Midrash Rabba are only a few selected from the numerous, sometimes repetitious, interpretations of the

[98]The final paragraph is included only in RuthR 5:6 (9d).
[99]SSR 2:3 §1 (16c-d). SML
[100]Intercalation of an extra month in a year to balance the calendar with the seasons of the year.

scripture in the five books of the Torah and the five scrolls. The commentary on the Song of Songs, which was a favorite book of Rabbi Akiba, has been traditionally understood in nationalistic, eschatological terms. This commentary reflected that concentration. The passages selected here fall roughly in three categories: Zion and the temple, the role of the Messiah, and Israel's bright future in the age to come.

The Lord was pictured as weeping over the destruction of the temple. He regretted having to allow the Gentiles to do it, but the Jews were so rebellious, the Lord had to enforce strict discipline. Now that the temple has been destroyed, all Jews pray only for its reconstruction. In the future, the Jews will be unashamed, because the Lord will rule again on Mount Zion. Then kings will come bringing gifts to the Messiah and the Shekhinah will fill the world completely.

When Jacob returned to meet Esau, he pacified Esau with advance gifts. In the future, Gentiles are required to return these to the sons of Jacob. Jerusalem will be the resting place for Jews, and it will extend all the way to Damascus. At the same time the Christian kingdom will pass, Israel's subjection to the Gentiles will pass, Elijah, the Davidic and Ephraimic messiahs, and Melchizedek will appear in Palestine, Jews will be redeemed, Gentiles will be cut off, the Christian kingdom will be destroyed, and the Davidic kingdom will be restored. Elijah, the Messiah of Ephraim, and the Messiah of David will appear together to redeem Israel.

Israel's future will be glorious after her sins have been cancelled. Gentiles will all be slaves to the Jews. Jews will infiltrate and control all the world, just as a vine climbs over the branches of the tallest tree. Israel's sins were all cancelled by the destruction of the temple, so Jews are free from sin. The Lord will not require full justice, but he will forego the deserved punishment, lighten Israel's sentence, and restore her to the land. The new exodus will be like the old, with a hidden messiah, a wilderness period of cleansing, and the provision of manna.

GENERAL SUMMARY

This unit contains some of the deepest longings and most basic convictions of medieval Judaism. Loyal, nationalistic Jews like Judah Halevy reflect the deep feeling Jews had for the promised land, the hostility they held toward the Christians and Moslems of their day, and their conviction that the Christians and Moslems would soon be banished or reduced to slavery while the Jews received their promised heritage of international rule from Jerusalem. These are consistent with the teachings of the rabbis that have been preserved in standard Talmudic and midrashic teachings. As in the first section, the choice of literature contained here, both by its nature and its authorship, reflects the feelings of medieval Jews in general and not the distorted views of one particular sect.

The next section contains various forms of apocalyptic literature. This has frequently been dismissed as "fringe literature," to be distinguished from the theology of "normative Judaism." The reader may judge for himself whether or not he thinks that the views contained in this literature are basically different from those of the rest of the literature of this book—the poetry, prayers, responsa of famous gaonim, and excerpts from the Talmud and Midrash Rabba.

HISTORY AND APOCALYPSE

Introduction

There are four variant forms of the text which is here called "The Book of Zerubbabel." The longest of these is better known as "Pirke Hecalot Rabbati," and at the beginning, is not paralleled by other texts. This is called "Part I." Part II is paralleled by three other texts, all of which are normally called "The Book of Zerubbabel." All four of these texts will be shown in as nearly parallel form as possible by dividing the text into units and numbering the units to keep the parallel sections together. Notes, accompanying the text, are intended to clarify the meaning. The texts which preserved the line and page division of the manuscript have the same divisions shown in the translation. When the translation could not divide the words exactly as the Hebrew did, this is shown by italicizing the words from the following line of the Hebrew text that are included in the previous line in the translation.

THE BOOK OF ZERUBBABEL

Text of Pirke Hecalot Rabbati (PHR)[1]

32:3 If your hearts observe the Torah, then Zerubbabel[2] Ben Shealtiel will answer the door[3] on the fourth of the seventh month, the month of the feasts.[4] He will stand on his feet as a turgaman[5] and interpret the names as a turgaman.
32:4 Zerubbabel said:
"Hurry, go above me, where the Rock of ages is!" He answered me from the doors of heaven and said to me, "You are Zerubbabel." I answered, "I am." He answered and spoke to me *just as a man speaks with his neighbor* (Ex 33:11). He spoke to me words of very great uprightness. 32:5) He said to me, "Who are you, Sir?" Then he said to me, "I am Mettatron,[6] general of the Lord's army," and he placed my name as his name,[7] and he showed me a man,

---

[1]Translated from the Hebrew text of S.A. Wertheimer (ed.), ספר פרקי היכלות רבתי (Jerusalem, 1890), 32:3 (10a)-40:2(12a). RPL

[2]The first ruler in Jerusalem after the return from Babylon (Zech 4:1-10). Traditionally, he, like Enoch, was believed to be kept in heaven until he returns as a Davidic messiah.

[3]The door of heaven.

[4]New Year's Day, Day of Atonement, and Feast of the Tabernacles.

[5]The person in a synagogue who translated and interpreted the Hebrew text into Aramaic for the understanding of the congregation.

[6] Mettatron is the mystical name for Enoch. See Gershom G. Scholem, *Major Trends in Jewish Mysticism* (New York, c1941), 67-70.

[7]This means he gave his apostolic authority or "power of attorney" to act in his name as authoratively as if Mettatron had acted himself.

like a pretty and handsome child. Mettatron said to me, "This is the Messiah of the Lord. He was born to the house of David, but the Lord hid him to become a leader over Israel. He is Menahem Ben Amiel,[8] who was born in the house of Nebuchadnezzar.

The spirit took him and placed him in Nineveh,[9] *The city of blood* (Ezek 22:2), which is Rome, until the time of the end.[10] 33:1) I asked him, "What signs does Menahem Ben Amiel perform?" Mettatron and Michael[11] said to me, "A year before one week [of years], the holy One blessed be He will send an emissary to Israel with confidence, quietness, joy, exultation, and rejoicing. That is a poor generation which has no virtue,[12] but [others] will stand opposite them and be shocked with panic. They will jeer them in the market places and streets, calling them 'brigands' and 'apostates,'"[13] saying words about them that ears cannot stand to hear. 33:2) At that time the holy One blessed be He will say, 'They still have not become subject. They are asking for still more [punishment].' Suddenly the holy One blessed be He will become angry, and he will tie up the Messiah [hand and foot] for eight years of privation, corresponding to the eight days of circumcision. Just as this child for eight days, when he is not circumcised, is not permitted to enter the congregation,[14] so also during those years when the Messiah is fettered, the holy One blessed be He will hide his

---

[8]"Amiel" means "people of God." Amiel was the representative of the tribe of Dan sent by Moses to spy out the land of Canaan (Num 13:12). A later Amiel was a friend of Saul's family (II Sam 9:4).

[9]Nineveh was for the Samaritans what Babylon was for the Jews in antiquity. It was the capital city of the country that took them into captivity. To understand how some North Israelites felt about Nineveh, see Nahum; to learn how some Jews felt about Babylon, see Ps 137 and Obadiah. The popular view that Nahum was written initially by Jews is not sound. It has been Judaized by the addition of the Isaianic verse, 2:1, and maybe chapter one as well.

[10]The end of the "captivity" at the national jubilee when Palestine would be returned to the Jews free from foreign rule.

[11]In function Mettatron and Michael were almost interchangeable. It appears as if the editor of this text had before him two texts, one of which had one name and the other, the other. Rather than choose between them, he included both.

[12]The generation that has no virtue is one that has added no merit to the treasury of merits so as to reduce Israel's sentence.

[13]"Brigands" were those Jews whom other Jews insulted by identifying their political, guerilla raids with ordinary robbery. They were the very zealous, militant Jews. On the opposite side of the spectrum were the ones who associated with the enemy Romans. They were called "apostates." They were also called "harlots" and "sinners" (Mt 9:10; 11:18-19; 21:31).

[14]Because the child, like the mother who bore him and thereby defiled him, is defiled for seven days after birth. After that, both may be baptized, and therefore purified from the baby's original defilement. Only then, after he is cleansed, may he be admitted to the congregation. See *Consequences*, 215-22.

face from him.[15] 33:3) Afterward the holy One blessed be He will give the Israelites the opportunity to speak. One will say to the other, "You know that that man was leading Israelites astray and injuring them. Did not Pharaoh fetter Moses, whom, like this emissary, they fettered?"

33:4)   In the first year that he was shackled, they used to proclaim in all the cities of Israel concerning him. The mighty men of the Torah were planning and conjuring a conspiracy because of him, as it is said, *The man defaced his appearance* (Isa 52:14). There will not be many [living people] in his behalf, but those who sleep in the dust [will support him], as it is said, *Many who sleep in the dust will awake* (Dan 12:2). The dead of the world will say to one another, "Perhaps our hope is gone, and the mission of the *bat qol* has ceased." Then he will say, "Do not fear. You will arise in his merit."[16] 33:5) In those years when he is fettered, the mighty men of the Torah who are in the city will die; the men of faith will cease; the wisdom of the cities will come to an end; and the generation will stand empty.[17] There will be no deans of academies to defend you and no faithful shepherds[18] and *hasidim*[19] to annul the [anti-Jewish] decree. The heavens will be locked,[20] and the gates of provision will be closed all those seven years; but the last year, when the Messiah goes out from prison, the generation will go and fall into a grave alive because of the [anti-Jewish] decrees which are decreed against it.[21] Many will die untimely deaths in servitude. 34:1) The first decree is the uprooting of mountains.[22] Whoever has a son, the son will rebel against his father; whoever has a field will rebel against it. This first decree is wicked Edom who is destined to rule over the Israelites for nine months, as it is said, *I have sworn to the house of Eli* (I Sam 3:14). This teaches that the holy One blessed be He has sworn that wicked Edom will rule in the last dispensation over the entire world,[23] and you will

[15]As if he, like the unbaptized baby, were defiled.

[16]Even those who died beforehand will be redeemed from their sins by the merits of the Messiah's suffering, which contributed to the treasury of merits.

[17]I.e., empty of merits in the treasury of merits.

[18]Kings and high priests.

[19]The laymen who were specially pious.

[20]So that they will not allow rain to fall. Paul (II Cor 12:2) knew of three heavens. Enoch went through all seven heavens (Enoch, *Passim.*).

[21]There were many anti-Jewish decrees made by Christian and Moslem governments during the Middle Ages. They required heavy taxation, expulsion, conversion, forfeiture of property, or other discriminatory demands.

[22]I.e., just as mountains cannot be moved, so this decree cannot be observed. It is impossible.

[23]The last Gentile dispensation before Israel gains control of the world. It plays the role of

have to learn what those decrees are—doubled[24]—if, concerning the mighty men of the Torah, concerning the eleven, everyone who lists [his wealth at] ten dinars of silver, they will try to get from him ten dinars of gold; everyone who has none, they will decree from his flesh [to take] ten dinars [worth] of flesh.[25] They will decree that they must not circumcise their sons; they must not observe menstrual purity; and if someone mentions the name of the holy One blessed be He, they will cut off his head. 34:2) The third [anti-Jewish] decree is when they are not required to make war, but they all die from their rebelliousness. They have seven eyes: two like every man, plus one in his head, one in his forehead, one between his shoulders, one in his heart, and one in his navel,[26] as it is said, *For behold the stone which I have given to Joshua—upon one stone there will be seven eyes* (Zech 3:9). In that time, the righteous ones of Israel will say with one voice, "Blessed is he who was not created; blessed are the first generations who have not seen anything like this!" All this will come because the mighty men of the Torah did not believe from the beginning, and they did not remember the Lord.[27]

34:3) The first of all the [anti-Jewish] decrees is the kingdom of Gog and Magog[28] which all the Torah and commandments do not require; but in that hour every single one from Israel will be ruled by it five hundred, eighteen thousand years, as it is said, *The kings of the land will be established* (Ps 2:2). In *gematria*, Alas! the maximum! 34:4) Even the holy One blessed be He will not be shaken from his place. In that hour the seven winds will encircle the world, and not a single one from Israel can escape, as it is said, *Where can I go from your spirit* (Ps 139:7)? This is when they will say, "Woe for the generation in which the Messiah is revealed!"[29]

---

the fourth beast before the saints of the Most High and the son of man both receive the kingdom, power, and glory (Dan 7:14, 27).

[24]Because, according to sabbatical rules, the debtor was required to work off his debt at half wages, paying double for all his sins.

[25]In all cases they will try to take more than the Jew would be able to give.

[26]The governments of the Christians or Moslems have spies everywhere, trying to obstruct all fifth columnist activity.

[27]The ancient ones ran up a very high bill in the heavenly account.

[28]The hostile forces from the North about which Ezekiel wrote (Ezek 38:1-39:16). Later Jews and Christians used it as a symbol for the entire assembly of Gentile forces lined up against Jerusalem for battle where they will be defeated just before the Israelites overthrow the Gentiles completely. During the Middle Ages, these forces were the Christians and/or the Moslems, from the Jewish standpoint.

[29]Because Jews who are alive then will be involved in the fierce military conflict ("birth pangs") necessary to defeat all the Gentiles.

34:5) Then the holy One blessed be He will arise and bring out the Messiah who will be alone in prison, as it is said, *You will go forth to save your people* (Hab 3:13), and it is written, *He will go out from the prison to rule* (Eccles 4:14). But when he goes out from prison and sees all the troops which will be gathered because of him, he will tremble and say, "Who is able to stand against all these troops?" In that hour he will gather the troops of Israel and go to Babylon and request mercy. All the Israelites will mock the *haverim* turning away from him, and they will say, "Woe, because of the one who was shackled for eight years!" He will say, "I am an emissary,"[30] and now since he has brought me out from prison, I am now requesting mercy." With the same scorn as those who jeered him, the holy One blessed be He will vindicate him, as it is said, *I know that the Lord will save his Messiah* (Ps 20:7). Everyone will fall under him, as it is said, *They will bow and fall down* (Ps 20:9).

35:1) After that the holy One blessed be He will return him to his bosom. He will embrace him and kiss him, and his splendor will minister throughout the entire world. The mighty men of the Torah and all the Israelites will say to one another, "How far we have gone astray! The sufferings of our iniquity, and we did not know, as it is said, *All we like sheep have gone astray*" (Isa 53:6). After that they will comfort him and those who mourn for him, as it is said, *I have seen his ways, and I will heal him* (Isa 57:18) and *announce the year of the Lord's favor* (Isa 61:2). Through Zechariah, it is said, *Behold the day of the Lord comes* (Zech 14:1).[31] With respect to what do they say [this]? It is only with respect to that week [of years] in which the Messiah comes, because he will be hidden.[32] Then all those generations will come, and a deep sleep will fall upon them, but when the Messiah is driven from them, and when the holy One blessed be He wants him, he will shake the four corners of the world (Job 38:13). He will come and promise the Israelites and say to them, "Redemption is already [here]!" Then men, women, and children will be gathering together, seeking great mercy, as it is said, *For a short instant I have forsaken you* (Isa 54:7).

[30]An emissary or agent has complete authority of the one who sent him—power of attorney. The Messiah claimed to be the agent, emissary, or apostle of God (Ber 5:5; Mt 10:40-42; Jn 13:20; 14:9; 14:28; Sifra, *behukkotai*, perek 8:12; Lev 26:46; Assump. Mos. 11:17; I Cor 5:1-5; see also *To The Hebrews*, 7.

[31]These two terms belong together. The day of the Lord's favor is the day of the Lord, when the Messiah will defeat the Gentiles in war, comfort the Jews, redeem Israel, or cancel her sins.

[32]Not available yet to advance the "redemption."

35:3) At that time six million from Israel will turn in repentance, and all the Gentiles will gather and beg to return in repentance when they see that Israelites are seeking the synagogues and houses of study. They will request mercy in a loud voice, and they will see that whoever does not see and hear, the Gentiles will see and shame.[33] 35:4) They[34] will sit and worry and say, "Surely there is redemption for the Israelites, but we have scorned them, as it is said, *They will lick the dust like a snake* (Micah 7:17). It is scriptural to say they have gone out from us. How does the scripture say they are really afraid of the voice of the Messiah? In that hour, when they hear his voice, when he stands on the wheel of the chariot of the holy One blessed be He, the world will say, "God forbid! For this one is born of a woman and we cannot stumble at his voice." 35:5) Then the Gentiles will return in repentance. At once the Messiah's general will stand and praise the holy One blessed be He and say to him, "Master of the age, if you have punishments greater than these, punish me [with them]. Then none of the Gentiles will see or enjoy the hidden favor of the Israelites.[35] The holy One blessed be He will say to him, "Ephraim, my righteous Messiah, I also want to do this, but I have been considerate of your honor." At once the holy One blessed be He will take two chains of iron and place them on the Messiah's shoulders and say to him, "One is for the iniquity of your generation, and one, that there may be no Gentiles in that hour, [no] Israelites turning to another view, and [no] scorners of the Messiah. They will say, "Woe to us! for we have gone astray after this crazy one!" The holy One blessed be He will say to them, "Do you call him crazy? Now you will see his light which illumines his environs, as it is said, *Round about him is a mighty tempest* (Ps 50:3). None who believes in him will be blotted out of the book of life, as it is said, *In that day your people will [just barely] escape* (Dan 12:1). 36:1) In the last year there will be severe punishments, many [anti-Jewish] decrees, heavy enslavement, and many illnesses. The world will be changed, and an [anti-Jewish] decree will be given for everything. They will be very expensive; there will be no going or coming in peace; and the masters of faith will die. At once the Messiah will be revealed.

[33]Even the Gentiles will promote activity in Jewish study and worship. They will shame non-observant Jews.

[34]The Gentiles.

[35]Since the more righteous Israel is, the more the Gentiles must suffer, the Messiah wants to suffer still more to cancel all of Israel's sins, so that there will be no reward left for the Gentiles. Compare the Messiah's willingness to suffer all available pain to Christian profession that Jesus descended into hell, etc. See *Consequences,* 18-37.

36:2) In that hour when the Messiah goes out of prison, he will occupy himself against the Gentiles before every people. They will say to him, "Why do you want to uproot seventy nations for the sake of one nation? All the evil things which are among our people are among your people. There are thieves among our people; there are thieves among your people; there are murderers among our people; there are murderers among your people; there are lewd people among our people; there are lewd people among your people. 36:3) At that time he will be silenced, and there will be no reply for the Messiah. Even Michael, the great prince will be silenced and have no reply, as it is said, *Shall I wait when they have not spoken* (Job 32:16)? At once the holy One blessed be He will flow down upon the Messiah and answer him in the day of trouble. He will say to them, "Fools who are in the world! Do you give any thought for my children at all? Are there among you any who recites the *shema*[36] at dawn like my sons?" Concerning that hour it says, *I will tell your righteous deeds, [but they will not help you]* (Isa 57:12). Do not read *your deeds* (אֶת מעשיך) but *those deeds of yours* (אוֹתָן מעשיך) (Isa 57:12).[37]

36:4) *Who has heard anything like this? Who has seen anything like this? [Can a land be born in one day? Can a nation be brought forth in a moment? For as soon as Zion was in labor she brought forth her sons]* (Isa 66:8). In the beginning, it was the plan of the holy One blessed be He to make the Israelites wander in the wilderness six months, from Nisan to Tishri. Every time we meditate on the affliction of the Messiah, all these years suddenly come at once to his temple.[38]

36:5) Another interpretation: Because Israelites say, "In that generation the world follows its own practices;" and "there will be redemption during this year;" but they do not know that he will come suddenly.[39]

37:1) Another interpretation: For behold the day will come for the days of the Messiah [when] the Gentiles will be converted [to Judaism] and enter [the community] with Israelites. They will fulfill the commandments of Sukkah, circumcision, prayer, and fringes. They will enter and depart with the Israelites for forty years, as it is said, *Rule over the world of many nations.*[40] After

---

[36]Dt 6:4-5, recited together with the Eighteen Benedictions.

[37]Those *particular* deeds—reciting the *shema'*, which deserves special praise.

[38]The meditation itself is considered in the treasury of merits system as meritorious as the deeds themselves, so meditation is an easy way of piling up treasures in heaven.

[39]Therefore Jews must be prepared and sinless at every moment (Mt 24:45-51; 25:13).

[40]This seems not to be an exact quotation, but it is treated as if it were. Possibilities might be Ps 47:9, Micah 4:7, or some liturgy.

forty years Gog and Magog will come against Israel, he and all the kings of the East and the West, the cities of Gomer and all her flanks, as it is said, *Gomer and all her flanks* (Ezek 38:6).[41] When the proselytes who have been converted [to Judaism] see Gog and Magog and all his troops which come with him, they will ask and say to them, "Where are you going?" They will say, "*Against the Lord and his Messiah* (Ps 2:2)." At once they will tear off their fringes [and throw them] on the ground; they will trample down their sukkoths, take down their muzzuzahs, and go with them [the troops of Gog and Magog] against the Israelites, as it is said, *Tearing out their traditions, [let us cast their cords from us]* (Ps 2:3).[42] In that hour the holy One blessed be He will sit and laugh at them, as it is said, *He who sits in the heavens will laugh* (Ps 2:4). Every man from Israel will surround for himself nine thousand, five hundred swords,[43] as it is said, *The Gentiles rage, [and the people plot in vain]* (Ps 2:1). In *gematria*, the maximum!

37:3) *Behold the day is coming for the Lord* (Zech 14:1). That day when Gog and Magog come against the Israelites, the earth and the heavens will rage, and there will be a great earthquake in Israel. Those who come to conquer Jerusalem, as it is said, *I will gather all the nations against Jerusalem* (Zech 14:2). In that hour he will make war against Gog and Magog, and they will bring out with him seven shepherds and eight princes of men, as it is said, *You will raise up against him seven shepherds and eight princes of men* (Micah 5:4), [with] David in their midst. Adam, Seth, Enosh, Methusaleh on his right; [and] Abraham, Isaac, Jacob, Moses, and Aaron on his left. Eight princes: Saul, Samuel, Amos, Zephaniah, Elijah, Melchizedek, Jesse, and Hezekiah. In that hour the knowledge of the ministering angels will become cold before the holy One blessed be He. In that hour the holy One blessed be He will trample down Rome; he will only trample it by himself, *I have trampled the wine press alone* (Isa 63:3). The ministering angels will say to the holy One blessed be He, "Master of the age, from where have you come?" He will say to them, "From heaven." They will say to him, "Why are your garments scarlet?" He used to say

[41]The text continues: *Beth Togarmah from the uttermost parts of the North with all her flanks—many peoples are with you.* Gomer must be a city either from the South in contrast to the North or else someplace far east of Beth Togarmah, to form a merismus similar to East and West.

[42]Many Jews and early Christians believed converts from Gentiles could not be trusted (Mt 7:6; 21:31; Lk 15:11-32; Philip. 3:2; II Peter 2:22). See also *Consequences*, 184-89. The troops may refer to the Crusaders who sometimes gave Jews the option of conversion or death.

[43]Meaning 9,500 *men* who are armed with swords.

to him, "Master of the age, is there ever a king who goes to war without horsemen? Why have you not requested us to go with you?" He will say to them, "The olive press is small, and you have not been necessary to me." Even so, their conviction will not grow cold. He will say to them, "Wait awhile. I have another large olive press, and you will be necessary to me, as it is said, *The valley of my mountains will be stopped up, for the valley of the mountains will touch the side of it; and you will flee as you fled from the earthquake in the days of Uzziah, king of Judah* (Zech 14:5).

37:5)   When Gog and Magog come against Israel, the holy One blessed be He will go out with all kinds of punishments to fight with him. Then the ministering angels will go out, as it is said, *I will judge him with pestilence and blood* (Ezek 38:22). The holy One blessed be He will strike them a severe blow, and they will all fall before him, as it is said, *This is the plague [with which the Lord will strike all the Gentiles that wage war against Jerusalem: their flesh will rot while they are still on their feet; their eyes will rot in their sockets; and their tongues will rot in their mouths]* (Zech 14:12). It will not be necessary for the Israelites to cut wood, but [they can gather wood] from their supplies and from their weapons (see Ezek 39:10). After Gog and Magog, the Israelites will dwell securely, as it is said, *And they will dwell in it, and there will be no more destruction* (Zech 14:11), and it is said, *A redeemer of Israel is the holy One* (Isa 49:7).

38:1)   Another interpretation: *Thus said the Lord, a redeemer of Israel is the holy One* (Isa 49:7). With respect to whom did Isaiah say this scripture passage? They only spoke with respect to the Israelites whom the Lord dispersed among the seventy nations, as it is said, *Israel is holy to the Lord, the first fruit of his produce* (Jer 2:3), but our iniquities, which have multiplied, they fell to the depths of the earth, *Fallen, no more to rise is the virgin daughter, Zion* (Amos 5:2).[44] Who is destined to exalt her? the Messiah, when he dresses all his enemies with shame and reproach. When the nations of the world see, they will bow down and prostrate themselves to him, as it is said, *Kings will fear and arise* (Isa 49:7).

38:2)   You will have to learn the Messiah when he is revealed. Will he be revealed as flesh and blood, or will he be revealed as an angel? This is already interpreted by Daniel, *Behold one comes like a son of man with the clouds of heaven* (Dan 7:13).[45] This

[44]This is a paraphrase of Amos 5:2: "Fallen, no more to rise is the virgin daughter, *Israel*"—not Zion.

[45]Since he is in heaven, he must be an angel. This is a misinterpretation of the Danielic theophany. See *To The Hebrews*, 157-62.

teaches that they will deliver to him five million wheels of light and with it the holy beasts, seraphim, and cherubim.[46] When the nations of the world see him, they will say to one another, "Perhaps this is the one about whom they say that he is the Messiah." Then he will say to them, "I am the Messiah under the soles of whose feet they will all fall, as it is said, *I will beat down his enemies before his face and I will strike down those who hate him* (Ps 89:24). *I will beat down his enemies before his face* (Ps 89:24). These are the Persians who watered the spirits of the Israelites like good news in the midst of gloom.[47] *I will strike down those who hate him* (Ps 89:24). These are the kings of wicked Edom, whose recompense the holy One blessed be He is destined to turn back upon their own heads, as it is said, *I will wreak vengeance upon my oppressors, and I will pay back those who hate me* (Dt 32:41). 38:3) *He who sits in heaven will laugh* (Ps 2:4) at what the Messiah, because of the fraud which he is destined to [execute], will do to the Gentiles.[48] At that time when they see him, they will be ashamed and say, "What shall we do?" He will say, "Of whom are you afraid? Go to their idolatry, and it will rescue you." Every single one will go to this religion, and they[49] will fall at once. They will say to one another, "In vain and for nothing we have worn ourselves out all these years!"[50] They will return and go to the Messiah and say that there was nothing substantial to their religions. He will say, "Do not be afraid. You do not have gods more severe than these, the sun and the moon."

At once they will walk to the sun and the moon, and they will see them when their light is extinguished, as it is said, *Then the moon will be ashamed and the sun confounded* (Isa 24:23). They will return to the Messiah and say to him, "The light of the sun and moon were extinguished," as it is said, *The Gentiles rage; the kingdoms totter* (Ps 46:7). 38:4) At once they will say to one another, "Now, what remedy is there for us? At once they will bring a gift and come to him, as it is said, *Sheba and Seba will offer a gift* (Ps 72:10). He will say to them, "What am I and what is my kingdom?

[46]This means the heavenly forces will be at his disposal (Jdgs 5:20-21; 1QM 10:3-12; 12:1; 17:6-9).

[47]The text reads בשר rather than בשרה, for "good news." During the sixth and seventh centuries Jews received strong support from the Persians in their efforts to crush the Christians. They considered the Persians their deliverers, just as Cyrus had been years before.

[48]The Lord will enjoy having the Messiah pull a "sleight of hand" trick on the Gentiles, leaving them surprised and embarrassed.

[49]The religions.

[50]Serving a false religion.

Come and draw near to the holy One blessed be He." They will
say to him, "Will the holy One blessed be He accept a bribe? Does
he not reject the one who accepts a bribe? Why do you transgress
his commandments and accept a bribe?"
38:5)   They will say to him, "What remedy is there for us?" He
will say to them, "There is a remedy, and its name is Gehinnom."
They will say to him, "What is it? What is it like?" He will say to
them, "There are good gifts in it: fire, brimstone, darkness, and
gloom." They will say to him, "Is there no mercy in your judgment? Is there no reduction of the hands of the holy One blessed
be He?" He will say to them, "Even I, with apostolic authority,[51]
judge you." He will say to them, "With the measure by which you
have acted toward my sons, thus I will act towards you." In that
hour the prince of Gehinnom will call to him, saying, "Ephraim,
my righteous Messiah, you have had enough conversation with
them." At once the Messiah will seize the four corners of the earth
and shake them into the midst of Gehinnom, just as a man shakes
his garment [to rid it] of dust, as it is said, *To seize the four corners
of the earth* (Job 38:13).

Part Two

That which follows in the text of PHR has more expanded parallels in the Bodleian Library text (BL)[52] and the texts of Wertheimer
(W)[53] and Jellinek (J).[54] The four texts will be shown here in a
somewhat parallel fashion:

W (1)

The word which happened to Zerubbabel Ben Shealtiel, *pehat*
of Judah on the twenty-fourth of the seventh month:[55] 1:1) I saw
this vision there, and I was praying in prayer before the God of
life. The vision of the appearance which I saw weighed upon me.

[51]Full authority of the one who sent him, namely God (see Jn 8:15-16).
[52]Bodleian Library no. 16716, Neuberg 2797.
[53]A.J. Wertheimer (ed.), בתי מדרשות (2 vols.; New York, 1968) II, 497-502.
[54]A. Jellinek (ed.), בת המדרש (6 vols.; Jerusalem, 1967) II, 54-57.
[55]The word, "Haggai," appears in the text after the word, "month." It seems to be a footnote reference to the book of Haggai: *In the second year of the king Darius, in the seventh
month, on the twenty-first day of the month, the word of the Lord came to Haggai"* (Hag
2:1). *On the twenty-fourth day of the ninth month, in the second year of Darius, the word
of the Lord came to the prophet Haggai* (Hag 2:10). The vision described here was placed
on a different day, but in the same intentional context and style as the visions of Haggai. It
was to have happened chronologically between these two visions reported in Haggai, and it
was to have happened *to* Zerubbabel, rather than *about* him.

Blessed are you, O Lord, who revives the dead. 1:2) It came to[56] my heart, saying, "Where is the Rock of Ages?" Then he answered me from the doors of heaven and said to me, "You are Zerubbabel." I said, "I am your servant." He answered and said to me, *just as a man speaks to his neighbor* (Ex 33:11). I heard his voice, but a form I did not see. I arose and prayed as at the beginning. Then I turned to my house.

On the eleventh day of the month of Adar, he was speaking with me there, and he said, "What shall I ask? My end is near, and my days are finished." He said to me, "I will make you live," 1:3) and he said, "Be alive!" Then the spirit raised me between heaven and earth, and it brought me to Nineveh, *the city of blood* (Ezek 22:2; 24:6, 9; Nah 3:1).

J	BL
The word which came to Zerubbabel, son of Shealtiel, *pahat* of Judah.	1:1) The word which came to Zerubbabel, son of Shealtiel *pahat* of Judah. On the twenty-1:2) fourth of the seventh month (see Ezra 3:4), the Lord
He showed me this vision: I was praying to the Lord when the vision of the appearance which I saw alongside the river *Chebar* (Ezek 1:1).[57] I was praying "Blessed are you, O Lord, Raiser of the dead." My heart roared over me,[58] saying, "What will be the form of the house of the ages?"[59] He answered me from the doors of heaven and said to me, "Are you not Zerubbabel, *pahat* of Judah?" I said, "I am your servant." Then a voice went out to	showed me this vision 1:3) there: I was prostrating myself in prayer before the Lord God. In a vision of 1:4) the appearance which I saw in *Chebar* (Ezek 1:1),[57] while they were saying, "Blessed are you, O Lord, Raiser of 1:5) the dead." My heart roared over me,[58] saying "[What] will be the form of the house of the ages?"[59] He answered me from the doors of 1:6) heaven and said to me, "Are you not Zerubbabel, *pahat* of Judah?" I said, "I am your servant." Then he spoke with

[56]Something has dropped out of the text. Jellinek and Bodleian Library texts have "My heart roared over me" in parallel. The W text may originally have read something like "[a great fear] came over my heart."

[57]The place of Ezekiel's vision. Daniel's vision came beside the Tigris River (Dan 10:4).

[58]See Dan 10:10.

[59]The temple at Jerusalem.

J

me

and spoke with me *Just as a
man speaks to his fellowman*
(Ex 33:11). His voice I heard,
but his appearance I did not
see.

Then I arose and prayed
as in supplication,
and I completed my prayer
and turned to my house.

On the eleventh day
of Adar, he was
speaking with me, and he
said to me,

"Come to me; ask from me."
I
said, "What shall I ask?
The days
of my time are short, and my
days are finished." Then
he said to me, "I will make
you live," and he said,
"Be alive!"

Then the spirit took me
up between heaven and earth
(Ezek 8:3) and made me
walk in *the great city* (Jonah
3:3) which is *the city of blood*
(Ezek 22:2; 24:6, 9; Nah 3:1).

BL

me and answered me

and spoke with me *Just as a
man speaks* 1:8) *to his fellowman*
(Ex 33:11). His voice I heard,
but his appearance I did not
see.

Then I arose to prostrate
myself 1:9) as in supplication,
and I completed my prayer,
and I went[60] to my house.

On the eleventh day of the
month of 1:10) Adar, he was
speaking with me there, and he
said to me, "You are my servant,
Zerubbabel." I said, 1:11) "I am
your servant." He said to me,
"Come to me; ask, and
I will inform you and answer." I
said, "What 1:12) shall I ask?

For my time is short, and my
days are finished."
He said to me, "I will make
you live," 1:13) and he said to
me, "Be alive!"

Then the spirit took me
up between heaven and earth
(Ezek 8:3) 1:14) and made me
walk in *the great city* (Jonah
3:3) which is *the city of blood*
(Ezek 22:2; 24:6, 9; Nah 3:1).

PHR

39:1)   Forty years before the Messiah son of David,[61] whose name
is Menahem Ben Amiel,[8] comes, Nehemiah Ben Hoshiel, a man of
Ephraim, son of Joseph,[62] will come. He will arise in Jerusalem,
and all the Israelites will be gathered there. He will gather each

[60] ואביא, "and I brought," is apparently a scribal error for ואבוא, here rendered, "and I
went."

[61] The Jewish Messiah.

[62] The Samaritan Messiah.

man and his house , and the sons of Israel will offer sacrifice, and it will please the Lord. The sons of Israel will be associated by their families (see Zech 12:10-14), and after forty years of Nehemiah Ben Hoshiel's [rule], Shiroi,[63] king of Persia, will come up and stab Nehemiah Ben Hoshiel in Jerusalem, and all the Israelites will mourn for him in a great lamentation and weeping. After that the wife of the prophet Nathan, son of David, Hafzi-bah, will come, and these signs will take place in the month of Ab. In the sixth of the month, Shiroi,[63] king of Persia, will stab Nehemiah in Jerusalem. He will cause Israel great lamentation. He will afflict them very much, and they will scatter themselves to the wilderness of Jerusalem to complete their mourning for Nehemiah.

For forty-one days his corpse will be thrown at the gates of Jerusalem, but no man, domestic animal, beast, or bird will be able to touch it. After forty days, the holy One blessed be He will bury him in the graves of the house of Judah.[64] 39:3)

I, Zerubbabel, continued to ask Mettatron and Michael, general of the Lord's army, concerning the covenant of the people of the saints. He said to me, *This calf—there it will lie down and consume its branches* (Isa 27:10). This city is the city of *Nineveh. The city of blood* (Ezek 22:2; 24:6, 9; Nah 3:1) is *great* Rome (Jonah 3:3). I said to him, "Sir, *When will be the wondrous end* (Dan 12:6)?[65] He held me tight and seized my hand (Isa 41:13). Then he brought me to the house of humiliation[66] and showed me there a stone which had a face like the appearance of a virgin which no man had known, and she was very beautiful. He said to Zerubbabel, "What do you see?" I said, "I see a marble image, whose face is like a beautiful woman." The man who was speaking with me answered and said to me, "This image was the wife of Beliel, and at the time when Beliel knew the image, she conceived and bore this Armilos,[67] who will be the chief of all idolatry. He is

[63]A king of Persia who ruled for a short time after A.D. 629. The text reads *Shidoi* (שידוי), evidently a scribal error for *Shiroi* (שירוי). Parallel texts all read *Shiroi*. According to Acts 13:21, Saul ruled 40 years before David.

[64]See Rev 11:3-12.

[65]Or "end of these wonders," meaning end of undesirable wonders. When will the rule of Gentiles be over and the Jews be given the kingdom?

[66]The "house of humiliation" may refer to a church in Rome. The stone which had the appearance of a virgin who gave birth to Armilos seems intentionally related to statues of the virgin Mary. In other contexts, Gentiles are shown worshiping this statue. The house of humiliation is once called "the house of humiliation, of scoffers" (W 37; BL 7:4).

[67]Armilos is a semitic form of Romulus, with the prosthetic *alef* to dissimulate the consonants differently. Romulus symbolized Rome, which also symbolized Christianity. From a Jewish point of view, Christianity was a monster that was born from pure Judaism but had strong Gentile influence.

all cut from one side, because half of him is from the stone and half from Beliel. The half which is from stone is cut like the appearance of a stone."

W (2)

When I said, "Woe to me, for my heart is grieved, and my spirit is troubled," I arouse quickly to pray to plead before my God. I confessed my transgressions and my sins (Dan 9:4), saying "You are the One who made everything with the breath of your mouth. [At] the word of your lips, the dead revive. He said, "Turn and go to the house of humiliation, the market place." 1:4) I went, just as I was commanded,[68] 1:5) and he said to me, "Turn farther on," so I went and turned. Then a despised man and a crushed spirit touched me. The despised man said to me, "Zerubbabel, what is your occupation in this [place]?" Then *I pitied the great city of Nineveh* (Jonah 4:11), and I answered and said, "You have thrown me in this [place]." Then he spoke with me straight forward and accurate words. When I heard [them], I was comforted. I asked the man, "What is the name of this place?" He said to me, "This is great Rome." Then I said to him, "What is your business in this [place]?" He said to me, "I am the Lord's Messiah."

J	BL
He troubled me very much	I said, "Woe to me, 1:15) for my heart is grieved, and my soul
I arose	burns me very much." I arose
from the trouble to pray and implore the face of the	from the trouble to pray and implore 1:16) the name of the Lord
God of Israel. I confessed my transgressions and my sin,	God of Israel. I confessed all my transgressions and my sins (Dan 9:4-5), for my heart was
and I said,	grieved 1:17), and I said,
"O Lord, I have sinned; I have transgressed; and I have been guilty (for my pains are grievous). You are the God of Israel who has made everything with the	"Ah, Lord, I have been iniquitous and I have sinned (for my heart was grieved). You are the Lord 1:18) God who has made everything by the

[68]"Was commanded" is conjectured from BL 1:21. There is a break in the text which requires something like this to make sense.

J

breath of your mouth. At
your word the dead come to
to life." Then he said to me,
"Go to the house of humiliation, the market place."[69] I
went as he commanded
me. Then he said to me,
"Turn further on;" I turned,
and he touched me, and I saw
a despised and wounded man.

The wounded and despised man
said to me, "Zerubbabel,
why are you here?"

I answered
and said, "The spirit of the
Lord raised me in a way I do not
know, and made me walk in
this place." Then he said to me,
"Do not be afraid, *for it is because of your vision you were
brought here*" (Ezek 40:4).
As I heard his words I was
comforted, and
I asked him,
"What is the name of this
place?" He said to me, "This
is great Rome in which I am a
prisoner, in jail until my
time comes."

BL

word of your mouth. At
your word *the dead* 1:19) come
to life." Then he said to me,
"Go to the house of humiliation, the market place."[69] I
went 1:20) as he commanded
me. Then he said to me,
"Turn further on;" I turned,
and he touched me, and I saw
1:21) a man whose face was despised, wounded, and crushed
from pain (Isa 53:3; San 98a;
PR 161b).
That despised man
said to me, 1:22) "Zerubbabel,
what is your business in this
[place], or who brought you to
it?" I answered
and said, "The spirit of 1:23) the
Lord raised me
and transported me to
this place." Then he said to me,
"Do not be afraid, *for it is because of your vision you were
brought here*" (Ezek 40:4).
As I heard his words I was
comforted, and my reason 1:25)
returned to me. I asked him,
"Sir, what is the name of this
place?" He said to me, "This
is great Rome in which I am a
prisoner (San 98a; Targ Jon on
Ex 12:42). Then I said to him,
"Sir, who are you, 1:27) and
what is your name, and what

are you looking for here, and what are you doing in this place?"
1:28) He said to me, "I am the Lord's Messiah, the son of

---

[69]For "Market place" (שוק), I. Levi, "L'Apocalypse de Zorobabel et Le Roi de Perse Siroes," *REJ* 68 (1917), 145 corrects to "place of frivolity" (שחוק), but it does not seem necessary.

Hezekiah, for I am a prisoner, in jail until the time of 1:29) the end."

W(3)

I was silent, and I hid my face from him. His anger burned within him, and I blushed before him. Then he changed his form.[70] 1:6) I turned and raised my eyes and gazed upon him, and I was afraid. He said, "Ask me." At his word all my limbs trembled. Then his hand reached out, and he held me. He said to me, "Do not be afraid, and do not let your heart melt" (see Jn 14:1). He encouraged me and said to me, "Why are you silent, and why did you turn your face from me?" I said to him, "Because you said, 'I am the servant and the Messiah of the Lord.'" He was the light of Israel, and he was like a handsome and attractive youth. I said to him, "When will you bring the redemption for the age?"

J	BL
When I heard this	When I heard this, I fell silent,
I turned my face away from him for a moment.	I turned my face away before him, and it burned inside me. 1:31) I arose and blessed him,
Then I turned back and looked at him. I turned away again, for I was afraid. Then he said to me,	but I was afraid. Then he said to me, "Draw near; draw near to me." While he was speaking 1:37) to me, my limbs trembled. Then he reached his hand down and held me tight. Then he said,
"Do not be afraid, and do not recoil.	"Do not be frightened, and do not let your heart be afraid." 1:32) He encouraged me, and
Why are you silent?"	said, "Why have you been silent and turned your face away?"
I said,	1:33) I said to him,
"I heard your report that you are the Messiah of my God."	"Because you said, 'I am the servant of the Lord, his

[70]Compare this to the transfiguration of Jesus (Mt 17:1-8). καὶ μεταμορφώθη ἔμπροσθεν αὐτῶν (Mt 17:2).

J	BL
	Messiah and the light of Israel.'''
At once he	Then he spoke 2:1) to me, and he
seemed to me like a pleasant	seemed like a youth, a hand-
man.	some and attractive man.⁷¹
I said to him, "When will the	I said to him, "When will the
candle of Israel shine?"	light of Israel come?"

PHR

39:4) This word was in the prophecy of the Lord to Zerubbabel, and my soul troubled me very much. I arose and went to the head waters, where the assembly of the Lord God of Israel was. He is the God of all flesh, and he sent his angel while the prayer was still in my mouth. I had not stopped when I saw that he had been speaking with me all the first words. Then I bowed down and prostrated myself to the Lord. He answered and said to me, "Ask, before I leave." I continued to ask him concerning the Messiah of the Lord, and I said to him, "When will the light⁷² of Israel come?"

W (4)

As I spoke, a man came to me, and he had six wings, and he said to me, "Zerubbabel, what are you asking the Messiah of the Lord?" I said to him, "Do I have to ask?" He said to me,⁷³ 1:7) "I will tell you." [I said], "Who are you, Sir?" He answered me with a pleasant voice and said to me, "I am Mettatron, prince of the presence, 1:8) and my name is Michael.⁷⁴ 1:9) He placed me to be over his people and over those who love him. I am the one who led Abraham from [sic.] the land of Canaan, and I blessed him in the name of the Lord. I am the one who redeemed Isaac, and I wept over him. 1:10) I am the one who wrestled with Jacob beyond the river. I am the one who led the Israelites in the wilderness for forty years in the name of the Lord God. I am the one who appeared to Joshua at Gilgal. 1:11) I am the one who brought out fire and

⁷¹Levi, "L'Apocalypse," 146, said this is the only place where an angel is transformed into a man in apocalyptic literature.

⁷²"Light" is conjectured from BL 2:1. The text reads יבוא יבוא—evidently dittography.

⁷³The text reads "He said to me, and I will tell you." There is apparently something missing from the text. Judging from BL 2:4, it may have read, "He said to me, "[Ask me], and I will tell you."

⁷⁴Note the problem of identifying Michael with Mettatron, which was evident also in PHR.

brimstone for the Lord from heaven. 1:12) He set my name as his name.[7]

You are Zerubbabel Ben Shealtiel Ben Yeconiah, king of Judah. Ask, and I will tell you." I answered and said to him, "Who is this man?" He said to me, "He is the Messiah of the Lord. He was born to the house of David, and the Lord has hidden him, so that he will be a leader of the covenant for the people. 1:13) This is Menahem Ben Amiel.[8] He was born when Nebuchadnezzar came against Jerusalem. 1:14) Then the spirit of the Lord took him up and set him in this place until the end of time."

J	BL
As I was speaking these words with him, behold a man with wings came to me,	2:2) As I was speaking to him, behold a man with wings came to me, and he had two wings. .
and he said to me that	He said 2:3) to me, "Zerubbabel, what are you asking of the Lord's Messiah?" I answered and said to him, "I am asking 2:4) when the time of salvation will come." He said, "Ask me, and I will inform you." I said to him, "Who are you, 2:5) Sir?" He answered and said, "I am Michael, who proclaimed the good news to Sarah (BM 86b).
he was the general of the army of Israel who fought with Sennacherib	I am the general of the Lord God of Israel's army who fought with Sennacherib, and I struck a hundred, 2:7) eighty thousand men (ExR 18). I am the general of the Israelites who fought the wars
and with the kings of Canaan, and that he was destined to fight the war of the Lord together with the Lord's Messiah	with 2:8) the kings of Canaan, and I am destined to fight the wars of the Lord together with the Lord's Messiah.

J

and against the king of fierce
countenance against
Armilos, the son of the stone.

Then Mettatron
continued and said to me, "I
am the angel who led Abraham
into the whole land of Canaan;

I am the one who redeemed
Isaac;
and I
struggled with Jacob at
the fording of the Jabbok.
I am
he who led the Israelites in the
wilderness forty years in
the name of the Lord. I am the
one who was revealed to Joshua
at Gilgal. I am he

whose name is like the name of
my Master,
and his name is within me.[76]

"Now you, Zerubbabel,

ask from me,

BL

This is [against] Rome 2:9)
which I will place before you
with the king of fierce
countenance (Dan 8:23) and
with Armilos, the son of Satan,
who came forth from a stone
dish. The Lord has set me over
this people and over those who
love the general (Dan 10:21) to
fight 2:11) with the generals of
the nations.[75]
Michael spoke and Mettatron
answered and said to me, "I
am the angel who led [Abraham]
into the whole land of Canaan,
and I blessed him in the name of
the Lord (Gen 22:17). 2:13)
I am the one who redeemed
Isaac and his house because of
him. I am the one who
struggled 2:14) with Jacob at
the fording of the Jabbok (Ps
Jon. Gen 32:25; GenR 76). I am
he who led the Israelites in the
wilderness forty years 2:15) in
the name of the Lord. I am the
one who was revealed to Joshua
Gilgal (Josh 5:13). I am the one
who rained over Sodom and
Gomorrah brimstone and fire.

Then the Lord put *Mettatron,*
2:17) his name, within me
(San 38b).[76]

"Now you, Zerubbabel, son
of Shealtiel, whose name is 2:18)
Jeconiah (I Chron 3:17), ask me,

[75]Before the word, "nations," there is a three letter word that is unclear. The first letter is
alef. It may have been אלף , "a thousand," or it may have been אלי, "these."

[76]This means he has been given apostolic authority. He can speak authoritatively in the
other's name and it is considered as valid as if the other person had spoken it himself.

J

and I will inform you what will happen[77] to your people in the end of days." He said to me, "This Messiah of the Lord is hidden here until the time of the end."

W (5) (Note change of texts)

"Then I, Zerubbabel, [asked] this Mettatron, 'What are the signs which [this] Menahem Ben Amiel will perform?' He said to me, "The staff of these[78] deliverances the Lord will give to Hafzi-bah,[79] the mother of Menahem Ben Amiel. The brilliance of Venus will go before her, and all the stars will descend from their courses of their wars.

"Hafzi-bah, the mother of Menahem, will go out and she will kill two

BL

and I will inform you what will happen[77] to your people in the end of days." 2:19) He answered and said to me, "This 2:20) Messiah of the Lord is hidden in this place until the time of the end, and this is the Messiah, son of David whose name is Menahem Ben Amiel (Num 13:12; II Sam 9:4; San 98b; JBer 5a). He was born in the days of David, king of 1:21) Israel. The spirit lifted him (JBer 5a), and I hid him in this place until the time of the end" (PR 49a; RuthR 2:14).

"Then I 2:22), Zerubbabel, asked Mettatron, general of the Lord's army,

and he said to me, "The staff of these[78] deliverances the Lord will give to Hafzi-bah[79] the mother of Menahem Ben Amiel, and a great star will begin to shine 2:24) before her, and all the stars will wander from their courses.[80]

Hafzi-bah will go out with 2:25) Menahem Amiel, and she will kill two

[77]Reading יקרה for יקרא. The pronunciation is the same for both.

[78]There is an intentional replay here of the situation in the exodus from Egypt, with plagues and miracles brought about by the staff of Moses and Aaron.

[79]Hafzi-bah means "my desire is in her." There was a woman in the OT by that name who was the wife of King Hezekiah. See II Kgs 21:1; San 94a.

[80]There were fallen meteorites during the Middle Ages which made people think the world was facing radical changes. Jews expected the Messiah to come then. The prominence of astrology during the Crusades would also prompt this kind of a statement.

W (5)

kings.[61] The hearts of the two kings are for evil.
The name of the one king will be Nof, king of Teman, who waved (*henif*-הניף) his hand over Zion 1:15), and the name of the second is Atras,[62] king of Antioch.
These signs will take place in the fifth year, in the third month, when the sons of Israel make the Feast of Weeks to the Lord,

after the destruction of Jerusalem,

BL

kings.[61] The hearts of the two kings are for evil (Dan 11:27).
The name of the two 2:26) kings are Nof, king of Teman, who waved his hand over Jerusalem. The name of the second is 2:27) Esarenan,[62] king of Antioch. This war and these signs will take place 2:28) in the Feast of Weeks, in the third month.

The word is true for the subjection of the city 2:29) and the sanctuary.[63] After four hundred and twenty 2:30) years, it will be destroyed a second time [A.D. 70], and after twenty years from the subjection

of the city of Rome, and seventy kings will rule it,[64] corresponding to the seventy 2:31) nations. With the completion of the ten kings, the tenth will come.[65] He will destroy 2:32) the fortresses and discontinue the continual offering. He will shatter the holy people and give them up to the sword and for plunder 3:1) and for trouble (Dan 11:33). Many of them will fall into their [the pagan] teaching. They [the Israelites] will abandon the teaching of the Lord, and they will serve their [the Gentiles'] idols 3:2), and when they [the Israelites] stumble, they will receive a little help (Dan 11:34). From the day they discontinue the continual offering (Dan 11:31), and the wicked ones set up that which they set up—

[61]The heroic role of Hafzi-bah, the mother of the Messiah, reflects the influence of the Roman Catholic belief in the virgin Mary at the time of this composition.

[62]There are no such kings associated with national powers of that period by these names. These are probably code names that give special meanings to Christians and Moslems or something like that.

[63]Levi, "L'Apocalypse de Zorobabel," 149, has noticed that there is a break here where a new unit is obviously joined to the material that precedes. He did not notice, however, that the unit beginning here concludes with 4:19, as the inclusion, "The word is true" indicates.

[64]Apparently a mythical number with no historical significance.

[65]Meaning the tenth will be the completion of the list, with nine before him.

W (5)

nine
hundred, ninety years (A.D.
1060). (From then on wait for
him) will be the salvation of
the Lord.

תשע מאות ותשעין שנה
תשועה לה׳

The staff which the Lord
will give to Hafzi-bah,
he will give it to Menahem Ben
Amiel, and that staff
which is granite is
prepared in Rakat, a city in
Naphtali (Josh 19:35). This is
the staff which God gave to
Adam, Seth, Noah, Abraham,
Isaac, Jacob 1:16), Moses,
Joshua, David, and Elijah.
It is the staff of Aaron which
he brought out and it grew
shoots."

J (note change of text)

Then Zerubbabel Ben
Shealtiel answered and said,
"Please, Sir,

BL

an abomination in the temple,
from the end of nine
hundred, ninety years (A.D.
1060)
will be the salvation of
the Lord.

An arm will shatter the holy
people (Dan 12:7), to redeem
them and to gather them by the
arm of the Lord's Messiah,
and the staff 3:5) which the Lord
will give to Hafzi-bah, the
mother of Menahem Ben
Amiel
will be from granite which is
preserved in Rakat 3:6) a city in
Naphtali (Josh 19:35). This is
the staff which the Lord gave to

Moses, Aaron
Joshua 3:7), and king David.
It is the staff which
blossomed and grew
shoots in the temple at the hand
of Aaron 3:8), and Elijah, son
of Elazar,[86] preserved in Rakat
a city in Naphtali, namely
Tiberias. And he preserved the
name of 3:9) a man whose name
is Nehemiah, son of Hoshiah,
son of Ephraim, the son of
Asaph.

BL

Then Zerubbabel
answered 3:10) and said to
Mettatron and to Michael, "Sir,

[86]This identifies Elijah with Phineas, son of Elazar.

J

when will the candle of Israel
come, and what will
happen after this? The
Messiah son of Joseph

said to me, "He will come five
years after Hafzi-bah, and he
will gather all the Israelites
together as one man. They will
remain in Jerusalem for forty
years
and offer
sacrifice.[88]

Then the king of Persia

will come up against
the Israelites, there will be a
great hardship in Israel. Then
Hafzi-bah, the wife of the
prophet Nathan,
will come out
with the staff which the Lord
will give her, and
the Lord will put among them
a spirit of confusion (Isa 19:14).
Then each man will
murder
his brother. There he will
slay the wicked.

BL

I want you to inform me
when 3:11) the Messiah of the
Lord will come, or what will
happen after all this? The
Messiah of the Lord, who is
3:12) Nehemiah Ben Hoshiah,
said to me, "He will come five
years after Hafzi-bah, and he
will gather 3:13) all the Israelites
together as one man. They will
go up forty years to Jerusalem[87]
(San 99a; PR p. 8), and *the sons
of Israel* will offer 3:14) a
sacrifice, and it will be pleasing
to the Lord. He will relate the
Israelites by their families (see
Zech 12:10-14), and in *the fifth
year* 3:15) of Nehemiah and of
the gathering of the holy ones,
Shiroi,[63] king of Persia, will go
up against Nehemiah 3:16) Ben
Hoshiah, and against
the Israelites. The hardship in
Israel will be great. Then
Hafzi-bah, the wife 3:17) of the
prophet Nathan, the mother of
Menahem Amiel, will come out
with the staff which the Lord
God of Israel will give her 3:18).
The Lord will put among them
the spirit of confusion (Isa
19:14). Then each man will
murder his neighbor,
his brother. 3:19) There he will
slay the wicked.

---

[87]Levi, "L'Apocalypse de Zorobabel," 151, amends the text to read "four," rather than "forty."

[88]See PHR 39:1.

W (6)

I, Zerubbabel, answered and said to Mettatron, "This Messiah of the Lord, when will he come?" Then he said, "Nehemiah Ben Hoshiel, who belongs to Ephraim Ben Joseph, will come in the fifth year before Hafzi-bah, the mother of Menahem Ben Amiel. He will arise in Jerusalem and gather all the Israelites into one congregation, each man and the men of his house, and the sons of Israel will offer a sacrifice to the Lord, and it will please him. The sons of Israel will be associated by their families (Zech 12:10-14). After Nehemiah Ben Hoshiel has been in Jerusalem for three months, and all the Israelites will mourn for him and weep for him. After this Hafzi-bah, wife of Nathan Ben David, the prophet, will come. These signs will strike. It will be in the sixth year and the fifth month, which is the month of Ab, on the sixth of the month, when Shiroi[63] 1:17) will stab Nehemiah, and it will grieve the Israelites very much. They will scatter to the wilderness of Judah to complete the mourning for Nehemiah. (All the Israelites will mourn for him and weep for him.) For forty-one days his corpse will be hurled at the gates of Jerusalem, but no man, beast, or bird will be able to touch it (see Rev 11:3-10). After forty-one days 1:18) the holy One blessed be He will bury him in a grave of the house of Judah."

Then I, Zerubbabel, continued to ask Mettatron, prince of the presence, concerning 1:19) the leader of the covenant of the holy people, and he said to me, *This calf will lie down [and he will cut off] its branches* (Isa 27:10). *This* city is *Nineveh, the city of blood, and it is great* Rome (Jonah 4:11; Ezek 22:2; 24:6, 9; Nah 3:1). Then I said to him, "Sir, how long before the end?" Then he came and held me tight (Isa 41:13), and took my hand and brought me to the armory and showed me there a stone, a marble stone, and it had the appearance of a virgin who had not known a man. He said to me, "What do you see?" I said, "I see a stone like a woman, and her face is that of a beautiful woman." The one who was speaking to me answered and said, "This stone is the wife of Beliel. When Beliel had intercourse with her, she became pregnant and gave birth to Armilos. She will be the chief of all idolatry."

J	BL
When I heard his words, I fell on my face and said to him, "Tell me the truth concerning	When I heard, I fell on my face and said, "O Lord, tell me what 3:20) is that

J

the holy people."

Then he held me tight (Isa
41:13),

and he showed me
a stone like the form of a
woman,

and he said to me,

"Satan will lie with
this stone, and Armilos will
come out of her.

He will rule over
the entire world.[90]

No one will be able to stand
before him, and everyone who
does not believe in him will die

BL

which the prophet Isaiah said
there, *There the calf grazes,
and there it will lie down and
consume its branches* (Isa
27:10). 2:21) He said to me,
"This calf is Nineveh, *the city of
blood. It is great* Rome" (Jonah
3:3; Ezek 22:2). There I continued 3:22) and asked about
the prince of the holy covenant.
Then he spoke to me and
brought me to the house of
humiliation, of scorn,
and he showed me there
a marble stone in the form of a
a woman, a virgin, and her appearance and form were 3:23)
beautiful, and very attractive to
see. He answered and said to
me, "This stone is the wife[89] of
Beliel, 3:24) and
Satan will come and lie with
her. A son will come out from
her whose name is Armilos. He
will destroy 3:25) the people,
and he will rule over
all [those who speak] in the
Hebrew tongue. His kingdom
will reach from one end of the
land 3:26) to the other end of
the land. There will be ten letters in his hand, and he will
serve foreign gods, 3:27) and he
will say he is meritorious.[91]
No one will be able to stand
before him, and everyone who
does not believe in him will die

---

[89]The text reads א י ש , "husband," but the sense requires א י ש ה , "wife."
[90]See PHR 39:3.
[91]Several blurred letters here.

J

by his harsh sword. He

will come to the land of Israel

with
ten kings to Jerusalem, and

they will kill the Messiah son of
Joseph there
together with sixteen righteous
men.
The Israelites will go
into exile in the wilderness,
but Hafzi-bah,
the mother of Menahem,
will be there. There
that wicked one will not come.

This war will be in the
month of Ab, and there will be
hardship in Israel, such that
none has been like it in
the world. They will flee into
towers, caves, and wilderness
areas.

All the Gentiles
will wander
astray after that wicked Satan,
Armilos, except those from
Israel. All the Israelites
will mourn for Nehemiah Ben
Ben Hoshiel who was killed.

BL

by his sword. 3:28) He will kill
many of them, and he
will come against the men of the
saints of the Most High (Dan
7:21, 25).[92]
There will be with him there
3:29) ten kings with troops of
great strength (Rev 17:12-14).
He will make war with the saints
and will destroy 3:30) them.
He will kill the Messiah son of
Joseph, who is Nehemiah Ben
Hoshiah. Sixteen 3:31) righteous
ones will be killed with him.
They will send the Israelites
into exile to the wilderness,
[in] three groups. Hafzi-bah,
3:32) the mother of Menahem,
will stand at the east gate. There
that wicked one will not come.
3:33) [This is] to fulfill that
which was written, *And the
people will not be cut off from
the city* (Zech 14:2).
This war 4:1) will be in the
month of Ab, and there will be
hardship in Israel, such that
none has been like it in
Israel. They will flee 4:2) into
towers, mountains, and caves,

but they will not be able to hide
from him. All the nations
of the lands 4:3) will wander
astray after him,
except the Israelites who will not
believe in him. All the Israelites
will mourn for Nehemiah 4:4)
Ben Hoshiel for forty-one days

[92]The Jews.

J	BL
	(Zech 12:11; Suk 52a; see Rev 11:7-9).
His corpse will be thrown before the gates of Jerusalem,	His corpse will be thrown before the gates 4:5) of Jerusalem.........(see Rev 11:7-9).[93]
and no beast or bird	and no beast, bird, or domestic animal
will touch it.	will touch it. Then the sons of *Israel* will cry aloud 4:6) to the Lord from much distress and great hardship, and the Lord will answer them.

W (7)

This word is the prophecy of the Lord to Zerubbabel. My soul grieved within me very much, and I went up [to] the head waters,[94] and I prayed there to the God of all flesh. He sent 20) his angel while the prayer was still within me, but I did not stop. 21) I saw him, and I knew that he was the one who had been speaking with me all the first words,[95] so I bowed down and prostrated myself before him. Again he touched me as he had the first time,[95] and he said to me, "What's wrong, Zerubbabel?" I told him that my spirit troubled me (Job 17:1) 22) concerning the Messiah of the Lord. He said to me, "By the life of the Lord who sent me, [I hereby swear] that I now will truly tell you the word of the Lord God, the holy One.

J	BL
When I heard his words,	When I heard 4:7) the word of the prophecy of the Lord to me, it troubled me very much,
it troubled me very much, and I arose to pray	me, it troubled me very much, and I arose and went to the water conduit, 4:8) and I cried

[93]Several blurred letters here.

[94]Or "Rosh Hamaim" may be the name of a known geographical location. It may refer to some "fountain" or "source," such as the head waters of the Jordan at Panias or Caesarea Phillipi. It was used frequently by medieval poets to symbolize the source of the water of life. It is parallel to "Emet Hamaim," or "truth of the water" in BL 4:7.

[95]At the beginning of the Apocalypse.

J

before the Lord.
He heard
and sent his angel to me,

and I knew that he was the
angel who had been speaking
with me,
and I
prostrated myself before him

He said to me, "What's
wrong, Zerubbabel?" I said to
him, "The spirit has terrified
us [sic.]"[96]
Mettatron stood up and
answered and said, "Zerubbabel,
ask [something] from me
before I leave you." I
asked him and said,

"When will the candle of Israel
come?"[97] He answered
me and said, "By the life of
the Lord who sent me,

[I swear] that I am telling you
the work of the Lord, for
the voice of the holy One
sent me
to tell you everything you ask."

Then Michael
said to me,

BL

out before the Lord God of
Israel, the God of all flesh,
and he sent his angel to me
while *the prayer* was still 4:9) in
my mouth, and I had not yet
finished when the Lord sent his
angel to me. Then I saw 4:10)
and knew that he was the
angel who had been telling
me all the first things.[95] 4:11)
Then I bowed down and
prostrated myself before him.
He continued and touched me
as in the first time, and
he said to me, 4:12) "What's
wrong, Zerubbabel?" I said to
him, "Sir, I am in pain from the
spirit of my womb (Job 17:1).
Mettatron
answered 4:13) and said to me,
"Ask me, and I will tell you
before I leave you." I continued
and asked him 4:14) and said,
"Sir Mettatron,
when will the light of Israel
come?" He answered and said
to me, "By the life 4:15) of
the Lord who sent me and who
made me prince over Israel,
[I swear] that I will tell you
the work of the Lord, 4:16) for
the holy God said to me, 'Go
tell Zerubbabel, my servant,
and whatever he asks you, tell
4:17) him."
Then Michael, who is Mettatron,
said,

[96]A *yodh* has been confused for a *waw*. הבהילנו for הבהילני . It initially read "terrified me."

[97]See PHR 39:4.

J	BL
"Please draw near to me and pay attention to what I am telling you, for the word is true in the name of the God of life."	"Please come here and pay attention to all 4:18) that I am saying to you, for the word which I am speaking to you is true by the words of 4:19) the God of life."[98]

PHR

(Repeat of page 354, parallel to W (3))

39:4) This word was in the prophecy of the Lord to Zerubbabel, and my soul troubled me very much. I arose and went to the head waters, where the assembly of the Lord God of Israel was. He is the God of all flesh, and he sent his angel while the prayer was still in my mouth. I had not stopped when I saw that he had been speaking with me all of the first words.[99]

Then I bowed down and prostrated myself to the Lord. He answered and said to me, "Ask [something] for yourself before I leave." I continued to ask him concerning the Messiah of the Lord, and I said to him, "When will the light[100] of Israel come?" He answered and said to me, "By the life of the Lord who sent me, who placed me over Israel, [I swear that] I will tell you the work of the Lord, for the holy God told them [the following statements] to me: 'Go and tell my servant Zerubbabel that which Israel....[101] 39:5) Then he said, 'Draw near to me, and I will tell you the word of God.'"

W (8)

Then he said to me, "Menahem Ben Amiel will come in the month of Nisan, suddenly, in the fourteenth of it,[102] 23) and he will come and stand over the Valley of Arabiel which belongs to Joshua Ben Saraph, and all the scholars of Israel who are left will go out to him, for they will be few because of the plunderers who plundered them. Menahem Ben Amiel will answer and tell the

---

[98]The inclusion, "the word is true" (BL 2:28) concludes here: "the word which I am speaking to you is true."

[99]See W (7).

[100]Name for the Messiah.

[101]An incomplete sentence. Something has been omitted.

[102]At Passover time, commemorating the exodus and deliverance through Moses.

elders that he is the Messiah of the Lord, "who sent me to proclaim the good news to you." The elders will look at him, because he will be despised, and his clothes will be filthy. 24) This anger will burn within him, and he will remove his garments and put on garments of vengeance. The prophet Elijah will come with him, and they will go together to Jerusalem. They will arouse Nehemiah Ben Hoshiel, who had been stabbed at the gates of Jerusalem.[103] Then all the Israelites will come and see him [Menahem] with Nehemiah coming with him, and they will believe in Menahem Ben Amiel.

J	BL
Then he said to me, Menahem Ben Amiel will come suddenly, in	Then he said to me, "Menahem Ben Amiel will come suddenly, in the *first month* 4:20) which is
the month of Nisan,	the month of Nisan, on the fourteenth day,[104]
and he will stand in the Valley of Arabiel.	and he will stand in the Valley of 4:21) Arabiel, which is the [the home] of Joshua Ben Yaho-zedek, the priest. All the wise
All the wise men of Israel will go out to him,	men of Israel who are left will go out to him, 4:22) for few will be left from the smiting and plunder of Gog and Armilos and from 4:23) the horses which fortify them. Then Menahem
and Ben Amiel will say to them, "I am the Messiah whom the Lord has sent to proclaim good news to you and to deliver you from the hand of your oppressors." The wise men will look at him and despise him,	Ben Amiel will say to the elders and wisemen, 4:24) "I am the Messiah of the Lord who sent me to proclaim good news to you and to deliver you from the hand of these enemies." 4:25) The elders will look at him and despise him, for they will see him, a man despised 4:26) and his clothes worn out, so they will

---

[103]But he was not buried there. He was removed after forty-one days to one of the tombs of the kings of Judah.

[104]Passover time for a group who celebrated New Year's Day in the Spring.

J	BL
just as you have despised him,	despise him just as you have despised him. Then his wrath will burn in him, 4:27)
and he will *put on garments of vengeance [as] a garment* (Isa 59:17).	and he will *put on garments of vengeance [as] a garment* (Isa 59:17) and wrap himself like a robe of zeal.
He will come to the gates of Jerusalem with Elijah, and he	He will come to the gates of Jerusalem 4:28) with Elijah the prophet, and they
will raise up and give life to Nehemiah,	will raise up and give life to Nehemiah Ben Hoshiah in the gates of 4:29) Jerusalem.[103] Then Hafzi-bah, the mother of the Messiah, will come and hand

over to him the staff 4:30) with which the signs were performed. Then all the Israelites, the elders of Israel, will come, and the sons of Israel will see that Nehemiah is alive. 4:31) Then he will stand on his feet.

J	BL
and they will believe in him.	At once they will believe in him as the Messiah.

PHR

Be informed that Menahem Ben Amiel will come on the fourteenth of Nisan,[104] and he will stand over my valley, and Menahem Ben Amiel will answer and say to the elders, "I am the Messiah of the Lord who sent me to proclaim good news to you." 40:1) The elders will see that he is despised with clothes worn out. They will despise him just as you despised the elders,[105] because he was despised. Then his wrath will burn in him, he will remove his clothes and *put on garments of vengeance [as] clothing* (Isa 59:17). The prophet Elijah will come with him, and they will go to Jerusalem, and he will revive Nehemiah Ben Hoshiel who was buried in the gates of Jerusalem.[103] They will walk to the council of Israel, and the sons of Israel will see him [and observe] that Nehemiah is with him, and they will believe in Menahem Ben Amiel."

---

[105] An "improvement" over the other parallel texts.

W (9)

This is the word of the Lord which Mettatron, general of the army of the Lord, spoke in truth, *Ephraim will not be jealous of Judah, and Judah will not oppress Ephraim* (Isa 11:13), and there will be a council of peace between them. 25) In the twenty-first of the first month after [the destruction] of Jerusalem, nine hundred, ninety years (A.D. 1060) will be the salvation of the Lord.

J	BL
Thus Mettatron swore to me that	Thus Mettatron, the general of *the army of the Lord* swore to me: 4:32) Truly this thing will take place, for [there is] a council of peace between them according to the prophecy of Isaiah,[106] 4:33) *Ephraim will not be jealous of Judah, and Judah will not oppress Ehpraim* (Isa 11:13), 4:34) and on the twenty-first of the first month
after the destruction of Jerusalem, nine hundred, ninety years (A.D. 1060), there will be salvation.	after the destruction of Jerusalem, nine hundred, 5:1) ninety years (A.D. 1060) there will be salvation of the Lord for the Israelites.

PHR

Mettatron and Michael, general of the Lord's army, said, *Truly Ephraim will not be jealous of Judah* (Isa 11:13), and there will be a council of peace between them. On the twenty-seventh of the first month after the destruction of Jerusalem, eight hundred, ninety years (A.D. 960), the salvation of the Lord [will take place]."

---

[106]Omitting the *waw* in Armilos, the value of the letters total 341, the same as those of the name Menahem Ben Amiel.

W (10)

Menahem Ben Amiel will come in the days of Armilos, whom the stone brought forth. This Menahem Ben Amiel, Nehemiah Ben Hoshiel, and Elijah Ben Phineas will go out and stand over the Great Sea, and they will draw out and bring up all the corpses which fell into the sea because of their enemies 26) and upon the waves of the Great Sea, and throw them into the Valley of Jehoshaphat, because there will be a judgment for the wicked and happiness for the righteous.

J	BL
Menahem	Menahem Ben Amiel, Nehemiah 5:2) Ben Hoshiah,
and Elijah will stand alongside the Great Sea, and they will read in his prophets, and all the corpses of the Israelites who had cast themselves into the sea because of their enemies will come forth.	and the prophet Elijah will come and be alongside the sea. [There] they will read the prophecies of the Lord. 5:3) Then every corpse of the Israelites who had cast themselves into the sea because of their enemies will come forth (Rev 20:3). 5:4) Waves will come up and overflow them, and they

will throw them alive into the depths of judgments alongside the Shittim Valley, 5:5) for there will be the judgment of all Gentiles (Joel 4:18).

PHR

40:2 Menahem Ben Amiel will go out (in *gematria* Armilos).[106] He, Nehemiah Ben Hoshiel, and the prophet Elijah Ben Elazar Ben Aaron, the priest, will go and stand together alongside the Great Sea. They will act and bring up the corpses which fell into the hands of their enemies, and the waves of the sea will cast them into the river Soter. There will be a judgment of the wicked and happiness for the righteous.

W (11)

In the second month, which is the month of Iyyar, the council of

W (11)

Korah, whom the land opened its mouth and swallowed, will come up with their houses and their tents in the Araboth[107] of Jericho, alongside the Shittim Valley (Joel 4:18).[108] On the eighteenth of it [Iyyar], the mountains and hills will quake, and the land and all that is on it, the sea and all that is in it will move about. On the first of the third month, the dead of the wilderness will come and associate with their brothers along the Shittim Valley.[108] On the eighteenth of the month of Sivan there will be a shaking as in the houses, walls, and towers, and the land and its inhabitants will tremble. Then Menahem Ben Amiel, Nehemiah Ben Hoshiel, the prophet Elijah, and all the Israelites, near and far, the living ones whom the Lord revived will come up to Jerusalem. In the month of Ab, on the very day they mourned for Nehemiah, they will rejoice with very great joy, and they will offer a sacrifice to the Lord God. The Lord will smell the sacrifice of his children, and he will rejoice with the Israelites very much and be glad.

J

Then
the council of Korah will come up

and
they will come to Moses, and the dead from the wilderness will come to life, and the banner of the Korahites will gather.

BL

In the second month, in Iyyar, *the council of Korah* will come up 5:6) in the Araboth of Jericho, alongside the Shittim Valley.[108]
They will go to Moses, and

he will add 5:7) the banner of the Korahites [to the camps of Israel]. On the eighteenth, the mountains and hills will rumble, and *the earth and all that are upon it* will quake, 5:8) the sea and all that is in it. On the first day of the third month 5:9) the dead of the wilderness will come to life

[107]The wilderness area in the Jordan Valley and also the south of the Dead Sea.
[108]The Shittim Valley was evidently a valley across the Jordan into Moab alongside the Dead Sea (Num 25:1; Micah 6:5). It is also called a Shittim meadow. The term was not used enough to define its limits. The medieval Jews who wrote these apocalypses thought it was near Jericho, and was related by a water channel to the temple area (Joel 4:18; Ezek 47:1-8). Wadi Qumran makes this connection with the Kidron Valley. The entire Jordan Valley may have been called the Shittim Valley, if not by biblical authors, then by medieval authors. The geography should make sense topographically. Allowing for miracles, the ancients usually related miracles to reasonable situations, such as the dead being thrown out of the Dead Sea all the way up the wadi to the Kidron Valley.

BL

and go with their families to the Shittim Valley.[108] On the eighteenth 5:10) of the month of Sivan, there will be a great turbulence in the land of Israel.

J	BL
Then the Lord will descend to the Mount of Olives, and the mountain will split from its outcry.	In Tammuz, the fourth month, 5:11) the Lord God of Israel will descend to the Mount of Olives, and the Mount of Olives will split open from its rebuke (Zech 14:4).
	Then the Lord will blow 5:12) *the great shofar* (Isa 27:13), and all foreign gods and the temples of idols will fall to the ground (I Sam 5:1-5), every wall and staircase 5:13) will fall to the ground, and......all their hors-
and he will fight those Gentiles *as a man of war, he will stir up* his *zeal* (Isa 42:13). Then the Messiah son of David will come. He will blow in the face of Armilos and kill him (Isa 11:4).	es,[109] and he will fight those Gentiles *as a man of wars* 5:14) *he will stir up zeal* (Isa 42:13). Then the Messiah of the Lord will come, who is Menahem Ben Amiel, and he will blow in the nostrils of Armilos 5:15) and kill him (Isa 11:4). Each man will put his sword to the throat of his neighbor, and there[110] they will fall [as] dead corpses. 5:16) The people of the saints will go out to see the salvation
All Israelites will see the Lord, eye to eye, as a man of wars when he returns to Zion with a helmet of salvation on his head,	of the Lord. All Israelites will see the Lord, eye to eye, as a man 5:17) of wars with a helmet of salvation on his head;

[109]Instead of "their horses" (סוסיהם), Levi, "L'Apocalypse de Zorobabel," 155, renders "their plundering" by changing a *samekh* to a *sin* (שוסיהם). The text is difficult to read because part of the letters are blurred.

[110]Blurred text.

J

wearing a coat of mail.
He will fight

with Armilos and his troops.
They will all fall [as] dead
corpses in the Valley of Arabiel.

Remnants will escape
and gather together at the rock
of the Lord, a thousand, five
hundred,
and those wearing
coats of mail, a hundred thousand. Five hundred men from
Israel with Nehemiah

at their head will kill them,

BL

he will wear a coat of mail
(Isa 59:17), and he will fight
in the war of Gog and Magog
5:18) and
with the troops of Armilos.
They will all fall [as] dead
corpses in the Valley of Arabiel.
All the Israelites will go out and
take 5:19) their booty and despise their despisers for seven
months, but some of
their remnants will escape. 5:20)
They will all gather together,
a wing of a thousand, five
hundred men from Israel
5:21);[111] and those wearing
coats of mail, a hundred thousand. Five hundred men from
Israel, together with Nehemiah
and Elijah and you, 5:22) Zerubbabel, at their head will kill them
all, and there *each man will
pursue a thousand* (Josh 23:10).
5:23) This will be the third war,
and there will be three in the

land of Israel, one 5:24) of which Hafzi-bah and also Shiroi, king
of Persia, makes.[112] One which the Lord God 5:25) of Israel and
Menahem Ben Amiel make with Armilos and the ten kings who
are with him and Gog 5:26) and Magog. The third will be with a
wing of a thousand which Nehemiah Ben Hoshiel and Zerubbabel
will wage. 5:27) The third war will be in the month of Ab.

J

"After this, Menahem Ben

BL

After [this],[113] Menahem Ben

[111]Kallir's version of this event calls for 190,000 men. See "In Those Days and in That Time."

[112]Apparently here Hafzi-bah was making war *against* Shiroi, because he was shown earlier stabbing Nehemiah.

[113]A blurred area equalling two words, one of the two letters and the second of three letters. The sense and the Jellinek parallel require something like כל זאת , "all this." This is possible but not clear.

J

Amiel,
Nehemiah,

and Elijah
will come.

In the month of Ab they will restore the ruins of Jerusalem,

and there will be great joy
for the Israelites. They will
offer their sacrifices
and they will receive favor
from the Lord, grain offerings
of Judah and Israel as at first.

He will smell our
fragrant aroma
and he will be very glad

with the splendor of the temple
that will be built above, and he
will extend it both in length and
width. It will go down *from* the
East and the Great *Wilderness to
the Last Sea [Mediteranean]* (Dt
11:24) and to the *Great River
(the river Euphrates)* (Gen
15:18).

BL

5:28) Amiel will come, together
with Nehemiah Ben Hoshiel,
and all the Israelites, and all the
dead will come to life, and Elijah
5:29) the prophet with them.
They will go up to Jerusalem,
in the month of Ab,

after they will have mourned
for Nehemiah, 5:30) because
Jerusalem was destroyed in it
[Ab].There will be great joy
for the Israelites. They will
offer a sacrifice to the Lord,
5:31) and the Lord will desire
and take delight in the gift of the
Israelites as at first and in
ancient times (Mal 3:4).
The Lord will smell 5:32) the
fragrant aroma of his people Israel, and the Lord will rejoice
greatly. The Lord will bring
down *to the land*
the temple
that is built above.

PHR

In the second month, the above mentioned stream will bring up
the council of Korah, whom the ground opened up and swallowed.

W (12)

Then the pillar of fire of incense which was in the temple of the Lord will go up to the heavens. 27) The Messiah of the Lord will come out and all the Israelites after him on foot, and they will stand before the gates of Jerusalem opposite Mount Gerizim.[114] The holy God will stand on the top of the mountain, 28) and terror will weigh over heaven and the heaven of heavens, over the water and its produce, over the mountains and their foundations. No creature will be found with breath and soul, for the holy One blessed be He will rise up against everything on the Mount of Olives. The mountain will split under it (Zech 14:4), and the exiles of Jerusalem will go up to the Mount of Olives. Zion and Jerusalem will see, and Zion will say, *Who gave birth to these for me, and from where did these come* (Isa 49:21)? Then Nehemiah will go up to Jerusalem and say, "Behold your children whom you bore and who have been exiled from you! *Rejoice greatly, daughter of Zion! Shout for joy, 29) daughter of Jerusalem* (Zech 9:9)! *Extend in width the place of your tent and the curtains of your dwellings*" (Isa 54:2).

BL

5:33) The pillar of fire and the cloud of incense will go up to heaven. The Messiah *and all the Israelites after him* will go out 5:34) on their feet[115] at the gates of Jerusalem, and the holy God will stand on the Mount of 6:1) Olives, and his truth and his glory will be above the heaven and the heaven of heavens, and all the earth and that which is underneath it, 6:2) all the walls and buildings on their foundations. No living being will be there, because the Lord God will be revealed 6:3)....everything on the Mount of Olives. The Mount of Olives will split open under him (Zech 14:4), and the exiles of Jerusalem will go up to the Mount of 6:4) Olives,

W (13)

Mettatron, who was speaking to me all these words, showed me Jerusalem in [its] length and width. He showed me its walls

---

[114]The Mount of Olives was evidently intended as BL 5:33-6:1 indicates. Mount Gerizim is several miles north of Jerusalem.

[115]Or "At their feasts."

W (13)

encircling (מקפים) its surroundings *from the wilderness and Lebanon and from the Great River, the river Euphrates, and as far as the Last [Mediterranean] Sea* (Dt 11:24). He showed me the temple and the palace built[116] on five mountain peaks. He said to me, "These are the mountains which the Lord chose [for dwelling]," and I answered and asked, "What are their names?" Then he said to me, "These are their names: Lebanon, Mount Moriah, Tabor, Carmel, and Hermon."

BL

and Zion and Jerusalem will be astonished: *Who bore these for us and from where are these* (Isa 49:21)? Then Nehemiah and Zerubbabel will answer Jerusalem and say to her, "Look, your sons whom 6:6) you bore[117] and who went into exile from you. *Rejoice very much, daughter of Zion* (Zech 9:9). I waited further and asked 6:7) Mettatron, general of the Lord's army, "Sir, show me Jerusalem—how long and how 6:8) wide [it is], and its buildings. Show me the walls of Jerusalem around it—the walls of fire *from* 6:9) *the great wilderness, the river Euphrates to the Last Sea [Mediterranean]* (Dt 11:24) *to the river Euphrates* (Gen 15:18).

J	
And also the temple of the Lord will be built on five mountain peaks." Then I asked, "What are their names?"	He showed me the temple. 6:10) The house and the temple were built on five mountain peaks,
	which, with the mountain of the Lord, [are places on which] to raise 6:11) his sanctuary: Lebanon, Mount Moriah, Tabor, Carmel, and Hermon.
He said to me: "Lebanon, Mount Moriah, Tabor, Carmel, and Hermon" (see PR 114b).	

W (14)

30) Mettatron answered and said to me, "This will be the sign, after the destruction of Jerusalem, nine hundred, ninety years (A.D. 1060) is the salvation of the Lord.

[116]Reading בנויי for בני.
[117]Text is blurred.

W (14)

If you inquire, inquire, come back again (Isa 21:12). In the fifth year Nehemiah Ben Hoshiel will come and gather the Israelites to Jerusalem. In the sixth year, Hafzi-bah, the wife of 31) Nathan Ben David, who was born in Hebron, will come, and she will kill the two kings, Nof and Atras. 32) In the seventh year, the root of Jesse will sprout forth, who is Menahem Ben Amiel. Before him will arise ten kings from the nations. A week and a half they will manage to rule year by year. These are their names and their cities: The first king is Silkom, the name of his city is Safrad; the second king is Artimos, and he is from the land of the sea; the third king is Talis, and the name of his city is Godia; the fourth king is Paolas, and the name of his city is Gilos; the fifth king is Mador and the name of his city is Martotania; the sixth king is Markilanos, and the name of his city is Italia; the seventh king is Iftonras, and the name of his city is Doris; the eighth king is Efarmos, and the name of his city is Aram-Naharaim; the ninth king is Shiron, king of Persia.

BL

Then Michael answered and said 6:12) to me, "After the final destruction of Jerusalem, nine hundred, ninety years (A.D. 1060) I will visit 6:13) salvation upon Israel."

Then he interpreted for me the word and vision after which he had spoken 6:14) to me at first, *If you inquire, inquire, come back again* (Isa 21:12). "In the fifth week,[118] *Nehemiah Ben Hoshiah will come* 6:15) *and gather all the Israelites.* In the sixth week will come 6:16) Hafzi-bah, the prophet Nathan's wife, who was born in Hebron and killed the two kings, Nof 6:17) and Esarvagan. At that year the root of Jesse, Menahem Ben Amiel, will go forth, and *the ten kings from the nations* will arise. 6:18) For a week and a half a week they will not cease ruling, 6:19) year after year.[119]

J	BL
These are the ten kings will rise up over the nations in	"These ten kings will rise up over the nations in

[118]Meaning the fifth of seven weeks of years, counting in terms of sabbath years and jubilees.

[119]Levi, "L'Apocalypse de Zorobabel," 157, observed that this sentence makes no sense.

J	BL
seven years:	*the second* week,[120] 6:20), and
	these are the names of their cities
The one	when they arose. The first is
	Silkom,[121] 6:21) and the name
	of his city is Safrad, which is
of Aspamia. The	Espania, a city of the sea. The
second is Armanos	second king will be Hartomos,
from the city of the sea;	6:22) and the name of his city
The third,	will be Gitania. The third king
Kilos	is Philimos, and the name of his
from Gita; the	city will be Philois. 6:23) The
fourth, Piluos	fourth king will be Galoas and
from	the name of his city will be
Gallia; the fifth,	Gallia. The fifth king will be
Romatros	Ramosharia, 6:24) and the name of
from Moratia; the	his city will be Moditica. The
sixth, Makalnos	sixth king will be Markalanos, and
from	the name of his city will be
Zaltia; the seventh,	Italia. 6:25) The seventh king
Aractonis	will be Aktinos, and the name of
from Adamim; the	his city will be Dormis. The
eighth, Mas-	eighth king 6:25) will be Maph-
palisnis from Aram-Naharaim;	lostos from Aram-Naharaim.
the ninth, Piros	The ninth king will be Shiroi, king
from Persia; the tenth	of Persia, 6:27) and the tenth
Armilos, son of	king will be Armilos, son of
Satan.	Satan, who came forth from the
	stone image. He 6:28) will rule
	over them all.

(No Corresponding Jellinek Text [15])

W	BL
He [Shiroi] will come and	He will come and stir
line up for battle in the Valley	up war in the Valley of
Arabiel.	Arabiel with the kings of 6:29)
	Kedar and the sons of Kedar, and

[120]Of years.
[121]Levi, "L'Apocalypse de Zorobabel," 158, said this is Seleucus Nicator.

W

BL

Nishrab will go out against him,
and he will come and rule in that
valley.

theirs will be the kingdom.
Then in his strength, he will go
up and attack 6:30) the whole
entire world. From there, in
Riblah, which is Antocia,[122]

He will begin to plant his
Asherahs,[123]

he will begin to plant 6:31)...all
the days of[123] the Gentiles and
to serve Baals

which [the Lord] hates, 33)
because in those days
there will be no wage
for man and no salary for a beast.
He will build
four altars and make the Lord
angry with his deeds.[124]
There will be a great famine

which the Lord hates on the face
of the land. 6:32) In those days
there will be no wages neither
for man nor beast.
He will build
four altars and make the Lord
angry with his evil deeds.[124]
The famine will be great and
very severe 7:1)

over the face of all
the land for forty-five days.
Israelites, their kings, and
their prophets 34) will go up
to the wilderness of Jerusalem,
and all the Israelites will go
up to the Shittim Valley.[108] For
forty-five days they will pick
salt bushes
to keep
alive day by day. 35)
A spring will go out
from the house of the Lord and
provide water for the Shittim
Valley (Joel 4:18; Ezek
47:1-10).[108]
36) The tenth king will be

upon the face of all
the land for forty days,

warming themselves from
salt bushes, leaves of broom 7:2)
bushes they gather to keep themselves alive.
In that day a spring will go out
from the house of the Lord and
provide water for the Shittim
Valley (Joel 4:18; Ezek
47:1-10).[108]
7:3)

[122]Like Antocia, Riblah is on the Orontes, but many miles away.

[123]This seems to be a sentence taken out of context, describing one of the Omayyid caliphs, but the text is too blurred to make sense of it.

[124]The way Balaam had done (Num 23:1-2, 29-30).

W	BL
Armilos, 37) the son of a marble stone	"He is Armilos. His mother is a stone from which he was born. He took 7:4) her
which is in the house of obscenity, of scoffers, and all the Gentiles from all the places will come and stand before that stone. They will burn incense, but they will not be able to see her face because of her beauty. Everyone who is arrogant enough to look at her will not be able to do so.	from the house of obscenity, of scoffers, and all the places, and all the Gentiles will come 7:5) and worship that stone, burn incense to her, and pour out libations to her. No one will be able 7:6) to look at her face because of her beauty. Everyone who does not pros- strate himself to her will die in anguish 7:7) as an animal.
This is the sign of Armilos, the son of the stone: The hair of his head is dyed; his hands [reach] to the soles of his feet; his face is a span long; His height is twelve cubits; his eyes are deep; and he has two heads.[125] He will go up and rule in Imos, the province of Satan, which his father took. All who see him will shudder. After this Menahem Ben Amiel will go to him from the Shittim Valley,[108] and he will blow in his face and kill him, just as it is said, *With the breath of his lips he will slay the wicked* (Isa 11:4). After this, *And the kingdom will be the Lord's* (Obad 21), and *the saints of the Most High will receive the kingdom* (Dan 7:18).	This is the sign of Armilos: The hair of his head is *yellow* gold, 7:8) and the soles of his feet are also green. His face is wide as a span, and his eyes are distorted. 7:9) He has two heads.[125] He will go up and rule his cities with terrors. [He is] Satan, the father 7:10) of Beliel. All who see him will shudder. "Menahem will go up from the Shittim Valley[108] and blow 7:11) in his nostrils and kill him, just as it is written, *With the breath of his lips he slay the wicked* (Isa 11:4), and *the kingdom will be* Israel's (Obad 1:21),[126] and *the saints of the Most High will receive the kingdom* (Dan 7:18).

[125]Perhaps an allusion to the head of the church at Rome and the other at Constantinople. Both affected the Near East.

[126]Note the variant from the text of Obadiah. The kingdom that was to be the Lord's was
expected to be Israel's at the same time.

W (16)	BL
These words which Mettatron, general of the Lord's army, told to Zerubbabel Ben Shealtiel, *pahat* of Judah in the midst of the exile in the days of the king of Persia, and Zechariah Ben Edoa and the prophet Elijah wrote them	These are the words which Mettatron spoke to Zerubbabel Ben Shealtiel, *pahat* of Judah in the midst of 7:14) the exile in the days of the kingdom of Persia. Zechariah Ben Anan and Elijah wrote them in the *complete exile* (Amos 1:6, 9). 7:15)

for the people who reach the final days, years, and seasons. [At] the time of the end, may all the congregation of Israel come with him. Words of peace. 38)

May the Lord make us merit seeing the house of the sanctuary with our children and see the Messiah quickly, in our days. Amen. Amen. Amen. Selah. Selah. Selah.

J

May our eyes see *the faithful city* (Isa 1:21),[127] which is delayed because of our sins. Until now the expectation is delayed.

PHR

With this word, he [Zerubbabel] complied and was opening up the names as a turgaman, one by one, with its name—here a crown and there a seal.

Summary

Content

Part one opens with Zerubbabel standing at the gate of heaven, knocking. Mettatron, the turgaman, came to the door. Just as a turgaman stands by the scroll in the synagogue and interprets the word of God from a scroll to the congregation, Mettatron stood at the gate of heaven and interpreted God's message for the Jews to be communicated to them by Zerubbabel. Mettatron opened the

---

[127]This seems to be an allusion to Isa 1:21, "the faithful city" (קריה נאמנה), but the text actually reads, "the poured-out city" (קריה הנסוכה), or possibly, "the city consecrated under libations."

door and fulfilled his role as an interpreter and commentator by answering Zerubbabel's questions and describing the future to him. The description of the future takes place on three fronts: 1) the lot of the Israelites, 2) the function of the Messiahs, and 3) the activity of the Lord.

The lot of the Jews. — During the seven years prior to deliverance, the Jews in the diaspora will be in difficult straits. Sons will rebel against their fathers; there will be increasingly severe anti-Jewish decrees issued, as there actually were in the Middle Ages; heavy taxes, enslavement, prohibition of required Jewish religious practices, such as circumcision, observance of menstrual purity, and Torah studies. Gentiles will keep Jews under strict surveillance to hinder their resistance movements. Many Jews will leave their faith and converts to Judaism will return to their former beliefs. When the Messiah of Ephraim appears, most Jews will despise him and not believe him. When it becomes obvious that he has a strong and victorious army, many Jews will repent, and many Gentiles will become converts to Judaism; Jews will repent; and all religious rules will be observed.

The function of the Messiahs. — The Messiah, son of Joseph, will be fettered in prison in Rome for eight years where he will voluntarily endure tremendous tortures to cancel Israel's indebtedness in the treasury of merits. He will suffer until the treasury balance for Israel is so great that Gentiles will be nothing by comparison. This means there will be no Gentiles in the world to come. When the Messiah is finally released from prison, a large army of Jews will be waiting for him. He will show no mercy on the Gentiles but will cast them into Gehinnom. He will overthrow all of the Gentile nations in the final war of Gog and Magog.

The activity of the Lord. — The Lord will direct all the events. He will punish the Jews with many afflictions, and he will shackle the Messiah. Later he will release him and restore him to his own bosom. He will become angry with the Gentiles. The Lord will gather the nations together to fight with him at Jerusalem, where he himself will trample them like olives in a press. He will also cast a plague upon them so that the Gentiles' flesh will rot while they are still alive.

Part two shows Zerubbabel receiving a vision just before he was scheduled to die, but an angel restored him to life. From the angel, Mettatron or Michael, Zerubbabel received a forecast of the future which involved the appearance of the Messiah of Ephraim, reestablishing the kingdom from Jerusalem and restoring sacrifices, until Shiroi, king of Persia, came and killed him and all Jews mourned for him.

Then Zerubbabel was transferred to the wicked city of Rome where he was shown Armilos and his virgin mother. Zerubbabel also saw Nehemiah, the Messiah of Ephraim, before he was killed in Jerusalem. Nehemiah was despised and wore ragged clothes before he was transformed and put on garments of vengeance.

The third scene pictured Mettatron coming to Zerubbabel in prayer and recounting his own heroic deeds in behalf of the Israelites during their long history. He gave Zerubbabel signs to authenticate the Messiah. This was the staff by which Nehemiah's mother would kill two kings. Mettatron also promised deliverance of Israel in the year A.D. 1060. A repeated account was given of Nehemiah's sacrifice and rule at Jerusalem, his death, the mourning of the Jews, and another description of Armilos. Then Menahem, the Davidic Messiah, will appear with Elijah, and the two will revive Nehemiah. Then they will revive the dead who drowned in the sea, the council of Korah, the wilderness generation. Then the Lord will fight the battle of Gog and Magog. Jews will renew sacrifices in the heavenly temple which will be brought down from heaven and restored to Jerusalem. All Israelites will be gathered at the Mount of Olives which will split open. Ten kings will rule, the Jews will spend forty-five days in the wilderness before the kingdom is restored.

The Literature

This is a composite collection of stories related to the period when there would be an end to the Gentile rule and Jews would take over the control of the world which was then ruled by Moslems and Christians. This was not just vicarious pipe dreaming. This literature was related to real history, on conditions that really existed. There was the biblical history of earlier deliverance on which to base their expectations. There was the present situation which Jews interpreted religiously, and there was the future which they really expected to develop in their favor, and they were working intensely to bring this about.

The composite nature of this literature is evident throughout. Not only are there four basic versions with some extensive variations, but each version is composed of several units, which are complete in themselves. In one case an inclusion shows the size of the unit (2:28-4:18-19). Sometimes there is hardly a transition sentence between one source and the other, so that the change in subject matter is very abrupt. Because of this scissors-and-paste type of composition, there is clearly no logical chronological sequence. The Messiah is seen killed, and the Jews mourn for him in one unit, but the next unit shows him alive in Rome, ready to be transferred to Jerusalem to be killed again.

The apocalyptic style of relating events in history to Jewish theological views that pictured heaven, angels, and God actively engaged in earthly activities, is similar to that of Daniel, Enoch, and the Book of Revelation. At least one unit within the sources was written before A.D. 1060, because that was the future date given for the end, and there were traditions included in all versions that were familiar to Saadia Gaon. On the basis of this given date, scholars like Graetz have conjectured an eleventh century date for this material, written from Rome. Levi (L'Apocalypse de Zorobabel) has opposed this late date and western provenance. He held that the significance of the Persian king Shiroi to this material relates it to the events of the seventh century, when Jews successfully helped Persia to get Jerusalem away from the Christians. Soon after, however, the Roman emperor Heraclius recovered Jerusalem from the Christians again. Levi believed that for the author of this apocalypse, Armilos was a symbol for Heraclius. Another point that would support Levi's position is the emphasis given here that the divided kingdom would reunite in the days of the Messiah just as Samaritans and Jews actually did to support the Persians.

Kallir's poem, "In Those Days and in That Time," is very similar in content to part of this material, some of it verbatim. Zunz has considered Kallir to be the source for the Book of Zerubbabel, but that was on the assumption that this apocalypse was composed in the eleventh century. Ibn Shmuel believed that *Pirke Hekhaloth Rabbati* was a seventeenth century forgery, related to the Sabatian messianic movement. This has not been established, but if it were, the question would still be what part of this text was finally added at that late date. It is possible for all the ingredients to have been written before A.D. 1060 with only a few editorial additions made in the seventeenth century. The composite nature of apocalyptic literature made it adapt well to religious needs and possibilities of medieval Jews in their disrupted history. It was the king of material that could be used and revised again and again. With each new movement, this literature might be revised, parts discarded, other units from other literature appended to form a new complete document. It is not likely that there was any one place or time where it was all composed. Levi's observation that the activity took place in the East rather than the West is an argument for a Palestinian origin, or at least an eastern origin, but it is not as strong as Levi indicates. Many medieval Jews were international merchants, traveling from East to West regularly. This made them good linguists and enabled them to keep Jews in one part of the world acquainted with other parts of the world. Through merchants, Jewish congregations kept in touch with one another from many parts of the world. This made migration easier when Jews were expelled from some country. They did not become immoveably located in any country of the diaspora. Therefore a Jew like Judah Halevy, who lived in the West, had his heart in the East and finally moved there from Spain. The migratory nature of merchandising also helped circulate literature quickly, so that a document that was finally discovered in Egypt by archaeologists may have been written in France, Spain, Persia, Greece, or Palestine. Therefore the place where this literature originated is enigmatic.

There are still other fragments of this material besides these translated here, but these are the main ones. The other variants in the fragments testify further to the composite and variable nature of this apocalyptic literature in the Middle Ages.

No attempt has been made here to solve the synoptic problem of the relationship that exists among these four texts, but there are clues apparent that would make progress toward a solution seem possible. This collection represents views that belong to medieval Judaism and shows how these materials accumulated, grew, and were used, altered, and preserved. They are valuable texts for Christians and Jews to read today.

The next apocalypse is also composite and has been preserved in three extant texts. Rabbi Shimon Ben Yohai was a second century Jewish zealot and mystic who spent thirteen years in a cave with his son, hiding from the Roman authorities. It was during those years that he offered the prayer that is here translated together with the responses he received. The prayer, of course is pseude-pigraphical and reflects historic events and expectations of the Middle Ages.

THE PRAYER, SECRETS, AND MYSTERIES OF RABBI SHIMON BEN YOḤAI[128]

I

Prayer

This was Rabbi Shimon who was hidden in an ancient cave before the time, because of Caesar,[129] and he was fasting forty days and nights, and he prayed to the Lord. This is what he said in his prayer:

Invocation. — "Blessed are you, Lord our God, the God of Abraham, the God of Isaac, and the God of Jacob, the great God, the mighty and fearful One, Creator of heaven and earth in his mercy, who lives and remains forever and to an eternity of eternities! May you be honored, praised, crowned, glorified, [and] distinguished, for you are the King of kings, and the Lord of lords. One is he whose name is with you, and with you is your name. You are hidden from the eyes of all life, and your name is hidden; you are marvelous, and marvelous is your name; you are singular, and your name is singular! You are he *who has chosen Abraham and brought him out from Ur of the Chaldees* (Neh 9:7) and informed him [of] the cruel subjection of the nations to which his children would be enslaved.[130] Now, I beseech you, Lord God, open for me the gates of prayer and send me an angel to inform me: When will the Messiah son of David come? And how will he gather the exiles of Israel from all the places where they are

[128]This apocalypse appears in three documents which are somewhat parallel: "The Secrets of Rabbi Shimon Ben Yoḥai," translated from the text of A. Jellinek, בית המדרש (8 vols.; Jerusalem, 1967) III, 78-82. SML. A similar text is "The Future Events of Rabbi Shimon Ben Yoḥai," translated from the text of Ch.M. Horowitz, בית עקד האגדות (Frankfort a.M., 1881), 51-55. SML. These two texts are shown here in related columns throughout. "The Prayer of Rabbi Shimon Ben Yoḥai," translated from the text of A. Jellinek, בית המדרש IV, 118-26, RPL, is more extensive than either of the other versions. In some places the parallels are not in the same sequence, and sometimes a different meaning is given to the same reference. At the beginning all three are shown in parallel, but where the sequence breaks, "The Secrets" and "The Future Events (or Mysteries)" are continued in sequence until their texts are concluded. Then "The Prayer" is resumed from the place where it was discontinued in parallel relationship to the other two texts.

[129]Rabbi Shimon Ben Yoḥai belonged to the second half of the second century. He was considered less than orthodox because of his mystical views. He was sentenced to death by the Romans because of his anti-Roman activity, so he fled for his life and lived, together with his son, Eliezer, in a cave for thirteen years. His mysticism, nationalism, and his thirteen years spent in a cave made him an ideal figure for apocalyptic heroism. Tradition added to his reputation by attributing to him the composition of the *Zohar* during those years. It was also then that he was held to have had the visions attributed to him in these midrashim.

[130]Gen 15:13-16.

scattered? And how many wars will pass over them after they are gathered? Explain this matter to me, in your goodness, O Lord God! until *the end of the marvelous deeds* (Dan 12:6)."

Secrets	*Future*
These are the secrets which were revealed revealed to Rabbi Shimon Ben Yoḥai when he was hiding	These (144) are some of the future events which were revealed to Shimon Ben Yoḥai when he was hidden for thirteen years (145) in a cave
because of Caesar, king of Edom.[131]	because of the king of Edom.[131] (146) When they were (147) decreeing destruction against Israel,
He continued in prayer for forty days and forty nights,	he continued in prayer and fasting for three days and three nights. (148) At the end of [that period], he
beginning thus: *O Lord God, how long will you be angry with the prayer of your* servant (Ps 80:5)?	began to say, *O Lord God, how long will you be angry with the prayer of your* servant (Ps 80:5)?

II

Response

Prayer

Rabbi Shimon said, "The gates of heaven were immediately opened for me, and I saw the appearance of God. Then I fell on my face, and behold, a voice [was] speaking to me, 'Shimon, Shimon!' I answered, and I said to the one speaking to me, 'What are you saying, Sir?' He said to me, 'Stand where you are!' When he spoke to me, I stood trembling, and I said to him, 'What is your name?' He said to me, *Why do you ask? It is a mystery* (Jdgs 13:18)? Then I said to him, 'When will a redeemer of Israel come?' He said to me, *God has seen the children of Israel, and God knows* (Ex 2:25). Immediately the Kenites[132] passed by. I asked him, 'Who

[131]Edom was a Jewish code word for Rome. It also applies to Christians.
[132]The Kenites lived in the Negev. Here they were interpreted to mean the Byzantine or Roman Christians who controlled Palestine before the Moslem conquest.

Prayer

are these?' He said to me, 'These are the Kenites.' Still he showed me the kingdom of Ishmael[133] who will be after the Kenites. I immediately wept intensely and said to him, 'Sir, has he two horns and two hooves with which to trample Israel?' He said to me, 'Yes.'

Secrets	Future
The secrets of *the end time* and *things sealed up* were at once revealed to him (Dan 12:4, 9). He began to ponder and explain: *Then he saw the Kenites*[132] (Num 24:21). When he saw the advent of the kingdom of Ishmael,[133] he began to say,	*Hidden and sealed things* about *the end* were revealed to him (Dan 12:4, 9). These he began to interpret and said,
	"Was this the decision of the holy One blessed be He to deliver the Israelites into the hand of the
"Is it not enough that the wicked kingdom of Edom[131] has done to us, but also the kingdom of Ishmael!"	kingdom of Edom[131]

to make them subject [to the Edomites]? Then they will begin to subdue them and distress them until they cause the holy One blessed be He much distress. Why will this distress the holy One blessed be He? As it is said, *I am with him in oppression* (Ps 91:15). It [also] says, *In all their oppression it afflicts him* (Isa 63:9)."

III

Prayer

"While I was still speaking with him, behold another angel touched me, whose name was Mettatron,[134] and *he aroused me as*

---

[133]The Arabs or Islamic kingdom.

[134]The name given to the resurrected Enoch. See G.C. Scholem, *Major Trends in Jewish Mysticism* (New York, c1941), 67-70.

Prayer

a man who awakens [someone else] from his sleep (Zech 4:1).
When I saw him I stood trembling, and my pains convulsed me,
and I could not bear it. The pains seized me like the pains of a
woman in travail (Dan 10:8, 16), and he said to me, 'Shimon!' I
said, 'Here I am!' He said to me, 'Be informed that the holy One
blessed be He sent me to you to inform you [about] your question
which you asked him. Now when you saw the Kenites and the
kingdom of the Ishmaelites, you wept, and you had no reason to
weep except for the kingdom of Ishmael alone, which at the end of
its kingdom will kill numberless Israelites, and it will decree severe
decrees against the Israelites, and say, "Everyone who reads the
Torah will be stabbed with a sword!" It will turn some Israelites
over to their judges, and the kingdom of the Kenites will come in
that time to Jerusalem, and subdue it and murder more than thirty
thousand in it. Because of the oppression which they oppress
Israel, the holy One blessed be He will send Ishmaelites against
them to make war with them, so as to deliver the Israelites from
their hand.[135] A foolish man and a master of wind (Hos 9:7) will
arise and speak lies against the holy One blessed be He, and he will
subdue the land, and there will be strife between them and the
children of Esau.'

Secrets

Future

Rabbi Shmuel says (149) concerning the words of Rabbi
Ishmael, that he used to say,

Mettatron, the minister of
the interior,[136] immediately
answered him and said, "Do not
be afraid, son of man, because   "Where do you find that

---

[135]Many peoples who had felt the heavy hand of the Byzantine Christians welcomed the
rule of the Moslems who followed them. The author here reasoned that God had raised up
the Moslems (Kingdom of Ishmael) to overthrow the Byzantines (Edomites) in preparation
for Jewish rule of the entire territory ruled by both. Maimonides conceded that both Jesus
and Mohammed fulfilled a divine mission in preparing the way for the Messiah who was to
come, since it was through them that a large part of the world population was brought to a
knowledge of God that led them well on the way to becoming Jews (see Margolis and Marx,
A History, 341). In his letter to Yemen and in his essay on the Messiah, Maimonides
emphasized his conviction that the Moslems were the necessary and last world rulers to
precede Jewish rule and domination.

[136]An angelic officer closest to God, the one allowed to enter the innermost room.

Secrets	*Future*
the holy One blessed be He is only bringing the kingdom of Ishmael in order to deliver you from this wicked kingdom [of Edom]. He will raise over them a	the holy One blessed be He will deliver the kingdom of Ishmael only to deliver Israel through it?"[135]

prophet,[137]according to his own will. He will conquer the land for them, and they will come and restore it to its former greatness. There will be a great terror between them and the sons of Esau."[138] Rabbi Shimon answered him: "How can [we know that] they will be [the instruments of] salvation for us?"

IV

Mohammedan Caliphs

Prayer

"I replied to Mettatron, and I said to him, 'Sir, will the Ishmaelites be salvation for Israel?' He said to me, 'Did not the prophet Isaiah say thus: *He saw a rider, a team of horsemen, a rider upon a donkey, a rider upon a camel* (Isa 21:7)?

"'*A rider*—This is the kingdom of Media and Persia; *a team*—this is the Greek kingdom; *horsemen*—this is the kingdom of Edom; *a rider upon a donkey*—this is the Messiah, as it is said, Meek and riding *upon a donkey* (Zech 9:9); *a rider upon a camel*—this is the kingdom of Ishmael, because in its days the kingdom of the Messiah will shoot forth (Isa 11:1). Therefore, *a rider upon a donkey* precedes *a rider upon a camel*, and *a rider upon a camel* rejoices at the coming of the Messiah, but the scholars will die, and the hands of the sons of Beliel will grow strong.'

Secrets	*Future*
He replied: "Did not the prophet Isaiah say this: [*Go, position a watchman. Whatever he sees, let him declare!*] *When he sees riders,*	As it is said at the hand of the prophet Isaiah: *When he sees riders,*

[137]Mohammed.
[138]I.e., war between the Moslems and the Christians (sons of Esau).

Secrets

horsemen in pairs, [riders on donkeys, riders on camels, let him pay attention, very close attention] (Isa 21:6-7).

Future

horsemen in pairs, riders on donkeys, riders on camels, [let him pay attention, very close attention] (Isa 21:6-7). [This text] teaches that in the beginning he will return as the driver of the seed of that nation who oppresses and afflicts (Jdgs 2:18) the world with heavy taxes. *Pay attention, very close attention* (Isa 21:7). (150) [What is the meaning of] *very close attention?* Rabbi Shimon says, "When Isaiah saw that there was peace in his mouth, he was happy." Rabbi Shimon explained, (151) "The verse: *When he sees riders, horsemen in pairs, riders on donkeys, riders on camels* (Isa 21:7), the *rider* is Babylon (Ezek 26:7); *pairs* is Media;[139] (152) *horsemen* is Greece; *riders on donkeys* is Edom;[140] (154) *riders on camels* is the kingdom of Ishmael; (155) when he saw the salvation was destined to rise, he said, *The oracle concerning Arabia: In the forest of Arabia you will lodge, caravans of the Dedanites* (Isa 21:13)." (156) Rabbi Shimon said, (157) "When Isaiah saw that there was destined to arise from it wicked kings [who] would oppress Israel and take from the living, the reward of life, and from the slain, the price of the dead,[141] he began to cry out, *very close attention* (Isa 21:7).

Secrets

Why did he mention *riders on donkeys* before *riders on camels?* He should rather have said, *riders on camels, riders on donkeys,* but when he goes out, he will be riding on a donkey.[142]

"Another interpretation: *Riding on a donkey.* When he rides *on*

[139]Medes and Persians are often mentioned together in pairs.

[140]Edom means Rome or Christians. Under Moslem rule, Christians and Jews were forbidden to ride horses and forced to ride on donkeys to symbolize their lowly status. From a Jewish point of view, this was a proper role for Christians—but not Jews.

[141]A reference to the taxation which the Moslems imposed on Christians and Jews in their countries.

[142]This could mean the Messiah (Zech 9:9), or it could mean, as B. Lewis, "An Apocalyptic Vision of Islamic History," *Bulletin of the School of Oriental and African Studies* 13 (1950), 322, holds that this alludes to the return to power over Jerusalem by the Christians after Moslem rule. This would imply the invasion of the Crusaders. It seems more likely to refer to the end of the Moslem rule. It entered on a camel and would leave on a lowly donkey. See also Lewis, p. 324.

Secrets

a donkey.[143] From this [we can deduce] that they are [instruments of] salvation for the Israelites, like the salvation of one who rides *on a donkey.*[144]

Rabbi Shimon said further that which he heard from Rabbi Ishmael that when he [later] heard that the kingdom of Ishmael was about to come, [Rabbi Ishmael said], "They were destined to measure the land into districts,[145] as it is said, *He will divide the land for a price* (Dan 11:39). They will make the cemeteries grazing places for flocks. When one of them dies, they will bury him in whatever place they can find. Then they will plow [over the top of] the grave and plant it [the field into crops], as it is said, *Thus the sons of Israel will eat their bread, unclean* (Ezek 4:13). Why is the *bet ha-peras*[146] not [sown, cultivated, harvested, and] threshed?

"[What does the verse mean]: *He saw the Kenite. [Then he took up his parable and said]* (Num 24:21)? What parable could that wicked man [Balaam] take up? When he saw that his grandchildren were destined to be enslaved to the Israelites, he began to be happy and say, *Steadfast* אֵיתָן *is your dwelling place* (Num 24:21). I see men partaking only of the commandment formulated by *Eitan* (אֵיתָן) *the Ezrahite* (Ps 89:1).[147]

"The second[148] king who will arise from the Ishmaelites will be a friend of the Israelites. He will patch up their breaches [in the walls] and those in the temple. He will level off Mount Moriah and make it a plain.

---

[143]At the time the Moslems ride on a donkey at the end of the Moslem era, just before the beginning of the Jewish rule.

[144]The Messiah (Zech 9:9). "The Future" has no reference to the hope of the Messiah coming on a donkey, and it may reflect a later composition, after the hope had failed.

[145]This was done under the administration of Omar I (A.D. 634-44).

[146]A *bet ha-peras* is a field where there may have been someone buried, but whose grave is now unmarked. A priest is not allowed to walk in such a field. Omar I decreed that Christians and Jews must keep their graves level with the ground, which made their location more difficult to record. (See M.W. Montgomery, "Omar I," *JE* 9, 396-97.)

[147]Ps 89 is attributed to Eitan the Ezrahite. It is a praise to God and a reminder of his mercy and his covenant with David to establish him as his son and destroy his enemies. The worshipper pleads with God to renew his mercy and uphold his promises. The midrashic author related the two references to *eitan*: One, meaning "firm" in Num 24:21, and one, a proper name, Ps 89:1.

[148]Most scholars take this to Omar I (A.D. 634-44), the second caliph after the death of Mohammed. He was followed by Abu-Bakr (A.D. 632-34). Lewis, "Apocalyptic Vision," 328, however, said this "can only be Muawiyya, to whom some of the actions of Omar in Syria during Muawiyya's governorship are erroneously attributed."

Future

Thus Rabbi Shimon used to say, "In the beginning of his kingdom, (158) when he goes out, he will seek to injure the people of Israel,[149] but important men of Israel will confer with him and give him a wife from among them, and there will be peace between him and the Israelites. He will conquer (159) all the kingdoms and then

Secrets	*Future*
He will build there [a place of] worship on the foundation stone, as it is said, *Your nest is set in the rock* (Num 24:21).[151]	come to Jerusalem and worship there (160).[150]
He will make war with the sons of Esau[152] and slaughter their troops, taking a large number of them captive.	He will make war with the Edomites[152] (161) and they will flee from him, and he will take the kingdom by force. After that he will die.[153]
He will die in peace and great glory.[153]	

[149]This may be an allusion to the dealings of Mohammed with the Jews of Medina. Afterward, Mohammed was given a Jewish wife. As Lewis suggests, the author may have added the achievements of Mohammed as well as those of Omar to the deeds of Muawiyya, who "died in peace and great glory," ("Apocalyptic Vision," 328) but this requires a lot of displaced credit. Omar was the first strong military leader and administrator after the death of Mohammed. He ruled for ten years (A.D. 634-44), during which time he expanded Moslem rule from Persia to Egypt, controlling the territory in between. He set up administration centers throughout the empire. On the promised land, he established a center at Lydda which was later moved to Ramlah, and another for the region around Galilee at Tabaryaho (see P.K. Hitti, *History of the Arabs* [London, 1970], 169). With the overwhelming victory in the Valley of Yarmuk, August 20, 636, he gained control of all Syria, and his control of Jerusalem followed promptly. During his visit to Jerusalem, he probably worshipped, but not necessarily according to Jewish beliefs alone. Sophronius, patriarch of Jerusalem, referred to Omar's presence in Jerusalem as the abomination of desolations in the holy place, about which Daniel spoke (Hitti, *History of the Arabs,* 154).

[150]Probably Omar after he captured Jerusalem.

[151]The "Rock" refers to the temple area where the "Dome of the Rock" was constructed. Omar was a Jewish convert to Islam. He was present at the conquest of Jerusalem and is said to have had the site of the temple mount pointed out to him. He ordered the clearing of the rock and the location was used as a place of prayer until the time of Abd al-Malik (685-705) who built the Dome of the Rock (see E. Basham, "Omar ibn al-Khattab," *Encyclopaedia Judaica* 12, 1382.

[152]Apparently Omar's successful combats with the Christians.

[153]Mohammed died a natural death in A.D. 632, possibly caused by the lingering effects of poison. Omar was killed in A.D. 644 by the poisoned dagger of a Persian Christian slave. Lewis, "Apocalyptic Vision," 328, said Muawiyya alone died in peace and great glory. This all depends on the point of view of the author, and we are not sure what that was.

Secrets

"A great king will arise from Ḥazarmawet,[154] and he will act for a few days.[155] Then the mighty men of Kedar will rise up against him and kill him.[156]

They will appoint another king,

whose name is Mario.[159] They will take him from behind the flocks and donkeys and elevate him to the kingdom (Eccles 4:14). Four "arms" will arise

Future

(162) "*Another* will arise from Ḥazarmawet (163) after him. Then another will arise (164) and kill him[156] (165) and [then] go up (166) to Jerusalem and cut off Mount Moriah and make it a plain.[157] Another will arise (167) and rule after him for [only] a few days.[158] Then another king will arise who will be greater than all of them. They will call him Marwan.[159]

Four dynasties will arise

---

[154]See Gen 10:27. This is a district in Arabia situated on the Indian Ocean. Today it is called Hadramaut. The caliph involved was probably Utman, who followed Omar and ruled twelve years (A.D. 644-56), or Ail (A.D. 656-660).

[155]Utman's twelve years is not nearly so brief a term as Ali's four.

[156]Both Utman and Ali were killed by the "mighty men of Kedar." Ali led a rebellion with these men against Utman, in the course of which Muhammed, the son of Utman's friend, Abu-Bakr, killed Utman in Utman's home, June 17, 656. In about a week (June 27, 656), Ali was proclaimed caliph. A few years later Ali was murdered. Some also accused Muawiyya II, who succeeded Ali, of complicity in his murder. The "Future" text made that assumption.

[157]Abd al-Malik built the "Dome of the Rock."

[158]Evidently Muawiyya II, who preceded Marwan, and ruled only three months (683-84), but after Ali and before Muawiyya were the long and effective reigns of Muawiyya I (660-80) and Yazid (680-83). The author of the Horowitz text ("Future") passed over these in silence or else understood that Ali accomplished more than he did. The latter possibility is strengthened by the fact that he also seems to have attributed to Mohammed the achievements of Omar or else the works of both to Muawiyya. Since Ali became a canonized martyr by his Shiite partisans who considered him a saint, his importance increased, and he became legendary (Hitti, *History of the Arabs*, 183). Muawiyya, rather than Ali, may have been the leader the author had in mind in relationship to Jerusalem, since he was proclaimed caliph in Jerusalem.

[159]Mario (מריאו) seems like an easy scribal error for Marwan (מרואן), as the parallel text suggests. Marwan's reign was short (A.D. 684-85) and not so great as his predecessors. During his reign the kingdom was extended to Egypt. His dynasty was greater than he. He was killed either by the wife of Yazid I or else died of a great epidemic that swept the East at that time.

Secrets	Future
from him,[160] and they will make a fence around the temple.[161] At the end of the king-dom of the four 'arms' another king will arise, who will diminish the weights,	from him,[160] (169) who will repair the walls of the temple.[161] (170) Still another king will arise, (171)

measures, and scales, and he will act for three years in tranquil-ity.[162] There will be strife in the world in his days, and he will send out many troops against the Edomites. There he will die of famine. They will have much food, but he will withhold [it] from them and not give them [any].[163] The sons of Edom will rise up against the sons of Ishmael and kill them. The Ishmaelites will burn up the food, and those who are left will seek refuge in flight.

Secrets	Future
"After this a great king will arise who will rule for nineteen years.[164]	and he will rule for nineteen years.[164]

These are his signs: He will be ruddy, squint-eyed, and will have three warts: one on his fore-head, one on his right hand, and one on his left arm. He will plant plants, rebuild destroyed cities, split open the depths in order to bring up water [with which] to irrigate his plants so that his num-erous great-grandchildren will have much to eat. Everyone who rises up against him will be given into his hand.

[160]The Hebrew word for "arms" is זרועות which is probably a scribal error for "seed" which is זרועים. The four children of Marwan are: 1) Abd al-Malik (685-705), 2) Sulayman (715-17), 3) Yazid (720-24), and 4) Hisham (724-43).

[161]Probably a reference to the construction of the Dome of the Rock, built by Abd al-Malik (685-705) in 691 (so Hitti, History of the Arabs, 220).

[162]It is not clear what is meant by diminishing weights, measures, and scales. Omar II (717-20), reduced tributes generally and thus pacified the restless nation by decreeing that a Moslem, whether Arab or mawla, need pay no tribute at all (Hitti, History of the Arabs, 219), a custom accepted as just in NT times (Mt 17:25-26). This might also refer to the fiscal measures imposed by Sulyman to cover the costs of his military campaign against Constan-tinople.

[163]This seems to be a description of the unsuccessful military attack of Sulyman against Constantinople. At that time food was short and Maslama burned the reserves. See Lewis, "Apocalyptic Vision,"327.

[164]This is Hisham (A.D. 724-43), whose activities in planting trees and constructing build-ings are well known. He is reported to have had a squint and numerous progeny. He over-came his enemies and established peace. The ruins of his palace can still be seen near Jer-icho. See Lewis, "Apocalyptic Vision," 327, and J. Sauvaget, "Remarques sur les Monu-ments Omeyyades," Journal Asiatique 131 (1939), 1-13. Abd al-Malik and Muawiyya I also ruled nineteen years.

Secrets	Future
The land will be quiet in his days and he will die in peace.	(172)
Another king will arise who will seek to cut off the waters of the Jordan.[165] He will bring distant people from foreign lands to dig and make a canal and bring up the waters of the Jordan [with which] to irrigate the land, but the excavation of the land will fall upon them and kill them. When their leaders hear, they will rise up against the king and kill 'him.	He will consume the tranquility of the Ishmaelites. (173) Another will arise, (174) and seek to cut off the waters of the Jordan,[165] (175) but his plan will not mature, for the princes of Kedar will rise up against him and kill him.

"Another will arise (176) who will reduce the weights, measures, and scales.[162]

"Another will arise (177) and will be cut down in the East and West.[166] (178) After this, (179) 'There is no peace,' says the Lord, 'for the wicked' (Isa 48:22).

"These are the kings (180) who will arise from them [the Abbasids or Omayyids]: First, *Ebed Moshalim*,[167] (181) as it is said, *Thus says the Lord...to a soul despised, abhorred by the Gentiles, Ebed Moshalim* (Isa 49:7). The second, from the seed of the kingdom;[168] (182) the third will arise in the midst of disputes;[169] (183)

[165]The caliph who followed Hisham was Walid II (A.D. 743-44) who evidently tried to divert the Jordan. Later literature referred to the canal he built. His activities in Palestine and his violent end at the hands of the princes of Kedar make him a likely possibility. Other caliphs who were interested in irrigation systems were Muawiyya I (660-80) and his son Yazid (680-83).

[166]This is evidently a reference to Marwan II's final conflict with the Abbasids before he was forced to flee to Egypt where he was killed.

[167]This seems to begin a separate unit, which most scholars consider to be another listing of four of the Omayyid caliphs, together with their identifying features. Abd al-Malik (685-705) means literally, "a servant of a king," hence a servant to rulers (*Ebed Moshalim*). Lewis, "Apocalyptic Vision," 329, however, took them to be Abbasid kings. Only two of the four persons he identified, however, were caliphs. The first leader, Abu Muslim, was a leader of Abbasid propaganda whom Lewis identified with *Ebed Moshalim* as an intentional pun.

[168]Seen as an Omayyid, the second would be a nickname for Al-Walid (A.D. 705-15), "the boy," or the "one born." Lewis chose instead the caliph Saffah, whose name has no noticeable relationship to "seed of the kingdom."

[169]The Omayyid caliph Sulayman, (A.D. 715-20) arose in the midst of disputes, but so did the Abbasid rebel Abdallah.

Future

the fourth will be the brother of the second.[170] In their days a shoot
will shoot forth (185) if the Israelites are meritorious. This is the
sign for you: (186) when you see a week [of years]: the first [year]
without rain; the second, with half a famine; the third with (187)
[a great famine; the fourth, no famine but (also) no plenty; and the
fifth] a great plenty.[171] Then the star of the Messiah will shoot
forth (Num 24:17). In the sixth [year] there will be voices; and in
the seventh, wars. At the conclusion of the seventh, the son of
David will come, if the Israelites are virtuous. If they are not [vir-
tuous, they will bear] the yoke of the fourth king, (188) a horn will
revolt from the south-west and send there *very many* armed
troops. (189)

Secrets

"Another king will arise vested with power. He will be a man of
war, and there will be strife in the world in his days.

Future

"In the first war, the westerners will be victorious (190) in the
second, the easterners will be victorious.[172] In that day the prophecy which Isaiah saw in a vision will be fulfilled, as it is said, *In
that day the Lord will whistle for the fly* (Isa 7:18).

Secrets	*Future*
This will be a sign for you:	
When you see that the western	When you see that *the western*
Gairun which is west of the	Gairun (191)
worshipping [place] of the sons	
of Ishmael in Damascus has	which is in Damascus has

[170]Yazid (A.D. 720-24) the brother of Al-Walid (A.D. 705-15). The Abbasid caliph
Mansur, however, was also the brother of the caliph Saffah.
[171]The bracketed portion is missing from the text and has been supplied from a parallel
narrative in San 97a.
[172]Marwan, one of the Omayyid westerners, led an attack across the Euphrates. After his
victory there, he entered Damascus, seized Homs, Baalbeck, Jerusalem, and other large
towns in Syria, restoring peace to all Syria. His second conflict with the Abbasids, however, was different. He was defeated at the upper Zab and forced to flee from one place to
another until he was finally killed in Bursiris, Egypt, August 5, 750. (So K.V. Zettersteen,
"Marwan II b. Muhammed," *The Encyclopaedia of Islam* III, 308-09.)

Secrets

fallen, his kingdom
will have fallen.[173]

Future

fallen, the kingdom of the easterners will have fallen.

Secrets

They will pay taxes to enter and leave, and the kingdom of Ishmael will also fall. Concerning them, he says, *The Lord has broken
the staff of the wicked* (Isa 14:5). Who is this? This is Marwan
Shaar.[174] The mighty men of Kedar will be with him. The northeast corner will rebel against him, and three of his large troops will
fall from him at the Tigris and at the Euphrates. He will flee from
them, but he will be trapped and killed, and his sons will be
hanged on a tree.[175]

Future

The westerners will come against the easterners and destroy [them]
and lay [them] waste. Those who are left will flee,[176] and they will
pass over *the pleasant land*[177] (Dan 11:41), and all of it will be in
their hand. The western kingdom will grow strong in Egypt, and in
Shihor to the Euphrates (Josh 13:3-5; Gen 15:18).[178]

Secrets

"After this,

Future

"After all this, if Israelites

[173]M. Steinschneider, "Apocalypsen mit polemischer Tendenz," *Zeitschrift der Deutschen Morgenlandischen Gesellschaft* 28 (1874), 638-45, has made a strong case for existence of a Gairun gate, the eastern gate of the mosque of Damascus. Although "Prayer" calls it the western Gairun twice and "Secrets" mentions it once as eastern and once as western, Lewis, "Apocalyptic Visions," 328, concurs that this is the gate meant here.
[174]Clearly Marwan II. This may be a scribal error, using Shaar (שער) for *Sheni* (שני) second."
[175]The death of Marwan II and his sons in Upper Egypt.
[176]Marwan II and his followers.
[177]Palestine on their way from Damascus to Egypt.
[178]There is a problem here that has no solution without difficulties: Who were the westerners and who were the easterners? If the westerners were the Omayyids who first attacked the Abbasids, laying them waste, as they did under the leadership of Marwan II, then later the easterners repelled the westerners and drove Marwan II and his followers to Egypt. This all works out well, with the eastern Abbasids in charge, but this text now turns the coin and shows the *westerners* as the victors. Others have said the crusaders were the westerners. Lewis opted for the Fatimids ("Apocalyptic Vision," 31-33), noting that the Fatimids came to Cairo from North Africa in the West, captured the East, went further and took Palestine, and later ruled the whole territory from Egypt. This makes good sense. Whatever identification is given here, it seems that "Future" 189-90 should be the same. Shihor, on the Nile Delta, and the Euphrates river to the north are two of the landmarks for the boundaries of the promised land. See *Consequences*, 91-109.

Secrets	Future
a brazen-faced king will arise	are not virtuous, a brazen-faced king will arise (192) who will kill the king of the easterners in the month of Ab.
for three months. He will rule over Israel for nine months,	He will issue decrees (193) against Israel. He will annul their festivals and Sabbaths,
as it is said,	as it is said, *He will think to*

change the times and the law, and they will be given into his hand for a time, two times, (194) and half a time (Dan 7:25). *A time* means a year; *two times* means two years; *half a time* means half a year. After this a king will arise, whose name is *Moshiv* (Restorer), and he will restore every idol worshipper, as it is said, *He will act indignantly against the holy covenant* (Dan 11:30). He will rule for nine months, (195) as it is said,

Secrets	Future
Therefore he will give them until the time required for a pregnant woman to bear (Micah 5:2).	*Therefore he will give them until the time required for a pregnant woman to bear* (Micah 5:2). How long is the time of pregnancy? Nine months.

Armilos

Future

"After (196) all this, Satan will descend and walk in Rome to the stone statue with whom he will have sexual intercourse. The stone will become pregnant and give birth to Armilos (197).[179] He will rule for forty days. His hands will be stronger than forty seahs, and he will decree evil against the Israelites. Men of action will cease, and *robbers* will multiply (198).

Secrets	Future
Then the Messiah son of	If the Israelites are virtuous, [then] the Messiah son of

[179]This account was repeated often in medieval Jewish literature. This is a caricature of the Christian church (Rome equals Romulus equals Armilos), Jesus, and the virgin Mary.

Secrets	*Future*
Joseph[180] shoot forth. He will take them up to Jerusalem and will build the house of sanctuary. He will offer sacrifices, and fire from will descend and consume their sacrifices, as it is said,	Joseph will shoot forth in Upper Galilee. The Messiah son of Joseph[180] will go up to Jerusalem and build the temple where he will offer sacrifices, and fire will descend [from heaven] and consume the sacrifices. The Israelites will [then] live securely all of his days.

The violent ones of your people will rise up [to establish the vision, but they will stumble] (Dan 11:14). If they [the Israelites] are not virtuous, the Messiah son of Ephraim[181] will come; but if they are virtuous, the Messiah son of David will come.

"A wicked king will arise, and his name will be Armilos. He will be bald, his eyes will be small; he will have leprosy on his forehead; his right ear will be deaf, and his left ear will be capable of hearing. Whenever someone tells him something good, he will incline his deaf ear to him, but if a person tells him something bad, he will turn to him his good ear. He will be a creature of Satan and of a stone.

Secrets	*Future*
He will go up to Jerusalem and stir up a war with the Messiah son of Ephraim at the east gate,	The army of Gog will go up and destroy Jerusalem and kill the Messiah son of Joseph.
	This is [the meaning of] what is written, *The kings of the land will establish themselves, [rulers will take counsel together against the Lord and against his Messiah]* (Ps 2:2). (199) The Israelites will mourn and weep [because of the death of] the

---

[180]The Samaritan Messiah, who, in Jewish opinion, would defeat the Romans, be killed and pave the way for the son of David Messiah.

[181]Same as the Messiah son of Joseph.

Secrets	*Future*
is said,	Messiah, as it is said,
They will look on him whom	*They will look on him whom*
they stabbed (Zech 12:10).	*they stabbed and they will*
	mourn for him (Zech 12:10).
	They will be divided after this
	into four groups,
Then the Israelites will go into	three of them will go into
exile	exile but one will remain, as it
	is said, *But the rest of the people*
	will not be cut off from the city
	(Zech 14:2).

to the wilderness of bulrushes to
pasture on saltwort and roots of broom grass for forty-five days.
They will be tested and purified, as it is said, *I will bring the third
through fire [and I will test them as testing silver, and I will test
them as testing gold]* (Zech 13:9). There the Messiah son of
Ephraim will die, the Israelites will mourn for him.

V

Messianic Victory

Secrets	*Future*
"After this the holy One	"After this the holy One
blessed be He will	blessed be He will go forth to
	fight with them, as it is said,

*The Lord will go forth and fight with those nations as when he
fights on the day of battle* (Zech 14:3). What is written there, *his
feet will stand on that day on the Mount of Olives* (Zech 14:4)?
*And this will be the plague [which the Lord will afflict on all the
Gentiles who fight with arms against Jerusalem: (Each man's) flesh
will rot while he stands on his feet; his eyes will decay in their
sockets; and his tongue will dry up in his mouth]* (Zech 14:12).

Secrets

reveal to them the Messiah son of David. The Israelites will try to
kill him and say to him, "You have spoken falsely, because already
the Messiah has been killed, and there is no other messiah destined
to arise! They will despise him, as it is said, *He was despised and
rejected of men* (Isa 53:3). But he will turn and hide himself from

Secrets

them, as it is said, *Hiding [his] face from us* (Isa 53:3). When the
Israelites will be in distress, they will return and cry out from
hunger and from thirst. The holy One blessed be He will immediately disclose himself to them in his glory, as it is said, *And all
flesh will see him together* (Isa 40:5). Then the messianic king will
sprout forth there, as it is said, *He comes with the clouds of heaven*
(Dan 7:13), and it is written after it, *to him will be given the sovereignty* (Dan 7:14).[182] Then he will hiss against that wicked
Armilos and kill him, as it is said, *With the breath of his lips he
will kill the wicked* (Isa 11:4), and the holy One blessed be He will
whistle and gather together all Israelites and bring them up to Jerusalem, as it is said, *I will whistle to them, and I will gather them*
(Zech 10:8).

VI

Return of the Exiles

Future

"The holy One blessed be He will sound a great shofar (Isa
27:13) and *say to the North, 'Give up,' and to the South, 'do not
hold back'* (Isa 43:6), and it says, *The ransomed of the Lord will
return* (Isa 35:10), and it says, *Saying to the prisoners, 'Come
forth!' and to those who are in darkness, 'Appear!'* (Isa 49:9). (200)
To the prisoners, 'Come forth!'—these are those who are in the
River Sambation,[183] who are like prisoners, *and to those who are
in darkness, 'Appear!'*—these are the nine and a half tribes who
dwell below the mountains of darkness.[184] (201) The holy One

[182]This text originally applied to Judas the Maccabee and the Jews of his time. See *To The Hebrews*, 38-51.
[183]Sambation River is a legendary river, believed to exist somewhere beyond Khazaria. D. Kaufmann, "Le Sambaton," *REJ* 22 (1891), 285-87, thought it was once a Sand River (נהר חול). Since חול means both "sand" and "week day," the name was confused, and the legend grew up around it that it was so named because it never ran on Saturday.
[184]Jews in the Middle Ages always anticipated some kind of miraculous deliverance. They were overjoyed to learn of the strong Jewish government in Khazaria. Merchants also told them of Jewish soldiers among the Mongols. With some imagination, these became thou-sands. They were all ears for the stories of a certain Eldad son of Mahli who claimed to be one of the many Danites as well as those from other Northern tribes now in Ethiopia and other distant territories. There was enough basis to make some of this seem credible. Samaritans existed in the diaspora in Egypt as late as the sixteenth century, and at least part of the time, were on good terms with the Jews. See A. Cowley, "Samaritan Dealings with Jews," *JQR* 16 (1904), 474-84. Also Graetz, *History* III, 581.

Future

blessed be He will gather them and bring them up to Jerusalem,
and he will comfort them doubly, (202) as it is said, *I, I am he who
comforts you* (Isa 51:12). The Israelites said before the holy One
blessed be He, 'Master of the age, we have sinned before you on
the mountains.' He will say to them, 'I will remove them [the
mountains], as it is said, *For the mountains will depart* (Isa 54:10).
Still they have said, 'We have blasphemed in [that we have wor-
shipped] the sun and the moon.' He will say to them, 'I will remove
them,' as it is said, *The moon will be disgraced, and the sun will be
ashamed* (Isa 24:23). The holy One blessed be He will send Elijah
who will make the hearts of the Israelites happy, as it is said,
*Behold I will send to you the prophet Elijah [...and he will turn the
hearts of the fathers to the children and the hearts of the children
to the fathers]* (Mal 3:23-24). He will announce to them the good
news of peace and prosperity, as it is said, *How beautiful upon the
mountains are the feet of him who brings good news, [who pub-
lishes peace, who announces good news of good, who proclaims
salvation, who says to Zion, 'Your God has become king!']* (Isa
52:7). This is the return to the house of David.

VII

Restoration of the Temple

Secrets

"Then a fire will come down from heaven and consume
Jerusalem until [only] three cubits [are left], and he [the Messiah]
will clear out the strangers, the uncircumcised, and the defiled
[Jews] from its midst. Then the perfected, rebuilt Jerusalem will
come down from heaven, in which will be seventy-two pearls
which will shine from one end of the world to the other. All the
Gentiles will walk towards its shining, as it is said, *Gentiles will
walk to your light* (Isa 60:3). Then the [already] constructed
temple will descend from heaven,[185] for it is bound to the celestian
abode, for this is what Moses (upon whom be peace) saw through
the Holy Spirit,[186] as it is said, *You shall bring it, and you shall
plant it [on the mountain of your inheritance; a place of your
dwelling you have constructed, Lord; a temple, Lord, your hands
have prepared it]* (Ex 15:17).

[185]See Rev 21:2.
[186]The Holy Spirit often speaks through scripture.

Secrets

Future

The ninth king: (203) This is the Messiah son of David who will rule from one end of the world to the other, as it is said, *He will rule from sea to sea, from the river to the ends of the land*

Then Israelites will dwell securely for two thousand years, and they will consume Behemoth, Leviathan, and Ziz,[188]

(Ps 72:8).[187] The Israelites will dwell securely for two thousand years. They will consume Behemoth, Leviathan, and beasts of the field. (204)

slaughtering Behemoth, and Ziz will tear open Leviathan with its claws. Then Moses will come, and the Almighty will slaughter Ziz.

"At the end of two thousand years, the holy One blessed be He will sit on the throne of judgment in the Valley of Jehoshaphat. At once heaven and earth will continue wearing away.[189]

"At the end of two thousand years, they will be gathered for judgment,

The sun will be disgraced, and the moon will be ashamed. The mountains will totter, and the hills tumble down, so that they will not be able to remind the Israelites of their iniquities.[190] The gates of Gehinnom will be opened at the brook of Joshua, and the gates of the Garden of Eden in the East,[191] [will open] on the third day,

Secrets

Future

as it is said,
After two days he will revive us
(Hos 6:2). These are the days of
the Messiah, which [will last]

as it is said,
After two days he will revive us,

[187]Ps 72 pictures a Messiah ruling the entire promised land from the Dead Sea to the Mediterranean Sea or from the Jordan River to the ends of the land at the Mediterranean (see *Consequences,* 104-06), but the author of this midrash interpreted the land to mean "world," and used the proof text to justify his messianic claim.

[188]Ziz was a fabulous bird.

[189]This is an awkward image, "At once...he will continue." The authors of these apocalyptic texts use the term "at once" as frequently as it is employed in the Gospel of Mark.

[190]In which they sinned in the mountains.

[191]Probably east of the Valley of Jehoshaphat in the area of the Mount of Olives.

Secrets	*Future*
for two thousand years. *On the third day*[192] *he will raise us, [and we shall live before him]* (Hos 6:2).[193]	*on the third day*[192] *he will raise us, and we shall live before him* (Hos 6:2).[193]
This is the day of judgment.	This is the day of judgment.
Woe to everyone who dies in it!	Blessed is the one who is meritorious in it. May the holy One

make us meritorious on [this day] together with all the Israelites. Amen and amen.

VIII

The Great Judgment

Secrets

"The holy One blessed be He will make all nations pass before him, and he will say to them, "You worshippers of gods of silver and gold, see if they are able to deliver you!" At once they will pass over and be burned, as it is said, *The wicked will return to Sheol, [all Gentiles who have forgotten God]* (Ps 9:18).

"After them, the Israelites will come, and the holy One blessed be He will say to them, "Whom do you worship?" They will say, *For you are our Father, for Abraham does not know us [and Israel does not acknowledge us; you, O Lord, are our Father, our Redeemer from an age is your name]* (Isa 63:16).

"The Gentiles from the midst of Gehinnom [will say], "Let us see if he judges his people, the Israelites, as he judged us." The holy One blessed be He will immediately pass the people, the Israelites, through the midst of Gehinnom, making them as cold water, as it is said, *Their king will pass before them, [the Lord at their head]* (Micah 2:13), and it says, *You will walk in the midst of fire, and you will not be burned. [The flame will not burn you]* (Isa 43:2). At that hour the transgressors of Israel will be poured off into Gehinnom for twelve months. After that the holy One blessed be He will raise them and they will dwell in the Garden of Eden and enjoy its fruits, as it is said, *All your people will be righteous* (Isa 60:21).

---

[192]The third millennium, considering a day as a thousand years.
[193]"Living" in convenantal terms meant living on the promised land with the Messiah.

IX
Resumption of the Prayer
Prayer

"But still, *He saw the Kenites* (Num 24:21). What riddle did the wicked Balaam see? When Balaam saw the *Kenite* tribe destined to arise and enslave the Israelites, he began to say, *Your dwelling place is firm* (איתן) (Num 24:21). I see that you will only eat at the musical instrument of *Eitan* (איתן) *the Ezrahite* (Ps 89:1).[147]

"The second king who will arise from the Ishmaelites is one who loves Israel, and he will enclose the broken parts of the temple and make war with the sons of Esau and will kill their troops.[194]

"A king will arise whose name is Marwan, and he will be a herder of donkeys, but they will take him from behind the donkeys and make him king (Eccles 4:14). The Edomites will rise up against him and kill him.[195]

"Another will arise in his place, and there will be peace from all his territories. He will be a lover of Zion,[196] and he will die in peace.

"Another king will arise in his place, and he will seize the kingdom with his sword and his bow, and there will be strife in his days: at one time in the East, then in the West, and again in the North, and then in the South. He will make war with everyone, and when the Gairun[197] in the West falls against the Ishmaelites in Damascus, the kingdom of the Ishmaelites will fall. Concerning that time, it is said, *The Lord has broken the staff of the wicked ones* (Isa 14:5). Still there will be with him mighty men, the sons of Kedar. A northeast wind will blow over him and many of his troops[198] will fall: the first alongside the Tigris, the second alongside the Euphrates, the third, between them. He will flee from them, but they will capture his sons, and they will be murdered and hanged from trees.[199]

"*It will happen on that day that the Lord will whistle to the fly*

[194]Probably Omar or Abd al-Malik.

[195]Lewis, "Apocalyptic Vision," 327, said this was Marwan I, and it referred to the obscurity with which he spent the last year of Muawiyya's reign. It might also be Yazid (680-83). Yazid's mother loved the rural life, so she sent her son out to the villages to live with the shepherds. When Yazid's father died, he was taken from the shepherd's tents and made king.

[196]Ibn Shmuel, *Redemption*, 272, corrects צאן (flock) to read ציון (Zion). Probably Abd al-Malik.

[197]For גירודן (gallows) read גירון (Gairun).

[198]Reading חיילים (troops) as in "Secrets" for חללים (slain).

[199]Marwan II.

Prayer

which is at the end of the Egyptian Nile and to the bee which is in the land of Assyria (Isa 7:18), and they will make war with the Ashkenazim.[200] The first king will lead them, and he who rebels against their Lord will go out, as it is said, *Thus says the Lord...to a soul despised, to a nation abhorred, to Ebed Moshalim* (Isa 49:7). *To a nation abhorred.* Who is this? He was saying, "This [represents] the Canaanites,[201] because they were *abhorred* by all nations." *To Ebed Moshalim (a servant of rulers)*—who will be a servant of rulers, and he will rebel against his Lord, and they will gather themselves to him, and the men who rebelled against their Lord will be gathered with them. They will make war with the Ishmaelites, and they will kill their mighty men, confiscate their wealth, and dispossess them. The men will be especially ugly and will wear black, and they will come from the East.[202] They will be *bitter and swift,* as it is said, *For behold, I will raise up the Chaldeans, the bitter and swift nation* (Hab 1:6). All of them will be horsemen,[203] as it is said, *Horsemen coming up* (Nahum 3:2), and they will come from a distant land, *to inherit dwellings that are not his* (Hab 1:6), and they will go up over high mountains, that is the high mountains of Israel (cf. Ezek 17:23; 20:40; 24:14), and they will break into the temple, snuff out the candles, and tear off the doors.[204]

"Still four other kings will arise: two of them known, and two others will rise up against them. In their days the son of David will shoot forth, as it is said, *In the days of the kings, [the God of heaven will establish a kingdom which (will last) for ages; it will not be destroyed]* (Dan 2:44).

"The appearance of the first king is that he is an aged man, but not very old.[205] The king will be humble, [with] attractive eyes, pretty black hair, and they will be made to stumble through him.[206]

---

[200]Either the Franks or Germans or as Lewis, "Apocalyptic Vision," 329, holds, following Krauss, the Khazars, as the Karaite commentators believed.

[201]Lewis, "Apocalyptic Vision," 329, identifies Canaan with Khurasan.

[202]Probably the Abbasids who overthrew the Omayyids in A.D. 750.

[203]Lewis, "Apocalyptic Vision," 329, identifies "horsemen" (*parashim*) with the Persians, as a pun.

[204]There was no Jewish temple throughout the Middle Ages. This may refer to the Dome of the Rock.

[205]Lewis, "Apocalyptic Vision," renders איש ישיש "experienced man" as Job 12:12; 32:6.

[206]Lewis, "Apocalyptic Vision," 330, said this is Suffah, who was described as "tall and fair, with an aquiline nose, a handsome face and curly, plentiful hair." He died at the age of 33.

Prayer

"After him another will arise in the midst of conflicts, and he will raise up many troops along the river Euphrates, and in one day his troops which are in the North and which are in the South will fall, and he will flee, be captured, and imprisoned. All the days which he will be in prison, there will be peace in the land.

"The fourth king will love silver and gold, and he will be old and tall of stature, but he will have a blemish on the big toe of his right foot. He will make coins of copper, conceal them, and hide them under the Euphrates with silver and gold, and they will be hidden for the messianic king, as it is said, *And I will give you dark treasures, things secretly concealed* (Isa 45:3).[207] In his days the fortunes of the West will arise, and they will send two armies, and they will kill some of the easterners, and he will send still others.[208]

X

The Week of the Messiah

Prayer

"In the beginning of the first week [of years], there will be no rain; in the second, there will be half a famine; in the third, there will be a great famine, and there will be no rain; in the fourth, moderate; in the fifth, there will be a great abundance; and in the sixth, a star will shoot out from the East, and at his head will be a staff of fire like a spear, and the Gentiles will say, "This star is ours." But it will not be so, but rather of Israel, as it is said, *A star has stepped out from Jacob* (Num 24:17). The time of his rising, in the first watch of the night until two hours, and he will continue to gather for fifteen days in the East, then circle around to the West, and act fifteen days,[209] and if more, it will be good for Israel.

"I again returned to my prayer and also to my fast for forty days until this angel was revealed to me, and said to me, 'Ask!' I said to him, 'Sir, what will be the end of these things?" The angel said, 'After all these things, the westerners will prevail with great forces, and they will come, mixed, and they will engage battle with the easterners who are in their land and they will kill them. Those who are left will flee from them and go to Alexandria, but some of the

---

[207]Perhaps Mansur, who was so thrifty he was called "Father of Farthings." So Lewis, "Apocalyptic Vision," 330.

[208]Lewis, "Apocalyptic Vision," 330, said this is a reference to Mansur's struggle with the Sufyani and Shiite uprisings in Syria and Arabia.

[209]Perhaps gathering troops and supplies with which to attack Jerusalem.

Prayer

westerners will pursue them. They will go, and there will be a great battle there, and the easterners will flee from there and come to Egypt, take it captive, take booty, and make it a desolation, to confirm that which is said, *Egypt will become a desolation* (Joel 4:19). They will pass over into the pleasant land[210] and evil doing will be at their hands, and no one taken captive [by them] will return until the Messiah comes.'

XI

Birth Pangs

Prayer

"When I heard this word, I wept very much. The angel said to me, 'Shimon, why are you weeping?' I said, 'Will there be any escape for the sons of Abraham, Isaac, and Jacob in his days?' He said, 'The matter is very harsh. If you put meat on the fire, you will not be able to be saved from its smell. Thus the Israelites will not be delivered, but everyone who goes into a room, flees, and hides himself will be delivered, as it is said, *Go, my people; into your rooms, [and close your doors after you. Hide for a short instant until the wrath passes over]* (Isa 26:20). *Everyone that is found will be stabbed, and everyone that is captured will fall by the sword* (Isa 13:15). They will pass over into the pleasant land,[210] and they will plunder [it], as it is said, *Go into the lands, plunder, and pass over* (Dan 11:40). They will *come in the desolate valleys* (Isa 7:10), and they will be in its midst. There will be a great war there, concerning which all the prophets have prophesied, rivers will be changed, and waters of the Euphrates [will become] blood. Those who are left will not be able to drink from it, and the kingdom of the East will be broken from there.

"'After these things, an insolent king will arise, and he will act for three and a half years. At the beginning of his kingdom, as he is arising, he will take the wealthy people, confiscate their wealth (Zeph 3:16), and kill them, but silver will not be able to save them (Ezek 7:19). Counsel and thought will not attend him. He will kill everyone who mentions, "Hear, Israel, the Lord your God...!" and he will murder everyone who says, "The God of Abraham." They will say, "Let us return, all of us, to become one nation, and let us abolish the sabbaths and festivals and new moons from the

[210]Palestine.

Prayer

Israelites, as it is said, *And he will think to change the times and the law* (Dan 7:25). *Times*—they are the festivals, and *law* is the Torah, as it is said, *a fiery law is theirs* (Deut 33:2). In his days there will be a great distress over Israel. Everyone who goes into exile to Upper Galilee will escape, as it is said, *For on Mount Zion and in Jerusalem there will be [a way to] escape* (Joel 3:5), until the Lord arrives. He will kill people of Israel until he reaches Damascus, and when he reaches Damascus, the holy One blessed be He will give help and success to Israel. In his days there will be strife and war in the world. Every city will engage in war with its neighboring city, state with state, people with people, and nation with nation, and there will be no peace for him who comes or for him who goes, as it is said, *I will distress mankind, and men will walk as blind men* (Zeph 1:17). The people of the Lord will be made to wander, and there will be distress over them for three years, and they will be given into his hand until the end of three years, as it is said, *And they will be given into his hands until a time, two times, and half a time* (Dan 7:25). *A time* means a year; *two times* means two years; *half a time* means half a year. This means he will annul the decree, and the folly for three years, as it is said, *From the time the continual offering is turned away, and the desolating sacrilege is set up twelve hundred, ninety* (Dan 12:11), which totals three and a half years.

"'A king will arise who will return them [the opportunity] to atone, as it is said, *They will place the desolating sacrilege* (Dan 11:31), and he will rule three months.

XII

Death in the Valley

"'After this the Ishmaelites will make war with the Edomites in the Valley of Acre , and at once the Syrians will come upon them and take them captive, as it is said, *Until Assyria [Syria] takes you captive* (Num 24:22), and *Ships from the hand of the Kittim* (Num 24:22). These are the Edomites who are destined to arise at the end of days, and when they leave, they will leave as thieves, as it is said, *If thieves come against you* (Obad 5); and they will make war with the Ishmaelites, and they will kill many of them. They will gather themselves at the camp of Acre , and the iron will break the clay (Dan 2:40), the legs [of iron] will break the toes [of clay], and they will flee naked without horses. Legions from Edom will be tested with them, and they will come and make war in the Valley of Acre, until the horse sinks up to his thigh in blood. Israelites will flee until they come to the Valley of Jericho, and there they will stop, and each man will say to his fellow, "Where can we, our wives, and our children flee? Let us return!" Then they will return and wage another war in the Valley of Megiddo. Edomites will flee and go up to [their] ships, and a wind will go out and bring them to Syria, and they will afflict the Syrians and those beyond the river (cf. Num 24:24).[211] At the end of nine months, the Syrians will go out and destroy the Israelites and the Romans, as it is said, *Until Assyria [Syria] takes you captive* (Num 24:22), and when you see Syrians going out and marching in the land of Israel, they will make peace, and Elijah (May he be remembered for blessing) will go out and proclaim to them the good news of peace, as it is said, This will be peace: *Syria, when it comes into our land* (Micah 5:4). The Italians will try to make war with them, and the Ishmaelites will return to them the kingdom, a small portion. But they will hardly be able to bring out their wives before Syria takes them captive. Immediately a *bat qol* will go out and proclaim in all the places where Israelites are captives, "Leave and vindicate the vengeance of the Lord in Edom, as it is said, *I will afflict vengeance against Edom by the hand of my people, the Israelites* (Ezek 25:14). At once young Israelite men will be gathered and heard, and they will enthrone a king from the seed of David, and a division will fall between these two groups, and citizens of the land of Israel will transgress against the seed of David, to fulfill that which has been said, *And the Israelites will sin against the house of David until this day* (II Chron 10:19). *Until this day*, that is the day when the messianic king will come. These two groups will come and be held fast, and a *bat qol* will go out and whisper, *Whatever has been is that which will be* (Eccles 1:9). He is the holy One blessed be He, who was before the creation of the age, and he is destined to be after the destruction of the age. *Whatever has been* done *is what will be* done (Eccles 1:9). She will reply and say, "Just as Joshua did to Jericho and its king, thus do with the Gentiles." Then he will say, "We do not have the ark of the

---

[211] This may refer to the famous battle of Acre in A.D. 1291 when Moslems succeeded in driving every Christian from the city. See the poem, "That Day" and M. Benvenisti, *The Crusaders in the Holy Land*, 90-93. Lewis, "Apocalyptic Vision," 336-37, interprets this story in relationship to the extension of Alptakin's authority after the departure of the Byzantines, but it is necessary to amend Israel to read "Ishmael" and Italia to read Tayya to make this at all credible as a tenth century apocalypse. Christians were "clay," and Moslems, "iron."

covenant with us as there was with Joshua." It will reply to them, "It was not the ark but two tablets of stone and their stamp of approval, 'Hear, Israel!'" Immediately they will shout with a loud shout, and say, "Hear, Israel, the Lord our God, the Lord is One!" Then they will surround Jericho and at once the wall will fall under it, and they will enter its midst and bring out the young men dead in its streets, to fulfill that which is said, *Therefore its young men will fall in its streets, and all her men of war will keep still* (Jer 50:30). They will kill [people] in its midst three days and three nights. After this they will collect all its booty to the middle of its streets. A report will go out concerning them from the land of Israel, and they will fear greatly.'

XIII

Israelite Victory

"Again I returned to prayer before the Lord, in fasting and sack cloth and ashes, until I looked and behold a hand touched me and raised me up on my feet and said to me, 'Ask, righteous man! Whatever you request, I will do.' I asked and said to him, 'In the last of these days, how will all the Israelites be gathered from the four corners of the earth? How will it happen that you will bring them out from under the hand of the kingdoms? If they go out, where will they go out? How will you make them walk? What will they be able to do? I want you to tell me these and all things like them until the end of everything.' He answered me from the doors of heaven and said, 'At the end of the kingdom of the Ishmaelites, the Romans will go out against Jerusalem, and they will make war with the Ishmaelites, and the land will be subdued before them. They will come into its midst, and they will kill many Ishmaelites in it and cause many to fall slain in it, and they will take a great captivity from the daughters of Ishmael, and they will take out brains from the little girls, and they will slaughter every day little Moslem girls.[212] In that time, it will be very grievous for Israel. In that time the Lord will arouse the tribes of Israel and they will come to Jerusalem, the holy city, and they will find written in the Torah, *The Lord will walk before them, a pillar of cloud by day* (Ex 13:21), and further it is written, *For the Lord will walk before you; the God of Israel will be your rearguard* (Isa 52:12). They will

---

[212]The Hebrew is ליש׳ תי נקות. The abbreviation could be taken to mean "for Israel" or "for Ishmael." Lewis, "Apocalyptic Vision," 318, renders it "children for Jesus."

walk in cloud and in darkness. They will make war with the
Edomites, and they will kill many of them in a great slaughter, and
their fame will go out into the world with the tribes to come. In
that time the passage will be fulfilled in Israel, *A time of distress
will come as never was from the existence of the nation until that
time. At that time your people will escape, all who are found
written in the book* (Dan 12:1). The Gentiles will rise up against
the Israelites and will kill many of them in a great slaughter, and
many of the people of the land will transgress, and they will torture many of the pious ones in chains so that they will forsake the
Torah of the Lord.

"While they are still in this distress a few days, the Lord will
bring a great and powerful wind and a great quaking and a cloud,
so black that there has never been seen anything like it in the
world, and from the midst of that wind, the holy One blessed be
He will scatter the tribes in every single city. Concerning them, it is
said, *Who are these flying like clouds* (Isa 60:8)? They will be
gathered from Israel to Jerusalem, a few men, and they will have
no bread, but the holy One blessed be He will change the sand into
flour for the Israelites.[213] Concerning that time, it is said, *There
will be an abundance of grain in the land on the top of the mountains* (Ps 72:16). Then Nehemiah Ben Hoshiel will arise and perform signs by the word of the Lord. A king will arise denying judgment, and he will make himself appear like one who serves the
Lord, but his heart is not right within him. Great wrath will go out
in the world, and all the world will be afraid of him. The Israelites
will be gathered to Nehemiah, son of Hoshiel. The king of Egypt
will make peace with him, and he will kill all the states which
surround Jerusalem, such as Tiberias, Damascus, and Ascalon.
The Gentiles will hear, and dread and fear will fall upon them. The
sign which will be in that time is that the stars will appear with
blood, and concerning that time, it is said, *The sun was changed to
darkness and the moon, to blood* (Joel 3:3). The holy One blessed
be He will send the Gentiles ten plagues as he sent in Egypt, to
confirm that which he said, *It will happen in that day the Lord will
put his hand a second time to acquire the remnant of his people*
(Isa 11:11).

XIV

Armilos

"They say there is in Rome a marble stone, and it is like a

[213]Compare this to the temptation of Jesus to transform stones into bread (Mt 4:1-4).

beautiful maiden, created from the six days of creation. The sons of Beliel of the Gentiles will come and lie with her, and she will become pregnant, and at the end of nine months she will split open, and a male in the form of a man will go out from her. His length will be twelve cubits and his width, two cubits, and his eyes will be bloodshot. The hair of his head will be red like gold, and the soles of his feet, green, and he will have two heads.[214] They will call him Armilos. Edomites will come to him, and he will say to them, "I am your Messiah. I am your God." Thus he will mislead them. At once they will believe him, and they will make him king. All the sons of Esau will associate with him and come to him, and he will go and proclaim good news to all the states, and he will say to the sons of Esau, "Bring me my teachings which I have given you!" At once the Gentiles will come, and they will bring a book, and he will say to them, "This is what I have put before you." He will say to them, "I am your God. I am your Messiah." In that hour he will send to Nehemiah and all Israel, and he will say to them, "Bring me your Torah and take an oath to me that I am God!" Immediately all the Israelites will tremble and be afraid. In that hour Nehemiah will arise and three of the Ephraimites with him, and they will walk with him, and the book of the Torah will be with them, and they will read before him, "I [am God] and you shall not have [another]." He will say, "There is nothing at all of this in your Torah! I will not give you rest until you believe that I am God, just as the Gentiles have believed in me." At once Nehemiah will stand up against him and say to him, "You are not God, but Satan!" He will say to them, "Why do you lie to me? I will command [my servants] to kill you!" Then he will say to his servants, "Seize Nehemiah!" At once will arise thirty. thousand mighty men from Israel, and he [Nehemiah] will make war with him and kill two hundred thousand from the camp of Armilos. The anger of Armilos will arise, and he will gather all the armies of the Gentiles and make war with the Israelites, and he will murder a million Israelites and even kill Nehemiah at noon. Concerning that time, it is said, *"And it will be, in that day,"* says the Lord, *"and I will make the sun set at noon, and I will make the land dark in daylight* (Amos 8:9). Those who are left of the Israelites will flee to the *wilderness of the peoples* (Ezek 20:35), and they will dwell there forty-five days without bread or water, but grass of the field will be their food. After forty-five days, Armilos will come, and he will fight with Egypt and capture it, as it is said, *And the land of*

---

[214]Probably an allusion to the two Christian "heads": Rome and Constantinople.

Egypt will not be [a place] for escape (Dan 11:42). Then he will return and set his face to Jerusalem to destroy it a second time, as it is said, *And he will pitch the palatial tents between the seas and the pleasant holy mountain, and he will come to his end, and no one will help him* (Dan 11:45).

XV

The National Jubilee

"'*In that time, Michael, the great prince, will arise* (Dan 12:1). He will blow the trumpet three times, as it is said, *It will happen on that day a blast will be made with a great trumpet* (Isa 27:13). That horn will be the right horn of Isaac's ram, and the holy One blessed be He will extend it until [it becomes] a thousand cubits [long]. He will blow a trumpet blast, and the Messiah, son of David, and Elijah will be revealed. The two of them will walk to Israel where they are in *the wilderness of the people* (Ezek 20:35), and Elijah will say to them, "This is the Messiah!" He will turn their heart and strengthen their hand, as it is said, *Strengthen the weak hands; hold steady the knocking knees; say to the faint hearted, "Be strong! do not be afraid!"* (Isa 35:3-4). Then all the Israelites will hear the sound of the trumpet, and they will hear that the Lord has redeemed Israel, as it is said, *For the Lord has redeemed Jacob [and delivered him from the hand of one stronger than he]* (Jer 31:10). *Those who were lost in the land of Assyria [and those who were rejected in the land of Egypt] will come* (Isa 27:13). The fear of the Lord will promptly fall upon the peoples and upon all the nations. Israelites will return with the Messiah until they come to the Wilderness of Judah. Then they will meet with all the Israelites, and they will come to Jerusalem and ascend the stairs of the house of David which remain from the destruction, and the Messiah will dwell there.

"'Armilos will hear that a king has arisen for Israel, and he will gather the troops of all the Gentiles, and they will come to the messianic king and to Israel. Then the holy One blessed be He will fight on behalf of Israel, and he will say to the Messiah, *Sit at my right hand* (Ps 110:1). The Messiah will say to the Israelites, *Gather yourselves together; stand firm; and see the salvation of the Lord* (Ex 14:13). At once the holy One blessed be He will go out and fight with them, as it is said, *The Lord will go out and fight with those Gentiles* (Zech 14:3), and it is written, *In that time I will bring you, and I will gather you, for I will give you for a*

name and a praise in all the peoples of the land (Zeph 3:20).
Amen.'''
May he bring near that time and that period!

Summary

Rabbi Shimon Ben Yoḥai was so highly respected for his
nationalistic zeal and piety that his works of supererogation were
believed to have a much greater value than the same works done
by others. In that perspective he was pictured in this apocalypse in
prayer which received immediate response from the Almighty. An
angel was sent to satisfy his needs and to answer his questions.
Like other apocalypses, this document is structured like disguised
responsa. During the Middle Ages Jews with burning religious
questions sent them to the great Jewish scholars of the world.
These were such men as Maimonides, Saadia Gaon, Hai Gaon,
and others. The responsa were the answers given by the scholars
to these questions. Many of these responsa, such as those published here of Rabbi Hai Gaon on salvation, dealt with the eschatological questions believed by medieval Jews. The apocalyptic
writers also proposed the questions asked by pious Jews about the
promised end of the Christian and Moslem rule and the beginning
rule of the Jewish government. Jews were asking, "How near is the
end?" "Are the events now taking place in history the final signs?"
"What can Jews expect?" "What should Jews do at this time?" Like
the *geonim* and other respected scholars, the apocalyptic writers
also gave answers or responsa to the questions raised, and their
answers were very similar to those proposed by the *geonim*. The
difference was in the style of presentation. The answers were
revealed by an angel or some divine medium. Rabbi Shimon received his answers from the "voice" whose name was a mystery.
The voice sent an angel whose name was Mettatron to Shimon to
mediate the answers. The angel Mettatron replied in terms of
scripture which he interpreted in relationship to the Moslem
caliphs of the seventh and eighth centuries. The "predicted"
decrees and hardships destined to be experienced by Jews during
this period were those with which Jews were already acquainted.
The angel explained to Shimon how these political events fit into
the divine plan of fulfilling for the Jews the promised restoration of
the Davidic empire and deliverance of Jews from any type of subservience to the Gentiles. This involved the advent of the Messiah,

the destruction of the Roman sons of Satan, and the reduction of power of the Moslems to humble subservience. The precise description of some of the caliphs shows that the author was well acquainted with the activity of these rulers and the effect of their rule on contemporary Jews. The promised future was not so clear and not directly based on known history. On the basis of scriptural promises the expected end was foreseen. Some historical allusions belonged to a period that took a knowledge of the Crusades and the Battle of Acre for granted and "predicted" them. This means that this document is composed of some earlier material and some later re-edited and reinterpreted material. An examination of the literary style shows that there were parts written by some authors and some written by others. The relationship among the "prayer," "secrets," and "future events" shows that apocalyptic authors utilized units that were popular at their time, quoted them verbatim, expanded them, compressed them, or brought them up to date, but they fit them into whatever larger design they had at the time. These popular apocalypses were not dropped when their predictions failed, but were instead reinterpreted to fit the eschatological needs and beliefs of a later period. The earlier writer was glad the Moslems overthrew the Byzantine Christians and understood that this was a necessary preliminary step to Israelite world domination. The composition of the document about Armilos (Roman and Byzantine Christianity) was also early, but may have been added to the apocalypse about the caliphs by a later editor after the Christians had again moved to take control of the Near East. Jews also saw this as a divine move to weaken the Moslems and provide an opportunity for the Jews to work themselves into power, but they needed to foresee the downfall of this Christian power which had oppressed them longer than the Moslems had. The description of the defeat of the Christians at the Valley of Acre reflected the ardent belief that this was the beginning of the end which Jews had long anticipated. The document concludes with the predicted end of Armilos and the installation of the Messiah.

This was the answer or response of the apocalyptic writer to pious Jews for whom the questions answered were important. The author probably was not as well known as the *geonim*, but he achieved an even greater authority for his work by testifying to its divine source through revelation to the great Rabbi Shimon Ben Yohai. Other authors attributed their works to Daniel, who also had dreams and saw visions.

THE VISION OF DANIEL[215]

1:3) This is the vision of Daniel which was revealed to him in the days of Cyrus, king of Persia, which is "The Vision of the Lord."[216]

I, Daniel, 4) was standing alongside the river Chebar (Ezek 1:1), and the awe inspiring vision appeared to me. It was glorious! I 5) was astounded at that vision, but Gabriel, general of the celestial army, came to me: "Take cognizance, O delightful man, 6) and hear! I have come to tell [you] that the mighty and holy One said to me, 'Go, Gabriel, and reveal to Daniel what 7) is destined to happen in the end of days:'

In those days, a king will arise, and the sign of his name will be the number one thousand, two hundred, three.[217] 8) The kingdom will be given to him, and they will be satisfied with the good things in his kingdom. He will blaspheme before God and *shame*[218] the congregation 9) of God. He will make mock priests and [thus] anger the Most High with his deeds.

The gods will destroy him and raise up 10) in his stead another king who will cut him off on account of the evilness of his actions. That tribe will exalt itself more than that which was before it. 11) The sign of his name will be two *Beths*,[219] and he will begin to build the congregation which the preceding tribe had despised. He 12) will make his kingdom rich and will subject nations and peoples to his rule. He will be content on account of his goodness and will set 13) his face towards the people of the saints of the Most High (Dan 7:18, 25, 27; 11:17-18). Then he will baptize them against their will amidst great hardship and force, after which 14) he will sell them for male and female slaves, but he will die in his bed with great pains. His tribe will be seized 15) by his son as a heritage. His name will be the sign of the kingdom of beasts, Leon,[220] and he will provide relief and freedom for the people 16) of the saints of the Most High (Dan 7:18, 25, 27). The Lord of lords will increase his kingdom, and a man of Kush without a crown of his own[221] will rule

[215]L. Ginsburg, "Midrashic and Haggadic Fragment," גנזי שעכטער I, 310-23. SML

[216]The Hebrew that has been rendered "Lord" is ייוד

[217]The number 1203 undoubtedly spells the name of some known king in *gematria*.

[218]Underlined words just before a new line are those that in Hebrew belong to the next line.

[219]King Basel, whose name in Greek is Βασιλεῦς Βάσιλ.

[220]Emperor Leo VI (the Lion) annulled a decree made by Emperor Basel about A.D. 874 coercing the Jews to be baptized. So A. Sharf, "Jews in Byzantium" *The World History of the Jewish People*, ed. C. Roth (Ramath-Gan, Israel, c1966) II, 61.

[221]Ibn Shmuel, *Redemption*, 250, said this is Romanus, sometimes called a Cushite.

with him 17) in peace for twenty-two years, one who will be strongly bound to him by his love. After his death, a man from Arabia will combat with him 18) and will prevail over him, but he will hold evil counsels and will not succeed. In his days, the humble people will be undisturbed, 19) but after that a king will arise[222] who will torture them with expulsion but not with destruction. He will act mercifully towards them and set his face toward the gods. 20) He will not succeed, for his kingdom will quickly change. A forty-four [year old] king[223] will rule with him with the crown 21) inherited from his father, but he will also die, and one of his descendants will rule with him.[224] Many will rise up 22) against him as those that lie in wait, but their counsel will be frustrated. It would be advisable for him to pay close attention at the beginning of his rule so that *his kingdom* should be exalted 2:1) and lifted up to heaven, but in the end of days his kingdom will be cut off and subjugated by Tyre, the powerful.

2) *You, Daniel, seal these words* (Dan 12:4) until they are destined to be proved and your words made crystal clear (Dan 12:9). 3) That which is destined to be, is revealed. Perhaps another who is like you or fears God will bring forth the reason of his deeds (Isa 41:21), 4) but the words which were revealed to you, Daniel, are trustworthy and true *until the time of the end* (Dan 12:9). Then the angel *raised* 5) *his hands to heaven and swore by the life of the age* (Dan 12:7) that the tribe[225] would arise, and its strength would be divided 6) peacefully and fill all the earth with good things. Then a transgressor, the son of a wicked man, will arise from the North and rule 7) over the city of Eptalopon[226] for three and a half years (Dan 7:25). He will commit great iniquity such as had not been done 8) from the creation of the world until its end, such as marrying sons with their mother, brothers 9) with their sisters, and daughters with their fathers. Great and severe will be the defilement, 10) much more than that [described] in the Torah. The Lord God will look on all the face of the land, and *a fire from heaven* will burn the guilty cities of Rome. 11) There will be no

---

[222]This is Romanus. So Sharf, "Jews in Byzantium," 62.

[223]This is Constantine VII Porphyrogenitus, the legitimate heir, who finally removed Romanus and his sons from office. So Ibn Shmuel, *Redemption,* 409 and Sharf, "Jews in Byzantium," 62.

[224]This is Alexander, Constantine's uncle. So Ibn Shmuel, *Ibid.*

[225]The tribe Constantine ruled, the Byzantines.

[226]Ginsburg, "Midrashic and Haggadic Fragment," 321, identified this city with Rome as the city of seven hills. This on the basis that ἐπτάλοφος means "seven hills." It was used by early secular writers with that meaning. There is a problem here, however, in the distinction made in 2:14 between Eptalopon and Rome (2:13).

salvation, either on sea or on dry land, from the wrath of the Lord of armies against their obscenities, and *the Lord God* 12) will kill the wicked tribe. Blessed is he who dwells in that day in Rome, Selonika, Cilicia, 13) Sicily, Riyah, Satriglion, Ashiniad, Aram...........14) and Istanbul. Happy are all those who dwell in these places, but in Eptalopon *many* peoples will wage war. 15) The Lord God will become very angry with those who dwell in all the islands and will lead them into exile and make them dwell in *the great*...16) The cattle and the grass of the field [will be destined] for leanness. There will be thunderstorms in heaven and *earthquakes.* 17) A great fire from heaven will inflame those who dwell in the land,[226a] and many will be the corpses strewn about without burial 18) on the face of the ground. Cattle, birds, reptiles of the land, and whatever is on the face of the ground will be carcasses. 19) The Lord God will be angry, and he will rain his fire upon it and pour out the water and violently stir up the seas, 20) making their waves roar and boil. Then there will be void, nothing, and emptiness, and he will cast them out and sink them in the deep, 21) so that those who dwell in the sea will swallow them and their fortresses. The land which [they will reach] will not be recognizable by those who will come from the distant parts of the sea to lament over it.........for.....they that were rich.... 23) will come to go with ships, and they will say to one another, "Is not this the city of which they have said, 'A crown 24) of beauty, a joy of all the land'"? They will mourn over it for many days. In those days the kingdom of Rome will be given. 25) ....of Ashpion, the gates and the fortresses.. 26) ....and they will judge. Then the [messianic king] will rule......

Summary

This apocalypse is centered around the Byzantine Christian rulers during the ninth and tenth centuries in a disguised language that is at least partly understandable to anyone who is familiar with this period. It reflects attitudes toward Jews that were critical—forced baptism, taxes, and expulsion as well as relief from some of these anti-Jewish decrees. The "vision" is couched in a literary style as if all of this history were foreseen by Daniel alongside the river Chebar in the days of Cyrus king of Persia. The last part of the document probably really is prophecy, predicting the destruction of Rome and all of the empire under its control.

[226a]I.e., non-Jews who live in Palestine.

Although most of this is general, anticipated destruction in color-ful language, the earthquakes and fire, some of it seems a little incoherent. For example, if Rome is to be destroyed, why would all of the Jews in Rome and its provinces be blessed? Is this because they will be able to escape and return to Palestine? Eptalopon seems to be Rome, but why is it contrasted to Rome in 2:14? The fragment ends with the arrival of the Messiah and his beginning rule. As with other apocalypses this vision describes the events with which the readers were familiar and a promise of redemption and restoration under messianic leadership. It was written in disguised language so that the fifth-columnist nature of the message could not be understood by Christians if they gained pos-session of the document.

THE LEGEND OF THE MESSIAH[227]

A star will step out from Jacob; and a scepter will arise from
    Israel.
It will smite through the corners of Moab and shatter all the
    sons of Sheth.[228]
Edom will become an inheritance, and also his enemy, Seir,
    will become an inheritance.
        Israel will do valiantly!
He will have dominion from Jacob and will destroy the
    remnant of the city (Num 24:17-19).
A star will step out from Jacob. The sages taught: 1) "During the week [of years] in which [the Messiah] David will come, there will not be enough food to supply everyone's needs during the first year. In the second [year], there will rage half a famine. In the third [year], a great famine will prevail. In the fourth [year], there will be neither hunger nor plenty. In the fifth [year] there will be plenty. A star will step out from the East (see Isa 41:2). There will be the star of the Messiah. He will dwell in the East for fifteen days; if he spends longer, it will be for the benefit of Israel.[229] In the sixth [year], there will be sounds and rumors, and in the seventh [year], wars [will break out]. At the end of the seventh, let [everyone] watch for the Messiah" (see San 97a; Gittin 88a-b). 3)

[227]Ch. M. Horowitz, בית עקד האגדות, 56-58. SML
[228]Here understood to be the Gentiles, as the commentary shows.
[229]Perhaps because he will be busy gathering still more troops with which to vindicate Jews and restore them to their land.

Then the inhabitants of the West will become arrogant.[230] They will come and establish a kingdom 4) without force. They will go as far as Egypt and take all [the residents] captive. In those days an insolent king[231] will arise over a poor and humble people, and he will *obtain the kingdom by flatteries* (Dan 11:21). Concerning that time, Isaiah said, *Come, my people! Enter your chambers [and close your doors behind you; hide yourselves for a little while until the wrath passes]* (Isa 26:20).

The sages said, "Rabbi Chiyah commanded his generation, 'When you hear that *an insolent king* (Dan 8:23) has arisen, do not dwell there [under his sovereignty], 5) because he will decree [that] everyone who said, "The God of Hebrews is one," will be killed. He will say, "Let us all become one tongue and one nation."[232] He will annul the times, appointed seasons [for feasts and holidays], [Jewish] Sabbaths, and the new moons, as well as the Torah from Israel, as it is said, *He will think to change the seasons and the law, and they will be given into his hands until a time, two times, and half a time* (Dan 7:25). *A time* means "a year"; *two times* means "two [years]"; and *half a time* means "half a year."'" They said to him, "Teacher, where will we escape?" He told them, "To Upper Galilee, as it is said, *For on Mount Zion and in Jerusalem there will be a [place of] escape* (Joel 3:5). *Mount Zion will be a [place of] escape, and it shall be holy* (Obad 17).[233]

He will smite through the corners of Moab (Num 24:17). Rabbi Huna said in the name of Rabbi Levi, "[This] teaches that Israel will be gathered together 6) in Upper Galilee and that the Messiah son of Joseph will watch over them there. They will go up from there, [the Messiah] and all the Israelites with him, to Jerusalem, to fulfill that which is said, *The children of the violent among your people will exalt themselves to establish the vision, but they will stumble* (Dan 11:14). Then [the Messiah] will go up and build the house of the sanctuary and offer sacrifices, and fire will come down from heaven [to consume them].

He will smite all the Gentiles. He will then come to the land of *Moab*, will slay half of [the people in] it, take the rest into captivity, and they will levy a tax for him.[234] Finally, he will make peace

---

[230]Either the Byzantines, coming from Europe or the Fatamids, coming from the western end of North Africa. See Dan 8:5.

[231]Perhaps Armilos.

[232]Decrees to this effect were made by Emperors Heraclius and Basil.

[233]A strange proof text for justification of advice to flee to Galilee—quite a distance north of Jerusalem.

[234]Jews looked forward to the time when they could levy taxes but not pay them.

with *Moab*, as it is said, *Yet I will restore the fortunes of Moab in the end of days* (Jer 48:47). [Israelites] will dwell securely for forty years, eating and drinking, *and the aliens will be your plowmen and vinedressers* (Isa 61:5). *And shatter all the sons of Sheth* (Num 24:17). He will *shatter all the* Gentiles, who are called *Sheth*, as it is said, *[She bore a son and called his name Sheth]*, for (she said), *God has appointed [shath] me another (or a foreign) seed* (Gen 4:25). 7)

After all this, Gog and Magog will hear and come up against him, as it is said, *The kings of the earth will establish themselves, and the rulers will take counsel against the Lord and against his Messiah* (Ps 2:2). He will enter and kill him in the outskirts of Jerusalem, as it is said, *There will be a time of hardship [such as has not been from the existence of the nation until that time]* (Dan 12:1). Then the Israelites will see this and say, "The Messiah has perished from us, and no other messiah will return to us again." Four families will mourn for him, as it is said, *The families of the land will mourn, every family apart:...1) the family of the house of David apart, 2) the family of the house of Nathan apart,... 3) the family of the house of Levi apart,...4) [the family of the Shemites apart, and their wives apart]* (Zech 12:12-13).

Then the holy One blessed be He will go out and fight with them, as it is said, *The Lord will go out and fight against those Gentiles* (Zech 14:3). The mountains will be removed, and the hills will totter, and *the Mount of Olives will be split in halves* (Zech 14:4). The holy One blessed be He will come down upon it, and Israelites will flee and escape, as it is said, *You shall flee to the valley of the mountains...[just as you fled from the earthquake in the days of Uzziah, king of Judah]* (Zech 14:5). *This will be the plague [with which the Lord will strike all the Gentiles who make war against Jerusalem: their flesh will rot while they are still on their feet; their eyes will rot in their sockets; and their tongues will rot in their mouths* (Zech 14:12). 8)

Israel will go into exile after this into the wilderness of swamps to pasture for forty-five days in saltry marshes and on broom-plants. Clouds of glory will surround them. There Israel will be hidden, and everyone who has in his heart an evil thought against the holy One blessed be He, the clouds will cast him off, and the Gentiles will murder him.[235] Many Israelites will go out to the Gentiles, but there will be no portion for them with the Israelites in the world to come. Those who are left in the wilderness are

[235]Reminiscent of the death of apostates from Essene Sect (*BJ* II [143-44]).

destined to be afflicted in salt marshes for forty-five days.

At the end of forty-five days, 9) a *bat qol*[236] will say to them, "Go down to Babylon!" as it is said, *You shall go to Babylon, for there you will be saved* (Micah 4:10). The *bat qol* will break out a second time, "Go down to Edom and there carry out my vengeance!" as it is said, *I will lay my vengeance on Edom by the hand of my people, the Israelites* (Ezek 25:14). Then the Israelites will come to Rome, and the *bat qol* will go out a third time: "Do to it just as Joshua did to Jericho!" They will surround the city and sound the trumpet blast. On the seventh time [around], they will shout loudly, *Hear, O Israelites, the Lord your God, the Lord is One* (Deut 6:4). Then the walls of the city will fall, and they will enter it. They will find its young men dead in its streets, as it is said, *Therefore its young men will fall in its streets* (Jer 49:26). After this they will gather all their booty, and *the Israelites will seek the Lord their God and David their king* (Hos 3:5). At once the messianic king will be revealed to them. He will say to them, "I am the messianic king, for whom you have been waiting." Then he will say to them, "Bring me the silver and the gold," and they will bring it and come up, as it is said, *A multitude of camels will cover you* (Isa 60:6).

Then a fourth *bat qol* will go out and say, *In the wilderness prepare the way of the Lord* (Isa 40:3). A fifth *bat qol* will say, *There will be no lion there* (Isa 35:9). A sixth *bat qol* will say, *I will put in the wilderness cedar, acacia, and myrtle* (Isa 41:19). The seventh *bat qol* will announce, *Comfort, comfort my people* (Isa 40:9). Then Elijah will proclaim good news to the Israelites, *Your God has become king* (Isa 52:7)! An eighth *bat qol* will announce and say, *Open the gates, and let the righteous Gentile enter* (Isa 26:2). A tenth *bat qol* will say, *Lift up your heads, O gates* (Ps 24:9)!

Then the dead will come to life, as it is said, *Your dead will live; [your] bodies will rise* (Isa 26:19)! Then the exiles will be gathered, as it is said, *And it will be on that day [that] there will be a blast with a great trumpet, and those who have been lost in the land of Assyria will come, and those who have been pushed into the land of Egypt, and they will worship the Lord on the holy mountain in Jerusalem* (Isa 27:13). Then will be fulfilled [the passage]:

> *A star will step out from Jacob [and a scepter will arise from Israel.*

---

[236]Literally, "daughter of a voice." This is an echo or a voice from Heaven, giving directions to covenanters.

*It will smite through the corners of Moab and shatter all the
sons of Sheth.
Edom will become an inheritance, and also his enemy, Seir,
will become an inheritance.
Israel will do valiantly!
He will have dominion from Jacob and will destroy the
remnant of the city]* (Num 24:17-19).
May it be the will of our Father in heaven that this verse may be
fulfilled: *He will raise a banner to the Gentiles and gather those
who have been purged out of Israel, [and the scattered ones of
Judah gather themselves from the four corners of the earth]* (Isa
11:12), in our days and in the days of all Israelites. Amen.

Summary

This small legend or haggadic narrative is a midrash on Num
24:17-19, which forms an inclusion at the beginning and end of the
midrash. This stylistic form shows that this is a complete unit,
although it has been preserved together with other material in a
larger unit called "The Ten Kings." The author of this midrash was
heavily dependent on scripture for his authority, but he was also
familiar with Jewish eschatological tradition, such as Armilos and
rabbinic testimony.

There is no certainty about the date or location of the composition, because the style is too general. It would apply to almost any
medieval period. The author never used such terms as "Ishmael"
or "Edom" to give away to the reader the identity of his opponents. If the inhabitants of the West were the Byzantines, it would
refer to a much earlier period than it would if they were the
Fatamids, but the author calls the opponents "Gentiles," which
would apply both to Christians and to Moslems from a Jewish
point of view. The expectation that the Messiah would reside in
the East was more popular at the time of the Crusades than earlier,
since there really were pretending messiahs, such as Alroy in the
East at that time.

THE BOOK OF ELIJAH

Buttenweiser Text (B)[237]   *Ibn Shmuel Text (IS)*[238]

He lay down and slept under a   He lay down and slept under a

[237]This text is from M. Buttenweiser, *Die Hebraische Elias-Apokalypse* (Leipzig, 1897),
15-26.
[238]The manuscript for this text belonged to Rav Y.L. Fishman, but it is no longer

B

broom tree, and behold this angel was touching him, and he said to him, "Arise, eat!" (I Kgs 19:5).

Michael, the great prince of Israel (Dan 12:1) revealed this mystery to the prophet Elijah on Mount Carmel: the end and the time which is destined to take place at the end of the four kingdoms.[239]

Elijah said:

The spirit of God took me up and brought me to the south of the world (Ezek 11:24; see also 3:12, 14; 8:3; 11:10),[240] and I saw there a high place,[241] burning with fire, and no creature was able to enter there.[242]

IS

broom tree, and behold this angel was touching him, and he said to him, "Arise, eat!" Then he looked and behold at the place of his head was a cake [baked on] coals and a flask of water, so he ate and drank and again lay down (I Kgs 19:5-6).

This is the mystery which Michael, the great prince of Israel (Dan 12:1) revealed to Elijah (May he be remembered for blessing) on Mount Carmel: the end and the time at which the end of the four kingdoms[239] was destined to take place.

Elijah said:

The spirit of God took me up and brought me to the east of the world (Ezek 11:24; see also 3:12, 14; 8:3; 11:10),[240] and I saw there a high place,[241] burning with fire, and no creature was able to enter there,[242] as it is said, *For no man will see me*

---

available. It is now preserved in Y. Ibn Shmuel, *Redemption,* 51-54. Dr. Ibn Shmuel frequently altered texts to improve the organization, logic, or to make them conform to other texts. Therefore this text may not be exactly like Rav Fishman's text.

[239]The four kingdoms are the four that ruled the Jews from the time of the Babylonian captivity until the restoration of the promised land under Hasmonean rule. The "end" expected there was the end of the foreign rule. Here the end expected is exactly the same, also to be followed by another restoration of the Jews on the promised land free from foreign rule. Symbolically the "fourth" kingdom is always the one in power, which the Jews are trying to overthrow, just before the Jews expect to gain control.

[240]In these paragraphs, B is more concise, but includes the basic content of the IS text. Either IS expanded or B summarized, or they used the same basic text differently. They differ in directions: B has "south" where IS has "east," etc. South probably refers to Egypt and east to Jerusalem.

[241]A temple area or place of worship.

[242]The holy of holies where no one may enter except the high priest.

B	IS
	and live (Ex 33:20).[243]
	Again *the spirit of God took me*
	up and brought me (Ezek 11:24)
	to the west of the world,[244] and
	behold many souls were

assigned to suffering, each according to his deeds. [The sinners] who rebelled excessively were judged publicly, as it is said, *"I will bring you for judgment, and I will be a witness quickly against magicians, adulterers, and those who take false oaths, and those who oppress the employee in wages, the widow, and the orphan, and turn away the stranger, and do not fear me,"* said the Lord of armies (Mal 3:5).

B	IS
Again *the spirit took me up and brought me* (Ezek 11:24) to the east of the world,[245] and I saw there stars battling, one against the other, and none of them resting.	Again *the spirit* of God *took me up and brought me to the south* (Ezek 11:24),[245] and behold there were seven stars making war with each other, and none of them was victorious over the other, as it is said, *From heaven they fought; the stars from their courses fought with Sisera* (Jdgs 5:20).[246]
Again *the spirit took me up and brought me* (Ezek 11:24) to the west of the world,[244] and I saw there souls judged by hardship, each according to his deeds.[247]	
Then Michael said to me, "The end is destined to take place	[Then] Michael said to me, "The end and the time which is destined to take place at the end of days will be at the end of the

---

[243]God was only to be seen through the smoke in the holy of holies by the high priest. See further *To The Hebrews*, 157-62.

[244]Probably Rome.

[245]East of the world is probably Jerusalem, and the south, Egypt.

[246]The battle of the stars resulted in a military victory of Israel against Sisera and the Philistines.

[247]As recorded in the treasury of merits.

B

in the last days of a king who is destined to be. His name is Harmelat (but there are some who say, 'Tarmila will be his name;[248] Rabbi Simai says, 'Hachsharat[249] will be his name'; Rabbi Elazar says, 'Hartaḥshasta[250] is his name'; Rabbi Judah Ben Batira says, 'Cyrus is his name';

Rabbi Shimon Ben Yoḥai says, 'Hachsera[251] is his name,' and the *halakhah is according* to Rabbi Shimon who said, 'Hachsera[251] will be his name.')"

A later king of Persia will go up to Rome for three years, one after the other, until the time he will strip it bare for twelve months. Then three mighty warriors will go up to meet him from the sea, but they will be delivered into the hands of a very despicable king, a maid's son, whose name is Gigit. [He will go up] to meet him from the sea. These will be his signs which Daniel saw in him: His face is long; there is baldness between his eyes;

IS

four kingdoms." He said further, "In that day, the last king is destined to take his stand. His name will be Tarmilat (but there are some who say Tacmilat;

Rabbi Eliezer, son of Jacob, said, 'His name is Koresh'; Rabbi says, 'Keshra is his name'; Rabbi Nehemiah says, 'His name is Artaḥshast'; Rabbi Shimon Ben Yoḥai says, 'Kasri is his name,' and the *halakhah* is according to Rabbi Shimon Ben Yoḥai who said, 'Kasri is his name.')"

The last king of Persia will go up to Rome for three years,

and three mighty warriors will come out to meet him from the sea, but they will be given over into his hand. One king, a nobody among kings, and the son of Sharani will go out to meet him from the sea. These are his signs:

His face is long; there is the long horn between his eyes which

---

[248]S. Krauss, "Der Romisch-Persische Krieg in der Judischen Elia-Apocalypse," *JQR* 14 (1902), 359-72, reads this to be Armilat.

[249]*Ibid.*, identifies this name with Artaxerxes.

[250]Krauss, "Der Romisch-Persische Krieg," 359-72, also identifies this name with Artaxerxes.

[251]*Ibid.*, Krauss identifies this name with Chosroes II (A.D. 590-628) who conquered Jerusalem in A.D. 614.

B

his height is very great; the
soles of his feet are high; and
his fore-legs are thin.[252]

He is destined to set his
hand one day against the faithful
people.
    On that day, there are
destined to be three disturbances:
All
the constellations will be
gathered to one place.[253]

[People] will exploit houses

and rob fields

and pervert justice of the
the orphan and the widow in the
market place, but if they do
penance,

they will be forgiven

    On the twentieth of
Kislev,[254] all Israelites will stand
in prayer and in crying before
their Father in heaven, and on

IS

Daniel saw (Dan 7:8); he has
two skulls; he has attractive
eyes; he is tall in stature;
and
his legs are thin; the soles of
his feet are long.[252]
He will begin to reach out his
hand against the
people of God.
    On that day, the world is
destined to witness three earthquakes: The sun, moon, and all
the constellations will be
gathered to one place at the end
of the fourth kingdom. All nations will be terrified there, and
there will be no peace.[253] The
Lord will say to the sons of
Ishmael, the sinners of Israel,

those who plunder one another,
those who rob each man his
neighbor, and those who take a
bribe, and pervert the justice of
the orphan and the widow falsely. But God said, "If they do
penance and pay attention to
the words of the Torah,
they will be forgiven,
as it is said, *Return, wayward
children. I will heal your
backslidings* (Jer 3:22).
    On the twenty-sixth of
the eighth month,[254]

[252]Description of Armilos, a caricature of Rome or the Christians.
    [253]These are reminiscences that suggest the astrological prophecy, "The Days of Tribula-
tion."
    [254]Differences of date and content suggest that these paragraphs may not be parallel, even
though they are parallel in order.

B

that day a sword will come
down and it will fall against the
Gentiles, as it is said, *Now one
and now another will the sword
devour* (II Sam 11:25).

On the twenty-second of
Nisan, the first exile will
go out from Babylon
with eighteen thousand men and
women
but none of them will perish.[255]

On the twenty-fifth of
Tishri, the second exile which is
in the river Sabation[256]
will go out
with seventeen thousand
but
twenty men and fifteen women
of their number will be killed.[257]

On the twenty-fifth of the
eighth month the third exile will
go out, weeping and crying out
for their brothers who have been
killed.

They will fast

IS

the world will shake violently
for its inhabitants, and the
earth will quake from its place,
as it is said, *Still once more, a
little while, and I will shake
the heaven, the earth, the sea
and the dry land* (Hag 2:6).

On the twenty-eighth of the
eighth month, the first exile will
go out into the wilderness
ten thousand men and eight
hundred, twenty women,
but none of them will perish.[255]

On the twenty-second of
of Nisan, the second exile

will go out into the wilderness,
eighteen thousand men and eight
hundred, sixteen women, but
thirty men and thirty-six women
of them will be killed, *and
escape will vanish from the
swift* (Amos 2:14).[257]

On the twenty-eighth of
Tishri the third exile will
go out into the wilderness,

sixteen thousand men and two
hundred, twenty women.
They will be hungry and thirsty,
and they will be pushed about,
weeping and lamenting over

[255]Note the differences of date and number of people.
[256]A mythical sand river somewhere in the East. The ten tribes were expected to return from the other side of that river and come to the aid of the southern two tribes. See p. 403, fn. 183.
[257]Note the differences of date and number of people.

B

IS

their brothers, and the righteous
in the wilderness for   will be in the wilderness for
forty-five days, and none of   thirty-nine days, without
them will taste anything, but   tasting anything at all, but
they will live by *that which*   they will live on all *that which]*
goes out of the mouth of the   *goes out of the mouth of the*
Lord (Dt 8:3).[258]   *Lord* (Dt 8:3).

"The first exile will not
go out from Babylon until the second reaches Babylon, as it is
said, *Be in pain and labor to bring forth, O daughter of Zion, [like
a woman giving birth, for you will go out of the city, and you will
dwell in the field, and you will come to Babylon. There you will be
delivered; there the Lord will redeem you from the hand of your
enemies]* (Micah 4:10).

(Elijah the prophet said):
"This is the Torah of which it is
said that *she is a tree of life
to those who lay hold upon her,*
and happy is everyone who holds her fast (Prov 3:18).

"On the twenty-sixth of Kislev, Israelites will stand in prayer
and supplication before their father in heaven. A sword on that
day is destined to fall on the Gentiles, as it is said, *The sword of
the Lord is full of blood* (Isa 34:6).[259]

"On the twentieth of Nisan   "On the ninth [of Nisan]
a king will go up   a king of Ishmael will go out.
from the sea. He will destroy
and disturb the world,

                                    He will leave all the world with-
and he will come to the top of   out food and come to the
the pleasant, holy mountain and   pleasant, holy mountain and
burn it.   burn it.
Cursed may his mother be among
women! He is the horn which   This is the horn which
Daniel saw.   Daniel saw: *From one of them
                                    will go out one small horn, and
                                    it will become very great, to-
                                    ward the South and to the East
                                    and to the pleasant [land]* (Dan

[258]Note the differences of date and number of people.
[259]See page 427, the text related to footnote 254, for an earlier parallel for this in B.

B

On that day, there will be
hardship   and
wars against Israel[260]

"Demetrius, son of
Porfos,[261] and Anfilipos, son
of Panfos,[262] will make a second
war, and with them will be ten
myriads of horsemen and ten
myriads of foot soldiers, and
they will be concealed in ten
myriads of ships.[263]

"On the twentieth of Elul,
the Messiah will come, and
his name
will be Yinon.
On that
day, Gabriel will come down
from nine to ten hours and
destroy ninety-two
thousand men from the world.[264]

"On the twentieth of
Tebeth, a third war will wage
from the border of Cirtilos,
including all their provinces,
a very great people, and from
the great valley as far as Yafo
and Ascalon.

IS

8:9). [On] that day, there will be
great distress in the world, and
there will be wars against Israel.[260]

"On the twenty-eighth of Elul,
the Messiah will go out from the
mountains of the age. His name
will be Yinon, and he will make
war with the Ishmaelites. In that
hour, Gabriel will go out with
him, and they will
destroy the enemy, ninety-two
thousand lives,
from three until nine hours.
Who will do it? Constantine
and Qartelius, and all the
camps with them until thirty
thousand myriads.[264]

[260]Note the differences of date. "The small horn" was the contemporary equivalent of
Antiochus IV Epiphanes, the Gentile king whose pressures against the Jews instigated the
Maccabean Revolt which led to the end of the age.

[261]Krauss, "Der Romisch-Persische Krieg," 359-72, identified Demetrius with Misitheus,
the prefect.

[262]Krauss, *Ibid.*, said this is Phillipus, the prefect.

[263]Krauss, *Ibid.*, reads, "There will be 30,000 concealed in ships."

[264]There are variants of date and hours Gabriel spent, but agreement on the number of
people killed.

B

IS

"On the twentieth of Shebat, the Messiah will come, and

"On the twentieth of Shebat, the Messiah will go out before them with thirty thousand myriads of righteous [soldiers], and they will confront each other. In that hour, the heavenly angels, and angelic saboteurs will go out and destroy them until not even one of them is left,[265] as it is said, *I will make my arrows drunk with blood, and my sword will consume flesh with the blood of the slain and captives, from the long-haired heads of the enemy* (Dt 32:42).

angelic saboteurs will come down and destroy all that mob, and they will not permit anything that breathes [to remain].[265]

"On the twentieth of Tebeth, in the seventh [year], a second war will take place. Demetrius, son of Phillip and nine myriads with him in a ship, ten myriads of horsemen and numberless infantry will shake [the world] violently. They will confront each other in a great valley, and he will pursue them until Yafo and Ascalon.

"On the first of Adar, the Messiah alone will go out before them. When each one of them sees the face of the Messiah, he and his horse will immediately be crushed, as it is said, *He will smite the land with the staff of his mouth; with the breath of his lips he will slay the wicked* (Isa 11:4).

B

IS

"At that time

the holy One blessed be He will say to Abraham, 'Your children are destined to be brought down, as it is said,

You shall speak out of the ground (Isa 29:4). After that they will be exalted above all the Gentiles, as it is said,

"On that day the Israelites will be like ministering angels, and the holy One blessed be He will remember for them his covenant with Abraham our father, because the Israelites will descend to the lowest degree, as it is said, *From the depths I have called to you, Lord* (Ps 130:1). Hence their horn will be raised, as it is said,

---

[265]B is much more succinct than IS, but holds the same basic content as IS.

B

The Lord your God will set you on high above all the Gentiles (Dt 28:1).[266]

"'After that, all the Gentiles will come and prostrate themselves before every single Israelite and lick the dust of his feet, as it is said, *Kings will be your foster fathers [and their queens, your nursing mothers; they will prostrate themselves before you and lick the dust of your feet]* (Isa 49:23).

"'On the twentieth of Adar, the Messiah will come and with him thirty thousand righteous [soldiers], as it is said, *Righteousness will be the girdle of his loins* (Isa 11:5). When the Gentiles see this, at once everyone of them will be crushed, he and his horse, as it is said, *This will be the plague with which the Lord will smite all the Gentiles* (Zech 14:22). At the time, the holy One blessed be He will say to the Gentiles, "Woe to you wicked ones, for all four of your kingdoms will be banished from the world."

IS

The Lord your God will set you on high above all the Gentiles (Dt 28:1).[266]

B

Then a *kor* of wheat will produce nine hundred *kors*, and the same will be true of wine and oil, and every single tree will be loaded with choice produce and fruits, as it is said, *You, Israel, behold your branches will produce [and they will bear fruit for my people, the Israelites]* (Ezek 36:8),

IS

"*It will be on that day that the mountains will drip sweet wine* (Joel 4:18). On that day one *kor* of wheat will produce nine hundred *kors*, and one *kor* of wine...

as it is said,

There will be in the land a handful of grain on the top of the mountains, and its fruit will shake like Lebanon (Ps 72:16),

because in the days of the Messiah, all the trees will be loaded with all kinds of fruit and all kinds of drink. Every hour the heavens

---

[266]Although some of the proof texts used are not the same, the same emotional content is contained in the texts.

IS

will be opened to him [the Messiah], and all secrets will be
revealed to him, as it is said, *Who has raised up one from the East,*
at whose step victory attends (Isa 41:2). [It is said], *The feeble*
among them will be in that day like David, and the house of David
like that of the gods, like an angel of the Lord before them (Zech
12:8). All the Gentiles will come and prostrate themselves before
every Israelite, and they will lick the dust of his feet,[267]

B	IS
and Israel will eat and drink for forty years. After this, the holy One blessed be He will bring up Gog and Magog and all his [military] flanks.	and [Israel] will eat and drink for forty years. After that, Gog and all his [military] flanks will come up against them, as it is said, *You will ascend and you will come*

like a storm; you will be like a cloud to cover the land, you and all
your [military] flanks and many peoples will be with you (Ezek
38:9).

On the twentieth of Iyyar, which is the twentieth year for the Messiah, there will be war. After all the peoples of the land	
	All the peoples of the land and the families of Babylon...when [there will be] two heads for
will have gathered and have sur-rounded Jerusalem	everyone, and they will sur-round Jerusalem, forty thousand camps. Every camp [will have] four hundred thousand towers, and for every tower, forty lad-ders. It will be one day for all, as it is said,
to fight against them,	*I will gather all the Gentiles to Jerusalem for war, and the city will be captured* (Zech 14:2).
The Messiah will come,	On that day the Messiah will go out before them, and over against him will be the righteous

[267]See page 432 for the earlier parallel in B.

B

and the holy
One blessed be He with his [the
Messiah's] help will wage war
with them, as it is said, *The
Lord will go out and fight with
those Gentiles as he fights in
the day of battle* (Zech 14:3).

IS

ones with him, and the holy
One blessed be He
will wage war
with them, as it is said, *The
Lord will go out and fight with
those Gentiles as he fights in
the day of battle* (Zech 14:3). It
also says, *The Lord will fight for
you, and you shall hold your
peace* (Ex 14:14).

On that day the mountains will quake, and the hills will dance; fortresses and towers will fall. Then the holy One blessed be He will bring every bird of heaven and the beasts of the earth to eat their flesh and drink their blood, as it is said, *The birds will summer on them, and all the beasts of the earth will winter on them* (Isa 18:6). The Israelites will heat [their houses] from the weapons for seven years, as it is said, *Those who dwell in the cities of Israel will go and make fires of their weapons and burn them for fuel, and they will make fires with them for seven years* (Ezek 39:9). They will bury them [the dead] for seven months, as it says, *The house of Israel will spend seven months burying them so as to purify the land* (Ezek 39:12).

"'These are the cities which will be destroyed: Jericho, Beirut,[268] Beit-horon, Sisrin,[269] Milkah, Arad,[270] Shallum, Samaria,[271] Beit-migdol,[272] Tyre, Beit-halsot, Lydda, Bux, Beit-einan,[273] Hamat-sefer, Hadashah,[274] Antioch, Alexandria, and Edom. All the cities of Israel they will surround with fire and angels of fire, as it is said, *"I will be to it,"* says the Lord, *"a surrounding wall of fire"* (Zech 2:9).

B

"'Then the last day
will come

IS

"What will happen on that
day? [In that day the world] will
be in turmoil together with all its

[268]Krauss, "Der Romisch-Persische Krieg," 359-72.
[269]Krauss, *Ibid.*, identified Sisrin with Susin.
[270]Krauss, *Ibid.*, identified Arad with Dora.
[271]Krauss, *Ibid.*, identified Samaria with Schimron.
[272]Krauss, *Ibid.*, changed Beit-migdol to read Magdiel.
[273]Krauss, *Ibid.*, took Beit-einan to be Einam.
[274]Krauss, *Ibid.*, took Hadashah to be Adasa.

B

which will endure for
forty days. The moun-
tains and the hills will totter
and quake

and the land will cry out against
the wicked ones and say, "In a
certain place, a certain person
killed a certain one," as it is
said, *And the land will reveal
her blood* (Isa 26:21).

IS

inhabitants. That period of time
will last forty days. The mountains and the hills will
quake, as it is said, *The mountains will be thrown down, and
the steep places will fall* (Ezek
38:20).

The sea and the depth will vanish, as it is said, *Deep calls to
the deep at the sound of your
cataracts; all your billows and waves have passed over me* (Ps
42:8). The towers will shake and fall, as it is said, *The Lord of
armies has a day upon all that are proud, and they will be brought
low* (Isa 2:12). All the world will tremble on account of Gog and
his bands [of soldiers]. Then stones from heaven will fall upon
them, hail stones and meteors which were prepared *for a time of
hardship, for a day of battle and war* (Job 38:23). [Israelites] will
keep a fire burning for seven years, as it is said, *The city dwellers
of Israel will go out and burn weapons, shields, bucklers, bows,
arrows, clubs, and spears, and they will light fires with them for
seven years* (Ezek 39:9). Then they will bury Gog and all his mob
for seven months, as it is said, *The house of Israel will bury them
for seven months so as to purify the land* (Ezek 39:12).

"The ministering angels will watch over the temple with a wall
of fire, as it is said, *'I will be with you,'* says the Lord, *'a surrounding wall of fire'* (Zech 2:9).[275] But the eye cannot see the greatness
and glory which the holy One blessed be He will provide his sons,
just as he did for our fathers in the wilderness, until they return
and inherit the land and the rest of his heritage, as it is said, *The
houses of Jacob will take possession of their possessions* (Obad
17), and it is said, *Therefore the Lord will wait to be gracious to
you, and therefore he will be exalted [so as] to be merciful to you*
(Isa 30:18), as he says, *For God will deliver Zion, and he will build
[the cities of Judah, where they will dwell and (which they will)*

[275]For the parallel see B, page 437-38.

IS

possess] (Ps 69:36). He also said, *[You will build] the walls of Jeru-salem* (Ps 51:20). After this the wicked and the heretics will be ashamed, and they will know that there is no one to worship [except God]. Those who worship idols will be ashamed and embarrassed, because they oppressed Israelites, as it is said, *Kings will be your foster fathers and their queens, your nursing mothers* (Isa 49:23). The sea of Tarshish will become a garden of pome-granites, and they will walk on it dry-shod, [because] *the Lord will destroy the tongue of the sea of Egypt, and he will wave his hand over the river with his scorching wind, and make [them] walk dry-shod over* (Isa 11:15). Then the Israelites will confess and praise the holy One blessed be He, as it is said, *We are your people and the flock of your pasture; we will give thanks to you for the age; for generation after generation we will tell of your praise* (Ps 79:13). They will say, *The Lord has become king; he is clothed in majesty; the Lord is clothed; he has girded himself [with] strength* (Ps 93:1).

B

Elijah said:

I see dead men drowned and their dust kneaded, and they became as they were at the beginning, [but] giving praise to God, as it is said, *See, now, that I, I am he, [and there is no God except me; I will kill and I revive]* (Dt 32:39). Thus [also] Ezekiel says, *I looked and behold upon them were sinews* (Ezek 37:8). The minis-tering angels will open their graves and put their breath within them, and they will live, and they will stand them upon their feet. Everyone who was guilty in judgment, they will oppress with great pain.[276] Its length will be two thousand cubits and its width, fifty cubits. Everyone who does not desire the Torah of the holy One blessed be He, the eyes of the righteous will see his downfall, as it is said, *And they went out and saw the corpses of the men who transgress against me* (Isa 66:24).

Elijah said:

I see fire and brimstone coming down from heaven against the wicked, as it is said, *He will rain snares, fire, and brimstone upon*

[276]There seems to be a break between the end of this sentence and the beginning of the next. The next sentence describes the measurements of something about which the reader was expected to know, apparently Gehinnom, but the context as now preserved is missing. This seems to be an abridgment or splicing of sources.

B

the wicked (Ps 11:6). Then the holy One blessed be He will move the temple a great distance away from the destruction of the age, so that the righteous will not hear the voice of crying of the wicked and seek mercy for them. They will be as if they never existed.
Elijah said:

I see Abraham, Isaac, and Jacob, and all the righteous sitting, and the land sown before them with all kinds of delicacies and that tree which the holy One blessed be He prepared in the midst of the garden, as it is said, *Alongside the river banks on both sides will grow every fruit tree; its leaf will not wither nor its fruit fail* (Ezek 47:12). Ships will come from Ain Gedi to Ain Eglaim,[277] loaded with great wealth for the righteous.
Elijah said:

I see a city [that is] beautiful and glorious, where splendor descends from heaven as it was when built, as it is said, *Jerusalem that is built like a city that is compact together* (Ps 122:3), built and perfected, and with it, perched in its midst, are three thousand towers, and between one tower and the next will be [a distance of] twenty *ris* [ca. 43 miles], and between each *ris* will be twenty-five thousand cubits of emeralds, precious stones, and pearls, as it is said, *I will make your windows of agates, [your gates of carbuncles, and all your borders of precious stones]* (Isa 54:12).
Elijah said:

I see houses and gates of the righteous, their thresholds and their doorposts of precious stones, and the treasures of the temple are opened wide, among them is the Torah of peace, as it is said, *all your sons will be taught of the Lord [and great will be the peace between you]* (Isa 54:13), and it says, *How great is your goodness which you have laid up for those who fear you, [which you have done for those who trust you]* (Ps 31:20).

Summary

Taking as his cue I Kings 19:5-6, the editor or one of his sources imagined that which Elijah saw in his dream while he slept. His dreams took him all over the world, as Enoch's did in his vision.

---

[277]Ain Eglaim is modern Ain Feshka on the eastern coast of the Dead Sea, north of Ain Gedi and south of Qumran. W.R. Farmer, "The Geography of Ezekiel's River of Life," *BA* 19 (1956), 17-22.

He first dreamed of general things, but later got to the point that interested medieval Jews—What will happen in the future to Israel to enable her to regain the promised land. The events related belonged to the seventh century, when Persia ruled Jerusalem. The last king of Daniel's fourth kingdom was identified with the "last" Persian king, Chosroes II. Familiar eschatological expectations, such as Armilos and the days in the wilderness as well as the advent of the Messiah were repeated also in this apocalypse. Israel will be exalted to its destined status and the Gentiles will be reduced to dire humility. The great battle will be fought near Jerusalem, with Jews victorious, the dead will be raised to face judgment, and Jerusalem will be reconstructed to even greater luster and majesty than before its destruction.

This apocalypse was mostly written about the seventh century, perhaps using earlier sources and possibly including a few later additions.

A LEGEND OF RABBI ISHMAEL[278]

Rabbi Ishmael said:

I set my mind to investigate and explore with wisdom and to consider the appointed times, 1) times, minutes, and end times, *A time* (עד), *two times*, and *an appointed time* (מועד), *two appointed times* (Dan 7:25 and 12:7), and I set my face to sanctify 2) the Most High in prayer and supplication,[279] with fasting and in sack cloth and mourning. Thus I was praying and saying, "Lord God of armies, God of Israel, how long will we be abandoned, scattered, and made for mockery and derision among the Gentiles? All who see us mock us and say, 'These are the people of the Lord! Why has he smitten them? Why has he cast them away from him? Because of the magnitude of their iniquity and the number of their sins. Look, he abhors and detests them. Therefore he has removed them from his presence and will never again restore them...'"

Rabbi Ishmael said:

Acatriel, Lord God of Israel, said this to me: 3)

"My friend, Ishmael, you know that I have only allowed all the Gentiles to enslave the Israelites 4) for one day of this age,[280] because they have forsaken me and sinned against me by

---

[278]Ch. M. Horowitz, בית עקד האגדות, 59-61. SML

[279]By reciting the qadesh.

[280]That is for a small portion of the whole, measured chronologically rather than spatially. Therefore it is this *age* and not this *world*, as many translators interpret.

worshipping other gods, and they have set up an image in my house and have removed my Shekinah from me, in which I have sworn to make my name dwell for the age. They have provoked me to anger and have rebelled against me, they, their kings, their princes, their priests, and their prophets. 5) They have separated from me for seven hundred years, and I have sworn that I would humble them under iron and clay. They will kill their princes, and they will destroy their kings. They have made their young men childless,[281] and they have torn their infants to pieces. They have made the yokes of their elders heavy, and they have attacked them until they have rotted away in their iniquities and in the iniquities of their fathers. Either 6) they return to me or the end will be fulfilled![282] Therefore I have sent through my servants, the prophets, [the message] that I am destined to visit upon them the days of the *baalim* to whom they have offered incense. Just as they have made me angry for seven hundred years, so will I make them angry and make them jealous through a foolish nation and through a nation to which I have not apportioned any kingdom 7) in the day when I cast the lots of all the peoples *just because [they spurned my ordinances, and their soul abhorred my statutes]"* (Lev 26:43).

Rabbi Ishmael said:

When I heard, *just because,* my hands became weak, and I fell full length on my face, and I was terrified. I had no strength either to speak or to answer. At once Mettatron, minister of the interior,[283] said to me, 8) "My friend, arise and stand up, and strengthen your loins, and understand and grasp the words which he will speak to you."

Then I heard a voice proceeding 9) from between the *Cherubim* and saying, "My friend, Ishmael, do not be afraid, because I will not 10) pay them back [in retribution] measure for measure, because I know that they do not have strength [enough] to stand [up to it] unless I act for the sake of my name, so I will create division 11) among the Gentiles [and set up] great animosity between Edom and Ishmael,[284] so that some will be incited against the others, and they will not [unite] so as to destroy my people, the Israelites."

[281]By emasculating them so that they could be sold as eunuchs.

[282]The exile will last for the fully prescribed sentence. There will be no suspension of the sentence, pardon, or any other release.

[283]The angelic officer in the most inward office, nearest to the Lord.

[284]The author here interpreted the rise of Mohammedism as the work of the Lord to destroy the Roman Christians. This would weaken the Gentiles generally, and Israel would be relieved. Apocalyptists have always seen international disaster as signs of deliverance. When there are wars and rumors of wars, then the end must be near when the covenanters

Rabbi Ishmael said:

I sat down, and I was calculating the sum total which was given to me the first time,[265] and I reckoned: 12) seventy years for Babylon, fifty-two years for Media, a hundred, eighty for Greece. I did not find a reckoning [for the time to be spent] in Edom until I stood in prayer and in fasting as I did at first,[265] day after day. 13) Immediately I heard a *bat qol*[266] go forth and say, "My friend, Ishmael, you know that if Israelites repented at once they would be redeemed, for I noted this for Isaiah, *In repentance* 15) *and rest you will be saved*" (Isa 30:15).

I responded to the word which he spoke and said, "This is the end of this wicked kingdom, but I am not able to pass on the revelation." I heard a *bat qol* proclaim, "My friend, Ishmael, after *the construction of the house of the king of Persia* is completed, 16) seven hundred years will pass, and everything on the face of the earth will be ended. [When] they are gone, he will purify their iniquities. Just as they have forsaken me seven hundred years and served *Baalim*, so I will abandon them into the hand of cruel men for seven hundred years with none to save them: no priest or teacher, no prophet or king, no leader or general until they return and repent with prayer and supplications. They will then seek my face, and I will find them and return them to their land."

I replied to the one who had spoken and said, 17) "If they do not repent, will they not be redeemed for the age?"[287] He replied, "I will raise up over them a king whose [anti-Jewish] decrees will be more severe than those of Haman. Against their will, and not out of the goodness [of their hearts] will they return to me. He will be the brazen faced king, 18) understanding riddles, 19) *and he will*

---

can get themselves into power. Apocalyptists become discouraged at international *detente*. When the report came back that the world was at peace, the angel of the Lord complained, "O Lord of armies, how long will you have no mercy on Jerusalem and the cities of Judah against which you have had indignation these seventy years" (Zech 1:12). In this author's judgment, Jeremiah's prophesied seventy years was up and the covenanters had a right to expect international disaster that would give the Jews a chance to gain possession of the land again.

[265]This implies that this story is only a part of a longer narrative in which Rabbi Ishmael had been given a list for calculation before. There are several apocalyptic narratives related to Rabbi Ishmael. Perhaps in other collections, several were put together. The present text, however, has no antecedent for this reference, unless 19-22 once was arranged before these lines.

[266]Literally a "daughter of a voice." Refers either to a lull, an echo, or a voice with a message from God.

[287]Either, will they not be redeemed before their sentence expires, having it reduced for good behavior? or will they not even be admitted into the messianic age when the time comes?

speak words against the Most High, and he will wear out the saints of the Most High. He will think he can change the times and the law, and they will be given into his hand for a time, two times, and half a time (Dan 7:25).

Rabbi Ishmael said:

I was calculating:[288] with a total of 20) seventy years for Babylon, fifty-two [years] for Media, a hundred and eighty [years] for Greece, about three hundred, fifty 21) [years are left to complete the seven hundred years after the destruction of the second temple [70+52+180+350=652 and not 700. 700 years after A.D. 70 (or 68) is A.D. 770 (or 768)]. I examined the books which Daniel had closed and sealed, and I found that which was written, 22) *Seventy weeks are decreed upon your people and on your holy city to complete the transgression, finish the sin, and atone the iniquity* (Dan 9:24). Soon (ועֶן עֵי) the righteous One of the ages will bring the Messiah who has been covered up and sealed to all the prophets. He will *anoint the holy of holies* (Dan 9:24).[289]

As it has been explained, 23) *Seventy weeks of years are decreed upon your people and upon your holy city* (Dan 9:24). These seventy weeks hint at the seven hundred years. When these [seventy weeks] are finished, these [seven hundred years] will be finished. 24) At evening time, immediately the light will come, as it is said, *It will be at evening time there will be light* (Zech 14:7).

Summary

This apocalypse was closely related to historical events. The author expected the scripture to be fulfilled, so he counted the years the Jews had been in captivity and calculated a scheme whereby the prophecy in Daniel was to be fulfilled shortly after the time he wrote. The Moslems drove out the Christians and took control of Palestine in A.D. 638. The early reaction of Judaism to the change of powers was favorable. Moslems allowed Jews to return to Jerusalem as the Christians had not. One of Mohammed's

[288]Note the parallelism between these lines and 11-15. The reference in line 11 to an earlier "first time" may mean that lines 19-22 were once organized in a position which placed them first and 11-15 second, but this is a conjecture.

[289]There are problems with this calculating. 70+52+180+350 equals 652, but the author wanted his total to concur with 700 to match the 70 years mentioned by Dan 9:24. 652 years after A.D. 68 would total A.D. 720 as the year the end time was expected. This means the author wrote before that time and did not want to extend the time to a full 700 years to make A.D. 770. By A.D. 770 most Jews did not look to the Moslems as hopeful deliverers of the Jews from the hands of the Christians.

wives had been Jewish. The author of this apocalypse interpreted the wars between Christians and Moslems to be the work of God who was dividing the forces of the Gentiles so that Jews could more easily conquer and rule all the Gentiles. The author expected Jews to be able to do this by A.D. 720 or 722, depending on whether he calculated from A.D. 68 or 70. Consistent with Jewish theology, the author believed Israelites were currently suffering because of their own sinfulness, and if they would just repent their sentence would be reduced and the end time would come much sooner.

THE JUDGMENT OF JEWS AND GENTILES[270]

The Lord will be King for an age and still (Ex 15:18).

Our sages (May they be remembered for blessing) said, "Moses said to the Israelites, 'You have seen the miracles and the mighty deeds which the holy One blessed be He did for you. More and more is he destined to do for you in the future, both in this age and in the age to come. In this age, wars, hardships, the evil impulse, Satan, and the angel of death have permission to rule in the world, but in the age to come, there will be no hardships, no sighing, no subjection, no evil impulse, no Satan, and no angel of death, as it is said, *The Lord God will wipe away the tears from all faces* (Isa 25:8), and it is written, *On that day he will say, "Behold, this is our God; we have hoped in him, and he will deliver us. This is our Lord; we have hoped in him. Let us be glad and rejoice in his salvation"* (Isa 25:9).

When the days of the Messiah arrive, Gog and Magog will go up against the land of Israel, because he will hear that the Israelites are without a king and that they are dwelling securely. At once he will take with him seventy-one nations and go up to Jerusalem. He will say, "Pharaoh was an idiot when he decreed to kill the males and spare the females. Balak was a fool when he wanted to curse them and did not know that their God was blessing them. Haman was [equally] crazy when he wanted to kill them but did not know that their God was able to save them. I, however, will not deal with them thus. I will go up and fight with their God first. After that, I will kill them, as it is said, *The kings of the land will establish themselves, and the rulers will take counsel together against the*

[270]The text is from the concluding section of " מדרש ויושע ," J.D. Eisenstein (ed.), אוצר מדרשים I (New York, 1956), 155b-156a. SML

Lord and against his Messiah (Ps 2:2). The holy One blessed be He will say to him, "Wicked one! Will you try to make war with me? By your life, [you will soon see how] I will deal with you!" Hailstones that are stored up in the firmament will descend upon them immediately, and he will strike them a mighty blow, as it is said, *This is the plague which the Lord will afflict on all the Gentiles who make war against Jerusalem. Their flesh will rot while they stand on their feet, and their eyes will rot in their sockets. Their tongue will rot in their mouths* (Zech 14:12).[291] After him another wicked and insolent king will arise and make war with the Israelites for three months. His name will be Armilos, and these are his signs: He will be bald, with one small eye and one large one. His right arm will be one span long, and his left arm will be two and a half cubits long. He will have leprosy on his forehead, and his right ear will be stopped up, but his left one will be open. When someone comes to tell him [something] good, he will extend to him his deaf ear, but if he wishes to impart evil things to him, he will extend to him his open ear. He will go up against Jerusalem and kill the Messiah son of Joseph, as it is said, *They will look at me whom they have stabbed. Then they will mourn for him as one mourns for his only son* (Zech 12:10).

After that the Messiah son of David will come with a cloud, as it is said, *One like a son of man will come with the clouds of heaven* (Dan 7:13), after which it is written, *And to him will be given dominion, glory, and a kingdom* (Dan 7:14). He will kill the wicked Armilos, as it is said, *With the breath of his lips he will kill the wicked* (Isa 11:4).

After that the holy One blessed be He will gather the exiles of Israel who are scattered here and there, as it is said, *I will whistle for them, and I will gather them, for I have redeemed them, and they will multiply as they multiplied [in the past]* (Zech 10:8). There will be suspended in Jerusalem seventy-two jewels that will shine from one end of the world to the other, and the Gentiles will walk by the aid of that light, as it is said, *Gentiles will walk by your light and kings at the brightness of your rising* (Isa 60:3). Then the holy One blessed be He will bring down the temple from heaven, just as the holy One blessed be He showed to Moses, as it is said, *You will bring them, and you will plant it in the mountain of your inheritance, the place of your residence, you have done the work, O Lord* (Ex 15:17).

[291] The Hebrew changes from singular to plural in this passage. To maintain consistency, the pronouns are kept in the plural throughout in the translation.

Israelites will dwell there for two thousand years, and they will eat of the Leviathan. At the end of two thousand years, the holy One blessed be He will sit on the throne of judgment in the Valley of Jehoshaphat. At once the heaven and earth will be changed. The sun and the moon will be ashamed, as it is said, *The moon will be disgraced, and the sun, ashamed* (Isa 24:23). From where do you find that on the third day [the third millennium] there will be the judgment? Because it is said, *On the third day he will raise us up that we may live in his presence* (Hos 6:2). This will be the judgment. The holy One blessed be He will bring [the people] of every nation and tongue and say to them, "Whom did you serve in the world where you walked, and whom did you worship?" They will answer, "Idols of silver and gold." The holy One blessed be He will say to them, "Pass through this fire, and if your gods are able to save you, let them save [you]." They will immediately pass through and be burned there, as it is said, *The wicked will return to Sheol, all the Gentiles who have forgotten God* (Ps 9:18). After that the Israelites will come, and the holy One blessed be He will say to them, "Whom did you serve?" They will answer, *You are our Father. We did not know Abraham nor did we recognize Israel. You, O Lord, are our Father [and] our Redeemer. From the age is your name* (Isa 63:16). The holy One blessed be He will immediately deliver them from the judgment of Gehinnom and place them in the Garden of Eden where they will enjoy its fruits, as it is said, *The humble will inherit the land and delight themselves in the abundance of peace* (Ps 37:11).

After that the holy One blessed be He will renew for them heaven and earth, as it is said, *For behold I will create a new heaven and a new earth* (Isa 65:17). The land which the holy One blessed be He is destined to renew will produce good trees and all kinds of choice things. Every living being will live for an age and ages of ages. May the one who will perform the miracles and wonders in those days perform also miracles and wonders in our days and in this time, and may he gather us together from the four corners of the earth and lead us to Jerusalem. May it be built and established quickly, in our days. Amen.

Summary

This portion of "Wayosha" is a unit as is indicated by the introductory and final references to miracles, forming an inclusion.

This eschatological story includes many of the standard *dramatis personae*: The two messiahs, Armilos, the war of Gog and Magog, the son ˹f man on the clouds of heaven, redemption of Jews and their restoration to Palestine, the final judgment, the millennial divisions of the future, the destruction of the Gentiles, and the age of bliss for Jews. There are no good historical clues to determine the place and time of its origin, but the imagery is consistent with other medieval Jewish concepts.

REDEMPTION AND WAR[292]

Open for me, my sister, my beloved (SS 5:2).

This refers to the days of Gog, when the Israelites are destined to be hidden in caves and holes [in the ground], and the holy One blessed be He will be knocking for them. 4)

Shimon Ben Shetah used to say, "When the holy One blessed be He will say to Israel, *Open for me, my sister* (SS 5:2), they will be looking and the Lord will be performing miracles for them. They will see the Messiah, standing on the top of the Wilderness of Moab and there will be four hundred men with him, and the Lord will give them redemption to confirm that which was said, *Therefore, behold, I will lure her and lead her to the wilderness, and I will speak to her heart; and I will give her from there her vineyards* (Hos 2:16-17). Then the cave will be opened for them from there [in] the Wilderness of Moab to Horeb, and the Israelites will go and take weapons from the Wilderness of Horeb, because the Name is written in it. They will [then] go and conquer Ammon and Moab to confirm that which is said, *They will put forth their hand against Edom and Moab, and the children of Ammon will obey them"* (Isa 11:14).

Rabbi Jose Ben Judah said, 5) "In the way which the legions made for them a desirable house, thus Horeb was made for the Israelites a desirable house."

When the kings of the North hear that the Ammonites and the Moabites have been slain, all of them will congregate and come and establish the kingdom in Damascus. The kings of the West and the South, even they, will congregate and come and hold counsel at Midian. 6) The Egyptian Israelites [will think] it is impossible to leave the scholars in Midian and to leave their brothers who are in

---

[292]The text is from S. Buber, *Midrasch Suta Hagadische Abhandlungen uber Schir ha-Schirim, Ruth, Eikah, und Koheleth* (Berlin, 1894), 33-34, 5:4-13. SML

Jerusalem [so they will come to their aid]. 7) The Lord will provide a way out for Elijah, and he will go out to Midian and leave the scholars whᴏ are in Jerusalem. What will Elijah do? He will make all the wilderness where he walks from Jerusalem to Midian, which is completely rocky and full of evil beasts, a place of miracles. Then he will come and stand before the Messiah in Midian. The Messiah will leave from there, but Elijah will remain. At that time he will bring out the *Book of Yashar*, from which all this Torah has only one song: *The land was opened...from under them* and *burned them, and there was for them there a large grave* (Num 26:10). This is the fulfillment of [the verse], *Open for me, my sister, my beloved* (SS 5:2).

The Messiah will come from Midian and take all of its booty. Then [he will go] to Damascus and take its booty, to fulfill that which was said, *The wealth of Damascus will be taken away* (Isa 8:4). [He will continue from place to place] until [only] the king-dom of Edom has not fallen. There will be a door from there to Rome, to fulfill that which was said, *There the calf will graze, and there it will lie down* (Isa 27:10). 8) *For my head is filled with dew* (SS 5:2). 9) The holy One blessed be He said, "The man is like this sleeper. I will arouse him." Look, the kings of the East will congregate at Tadmore, and the Israelites will come from Rome. 10) They will offer sacrifices in Jerusalem for seven days. Then the holy One blessed be He will restore the spirit and say to the Israel-ites, "Return to Tadmore against the kings of the East!" The kings of the East will say, "He is giving the Israelites permission to build the house of the sanctuary," and they will come to burn it. Then the holy One blessed be He will go out and fight with them, to ful-fill that which is said, *The Lord will go out and fight with those Gentiles* (Zech 14:3). 11)

The Messiah will come to him to Tyre, Sidon, Tadmore, Biria 12) to confirm that which is said, *They will put forth their hand against Edom and Moab, and the children of Ammon will obey them* (Isa 11:14).

All the Gentiles are destined to hear, and they will congregate near Pugah,[293] 13) and Acre. They will weep over the area spread out around Acre and all the Jordan. All the Israelites will show [them] this prison which is in pitch darkness.

Then the holy one blessed be He will tear open the heavens and show to the Israelites his glorious throne. They will pray, and he

---

[293] A place near Jerusalem.

will accept them, to fulfill that which is said, *Open for me, my sister, my beloved* (SS 5:2).

Summary

This is a typical midrashic unit. The topic is based on the text from the Song of Solomon which opens the discussion, is repeated twice within the unit, and also closes the topic, forming an inclusion of the narrative. Rabbis normally interpreted the Song of Solomon eschatologically, and this is no exception. The invitation to "open" suggested a situation whereby the Lord would be knocking at the door of the Israelites, waiting for them to open. It also suggested openings in the ground which swallowed up the enemies, provided underground passages, and caves for hiding. The battle of Gog and Magog is central to the thesis, with Israel fighting the Gentiles victoriously in all surrounding locations. The Israelites conclude the experiences with the enemies defeated and God opening up the heavens and showing the Israelites his glorious throne, indicating that now that the kingdom of Israel was established, he could rule from his throne.

ESCHATOLOGICAL LEGENDS

THE HIDDEN MESSIAH[1]

Rabbi Samuel Bar Naḥman said, "Wherever the words *wayehi* (ויהי-"and it has happened" or "and it will happen") occur, it signifies trouble, but wherever the words *wehayah* (והיה-"and it will happen" or "and it happened") occur, it spells joy, as it is said, *And it happened (wehayah) whenever the stronger of the flock were breeding* (Gen 30:21).[2] How joyous it was there when the righteous man received the reward of his toil! [For further examples], as it is said, *And it will happen (wehayah) in that day that the mountains will drop down sweet wine* (Joel 4:18); *[And it will happen (wehayah) in that day] living water will go out [from Jerusalem]* (Zech 14:8); *[And it will happen (wehayah) in that day] the Lord will set his hand a second time [to recover the remnant of his people]* (Isa 11:11); *[And it will happen (wehayah) in that day] a man will rear a heifer [and two sheep; and it will happen (wehayah) because of the abundance of milk which they will give he will eat curd]* (Isa 7:21-22); *[And it will happen (wehayah) in that day] that a great shofar[3] will be blown [and those who are lost in the land of Assyria and were dispersed in the land of Egypt will come and worship the Lord on the holy mountain at Jerusalem]* (Isa 27:13); *And it will happen (wehayah) that he who is left in Zion [and he who remains in Jerusalem will be called holy]*" (Isa 4:3).

They asked him, "But is it not written, *And it happened (wehayah) when Jerusalem was taken* (Jer 38:28)? [How about that?]" He replied "Even this is not distress, but happiness, for it was on that day that Menahem[4] was born, and it was on that day that the Israelites received compensation with respect to their iniquities." Rabbi Samuel Bar 131) Naḥman had said [on another occasion], "Israelites received a great compensation[5] for their iniquities on the days when the house of the sanctuary was destroyed, as it is said, *[The punishment for] your iniquity is accomplished, [daughter of*

[1]This is a variant and longer version of the legend from Lamentations Zuta. The text is from Ch. Albek, *Midras Beresit Rabbati* (Jerusalem, 1940), daf 84-85, pages 130, line 25-131, line 26. Commentary on Gen 30:41. SML

[2]This is a reference to the way Jacob out witted his father-in-law, Laban, to get the best of a business deal.

[3]As in jubilee to announce that all debtor slaves are to be liberated and the land sold for indebtedness by Jews, restored to the original owners.

[4]The traditional name given for the expected Messiah son of David. The name means "comforter."

[5]In the treasury of merits, many debts were cancelled.

Zion; he will no more extend your exile] (Lam 4:22). Where [do you find] that it was on the day that the Messiah was born? Because it is said, *Before she travailed, [before the birth pangs came upon her, she bore a boy]* (Isa 66:7).

Elijah (May he be remembered for blessing) was walking on the way on that day when the house of the sanctuary was destroyed, and he heard a *bat qol*[6] crying out, "The house of the holy of holies (131:5) is to be destroyed; the sons of the king will be sent into captivity; the wife of the king will be kept a widow (*daf* 85), as it is said, *How does the city full of people dwell alone? [How] has she become a widow"* (Lam 1:1)? When Elijah heard that, he said, "He has decided to destroy the whole world!" He went and found men who were plowing and sowing. He said to them, "The holy One blessed be He has become angry with his world, and he wishes to destroy his house and cause his children to be taken captive among the Gentiles, and yet you are busy with ephemeral matters?" A *bat qol* went out and said to him, "Let them alone, for already their deliverer (131:10) has been born!" He said to it [the *bat qol*], "Where is he?" [The voice] responded, "In Bethlehem of Judah."

He went and found a woman sitting at the door of her house, and her son was stained [with blood] and lying before her. He said to her, "My daughter, have you given birth to a son?" She replied, "Yes." He said, "What is the reason that he is stained with blood?" She replied, "Great is the evil, because on the [very] day he was born, the house of the sanctuary was destroyed." He said to her, "My daughter, arise and take hold of him, because already there will be a great salvation for you at his hands." She arose at once and took hold of him [the child]. He gave her garments with which to dress him (131:15) and ornaments with which to adorn him, but she did not want to accept [them]. He said to her, "Accept them from me, and I will come later to receive payment for them." He [then] left her and went away for five years.

After five years, he said, "I will [now] go and see the deliverer of the Israelites, whether he is growing up resembling kings or resembling ministering angels." He went and found the woman standing at the door of her house. He said to her, "My daughter, what sort of child has he become?" She replied, "Rabbi, did I not tell you that his fortune [would be] bad, because on the day when he was born, the house of the sanctuary was destroyed? (131:20) Although he has legs, he does not walk; although he has ears, he does not hear; although he has eyes, he does not see; although he

[6]Literally, "a daughter of a voice." It means a message from God.

has a mouth, he does not speak. See, he is lying [there] like a stone." While she was speaking, a wind from the four corners of the world blew and cast him into the Great Sea.[7] [Elijah] tore his clothes and plucked out his hair. Then he cried out and said, "Lord, the salvation of Israel has perished!" A *bat qol* went out and said, "Elijah, it is not as you think, but he will dwell for four hundred years in the Great Sea, and for eighty years after the smoke has gone up, near the sons of (131:25) Korah and for eighty years at the gate of Rome. The remaining years he will roam over all the great states until the time of the end."

Summary

Just as great leaders like Xerxes, Sargon, and Moses were attributed unusual birth narratives, so the Messiah was the subject of such creative narration. Two different narratives were attributed to Jesus' birth. In other traditions, it is the son of Joseph, Nehemiah, who was hidden in Rome, suffering for the sins of Israel. This entire composition was prompted by the expression, *wehayah*, which occurred in the text to which the commentator turned his attention.

THE BIRTH OF THE MESSIAH

Lamentations 1:2 Zuta[8]	Echa Rabbati[9]
It once happened when a	
	There is none to comfort her of all her lovers (Lam 1:2).
	They said: The day when the enemies entered the city and destroyed the sanctuary, there was outside of Jerusalem a certain Jew, plowing with his plow. He
man was plowing	saw that his cow with which he was plowing made herself fall to the ground. The man saw her and was very much alarmed. He

[7]The Mediterranean Sea.
[8]From Lamentations Zuta 452-62 (45a-45b), commentary on Lam 1:2.
[9]From Lamentations Rabbati 2:1-2, commentary on Lam 1:2.

Lam 1:2 Zuta	*Echa Rabbati*
	was hitting the cow so that she would plow, but she did not want to. She kept falling to the ground, and he kept on hitting her continually until he heard a voice
that his ox was mooing. An Arab passed by and said, "Who are you?" [The man] said, "I am a Jew." [The Arab] said to him, "Unharness your ox, and release your plow!" [The Jew] said, "Why?" [The Arab]	
replied, "Because the house of the sanctuary has been destroyed."	saying, "What are you doing to the cow? Let her alone, for she is crying out because of the destruction of the house and the sanctuary which was burned today."
[The Jew] said to him, "How do you know?" [The Arab] replied, "I know this from the mooing of your ox."	
	When the man heard he immediately tore his garments, plucked out his hair, wept, and put ashes on his head, crying, "Woe to me! woe to me!"ᶜ
While they were engaged in this conversation, the cow mooed a second time.	After two or three hours, the cow stood up on her feet, danced, and was happy. The man was very much astonished.
[The Arab] said to him, "Harness your ox and hitch up your plow, because the savior of the Jews is born."	He heard a voice saying, "Harness [the cow] and plow, for at this hour the Messiah was born." [When the man heard this] he washed his face, arose, and was happy.
[The Jew] said to him, "What is his name?" [The Arab] replied,	

Lam 1:2 Zuta	Echa Rabbati

Lam 1:2 Zuta

"Menahem is his name." [The Jew asked], "What is his father's name?" [The Arab] replied, "Hezekiah." [The Jew] asked, "Where do they live?" [The Arab] answered, "In an Arabian city of Bethlehem of Judea." The man went and sold his ox and his plow and took

to selling felt clothes for children. He entered and left city after city, until he reached that city [of Bethlehem]. All the villages were buying from him, but not that woman who was the mother of that

child.

He said to her, "Why do you not buy children's clothing from me?" She replied,

"Because it is hard for my child." He asked her, "Why?" She replied, "Because it was on his account that the house of the sanctuary was destroyed."

He said to her, "I trust in the Lord of the age that because of

Echa Rabbati

He went back to his house and took long strands of silk for children with which to make cradles.

He took them and went

to Jerusalem. As he came to the city; he took them in his arms and called out in the city street, "Who will buy a strand[10] for his son or his daughter?" The neighbor of the Messiah's mother heard and she said to him, "Go to that house, because there a child has been born." He went and entered the house and said to them, "Buy a strand for your son." She [the mother] said, "I will not buy [any] for him,

because he was born the day

when the temple was destroyed. Cursed be the day on which he was born!"

[10]The context requires "strand," but the text really says, "cow," as if he were selling the cow he used for plowing to be used for newly born children. This makes no sense. It must have been a scribal error.

Lam 1:2 Zuta

him it will be rebuilt."
 Then he said to her,

"You may take [anything] from

these children's clothing." She
said to him, "I have no money."
He said to her, "What does that
matter? Come and buy for him.
Later on I will come to your
house and collect your payment." She took [some clothing]
and left.
 After some time, he said,
"I will go and see that child
[to find out] how he is doing."

He came to
her [the child's mother], "How
is that boy doing?" She replied,
"Did I not tell you that he fell,
and that he has pain in his feet?
Since that time the winds and
whirlwinds have come; they
took him and left."

He said, "Did I not tell you that it
was on account of him (at his feet)
that it [the temple] was destroyed, and it will be because of
him (at his feet) that it will

Echa Rabbati

 The man immediately came to
the child and kissed him on his
head and gave him a strand. He
asked the mother about him [the
child] and went back home.

 Every year he went to Jerusalem in order to see him.

The name of the child was Menahem, son of Amiel. One year
when he came to Jerusalem and
entered the house,

the child's mother immediately
began to weep and, raising her
voice loudly, she said, "I have
no Menahem [comfort], be-
cause he has been hidden."[11]

---

[11]This is a play on the words of the text and the name of the Messiah. Traditionally, it
was the son of Joseph, Nehemiah who was hidden until he had suffered for the sins of
Israel.

Lam 1:2 Zuta	*Echa Rabbati*
be rebuilt?"[12]	

This is what is written,
*There is none to comfort her
[no menahem for her] of all her
lovers* (Lam 1:2).

Summary

Like "The Hidden Messiah" in Genesis Rabbiti, these texts are variant stories of the birth and infant death of the Messiah. In all three accounts, the Messiah was named Menahem and he was born on the day the temple was destroyed. In the accounts in Genesis Rabbati and Lamentations Zuta the death of the Messiah was believed to be meritorious and a part of God's plan to restore the temple when this hidden Messiah comes again. No such aspiration is reflected in Lamentations Rabbati. Lamentations Rabbati gives a literary unit enclosed in an inclusion formed by the text (Lam 1:2) at the beginning and end. In the Lamentations Rabbati account, the Messiah was born in Jerusalem, whereas in the Lamentations Zuta narrative, the Messiah was born in Bethlehem. The roles of the cows and the Arab are fanciful folk lore reflecting a story-telling culture.

THE MESSIAH REVIVES THE DEAD[13]

Rabbi Ishmael said:

Zeganzagel, the minister of the interior,[14] said to me, "The first [generations] were not accepted [for visions] to appear to them, but you are equaled in your generation to Aaron, the priest.[15]

"[In] the generation when the son of David comes, all the world will be like a woman giving birth. People will eat and drink, but their hearts will not be with them, for there will be wailing among the saints; a cry among the noble families; trembling will go up in

[12]Perhaps the author meant here that because of the atoning value of the Messiah's death the kingdom would be restored and the temple rebuilt.

[13]This document is from a manuscript which belonged to the late Rav Y.L. Ha-Cohen Fishmann and is no longer available. It has been copied and preserved by Dr. Y. Ibn Shmuel, *Redemption*, 326-27.

[14]Angelic minister whose office is in the innermost area, closest to God.

[15]And therefore, like Aaron, meritorious enough to receive a vision.

the cities; and terror will prevail in the provinces. The vine will not produce its fruit, and wine will be expensive. Olives will be smitten, and oil will be costly. When the Gentiles see this, they will order that all idolatry be eradicated, as it is said, *All idol worshippers who serve graven images will be ashamed* (Ps 97:7). When you see all these signs, you will know that it is the end time of the Messiah.

"After this, four nations,[16] will come from the four corners[17] of the world. These will be: the sons of Maskaria from one corner, the sons of Shabbor from another, the sons of Parthia from one corner, and the sons of Ethiopia and Margish from another. They will make war with one another and will kill one another. More than two hundred thousand of them will fall murdered. At that time one will say to the other, "Why do we make war among ourselves? Come, let us cast lots, and whoever triumphs will be king over us, and we will all be subject to him.'

"At that time the Messiah[18] will come out from prison with his staff and his bag. He will come to them and say, 'I want a personal confrontation with you.' Then they will say to one another, 'How can he conquer us? He has neither the appearance nor the form of a human being, and he has not the strength of a human being. We, however, possess wealth and troops; we are experts in war, and we are princes; so how can this man conquer us?' The Messiah will tell them, 'If you conquer me, [then] all Israel and I will be your servants.' When they hear that, because of their great desire to subjugate the Israelites, each one will say, 'Speak your words!' The Messiah will say to them, 'I have a small thing. I have no great word [to speak to you]: Whoever revives all these corpses will be king over us.' At this they will all be struck dumb; they will not be able to utter a word. Then the Messiah will be wrapped up in prayer.[19] He will gird himself as a mighty man before the One who spoke and the world came into existence, and he will say to him, 'Master of all the ages, remember my grief and sighing and the darkness and gloom in which I dwelled, my two eyes which saw no light and my two ears which heard great reproach. I wept alone, and my heart was broken within me. My strength became feeble with grief and sighing. May it be clear and known to you

---

[16]The four nations reported in Daniel were Gentile nations who ruled the Israelites and were hated for their position.

[17]Really, the four "winds," but that seemed awkward in the developing translation.

[18]The son of Joseph who suffered in hiding for Israel's sins and later was to overthrow the Romans before the son of David appeared.

[19]Wrapped in his prayer shawl.

that I have not done this thing for my glory nor for that of the house of my father, but for your glory, because of your truth, your temple, and your children who dwell in grief among the Gentiles.[20] Then those two hundred thousand [corpses] will stand upon their feet and say, 'We are from Israel! We are from Israel!' As it is said, *Many Gentiles will attach themselves to the Lord* (Zech 2:15). At that time, the Messiah will say to them, 'Go and gather all your brothers from all the nations!' Then they will go and gather together all the Israelites and place them before the Messiah, as it is said, *They will bring all your brothers from all the nations for an offering to the Lord'"* (Isa 66:20).
Rabbi Ishmael said:

Zeganzagel, minister of the interior, said to me, "All the Gentiles are destined to come to the Messiah and say to him, 'Have we not heard about you that you able to put to death and to make alive again? If you are willing, speak to the holy One blessed be He and [persuade him] to receive a gift from us.' He will say to them, 'What is the gift you would bring him?' They will reply, 'The house of his dwelling which we have destroyed, we will [now] rebuild!' Then he will say to them, 'Those men are wicked! He does not need your building, for thus it is written, *The Lord will build Jerusalem'* (Ps 147:2). They will say to him, 'Even so, let us gather in it precious stones...'"

Summary

During the medieval period, Moslem and Crusader forces were strong, and it seemed impossible to overthrow all these with military force. Nonetheless Jews believed that God would fulfill his promise to them, restore their land, and make the Gentiles subject to them. This would require a divine miracle, but Jews lacked no imagination in formulating possible miracles by which this could take place. This narrative is one of those imaginative eschatological solutions to this difficult problem. The Messiah would appear at an international wager, cast his lot in with the gamble, and win. The miracle enabled Jews to win control over the Gentiles very simply without conflict or cost. The narrative shows the Gentiles embarrassed, depreciated, rebuked, and humbly begging for the privilege of contributing something to the temple.

---

[20]List of the virtues the Messiah performed to cancel Israel's sin and therefore justify a miracle.

THE STORY OF DANIEL (Upon Whom be Peace)[21]

Israel's Deeds

Israel's sins. —I am Daniel, one of the sons of Jeconiah, king of the house of Judah. When I was in Jerusalem in the holy place, there was with us a man whose name was Jeremiah, son of Hilkiah, who walked in the fear of God. There were also many men in our midst whose hearts the fear of God had not touched and who did not mention the name of the Lord, and they were not willing to listen. Continually, day and night, they committed abominable, evil deeds. Idolatry, fornication, and lewdness increased in their midst. Then the Lord (May his Name be blessed) sent Jeremiah to them to condemn them for their evil and to bring them back to the fear of the Lord. At that time, King Zedekiah ruled, and Jeremiah spoke to them, saying, "Thus says the Lord, 'Return to me, and listen to my voice! For if you do not listen, then I will strengthen the hand of Nebuchadnezzar, your enemy, and I will bring him against you to make Jerusalem a desolation, and he will cut you off.'"[22] It came to pass as Jeremiah spoke these words of the Lord into the ears of King Zedekiah that [Zedekiah] said, "Go and do with this man Jeremiah as it seems good in your eyes." They seized Jeremiah and threw him into a narrow pit which had no water so that he was on the verge of dying, and because of this, the Lord became very angry with them. Nebuchadnezzar commanded the soldiers of his army to bring Jerusalem into a stage of siege, and he sent Nebuzaradan, the general of his army, to march at the head of his troops against Jerusalem. [Nebuzaradan] lived in Bagdad.

Israel's sacrifice. —There were, however, two *mitzwot* (commandments) in Israel's possession which rendered them inviolable against any external enemy. These are: The *Qorban* (sacrifice) and the *Milah* (circumcision). Were it not for these two, they [the Israelites] would not be able to perform even one of all the commandments of the Lord. This is what they do to sacrifice a *Qorban*: Every single day they put one drachma in a basket which they let down with a rope from the wall to the camp of Nebuchadnezzar to acquire from them a sheep for *Qorban*.

It once happened that an Israelite youth was standing on the wall of Jerusalem. When the Chaldeans saw him, they asked,

[21]Jellinek, בית המדרש V, 117-130. SML
[22]Not an exact quotation, but a summary statement of the message of Jer 21-22.

"What are you going to do with this sheep which you purchase from us every day?" The youth answered, "It is a gift for the Lord." From that day on, they would not sell another sheep, but they [instead] misled them. Instead of putting a sheep into the basket to draw it up on the wall, they put in it a pig. When they raised it on the wall, they shot it with deadly arrows, so that its blood poured over the wall, [with the result that] it was split in two. This happened to be on the ninth day of the month of Ab. When Nebuzaradan saw this sign, then he knew that God had given Israel into his hand, and he came to the city and went up to the house of the sanctuary. Zedekiah, king of Judah, fled and the officers of Nebuchadnezzar's army pursued him. They brought him to the king and said, "What do you wish [us] to do with him?" He commanded [them] to slaughter the two sons of Zedekiah before his eyes and to make him blind after that. Then Nebuzaradan killed a pig in the temple, because Nebuchadnezzar had not yet come to Jerusalem, but he was residing in Riblah, having sent Nebuzaradan before him at the head of his troops to Jerusalem. [Nebuzaradan] did everything which the king commanded.

The Boiling Blood

Livestock.—Near the threshold of the house of God, blood appeared continually boiling in the land. Then Nebuzaradan commanded [them] to bring the chiefs, elders, and Jeremiah together, and he asked them, "What is this blood?" They answered, "It is the blood of cattle and sheep which they offered to the Lord, but now they have discontinued the sacrifices." Nebuzaradan commanded [them] to bring many sheep and cattle and to slaughter them over this blood, but the blood did not stop boiling, but rather increased in intensity. Then Nebuzaradan said, "This blood is not the blood of sheep and cattle. If you do not tell me the truth, then I will kill all of you."

Israel's choice people.—Then Gedaliah, son of Aḥiqam, said in reply, "Alas, Sir, what can I say? Our shame is greater than our deed. There was a man in our midst whose name was Zechariah, priest and prophet of the Lord, but they murdered him on the Day of Atonement in the temple of the Lord; because he rebuked us, they rose up against him and killed him, and this is his blood which answers against us before you." Nebuzaradan became very angry, and he commanded [them] to bring three thousand scholars. He slaughtered them over this blood, yet the boiling of the blood did not cease. Then he slaughtered three thousand priests, but the boiling of the blood did not cease. They then brought another two thousand Levites and slaughtered them, but the blood did not cease its boiling. They further brought two thousand bridegrooms and brides and slaughtered them over the blood, but the boiling of the blood [still] did not cease. Then they brought two thousand school children and bound them with the scroll of the Torah and threw them into the fire, yet the boiling of the blood did not cease even then. [It was] then [that] the pity of the torturer was stirred, and he said, "O Zechariah! Do you really want all the Israelites [to be slaughtered] because of your blood?" But the blood has not rested even now, from its boiling.

Daniel and Nebuchadnezzar

Solomon's throne. —I, Daniel, was then in the house of study, and a warrior came in to kill us, but God gave Hananiah, Mishael, Azariah, and me favor in his eyes, so that they spared us, but they led us captive, together with all the [other] Israelites with their wives and children, as well as with the vessels of the house of the Lord and the throne of King Solomon (upon whom be peace). They took the garments of the priests, brought them to Bagdad, and put them into the treasury of the king. [The king] resolved to sit on the throne of Solomon. The throne was of ivory with its legs different one from the other; one was like an ox; the second, like an eagle; the third was like a lion; and the fourth leg was like a man. The lion was situated opposite the ox; the ox, opposite the eagle; and the eagle, opposite the man. When Nebuchadnezzar wanted to get upon the throne, he fell and his right leg was broken. He became very much afraid, because he knew he had sinned against the Lord.

Nebuchadnezzar's leg healed. —Then he called me, Daniel, and said, "Daniel, this accident has happened to me. Now, pray to the Lord so that my leg might be healed, and I will surely treat you and all your friends well." Then I prayed to the Lord that he might have compassion on Nebuchadnezzar. God sent his angel and said to me, "Daniel, my friend, everything you ask of God will be given you." I fell on my face before the angel, and I prayed in behalf of Nebuchadnezzar, saying, "Do save this wicked man. Please heal his broken leg!" God answered, "Daniel, arise and walk, for the leg of the wicked one is already healed." When his leg was healed, he increased benefits for my friends and me and proclaimed that whoever saw them should honor them for the sake [of the king].

The fiery furnace. —Nebuchadnezzar made a gold image and commanded that every man who loved the king in his heart should honor this image, but my friends and I, Daniel, did not honor him. As a result they slandered and denounced us to the king, saying, "May the king live for an age! There are some men who do not perform your commandment and do not honor your image. When I, Daniel, heard this accusation, I built for myself a house which overlooked the sanctuary in Jerusalem. Hananiah, Mishael, Azariah, and I prayed every day. The king became very angry with us and commanded [his men] to prepare a fiery furnace in which he cast Hananiah, Mishael, and Azariah. This they did, but God sent his angel and delivered them and did not allow the fire to touch them so as to hurt them. Then Nebuchadnezzar fell on his face before the angel and gave praise to the Lord.

Temple vessels. —After these things, Nebuchadnezzar died, and his son, Belshazar succeeded the throne of his kingdom. It happened one day that he commanded [them] to bring him the holy vessels and the holy garments, because he had prepared a banquet and wanted to drink wine [in the holy vessels]. He put on the holy garments and sat on his throne. Then Belshazar, together with his friends and principal men, drank wine in the [holy] ministering vessels. God then sent his angel, and where they sat, a hand went out from the wall and wrote on it: "O king, because you have done this thing, you have destroyed your kingdom." When the king saw the hand, he was very much afraid and commanded every magician and scholar to come before him, but none of them was able to read the writing. The king's mother suggested, "There is a man among the Jews [who] knows how to decipher and interpret it. Then they rushed me, Daniel, there and commanded me to read the writing and tell its meaning. When I saw this writing, I said, "May the king live for an age! but I refuse to read this writing lest you put me to death." The king answered, "I will not slay you if you tell its interpretation." At this, I, Daniel, said, "Because you have done this thing, and you have worn the holy garments, and you have drunk wine in the [holy] ministering vessels, your kingdom will be taken from you and given to your enemy."

Daniel and Cyrus

Daniel's prayer. —On that day Belshazar went out to war; and I,

Daniel, fled to Shuster to Cyrus. When he saw me, he was glad and said to me, "From where have you come?" I answered, "From Bagdad have I come, where Nebuchadnezzar exiled us." Then Cyrus said, "How have your fathers sinned so much that the Lord has given them into the hand of Nebuchadnezzar?" I answered, "They have sinned before the Lord [in that] they have killed the prophets; they did not walk in the way of the Torah; and they have done evil in his eyes. Therefore he has handed them into the power of the enemy." Then Cyrus said to me, "Daniel, pray now to the Lord that he may give Masul into my hand, and I will go and bring back the holy vessels and vestments to Jerusalem." So I prayed to the Lord and said, "Please, Lord, deal kindly with Cyrus. May his hand be [capable of] killing the king, Masul, and returning the holy vessels and vestments to Jerusalem." Then the Lord answered, "Daniel, I have heard your prayer on behalf of Cyrus. Now go and tell him that he should go to Baghdad, and he will capture it and do what seems good in his eyes to Masul. Only let him return the holy vessels and garments." I said to Cyrus, "Go to Babylon, for God has already given the kingdom into your hand."

Return to Jerusalem. —Then Cyrus arose and took with him four thousand men and went to Babylon, and he fought with King Masul and killed him and his army. He took the holy garments and vessels of silver and gold, and also the throne of Solomon. These he brought to Shustar and left them there, as it is written, "Cyrus commanded [his servants] to return the holy garments and vessels to Jerusalem, and the throne of Solomon he took for himself and sat on it." Then God said to me, "Daniel, arise and cry aloud in all the cities, 'Arise and let us build the temple a second time, for already the seventy years have been ful-filled.' You, Daniel, shall say to Cyrus, 'Thus said the Lord (May his Name be blessed): "Go and build again the sanctuary!"'" Bring Ezra the scribe, and Zerubbabel, the son of Shealtiel, before Cyrus." Then Daniel said to Cyrus all that which the Lord had commanded him. Yet this house would not be constructed before the tribes of Israel and the tribe [of Judah] and half the tribe [of Benjamin] returned.

The temple. —Ezra went through all the cities and proclaimed: "Arise and go to the temple so that we can return [and] build it again!" But the Israelites did not go because they thought Ezra was telling a lie, and they tried to kill him. The matter was made known to Ezra, and he prayed to the Lord, and the Lord heard him and hid him. The tribe and a half of the Israelites returned to the holy place, and they offered sacrifices which were pleasing to the Lord, and he blessed them.

Daniel and Darius

The invitation. —After a year had passed, Darius came and fought Cyrus in battle and captured him, slew him, and took away his kingdom, ruling in his place. When I, Daniel, saw all that happened, I was afraid of Darius, and I fled from him and came to Persia alongside the mountain beside the Ahavaz River. There I dressed in sack cloth and wallowed in the dust and ashes and prayed to the Lord, and said, "O Lord, how long will you burden me [with] this trouble and distress? My ancestors have died; your temple is destroyed; and before my eyes they have killed priests, Levites, and prophets." I, Daniel, was thus before the Lord fourteen days. For four days I neither ate nor drank, night and day. I sat on the ground, weeping and mourning, except for the days when I stood on my feet. [I continued in this fashion] until the Lord heard my prayer and sent an angel who said to me, "Daniel, why are you weeping, and why do you sigh?" I answered, "Because I am afraid of King Darius." Then he said, "Do not be afraid, for I will not give you into his hand."

In Darius' palace. —After several days, Darius commanded [his servants] to bring me before him. He sent me a letter of peace in these words: "Arise, Daniel, come to me, and do not be afraid, for just as Cyrus was generous to you, so will I be even more generous with you. After I read the words of this letter, I hurried and went to Shustar. When Darius saw me, he was happy to meet me and said, "Daniel, why have you refused to believe that I am able to do good with you just as Cyrus did?" I answered, "May the king live for an age! Because I was afraid lest they would slander me to you." He said, "Do not be afraid! Come near to me and sit down." So I came near to him, and I sat down before him, and peace was mine. The days of this peace increased, as it is written in the book, for God gave me favor in the eyes of the king, and he honored me more than the greatest men in his kingdom. I praised God and sat before the king.

Holy garments and the king's blindness. —It happened one day that Darius could not find a thing which he wished to do. He told [his servants] to bring the holy garments before him. They looked for them, but they were not [to be] found. His principal men and generals told him: "We do not know where they are." The king commanded [them] to rush me to him and said to me, "You know where the holy vestments are, do you not? Now tell me! Show them to me!" I answered, "I do not know." He said, "I have asked you to tell me so that I could fulfill [my promise of doing] good to you, but if you will not tell me, then I will punish you." I answered, "I do not know." So he put me in prison, shackled my feet with bands of brass, and placed a guard over me. Then I prayed to the Lord and said, "Almighty God, how long will they inflict such tortures as these on me? Forgive me, and hear the voice of my prayer; deliver me from the hand of this wicked man; and do not put the holy garments into his hand." God heard my prayer and sent an angel who blinded the eye of Darius and said to him, "Why have you injured Daniel and placed him in prison because of the holy garments?" King Darius replied, "I have sinned against the Lord and have acted wickedly. Forgive me, and return to me the sight of my eye." The angel said to him, "If Daniel will pray for you, I will return to you the sight of your eye." Darius commanded [them] to rush him from prison and said to me, "Come with me, and let us go to the place of the sanctuary and pray there for me to God that he will return to me the sight of my eye."

Then the king took with him a thousand horsemen and me, and he traveled to the holy place. When I saw the temple, I cried, "How long will the house of God be desolate and the Israelites scattered?" Again the angel of God said to me, "The house of God has been desolate until now, and it will remain desolate until [the Israelites] repent. When they know that they are sinners against the Lord and forsake their sins, then God will forgive them, and they will return [and] rebuild the temple.

I blessed the Lord, and I prayed to him in behalf of this wicked man that he should return the sight of his eye. The angel of the Lord said to me, "I have heard your prayer." He said further, "Go and make Darius stand alongside the river of water and wash his eye with the water, and after that he will be healed, for God will restore to him the sight of his eye." Then Darius washed his eye, and it was healed; by a divine miracle was the sight of his eye restored. Then he blessed the Lord and said, "May the Name of the Lord God of Daniel be blessed, for he is the Creator of heaven and earth. None is like him, and none resembles him, who exalts the humble and heals the blind. Through Daniel, he found healing for my eye, and he healed it."

God put it into his heart, and he opened his treasury and gave the tithe to the priests, Levites, and orphans, and to me, Daniel, he gave much wealth. He turned to go back to Shustar, and he took me with him. We passed our way in peace, and when the men on the way who had seen King Darius when he was blind and that now he could see, many of them became proselytes to Judaism through Daniel. We came to Shustar, and the king once again took the rulership into his hand as at first.

I, Daniel, dressed in sack cloth and sat on the earth for many days. I did not eat meat nor drink wine. I wept day and night, and my eyes were like a fountain of water because of the house of God which was destroyed. Then God sent an angel who said, "Daniel, why are you weeping bitterly?" I answered, "For the house of God I am weeping; for I have seen it, and it is laid waste. In my days they have killed priests and Levites. These evil things have brought me low, and their hand is against me, even now." When I became silent, God said to me, "Daniel, listen carefully, and I will show you that which will happen to the Israelites when the end time comes—how many kings will rule them; how long they will be in captivity; and how they will be redeemed. [Also] the good things which will come upon them in the last days [of the captivity], and how long each individual king will rule over them."

The angel showed me all these things and also all the sins which the Israelites would commit during those times. "Daniel," he said to me, "Tell the Israelites, 'Blessed will you be if you observe the commandments of the Lord and repent sincerely, day and night, fasting and praying to the Lord every time he has commanded you. Seek the Lord always, and do his holy will.'" God said further, "Daniel, be glad and thank the Lord, and say to the Israelites, "Happy will you be if you walk in the way of the Lord. Daniel, behold I have shown you how many kings will be over every people and every faith and how long the rule of these kings will last. Now I will tell you how all these things will happen.

"Daniel, in your days a wicked king will arise and he will rule for one year and die.

"After him a king will arise who will not know the Lord. His appearance will be ruddy, and many evils will befall mankind. He will teach them the way in which they must walk, and he will make them walk according to the desire of his heart.

"After him another king will arise and all men will become wise. They will have intercourse with their mothers and sisters, and they will institute the worship of the sun. Prayer and the blessing of peace will go out into all the land in their days. The king will do many good things for mankind. Scholars of Israel will be at peace with them and acquire wisdom from them while they [the Gentiles] will seek the words of God from the Israelites, but there will be no peace in those days. There will be war in their midst, and each man will kill his brother for four hundred years."

The angel of God said to me further, "Another king will arise who will not fear God. Human beings will be impudent. A man will not be ashamed of another; there will be no curbing of their lusts, and they will reject the word of God. Stealing and plunder will increase; creeds and sects will flourish; and in their ways there will be bloodshed and oppression. There will be a wicked king who will compare himself to God and who will call men to stand before him; but suddenly they will fall down in dread and will never rise again."

I, Daniel, have seen that in their days a king will arise of short stature and ruddy appearance; he will have no treasuries; and he will not observe the written words of God, but he will say that he is a prophet. He will come and go on a camel, for he will be a driver of camels. He will come from the South, and he will subdue mankind. At his hands Israelites will be oppressed, and a number [of them] will surrender to him and to his faith.

"You, Daniel, warn the Israelites not to pay attention to him and not to forsake the Torah of Moses, but to hold fast to the faith of Israel. The men among them who will come from the South on the camel will say that he is a prophet. With reference to him, Daniel, tell them that no prophet will arise from the South, and that which he says is lie and falsehood. From him and those who cleave to him will go forth many distresses to men, and the days of their kingdom will continue for eleven years, after which he will die in the South.

"After him will arise another king, tall of stature with a long beard and black hair who will set his rule over all men and who will become great. He will rule for thirteen years, and afterwards, he will die.

"After him another will arise, short of stature, and possessed of a hard countenance. He will be a mocker, and many evils will befall mankind in his days. He will proudly say that he is a prophet, and he will seek to turn men to him, and Israel will bear many hardships. He will rule for ten years, and then he will die.

"After him another will arise, tall of stature, wise, but blood-thirsty, and he will plan wars. He will come from the West, and will shed much blood. He will rule for twelve years, and he will be killed in the East.

"After him another will arise in whose days there will be hunger and poverty, and disaster will come over every man. He will rule for fourteen years and fifteen days, and then he will die.

"After him, another will arise and rule in his place. He will be wicked; he will not fear God; and men will suffer a great famine. He will rule fourteen years and five months and afterwards die.

"After him another will arise. There will be terror and dismay for two years, and afterwards he will die.

"After him will arise another. Men will find rest, and they will have much silver and gold, and Israel will succeed greatly. He will rule twenty-three years, and afterwards he will die.

"After him another will arise in whose days there will be great dismay; there will be famine and pestilence in the world. He will rule twenty-five years and three months, and afterwards he will die.

"After him will arise another from the East, and he will extend to the West. He will subdue all the world; he will deal kindly with men; and he will rule over all the world for ten years and five days. Afterwards he will die.

"After him another will come from Babylon. Men will live in peace, and it will be good for Israel. He will rule thirteen years and afterwards will die.

"Afterwards another will arise who will build mosques and minarets. Men will pray five times a day. He will be exalted as a prophet and will seek to gather all men around him. He will rule for a year and a half, and afterwards he will die.

"After him another will come who will be a wise man. He will collect much silver and gold, and he will draw men near with loving kindness. There will be peace in all the world, and he will regard Israel with favor. He will die in his house at the end of three years of his kingdom.

"After him, his son will arise. He will be a wise man, who will know God. He will distribute gold and silver to men and judgment, righteousness, and tranquility will fill the land. Israel will prosper greatly. He will go to the East, and there he will die at the end of twelve years of his rule.

"After him, his son will arise. He will be depressed, mentally deranged, and a Nazarite. He will want to destroy the world. He will rule a year and five months, and afterwards he will die.

"After him his son will arise. He will commit acts of violence, and in his heart he will think of killing the Ishmaelites and of making all men subject to his rule. Many evil things will happen to men. He will go from the East to the West, and there will be war and bloodshed in the land. He will establish the throne of his kingdom in Babylon. Then he will arise and go to Greece and will fight with its inhabitants. There will be fear in the world, and evil will come upon mankind. When he returns from Greece, he will go to the East. There he will make wars and there he will remain. He will rule for twenty-three years, and afterwards he will die in the East.

"He will have three sons: one will go to the East; the second, to the West; and the third, to Babylon. One will not find [anyone] paying [sufficient] attention to him, and the one who is in Babylon will not rule. This [son] who is in the East will raise himself up and go to the West and take it [the country] from his brother's hand. Much blood will be shed in the land, and afterwards he will die.

"After him another will arise who will command [men] to wear white garments, and the black [garments] will be destroyed from the land. Many Arabs will be killed. Men will flee from land to land, and Israelites will be in distress. For twenty years he will rule, and afterwards he will die.

"Then a king will arise from the Romans, and he will wear red garments. He will set out to engage in wars as far as Damascus. He will kill the mighty and glorious men and the leaders of the Ismaelites, and greatness will cease from the Ishmaelites. He will destroy the mosques and the minarets, and no one will again mention the name of Beliel. He will remove the kingdom of the Ishmaelites from the land so that it will not raise its head again. The rest of the men will attach themselves to him and will obey his wishes all the days of his life. Whoever disobeys him will be killed. The Israelites will beg and suffer great travail and much evil. He will prohibit them from circumcising the flesh of their foreskins and forbid the observance of the Sabbath so as to desecrate it. He will not permit them to read the Torah or to offer their prayers, and he will kill many Israelites. But happy will be he who holds fast to his Jewish faith in that evil time and does not submit to him. Because of this distress which they will suffer, all Israelites will of one accord turn to the Lord, and he will deliver them and make them prosper. The one who will conquer all the world with his power will rule only for nine months and afterwards will die.

"Afterwards another will arise from Magrav, more wicked and oppressive than [those] before him. This will be his distinguishing mark: He will be a hundred cubits and eleven spans tall, ten spans wide, and he will have hair on his face. He will conquer all the West. There will be many wicked men and those who love war in those days, and they will gather themselves to him from every land. They will tell him that he is the Messiah. This report will go out into all the world, and every land will surrender to him. He will kill anyone who does not surrender to him. Israelites will suffer hardship and distress in those days, and they will flee from before him. There will be suffering in all the land, and they [the Israelites] will go into the mountains, and they will reach their peaks. Then the army of Gog and Magog will join the king and will walk with him. This is how those who see them will recognize them, because they will all have four eyes each, two before and two behind. Men will bear and suffer hardship and great distress, but the Israelites more than [the rest] of them."

Then I, Daniel, said, "O God, will all these hardships come upon the Israelites?" I wept and made supplication for them and said, "Blessed is he who is not born and will not see all this distress!" Then God sent an angel to me who said, "Blessed are those Israelites who trust in the Lord and in the faith of Israel and who will die in the fear of God. They will not perform the wicked deeds of the religion of those days, and they will not revolt against the faith of Israel."

After this, another man will arise and make peace with them; they will so destroy their ways that there [will be] none like them in all the land. A man will have intercourse with his neighbor's wife...and they will kill men. They will go to Damascus, to that wicked one who will say, "I, I am he," and they will follow him. He will bring up a fish from the sea and feed him from the flesh of the Israelites. Great suffering and grief will come upon them, but all those who come from the seed of the righteous will not surrender to them. Then the word which the Lord has spoken concerning them will come to pass.

The False Messiah

Then a man will appear there in a certain distant place, and all Israelites will abandon their place and congregate to him. That man will be from the sons of Ephraim. They will walk together to that wicked man who says, "I am the Messiah, your king, and your wealth." The Israelites will tell him, "We ask from you three signs, so that we may know your true credentials." He will say, "What are the signs which you ask? Tell me!" They will tell him, "We are seeking these signs: 1) This stick which Moses our master changed into a snake before Pharaoh—you [use it to] do the same.

2) That staff of Aaron which was a withered branch should now produce before our eyes new leaves and bear fruit. 3) The last [sign] which we request is that you bring forth the jar of manna which Aaron left as a preservation, and show it to us. Perform these three signs and we will know that you are speaking the truth."

But this evil one will not be able to perform even one of these signs. Then all the Israelites with their leaders will congregate and go to the wilderness of Ephraim, dress themselves in sack cloth, sit on the ground, and cry out to the Lord and say, "O God, redeem us from this distress, hardship, and oppression. Do not visit upon us our iniquities, but forgive us." Then God will send an angel, and he will say, "Do not be afraid! For I will not give you into the hand of this wicked one. But you, Israelites, go directly to him and say, 'If you are the Messiah, now revive the dead so that we can be convinced!'" But because he will not be able to do [so], he will become angry and command [his servants] to kill them. The Israelites, with their wives and sons, will flee together to the wilderness [where] they will give way to weeping and lamentation, sit on the ground, cry aloud to the Lord, and engage in great mourning for forty days. Then God will send them his mercy and open the windows of heaven. A month will pass as a week, a week as a day, and a day as an hour. God will do good to the Israelites and fulfill the covenant he made with their fathers. After this darkness, he will provide light, and the Israelites will rejoice and prosper by the will of God.

Then Michael and Gabriel will place themselves before God and make supplication to him, saying, "How long will you abandon the Israelites in captivity? If their fathers have sinned, have they not already been punished [sufficiently] for their sins? Now hasten to redeem them, O Lord. [Send them] deliverance and salvation, and fulfill the covenant which you made with Abraham, Isaac, and Jacob. Remember for them the righteousness of Moses who walked before you a hundred and twenty years and was a shepherd to the Israelites." Then God will say to Michael and Gabriel, "Go and tell the Israelites, 'Blessed are you that you did not abandon the statutes of God and his teachings, and you did not follow that wicked one.' To those who followed him, say, 'Woe to you! You have become defiled! Now, remember the Lord, the God of Israel and your God. You have banished your souls and betrayed the Torah of Israel.'"

Then Michael and Gabriel will come to the camp of the Israelites and will see all of them lying on the ground in suffering and distress, crying to the Lord. [Michael and Gabriel] will speak these words, "Arise and lift up your heads from the ground! Praise the Lord, for he will redeem you and give salvation to your souls from the hand of this wicked one, and he will bring you out from darkness to light, and from light to rule." When the Israelites will hear these words, they will be comforted and thank the Lord and praise him.

Afterwards they will rise up against the man who said he was the Messiah, and they will kill him. The Lord will appear from heaven; a great noise will go out from Zion and from the holy place; and a mighty voice will be heard. All the Israelites will find favor in the eyes of God. Instead of Jerusalem destroyed, he will bring down from heaven a Jerusalem rebuilt, and *a shoot will appear from the stock of Jesse* (Isa 11:1).

Days of the Messiah

He will be the son of David, and he will appear, as it is written in the book, *With the breath of his lips he will kill the wicked* (Isa 11:4). Then the Messiah son of Joseph will be killed, and the flag of the Messiah son of David will be raised aloft. He will kill all the military force of Gog and Magog. Elijah will come and proclaim the good news to Israel, both for the living and the dead. He will return and build the temple of the Lord; Egypt will become desolate; and the temple of God will be established in its position.

The Messiah son of David, Elijah, and Zerubbabel will go up to the top of the Mount of Olives, and the Messiah will command Elijah to blow the trumpet. The light of the six days of creation will return and appear. The light of the moon will be as the light of the sun, and God will send complete healing to all the sick in Israel. The second trumpet blast which Elijah will send will revive the dead. They will arise from the earth, and each man will recognize his neighbor; husband, his wife; father, his son; and brother, his brother. They will all come to the Messiah from the four corners of the earth, from the East, West, North, and South. The Israelites will fly on the wings of the eagle and will approach the Messiah. A pillar of fire will go out from the sanctuary, and it will be a sign to all who see it that the sanctuary has now been reconstructed, so that they will know and be convinced. At the third trumpet blast, the splendor of God will appear, and at the fourth blast, the mountains will become a valley, and the surface of all the earth will become a plain. Tabor, Carmel, Hermon, and the Mount of Olives. There will be a distance of eight parsangs between the mountains. The sanctuary will appear just as Ezekiel had prophesied, with the Golden Gate hidden in the ground. Two angels, carrying the commandments of God will raise it [the Golden Gate], and they will establish it just as it was in the former days.

Abraham, our father, will stand on the right [of the Golden Gate], and Moses, our master, with the Messiah son of David, will stand on the left, and all the Israelites will be stationed there. Then the Messiah will say to Abraham, "Are these your children?" To Moses, our master, he will say, "Is Israel your friend?" Then Abraham will look into the face of the Israelites and say to the Messiah, "These are my children, just as it is written, *the seed of Abraham, my friend* (Isa 41:8).

The Israelites will be happy, and they will bless and praise the Lord and say, "The Lord is righteous; everything which he promised concerning us, thus has he done for us."

They will rejoice with the joy of the Messiah for a thousand, three hundred years, and the sanctuary will be completed. For all the peoples will hear that which has been done with Israel, and they will come in tens and twenties to the Israelites, and they will say, "In what way have we sinned? In what way have we transgressed that you have not invited us to rejoice in your happiness?" These will be those who come from among the righteous Gentiles. Whenever they will see an Israelite, they will bow down before him and give him honor, and they will carry him on their shoulder and hurry to bring him to the messianic king. In this way all Israelites will be gathered before the Messiah in the holy place. Those who have transgressed against the faith of Israel will be [destined for] shame and disgrace until everyone who sees them will recognize them, and people will point them out with their finger, as it is written, *And they will go out and see the carcasses of the men [who sinned against me, for their worm will not die, and their fire will not be quenched, and they will be a disgrace to all flesh]* (Isa 66:24). But these men who bore the yoke of the exile and kept the faith of Israel will be happy and charitable. The transgressors will be excommunicated from their midst, and they will tell them, "Depart from us, for we hate you!" Their faces will be changed to black, and they will be [destined] to fear and horror. Then they will go down to the Valley of Jehoshaphat, and there they will be until the great day of judgment comes.

The days of the Messiah will last for a thousand, three hundred years. For Israel there will be holidays and festivals, wealth, greatness, and glory until the great day of judgment. Nevertheless, that day will be a day of terrible darkness and dread, when the glitter of the burning torches shines, for then the holy One blessed be He will reveal the Garden of Eden and Gehinnom, both of which he created before the world. To Eden, there will be seven gates, and to Gehinnom, three. In the day of judgment, all the peoples will be gathered before the Shekinah of God. Every man who is found guilty will stand before an Israelite who has held fast to his faith. Near the three gates of Gehinnom, Abraham will stand at the first, Isaac, at the second, and Jacob, at the third. They will pray and say, "Please, Lord, remember that which you said and the covenant which you made, as it is written in your holy scriptures, *I will remember my covenant [with] Jacob, also my covenant [with] Isaac, and also I will remember my covenant [with] Abraham* (Lev 26:42). Then the holy One blessed be He will hear their prayer and will forgive them for their sins. He will give to Abraham all those who have come from the true seed, and all the Israelites will go into Eden. Then the sinners will say to them, "Woe to [you] prophets! Have you not descended from us? Yet you have now put us at a distance. They [the prophets] will not answer them a word, but they [the sinners] will all be sent to Gehinnom at once.

Gehinnom

Gehinnom will be divided into seven departments. In the lowest, all those who have changed the Torah will dwell. In the second, the sinners; in the third, all those whose faith in the Jewish religion has not been a complete faith; in the fourth, whoever has not believed and has not heard the voice of God; in the fifth, the transgressors of Israel who committed fornication and adultery; in the sixth, all the Gentiles who prayed hypocritically and acted falsely and deceitfully; and in the seventh, all those in the midst of Israel who were arrogant and destructive and did evil deeds. All the rest of the Israelites will merit the life of the age to come. Thus [God] will condemn all the wicked Israelites in Gehinnom. After this, they will be rescued from the judgment of Gehinnom, and they will return and be united with their brothers. For the descendants of Abraham, Isaac, and Jacob will not perish. "God is with them," as if to say, "The Shekinah of God is in their midst."

Negarsagel, who is the superintendent of Gehinnom, will stand before the Lord and say, "Creator of the ages, you have put into my hand all peoples and all nations for me to burn with fire. What is the reason that you have withheld from me this one people, the Israelites?" Then God will answer him, "All the peoples and nations I have given into your hand except the Israelites, over whom you have no authority." Gehinnom will ask, "Why is this?" Then God will answer, "Because of this. Because they have read my Torah and because I love them for ages of ages, as it is written, *The Lord appeared to me from afar; I have loved you [with] a love of the age. Therefore I have continued loving kindness to you*" (Jer 31:3). Furthermore, because the Shekinah has chosen its dwelling in your midst, as it is written, *They will make for me a temple, and I will dwell in their midst* (Ex 25:8).

The Lord, blessed be He, in his abundant mercy, great loving kindness, and faithfulness, may it be his will to gather the dispersed of Judah from the four corners of the earth and unite them in the near future. Say, "Amen." May he fulfill for us the verse which is written, *The Lord will build Jerusalem, and he will gather the scattered of Israel* (Ps 147:2). May the Lord be blessed for the age. Amen and amen.

Summary

"The Story of Daniel" is a collection of various legends, apocalyptic units, and narratives that are only loosely related. The document begins with an explanation of Israel's sins that caused the captivity. This is followed by an account of the way the *Qorban* sacrifice was stopped. The narrative about the boiling blood seems to have no eschatological message, but was included because it was about Nebuzaradan. An important theme is the attempts of foreign kings to use Solomon's throne, the sacred vessels, or the priest's robes. Every time this was attempted the king involved was stricken with some physical problem which required Daniel's prayers for recovery. The hero throughout was Daniel who survived three foreign kings. It was because of his effective prayers and his skill at negotiation that Jerusalem was restored. Daniel was supposed to have foreseen many kings who were to arise. Most of these cannot be identified. One of the early ones was Mohammed, the prophet who came from the South. Much later the king who was to arise from the Romans and kill many Ishmaelite leaders must have been the early Crusaders, but in between were many Moslem kings and caliphs together with the lengths of time they ruled, but these do not coincide with periods of time for the respective caliphs, and the descriptions, even when recognizable, do not seem to be in the proper relationship to one another. The importance of this predicted history like other similar lists of kings was to anticipate the final war of Gog and Magog that was soon to follow. The false Messiah described may have been Alroy, but that is not certain. In the days of the Messiah the dead would be awakened by Elijah and the temple would be brought down from heaven. Judgment would be held and the variously qualified people would find their appropriate places in the Garden of Eden or Gehinnom.

These literary units have probably been composed at different times and in different places. The final editor lived during the times of the Crusaders, and he looked forward to their final destruction and the exaltation of Israel.

HOW THE ANTI-JEWISH DECREES WERE ANNULED[23]

These are the secrets and the revelations which were revealed to Rabbi Shimon. This is the Rabbi Shimon Ben Yoḥai whom [the Lord] sent from Jerusalem to Rome to Caesar, and when he was in the ship, Ashmedai, prince of shades,[24] appeared to him in a dream and said to him, "Ask what I should do for you." Rabbi Shimon said to him, "Who are you?" He replied, "I am Ashmedai, whom the holy One blessed be He sent to perform a miracle for you." He said, "Master of the age, you have appointed an angel to Hagar the handmaid of Sarah, but to me you have sent the prince of shades!" Ashmedai said to him, "The miracle may come from any place. Your desire may be achieved either from an angel or from me." Ashmedai said to him, "Behold, I am going right now, and I will enter the daughter of Caesar, and I will weaken her, and I will call out your name, 'Rabbi Shimon! Rabbi Shimon!' until you come and they will ask you how you can appease me, so I will leave this daughter. Then I will say that I will not leave her until they do the will of Rabbi Shimon." Then Ashmedai went to the house of Caesar and did all that he said to Rabbi Shimon, and Caesar's

---

[23]This narrative is ordinarily classified as the introduction of "The Prayer of Rabbi Shimon Ben Yoḥai," but it clearly has nothing to do with the prayer. It is a separate legend. The text is found in Jellinek. בית המדרש IV, 117-18. RPL

[24]Demons.

daughter arose, and he entered into her. When he entered her, she broke all the vessels which were in the palace of her father, and she was crying out, "Rabbi Shimon! Rabbi Shimon Ben Yoḥai!"

After a few days a ship came and in it was Rabbi Shimon! They went and reported the good news to Caesar. Caesar sent after him and said to him, "What do you want?" He replied, "The Jews who are in Jerusalem have sent a gift to you." He said, "I will not accept anything from you, and I do not want anything from you except that you drive out this shade from my daughter, because I have no one who will rule after me except her. I have no other children."

Rabbi Shimon went and said to him, "Ashmedai, leave this girl!" [The shade] said, "I will not leave until they do everything for you that you want." He said this many times, "I will not leave until they do what you wish." The king went and sent to all his elders, generals, and servants, and he said to them, "What do you say I should do to my daughter whom the shade has entered, and we have decreed against the Jews that they may not circumcise their sons, and they may not observe the Sabbath, and their women may not observe menstrual purity. The custom of our kingdom is that when we decree something, we do not change [it] for the age.[25] If [a king] changes it, they remove him from his kingdom, according to the law of the Medes and the Persians." One of his counsellors arose and said, "Your majesty, I will tell you something, by which your daughter may be healed, and you may pass over all your decrees, because this decree against the Jews is evil for us and for you." He said, "Speak!" He replied, "He who has an enemy, what does he want [his enemy] to be? that he will be poor or rich?" The king said to him, "Poor." The counsellor said, "It is the custom of the Jews to keep themselves employed all the week and acquire money, but on the [end of] the sixth day, they spend everything because of the honor of the Sabbath. But now that you have prevented their Sabbath, there is left over for them all the expenses of the Sabbath, and they gather money and rebel against you. If, however, you return their Sabbath, they will stop [working] on it, and [by] spending much money, they will become poor." The king said, "Return their Sabbath!" The counsellor told him further, "If a man has enemies, what will he want of them, that they multiply or diminish?" The king replied, ["That they] diminish." He said, "Your majesty, the Jews perform circumcision

[25]An age frequently referred to the period of one king, one dynasty, one country's rule. Since the law could not be changed for an age, the change required the king to leave office, because this change marked the end of his age.

on their sons when they are eight days old. For everyone of them who survives, a hundred die." The king said, "Also return their circumcision!" He added further, "Your majesty, also it is with menstrual purity. If you allow Israelite women to observe menstrual purity, they will not be able to multiply seed, because they observe seven days [as] menstrual days and seven days for cleanliness." The king said, "Allow their laws on menstrual purity to be just as they were!" The king said to Rabbi Shimon, "I have fulfilled your request. Go, tell the shade to leave my daughter!" Rabbi Shimon decreed against Ashmedai, and he left the king's daughter. The king returned to Rabbi Shimon the gift which he brought him, and he gave him many gifts also, and he wrote for him a letter of approval to the governor which was in Jerusalem. Then Rabbi Shimon went to Jerusalem, happy and in a good mood, and the decrees were annuled.

Summary

This narrative is legendary, certainly not historical; that which is true is the nature of the decrees that Roman and other governments made against Jews, as also against Christians in similar circumstances. The reason for the decrees was that the king wanted to restrict the Jews so that they could not rebel against him, as the counsellor in the legend discloses. It is necessary to understand the fifth column aspect of Judaism and early Christianity to make sense of all the persecutions faced in relationship to various governments. The problems were political, and apocalyptic literature reflects this military, political background. This legend is typically Jewish, showing the rabbi victorious over the king with superhuman powers at his disposal.

THE LAST DAYS

DAYS OF TRIBULATION[1]

The scholars of Egypt announced signs that at a future time there would be a congregation of all the planets and the tail of the dragon [would meet] with them in the sign of the scales[2] in the month of Elul, on the twenty-ninth of that month, following [the reckoning of] the Hebrews, the 4946th year of the beginning of the world [A.D. 1186), the day of the Lord,[3] the next night about midnight. The following signs would begin and continue up to the fourth feast day in the afternoon.[4]

For there will rise from the sea a very strong great wind, terrifying the human heart, and it will pick up sand and dust from the surface of the earth, so much that it will cover up trees and towers. This, therefore, [will happen] because that meeting of the planets will be in Libra, that is to say, in the sign of air and wind. Following that which those scholars determined, that conjunction will point out a very strong wind, breaking into pieces mountains and rocks (I Kgs 19:11). [There will be] noises, thunder, and voices[5]

---

[1]The Latin text is from Fritz Baer, "Eine judische Messiasprophetie auf das Jahr 1186 dritte Kreuzzug," *MGWJ* 70 (1926), 114-115.

[2]Latin *Moraniam.* Baer, "Eine judische Messiasprophetie," 115, follows Grauert, "Meister Johann von Toledo," *Munchner Academie der Wissenschaften.* phil.-histor. Kl. 1901, 111-325, in taking this word as a transliteration of the Hebrew, מאזנים. Baer suggested many other similar transliterations in the prophecy.

[3]Sunday, evidently a Christian interpretation. Jews would not be likely to call the first day of the week, "the Lord's Day." Other evidence points to Jewish composition.

[4]Baer has convincingly argued that this prophecy was originally Jewish and written in Hebrew. The locations which he deduces to be all Near Eastern oriented places correspond with many of the locations mentioned in the Elijah apocalypse. He also noted the surprising agreement of the astronomical date with the Jewish calendar. April 5, 1186, was the 14th of Nisan. April 22 was the first of Iyyar, 4946. The principal date was the 29th of Elul, 4946, or, according to another version of the text, Sept. 16, 1186, which was the first of Tishri, 4947. This would seem like a good time to expect something unusual to happen: at the turn of the year, 4946/47, *Rosh Ha-Shenah* or the birthday of the world (Baer, 118-19). On *Rosh Ha-Shenah*, Jews, like other Near Eastern peoples, believed the Lord sat in judgment, looking over the records of Israel's sins and virtues. Jews had through the Day of Atonement to repent and balance the books if there was only a slightly overdrawn account. If Israelites should show "a balance on hand" and appear sinless before the Lord, then he would redeem them at once, restoring the land. Taking the land away from the Crusaders in the twelfth century would require some sort of major catastrophe or military revolution. The prophet who composed this prophecy expected the "end" of the Roman era to take place that particular year. At that time David Alroy was gathering troops in Persia, and Saladin was preparing for his major victory at the Horns of the *Ḥittim*, which actually took place July, 1187. Zunz, *Gesammelten Schriften* III, 224-231, noted that there were at least 75 recorded and identifiable messianic movements between the second and the twentieth centuries.

[5]"Voices" may render the Hebrew קולות used to describe various sounds; human voices, trumpet blasts, and thunder. Human voices would not be expected along with all these other natural sounds.

heard in the air, striking terror into human hearts. All cities will be covered up with sand and dust, that is to say, [those] in the fifth climate; for that wind will begin from the western corner and extend all the way to the eastern corner [of the earth], taking in all the cities of Egypt and Ethiopia, that is to say, Malkah,[6] Bazara,[7] Aleppo,[8] Shinar,[9] the land of Arabah,[10] all the land of Elam.[11] Rama,[12] Carmel (Josh 15:55),[13] Segestan, Calla, Norozastan, Chabul (Josh 19:27),[14] Tanbrasten, and Beirut (Josh 18:25),[15] all of which cities or regions are included under the sign, Libra, and even the Roman lands.[16] After so much violence of the winds, five miracles will follow, one after the other.

First: There will arise from the east a certain very wise man with unusual knowledge, that is, with wisdom which is superhuman, and he will walk in justice, and he will teach the true law and upright character and right conduct. Many will turn back from the darkness of ignorance and faithfulness to the way of truth. He will teach sinners the ways of righteousness (Ps 25:8; Prov 16:31), but he will not extol himself [to accept a status] which is numbered among the prophets.[17]

Second: A certain man will go out from Elam and gather many and powerful troops (Dan 11:10), and he will bring about a great defeat among the Gentiles (Zech 14), but he will not live very long.[18]

Third: A certain other man will arise, saying that he is a prophet, holding a book in his hand and saying that he is sent from God [and that his mission was foretold] through his prophets.[19] Through [his] proclamation, he will make many Gentiles err and will seduce [still] more, but that which he will prophesy to the Gentiles will be turned upon his own path, and he also will not live long.

[6]Baer's rendering of *Mecha* (Baer, 116).
[7]Latin, *Balsara (Ibid.).*
[8]Latin, *Habeb* = Aleppo *(Ibid.).*
[9]Latin, *Sennaar (Ibid.).*
[10]Latin, *Terras Arabum (Ibid.).*
[11]Latin, *Helam (Ibid.).*
[12]Latin, *Roman (Ibid.).*
[13] Latin, *Carmen (Ibid.).*
[14]Latin, *Chebil (Ibid.).*
[15]Latin, *Barach (Ibid.).*
[16]Baer suggests that "Romans" should be rendered "Edom" here and considered the people populating the land south of Judah (Baer, 116).
[17]Possible Alroy, a messianic pretender in Persia at the same time.
[18]This may allude to Saladin's preparation against the Crusaders.
[19]This is Mohammed, who lived many years earlier, but whose movement was very much alive in Crusader times.

Fourth: Comets will be seen in the sky, that is to say, a hairy star or tail, and this appearance will indicate consumations, tumults, conflicts, hardships, withholdings of rain, droughts on the land, fierce wars, and the pouring out of blood. [This will happen] in the land of the East and through the river Chebar.[20] It will extend all the way to the end of the West, to such an extent that they will be oppressed, and persecutions will be endured by just and religious men who will be disrupted [in] the house of prayer.

Fifth: There will be an eclipse of the sun with so much brightness of display that the whole body of the sun will be darkened, and it will be so dark over the earth at the time of the eclipse that there will be as much sunlight as [there is] about midnight when the moon does not shine at the rainy season.

THE DAY OF THE LORD[21]

Rabbi Akiba

Shin: This refers to the teeth of the completely wicked ones whom the holy One blessed be He is destined to break three times, once in this world, once in the days of the Messiah, and once in the age to come,[22] for just as this shin (ש) has three branches, thus also will the holy One blessed be He break the teeth of the wicked three times, as it is said, Arise, O Lord; deliver me, O my God; for you have struck all my enemies [on the] jaw; you have broken the teeth of the wicked (Ps 3:8).[23] This is none other than the teeth of those who consume the wealth of the Israelites that are destined to protrude from their mouths for the days of the Messiah, for twenty-two cubits, and all those who enter the age will see and say, "In what way have these sinned that their teeth protrude from their mouths?" They will reply, "Because they consumed the wealth of the Israelites who are as holy to the Lord as terumah,[24] of which everyone who eats is guilty of a sin punishable by extinction, as it is said, Israel is holy to the Lord, the first fruits

[20]Latin, Heberi (Baer, 115).

[21]Text from S.A. Wertheimer, מדרשות בתי (Jerusalem, 1968) II, 392-94. SML

[22]Note the chronological order of the events: 1) this world or age, 2) the days of the Messiah, and 3) the age to come.

[23]This injury involved a "sock" with a fist on the jaw hard enough to break the recipient's teeth.

[24]See Kid. 53a; ExR 15.5(49b). Terumah is a "wave offering" which only priests are permitted to eat.

of the harvest; all who devour him [Israel] will be guilty; evil will come upon them (Jer 2:3).

Why does the holy One blessed be He break the teeth of the completely wicked three times? This teaches that the holy One blessed be He also separates the princes and the troops in the heaven above and says to them, "My princes, my troops; look at these completely wicked people who have decreed and wronged my children. They have devoured my people!" The princes and troops will reply, "Master of the ages, you are the Ruler over your age and over all the works of your hands, [all of] which you created in the world declare that you are their sovereign. Who in the world can tell you what you should do? as it is said, *When the word of the king rules, who will say to him, "What are you going to do"* (Eccles 8:4)? The holy One blessed be He will answer them, "If so, then you and I will first break their teeth, and after that, take them out of the world! My troops, I have appointed you over them in the world, that you become bound with them, break their teeth, and take them out of the world, as it is said, *The destruction of the transgressors and the sinners will be together; [those who abandon the Lord will be consumed]* (Isa 1:28). He will say to the princes, "I have appointed you over them for the days of the Messiah that you bind yourselves to them, break their teeth, and take them out of the world, as it is said, *Let those who persecute me be embarrassed, but let me not be ashamed; let them be dismayed, but let me not be dismayed. Bring upon them an evil day, and destroy them with double destruction* (Jer 17:18). I myself will also be bound to them, break their teeth, and expel them from the world, as it is said, *The Lord has broken the staff of the wicked, [the scepter of the rulers]* (Isa 14:5).

How do they break their teeth in this world? This teaches that troops descend from heaven and associate, one by one, with every single wicked person, break their teeth, and banish them from the world, as it is said, *The voice of the Lord breaks the cedars* (Ps 29:5). These are completely wicked ones who are compared to the cedars of Lebanon in this world because of their pride, as it is said, *I destroyed the Amorite before them, whose height was like the height of the cedars, [and who was as strong as the oak. I destroyed his fruit from above and his roots from below]* (Amos 2:9). *His fruit?* That is the body. *His roots?* That is the soul.

When the Messiah comes to Israel, Michael and Gabriel, princes of the troops and officers of the saints and noble ones, will come down and make war with the wicked man from the third and ninth hours. They will kill nineteen thousand myriads of the totally wicked among the Gentiles, as it is said, *Let the sinners be consumed from the land [and the wicked be no more]* (Ps 104:35).

When will the praise of the holy One blessed be He be increased in the world? When the wicked are exterminated from the land, as it is said, *When the wicked perish there is joy* (Prov 11:10). Also in the age to come, the holy One blessed be He will come down from heaven and execute judgment against the wicked and break their teeth with a fiery staff and destroy them from the world,[25] as it is said, *He strikes the peoples in anger, and with an incessant stroke* (Isa 14:6). There is no anger to compare with the judgment of Gehinnom, as it is said, *A day of anger is that day; [a day of anguish and distress, a day of ruin and devastation, a day of clouds and darkness]* (Zeph 1:15).

Summary

When Rabbi Akiba prepared his "Alphabet," with one topic of discussion for each letter of the Hebrew alphabet, the letter *shin*, which means "tooth," reminded him of the passage, "You have broken the teeth of the wicked" (Ps 3:7). Therefore the dissertation on *shin* deals with the punishment of the wicked. The wicked ones are those who have treated Jews unfavorably. On the day of judgment, the Lord with his angels will break their teeth and then drive them out of the world, leaving only the righteous Israelites to rule the world. This is part of the standard Jewish eschatology.

Another part of Jewish eschatology was the expectation that there would be signs in the world which would alert the faithful of the events that were to come. In the following documents, these signs were given in the order in which they were expected to occur.

SIGNS OF THE MESSIAH

Introduction

Higger's Text (H)[26]   *Jellinek's Text (J)*[27]

Ten signs will come to
the world before the end:

---

[25]The age to come is not distinguished by location but by time and nature. It is in the future, but God will still be in heaven and human beings on earth. God will come down to destroy them.

[26]M. Higger, הלכות ואגדות (Brooklyn, 1933), 127-30. SML

[27]A. Jellinek, בית המדרש II, 58-63. SML

The First Sign

The holy One blessed be
He is destined to
send three angels with the three
winds of the world.
They will
deny the [very] existence of
God and show themselves to
the sons of man as if they were
serving him,

and they will subdue
humanity.
At the end of days all the Gentiles
will deny the [very] existence
of God, as it is said, *The idols
shall utterly be cut off,*[28] and
the idols will utterly pass away
(Isa 2:18), because the holy One
blessed be He will display
troubles in the world, each different from the other.

The holy One blessed be
He is destined to

raise up three kings who will
deny their religion and be hypo-
crites who will make themselves
appear to others as if they were
serving the holy One blessed be
He when actually they are not.
They will lead astray and con-
fuse all the people, and infidels
among the Gentiles so as
to become heretics to their religion.

Also those transgressors of
Israel who have given up all
hope of redemption will reject
the holy One blessed be He and

give up revering him. Concerning that generation, it is said, *The
truth will be lacking* (Isa 59:15). What is the meaning of *will be
lacking*? It means that the faithful people will break up into herds
and persist in fleeing and hiding in the caves and caverns of the
earth. Then will all the faithful men and mighty men of the generation die; the gates of wisdom will be hidden; and the world will be
changed. In that time there will be no king or leader in Israel, as it
is said, *For many days Israel will live without king or prince,
without altar or pillar* (Hos 3:4).[29] There will be no deans of the
academies and no pride of Jacob, no faithful shepherds, no pious
ones, no famous scholars. The doors of heaven will be locked, and
the gates of sustenance and livelihood will be closed.

[28]This text is not apparently from the scriptures, but the author thought it was.

[29]The word translated "pillar" is מצבה which is a stone slab used by pagans as well as
Hebrews in antiquity as part of the furniture in the holy of holies.

J

When the Messiah will be revealed in all his might, then the generation will lose its courage because of the harsh, strange, and terrifying [anti-Jewish] decrees which those three kings had decreed. They will issue further decrees [with which] to deny the temple, the Lord, and the Torah. The holy One blessed be He has decreed that the wicked kingdom will rule for nine months, from vaulted chamber to doorway, as it is said, *Therefore he will give them until the time that she gives birth* (Micah 5:2). *Therefore* (לכן) is used only in an oath, as it is said, *Therefore, I have sworn concerning the house of Eli* (I Sam 3:14). All these nine months, one decree after another will be instituted, each one more severe than the one previous, and the tribute which Israelites will have to pay will be multiplied tenfold. Thus everyone who used to pay ten will pay a hundred, and everyone who used to pay eight will pay eighty, and the one who cannot pay will be beheaded.

Then men from the end of the world who are extremely repulsive will go forth, and everyone who sees them will die from terror. They will not have to make war, for they will slay everyone out of sheer fright. To each of them will be two heads and seven eyes that will burn like fire, and their pace will be as swift as a deer. In that hour, the Israelites will cry out and say, "Woe, woe!" Little Jewish children will be terrified and will hide themselves, each one under [the gowns of] his father and mother, saying, "Woe, woe, father! What shall we do?" Then will their father answer them, "Now we are near to the redemption of Israel."[30]

H   J

The Second Sign

The holy One blessed be He will bring out the sun from its sheath,	The holy One blessed be He will bring heat to the world from the heat of the sun together with wasting disease, fever, many evil diseases, pestilence, and plagues
and with it he will burn each day thousands of thousands of	will kill a million people of the

[30]This is part of the religious understanding of hardship by apocalyptists. The worse things become the better it is. Covenanters should rejoice in their sufferings. This follows the typology of the Exodus from Egypt.

H

Gentiles

until all the Gentiles will weep
and say, "Woe to us! Where
can we flee?"
They will dig

up all the caves in the land

to find relief for
themselves, as it is said,
*They will go into caves of the
rocks* (Isa 2:21).
One will say to the other,

"Come into the rock and hide in
the earth!" Concerning that sun,
Malachi prophesied, as it is said,
*For behold the day of the Lord
[is coming], burning like
an oven* (Mal 3:19), but that
sun will bring healing
for the Israelites, as it is
said, *For those of you who fear
my name, the sun of righteousness will rise, and healing will
be in its wings* (Mal 3:20). Concerning those hardships, the
wicked Balaam prophesied, as it
is said, *Alas, who will survive after God has appointed him*
(Num 24:23).

J

Gentiles every day. Then all the
wicked ones of Israel will die.
[These evils will continue]
until the Gentiles will weep
and cry out, "Woe to us! Where
can we go? Where can we flee?"
Then each one will dig his own
grave while he is still alive,
and they will wish that they
could die. They will hide
themselves in deserts, underground chambers, and briar
patches in an effort to cool
themselves.
They will enter caves and
caverns of the earth.
Should one say, "Where will the
righteous save themselves from
the heat of the sun?"

The holy One blessed be He
will provide them with healing
against that heat, as it is
said, *For those of you who fear
my name, the sun of righteousness will rise, and healing will
be in its wings* (Mal 3:20). Concerning that time, the
wicked Balaam prophesied,
*Alas, who will survive after
God has appointed him*
(Num 24:23).

The Third Sign

The holy One blessed be
He will cause dew of

The holy One blessed be
He will bring down a dew of

H

blood to descend for three days. It will appear to the Gentiles to be a dew of water, so they will drink of it and die.[31] Even the transgressors of Israel

will drink of it and die. The moderate [sinners] will become ill, and

the world will be in great distress during those three days, as it is said, *I will provide wonders in heaven and on earth, blood, fire, and pillars of smoke* (Joel 3:3).

J

blood. It will appear to the Gentiles as water. They will drink of it and die.[31] Even the wicked ones of Israel, who have given up all hope of redemption, will drink of it and die,

but the righteous ones, who have held fast to the faith of the holy One blessed be He will not be harmed at all, as it is said, *Those who teach will shine like the brightness of the firmament* (Dan 12:3). The entire world will wallow in blood during those three days, as it is said in Hosea [*sic.*], *I will provide wonders in heaven and on earth, blood, fire, and pillars of smoke* (Joel 3:3).

Marmorstein (M)[32]

The Third Sign (unique to M)

The holy One blessed be He will produce three rainbows in heaven, and they will remain there for three days and three

[31]M.L. Margolis and A. Marx, *A History of the Jewish People*, 404, told that during the "Black Death" epidemic that was imported into Europe from India and carried off more than one third of the population, the notion arose that Jews were causing the disease by poisoning the wells and rivers that supplied the drinking water. Since Jews drank the same water, theological views such as these may have given rise to such suspicions. If Jews believed God would provide water that would cause Gentiles to die and Jews to survive, a serious plague might suggest to Jews as well as to Christians that this was actually happening. Since Jews were international merchants, it was probably they who brought the disease to Europe from India, but they also died from it. In this age when all people were superstitious, it is not reasonable to expect that people could have deduced the real cause of the disease. It was normal both for Jews and Christians to find religious explanations for the disease.

[32]This text is taken from page 181-183 of Marmorstein, "Le Signes du Messie," *REJ* 52 (1906),176-86. This is a text from Cairo Geniza which is damaged at the beginning and in some places throughout the ms. It originally had ten signs, and parts of the second sign survive, but the clear text begins with the sign three. The lacunae are shown by brackets [].

M

nights.³³ Their beginning will be at one end of the world and their end
at the other end. One [   ]. All peoples and tongues will be
terribly frightened [at the sight], and they will think that the holy
One blessed be He is bringing a flood into the world, and they
will repeat the question, ["Will the Lord] bring a flood [into the
world?"] [   ]. Just as he has sworn [that he would not bring
a flood], thus he has sworn [that] he would not be angry with the
Israelites, as it is said, *I have sworn not to be angry with you nor
rebuke you* (Isa 54:9). The holy One blessed be He [   ]
will *gird on* the Israelites [with] *strength*, as it is written, *The bow
of the mighty will be broken, [but the stumbling ones will gird on
strength]* (I Sam 2:4).

The Fourth Sign (parallel to HJ third)

Rain will come down from heaven for three days and three
nights, but it will not be water but blood. The eighty thousand
Israelites who went astray after the three apostles of falsehood will
drink from that rain [and die].

The Fourth Sign (HJ)

H

The holy One blessed be He
will bring down healing dew
for three days and three nights
to heal the blood. All moderate
[sinners] will drink from it.
The sick will be healed,
as it is said, *I will be as the dew
to the Israelites. They will blossom as the lily, [and cast forth
their roots like a (cedar) of
Lebanon]* (Hos 14:6).

J

The holy One blessed be He
will bring down healing dew

to heal the blood. All moderate
[sinners] will drink from it,
and their diseases will be healed,
as it is said, *I will be as the dew
to the Israelites. They will blossom as the lily, and cast forth
their roots like a [cedar] of
Lebanon* (Hos 14:6).

The Fifth Sign (M)

The holy One blessed be He will bring down dew from heaven

---

³³A physical impossibility. The sunlight reflected on the moisture in the air creates a
rainbow. Therefore in the night time there could be none. In some areas and seasons there
are Northern Lights at night.

M

for three days and three nights and heal the previous [condition], but it will endanger all the world. People will think that it is [water] and is nothing but dew, as it is said, *I will be as the dew to the Israelites. [They will blossom as the lily, and cast forth their roots like a (cedar) of Lebanon and their roots will extend and their glory shall be like the olive]* (Hos 14:6-7)...*and they will sit in its shade, [and their grain will live]* (Hos 14:8).

The Sixth Sign (M)

The sun will grow dark for three days and three nights over all the Gentiles, but over the Israelites there will be light, as it is said, *For behold darkness will cover the earth [and deep darkness, the Gentiles, but the Lord will shine upon you]* (Isa 60:2).

The Gentiles will be very much afraid,

and they will come, prostrate

The Fifth Sign (J)

The holy One blessed be He will turn the sun into darkness for thirty days,

as it is said,

The sun will be changed to darkness and the moon into blood (Joel 3:4) After thirty days, the holy One blessed be He will restore it to its previous state, as it is said, *They will be gathered together as prisoners in the dungeons, and they shall be shut up in prison, and after many days, they will be [still further] punished* (Isa 24:22). The Gentiles will be very much afraid and embarrassed, for they will know that all these signs [happened] because of the Israelites. Many of them will become Jews in secret, as it is said, *Those who regard lying vanity forsake their own mercy* (Jonah 2:9).

M   J

themselves before the Israelites
and say, *Let us go with you, for we have heard that God is with
you* (Zech 8:23).

The Fifth Sign (H)

A king will arise in Rome, and he will destroy great states, and
he will conquer Egypt, as it is said, *He will stretch out his hand
against the North* (Zeph 2:13).[34] In his anger, he will turn against
the Israelites and impose a heavy tribute upon them, and he will
wish to destroy them from the world, as it is said, *He will turn his
face to the strongholds of the land* (Dan 11:19). These [the strong-
holds] are the Israelites, because they are the strongest among the
nations, and *his face* refers to his anger and wrath which he will
place upon them.

The Seventh Sign (M)

The king of Edom will go out and come to Jerusalem. All the
Ishmaelites will flee before him [   ] a great army, and there
will go out [   ] with them a man whose name is "Mantzur,"
and he will rule over them. They will go to Bazrah, and when the
king of Edom hears [of this] he will go after them. These [groups]
will make war with each other, as it is said, *[There is] a sacrifice in
Bozrah, [a great slaughter in the land of Edom]* (Isa 34:6), and it is
said, *"Eating pork and the detestable thing, and the mouse will be
consumed together," says the Lord* (Isa 66:17). Mantzur will kill
many from Edom. The king of Syria will flee before him, and
Mantzur will die. Then the king of Edom will return a second time
to Jerusalem and will enter the place of foundation stone, and he
will take the crown which is on his head and place it on the
foundation stone and say, "Master of the ages, I have returned
that which my fathers have taken."[35] The Israelites will suffer great
hardship in his days.

[34]This text is difficult or impossible to follow. Egypt was not from the North, either for
Roman Christians or Arabian Moslems, although it more nearly applies to the latter,
particularly with reference to the Fatimids who began in Yemen (A.D. 901), conquered
Tunisia (A.D. 908), and finally Egypt (A.D. 969). From there, they moved still further
north and east until they conquered Baghdad itself, taking Palestine on the way.
[35]Marmorstein conjectured that this was Heraclius (A.D. 610-41).

The Sixth Sign (J)

The holy One blessed be He will make the wicked Edom to rule all the world, as we have said above. Another king will arise in Rome and will rule over all the world for nine months. He will destroy many countries, and his anger will burn against Israel, and he will exact from it a heavy tribute. At that time the Israelites will endure great hardship, greater because of the many [anti-Jewish] decrees and tribulations that daily will be inaugurated against them. Israelites will be decreased and weakened at that time, and there will be no one to help the Israelites. It was concerning that time that Isaiah prophesied and said, *He saw that there was no one, and he was astonished [that no one interceded]* (Isa 59:16).

At the end of nine months, the Messiah, son of Joseph, will be revealed, and his name will be Nehemiah Ben Hoshiel. With him the tribe of Ephraim, Manasseh, Benjamin, and part of Gad will also appear. Then Israelites in every country will hear that the Messiah of the Lord has come, and they will gather themselves to him, a few from every province and city, as it is said in Jeremiah, *"Return, O backsliding children,"* says the Lord, *"for I am your Lord, and I will take you, one from every city and two from every family, and I will bring you to Zion"* (Jer 3:14).

Then the Messiah son of Joseph will incite a battle with the king of Edom and will conquer the Edomites and murder large numbers of them and kill the king of Edom. He will destroy the country of Rome, bring out the vessels of the temple which were stored in the house of Julianus Caesar, and will come to Jerusalem. Then the Israelites will hear and congregate to him. The king of Egypt will make peace with him, and he will kill all the men of the countries which surround Jerusalem as far as Damascus and Ascalon. Then everyone in the world will hear, and a great dread will fall upon them.

The Sixth Sign (H)

The holy One blessed be He will in that hour bring out the Messiah son of Joseph, whose name is Nehemiah Ben Hoshiel, and with mighty men from the sons of Zerah, son of Judah.

The Eighth Sign (M)

The holy One blessed be He will bring forth Nehemiah Ben Hoshiel, [who is] the Messiah son of Joseph

H   M

as it is said, *"Suddenly, the
Lord whom you are seeking, will come to his temple. [The messenger of the covenant in whom you take delight, behold, he is
coming," says the Lord of armies]* (Mal 3:1).

H   M

All the armies of Israel who
are in those places will accom-
pany him and war will be waged   He will make war
against the king of Edom.   with the king of Edom and kill
                                  him and wear the crown which
                                  the king of Edom left on the
                                  foundation stone,

The rest will flee and come
to Jerusalem and capture it. All the Israelites will hear and gather
themselves to him. The king of Egypt will make peace with him,
and he will slay all the Gentiles that are around Jerusalem.

H   M

Then all the nations will hear,   and the fame of Nehemiah will
                                   go out from one end of the world
                                   to the other

and great dread will fall upon
them.

The Seventh Sign

J

The holy One blessed be He, the Master of wonders, will perform a miracle in the world. They say that there is in Rome a
marble stone whose appearance is like a very beautiful woman.
She was [a statue] not made with human hands, but the holy One
blessed be He created her thus in his power. Then the wicked
Gentiles, sons of Beliel, will come and fall passionately in love
with her and cohabit with her. The holy One blessed be He will
keep their sperm inside the stone. He will then create inside
her a creature; he will form a son. [The stone] will

H

Armilos will come forth from that stone of a woman which is in Rome, and they will say of him that a stone gave him birth.

His length will be twelve cubits and his width, two cubits. There will be a distance of a span between his eyes.

He will be the Messiah of the sons of Esau.

He will gather all the nations and say to the sons of Esau, "Bring me the Torah which I gave you."

J

break open, and the one born from her will

appear like a man. His name will be Armilos, the tempter (Satan). This is the one whom the Gentiles [Christians] call the anti-Christ. He will be twelve cubits long and two cubits wide, and his eyes will be a span apart and be deep and bloodshot. His hair will be like gold dye. The soles of his feet will be greenish yellow, and he will have two heads.[36]

He will come to the wicked Edomites and say to them, "I am the Messiah; I am your God." Immediately they will believe in him and make him king over them. All the sons of Esau will join his followers and come to him, and he will proceed to conquer every country. He will say to the sons of Esau, "Bring me my Torah which I gave you." They will bring him their follies. Then he will say to them, "This is true which I have given you." He will say to the Gentiles, "Believe in me, for I am your Messiah!" At once they will believe in him.

H

J

At that time he will send to Nehemiah Ben Hoshiel and to all the Israelites and say to them,

---

[36]Heads of the church, one at Rome and the other at Constantinople.

H

At once all Israelites will
be startled,

Nehemiah Ben Hoshiel will rise
up, he and thirty [thousand]
mighty men with weapons of
war under their garments.

They will take the Book of
the Torah, and they will come
and read to him,
*You shall have no
other gods before me*
(Ex 20:3). He will say to them,
"Is this nothing at all?"

Nehemiah will
say to him,

"You are not god, but Satan!"
He will take to flight, and
[Armilos] will say to those
who serve him, "Search for
him and hang him!" [Nehemiah]
will make war with him and
smite down many of
them.
    Immediately the anger
of Armilos will
kindle, and he will gather
all the Gentiles
and come to
fight with the Isra-
elites between the sea...

J

"Bring me your Torah and
testify that I am God!" They
will immediately become frightened and bewildered. Then
Nehemiah Ben Hoshiel will rise
up with thirty thousand
warriors

from the soldiers of Ephraim,
and they will take the Book of
the Torah
and read it to him, *I am the Lord
your God...You shall have no
other gods before me*
(Ex 20:2-3). He will say to them,
"There is nothing at all in this
Torah of yours, but come, bear
witness to me that I am God,
just as all the Gentiles have
done." At once Nehemiah will
stand up and say to his servants,
"Seize him and tie him up." Immediately Nehemiah Ben
Hoshiel and the thirty thousand
who will rise up and

make war with him and
kill two hundred thousand of
his [soldiers].
    Immediately the anger
of the wicked Armilos will
be aroused, and he will gather
all the troops of the Gentiles
to the Valley of Decision. He
will join battle with the Israelites,

H	J
and the holy…The Israelites	
	and numerous of his soldiers
will smite them mightily, and	will be injured.
he [Armilos] will kill	He will slay
the Messiah	the Messiah of the Lord, and
	the ministering angels will
	come and take him and hide him
	with the patriarchs of the age.
When the Israelites see the	
Messiah has been killed, their	Suddenly the
hearts will melt,	hearts of the Israelites will melt,
and they will flee.	and their strength will weaken,
	but the wicked Armilos will not

know that the Messiah is dead, because if he knew, there would not be left from the Israelites a remnant or fugitive. At that time, all the Gentiles will drive the Israelites out of their countries, and they will not permit them to live with them in their countries. They will say, "Do you see this despised and defeated people who rebelled against us and set up a king?" There will be for the Israelites *harder times than there have ever been up to that time* (Dan 12:1).

H

The world will be in great distress. For twenty-five days, there will be those who will hide themselves in caves and holes. Those who are left will be locked in the midst of Jerusalem. He will set his face to fight against it and destroy it a second time, but he will not be successful.

J

At that time, Michael will stand up to purify the wicked ones in Israel, as it is said, *At that time Michael, the great prince who stands for the children of your people, will arise, and there will be a time of hardship such as there never has been [from the existence of the nation until that time]* (Dan 12:1). Quickly all will resort to the Gentiles and ask, "Is this the redemption for which we have been waiting, when the Messiah will be murdered?" But everyone who has not looked forward to the redemption will be embarrassed

J

by it and will defect to the Gentiles. At that time the holy One
blessed be He will test the Israelites and refine them like silver and
gold, as it is written in Zechariah, *I will bring the third part
through the fire, and I will refine them as silver is refined* (Zech
13:9). For it is written in Ezekiel, *I will purge you out from among
[the rebels and those who transgress against me]* (Ezek 20:38), and
in Daniel it is written, *They will cleanse themselves and make
themselves white, and many will be refined, but the wicked will
act wickedly* (Dan 12:10).

Then all the remnant of the Israelites, the saints and the pure
ones, will be in the Wilderness of Judah for forty-five days. They
will be shepherds and will eat [only] salt-wort and the leaves
plucked from shrubs. In them will be fulfilled that which is said in
Hosea, *Therefore, behold I will allure her and lead her into the
wilderness, and I will speak tenderly to her* (Hos 2:16). Where [can
you find scriptural proof] that it will be forty-five days? As it is
said, *From the time the continual burnt-offering is taken away and
the abomination of desolations is set up, [there shall be] one thous-
and, two hundred, ninety days* (Dan 12:11). It also says, *Blessed is
he who waits until [the time] arrives, one thousand, three
hundred, thirty-five days* (Dan 12:12). The difference between one
figure and the other is forty-five days [i.e., 1,335−1,290=45]. At
that time, the wicked ones of Israel who were not considered
worthy to see the redemption, will die. Then Armilos will come
and fight with Egypt and capture it, as it is said, *The land of Egypt
shall not escape* (Dan 11:42). He will turn his face toward
Jerusalem and destroy it a second time, as it is said, *He will pitch
his palatial tents between the seas and the mountains of the glorious sanctuary, and he will come to his end, and no one will help
him* (Dan 11:45).

The Ninth Sign (M)

A man will go out from the province of Rome, and his name will
be Armilos, son of the statue. [The statue] will be female, and
Satan will go, and he will cohabit with her. Then she will become
pregnant and give birth to him [Armilos]. A hundred years will
pass since his birth, and he will go out and make war with
Alexandria and destroy it. He will destroy the whole sea shore.
Woe to the man who [is alive] in his day! He will come to the city

M

of Emmaus, the city of his father, and he will place his throne upon it. [These are] his signs: His height will be twelve cubits, and his eyes, blind-folded. When he sits down, he will insult and blaspheme, saying, "I am God." He will tempt the sons of Esau and tell them, "Bring my Torah which I have given [you]!" They will then bring their images and their idols, and he will say to them, "The Torah which I have given you is true." Then he will say to the Ishmaelites, "Bring [me] your Torah," and they will bring their scriptures. He will [then] say to them, "The Torah which I have given you is true." Then he will say to the sons of Israel, "Bring [me] your Torah." When they bring him the book of the Law, he will say, "We do not believe this Torah." They will say, "If you do not believe this Torah, you are only Satan. You are the man to whom the scripture refers, *[May God] rebuke you, Satan* (Zech 3:2). He will take the thirty men who will have come with Nehemiah and will burn them together with the Torah. Then he will turn and say to Nehemiah, "Do you not believe in me?" Nehemiah will say to him, "I believe only in the God of Israel who has given the Torah through Moses, the son of Amram and in the prophet whom he will suddenly raise to his feet in his temple. I killed the king of Edom in whom I believe, but I do not believe in you. Armilos will then say, "Take Nehemiah and kill him in the house of his God." They will slay Nehemiah, and his corpse will be cast [in Jerusalem] for forty days and forty nights, and no one will come near it. The Israelites will then mourn for him, as it is said, *They will mourn for him as one mourns [for an only child, and weep bitterly over him as one weeps over a first born]* (Zech 12:10). He said, *The land will mourn, each family [by itself; the family of the house of David by itself; their wives by themselves; the family of the house of Nathan..., of Levi..., of the Shemites ..., and all the families that are left, each by itself, and their wives by themselves]* (Zech 12:12-14).

At that time the Israelites will be in great trouble. Some of them will hide themselves in caves and pits, and those who remain of them will flee to the wilderness of Ammon and Moab. *The outcasts of Moab will dwell in you* (Isa 16:4), and they will wander about there for forty days, eating broom bushes and salt wort, as it is said, *Those who pluck salt wort with wormwood, [and roots of broom bushes are their food]* (Job 30:4).

Then Armilos, the son of Satan, will go to the wilderness of

M

Moab (That is Armilos the son of the stone, as it is said, *He will bring forth the top stone* [Zech 4:7]). The Israelites will cry out bitterly to Heaven, and *Michael the prince* of the throne of glory, will provide mercy for them. He will *stand* in prayer before the holy One blessed be He, as it is written, *In that time Michael, the great prince who stands for the sons of your people, will arise* (Dan 12:1). The word *standing* (עומד) applies only to prayer. He will say to him, "Master of all the ages, remember that which you have sworn to their fathers and to them, and that which you have said to Moses your servant, *I have forgiven them according to your word* (Num 14:20), and further, *I will pardon those whom I leave as a remnant* (Jer 50:20). You have called them *saints*, as it is written, *You shall be my saints* (Lev 20:26) and separated for your name." Then the holy One blessed be He will hear the prayer of Michael in behalf of the Israelites.

The Eighth Sign

H	J
At that time Michael, the great prince, will arise (Dan 12:1).	*Michael will arise* (Dan 12:1) and sound the shofar three times, as it is said, *On that day a great*

shofar will be blown (Isa 27:13). For it is written, *God will blow the shofar and will come with the whirlwinds of the south* (Zech 9:14).

H	J
Then Elijah will come with the Messiah son of David to fulfill that which was said, *He will turn the heart of the fathers to the children and the hearts of the children to the fathers* (Mal 3:24).	At the first blast, the Messiah son of David

J

and the prophet Elijah will be revealed to those refined and righteous ones of Israel and those who had fled to the Wilderness of Judah. At the end of forty-five days, they will take courage, and

J

support their trembling hands and make steady their knocking knees (Isa 35:3).

The rest of the Israelites in all the world will hear the sound of the shofar, and they will know that the Lord has visited them and that the complete redemption has come. Then they will gather together and come, as it is said, *Those who are lost in the land of Assyria [and those who are dispersed in the land of Egypt will worship the Lord in the holy mountain at Jerusalem]* (Isa 27:13).

At that sound, fear and trembling will fall over the Gentiles, and grievous illness will fall upon them. The Israelites will gird their loins and get ready to leave. Then the Messiah son of David and the prophet Elijah will come to Jerusalem with the righteous ones who have lived in the Wilderness of Judah and with all the Israelites who have congregated, and he will go up the remaining stairs of the temple and dwell there.

Then Armilos will hear that a king has arisen over Israel, and he will say, "How long will this despised and broken nation keep on doing this?" At once he will gather all the troops of the Gentiles and will come to fight with the Messiah of the Lord. Then the holy One blessed be He

H	J
The Messiah will not be required to fight. He will fix his gaze on Armilos and destroy him from the world, as it is said, *With the breath of his lips he will slay the wicked* (Isa 11:4)	will not require him to fight,

but will say to him, *Sit at my right hand* (Ps 110:1). He will say to the Israelites, *Stand still and see the salvation of the Lord which he will bring about for you today* (Ex 14:13). At once the holy One blessed be He will engage in conflict with them, as it is said, *The Lord will go forth and fight those nations as when he fights on the day of battle* (Zech 14:3). The holy One blessed be He will bring down fire and brimstone from heaven, as it is said, *I will plead against him with pestilence and blood, [and I will cause to rain upon him] an overflowing shower, [hailstones, fire, and brimstone]* (Ezek 38:22).

Suddenly the wicked Armilos will die together with all his

J

troops, and the wicked Edomites who destroyed the temple of our God and drove us into exile from our land. Then the Israelites will wreak great vengeance upon them, as it is said, *Then the house of Jacob will become a fire, and the house of Joseph, a flame, and the house of Esau, stubble* (Obad 18).

The Ninth Sign

H

The Messiah will seek from the holy One blessed be He to restore life to the dead,

and the Messiah son of Joseph

will be the first to come to life again. He will be the agent of the Messiah son of David. [The son of David] will send him [the son of Joseph] into all the lands where there are Israelites.

J

Michael will sound forth a great blast, and the graves in Jerusalem will be opened, and the holy One blessed be He will revive them [the corpses]. Then the Messiah

son of David and the prophet Elijah will go and revive the Messiah son of Joseph who was buried at the gates of Jerusalem.

The Messiah son of David will send him out

for the rest of the Israelites who are scattered in all the lands. Immediately the Gentile kings will carry them on their shoulders and bring them to the Lord (see Isa 49:22-23).

They will be gathered from all the corners, and he [the son of David] will send him [the son of Joseph] beyond the river Cush, and he will bring out the ten tribes,[37] and he will bring out the

---

[37]There was a deeply imbedded belief in medieval Judaism that the ten lost tribes were

H

vessels of the temple of the Lord from Rome. Every place where the Messiah son of Joseph enters there will be dead Israelites. He will revive them. All of them will come with him, as it is said, *Behold these will come from afar* (Isa 49:12).

J

Michael will sound forth a great blast,[38] and the holy One blessed be He will bring out all the tribes from the river Gozen and from Halah and from Habor, and from all the cities of Media. [All the tribes] will come together with the sons of Moses, too many to be counted or estimated. The land before them will be like the Garden of Eden, but behind them, a flaming fire [will burn] so that no living being will remain of the Gentiles. When the tribes depart, clouds of glory will surround them, and the holy One blessed be He will go before them, as it is said, *The breaker has gone up before them* (Micah 2:13). The holy One blessed be He will open for them fountains of the tree of life, and he will provide them with water to drink on the way, as it is said in Isaiah, *I will open rivers on the high hills, and fountains in the midst of the valleys. I will make the wilderness a pool of water, and the dry land springs of water* (Isa 41:18). For it is written, *They shall neither hunger nor thirst, and neither scorching wind nor sun will smite them* (Isa 49:10).

May the holy One blessed be He make us worthy to see the redemption speedily, and make us worthy to see the chosen house and fulfill in us the scripture where it is written, *Behold I will return the captivity of the tents of Jacob, and I will have mercy on his dwellings; the city will be built on its tel, and the palace will be inhabited in its customary place* (Jer 30:18).

May he confirm for us all his comforts and promises which were told through his prophets, as it is written, *In that time I will bring you, and at that time I will gather you, for I will make you to be a name and a praise* (Zeph 3:20).

---

hidden in Africa and the East. In the days of the Messiah they would present themselves with thousands of well trained and armed troops to defeat the Gentiles, thus running interference for the Jews.

[38]Announcing the nationalistic jubilee (Isa 27:13).

The Tenth Sign (M)

He will bring forth [Menahem Ben] Amiel, the Messiah son of David from prison, *for he will go out from prison to rule* (Eccles 4:14). He will mount him on a cloud, as it is said, *He will come with the clouds of heaven* (Dan 7:13). [This is] the sign of the messianic king: He is tall; his neck is thick; his face is [round] like the sun; his eyes are aflame; the hooves of his feet are thick; his back is wrinkled. He will rule over all the countries, and he will be given the kingdom, the glory, and the greatness (cf. Dan 7:14). Then Armilos will arise and with him [the troops of] seventy tongues will be gathered, as it is said, *The kings of the earth will be gathered* (Ps 2:2). Everyone who resists him will become attached to him. [Then the Messiah son of David] will kill [them], as it is said, *With the breath of his lips he will slay the wicked* (Isa 11:4). He will slay Armilos the son of the stone and save Israel. His fame will go forth from one end of the world to the other.

The Tenth Sign (H)

The coming of Gog and Magog, as it is written in the Book of Ezekiel (Ezek 38-39).
May the holy One blessed be He grant us merit to see [him].
Amen! and quickly, in our days!
May this be his will
Amen!

Summary

Patterned, perhaps, after the ten plagues that afflicted Egypt before the end of the captivity in Egypt and the defeat of the Canaanites, Philistines, and the Amorites before gaining possession of the promised land, the unknown authors who prepared these various versions of this document listed ten events that would take place before the Gentiles would be defeated in the war of Gog and Magog and the Jews would be reestablished in the promised land. The signs included the activity of God, his angels, the Jews, and the Gentiles. Although Jews also faced some of the afflictions, most of these signs were directed in their favor as punishment to the Gentiles.

There is a synoptic relationship among these documents,

showing that one used the other or a source of the other. This is most obvious in the seventh sign. Higger's text is clearly parallel to Jellinek's, but Higger's text has omitted parts that leave the narrative incoherent and dependent upon Jellinek's or Jellinek's source. The sons of Esau were ordered to bring their Torah to Armilos, to which the *Israelites*, rather than the Edomites, responded. Jellinek's text shows the omitted conversation that prompted the Israelites' answer. This indicates the secondary nature of Higger's text.

There is little in the documents to indicate a date of origin. In Marmorstein's text, there is a certain king, named Mantzur, which, if identified, would be helpful. It is not even certain whether he represented the Ishmaelites or the Edomites. Marmorstein suggests Omar I (A.D. 634-41) as a possibility, but thought the Christian, Heraclius (A.D. 610-41) more likely. Either one requires a seventh century date. Additions may have been made to all the texts after their original composition.

THE COMFORTS OF THE MESSIAH[39]

Corresponding to these ten signs [of the Messiah], the holy One blessed be He is destined to establish Jerusalem with ten kinds of precious stones; namely, ruby, topaz, emerald, beryl, onyx, jasper, turquoise, sapphire, diamond, and gold. This totals ten. The holy One blessed be He will add two more in the building of the house of the sanctuary: the jacinth and carbuncle stones, as it is said, *I have set your pinnacles of jacinth and your gates of carbuncles, [and all your wall of precious stones]* (Isa 54:12).

Corresponding to them the holy One blessed be He is destined to restore to the Israelites ten things of which he had deprived them and which were missing in the second temple, as it is said, *I will be pleased with it and I will be glorified* (Hag 1:8). These are they: the ark and the cherubim, the anointing oil, the ranked wood [for the altar],[40] urim and thummim, and the Holy Spirit. There are five others which the holy One blessed be He is destined to add, such as the light of the sun [increased] three hundred, forty-three times its present light, as it is said, *The light of the moon will be as the light of the sun, and the light of the sun will be seven times the light of*

---

[39]The text is from A. Jellinek, בית המדרש VI, 118-20. SML
[40]Since a fire had to be kept burning on the altar continually, there was always firewood ranked nearby.

seven days, in the day that the Lord binds up the wound of his people and the stroke of their wound he will heal (Isa 30:26). Where do we find that the [number] is three hundred, forty-three? This we infer from the interpretation of Jonathan Ben Uzziel: "The light of the moon will be as the light of the sun, and the light of the sun is destined to shine about three hundred, forty-three times as bright as the light of the seven days." When you multiply seven times seven, the total is forty-nine. Multiply the total by seven, as it is said, *as the light of the seven days* (Isa 30:26). [When you multiply forty-nine times seven] the total is three hundred, forty-three. Thus the holy One blessed be He is destined to make the righteous shine according to this number, as it is said, *Those who love him like the sun in its power* (Jdgs 5:31). We interpret this to mean that the deeds of the righteous are destined to shine in splendid brilliance three hundred, forty-three times as much as the brilliance of the sun in its power. These are the seven which the holy One blessed be He is destined to restore and which Moses merited to receive, as it is said, *[Moses took] the tent [of meeting]* (Ex 31:7). The holy One blessed be He is destined to restore them, as it is written, *The joy of the age[41] shall be upon their heads* (Isa 35:10; 51:11). *Again you will be adorned with timbrels and go forth in the dances of the merrymakers* (Jer 31:4). There are ten blessings of corn and tallow.

Corresponding to these are the ten comforts of redemption and the promises of which the holy One blessed be He assured Israel and which are [incidentally] the most important comforts, the rest being consequential to them. The first is the coming of the redeemer, as it is said, *Behold your king comes to you* (Zech 9:9). Second, the gathering of the exiles, as it is said in Jeremiah, *Behold I will bring them from the land of the North, and I will gather them from the uttermost parts of the earth and with them the blind and the lame, [the pregnant woman and the one who is in labor, a great congregation will return here]* (Jer 31:8). Who are *the blind and lame?* This teaches that every righteous person will return just as he had departed from this age; that is, whoever was blind [in this age] will return in the resurrection, blind; whoever was lame [in this life] will also return in his resurrection, lame, and so on with all the blemished ones. [This is so] that everyone of them will be able to recognize his fellow and no one will be able to say, "These are different creatures!" After this the holy One blessed be He will heal them, as it is said, *Then the lame man will leap like a*

---

[41] The age when the land is restored.

hart and the tongue of the dumb will sing (Isa 35:6). Third will be the resurrection of the dead, as it is said, *Many who sleep in the dust of the earth will awaken* (Dan 12:2). Fourth will be the rebuilding of the house of the sanctuary. Its construction will be like the appearance of the building which Ezekiel saw in its full splendor. The fifth [comfort] will be that the Israelites are destined to rule over the entire world completely, from shore to shore, as it is said, *For the nation and the kingdom that will not serve you will perish [the Gentiles will be completely destroyed]* (Isa 60:12). The whole world will return to the judgment of the holy One blessed be He and to his Torah, as it is said, *Then I will turn to the Gentiles [so that they will all speak] a pure language, so that all of them may call upon the name of the Lord [to serve him (with) one shoulder]* (Zeph 3:9). Sixth, the holy One blessed be He is destined to destroy all the enemies of his people and wreak vengeance upon them, as it is said, *I will wreak vengeance with Edom through my people Israel* (Ezek 25:14). Seventh, the holy One blessed be He will remove every illness and every affliction from the Israelites, as it is said, *The inhabitant will not say, "I am ill," The people who dwell there will be forgiven [their] iniquity* (Isa 33:24). Eighth, the holy One blessed be He will extend the days of the Israelites like a tree, as it is said, *For the days of a tree will be the days of my people* (Isa 65:22), and it is written in Isaiah, *For the youngest will die at the age of a hundred, and the sinner, being a hundred years old will be accursed* (Isa 65:20). It is [also] written, *He will swallow up death forever, and the Lord God will wipe away tears from all faces* (Isa 25:8). Ninth, the holy One blessed be He is destined to reveal himself, eye to eye, to the Israelites, as it is said, *The glory of the Lord will be revealed, and all flesh will see it together, for the mouth of the Lord has spoken* (Isa 40:5). He is destined further to make all Israelites into prophets, as it is said in Hosea [*sic.*], *It will be after this, that I will pour out my spirit on all flesh, and your sons and your daughters will prophesy, [and your old men will dream dreams and your young men will see visions]* (Joel 3:1). Tenth, the holy One blessed be He is destined to remove the evil impulse and every other evil thing from Israel, as it is said, *I will give you also a new heart, and I will put a new spirit within you. I will remove the stoney heart from your flesh, and I will give you a heart of flesh* (Ezek 36:26).

Summary

This essay is the second half of a document called "The Wars of the Messiah." This portion takes for granted the knowledge of the ten signs of the Messiah which was evidently circulated very widely. Just as the signs of the Messiah are mostly signs of affliction and hardship that are the necessary birth pangs of the Messiah, so these are corresponding comforts that Israelites are destined to receive after the birth pangs are over. Although these are all exaggerated and utopian in nature, they are all normal parts of Israel's hope related to the restoration of the land and world rule.

KARAITIC CALCULATIONS[42]

Ps 90:3-4:

You turn back to the dust, and say, "Turn back, O sons of man."
For a thousand years in your eyes are but as yesterday when it is
past, or as a watch in the night.

41 *verso*) Moses said: "Lord God of Israel, I have seen with the *eye of prophecy* that *Behold the days are coming* (Amos 8:11) [when] *you turn man back* into exile *to the dust. You say, "If you wish,* [then] I will gather you together." *Turn back, O sons of man to me, and I will turn back to you* (Mal 3:7)...I have seen by means of the Holy Spirit[43] that the Israelites will be *a thousand years* in exile, but they [the years] will be *in your eyes*, O Lord, *but as yesterday*, because you live and exist. When the prophets and righteous men will entreat and call to you in their behalf, [then] you will pay attention at its proper season and its day.[44] They will call it exile and say, "Deliver your people, O Lord our God." You will not pay attention to this, however, because Israel will transgress your covenant and your Torah.

42 *recto*) There are not only *a thousand years* but *a thousand years and a watch*. Bear in mind that *a watch* is a third of *the night*, and they are therefore a third of *a thousand*,[45] [i.e.,] three hundred, thirty-three. The total is that the whole [period] is one *thousand*, three hundred, thirty-three years. The mourners for Zion say that their beginning will be from the destruction of the first house of the Lord [ca. 586 B.C.] until this day, when I wrote this book, i.e., the year one *thousand*, three hundred, [thirty] six years,[46]

[42]The text is from J. Mann, "Karaite Settlement in Jerusalem," *Texts and Studies* (New York, 1972) II, 100-102. SML

[43]As is often the case, the Holy Spirit speaks through the scripture.

[44]In the predestined time.

[45]Since a watch is a third of a day, and a day equals a thousand years, a watch equals three hundred, thirty-three and a third years.

[46]Which is the basic figure used and not three hundred, thirty-three.

according to the calendar of the Greeks of Alexander, in the month of Tishri, the sixth Rosh ha-Shenah, i.e., one *thousand,* three hundred, [thirty] six years (1336 Sel = A.D. 1024).

Note that from the day when the temple was destroyed (586 B.C.) until the kingdom of Alexander (331 B.C.),[47] [the period] was one hundred, six years. [Of] these, twenty-five were for Nebuchadnezzar; for his son Avil, twenty-two years; for Belshazzar, his grandson, three years; for Cyrus, three. For Darius, the Mede, ruled one year. To complete the Babylonian [rule] of seventy years, Ahashverus [ruled] thirteen [years]; and Artahshasta, the young, one year $[25+22+3+3+1+13+1=68]$. Darius the Persian, six years, and Artahshashtah the great, thirty-three. In his days, Alexander came into the West, and took the kingdom of Artahshashtah. The entire [Median and Persian rule] was one hundred, six [years].

I have stated that from the kingdom of Alexander until now is one *thousand,* three hundred, thirty-six. The whole is one *thousand,* four hundred, forty-two. How will there be a *watch* of three hundred, thirty three? Have not nine years already passed, and salvation has not yet come?

The answer: It has been said that until there will be in Israel those who teach [who] will pray this prayer, [the end will not come]. [The prayer] says: *For a thousand years in your eyes... and a watch in the night* (Ps 90:4) [will elapse during which] you will not listen to the prayer of the Israelites. After this, the prayer of those who teach, who will repent of their sin, will be heard. There will be great hardship, and times of the birth pangs of the Messiah, and they will be saved and prosper, as it is said, "He did not say *a thousand and* half *the night,* but he said, *[a thousand years]...*and *a watch in the night*(Ps 90:4). *Night* in winter is longer than day by three hours, more or less. Therefore it says, *in the night* which is proof for the day which *is a thousand years.* [If it were calculated for the long night of fifteen hours rather than for a watch in the day of less than twelve hours], there is left a little [time] for salvation.

May the God of Israel teach us and all those who are anxious at his word. Amen.

Summary

This great concern for calculations of the end time on the part of

---

[47]Alexander became king of Macedonia in 336 B.C. He conquered Persia in 331 B.C. The Greek period is usually dated from 312 B.C.

a Karaite commentator shows how deeply and thoroughly this concern for redemption had permeated Jewish thought. It was not only expressed by scholars like Saadia, Maimonides, Naḥmonides, Ḥiyya, and the author of *Pesikta Rabbati* 34-37, and poets like Kallir, Halevy, Gabirol, and Ibn Ezra, authors of numberless standard prayers, and the authors and editors of basic theological teachings like the Talmudim and many of the midrashim, but it even captured the attention of a Karaite commentator. There seems to have been no sect in Judaism for which this so-called fringe literature was not central. He did not comment on Daniel, but he picked a psalm that was frequently used by other Jewish calculators of the end times.

The author's text was Ps 90:3-4, from which he deduced that there should be one day of a thousand years elapse after the fall of the first temple—plus one watch—until the end of Israel's exile came. A watch is normally considered to be eight hours, or a third of a day. A third of a thousand year day would be three hundred, thirty-three years. When this number was measured from 586 B.C., he found that the time for the end had already passed at the time he wrote (A.D. 1024). This required recalculation. Closer observation reminded him that this particular watch to be measured was a night watch. In winter, the night is longer than the day by three hours. This means that there are still some more years left until the prophesied end is to be fulfilled. The promised deliverance had therefore not failed. Of course, by the same token it could be just as cogently argued that the night was in summer and therefore three hours shorter, but this would not have been satisfying. The author quoted one of the prophets to introduce his text (Amos 8:11).

THE SAMARITANS IN THE DIASPORA[48]

They will enter into the Sambation river,[49] and it will surround them for [the distance of] a three month's walk. Before them and behind them a flame will burn, and seven clouds of glory will

[48]The text is from J. Mann, "Glanures de la Gueniza," *REJ* 74 (1922), 150-54. T.-S 8 J. 33:2 *fol.* 1 *recto-fol.* 4 *verso*, p. 14.   SML

[49]D. Kaufmann,"Le Sambation," *REJ* 22 (1891), 285-87, conjectured that the legendary Sambation river was originally called a Sand river (נהר חול). Since חול means both "sand" and "working days," the river became called the "common river," and a legend developed that it ran only on week days—never on the Sabbath day. The same kind of confusion was possible with Beersheva, which could mean both "Oath Well" and "Well No. Seven." Legends developed for both (Gen 21:22-34).

surround them.[50] Now he knows how to bring you up, our brothers who are under the hand of exile of Edom[51] and Ishmael,[52] scattered among the Gentiles, pining and broken. And now he has sent us as several emissaries from him, mighty men and of great strength to spy out the land (Josh 14:7; II Sam 10:3) and to look around[53] [to find] from which place we should enter the land of Israel and from which city we should begin [our attack], because already the Sambation river has ceased [to flow], and it is dried up. Our brothers of the tribe of Moses will go out in countless numbers. We will all be gathered together, and we will come to one city which is called Ancone, [Italy], and we will make Joseph Ben Solomon, from the seed of Jesse, king (May his praise be exalted and his height magnified). He will bring out for us four flags upon which will be written the ineffable Name and the ten commandments in Assyrian script. The flag of the camp of Reuben, Gad, and Asher, registering them from twenty years old and older. There will be, altogether, three hundred, twenty thousand mighty men of valor, of great strength and [skill in] war. Those camping above them [will be under] the flag of Zebulun, Dan, and Naphtali, registering them from twenty years old and older, twenty-six thousand, all mighty men of war. Those who camp above them will be Ephraim, Issachar, and half the tribe of Manasseh, registering thirty-seven thousand, five hundred, all of them mighty men of valor.[54]

The tribe of Levi will be facing them all, five times [their number] and more than can be counted, all mighty men, armed with the sword and experienced in the strategy of war. *One will pursue a thousand, and two will make a myriad flee* (Dt 32:30). In our iniquities, however, there are only left from us the tribe of Judah, Benjamin, and half the tribe of Manasseh, who are now under the exile of Edom and Ishmael.[55] The fourth flag is deposited in the ark until King Joseph brings it to the tribe of Judah and Benjamin who are in exile. We have many cattle, horses, and camels. We have so much silver and gold that it is never completely counted. We have ten kinds of precious stones. They are: ruby, topaz, emerald, crysolite, beryl, jasper, turquois, sapphire, diamond, and gold

---

[50]Reminiscent of the Exodus from Egypt.

[51]The Roman or Byzantine Christians.

[52]The Moslems.

[53]Literally, "to look around in the age or world" (ולראות בעולם). The עולם in this case, is the promised land. In what sense is that the "world" or the "age?"

[54]Variation of Num 2.

[55]Since both Christians and Moslems were strong powers, this seems to have been written after A.D. 622.

with which to lay the foundation stone for Jerusalem. We have hidden in the house of the sanctuary a jar of manna and a shofar, the ark and the cherubim, the anointing oil, urim and thummim (Yoma 52b; Heb 9:2-5). Soon we will have to rule over all the entire world, from shore to shore, and we will wreak a great vengeance upon the Gentiles. They will all be slaves of the congregation of Israel, as it is said, *For the nation and kingdom which does not serve you will perish. The Gentiles will be completely destroyed* (Isa 60:12). The entire exile will go up when we all come together to the city of Ancone. From there we will divide the land into a lot for the tribes of Reuben and Gad. Asher's lot will fall for wicked Rome. We will camp in the wilderness, a four days' walk from the city of Rome. We will wait for an opportune moment; we will make an annihilation of Edom; and we will destroy Rome. We will bring out from there the vessels of the house of the Lord, and the scriptures will be fulfilled, *I shall wreak my vengeance against Edom by the hand of my people, the Israelites* (Ezek 25:14).

The tribe of Zubulun, Dan, and Naphtali will go out to subdue Mount Karan,[56] Mecca, and Yedda whose lot fell to them. Ephraim, Issachar, and Manasseh will go to the West to gather the Israelites and to wreak vengeance against the Gentiles. The tribe of the sons of Moses will go to the side of Aden to bring our brothers who are there in the exile. Among them will be found the prophet Elijah (upon whom be peace). We need have no permission to do anything except at the direction of the Lord and from the mouth of Elijah (upon whom be peace).

We will not leave any substance to the Gentiles who are there under our control. We will kill them all with the sword. After a year and a half, we will leave there[57] and go to the city of Ancone, and there we and our cattle will dwell in tents. Woe to the Gentiles when we come against them! There will not be left for them any substance. There will be no remnant and no fugitive.[58] Blessed is he who waits and comes to [the time], for the time is near and the coming salvation.

Therefore, our brothers, our chiefs, our informants—all the entire congregations that are in all the lands, including our lord and teacher, the great instructor Abraham will be delivered from destruction. He will be like a watered garden from our lord and king Joseph (May his praise be exalted) who is from the stock of

---

[56]A mountain somewhere on the route from Medina to Mecca.
[57]Apparently from the East, near the Sambation river.
[58]Patterned after the experience in the wilderness, just before taking Jericho.

Jesse, the father of David (upon whom be peace), declaring and witnessing to the roots of truth and righteousness, a flower of the shoot of David, a blossom of the crown of Naaman. From the fountain of loving kindness there will flow a great river with which to water all the gardens, to make the flowers bloom which are seen in the land of Judah and Jerusalem. Look, it flows slowly and speaks to every weary and thirsty person in the wilderness of Judah as it flows along. How they will long to see the faces of our brothers who are scattered in the exile awaiting the year of redemption.[59] We are in Calachene and Chabur and the River Gozen, and we have left the river Sambation. Therefore, it is our desire that we not be killed, and that he[60] dwell among us about a year until the sons of *Adbeal and Mibsam* (Gen 25:13)[61] come, and we will send him with them, but he said that he was living on the street of the Jews and that he still would recognize some words of the holy language.

Now as for us, we Israelites are waiting eagerly for you to rescue us, because you are stronger than we are. The tribes of Judah and Benjamin [are strong], for of Judah, it is said, *Judah is a lion's whelp* (Gen 49:9), and of Benjamin it is said, *Benjamin is a wolf; he will tear [the enemy] to pieces* (Gen 49:27).

Weakness [has prevented us] from coming to you.[62] Moreover, you live in the holy place, and the Shekinah has not departed from its place, and the Western Wall still stands.[63] Now, our brothers, sons of Israel, you must arise and help us with repentance, righteousness, and good deeds, so as to redeem the presence of our strength. Then we will return to the Lord our God, and he will have mercy upon us.

We have heard several bad reports about you, that you plunder, steal, perform lewd acts, shed blood, drink the wine of libations [to idols], and many [other] evil deeds, [such as] hating without cause, and particularly about Jews who live in the cities of Edom and who have taken foreign wives and have mingled with the Gentiles and adopted their ways.

When will you wake up from your sleep? Do you not remember what Sennacherib did for us, and Nebuchadnezzar who destroyed our sanctuary, and burned our temple, and carried away the vessels from the house of our sanctuary and our [other] precious

[59]A memorized eulogy used in letters.
[60]The antecedent is not clear.
[61]Sons of Ishmael, and therefore a symbol of the Moslems.
[62]In other words, they are *not* as strong as the author indicated earlier.
[63]The so-called "wailing wall" in Jerusalem—a place of worship.

things? Do you not remember what the wicked Titus did? Still you [are behaving on the principle]: *Each man does that which is right in his own eyes* (Prov 21:2-3). You give power to the Gentiles to overpower us. We and you are scattered to the four winds of the world in cities of Spain and cities of Italy, among the Philistine "dogs"⁶⁴ who behave as if they were nothing. You see that the sons of Gad and the sons of Reuben are two tribes over against seven nations: The Hittites, the Perizites, the Girgeshites, the Kadrites, etc. Also the sons of the Ammonites have come many times to line up for war with us.⁶⁵ With the help of our God there is no war that should not leave slain sixty thousand and many more thousands of them. Heaven forbid that a man should line himself up for battle against us. We know clearly that each man will die in his own sin. Thus also *Adbeal and Mibsam* (Gen 25:13)⁶⁶ who walk in glory and tell us that there are Jews also there making war with the sons of Kedar. The Jews executed a great slaughter among the sons of Kedar, and the sons of Kedar were made subject to the Jews and to the Jewish judges and police. We do not allow the sons of Kedar to possess weapons.

As for you, thus you are in exile, and you are mightier than we and you live in the holy place, the haven of Jerusalem. May it be constructed and established quickly, in our days.

As for us, nothing unclean comes to us, and we have no unclean livestock or wild beast. We have no falsehood, lie, plundering, stealing, lewdness, shedding of blood, and hatred without cause. We are all of one mind and one soul, as one man, and everyone has immeasurable wealth, and male and female slaves to do our work and to till our ground. We are all living in princely abode. All sides of the river Gozen are full of fruits and whoever wants to take [them] comes and takes [them]. The sons of Çain live at our right side and the sons of Yehonadab Ben Rechab on the other side. When ships arrive in the port, we all leave our locations until summer passes, but our property is left in place. Also the sons of *Adbeal and Mibsam*⁶⁷ come among us, and there is none of us who has not seven male and female slaves and more.

You, our brother Israelites, the sons of Abraham, Isaac, and

---

⁶⁴An insulting name for Gentiles (Dt 23:17-18; Mt 7:6; 15:26//Mk 7:27; Clem. Hom. II.xix; Clem. Rec. III; *Consequences*, 184-89).

⁶⁵The fictional nature of this account is apparent here. Geographically, the author has switched from the East to Italy, and here writes as if he were in Samaria during the time of the divided kingdoms.

⁶⁶Moslems.

⁶⁷Moslems.

Jacob, fortify yourselves, each the other. Let the weak man say, *"I am a warrior; if I am not for myself, who is for me?"* (Joel 4:10; PA 1:15). *Thus says the Lord, "Observe the statutes; do justice, for my salvation is soon to come, and my righteousness, to be revealed"* (Isa 56:1).

May he build the house of our sanctuary and our splendor. May he complete our temple quickly, in our days! May you all, the congregation of Israel, [see it] in your lifetime, quickly and in the near future. May a redeemer come to Zion. May we arise and go up to the house of God. Amen. May this be his will. Amen, eternally, Selah, and to [the age].

These are the words which have been copied. *A prayer of the afflicted when he fails and pours out his complaint before the Lord* (Ps 102:1). May the Lord make us worthy to see their faces, for *they will see the Lord returning to Zion, eye to eye* (Isa 52:8). Prayer and praise be to God, Creator of the age.

Summary

The audience for which this letter was intended is apparently the congregation of Jews in Palestine. The author intended to reprimand them for their loose character, urge them to be carefully observant, and to remind them that the end of the exile was near. At that time, the subservient Gentiles will become slaves, and the rebellious ones will be destroyed in war. The Messiah of Joseph has already been identified, and troops have been organized.

The pseudepigrapher fabricated the situation surrounding the author and his conditions. He even changed them to conflict with each other in order to support his arguments. He pretended to be one of the Samaritans in the diaspora, but he never mentioned Mount Gerizim. The point of view of the author is pro-Jewish, not pro-Samaritan. He was of the vicinity of Persia, but he seemed to be from Italy. At one time he wrote as if he were in Samaria dealing with problems of OT times. Following Num 2, he told of troops being organized to be dispatched to various parts of the world to conquer the entire world and set the Jewish exiles free. He and the Samaritans were absolutely free from any moral misdemeanor, and they lived in extreme prosperity with Moslems as slaves. They lacked nothing, but still they needed to be rescued by the Jews from Jerusalem. The letter is not complete, so it lacks even more coherence than it would if it were. The date of its composition is not precise. It presumes the power of the Moslems who rose to power in the seventh century.

Even though it is pseudepigraphical, the letter reflects accepted theological and eschatological views. The author and his readers expected the end soon. This would involve the destruction of the Gentiles, complete rule of the world by both Jews and Samaritans, the reestablishment of Jerusalem as the capital city of the world, the reconstruction of the temple at Jerusalem (not Gerizim), the necessity of a terrible war between Jews and Gentiles before Israel would become dominant, and the belief that the Lord would organize the ten lost tribes to come to the aid of the Jews and be responsible for most of the destruction before the kingdom was reestablished.

THE TORAH AND THE MESSIAH[60]

Rabbi Ishmael said:

In the future the holy One blessed be He will call the Garden of Eden "Zion," as it is said, *The Lord loves the gates of Zion more than all the dwellings of Jacob* (Ps 87:2). The holy One blessed be He is destined to call Zion "The Garden of Eden," as it is said, *The Lord will comfort Zion; he will comfort all her ruins; he will make her wilderness like Eden and her desert like the Garden of the Lord* (Isa 51:3). The holy One blessed be He is destined to build Jerusalem in the heavens and call it "The Lord's Throne," as it is said, *At that time they will call Jerusalem "The Lord's Throne"* (Jer 3:17). The righteous who are left in Zion and the pious ones who remain in it, the holy One blessed be He is destined to place each of them on the throne of glory, as it is said, *He will make them inherit a throne of glory* (I Sam 2:8). There will be a crown on the head of every one of them and the brilliance of the Shekinah on their faces, as it is said, *Those who love him [will be] like the sun when it goes out in its might* (Jdgs 5:31). He will make three groups of ministering angels stand before each one of them, who will say, *Holy, holy, holy* (Isa 6:3), just as the ministering angels proclaim in the heavens, as it is said, *It will be that the one who is left in Zion and the one who remains in Jerusalem will be called "holy,"everyone who is written for life in Jerusalem* (Isa 4:3). What does

---

[60]This narrative is from a manuscript belonging to the late Rav. Y.L. Ha-Cohen Fishmann of Jerusalem. It is no longer available, but this has been copied by Dr. Ibn Shmuel, *Redemption,* 348-50. SML

everyone who is written for life in Jerusalem mean? [This] teaches
that the holy One blessed be He is destined to write the name of
every righteous person for a good *life* and for years of blessings of
the days of the Messiah,[69] in order to see the joy and gladness in
the rejoicing of *Zion* and the gladness of *Jerusalem*, as it is said,
Rejoice with Jerusalem and be glad for her, all you who love her
(Isa 66:10).

The holy One blessed be He is destined to place the Messiah son
of David in the dwelling above, and they will address him, *O
Lord*, just as they address the Creator, as it is said, *This is the name
by which he will be called, "The Lord is our righteousness"* (Jer
23:6). Jerusalem, the Messiah, and the holy One blessed be He are
called *Rock*, as it is said, *The Rock, his work is perfect* (Dt 32:4).
Also Abraham is called *Rock*, as it is said, *Look to the Rock [from
which] you were hewn, and quarry [from which] you were dug.
Look to your father Abraham* (Isa 51:1-2). The holy One blessed
be He is called *Good* as it is said, *The Lord is good to all* (Ps
145:9). Even Moses is called *Good*, as it is said, *When she saw that
he was a goodly child* (Ex 2:2). The holy One blessed be He is
called God, as it is said, *God sits on his holy throne* (Ps 47:9). Israelites also are called *God*, as it is said, *I have said, "You are God"*
(Ps 82:6). The holy One blessed be He is called *The Lord's throne*,
as it is said, *The hand upon the Lord's throne* (Ex 17:16). Also
Jerusalem is called *The Lord's throne*, as it is said, *In that time they
will call Jerusalem, "the Lord's throne"* (Jer 3:17). The holy One
blessed be He is called *the Lord*, as it is said, *The Lord our God,
the Lord is one* (Dt 6:4). The Messiah is called *the Lord*, as it is
said, *This is the name by which he will be called, "The Lord is our
righteousness"* (Jer 23:6).

The Messiah is destined to sit in an academy and all those who
come into the age[70] will come and sit before him and hear a new
Torah, new commandments, and deep understanding which he
will teach the Israelites, as it is said, *You will draw water with joy
from the wells of salvation* (Isa 12:3). Elijah (May he be
remembered for good) will stand before him [as] a Turgaman,[71]
and when he interprets, his voice will carry from one end of the

[69]For the days of the Messiah it is not expected that the saints will live forever, but that
they live for "[many] years of blessings."

[70]Here "age" does not mean "world" but the age of the Messiah. Those who enter this age
are not "all those who enter the world," but only Jews whom the Messiah will teach at that
time.

[71]A Turgaman was a leader in a synagogue who interpreted the Hebrew scripture into
Aramaic and then illustrated it further to make it clear.

world to the other, as it is said, *The spirit of the Lord will rest upon him, the spirit of wisdom and understanding, the spirit of counsel and might, the spirit of knowledge and the fear of the Lord* (Isa 11:2). *The spirit* (רוח) *of the Lord.* This is the west wind (רוח) as it is said, *from the west they will fear the name of the Lord* (Isa 59:19). *The spirit* (רוח) *of wisdom and understanding.* This is the south *wind* (רוח), from which the Torah was given to Israel who is called *wisdom* as it is said, *The beginning of wisdom is this: Get wisdom, and whatever you get, get insight* (Prov 4:7). *The spirit* (רוח) *of counsel and might.* This is the east *wind* (רוח) from which the sun, moon, stars, and planets which lighten the world go out, as it is said, *Those who love him are like the sun going out in its might* (Jdgs 5:31). *The spirit* (רוח) *of knowledge and fear of the Lord.* This is the north *wind* (רוח), in whose midst the Garden of Eden is planted, because all those who fear God are to be found in its midst to receive the reward of good deeds they performed, as it is said, *Arise, O north [wind], and come, O south [wind], blow upon my garden that its spices may flow out* (SS 4:16).

What will be written [in the book of life] in that hour? Abraham, Isaac, and Jacob will be written; Joseph and all the tribes will be written; Moses and all the prophets will be written; Aaron and all the ministers will be written; Samuel and all the seers will be written. David and all the kings will be written; Solomon and all the wise will be written; Daniel and all the pious men will be written; Mordecai and all the learned ones will be written; Ezra and all the scribes will be written; the Hasomoneans and all the mighty men will be written; Nehemiah and all the instructors will be written; all the righteous will be written. They will arise from their graves through the Holy Spirit and sit in the academy before the Messiah in order to hear from him commentaries and rules. The academy of the Messiah is destined to be eighteen thousand *parsangs* [in circumference], as it is said, *Around eighteen thousand* (Ezek 48:35). The holy One blessed be He will reveal to them through the mouth of Elijah (May he be remembered for blessing) the *halakhoth* of life, peace, cleanliness, abstinence, piety, and righteousness, as it is said, *His delight shall be in the fear of the Lord, and he will not judge by the sight of his eyes* (Isa 11:3). All who hear *midrash* from the mouth of the Messiah will never forget it,[72] because the holy One blessed be He

[72]This is probably the interpretation of the author of Jer 31:33: *But I will put my law within them, and I will write it upon their hearts (or minds).* If, instead of writing it on

will be revealed in the *bet ha-midrash* of the Messiah, and he will pour out his Holy Spirit on everyone who comes into the age of his *bet ha-midrash*. His Holy Spirit will be on every single one. Each member of his *bet ha-midrash* will understand *halakhoth* of his own accord, *midreshoth* of his own accord, *tosephoth* of his own accord, and *haggadoth*[73] of his own accord, and instruction of his own accord, as it is said, *It will be after this that I will pour out my spirit on all flesh, and your sons and your daughters will prophesy. Your old men will dream dreams, and your young men will see visions* (Joel 3:1). Even upon male and female slaves of the Israelites who have been purchased with money from the Gentiles, the Holy Spirit will dwell upon them, and they will interpret of their own volition, as it is said, *Also upon your male and female slaves in those days, I will pour out my Spirit* (Joel 3:2). For everyone there will be a *bet ha-midrash* in his dwelling place, a temple of the Shekinah .

Summary

This eschatological narrative anticipates the future for Israel in the Garden of Eden. The Garden of Eden would be located in Zion after all of her ruins had been reconstructed, and the pious Jews would live there in prosperity and happiness. The Messiah, Abraham, Moses, and the Israelites would all be called divine names. The main part of the narrative is devoted to the new Torah which the Messiah would teach in the days of the Messiah. Without using the text, this prophecy was evidently based on the promise of a new covenant by Jeremiah: *"Behold the days are coming," says the Lord, "when I will make a new covenant with the house of Israel and the house of Judah...This is the covenant which I will make with the house of Israel after those days," says the Lord: "I will put my law within them, and I will write it upon their hearts, and I will be their God and they will be my people"* (Jer 31:31-33).

The close identification between the covenant and the Torah made the need for a new Torah in the new age obvious. The Messiah, like the dean of an academy, would teach all the various kinds of Jewish literature to all the Jews in the Garden of Eden.

---

stone it were written upon the minds of the believers, then it would not have to be learned and it could not be forgotten It would be memorized, and no one would have to teach it further.

[73]Narrative portions of Rabbinic literature, as distinct from the legal material or *halakhoth*.

With the reception of the new Torah, the Jews in the days of the Messiah would receive the Holy Spirit and become prophets in their own day. This is similar to the Christian interpretation of Jeremiah 31 and Joel 3.

A NEW TORAH[74]
Rabbi Akiba

Zain: This [*zain*] is the name of the holy One blessed be He, because he provides (*zan*) and supplies the needs of all his creatures from the horns of the wild ox until the eggs of lice, as it is said, *He waters the mountains from his heights; from the fruits of your works, the earth is full* (Ps 104:13). He [also] says, *You open your hand and satisfy the desire of every living being* (Ps 145:16). How many keys has the holy One blessed be He? (70) He has the key of woman, as it is said, *He opens the womb* (Gen 29:31). He has the key of rain, as it is said, *The Lord will open for you his good treasures* (Dt 28:12). He has the key of the resurrection of the dead, as it is said, *You will know that I am the Lord when I open your graves* (Ezek 37:13). He has the key of sustenance, as it is said, *You open your hand and satisfy with favor every living being* (Ps 145:16). He has the key of femininity, as it is said, *He bows down quickly to open* (Isa 51:14). He has the key to manna, as it is said, *He commands the heavens above and opens the door of heaven, and he rains down upon them manna to eat* (Ps 78:23-24). He has the key of the renewal of the kingdom, as it is said, *Your gates will be open continually; [day and night, they shall not be closed]* (Isa 60:11). He has the key of the eyes, as it is said, *Then the eyes of the blind will be opened* (Isa 35:5), and it is written, *The Lord opened the eyes of Balaam* (Num 22:31). (71) He has the keys of silence, as it is said, *The ears of the deaf will be unstopped* (Isa 35:5). He has the key of the lips, as it is said, *Lord, open my lips, [and my mouth will show forth your praise]* (Ps 51:17). He has the key of the mouth, as it is said, *He opened the mouth of the donkey* (Num 22:28). He has the key of the tongue, as it is said, *From the Lord is the answer of the tongue* (Prov 16:1). He has the key of prisoners, as it is said, *The Lord sets the prisoners free* (Ps 146:7). He has the key of the land, as it is said, *The land will be open, and salvation will shoot forth* (Isa 45:8). He has the key of the Garden of Eden, as it is said, *Open for me, O righteous gates*

[74]S.A. Wertheimer, בתי מדרשות II, 367-69. SML

Ps 118:9). He has the key of Gehinnom, as it is said, *Open the gates and let the righteous Gentile [who] keeps faith enter* (Isa 26:2). Do not read, *keeping faith* (שומר אמונים) but *he who responds, "Amen!"* (שהוא אומר אמן), (72) for it is because of one "amen" which the wicked answer from Gehinnom [that] they are delivered from Gehinnom. How is this?

The holy One blessed be He is destined to sit in the Garden of Eden and interpret. All the righteous of the world will sit before him with the whole household of heaven standing on their feet. At the right hand of the holy One blessed be He will be the sun and the planets, the moon, and all the stars at his left. (73) The holy One blessed be He will expound for them the reasons of the new Torah which the holy One blessed be He is destined to give them at the hands of the Messiah.

When he comes to the *haggadah*, Zerubbabel, son of Shealtiel (74) will stand up and say, "May he be magnified and sanctified!" His voice will carry from one end of the world to the other, and all those who enter the world will answer, "Amen!" Even the wicked ones of Israel and the righteous Gentiles who will be left in Gehinnom will all answer and say, "Amen!" from Gehinnom, as it is said, *The righteous Gentile [who] keeps the faith will enter* (Isa 26:2), until the world will be completely filled with the noise. Then the sound of their words will be heard by the holy One blessed be He, and he will ask about them and say, "What is that very loud noise that I heard?" The ministering angels will reply, "Master of the ages, these are the wicked ones of Israel and the righteous Gentiles who are left in Gehinnom, who answer, 'Amen!' from Gehinnom." (75) The mercies of the holy One blessed be He will immediately roll down abundantly, and he will say, "What can I do more to them than this judgment? It is their evil impulse that has caused them [their fate]. (76) At that time the holy One blessed be He will take the keys of Gehinnom and give them to Gabriel and Michael (77) before all the righteous and say to them, "Go and open the gates of Gehinnom and bring them up from there, as it is said, *Open the gates and let the righteous Gentile [who] keeps the faith enter* (Isa 26:2).

Gabriel and Michael will at once go and open forty thousand gates of Gehinnom and bring them up from Gehinnom. How will they bring them up from Gehinnom? This teaches that every single Gehinnom is three hundred *parsangs* long and three hundred wide. Its thickness is a thousand *parsangs*, and its depth is a thousand *parsangs*, (78) and every wicked person who falls into it is not able to come out from it. What will Gabriel and Michael do at that time? They will take each one by the hand and raise him up as a man raises his fellow from a deep pit with a rope, as it is said, *He brought me up also out of the bottomless pit, from the miry clay* (Ps 40:3).

Gabriel and Michael will then stand over them and wash, care for, and heal them from the wounds of Gehinnom. They will dress them in beautiful and good garments, take them by the hand, and bring them before the holy One blessed be He and before all the righteous ones where they will be dressed in clean, pressed garments, as it is said, *Your priests, Lord God, will be clothed with salvation, and your saints will rejoice in goodness* (II Chron 6:41). (79) *Your priests?* These are the righteous Gentiles who have served the holy One blessed be He as priests in the world, such as Antoninos Ben Asverros (80) and his colleagues. *Your saints?* These are the wicked ones of Israel who are called "saints," as it is said, *Gather to me my saints* (Ps 50:5).

When they reach the gate of the Garden of Eden, Gabriel and Michael will enter first and consult with the holy One blessed be He. The holy One blessed be He will say to them, "Permit them to enter! Come and see my glory!" When they enter, they will fall on their faces and prostrate themselves before him and bless and praise the name of the holy One blessed be He in the congregation of the perfectly righteous and upright ones who will be sitting before the holy One blessed be He, (81) as it is said, *Surely the righteous will give thanks to your name, and the upright will dwell in your presence* (Ps 140:14).

Summary

This unit is only a part of a whole alphabet with theological importance given to each letter. The letter *zain* reminded the commentator that God was a great provider, from the root *zwn*, which means "to nourish, feed, or provide." As the Provider, God has lots of keys to enable him to meet all the needs. Therefore the commentator accumulated many proof texts to show that this was true. The one text dealing with "keeping faith" which could be reinterpreted to mean "saying 'Amen'" led to the major discussion. The important argument was to show the way it was possible for sinners in Gehinnom to be allowed to enter the Garden of Eden.

This could be done by saying, "Amen." The purpose of the narrative was to encourage Jews to participate in worship services. In other narratives Jews were judged meritorious when Gentiles were not, even though the ethics of both were the same. The difference was that the Jews said the *shema'* every day. In most narratives dealing with Gehinnom, its inhabitants include the most virtuous of the Gentiles who have about the same rating as the most sinful Jews.

Jews speculated about the future frequently in terms of the Garden of Eden, the new Jerusalem, Gehinnom, the promised land, and heaven. The next section deals with that particular topic.

HEAVEN AND THE LAND

HEAVENLY JERUSALEM[1]

This is none other than the house of God (Gen 28:17).

Our rabbis said: "That day when the death of Moses, our teacher, had drawn near, the holy One blessed be He took him up to the exalted heavens and showed him his reward as well as that which was destined to take place. The attribution of mercy stood before Moses, our teacher (upon whom be peace), and said, "I will announce good news to you in which you will rejoice. Turn your face toward the throne of mercy and look!" He turned his face toward the throne of mercy and saw the holy One blessed be He building the house of the sanctuary with precious stones and pearls, and among all the stones was the splendor of the Shekinah, which was better than pearls, and the Messiah son of David was standing in the midst with his brother, Aaron, standing up and wearing his robe. Aaron spoke at this time with Moses, "Do not touch me, for I am afraid concerning you because of the Shekinah; since a man cannot enter there until he tastes the taste of death and gives his soul to the angel of death.[2]

When he heard the words of Aaron, he fell on his face before the holy One blessed be He and said, "Master of the age, give me authority to speak with your Messiah before I die." The holy One blessed be He said, [apparently to an angel] "Go, teach him my great Name, so that the flame of the Shekinah will not consume him, when he sees that Messiah son of David. Then inform Aaron, his brother, that the Lord has taught him his great Name." The Messiah and Aaron stood before him and said to him, *Blessed be he who comes in the name of the Lord* (Ps 118:26).

Moses asked the Messiah son of David, "Tell me, will the holy One blessed be He build the house of the sanctuary on earth for the Israelites, and may I see him building the house of the sanctuary in heaven with his hand?" The Messiah said to Moses, "Moses, your father Jacob saw the house which he will build on the land, and he saw the house which the holy One blessed be He will build in heaven with his hand, and he understood with all his might that the house which the holy One blessed be He will build with his hand in heaven will be with precious stones and pearls and with the splendor of the Shekinah. [This] will be the house

[1]The text is from Ch. Albek, *Beresit Rabbati*, daf 89-90, pages 136, line 3-137, line 18. SML

[2]Since Aaron was a priest he was not permitted to defile himself by touching a dead person.

which will exist for the Israelites for an age and for ages of ages[3] until the end of all generations. Thus he said at night when he was sleeping on the stone and saw Jerusalem built on the earth and Jerusalem built in heaven. While the holy One blessed be He was standing he saw Jacob our father and said to Jacob, "Jacob, my son, I am now *stationed above* you until your sons are established before me, as it is said, *Behold the Lord was stationed above him* (Gen 28:13). [Regarding] the Israelites, *they are stationed at the foot of the mountain* (Ex 19:17), and it says, *[All of] you are stationed this day* (Dt 29:9). When Jacob saw Jerusalem, once on earth and once in heaven, he said, "This is not anything at all which is on earth, as it is said, *This is nothing but the house of God* (Gen 28:17). *This* is not *the house* which will stand for my sons for generations of generations, but rather that *house of God* which he is building with his hands.[4] Should you say, "The holy One blessed be He will build for himself a *house* of the sanctuary with his hands [in heaven], thus will he build it with his hands on earth, as it is said, *The sanctuary, O Lord, your hands have established it* (Ex 15:17).

When Moses our teacher (upon whom be peace) heard these words [in the presence] of the Messiah son of David, he rejoiced greatly and turned his face toward the holy One blessed be He and said, "Master of the age, when will you bring down this Jerusalem which is now being built?"[5] The holy One blessed be He said, "That which I have not disclosed to any living being, neither to the first ones nor to the last ones, shall I tell you?" [Moses] said to him, "Master of the age, give me a hint of what is being done." The holy One blessed be He said to him, "I will scatter the Israelites at first in a dispersion within the gates of the earth, and they will be scattered to the four corners of the earth among all the Gentiles, so that in them the scripture may be fulfilled, where it is written, *Even if your outcasts [are in the uttermost parts of the heavens, from there the Lord your God will gather you and from there he will fetch you]* (Dt 30:4). My hand will gather a second time, and I

---

[3]Ages here refer to temporal units, like generations.

[4]A pagan altar was one made with hands *(sacrarium manufactum,* Pseudo-Philo 22:5). The future temple was thought to be built with God's hands also in 4Q Florilegium. Paul is reported to have said God would not dwell in a temple made with hands (χειροποιήτοις ναοῖς). Zion is expected to be rebuilt without hands *(aedificata...sine manibus,* IV Ezra 13:36). This apocalypse is consistent with the view that the true temple will be built, not with human hands, but with God's own hands.

[5]This is the burning, eschatological question. The important point of God's work in heaven is how it is related to Israel, the land, and the temple.

will bring back those who went with Jonah Ben Amiti[6] to the land of the Pathrosians and who will be in the land of Shinar, Ḥamath, Elam, Ethiopia, etc., as it is said, *[It will happen in that day that the Lord will set his hand again to receive the remnant of his people who will remain in Assyria, Egypt, Pathros, Ethiopia, Elam, Shinar, Hamath, and the isles of the sea]* (Isa 11:11).

Moses then came down from heaven, happy. The angel of death descended after him, but he did not give his spirit and his soul to the angel until the holy One blessed be He had revealed himself to him. Then he gave up his soul to the holy One blessed be He with a perfect heart and a longing soul. This is the meaning of [the verse] *This is none other than the house of God* (Gen 28:17).[7]

Summary

This little apocalypse is a complete unit whose boundaries are indicated by the text (Gen 28:17) at the beginning and end which form an inclusion. The events within the narrative are mostly located in heaven, but the real concern of the author was with the eschatological question, "When will you bring down this Jerusalem which is now being built?" The seer who composed Rev 21:2 visualized "the holy city, new Jerusalem, coming down out of heaven from God, prepared as a bride adorned for her husband," and the author of Hebrews 9:11 associated Jesus with a temple "not made with hands." See *To The Hebrews,* 133-36, 46-47.

TREASURIES OF TORTURE AND COMFORT[8]

Rabbi Ishmael said:

Segansagel, minister of the interior,[9] said to me, "My friend, sit at my bosom, and I will tell you what will take place concerning Israel." When I sat at his bosom he looked at me and wept, with the tears running down from his eyes and falling on my face. I said to him, "Splendor of the exalted Glory! Why are you weeping?" He replied, "My friend [J omits], come and I will bring you in and

---

[6]This is probably an error for Yoḥanan Ben Korah, (Jer 43:5).

[7]This conclusive allusion to the introductory text provides an inclusion to set this narrative apart as a separate unit, distinct from the surrounding literature.

[8]Text is from S.A. Wertheimer, פרקי היכלות רבתי (Jerusalem, 1890), 6:3-7:2 (3b-4a). The variants are from Jellinek, בית המדרש V, 167-68. SML

[9]The angelic officer in the innermost position, closest to the Lord.

inform you what is hidden for Israel, the holy people." He took hold of me and brought me into rooms [within] rooms and hiding places [within] hiding places and into treasuries where ledgers were kept. He opened [them] and showed me the sorrows [there] recorded [J the rooms (within) rooms and the hiding places (within) hiding places. He took the ledgers and opened (them), and he showed me the letters written of sorrows], all differing from one another. I said to him, "For whom are these?" He said to me, "For the Israelites." I said to him, "Will they [J the Israelites] be able to survive them?" He said to me, "Come tomorrow, and I will let you know of other hardships differing from these." The next day, he [again] brought me into rooms [within] rooms and showed me hardships [even] more severe than the first. Whoever [is destined] for the sword, the sword; whoever [is destined] for famine will receive famine [J whoever (is destined) for disgrace, disgrace], whoever [is destined] for captivity, captivity.[10] I said to him, "Splendor of [J exalted] Glory! Have the Israelites alone sinned?" He replied, "Everyday there are added to them [J omits] hardships more numerous [J severe] than these, but when they enter the synagogues and respond, 'Amen! May his great Name be blessed...' we do not allow them to leave the rooms [within] rooms."

When I went down from before him, I heard a voice speaking in Aramaic, saying, [J This was what he was saying]:

The sanctuary [is destined] for desolation.
virgins and young men to disgrace;
sons of the king [are destined] to be killed;
the dwellings of the king are reserved for [his] widow;
the altar [is destined] for decay;
Beel-zebub will disgrace the prepared table.
Jerusalem [is destined] for banishment,
and the land of Israel for trembling.[11]

---

[10]Rev 22:10-11: "He said to me, 'Do not seal up the words of the prophecy of this book, for the time is near. Let the evildoer still do evil; let the filthy be filthy still; let the righteous be righteous still; and the holy, holy still.'"

[11]The following is according to Jellinek's text:
The sanctuary is sanctified for destruction;
The temple [is sanctified] for flame;
the dwellings of the king are reserved for desolation;
virgins and young men, for disgrace;
the sons of the king, to be killed.
The undefiled altar [is destined] to decay.
Beel-zebub will disgrace the prepared table.
Jerusalem [is destined] for ruins,
and the land of Israel, for trembling.

When I heard [J this] strong voice, I was frightened and trembled. I fell backwards until [J the] Darniel, the prince, came and restored my strength and breath. Then he raised me to my feet and said, "My [J omits] friend, what has happened to you?" I told him, "Splendor of the exalted Glory! Perhaps there is not any cure for the Israelites."

He responded, "My friend, come and I will bring you into the treasures of the comforts and *the treasuries of* [J omits] salvation [J for Israel]. He brought me into *the treasuries of comfort and the treasuries of salvation* [J omits] and showed me groups [J (and) groups] of ministering angels, sitting and weaving garments of salvation and making crowns of life and fixing precious stones and pearls to them *and compounding all kinds of spices and sweet wines* [J omits] for the righteous. [J I said to him, "For whom are these?" He replied, "for the Israelites."] Then I saw another crown, different [J from all other crowns], the sun and moon and twelve constellations were fastened to it. I said to him, *"Splendor of the exalted Glory! For whom are these [sic.] crowns [sic.]?"*[12] [J This glorious crown. For whom is it?] He said to me, "For David, king of Israel."

I said to him, "Splendor of the exalted Glory! Show me the glory of David." He replied, "My friend, wait [J three] a few hours until David, king of Israel, comes here, and you will see [J him] in his greatness." He took hold of me and made me sit at his bosom. He then said, "What do you see?" I told him, "I see seven bolts of lightning that are running together." He said to me, "My son, close your eyes, so that you will not be terrified [at the sight], for they [J These are those who] are going out to meet David." Suddenly all the Ophanim, Seraphim, holy Hayot, treasuries of snow, clouds of glory, constellations, stars, ministering angels, *and flames of azure* [J omits] [all] said: (For the leader, a Psalm of David)

The heavens declare [the glory of God],
and the firmaments show the work of his hands (Ps 19:2).

David, king of Israel, was at the head, and all the kings of the house of David followed him, everyone with a crown on his head, but the crown of David was brighter and more glorious than all the [other] crowns. His splendor shone from one end of the world to the other. *When* [J omits] David went up to the house of the sanctuary which is in the firmament, there was prepared for him a throne of fire that was forty *parsangs* high. Its length and breadth

---

[12]The plurals evidently include all the crowns, even though the immediate antecedent is the crown of David. J's text is consistent on this point.

were each twice that. When David comes and sits on that throne which is prepared for him, facing the throne of his Creator, all the kings of the house of David will sit before him with the kings of Israel standing behind him. David will immediately stand up and recite poems and praises which no ear has ever heard. When David begins, he will say:

> *The Lord will rule for the age,*
> *[your God, O Zion for generation after generation,*
> *Halelujah]* (Ps 146:10)!

Mettatron will begin, and all his choir will say,

> *Holy, holy, holy is the Lord God of armies;*
> *[all the land is full of his glory]* (Isa 6:3).

Then all the holy *Hayot* will sing praises and say,

> *Blessed be the glory of the Lord from his place* (Ezek 3:12).

Then the firmaments will say

> *The Lord will reign for the age* (Ps 146:10),

and the earth will say,

> *The Lord has become king; the Lord has become king!*
> (Ps 97:1)

and all the kings of the house of David will say,

> *The Lord has become king over all the land* (Ps 96:9-10).

Summary

This apocalypse assumes the doctrine of the treasury of merits, and vividly pictures the way the tortures and comforts are stored to be applied to Israel at the proper time. The eschatological hope of the author is seen when David is pictured with a glorious crown on his head. The author and his readers all looked forward to the time when the treasures of comforts would be applied to Israel, when the land would be restored, the temple rebuilt, and the Messiah placed on David's throne in Jerusalem with a glorious crown.

SIN AND SALVATION[13]

Rabbi Ishmael said:

Mettatron said to me, "Come and I will show you the souls of the wicked. [Continues a list of souls of wicked together with their sins. Then follows:]

---

[13]Text from Jellinek, בית המדרש V, 186-87. SML

Then I saw the souls of the patriarchs of the age:[14] Abraham, Isaac, Jacob, and the rest of the righteous ones as they were raised from their graves and brought up to the firmament to pray thus before the holy One blessed be He:

"Master of the age, how long will you sit on your throne like a mourner who sits in the days of his mourning with your right hand behind you? Are you not going to have mercy on your children whom they use as slaves among the Gentiles while with your right hand, which is behind you, you once reached out and struck the heavens and the heaven of heavens? Are you not going to show compassion?"

In that hour the holy One blessed be He will reply to every one of them individually: "Because of these wicked ones who have sinned before me, thus and thus and have transgressed before me thus and thus, how am I able to save my sons from among the Gentiles and reveal my kingdom in the age before the eyes of the Gentiles to save with my great right hand which is falling and defeated by them?" Then Mettatron called to me and said: "My servant, take up the books and read their deeds, and the thirty-six *kritot*[15] which every single wicked person has transgressed. Moreover they have transgressed all the letters of the Torah, and all Israelites have transgressed your Torah. Concerning *your Torah* [only] it is not said,[16] but *your Torah which they have transgressed* from A to Z. Concerning the thirty-six *kritot*, [they have offended] every single letter." As soon as [they heard this], Abraham, Isaac, and Jacob each wept inwardly. After this the holy One blessed be He said to them, *Abraham, my friend*, Isaac, my *chosen one*, and *Jacob*, my *first born* (Isa 41:8), I cannot now save them from [their exile] among the Gentiles. Then Michael the prince of the Israelites will come at once and weep in a loud voice, *Why, O Lord, do you stand afar off* (Ps 10:1)?

Summary

This narrative was designed to reflect the feeling of injustice known to Jews in the diaspora and to give a theological justification for it. The question related is, "Why does God allow the Jews to be subject to the Gentiles when it is clearly understood by Jews

---

[14]These patriarchs are usually called the "ancient patriarchs," but the use of the term "age" may refer to the age of righteousness in which they lived.

[15]These are the thirty-six offenses that Israelites might commit for which the punishment is excommunication or being "cut off" from the community. See *Consequences*, 305-315.

[16]The place where this was said was evidently the books where the deeds were recorded.

that Gentiles should be subject to them?" The explanation given is that both God and his angels are deeply sorry about the situation, but they are helpless to do anything about it so long as there are so many sins piled up in the treasury of merits that have never been cancelled by a corresponding number of good works. Until that takes place, the exile will go on, and God will not assert himself by vindicating the Jews.

BIRTH PANGS AND DELIVERY[17]
Comforts and Curses

Once the prophet Elijah (May he be remembered for blessing) came to Rabbi Jose's house of study. When Rabbi Jose came, he found Elijah (May he be remembered for blessing) looking sad. Rabbi Jose asked, "Why are you sad?" He replied, "I have come from before the holy One blessed be He, and he and the Messiah were discussing the comforts [given by] the prophet Isaiah, but Samael, prince of Rome, came and accused the Israelites of being guilty. I said to him [Elijah], "The holy One blessed be He and his Messiah are discussing the comforts [promised by] Isaiah, and you [now come] denouncing [them]?" He slapped me in the face and drove me away but did not say a word to me at all.

[Finally] he began [and] said, *I will tell of your righteous deeds and all his works, but they will not help at all* (Isa 57:12). *I will tell of the righteous deeds* of Israel *and all the works* of Samael *will not help at all.*

Jews and Gentiles

Another explanation: Afterward the holy One blessed be He will hand over Samael into the hand of Michael. [Samael] will say to the holy One blessed be He, "Why did you give me over into the hand of Michael? Let him come and dispute the case with me before you!" At once the holy One blessed be He said to Michael, "Go and dispute the case with him!" Samael answered and said, "If the Gentiles commit sins, then so do the Israelites; if these are immoral and lewd, so also are these; if these shed blood, so also do these shed blood." At once Michael was forced to silence. The holy One blessed be He said to Michael, "You are silenced? Well, I will defend my children, *and all the* [devilish] machinations of

[17]Text from Jellinek, בית המדרש III, 68-78. SML

Samael *will not help* him." Hence it is said, *"I am speaking in righteousness, [mighty to save]* (Isa 63:1), and I will *save* them [the Israelites] in the day of judgment." What is this *righteousness?* When the Israelites received the Torah on Mount Sinai, which, if they had not received, he would have destroyed the whole world, the whole family of heaven responded, *Mighty to save* (Isa 63:1). *Mighty* is this merit to *save* them from Gehinnom. Because of this it is said, *In that time your people will escape, all who are found written in the book* (Dan 12:1). By virtue of what will they escape? By virtue of the Torah, concerning which they received everything *written in the book* [of the Torah]. The Israelites used to say, *I will witness against you* (Ps 50:7). *Against you* (בך). In *gematria,* twenty-two, according to the number of letters by which the Torah was written. This is to teach you that the holy One blessed be He will bear *witness* to the merit of the Israelites that they received the Torah when it was given in the twenty-two letters of the Hebrew alphabet.

To tell of the greatness of the King of kings, the holy One blessed be He. Since he loves the Israelites more than the ministering angels, is it necessary to say [that he loves them] more than the Gentiles? A king of flesh and blood has sons, servants, and friends, and they can be distinguished according to [the degree of] his love for them, but among sons, it is not possible [to do this since the father loves them all equally]. The holy One blessed be He is not thus. He has creatures above and below, but he does not love any of them except the Israelites. Who is the most beloved among sons? The one whom the king dresses with his own garment, mounts him on his own horse, places him on his throne, and sets a crown upon his head, proclaiming, "This is the king's beloved!" Thus the holy One blessed be He, so to speak, put his *garment* on the Israelites, as it is said, *For he has dressed me with garments of salvation* (Isa 61:10). That refers to the past. How about the future? As it is said, *Splendor and majesty are his garment* (Ps 21:6). He mounts them, so to speak, on his horse, as it is said, *He made him ride on the high places of the land* (Dt 32:13). This applies to the past. How about the future? As it is said, *I will make you ride on the high places of the land* (Isa 58:14). He sets them, so to speak, on his *throne,* as it is said, *Solomon sat on the Lord's throne* (I Chron 29:23). This refers to the past. How about the future? As is is said, *They will call Jerusalem "the Lord's throne"* (Jer 3:17). He takes his crown so to speak, and places it *upon their heads,* as it is said, *There shall be joy of the age upon their heads* (Isa 35:10; 51:11), and he says, *Their king will pass before them, the Lord will be at their head* (Micah 2:13).

When the Gentiles see all the praise and all this glory, their eyes will immediately bulge out, and their faces will turn green; their knees will knock against each other, and water will run down their thighs. The might of the Israelites will be like the mighty [blazing] sun on which no one is able to look, as it is said, *His friends are like the sun as it goes out in its might* (Jdgs 5:31). What is this *might of the sun*? They used to say, "In the month of Tammuz." All the Gentiles are destined to *prostrate themselves before* the Israelites *and lick the dust of* their *feet*, as it is said, *Their kings will be your tutors [and their princesses, your nurse mothers; they will prostrate their faces to the ground before you and lick the dust of your feet]* (Isa 49:23). Should a Gentile or heretic ask you, "How can this be?" tell him that this was already before the days of Nebuchadnezzar, as it is said, *He bowed down to Daniel* (Dan 2:46).

Praise and Glory

It is said in praise of Jerusalem that it is destined to be built of twelve precious stones and onyx, as it is said, *I will make your pinnacles of agate [and your gates of carbuncles]* (Isa 54:12). Also *the boundaries* of Israel are destined to be filled with *valuable stones*, as it is said, *All your border of precious stones* (Isa 54:12). If a Gentile or heretic asks you, "How is this possible?" tell him that it was [thus] already in the days of Solomon, as it is said, *King Solomon put silver [in Jerusalem] like stones* (I Kgs 10:27). Now we have told of the praise of Jerusalem.

It is told in praise of the house of the sanctuary that it is destined to be built with twelve onyx stones, as it is said, *And Elijah took twelve stones, according to the number of the tribes of Israel* (I Kgs 18:31). Is not this an *a fortiori* argument? If the altar, which is but one of the ornaments of the house of the sanctuary, is built of twelve stones, how much more so the [entire] house of the sanctuary, which is the praise of Israel, the praise of those above and those below, and the praise of the holy One blessed be He. The whole world shone because of the brilliance of the house of the sanctuary, a light which embraced and ascended to the firmament, the heaven, Ḥayot, the chariot, and the throne of glory. The altar was placed in the center, before the throne, and Jerusalem is below the throne of glory. This is what the prophet prophesied,

The throne of glory, on high from the beginning, the place of our sanctuary (Jer 17:12).

In praise of the Lord, blessed be He: Who can tell one of a thousand thousands and a myriad of myriads of the good things which he brings to Israel and [thus] makes [both those on] the heights and [those] below happy? It is like a king who brings a gift from a province and makes the members of the palace household happy. Thus the holy One blessed be He makes the [celestial] spheres above and those below happy, as it is said, *Sing for joy, O heavens, for the Lord has acted; shout, O depths of the earth* (Isa 44:23).

Now, let it be told in praise of the messianic king who is destined to come *with the clouds of heaven* (Dan 7:13) with two seraphim on his right and left, as it is said, *Behold, he comes like a son of man with the clouds of heaven* (Dan 7:13). In the generation when the son of David comes, fiery seraphim will be sent into the temple, and stars will appear like fire in every place, and there will be pestilence of three years' duration, one after the other. This will be sent by the holy One blessed be He, as it is said, *A pestilence will go before him, and a plague (רשף) will go out at his feet* (Hab 3:5), as it is said, *Her flashes (plagues - רשף) are flashes of fire* (SS 8:6).

In the third year of the pestilence, those in the exile will be atoning for it. At the end of that year, the king will be killed, and [people] will flee into the wilderness areas. The land will cry out from its place and disciples of the wise will die. *The treacherous will deal treacherously; the treacherous will deal very treacherously* (Isa 24:16). Another scripture passage will confirm it: *[If there is] still a tenth of it, it shall again be eaten up* (Isa 6:13). When the fifth year comes, they will be exiled into all the nations.

The Hound of Heaven

All the kings will provoke one another [into combat]: the king of Persia with the king of Arabia, and he will destroy it, as it is said, *They will fight, each man with his brother [and each man with his neighbor, city with city], kingdom with kingdom* (Isa 19:2). At that time Edom will fall; heaven and earth will shake [from the noise of its fall], and half of the world will be seized because of it, as it is said, *The Lord from on high will roar; from his holy dwelling he will utter his voice* (Jer 25:30). Then the holy One blessed be He is destined to gather crowds of people and give them over into the hand of the Israelites, as it is said, *I will exact my vengeance on Edom by the hand of my people, the Israelites* (Ezek 25:14).

The holy One blessed be He is destined to bring the prince of Edom and smite him. The prince of Edom will say, "Where can I flee? If I go to *Egypt,* the Shekinah is there, as it is said, *Behold the Lord rides on a swift cloud and comes to Egypt* (Isa 19:1). If I flee to *Edom,* the Shekinah is [also] there, as it is said, *Who is this coming from Edom* (Isa 63:1)? If I flee to *Babylon,* the Shekinah is [also] there, as it is said, *For your sakes I have sent you to Babylon* (Isa 43:14). If I flee to *Elam,* the Shekinah is there [also], as it is said, *I have placed my throne in Elam* (Jer 49:38). It may be compared to a fox to whom the lion said, "Pay me tax!" The fox got up and fled [for a journey of] three days. Despite this, the lion seized him and said, "Pay me the tax, even in this place." [The fox] said to him, "I have fled from you." [The lion] replied, "But you are still standing in my place." Thus the holy One blessed be He is destined to say to the prince of Edom, "*Is it because* you have [a place] to hide?" Then the holy One blessed be He will give him into the hands of the Israelites.

Distinctive Uniforms

The holy One blessed be He is destined to wear clothing of *vengeance* (Isa 59:17) so as to take vengeance on the seventy nations, as it is said, *Mine is vengeance and recompense* (Dt 32:35). He will wear ten garments, so as to conform with the ten times when the Israelites were called *a bride* for the Lord. These are they: *I have come to my garden, my sister, my bride* (SS 5:1); *Come with me from Lebanon, [my] bride* (SS 4:8); *a garden locked is my sister, [my] bride* (SS 4:12); *How nice is your love, my sister, [my] bride* (SS 4:10); *Your lips distil nectar, [my] bride* (SS 4:11); *You fascinate me, my sister, [my] bride* (SS 4:9); *the voice of the bridegroom and the bride* (Jer 7:34); *you will bind them as a bride does* (Isa 49:18); *rejoice as a bridegroom over a bride* (Isa 62:5); *as a bride puts on her jewels* (Isa 61:10).

These are the ten garments: *The Lord has become King; he wears pride* (Ps 93:1) (when he created the age); *the Lord is clothed and girded with strength* (Ps 93:1); (on the day he gave the Torah). *He put on righteousness as a breastplate* (Isa 59:17) (on the day he gave over the Gentiles to the Israelites [as slaves]). *He will put on garments of vengeance for clothing* (Isa 59:17) (on the day Edom falls). *Crimson garments from Bozrah* (Isa 63:1) (on the day he makes war with the Gentiles). *He is glorious in apparel* (Isa 63:1) (on the day of Gog and Magog). *When he sprinkled their life blood on my garments* (Isa 63:3) (in the war of Italy). *You are clothed with honor* (Ps 104:1). These are the two garments [worn] on the day when the dead are raised to life, as it is said, *Bless the Lord, O my soul! [O Lord my God, you are very great! You are clothed with honor and majesty]* (Ps 104:1).*Why is your apparel red* (Isa 63:2)? On the day when the holy One blessed be He takes hold of his sword and makes war, as it is said, *I will make my arrows drunk with blood; my sword will consume flesh* (Dt 32:42), *and I will wreak vengeance upon Edom through my people, the Israelites* (Ezek 25:14).

Before Rome Falls

Before Edom falls, ten places will be destroyed and in ten places revolution will take place; ten shofars will blast, and ten voices will be heard; [the people of] fifteen cities will be killed; there will be ten eruptions; and ten evil things will range. A brazen faced king will arise and issue evil, [anti-Jewish] decrees in his kingdom. A great king will go out against Alexandria with an army, and there will be great evil in the world. For three and a half years he will rule and rebel, and the princes of Edom will fall. There will be ten wars, and Israel will prevail over all the Gentiles, *and I will wreak vengeance on Edom [through my people, the Israelites]* (Ezek 25:14). Ships from the land of Israel will sail forth from Edom, and Israelites will say, "What do we have to do with Edom?" As it is said, *Who will bring me to a fortified city; who will lead me to Edom* (Ps 60:11). Israelites will go and pitch their camp against Tyre for forty days. At the end of forty days, they will stand up at the time of reciting the *shema'* and say, *Hear, O Israelites, the Lord our God, the Lord is One* (Dt 6:4). Then the walls of the city will fall, and the city will be conquered before them. They will flee, [leaving behind] in its midst all the silver and gold. They will plunder that which is left, [marching] from there to Rome, they will bring [back] the vessels of the house of the sanctuary. King Nehemiah will go out with them and bring them to Jerusalem.

Arabs and the Temple

Israelites will say to the king of the Arabs, "The house of the sanctuary is ours. Take the silver and gold, but give up the house of the sanctuary!" The king of the Arabs will say, "There is nothing at all that is yours in this sanctuary, but if you choose for yourselves at first a sacrifice such as you used to employ earlier, [then] we will also offer sacrifices. If this sacrifice is received, we will all become one nation. The Israelites will then sacrifice, but their offerings will not be accepted because Satan will accuse them before the holy One blessed be He. Then the sons of Kedar will sacrifice and their offerings will be received, as it is said, *All the flocks of Kedar shall be gathered to you* (Isa 60:7). At that time, the Arabs will say to the Israelites, "Come and adopt our faith!" But the Israelites will reply, "We would rather be killed than deny the existence of God!" At that time swords will be drawn, bows will be bent, and arrows will fly and cause men to fall slain from the Gate of Ephraim to the corner gate, and Nehemiah will be killed with them. Those who will escape will flee to the Wilderness of Moab and to the land of the Ammonites. There those refugees of Israel will wait, and the Lord will perform miracles for them there, and a spring will come out for them from the depths, as it is said, *My outcasts will sojourn in you, Moab* (Isa 16:4). There they will eat roots of broom grass for forty-five days.

Elijah's Miracles

At the end of forty-five days, the Lord will make Elijah shoot forth there and the messianic king will be with him. There Elijah will proclaim good news to them and say, "What is the matter with you Israelites here?" The Israelites will reply, "We are lost; we are destroyed." Elijah will say to them, "Arise, for I am Elijah, and this is the messianic king." They, however, will not believe him, because of Nehemiah who came to them and was killed. He will then say to them, "Perhaps you are looking for a sign like [the one] Moses [gave]?" They will say, "Yes." He will then perform seven miracles. *The first miracle:* He will bring to them Moses and his generation from the wilderness, as it is said, *Gather for me my pious ones* (Ps 50:5). *The second miracle:* He will raise for them Korah and all his fellow conspirators, as it is said, *You will revive me again; from the depths of the earth you will bring me up again* (Ps 71:20). *The third miracle:* He will raise up for them Nehemiah who was killed. *The fourth miracle:* He will reveal to them the hidden things of the earth, and the jar of manna and the anointing oil. *The fifth miracle:* The holy One blessed be He will put a staff of strength in his hand, as it is said, *[A staff] of your strength, O Lord, [the Lord will send from Zion]* (Ps 110:2). *The sixth miracle:* He will grind all the mountains of Israel like flour, as it is said, *I will destroy the mountains and the hills* (Isa 42:15). *The seventh miracle:* He will reveal for them the secret, as it is said, *This is the sign of the covenant* (Gen 9:12, 17).

When they see these miracles, they will send messengers who will say to all the princes who mocked Jerusalem, "Come and fight with them!" They will go out after the Israelites, fully prepared [armed]. The Israelites will say to the messianic king, "Is it not better for us to dwell [as we were]? Why have you come to stir up war among us?" The messianic king will reply, *Stand firm and see the salvation of the Lord* (Ex 14:13)! He will blow on them with the breath of his mouth, and they will all fall slain before him, as it is said, *With the breath of his lips he will slay the wicked* (Isa 11:4). Go and learn from Sennacherib, as it is said, *Behold they were all dead corpses* (Isa 37:36).

Good News

At that time Elijah will fly all over the world and proclaim the good news to the Israelites, as it is said, *Behold I send you Elijah, the prophet, [before the day of the Lord comes, the great and terrible day]* (Mal 3:23). That day will be a day of cruelty and wrath. That day will separate the two ages.[18] The wicked will say, *Ah for the day, for the day of the Lord is near* (Joel 1:15), and [Amos] will say, *Woe to those who desire the day of the Lord* (Amos 5:18). Jerusalem will be wide and spread out all the day, as it is said, *The day will be one (it is known to the Lord) [not day and not night, and it will happen at evening there will be light...all the land will be turned and become like an arabah from Geba to Rimmon, south of Jerusalem, and it will be elevated and will dwell under it]* (Zech 14:7, 10). Gog and Magog will come up against him on that day, and they will pitch their camp alongside Jerusalem for seven and a half days until they take Jerusalem. The congregation of Israel will then say to the holy One blessed be He, "Master of the age, every nation has despised me. I am positively ashamed to return to it. He will take that which they plundered from her hands. Then the holy One blessed be He will reply, *I will gather them all into your midst*, as it is said, *Behold the day of the*

---

[18]The age of Edom, Ishmael, the Gentiles, etc., and the new age of Israel's rule, called the age to come.

Lord comes, and your spoil will be divided in your midst, and I will gather all the nations to Jerusalem for war (Zech 14:1-2).

These are they: Gomer, Agapeiha, Togarmah, Africa, Germit, Germamia, Cappadocia, Barbaria, Italia, Ethiopia, Andalos, Saba, Hermon, Dolim, Aharson, Sasonia, Galatia, Gozia, Lombardia, Kalbariah, Pentapoli, Tripoli, Tyre, Macedonia, England, Monakak, Zipori, Nero, Nuzan, Daronia, Osiah, Talkia, Tarsus, Elam, and all their suburbs.

Citizens of their provinces will come out with spears, swords, and bows, and every one of them will strengthen his fellow with a door fastened with nails, as it is said, *They will help, each man his neighbor* (Isa 41:6). Each will be divided into three groups: the first group will drink all the water of Tiberias; the second will drink [the dregs of] the old wine; the third will pass over on foot and say, each man to his neighbor, "To whom does this place belong?" They will then grind the stones of the mountains of Israel with their horses. Jerusalem will be given into their hands, and although they will conquer the city, they will not kill anyone, as it is said, *The city will be taken captive and the houses plundered, and the women raped* (Zech 14:2), and they will humble two women in its midst from two families. Rabbi Yohanan said, "They will be raped."

It is written, "To what can this be compared? To a king into whose palace thieves had entered. The king said, 'If I seize them in my house now, they will say, "The king has no power except in his house!" but I will wait until they go away. [Then I will capture them].' Thus did the holy One blessed be He say, 'If I kill them in Jerusalem now, they will say, "He has power only in Jerusalem." I will wait until they depart to the Mount of Olives.'" There the holy One blessed be He will be revealed to them in his glory, and he will make war with them until there is not a single one of them left, as it is said, *The Lord will fight with those nations as in the day of battle, in a day of war* (Zech 14:3). The holy One blessed be He will gather all the beasts of the field and birds to eat their flesh, as it is said, *Say to every winged bird and every beast of the field, "Congregate and come, gather yourselves around my sacrifice which I slaughtered for you, a great sacrifice on the mountains of Israel; eat flesh and drink blood"* (Ezek 39:17). For seven years Israelites will burn the wood from their bows, shields, and spears (Ezek 39:9).

The Beauty of Israel

At that time the holy One blessed be He will clothe the Messiah

[with] a diadem, and he will place a helmet of salvation on his head and gird him with brilliance and splendor. He will [also] adorn him with glorious garments and place him on a high mountain, and he will proclaim good news to the Israelites. He will announce with his voice, "Salvation is near!" The Israelites will then say, "You are the one whom the holy One blessed be He called *Ephraim is my first born son* (Jer 31:9). *Is not Ephraim a dear son to me* (Jer 31:20)? Then he will say to them, "Yes." Israel will reply to him, "Go and proclaim the good news to those who sleep at Machpelah, for they will be the first to rise." At that time, he will go up and proclaim the good news to those who sleep at Machpelah and say to them, "Abraham, Isaac, and Jacob! Arise! You have slept long enough." They will reply, "Who is this who uncovers the dust from our eyes?" He will say to them, "I am the Messiah of the Lord. Salvation is near! Salvation is near!" They will reply, "If this is really so, go and proclaim the good news to Adam that he may be the first to arise." He will then say to Adam, "You have had enough sleep!" He will reply, "Who is this that drives sleep from my eyes?" He will say, "I am the Messiah of the Lord, one of your descendants." Adam will immediately stand up with all his generation, as well as Abraham, Isaac, and Jacob, and all the righteous, the judges, and all the generations from the beginning of time to the last day, and they will loudly chant the psalms and joyful songs, as it is said, *How beautiful upon the mountains are the feet of him that brings good news* (Isa 52:7)! Why *upon the mountains*? Because *how beautiful* are Moses and his generation who came from the wilderness.

Another explanation: *How beautiful upon the mountains!* It can be compared to a king who had two sons and one of them died. All the people of the city wore black. The king said, "You are wearing black now with the death of my first son; I will make you wear white with the joy of my second son!" Thus the holy One blessed be He said to all *the mountains:* "Since you wept for my children when they went into exile from their land, as it is said, *I will take up weeping and wailing on the mountains* (Jer 9:10), I will bring the joy of my sons *upon the mountains,* as it is said, *How beautiful upon the mountains [are the feet of the one who proclaims good news]* (Isa 52:7).

How beautiful is the messianic king proclaiming *good news* to Israel! *The mountains* leap like calves before him, and *the trees of the field will be clapping their hands* at the salvation of the Israelites, as it is said, *For you will go out in joy [and be led forth in peace; the mountains and the hills will break out into singing before you; and all the trees of the field will clap their hands]* (Isa 55:12). *How beautiful* are *the mountains* of Israel, flowing out milk and honey that gush forth like rivers of water, as well as will rivers of wine, as it is said, *On that day the mountains will drip juice, and the hills will produce milk, and a spring from the house of the Lord will go forth and water all the valley of Shittim* (Joel 4:18).

Why is the *spring* compared to that which *goes out* from *the house* of the holy of holies to the threshold of *the house*? [Because] in the beginning it was compared to the threads of a warp; until the courtyard it was compared to the thread of a woof; the court was compared to the horns and rams horns until the altar it was compared to the horns of a grasshopper; until the temple court it was compared to a small vessel, as it is said, *Behold water from a vessel* (Ezek 47:2). From there it will go down like a river flowing, and it will cleanse with respect to whole burnt-offering, menstrual defilement, and sin offering. Even the angel of death will not be able to cross it, as it is said, *A mighty boat* (Isa 33:21) will not be able to cross it, and even a fleet will not be able to cross it. It will descend to the Sea of the Arabah in order to increase the fish for the Israelites. There is salt for them from that place, as it is written concerning it, *Its swamps and marshes will not be healed; they are left for salt* (Ezek 47:11). There will grow up alongside it all the precious trees of Lebanon, as it is said, *Along the river, and along its banks on either side will grow all kinds of trees for food. Their leaves will not wither, and their fruit will not fail, but will be choice for its months* (Ezek 47:12). This latter refers to the ethrog which will produce ripe fruit every month. This is a tree of which its leaves are eaten as well as its fruit, as it is said, *Its fruit will be for food and its leaves for healing* (Ezek 47:12).

How beautiful is the house of the sanctuary, descending and built on its *tel*, as it is said, *a city built on its tel* (Jer 30:18).

The New Jerusalem

Jerusalem is destined to be built [with] a thousand suburban castles, a thousand defense towers, a thousand country residences, a thousand mansions, and everyone will be like Sepphoris in its prosperity. (Rabbi Jose said, "I remember Sepphoris in its prosperity when it used to produce eighty thousand spiced puddings.") There is destined to be in Jerusalem three thousand towers and every tower will have seven thousand stories. (It will be perched on three mountains: Sinai, Tabor, and Carmel.) Every story will have seven thousand divisions, and every division will be sixty-two cubits. It will be perched on the top of thirty-three slopes, and the house of the sanctuary will be on top of them all. How will they be able to ascend it? Like clouds and winged doves and flying beings [they will become], as it is said, *Who are these, flying like a cloud of doves to their windows* (Isa 60:8). The house of the sanctuary will extend in width to Damascus, as it is said, *The word of the Lord is raised against the land of Hadrach and will rest on Damascus* (Zech 9:1).

Seven walls will surround Jerusalem: of silver, gold, precious stone, puk, sapphire, carbuncle, and fire. Its brilliance will shine from one end of the world to the other. The house of the sanctuary will be built on four mountains of gold: refined gold, smelted gold, beaten gold, and gold of Parwaim (like gold which makes fruit *[perot]*), and it will be founded on a sapphire distinguished by its size. Its height will reach heaven, the stars, and the turning wheel of the chariot, as it says, *On the peaks of the high places of the town* (Prov 9:3). The Shekinah of God and his glory will fill the temple. There he will appoint every angel over his work, Gabriel over his thousands and Michael over his myriads. Huge crowds will enter its midst, and there they will set aside *some for life in the age and some [will be singled out] for reproach and contempt of the age* (Dan 12:2). They will open the gates of the Garden of Eden from its midst, as it is said, *You will be in Eden, the garden of God* (Ezek 28:13). Gehinnom will be opened and there the holy One blessed be He will bring down his throne and set it in the Valley of Jehoshaphat, and there he will make every nation and its idols pass by. When the Gentiles pass by there, they will fall into it, as it is said, *Like sheep appointed for Sheol; death will shepherd them, [and the righteous will dominate them in the morning, and Sheol will consume their form from his dwelling]* (Ps 49:15). Who caused this for them? Because their hands stripped the [heavenly] abode, as it is said, *A building I have built; a house of the abode for you, [a residence for your habitation for the ages]* (I Kgs 8:13). When a man sins against the throne of glory and repents, they will forgive him, as it is said, *Return, O Israelites, to [the Lord your God]* (Hos 14:2), but the Gentiles will pass into Gehinnom and will fall into it. The rebels and law breakers of Israel will be delivered [from] Gehinnom because of their tears, as it is said, *They will pass through the Valley of Baca; they will make it a spring* (Ps 84:7).

When the law breakers and the rebels fall into Gehinnom, the fire of the Lord will burn their bodies, and their teeth will fall out of their mouths, as it is said, *You will break the teeth of the wicked* (Ps 3:8). Do not read, *You will break* (שברת), but *You will strengthen* (שריבבת).

The Israelites and Gehinnom

Rabbi Eliezer Ben Jacob says, "The house of the sanctuary of the holy One blessed be He for the age to come will be eighteen thousand, five myriads of *parsangs*. The holy One blessed be He will sit on the throne of judgment, and David will sit in front of him, as it is said, *His throne, like the sun, will be opposite me* (Ps 89:37). All the women who were at ease because they had paid [others] to teach their sons Torah, Bible, and Mishnah will stand in a compartment made of reeds, like a fence. When they hear the voice of Zerubbabel Ben Shealtiel who interprets before the holy One blessed be He, they will answer after him, "May his great Name be blessed and sanctified for the age and for ages of ages." The righteous will say, "Amen!" [Even] the wicked who are in Gehinnom will say, "Amen!" The holy One blessed be He will say to the ministering angels, "Who are these who say, 'Amen' in Gehinnom?" The ministering angels will reply, "Master of the age, these are the rebels and the law breakers among the Israelites, who even though they dwell in grief, answer, 'Amen!'" The holy One blessed be He will say to them, "Bring them up from there!" When they bring them up, their faces will be as black as the rim of a pot. They will say to him, "Master of the age, you have judged well; you have inflicted fair punishment; you have done well to make us as a symbol for all the Israelites." At that time, the holy One blessed be He will open the gates of the garden of Eden and admit them to [the other] Israelites, as it is said, *Open the gates so that the righteous Gentiles that keep faith may enter* (Isa 26:2).

The Great Banquet

Then Gabriel will come to the Garden of Eden and proclaim, "Be established, O righteous, by the work of your hands!" They will say to him, "Who are you?" He will reply, "I am Gabriel." The Israelites will say, *Welcome in the name of the Lord* (Ps 118:26). Gabriel will reply, *We bless you in the name of the Lord* (Ps 118:26).

The holy One blessed be He will then prepare the tables and slaughter Behemoth, Leviathan, and Ziz Shadai, and he will make a great banquet for the righteous. He will seat everyone of them according to the respect due to him. The holy One blessed be He will say to them, "Do you want cider or citrus wine to drink? Or do you want pomegranites or grape wine?" The righteous will say, "It is in your power to do whatever you wish." Then the holy One blessed be He will bring them wine that had been preserved from his grapes from the six days of creation, as it is said, *I will serve you spiced wine* (SS 8:2). The holy One blessed be He will do the will of the righteous, leaving his glorious throne and sitting with them, as it is said, *I have come to my garden, my sister [my] bride* (SS 5:1). The holy One blessed be He will bring all praiseworthy things of the Garden of Eden, and he will bring every just person so that he will see his [God's] glory. Everyone will point his finger and say, *This God is our God* [for] *an age until [another age]* (Ps 48:15). They will eat and drink and be happy until the holy One blessed be He commands [them] to raise the cup of blessing. The righteous will say to Abraham, "Stand up and bless!" Abraham will reply, "Ishmael accuses me." They will [then] invite Isaac [to do the same], and he will reply, "Esau accuses me." They will then say [the same] to Jacob, and he will say, "Two sisters are my accusers." They will say [the same] to the tribes, but they will reply, "The testimony of Joseph accuses us." [They will continue] until they come to David, [and he will accept the invitation]. Then they will put four glasses into his hands. These are: *The Lord is the serving of my portion and my cup* (Ps 16:5); *my cup overflows* (Ps 23:5); *I will raise the cup of salvation* (Ps 116:13)[19]. The cup of blessing will be two hundred, twenty-one logs. How much is a log? An egg and a half in volume. David will say, "It is *beautiful* for me to bless; it is *beautiful* for me to praise." Then he will stand up and bless and praise and glorify with every kind of song, as it is said, *I will give thanks to the Lord according to his righteousness* (Ps 7:18). At that time the holy One blessed be He will take his crown and put it on David's head and on the head of the Messiah, the son of David, and recite their praise and *righteousness* until the end of all generations. Israelites will be seated in tranquility and confidence, and they will make a canopy and a dwelling for every righteous person according to his rightful place, and he will walk with the righteous, and they will raise his hand as a man who

---

[19]Only three "cups" are listed. Perhaps something has dropped out of the text from scribal copying.

tenderly nurses his joy, for thus Isaiah said, *The Lord has lifted up your hand, but they do not see [it]* (Isa 26:11). The holy One blessed be He said, I said, *"Let them see and be ashamed"* (Isa 26:11). The Israelites will say, "Master of the age, let it be as you have said, *Let them see and be ashamed."* The holy One blessed be He will raise the stature of the Gentiles above the walls of the Garden of Eden and they will *see* the joy of the Israelites and *be ashamed.* A fire will proceed from the mouths of the righteous and burn them up, as it is said, *You will consume even the fire of your opponents* (Isa 26:11).

The holy One blessed be He is destined to put to shame the brilliance of the sun and the moon, and he will bring the skin of Leviathan and make from it *sukkoth* for the righteous, as it is said, *Can you fill with sukkoth his skin* (Job 40:31)? They will make a *sukkah* for everyone who merits it; for giants they make a necklace; for everyone who deserves a diadem, they will make a diadem, and whatever is left of it [the skin of Leviathan], they will provide for the roof of the house of the sanctuary. Its brilliance will shine from one end of the world to the other. Israelites will sit, eat, drink, be fruitful, multiply, and enjoy the splendor of the Shekinah. According to Rabbi Shimon, the holy One blessed be He will raise the stature of every one of them two hundred cubits. Rabbi Judah said, "A hundred cubits, as was the height of Adam." All this about men, but what do you find about women? It is said, *May our daughters be like corner pillars* (Ps 144:12). Every single Israelite will give birth to children every day. How much more chickens! Do not be surprised about this, for you may go and learn from the vine. Every single vine in the days of the Messiah will have produce for at least one male donkey, as it is said, *Binding his colt to the vine* (Gen 49:11). Every barren tree that has never borne fruit will bear fruit then—[produce enough] for a colt's load, as it is said, *and his donkey's colt to the choice vine* (Gen 49:11). Lest you say, "There is no [strong] wine in it," we are told, *He washes his garments in wine* (Gen 49:11). Lest you say, "It is not red," the scriptures say, *His vesture* (סותה) *in the blood of grapes* (Gen 49:11). Lest you say, "It has no intoxication," the scriptures say, *Its incitement* (סותו) [20] *[in the blood of grapes, his eyes shall be red with wine]* (Gen 49:11-12). Lest you say, "It has no taste," the scriptures say, *red* (חכלילי). Every palate (חיך) that tastes it will say, "For me! for me!" (לי, לי). Perhaps you will say, "For young men it is good, but not for old men." Hence the scriptures say, *His teeth*

---

[20]Massoretic text reads סותה.

white with milk (Gen 49:12). Rabbi Yohanan says, "Wine *for* old men is *better than milk* for sucklings. If a Gentile asks you, 'How can this be?' tell him, 'Wicked one, go and learn from Obed Edom the Gittite, whose mother-in-law and his eight daughters-in-law produced sixty-two children in three months, six sextuplets in one womb.'" In the case of wine, once when Rabbi Aha Bar Ada was a teacher of the young children of Rabbi Shimon Ben Lakish, he left the children and came to him [Rabbi Shimon], and [Rabbi Shimon] said, "Why have you left the children?" He replied, "My father left for me one branch; the first day I gathered from it three hundred bunches [of grapes and the juice of] each filled one jar. The second day I gathered three hundred bunches [of grapes and the juice] of two filled one jar. The third day, I gathered three hundred [bunches of grapes and the juice of three] filled one jar only half full." In the age to come it will not be thus, for a man will bring his grapes in a wagon or boat and his family, as it is said, *You shall drink the blood of the grape* (Dt 32:14). The vine is destined to be continued there and grow to the top of the mountains like a staff. Lest you say, "It will be hard to harvest it," the scripture says, *Its fruit will rustle like Lebanon* (Ps 72:16). The holy One blessed be He will blow wind against it, and its fruit will fall [off], and every Israelite will take and bring provision for himself and his family.

The Prophesied Future

The holy One blessed be He is destined to make for every righteous one seven canopies: a canopy of cloud, of smoke, for the day, a canopy of fire, of brilliance, of flame, and a canopy for the night. Why does the scripture say, "Canopy of smoke?" To teach that everyone who was parsimonious towards the students of the wise, smoke will go out from the canopy of the righteous and blind his eyes. From where do we learn about "the canopy for the day"? Because it is said, *The light of righteous is like a shining light* (Prov 4:18). How about "a canopy of *fire*"? Because a *fire* is destined to go out from the canopy of the righteous, and the wicked will be burned by it, as it is said, *He will rain on the wicked coals [of fire and brimstone]* (Ps 11:6). How about "a canopy of brilliance"? Because it is said, *Brightness there will be like light* (Hab 3:4). Where do we find "a canopy of *flame*" that burns the wicked? Because it is said, *The voice of the Lord flashes forth flames of fire* (Ps 29:7). Where do you find "a canopy of *night*"? Because it is said, *Night will be like the light of day* (Ps 139:12). None of these canopies will touch the other.

Jeremiah says, "I have seen him gathering bridegrooms to brides," for it is said, *The voice of the bridegroom and the voice of the bride* (Jer 7:34).

Hosea says, "I have seen him multiplying Israelites *like sand*," as it is said, *The number of Israelites will be like the sand of the sea* (Hos 2:1).

Joel says, "I have seen him wreak vengeance from his enemies," as it is said, *I will hold innocent the blood which I have not held innocent* (Joel 4:21). The holy One blessed be He says, "Even if the Gentiles give all their treasures, they will not be able to give back the blood of Rabbi Akiba and his colleagues."

Amos says, "I have seen him visiting upon the Gentiles their iniquities," as it is said, *For three transgressions of Edom [and for four, I will not revoke the punishment]* (Amos 1:11).

Obadiah says, "I saw him wearing the crown of *the kingdom*," as it is said, *Saviors will go up to Mount Zion [to judge Mount Esau, and the kingdom will be the Lord's]* (Obad 21).

Jonah says, "I have seen him receiving the prayers of his people with mercy," as it is said, *He prayed to the Lord [and said..."For I knew that you were a gracious God and merciful, slow to anger, and abounding in steadfast love]* (Jonah 4:2).

Micah [sic.] says, "I saw him returning *to Jerusalem with mercy*," as it is said, *I have returned to Jerusalem with mercy* (Zech 1:16).

The rest of all the prophets, everyone of them, brings the comforts of his people, and the holy One blessed be He will raise them up before him, from the first generation to the last generation, and say to them, "Come and see the good which I have kept in store for you!" as it is said, *How great is your goodness which you have stored up for those who fear you* (Prov 31:20).

Summary

The major points of this narrative were the future expectation of blessings of prosperity, power, glory, honor, prestige, and comfort for the Jews at the same time the Gentiles received tortures and punishment. Throughout, the different themes are held together by the prophet Elijah expounding on the parts of Isa 47:12: *I will tell of your righteous deeds and all his works, but they will not help at all.* This involves the *righteous deeds* of Israel, and the demonic *works* of the Gentiles being weighed in the scales of justice and each receiving its just recompense. These themes were elaborated and expanded by normal messianic expectations, the day of the Lord, the restoration of Palestine as the Garden of Eden and Jerusalem exalted. Sinners in Gehinnom who say, "Amen!" will be restored to the Garden of Eden where a great banquet will be held.

HEAVEN, EARTH, AND JERUSALEM[21]

More beloved is everything which is below than that which is above. You know that he left that which was above and descended to that which is below, as it is said, *Make me a sanctuary, and I will dwell in its midst* (see II Chron 2:3-4). [It says], *All that is in heaven is in earth* (I Chron 29:11),[22] and it says, "*Mine is the silver, and mine is the gold," says the Lord of armies* (Hag 2:8).[23]

With respect to heaven, [it says], *Let there be a firmament in the midst of the water [and let it divide the waters from the waters]* (Gen 1:6). With respect to the earth, [it says], *And a veil shall divide for you [the holy from the holy of holies]* (Ex 26:33). With respect to heaven, [it says], *[Then Solomon sat on] the throne of the Lord* (I Chron 29:23).[24] With respect to the earth, [it says], *Throne of glory, exalted from the first, the place of our sanctuary* (Jer 17:12).[25]

Rabbi Berechiah said, "The love which the holy One blessed be He loved the Israelites, as it is said, '*I have loved you,*' says the Lord (Mal 1:2). What does *until it please* (SS 2:7) mean? The kingdom which is above. When the attribute of justice reverses its position, I will bring it [down] with the voice of voices, and I will not hinder. Therefore, it is said, *until it pleases.*[26]

In your midst [I am] the holy One, and I will not enter the city (Hos 11:9). Rabbi Yoḥanan said, "The holy One blessed be He

---

[21]Except for the first three, these examples have been collected by Ibn Shmuel, *Redemption,* 12-13. The original document is shown at the end of each unit. SML

[22]This involves a slight distortion of the text, which reads, "All that is in heaven *and* on earth."

[23]ExR 33:4 (61d).

[24]In context this scripture referred to Solomon sitting on the throne of his father David in Jerusalem, which was called the throne of the Lord, and the United Monarchy was called the Kingdom of the Lord (I Chron 17:12-14; II Chron 13:5, 8).

[25]ExR 33:4 (61c).

[26]SSR 2:7 §1 (16c).

said, *I will not enter* celestial Jerusalem until *I enter* terrestrial Jerusalem."[27]

Resh Lakish said, "[There are] seven [heavens], and they are these: Vilon, Rakiah, Shehakim, Zebul, Maon, [and] Arabot...Zebul, in which Jerusalem, the temple, and the altar have been built, and Michael, the great prince, stands and offers a sacrifice upon it. What does he sacrifice? ...The souls of the righteous."[28]

> *The place of your dwelling, you made, Lord;*
> *a temple, Lord, your hands prepared* (Ex 15:17).

This is one of the scripture passages which says that a terrestrial throne is prepared over against a celestial throne.[29]

Rabbi Nathan says, "Beloved is he who makes the ark like a throne of glory which is above,...because the temple which is above is prepared as a counterpart for the temple [which is below], and the ark is prepared as a counterpart for the throne of glory which is above."[30]

Those who stand and pray outside the land turn their faces toward the land of Israel. Those who stand and pray in the land of Israel turn their faces toward Jerusalem...Those who stand and pray in Jerusalem turn their faces toward the temple mount...Those who stand and pray on the temple mount turn their faces toward the holy of holies. To what holy of holies? Rabbi Hiyya Rabba: "Over against the holy of holies which is above," Rabbi Simon Ben Halaphta said, "Over against the holy of holies which is below." Rabbi Pinhas said, "Nobody differs on that. The holy of holies which is below is prepared as a counterpart for the holy of holies which is above.[31]

Seven things precede [the creation of] the age [by] two thousand years: The Torah, the throne of glory, the Garden of Eden, Gehinnom, repentance, the temple which is above, and the name of the Messiah.

The Torah is written in black fire on white fire and is placed on the knees of the holy One blessed be He, and the holy One blessed be He sits on the throne of glory...The Garden of Eden is at his right hand; Gehinnom, on his left; and the temple is prepared before him. The name of the Messiah is engraved on precious

[27]Ta'anit 5a.
[28]Hag 12b; *Ain Yaakob, loc. cit.* See also Rev 5:8; 6:9-11.
[29]Mekilta, *Beshelah,* 10.
[30]Tanhuma, *Vayakahel, siman* 7.
[31]JBer IV (5b-c).

stone on top of the altar, and a *bat qol* will announce, "Return, sons of man!"[32]

When the temple was standing, there was a high priest sacrificing and burning incense in the temple which is below, and Michael, as a counterpart, was standing and sacrificing in the temple which is above. When the temple which is below was destroyed, the holy One blessed be He said to Michael, "Michael, since I have destroyed my house, burned my temple, made my sanctuary desolate, and destroyed my altar, do not sacrifice before me: not in the likeness of a bull, not in the likeness of a sheep, not in the likeness of a goat." [Michael] said before him, "Master of the age! Your children! What will happen to them?" The holy One blessed be He said, "The sacrifice which you shall offer me [consists of] their good deeds, their prayers, and the souls of the righteous which are stored under the throne of glory,[33] and the children of school age.[34] With them, I will atone for the iniquities of Israel. While this joy prevailed below, joy also prevailed above. Now that lamentation is below, there is also lamentation above. When this which is below is built, the one above is also built, as it is said, *Behold, I will return the captives of Jacob's tents, and on his dwellings I will have mercy, and the city will be built on its own tel, and the palace will sit on its own position* (Jer 30:18). It does not say, "tent," but *tents*—one below, and one above, and it does not say, "his dwelling," but *his dwellings*—a dwelling above and a dwelling below. *The city will be built on its own tel.* This is Jerusalem which is below. *The palace will sit on its own position.* This is Jerusalem which is above.[35]

Summary

These passages show the close relationship between the theology of heaven and that of Jerusalem and the temple. In Christian and Jewish thought, heaven is the counterpart of the temple and

---

[32]Mid. Ps 90:3, Buber edition.

[33]Rev 6:9-11: "When he opened the fifth seal, I saw under the altar the souls of those who had been slaughtered for the word of God and the witness which they held. They cried out in a loud voice saying, 'How long, O Lord, holy and true, will you not judge and vindicate our blood from those who dwell on the land? There was given to them a white robe, and it was told to them that they must rest a little longer, until also their fellow servants and their brothers, who were about to be killed as they had been would fill up [the deficiency in the treasury of merits]."

[34]Prior to their bar miṣwah, before they had been responsible for any sins. Therefore their deaths would be complete credit in the treasury of merits.

[35]Midrash *Arakim* and Midrash, *The Lord in Wisdom Established the Land.*

Jerusalem. Michael corresponds to the high priest, and other angels correspond to the Levites and other priests who have duties in the temple, singing, standing guard, serving in the army of the Lord, interceding for sinners. Heaven has a temple, altar, cherubim, lampstands, and other temple facilities. Like Jerusalem, it has gates, streets, and other municipal requirements. Since the pillar of fire and cloud united the temple to heaven, the two were thought to be nearly identical (see *To The Hebrews*, 157-62). The Lord condescended to come from heaven and dwell in the temple at Jerusalem. When the temple was destroyed, the Lord withdrew to heaven. When it should please him, he would bring down the kingdom which is above to Jerusalem again. The Lord refused to enter the celestial temple until the terrestrial temple was restored. The temple above was created before the age or the world, before time began. Michael was not permitted to sacrifice in heaven so long as there was no temple on earth where Jews could sacrifice.

RABBI JOSHUA IN THE GARDEN OF EDEN[36]

Our sages (May he remember them for blessing) said:

Rabbi Joshua Ben Levi was a perfect saint, and when his time to depart from the world came, the holy One blessed be He said to the angel of death, "Fulfill all his requirements, and whatever he requests of you." [The angel of death] went to him [Rabbi Joshua] and said: "The time has come [for you] to depart from the world; but everything you request of me [beforehand], I will do for you." When Rabbi Joshua heard this, he said, "I request of you that you show me my place in the Garden of Eden." [The angel of death] said to him, "Come with me, and I will show you."

Rabbi Joshua went and searched all over the Garden of Eden, and he found seven houses there. Each house was a hundred, twenty thousand miles long and a hundred, twenty thousand miles wide [120,000 miles square], and the rest of its measurements, its length being equal to its width.

The first house was opposite the first gate in the Garden of Eden. In it dwelled those who had become proselytes of their own accord, not having been compelled to do so. Its walls were of glass and were firmly made. When I came to measure it, all the proselytes arose and wished to pass through. Obadiah, the righteous, who had been appointed over them, said to them,

[36]Jellinek, בית המדרש II, 48-51. SML

"What is your merit that this one [Rabbi Joshua] dwells with you?" Whereupon they permitted me to measure it.

The second house was opposite the second gate in the Garden of Eden. It was made of silver, and its walls were of cedar. The repentant ones dwelled there, and Manasseh, son of Hezekiah, was appointed over them.

The third house was opposite the third gate in the Garden of Eden and was constructed of silver and gold. In it lived Abraham, Isaac, and Jacob, and all the Israelites who came out of Egypt, all of the generation of the wilderness, and all the kings' sons except Absalom. There were David, Solomon, Caleb son of David, and all the kings of the house of Judah, except Manasseh son of Hezekiah, because he had been appointed over all those who had repented. Moses and Aaron were appointed over them [this group]. There all the vessels were of gold, precious silver, and all [other] good things [were there] such as oils, stones, canopies, beds, chairs, candlesticks of gold, precious stones, and pearls. I asked, "For whom are all these [treasures] designates?" David answered, "For all those who have lived in the world from which you came." I said to him, "Perhaps there are some Gentiles [also], even from the sons of Esau, my brother?" He replied, "No, because all the good deeds which they do in the world, the holy One blessed be He pays them their reward in their lifetime in that world, and at the end, they inherit Gehinnom. With reference to the Israelites, however, the wicked among them receives [his punishment] in this world and in his lifetime. Then he merits the age to come, as it is said, 'He repays those who hate him.'"

The fourth house is opposite the fourth gate in the Garden of Eden and is constructed as beautifully as [it was for] Adam. Its walls are of olive wood and in it [dwell those who are] completely righteous and loyal. Why of olive wood? Because their days were as bitter as olives.

The fifth house is built from silver and gold, gold ornaments, and refined gold, glass and crystal. The river Gihon flows into it, and its walls are of silver and gold. The smell of Lebanon pervades all the various beds of silver and gold and spices. The blue and purple are from the weaving of the hamlet, and the crimson and goat skins are from the weaving of the angels. In it dwells the Messiah son of David and Elijah (May he be remembered for blessing). The canopy is from the wood of Lebanon. *He made its posts of silver, its back of gold, its seat of purple* (SS 3:10). Inside the canopy dwells the Messiah, [the canopy] which [is made with] *the love from the daughters of Jerusalem* (SS 3:10).

Elijah (May he be remembered for blessing) takes the head of the Messiah and places it in his bosom and says to him, "Keep still, for the end is near!" The patriarchs of the age, all the tribes, Moses and Aaron, David and Solomon, and every single king of Israel; and from the house of David, every second and fifth, every Sabbath and festival will come to him and weep with him. They will strengthen him and say, "Keep still and lean for support on your Creator, for the end is near!" Korah and his fellow conspirators, Dathan and Abiram, and Absalom will also come to him every fourth day and ask him, *When will be the end of these wonders* (Dan 12:6)? "When will you raise us and bring us up from the depths of the earth?" Then he will say to them, "Go to your patriarchs and ask them." But when they hear this, they will be [too much] ashamed to ask the patriarchs.

When I came to the Messiah, he asked me, "What are the Israelites doing in the age from which you came?" I replied, "They are waiting for you everyday." Whereupon he raised his voice and burst into tears.

The sixth house is one in which those who died in the performance of a good deed live.

The seventh house is the one where those who died of illness on the account of the iniquities of Israel dwell.

Rabbi Joshua said, "When I saw all these things, I returned to the Garden of Eden and wrote down all these words and sent them to Rabban Gamliel and the elders of Israel, and I informed them [of] all that I saw in the Garden of Eden and in Gehinnom. May the Lord in his mercies deliver us from the punishment of Gehinnom and give us a portion in the age to come with the righteous and the pious. Amen.

Summary

This apocalypse was brief but typical. One of the saintly rabbis, because of his virtue, was supposedly given an introduction into the future life, and he recorded his insights for posterity. A still more involved description of the Garden of Eden is given in the following narrative.

THE GARDEN OF EDEN AND THE WORLD TO COME[37]

Walls of Fire

Outer wall. —There are three walls around the Garden of Eden, and all are of fire. The outer wall is of black fire which is both visible and invisible. The flaming sword around the outer wall turns itself around it (Gen 3:24). There are four gates in the outer wall with a distance of one hundred, twenty cubits from one gate to the other. The flaming sword revolves all day and night, is never still, and consumes all green grass and everything within a mile's distance from the garden. There is a distance of six hundred cubits between that outer wall and the second wall. There are the pious of the Gentiles, their kings who have rescued the Israelites, and those proselytes who do not fittingly implement the fear of the Lord in all its implications. From the time of the afternoon sacrifice onwards, the angels of destruction are gathered together to take them away from there and lead them to Gehinnom. All will be crying aloud when the angel appointed over them, whose name is Azriel, will come and seize them and deliver them from their hands. They will return from the afternoon sacrifice and before the evening prayer three times, and they will cry to Abraham in a loud voice. That angel will then return and seize them as in the beginning. All this is so as to afflict them. There in that outer wall will also be those who do righteousness in public, but not in the name of Heaven. These will be sorry for themselves three times a day, and two angels will seize them and rescue them from the hands of the destroying angel. All those who have received their punishment in Gehinnom and are coming out from there will be accompanied by three ministering angels who will bring them to the place of the revolving, flaming sword. There they will receive their purification and enter into this outer wall, and there they will stand and enjoy a trifle of the luster of the countenance of the righteous who are within, but they will not cause them distress. All those wicked ones who were contemplating to do repentance before they left the world and after they had received their punishment will enter this wall and wait there until the sanctifying of the day on the eve of the Sabbath. The breezes inside the Garden of Eden will go up from the angel Hariel who brings all these in and shows them their designated places of pleasure. When

[37]Text is from Jellinek, בית המדרש III, 131-40. SML

the winds go up towards the crevice of the rock, he [the angel] gives them a place which they enter at the termination of the Sabbath. At the time when the Israelites are saying the prescribed holy prayer, all the winds descend to their dwelling places, each one knowing his appointed place and his exact location.

The second wall. —The second wall is of green and red fire, and the angel Peniel is appointed over them. There, within that wall, are those who enabled their sons to learn Torah. Although they [the children] did not succeed, yet they [the parents] tried [to impart learning] to them. There are those who were men of action, who were immediately ready to listen to the words of the Torah and moral teachings. There the light from the pleasantness of the righteous remains with them only for an instant and immediately vanishes. All those who expect the Messiah and all those who see the Messiah from there once every day [are there]. On the sixth day, at the time when the Israelites try to rest, all the palaces in the Garden tremble. The inner palace where the Messiah is is called "the bird's nest." The Messiah goes out from there with all the righteous ones accompanying him. He wears garments of vengeance which are destined for the salvation of Israel. All enter with him and the fathers when he goes out from there and stands in the midst of the garden, in the place of the pillar which is in the center. He will take hold of the four signet rings which are in the four corners of the garden and will shout so loudly as to cause the firmament which is above the garden to tremble.

The Garden of Eden and all its effects were created before the world was created—all its plants, the firmament which is over them, and the ground under it. After one thousand, three hundred, sixty-one years, three hours, and two minutes, heaven and earth were created. The ground of the garden [came into existence thus]: When the holy One blessed be He created the Garden of Eden, he took snow from under the throne of glory from which he called into being the ground of the garden. This ground of the garden both touches and does not touch the land which is above all the countries. The firmament which is over the garden reflects all the colors of a paved work of a sapphire stone (Ex 24:10). The name of the holy One blessed be He is engraved in the middle of the firmament. There are four signet rings at the four corners of the firmament and four *Ophanim* in every signet. In the midst of the firmament is a pillar, and this pillar projected from the ground of the garden until it is seized before the throne of glory and is covered by the cloud of glory. The angel Gabriel, dressed in linen, stands over it. Once a day he seizes the signet rings of the firmament, and the pillar which revolves, and the firmament surrounding [it on which are engraved] the letters of the ineffable Name protruding, glittering, ascending, and descending. A voice proclaims, "Prepare yourselves, O righteous saints. Blessed are you that you have merited this. Who has heard or seen [things] like these?" When the music sounded, the firmament was moved by the man dressed in linen. It removes itself, stands still, and the pillar sounds its note, going up and down while the light continues shining, a pleasant light from above that pillar. The righteous will stand before that light and enjoy it until midnight. At midnight, when the holy One blessed be He comes to enter with the righteous, they will hear a voice encircling the firmament. Then the pillar will sound its note, the ground of the garden will be raised, and the righteous will arise from their canopies to meet their Maker. The whole garden will be filled with his glory. At that hour the male and female spirits will be mated as when they were created. From that pleasant desire of theirs to see the pleasant one of the Lord, all bearing fruit, and their fruit will produce spirits for proselytes just as Abraham and Sarah produced spirits for proselytes. Blessed is he who merits in this age to be found in that hour with the joy of the Torah!

The light of the brilliance of the holy One blessed be He will remain in the Garden of Eden, but it will ascend and all the righteous ones will sing at its ascent in the morning. From the covering of the ground of the garden and from the dew with which the holy One blessed be He is destined to revive the dead, and the righteous ones will go out and be nourished from it, just as are the heavenly, ministering angels. At that time when the Messiah goes out and seizes the four signet rings and shouts loudly, shaking all the firmament which is over the garden, the seven angels attending him will say, "Keep still, O chosen one of the Lord, for the time has already arrived when the wicked kingdom will be uprooted from its place." The voice will be heard from the synagogues and houses of study, where [the worshippers] will say with all their might, "Amen! May his great Name be blessed for the age and for ages of ages!" Then the holy One blessed be He will shake the firmaments and two tears will fall to the Great Sea. The righteous will enter together with the Messiah into that palace called "the bird's nest."

Third wall. —The third wall is composed of light mixed with darkness, and it is before the Garden of Eden. From there on the interest of the garden is in its ascents, pleasures, and buildings. It is like the paved work of sapphire stone whose plant ascends for the benefit of the spirits of the four winds which blow upon it from the four corners. These spirits are from the subject of the [living] beast which is under the God of Israel. This is the beast which the waters breed from the Upper Eden which *eye has not seen, O God, except you, who works for those who wait for him* (Isa 64:3). Inside this wall is the brightness which has appeared like the glory of the Lord. From there on the righteous, who are the spirits, dwell. When they enter there they are immediately embodied by the upper air which blows in the garden, and they are dressed in it like a pure and holy garment. That garment is of the same pattern which was in this age. With this garment, they walk and recognize each other, each as it befits him.

The Seven Degrees

First Degree.—There are seven degrees of the righteous in the Garden of Eden, with seven canopies separated from each other according to their degrees. The first degree of those who are called righteous, and they are all those who keep the holy covenant in this age and who controlled their evil impulses and faithfully observed the commands of the Torah. Opposite them from above were those angels named *Aralim*. The chief of this degree is Joseph the righteous, son of Jacob. He ministers in the first canopy, which is the first palace in the Garden of Eden.

Second degree.—The second degree is of those who are called the upright. They are just in their ways and all the things they do in this age [they do] with an upright heart. They have no thoughts of evil things, for all their deeds are upright before their Creator. Facing them above are those angels who are called *Hashmalim*. These are in front of the degree of the righteous. Concerning these two groups, it is said, *The righteous will praise your name; the just will dwell before you* (Ps 140:14). The chief of this degree is Phineas, the son of Elazar who ministers in this canopy which is the second palace in the Garden of Eden.

Third degree.—The third degree consists of those who are called perfect and who pace this age with a perfect heart and do not entertain impure thoughts of the ways of the holy One blessed be He. They have tried to attain the degrees of the first ones in righteousness and equity within their hearts, and they have kept the words of the Torah and the commandments. Facing them above are those angels, the ministers of the Most High who are called *Tarshsishim*. The head of this degree is Elazar, son of Aaron the priest who ministers in this canopy which is the third palace in the Garden of Eden.

Fourth degree. — The fourth degree is of those who are called holy. They are the ones of whom it is written, *They are for the holy ones who are in the land, my noble ones. All my desire is in them* (Ps 16:3). These possess all the keys of the gates of the Garden of Eden. When the pillar which is in the center of the garden moves and plays of its own accord, then the firmament which is over the Garden of Eden returns. Those who went out first to meet their Creator draw near to the pillar. The man dressed in linen seizes the four signet rings which are in the firmament, and the pillar of the firmament strikes the signet ring which is in the east of the firmament. Then all the trees in the garden sing for joy and burst forth in paeons of praise, and the glory of the God of Israel comes, concerning whom it is said, *Behold the glory of the* Lord *God of Israel comes from the* holy *way, and the land will reflect his glory* (Ezek 43:1). This is the Garden of Eden. The degree of these holy ones began first by saying, *Holy, holy, holy is the Lord of armies.* (Isa 6:3; Ps 72:19). Over the degree of these holy ones is Aaron, the priest of his holy God.

Fifth degree. — The fifth degree is of the repentant who broke the brass doors and returned to their Creator in a fitting manner. Facing them above is the degree of the attendants of the holy One on high. The place of their degree is called *Ophanim* and there is none who can reach their degree, because it is very high. The pleasant one of the Name reaches them because of the brilliance of the repentance from on high which *eye has not seen* (Isa 64:3). All the righteous ones are scorched by the canopy of these. Even the wicked ones in Gehinnom see the brilliance of their degree and cry out, "Master of the ages, there is favoritism in this, for both we and these in this great canopy have all sinned together and have transgressed the Torah. Why do they enjoy this great degree while we live in the thick darkness of the pit of Gehinnom?" At once the angel *Barkiel* appears for them and says, "Fools that you are! When you were in the age, you were content not to leave it for the age. These of your fellows who sinned like you finally meditated repentance and turned to their Creator. Hence they merit all this glory." Manasseh, king of Judah, is appointed over them.

Sixth degree. — The sixth degree is that of the school children who have not sinned. This is a more intimate degree than the others, and every day Mettation, the minister of the interior, descends by way of the pillar and teaches them the Torah. Their compartment is greater than all of the others. At midnight, they go up to the academy above, and the holy One blessed be He [himself] teaches them Torah in which they take delight. Facing them above are those called *Cherubim*, of whom it is said, *Who teaches knowledge and who understands the report? Those who are weaned from milk, taken from the breast* (Isa 28:9). The chief of this division below is Joshua, the young man who was the attendant of Moses.

Seventh degree.—The seventh degree is one whose members are called *Hasidim* and which is the most inward of all. Facing [the members] from above is the degree of the *Hayot* that are called the "holy *Hayot*." Over it [the degree] are appointed Abraham, Isaac, and Jacob. The name, Adam, has been placed over the door of this palace. There are seven gates in this seventh wall, corresponding to the seven degrees. Each of these degrees enters into a gate above that degree, and guards stand over every gate. The group of righteous enter through their own gate; the group of the just enter through theirs; and thus [it is with] every single degree of these seven degrees.

Contents of the Garden

In the Garden of Eden, from the wall inward, there is a thick cloud, but its surroundings are brilliant. On the north side, there is a curtain that is separated from the brilliance and a greenish fire divide them from the rest of the spirits of the garden. There the palaces are hidden because of the righteous and pure women that were in Israel. On the side of the east wind there is a palace that is hidden and closed. It is called the palace of splendor. This palace is built like heaven itself for purity, and surrounding all its walls are signs projecting and dazzling, some ascending and some descending. These wing their way from here and descend there on the other side. Whereas those letters which are on the other side fly from there and rest here, changing with each other without erring for the age. No one can stop them, because they do not cease even for an instant. Flowers [in the form of] lattice work display four colors of dazzling brilliance there. On the Sabbath day, the Messiah with the patriarchs enters there, and the letters chip themselves off. Those who read them are very glad, and no one knows how this happens.

In that palace, and before that open gate, and there inside that

curtain are statues of those killed at Lydda and the ten martyred
by the Romans. It is from there that the Messiah rises and enters.
When he sees those statues he will raise his voice and roar like a
lion. All the garden and all the righteous will tremble. The pillar in
the center of the garden will tremble and ascend and descend. The
four *Ophanim* will be summoned there, and they will seize the
four signet rings. The firmament will revolve, and the voice will be
heard on high. The holy One blessed be He will shed two tears on
the pillar below. The *Ophanim* will enter [the palace of] the
Messiah, and all the patriarchs will enter the door of the front gate
which is in that palace. There they will see all the degrees of the
righteous ones of Lydda and the ten martyred by the Romans.[38]
They will all, including the Messiah, be standing, and the
Ophanim will ascend to the King of kings of kings, the holy One
blessed be He. He will swear to them that he will wear garments of
vengeance and wreak their vengeance on the Gentiles, as it is said,
He will judge those nations, filling them with corpses (Ps 110:6).
They will return to the Messiah. They and the patriarchs will
approach [the palace of] the heads of the academies who are there
and will rejoice at the new interpretations of the Torah which
rejuvenate every individual in this age. From there all the deans of
all the academies will go to the academy of our teacher Moses
(upon whom be peace). Moses and all the righteous ones who
belonged to the generation of the wilderness will sit before him and
learn the Torah. He will interpret for them the reception of the
Torah according to that which he received from on high.

The Seven Dwellings

First dwelling.—In the Garden of Eden, on the north side, are
seven prepared dwellings and palaces for the righteous women in
Israel who performed meritorious deeds for God by giving charity
and from the merits of the Torah for their children. In the first
dwelling will be found Batyah, the daughter of Pharaoh. How
many will be righteous women that are there? All those who
reared orphans, showed kindness to scholars, showing the hospitality of their husbands, and giving charity secretly. Everyday
they are crowned with a shining crown of the splendor of the
Shekinah,   and they proclaim over it [the house], "Blessed are you
who fortify and continue the growth of the branch of splendor in
the age."

[38]At the time of the Bar Cochba revolt. Rabbi Akiba and his friends.

Second dwelling.—In the second dwelling there are many righteous women of Israel. There is Jochabad, the wife of Amram, who is chief over them. Three times a day they proclaim with respect to her: "Blessed are you that you have merited bearing a son whose head and feet stood among the thick cloud.

Third dwelling.—In the third dwelling there is Miriam the prophetess, with whom the righteous women stand. All those who encouraged their husbands [to walk in] the good way and in the service of their Creator. In every dwelling, there are canopies of tranquility, and well-known angels have been appointed over every dwelling.

Fourth dwelling.—In the fourth dwelling is Hulda the prophetess and many pious women who reside in that division.

Fifth dwelling.—In the fifth dwelling there is Abigail, and with her are many righteous women, dwelling in confidence, each in her own canopy.

From there on are those of the matriarchs: Sarah, Rebecca, Rachel, and Leah. At midnight when the holy One blessed be He enters with the righteous, a voice calls in the garden: "You are righteous, prepare yourselves to meet your Maker! Blessed are you who have merited all this glory." At that time, the souls will blossom forth and each of them will be paired together suitably and according to the degree of their works. They will see and attain their degree with joy, *Eye has not seen, O God, except you [who works for those who wait for him]* (Isa 64:3).

Scholars

In the Garden of Eden there is a dean of the academy in the palace of the nut. That is the palace of splendor which is closed up and hidden. Near it is the palace of "the bird's nest" (see Ber 5:3) and is called "[The academy of] Rav Gadeil, the youth." He reveals all the deep and secret things of the Torah which are made crystal clear by him. All the righteous ones desire to be near him. He was born in the days of the religious persecution [of Hadrian] and was studying the Torah in a cave when he was only seven years old. The enemies came and found him and cut him up into pieces. His soul ascended to heaven. It is said that like the appearance of a rainbow which is in a cloud on a rainy day, so is the radiance which surrounds this place. It is like the appearance of the glory of the Lord. The holy One blessed be He raised him [Gadiel] before him and swore to him that he would cause him to inherit the palace of splendor and that he would reveal in the Garden of Eden the secret and deep things which are in the Torah and which had not been disclosed previously. All the righteous ones who are in the Garden of Eden long eagerly to see him and to hear from him the deep things in the Torah and its secrets.

When he goes out, the letters of the ineffable Name protrude and dazzle over his head, and all the righteous ones are happy. He entered, fell on his face, and wept bitterly because he did not merit having a son in this age. Then Joshua Ben Yehozedek, the high priest, stood over him and seized him and made him stand on his feet. Then he said to him, "Arise! My associates are yours. My associates are your sons!" Rabbi Yoḥanan Ben Zakkai fasted seven fasts so that he might see him. They showed him the hidden things of seven firmaments in a dream. Finally, all of them had seen him like the brightness of the firmament; seventy angels surrounded him; and there were fifty keys in his hand. There were many groups of righteous ones before him and the letters of the ineffable Name hovered over his head. They were soon hidden, and no one could any longer see him. They used to ask him, "How long will you permit us to see this version of the bow which is in the cloud?" The sages returned to his father and found that he had never looked at the physical form of a man or at the rainbow of his covenant, that his hand never reached [the area] from his navel downwards, and that he did not arise from the study of the Torah in order to pursue the ways of the world. There was no other righteous man in the age who suffered such hardship and yet did not say a word outside of the Torah or the ways of the Torah. He fathered this son, and he died. When his mother gave him birth, she died and he was left an orphan. He grew up amidst hardship; yet he studied much Torah, and because they killed him, he merited all this [splendor].

The Righteous

All the righteous will see each other, and they will know and recognize with a mature knowledge which lacks nothing. When the souls ascend on the evening of the Sabbath to the heavenly Garden of Eden above, they proclaim many announcements above and below. They all strip themselves of that garment and go up to heaven. There in the firmament of the heavens stands Michael the great prince. There is an altar before him, and all the souls of the righteous will sacrifice on that altar. Then will come a spirit of fragrance because they performed [good] deeds in this age. The holy One blessed be He will restore to [each man] his spirit, for with the spirit with which they depart will they come into this age. That spirit returns and is restored to him. For this reason human beings return to their first cause. At that time, when Michael offers the sacrifice of the souls, he restores [each man's] spirit to him, and they bring him inside. There is a time when the holy One blessed be He restores [a man's] spirit to him, but he does not bring him inside. In the later case, the spirit returns here and there and roams to and fro to Gehinnom. When he brings him inside, to his bosom, he enters the earthly Garden of Eden. Once inside there, they [then] bring him into the heavenly Garden of Eden. If you are surprised that a man's soul goes out of his mouth, it is written, *He breathed into his mouth the soul of life* (Gen 2:7). He raises [the soul] from the altar with the love of the fragrance and brings it forth from its midst to the heavenly Garden of Eden.

The Heavenly Garden

The heavenly Garden of Eden is that which the Lord God planted, a place of Upper Eden, as it is written, *The Lord planted a garden in the east of Eden* (Gen 2:8). That garden is to the north side of heaven as is earthly Jerusalem, as it is said, *Mount Zion, in the far north, [the city of the great king]* (Ps 48:3). The heavenly Garden of Eden is beneath a screen under the God of Israel. It is square at the four corners of the firmament, which is like the terrible frost. Six mirrors brightly shine around it, and the sixth planet [Venus] resembles a river which flows into the midst of the garden. It goes out from the Upper Eden and enters the midst of the garden. From there is divides and becomes four heads. One head is [that of] Michael the great prince and faces Pishon, the first [river] which is beneath the earthly Garden of Eden. The second head is [that of] the man Gabriel, dressed in linen. He faces the second river which is in the earthly Garden of Eden, named Gihon. The third head is [that of] Nuriel which faces the river Euphrates. In the earthly Garden of Eden, a river goes out from Eden which is closed and hidden. It enters the Garden of Eden and waters all those plants. From there, that river divides and becomes four, just as it is in heaven. In the earthly Garden of Eden, there is a tree of life in the midst of the garden, and close to it is the tree of the knowledge of good and evil. In the tree of life, there are things that are closed off and hidden. When the holy One blessed be He enters the garden with the righteous, the tree of life gives forth a fragrance which permeates the whole garden. That fragrance [means] life for all the righteous who are there. It all spreads out, and the leaves shout for joy. The righteous dwell in its shade. Every New Moon and festival they sit down [to eat] of delicacies. Its fruit is life and rest. *Its leaf does not wither. In all that it does, it prospers* (Ps 1:3). How is it said, His *leaf does not wither, and all that* he *does prospers?* What does the holy One blessed be He do, entering the nut garden which is before the garden, and his beloved ones who are in the ten degrees and the righteous ones sit in the shade of the tree? A fountain of blessing cascades and falls upon the head of every righteous person. When the dew falls upon him, he goes and stands in the eastern gate before the nut garden and there he prostrates himself before the cloud of his glory. The holy One blessed be He asks and he answers, learns whatever he learns, and departs. Thus every righteous man does. The holy One blessed be He rejoices very much with them. He comes and stands near that tree of life. The cloud turns away, and the righteous come and prostrate themselves before that shining light of his glory above.

While on this subject, there are three walls [around] the heavenly Garden of Eden. One is called the "Secret Whisper"; the second is called "The Movement of the Lord's Laborer"; the third is called "The Garden of the Royal Cloak." The names of the holy One blessed be He are on every wall. The first wall is called "The Whisper of the Secret Staircase." It is that of which Solomon said by way of parable, *My dove is in the cleft of the rock, in the covert of the cliff* (SS 2:14). No soul enters the heavenly Garden of Eden except on Sabbaths and festivals which are called "the Sabbath of the Lord," because in them souls take delight, as it is written, *You shall call the Sabbath "a delight"* (Isa 58:13). This wall is of fire that consumes fire, and there are angels which were created on the second day. When they draw near to this wall they sing a song. They draw near to enter, and they are scorched by the licking of that fire. They return at the New Moons as at the beginning. Concerning them, it is said, *They are new every morning. Great is your faithfulness* (Lam 3:23)! The secret of the flaming sword revolves around this wall, and two Cherubim guard the garden. Between all the walls, there stand Seraphim, according to their kind, guarding and holding vigil. There the river Dinur surrounds winds around, leading and going forth with thousands of thousands and myriads of myriads using it. All the angels who are appointed over the nations [stay] around that river until the river [reaches] a high place and the ladder which Jacob saw in a dream is seen in it (Gen 28:12). That ladder is the one used by the young man Mettatron who is placed higher than his colleagues, a distance of five hundred years. All the princes appointed over the nations approach the ladder: some ascend while others descend. All who go up have a kingdom; all who go down enter into the river Dinur and are licked up there, and the kingdom departs from them.

The second wall is called "The Lord's Laborer." It is a light shining for the righteous, and the holy One blessed be He labors continually in this light which *eye has not seen, O God, except you, laboring for those who wait for him* (Isa 64:3). This Garden of Eden is above three hundred and ninety firmaments. The first veil and firmament [contain] clouds and a dwelling in which are Jerusalem, the house of the sanctuary, the altar, the dwelling, the abode, and the heavens. In the heavens are the seven hidden things of life as well as mysteries of peace and blessing. The souls of the righteous are higher than all those firmaments.

The Firmaments

Come and see how many numerous firmaments the holy One blessed be He created. There is neither number nor place for the heavens of the Most High. They are the place of all ages and all firmaments, *Eye has not seen, O God, except you* (Isa 64:3). Every single age is an age by itself, and every age is divided into a thousand ages except for the veil where there is time that exceeds a thousand [ages] and also which does not exceed a thousand. The remaining six which are six thousand ages and are held to each other three times; they are eighteen thousand ages. No one enters them except the holy One blessed be He, as it is said, *The chariots of God, twice ten thousand thousands doubled* (Ps 68:18), which are non-existent, because no one knows them except the one who ascends. This Garden of Eden is directed towards the clouds, where they grind manna for the righteous, and their mills are placed in the clouds, where they grind the manna. The clouds enter the garden and above toward the tree which is the secret of the central pillar in the Garden of Eden below. This pillar is in the midst of the garden above and leads downward. From it are drawn all the good things of the garden and all its delicacies. This pillar is bounded by twelve diagonal borders, and that tree is the place from which souls come forth. All twelve of its boundaries and this tree have their roots in Lebanon where is the throne of glory above. Lebanon faces the Lebanon above and it has seventy-two roots planted in the house of the Lord. There are forty-two branches, and all the princes of the age are suspended from it. There are thirty-six diagonal lines altogether, and it [the tree] is bounded by the corners of the age. The wind has nine in the East, nine in the North, nine breezes in the South, and nine in the West. In the middle of the garden where the trunk of the tree is, the holy people are held, and they took their lot. On this tree there are fifty gates, and each of them is a gate for those who are righteous in their faith to enter. From the trunk of the tree which is in the midst of the garden the souls blossom forth. There are no winds, because the winds are on the other tree below, and the souls from the upper tree are hidden, as we have said.

Summary

This is the end of this document. It is rather abrupt with no warning that there is no more to follow. The document, however, is rather extensive and describes in detail various parts and implications of the Garden of Eden. The eschatological reasoning that is behind this document is that the same typology which is considered historically is applied to the very beginning and to the very end of creation. There is also a perpendicular typology relating heaven to earth. The Garden of Eden in which Adam and Eve lived in righteousness before they sinned would be restored for the final dwelling of the righteous. People would be ranked there according to the kind of ethics they observed before they died. The better the ethic the higher the rank and the better the quarters. This eschatology was expressed mystically, but it was not divorced from the Messiah, the patriarchs, and the promised land. This was true of the entire section. Future expectations involved the restoration of the promised land and the temple restored, but the mysticism of the theology pictured a heavenly Jerusalem in very close relationship to the earthly Jerusalem and its temple. Narratives were invented with Elijah, the Messiah, and Moses as the chief characters. Heavenly activity was prominent, but that was primarily to show what would soon happen on earth.

Like other eschatological expectations, this collection also has its end. Many documents have been presented to show the reader the kind of expectations that were prominent from the time of the NT to the end of the Crusades, in doctrine, letters, poetry, prayers, and various kinds of apocalypticism. The Christian scholar of the NT for whom this literature is new will have reached his own conclusions now and will be prepared to compare his conclusions with some of the following which seem to be only some of the very obvious implications of this literature to NT study.

CONCLUSIONS

The Literature

Apocalypticism. —Medieval Jewish apocalyptic literature belongs to a classification called "redemption literature." That redemption literature which is apocalyptic is very similar to earlier apocalyptic literature, such as Daniel, Enoch, The Assumption of Moses, and Revelation. The author of each of these apocalyptic pieces was supposed to have been one of the ancient saints, such as Zerubbabel, Daniel, or Rabbi Shimon Ben Yoḥai, who received his information through a divine communication. Apocalyptic seers were either transported to heaven where they were shown the heavenly treasuries which implied to them what would happen to Israel in the future, or they were sent a special heavenly emissary, such as Michael, Mettatron, or some unnamed angel who told them what would happen in the future.

Apocalyptic editors. —Final producers of this literature were more skilled in editing than in composing, because their productions are notably composite, including prose and poetic units that were once independent documents or parts of different documents. Certain of these units were popular and used interchangeably by several different apocalyptic editors. Traditions such as Armilos, the relationship between the two Messiahs, the Garden of Eden and Gehinnom, and the bases for calculating the end appear not only in apocalyptic prophecies, but also in responsa, sermons, poetry, and letters.

Tracts for diaspora Zionists. —Apocalyptic documents have often been called "tracts for hard times," because they have been attractive to religious people in times of financial depression, hardship, or oppression. They might be more aptly called "tracts for diaspora Zionists," because they did not apply to all peoples or all kinds of hard times. The religious people for whom these were written were not poverty-stricken people. Medieval Jews underwent many very difficult times, involving mass murder, expulsion, and the confiscation of property, but these were not the kind of hard times Americans usually associate with an economic depression. Every time there was an expulsion of Jews from a country, the poor and uneducated Jews were culled out, because they were not well enough equipped financially or culturally to move and readapt to another country, language, and culture. They would have converted to Christianity, Islam, or have been killed. Surviving Jews continued to be those of the upper class, and the kind of hard times they suffered would be hard for *rich* people. There were not many medieval Jews who suffered from malnutrition or starvation. Times were hard for them because their aims had been frustrated. They were not in political control of the world, which they believed should have been centered around Jerusalem, Zion, the chosen people, and the promised land. Although it made good sense in relationship to their beliefs and historical situation, some of the language used is confusing to the uninitiated, because the authors regularly spoke of their local situation as if they were reliving parts of their nation's past history, such as their exile in Egypt, Babylon, or the Roman Empire. This meant that individuals or groups of people in their contemporary world were labeled by the name of some corresponding group or persons in the past. This code and style of literature was heavily based on the OT, which medieval Jews accepted as God's word which held the key to their code.

Non-apocalyptic literature.—Redemption literature is not limited to apocalyptic literature. The central point of description is not the form but the doctrine. Like other apocalyptic literature, medieval apocalyptic literature has as its primary reasons for existence the redemption or deliverance of the Jews from their "captivity" in the diaspora and the restoration of these coven-anters to their promised land which was liberated from foreign rule at the same time. Other literature which expresses this goal includes poetry, prayers, responsa of important leaders to questions of pious Jews of their day, letters, doctrinal formula-tions, and narratives of historical events related to messianic movements.

Relationship to the Old Testament

Typologically.—Basic to the idea that the future could be predicted was the belief that God worked according to certain patterns which could be discerned in history. It was partly from this perspective that apocalyptic literature came into existence. It was typological thinking that produced a style that attributed current literature to some important figure in the past. In the past it was possible to interpret events in a cause-effect relationship, assuming that God brought about the effect in the past and would do it again whenever human beings produced the same cause. In partial contradiction to this was the belief that all events were predetermined and destined to take place at certain specified times, regardless of human effort. Tied together with the Exodus from Egypt, for instance, was the persecution of Hebrews by Pharaoh, the establishment of a Hebrew in a top position of the government who was more loyal to his Hebrew kinspeople than to his country. Jews worked arduously to get their members into such positions, but they believed that God would raise up such people even if they failed. A targumist (*Yerushalmi*) in Ex 12:42 said: *"The fourth night:* When the age will complete [the appointed time until] its end to be redeemed, the fetters of the wicked ones will be destroyed and the yoke of iron will be broken. Moses will go out from the midst of the wilderness, and the messianic king [will go out] from the midst of Rome. The one [Moses] will lead [while sitting] on the top of a cloud (Ex 19:9, 19-20), and the other [the Messiah] will lead [while sitting] on the top of a cloud (Dan 7:13), with the Memra of the Lord leading between the two of them, and they will walk together. *This is Passover night before the Lord, kept and appointed for all Israelites for their generations"* (Ex 12:42). Hebrews escaped at night at the time of a feast, accompanied by miracles, under the leadership of Moses. If, then, at an appointed time in the future, Jews could succeed in structuring the same situation at the same feast, they could expect God to perform the necessary miracles and plagues to provide his chosen people another leader and an escape from the diaspora so that they could return to Palestine. The messianic king would do that which Moses had done. Although Jews worked zealously to bring about these conditions, they still accepted them as predestined events. II Isaiah had previously assumed the same kind of typology, so he foresaw Jews escaping from Babylon after they had been adequately persecuted by the Babylonians, similar to the way Israelites left Egypt. This would require the same kind of wilderness experiences that took place in the wilderness between Egypt and Palestine. God, in turn, would perform the same kind of miracles—water in the wilderness, healing for the sick and maimed, adequate provision for food, and release of the promised land from foreign control. Not only in NT times but also through the Middle Ages, Christian and Jewish covenanters looked for the restoration of the land in relationship to the patterns of establishment known both after the exodus from Egypt and the exodus from Babylon. The typology included a comparison of the Garden of Eden with the new Garden of Eden at the end of the Roman age, but most typologies were related to past events related to the captivities of Egypt and Babylon and the subsequent redemptions. Saadia Gaon compared the enslavement of Egypt and Babylon to that of his own day. He assumed that the redemption that would follow in his day would be similar, but more glorious, than the redemptions from Egypt and Babylon. Such a redemption would involve messianic leadership, committed covenanters, proper timing, ritualistic imitation of the wilderness experience, miracles, and gathering of exiles to Palestine. John the Baptist began his organizational movement in the wilderness of Judah. Before the destruction of Jerusalem, a certain Theudas led the masses to the Jordan, promising to command the water to be divided, as Joshua had done, so they could cross over on dry land. Fadus stopped the experiment with troops (*Ant.* XX [97-99]). One of the recurrent themes in medieval redemption literature is the forty-five days spent in the wilderness by Jews who understood that this would be the last event before they were restored to the promised land (see also *BJ* II [261-63]; Mt 24:26). They tested Messiahs for their validity by demanding a miracle. Some were supposed to have healed diseases, and others crossed streams without a boat. This was necessary for them to fit into the typology of Moses and Aaron both in Egypt and in the wilderness.

Midrashically.—The authors of redemption literature not only understood the basic types in the OT against which to anticipate the future, but, like their readers, they had memorized large portions of it so that they could just allude to a passage by quoting a few words, and expect it to be understood. In his personal introduction to the letter to Yemen, for instance, Maimonides said, "*If it had not been that the Lord was for us* (Ps 124:1), and *our fathers have told us* (Ps 78:3), I could not have achieved the little which I have accumulated and from which I draw continually."[1] Of course, Maimonides did not bother to document his biblical quotations, but his readers understood the whole passage intended by Ps 124:

> If it had not been the Lord who was on our side, let Israel say,
> if it had not been the Lord who was on our side
> when men rose up against us,
> then they would have swallowed us alive.
> When their wrath was incited against us,
> then the flood would have carried us away,
> the current would have covered us;

---

[1]Kafih, *Rabbi Moshe Ben Maimon, Letters.* 17 (in Hebrew).

then over us would have rushed the raging waters.
Blessed be the Lord who has not given us a prey to their
    teeth.
We have escaped as a bird from the fowler's snare;
the snare was broken, and we got away!
Our help is in the name of the Lord, who made heaven
    and earth" (Ps 124:1-8).

The short quotation, *our fathers have told us*, begins the third of a seventy-two verse narration of God's mighty acts which he performed for his rebellious people in the past, favoring Judah to Ephraim. Maimonides pointed to both of these passages to reinforce his testimony that the Lord had enabled him to achieve all of his accomplishments, in the face of severe difficulties. In Judah Halevy's beautiful poem, "Longing for Zion," he said,

When I dream of the return of your captivity, I am a
    harp for your songs;
my heart will throb loudly for Bethel and Peniel,
for Maḥannaim, the meeting places of your pure ones.

To get the point of this poetry, the reader must understand that "captivity" refers to those Jews of the diaspora who resented their existence away from the promised land. Halevy dreamed they were all returning to the promised land. This dream stirred him to musical rapture; he compared his heart beat to the strumming of strings on a harp when he thought of these three geographical locations in the United Kingdom. The reader, then, was expected to know that these were all places where Jacob had encountered heavenly angels—at Bethel, where he saw the angels going up and down from earth to heaven on a ladder (Gen 28:12-19) as he was leaving the promised land for the diaspora, Peniel, where he wrestled with the angel at the river Jabbok and received the name "Israel" (Gen 32:24-31) as he was returning to the land from "captivity" to recover his heritage from Esau, and Maḥannaim, where he met the army of angels after he had become safely separated from Laban (Gen 32:1-3) on his return to the promised land. He had left the land with angels reminding him that this was the gate of heaven, and he returned with the help of an angelic troop, escaping injury from his enemy, and unimpeded by Esau. All this was a part of the message Halevy intended in these few lines.

In addition to allusions to scripture, medieval preachers also interpreted texts, such as the following midrash:

"Another interpretation: *Rejoicing, I will rejoice* (Isa 61:10).

Rejoicing in the days of the Messiah; *I will rejoice* with the downfall of wicked Rome. *My soul will delight in my God* (Isa 61:10). This is the war of Gog and Magog" (Pesikta Rabbati 37).

To get the impact of the number of OT passages quoted, used as texts for commentary or as media for allusion, it is only necessary to skim the literature translated here and observe the percentage of material in italics. To observe how similar this is to NT composition, just glance through a Nestle or Nestle-Aland edition of the Greek NT, which prints every OT reference in bold face type, and note the number of OT passages in Romans 9 and 10, the Book of Hebrews, or the Book of Revelation. Closer examination will call attention to the similarity in method and goal even on points of detail. Students unfamiliar with this redemption literature. in medieval Judaism might miss the point of redemption literature in the NT, but those who can capture all of the allusions and significance of Halevy's poetry can also untangle much of the mystery of apocalyptic literature.

Speaking of the ten commandments, the OT preacher said, *For this commandment which I command you this day is not too difficult for you, nor is it too far away. It is not in heaven, that you should say, "Who will go up to heaven for us and bring it to us, that we may hear it and perform it?" Neither is it beyond the sea, that you should say, "Who will go across the sea for us, and bring it to us, that we may hear it and perform it?" But the word is very near you, in your mouth and in your heart, so that you may perform it* (Dt 30:11-14). From this Paul composed the following midrash:

"*Do not say in your heart, 'Who will go up to heaven,* this is to bring the Messiah down, or 'Who will go down to the abyss?' that is to lead the Messiah up from the dead. But what does it say? *The word is near you, in your mouth and in your heart.* This is *the word* of faith which we preach. Because if you confess *in your mouth,* 'Jesus is Lord!' and believe *in your heart* that God raised him from the dead, you will be saved" (Rom 10:6-9).

Like the NT, the medieval redemption writers wove the OT into their formal and informal writing—poetry, prayers, letters, or sermons. This enables those who work in one body of literature to learn from the other, and vice versa.

Prophetically.—Like NT writers, medieval eschatologists assumed that everything that is in the world is in the scripture. Therefore they had only to search the scripture carefully and apply it properly to learn from it the directions they needed for their day.

There was no attempt to study the scripture analytically, but only doctrinally, eisegetically, as material necessary to prove a point of which they were already convinced. They twisted the scripture through *gematria,* astrology, allegory, or mathematics. When they calculated to discover the date at which administrations of political force would change in their favor, they changed days to years, days to thousands of years, or weeks to weeks of years. They could add or omit whatever factors they needed to prove their point mathematically. In one way or another, however, they had to assume that all of the OT prophecy was to be fulfilled in their time. The words "rejoicing" and "delighting" called to the attention of the preacher reported in Pesikta Rabbati the days of the Messiah, the downfall of Rome, and the year of Gog and Magog—none of which occurred to II Isaiah. Paul interpreted the word, which in Deuteronomy meant the commandment, to mean the word of faith which Christians preached. This use of the scripture both was accepted as valid, and it was also necessary to religious people who considered the OT central for understanding the meaning of life.

The Chosen People

Choice names and benefits. —Basic to an understanding of redemption literature is the conviction that the authors belonged to the Lord's chosen people. The poets referred to Jews as the Lord's "dove," his "flock," "graceful doe," his "delicate ones," "the people he chose for an inheritance," his "lamb," "beloved," "afflicted one," and many other such tender names that expressed the authors' beliefs that Jews were the Lord's true heirs and were destined for his richest blessing. It was God's will that they all live like princes and princesses as the envy of all other peoples. When they farmed, their land should produce miraculous crops; when they engaged in business, they were meant to prosper, and people from all over the world should come to them and pay generously for their merchandise. They were to be so highly favored that others would be glad for the privilege of bringing Jews excessive gifts.

Frustrations and figures. —The problem that medieval Jews faced was that these dreams had not been fulfilled. Instead of ruling the world from the promised land, they lived under rule they considered pagan in foreign countries. Sometimes they were severely persecuted, and those destined to be princes were treated like slaves. This they resented, but it did not change their beliefs. They understood that they were being punished for their sin, while serving out a prison term as "captives" in the diaspora. The hardships they faced were considered "birth pangs" necessary as the last of the punishment was received before they were to be set free. The more painful the "birth pangs," the closer they were to giving birth to the Messiah who would deliver them from all these misfortunes. They understood their captivity in terms of "sabbatical eschatology" and tried very hard to learn from the scripture and the signs of their times how long it would be before their prison term would be over. Many set themselves to calculating, usually arriving at some date in the very near future. When this date came and went without a noticeable change in fortunes, they just assumed that they had overlooked some factor in the calculation, so they worked again at the task. They also fasted, prayed, let themselves be punished unjustly, and suffered voluntarily in an effort to pay off the debt of sin that hung over them. These voluntary sufferers or "mourners for Zion," "the poor in spirit," or those who were "persecuted for righteousness" were trying to relive the experiences of the first generation of Jews in Babylon, personified as "the servant," who suffered and paid for the sins of all the Jews who had lived before it so that their children could return to the promised land.[2] Like Christians, medieval Jews assumed that the Messiah, when he suffered, was judged on a different scale of merit from others. Therefore he was pictured as paying off all Israel's sin by his undeserved, vicarious suffering. This suffering was no end in itself, but it was a necessary step on the way to achieving their destined reward of receiving their promised inheritance. It seemed unfortunate and unfair to these chosen people that the rest of the world's people did not recognize at once their superiority and clear the way for them to receive immediately their destined position of privilege. The more reluctant others were to accept this conviction as fact, the more resentful the chosen people were to the rest of the world, which they described in very uncomplimentary terms.

The Gentiles

Insults and ideology.—The same people who thought of

[2]See *Consequences*, 128-30.

themselves as the Lord's favorites thought of others (Gentiles) in hostile terms, such as "enemies," "oppressors," "violent men," "wicked ones," "evil seed," "ignorant people," "goats," "vultures," "dogs," "uncircumcised," "defiled," "scorpions," "thorns," and "thistles." The Gentiles who confronted Jews most often in the Middle Ages were Moslems and Christians. Moslems were called "Ishmael," and Christians were called "Edom" or "Esau." Together with this identification of Moslems with Ishmael was the conviction that they were descendants of a servant, and medieval Jews had the same feeling toward them that Sarah had toward Ishmael after Isaac was born. Esau and Edom not only represented Isaac's stupid elder son, but also the Edomites who helped the Babylonians capture Jerusalem. Medieval Jews felt the same hatred toward contemporary Christians as the author of Obadiah and Ps 137 felt toward the Edomites. The names Jews gave themselves and others did not so much describe either as they actually were, but they indicated how medieval Jews *thought* they were or should be. They further characterized Jesus, the leader of the "Edomites," as Armilos. Armilos was a monster born of a pure Jewish virgin and a satanic Gentile father. The earliest datable recorded legend of Armilos is in the writings of Saadia Gaon, but he was also mentioned in Targ. Isa 11:6 and much earlier a first century apocalyptist pictured the last leader of Rome (II Bar 39:3) leading his troops against Mount Zion, where the Messiah would convict him of his evil deeds and then kill him (II Bar 40:12). As a fulfillment of Isa 61, many medieval Jews believed all Gentiles were destined to be their slaves. Saadia Gaon went so far as to subdivide the servile tasks that various Gentile groups and nations would do for Jews, everything from caring for their children to producing their food and paying their taxes. An earlier eschatologist gave Isa 61 the same interpretation, although with less detail: "Some of every nation will be subjected to your people" (II Bar 72:5). Others were still more hostile and looked forward to the war of Gog and Magog when all Gentiles would be destroyed from the face of the earth. This anti-Gentilic feeling was evident even earlier (Rev 17-19; Enoch 61:6-63:12; PsJ Gen 49:10-11; Ex 17:16; 40:11; Dt 25:19; Onkelos Num 24:24; Jon Hab 3:17).

Christian insults.—These feelings of superiority and hostility toward Gentiles were not unique to medieval Jews. Christians had the same feelings toward non-Christians, and in their early history, about Gentiles, calling them "swine" and "dogs." On the other hand, Christians also considered themselves God's chosen people, called "the light of the world," "the salt of the earth," "a kingdom of priests and a holy people," and "God's church." In the Middle Ages, however, Christians at least had the outward appearance of being rulers of a kingdom, whereas for Jews this deep religious, political need was unfulfilled. Redemption literature provided an interpretation for this condition and also scriptural bases for believing that the condition would soon be reversed.

A first century Jewish eschatologist compared the change of administrations to the birth of Jacob and Esau. Esau came first, but Jacob held him by the heel. This symbolized the two ages. Just as the beginning of a man is his hand, so the end of a man is his heel. The age of Esau-Edom-Rome must end before the age of Jacob-Israel-the Jews can begin. The eschatologist advised: "Do not bother, Ezra, to find out about anything between the heel and the hand" (IV Ezra 6:10), but eschatologists continued to speculate about the very steps necessary to bring about the end of one age and the beginning of the next. In between were miracles, judgment, the battle of Gog and Magog, the resurrection, and the administrative leadership of the two messiahs.

Change of Administration

Miracles.—Consistent with the OT, medieval Jews believed God would perform miracles that would rescue them and restore them to the ruling position among nations (Targ Jon II Sam 22:32; Hab 3:18; Zech 3:8; Targ Ps 18:32; EcclesR 1:11). The mother of the Messiah would wave a wand or staff that would perform the same kind of miracles the staff of Aaron and Moses did in Egypt and the wilderness (Targ on Song of Songs 4:5; 7:4; Targ Lam 2:22; Targ Jon Isa 11:16). When the shofar blast was sounded, announcing the Jewish jubilee, all foreign gods and temples would fall. When the Messiah stood on the top of the Mount of Olives, the mountain would split open. The Messiah of David would destroy Armilos simply by breathing on him; Jericho would fall miraculously as it had before at the hand of Joshua. Sand would be changed into fine flour for Jews. Mountains would be leveled at the right time, and waters would spring out. Moses would be restored, and the company of Korah would be revived. The Messiah of Ephraim would be the first raised, but the sea would also cast up its dead to receive life. Miracles of healing would take place. Diaspora Jews would fly to Palestine on the clouds of heaven. One Jewish leader promised that he would divide the Mediterranean Sea so that the Jews there could walk from Crete to Palestine on dry ground. Another messiah promised that with his magic myrtle branch no enemy could touch their army. Still another pretender broke out of jail, supposedly by magic, and crossed a river on his scarf, with no aid of a boat. These were some of the same kinds of miracles expected by early Christians and attributed to Jesus or his apostles. Like the followers of Jesus, these medieval Jews expected miracles to bring about the fall of the then existing governmental administration and the establishment of a new government in which they would have key positions. There were other necessary events destined to take place before the great shift in powers. One of these was the great judgment.

Judgment

Literature.—A first century patriot reported his anticipation that, at the right time when the millennium was completed, there would be a great judgment. God would sit on his great white throne and judge all of the world's dead which would be raised for the occasion. The books would be opened which listed all the good and bad works of each. There was also a book of life which included all the membership of the true covenanters. Those whose names had not been recorded here would be judged negatively and cast into the lake of fire. This would include all of the Gentiles and those covenanters who had not been faithful, according to the other book, listing the various works performed (Rev 20:11-15; see also Targ. Jon I Sam 2:7). This is very similar to the judgment scene in Enoch (47:3; 90:20-27), with the books open (see also Enoch 89:61-69) and the wicked cast into the fiery abyss. The judgment scene is based on the OT conception of God acting as judge on a throne (Dan 7:9), judging human beings for their innermost thoughts (Jer 17:10; Ps 28:4; 62:13; Enoch 49:4). Basically the same kind of judgment scene was pictured by II Bar (24-25; 59:5-12); and IV Ezra (6:18-23; 9:1-13) with the additional association to the jubilee trumpet. Saadia Gaon was convinced that the great judgment would punish Jewish oppressors (Christians and Moslems) and give Jews great wealth (above, p. 38). One medieval preacher pictured the Messiah as judge, vindicating the humble "mourners for Zion" and avenging, but later admitting, transgressors who repent (PR 158b), but punishing severely the Gentiles (PR 162b). Some unknown thirteenth century poet evaluated the Battle of Acre as the Battle of Gog and Magog to be followed by the appearance of the Messiah, comforting the Jews and condemning the wicked (Christians and Moslems) ("That Day"). In an allegorical, mystical poem, Abulafia spoke of a judgment after a war of three powers in which Israel and the Messiah survived ("The Book of the Sign"). Rabbi Aḥa said that when the exiles returned, the judgment would make the wicked subject and the righteous happy. The wicked would include the Gentiles and the heretics who had been subject to the tyrants. The righteous would include faithful Jews and proselytes (JBer II, 17a). Rabbi Ishmael said that after two thousand years the Lord would sit in judgment in the Valley of Jehoshaphat. At that time the mountains would totter and thus be unable to bear witness to the sins of the Jews. The two thousand years would be days of the Messiah, after which the judgment would be accompanied by the resurrection. The Gentiles would be cast into burning fire. Transgressors of Israel would be punished in Gehinnom for twelve months before they could enjoy the bliss of Eden with the righteous of Israel ("The Prayer, Secrets, and Mysteries of Rabbi Shimon Ben Yoḥai"). Another medieval author anticipated the judgment after the war of Gog and Magog in the third millennium together with the resurrection. At that time the Gentiles would be destroyed, and the Israelites would live miraculously in the Garden of Eden at Jerusalem for countless ages ("The Judgment of Jews and Gentiles"). Still another eschatologist associated the judgment with the destruction of the Gentiles and the world rule of Israel ("The Comforts of the Messiah").[3]

Judgment and politics.—For medieval Jews judgment was no remote, speculative, metaphysical concept unrelated to local, historical events. The judgment of God was internationally oriented and would be the deciding factor in the change from Roman, Moslem, or Persian rule of the world to Jewish rule from Jerusalem. Because of the impending judgment, Jews would soon be granted the superior political and economic status they believed they deserved. They expected miracles to take place in making this change, but they were also practical enough to realize that the strong man must first be bound before they could plunder his goods (Mk 3:27). This would involve a major war—not just

[3]Targumists believed the Messiah would conquer both Rome and the territory around the Mediterranean Sea and the countries east of Palestine (Targ. Onk. Num 24:24; PsJ Num 24:17; Jon. Hab 3:17).

against spiritual forces or moral standards—but against national powers that sent real, armed soldiers into the fields. This is what Ezekiel himself anticipated (Ezek 38-39).

The Battle of Gog and Magog

Identities and relationships. —The NT seer expected the battle of Gog and Magog to take place after the millennium, when the Gentiles would be gathered, like sand of the sea, surrounding the saints at Jerusalem. At that time, God would send down fire from heaven to consume them, destroying the Gentiles together with the beast and the false prophet before the great judgment was held (Rev 20:7-10). This battle, according to Saadia, will take place in the Valley of Jehoshaphat or the Valley of Decision. Maimonides said the battle of Gog and Magog would take place after the revelation of the Messiah. Hai Gaon concurred, noting further that the Messiah would rule in peace with the faithful Jews at Jerusalem before this war took place. He also identified the forces of Gog and Magog with the "Edomites." In addition to the armed Jews, Gog would bring against the Gentiles (Christians) earthquakes, torrential rains, and the plagues described by Zech 14:12-13. This would be followed by the Gentiles returning the Jews to Jerusalem, the sound of the trumpet, and the resurrection of the dead. An unknown thirteenth century author described the battle of Acre (A.D. 1291) as the battle of Gog *against* Magog, one being the Christians and the other the Moslems ("That Day"). The Book of Zerubbabel describes the Jews living in peace and making proselytes for forty years before the battle of Gog and Magog, when the proselytes would abandon Judaism and join the ranks of the enemy. Together with the earthquakes and storms, the Lord would send plagues to defeat the enemy, which is "wicked Edom" (Christians).

The Messiah and Armilos. —During the battle against Edom, the Messiah would be revealed and lead the troops (Book of Zerubbabel). In that war, Armilos would also be killed by the Messiah. Armilos and the ten kings and their troops who would fight in the Valley of Arabiel would all be killed. Rabbi Ishmael identified the troops of Gog and Magog with the ones who killed the Messiah of Ephraim in Jerusalem ("Prayer"). One messianic legend shows the Messiah killed by someone associated with Gog and Magog, without identifying the subject. As in other versions in which this subject was identified as Armilos, this happened after the Messiah of Ephraim had destroyed many Gentiles and reestablished the Jewish community at Jerusalem. The conflict which followed, however, that was led by the Messiah of David, was not called the battle of Gog and Magog ("The Legend of the Messiah"). Another narrative describes Gog and Magog as if the two constituted one person who led seventy-two nations against Jerusalem. It was after he was destroyed by plagues that Armilos appeared ("The Judgment of Jews and Gentiles"). Still another eschatological document showed Jews fighting with Gog and his bands and defeating him ("The Book of Elijah"). No mention was made of Magog (see also Targ PsJ Num 24:17; J I Sam 2:10). As with the poem "That Day," the author may have considered Gog to be one of the forces and Magog the other, one representing Christianity and the other Islam, but have been concerned for only one. Another possibility is that they thought of Magog as a ruler and Gog as a region he ruled as earlier Jewish authors did (Jub 7:19; 8:25). Another author showed the Messiah killing, not Armilos, but a false messiah with the breath of his mouth and rebuilding the temple of the Lord which was considered to be the temple brought down from heaven. In between these events he would kill all the troops of Gog and Magog ("The Story of Daniel"). One version of "The Signs of the Messiah" lists the coming of Gog and Magog as the tenth sign, but does not elaborate. Another author considered the Day of the Lord to be the dividing line that would separate the two ages. At that time Gog and Magog would appear, and a great battle would be fought between the Jews and Gentiles in which every Gentile there would be killed ("Birth Pangs and Delivery").

According to Jubilees, Magog was one of the sons of Japeth (Greece) (7:21), and Gog is listed as a region in the Northeast (Jub 8:25), but in the Middle Ages they were only symbolic names mentioned in Ezekiel. Whatever they represented to Ezekiel, to medieval Jews they meant their political enemies—the Christians, Moslems, or both. In the Book of Revelation, these forces were evidently the Romans, and there is no distinctive difference between the way the NT seer used this symbol from that of medieval Jews. Gog and Magog were not philosophical terms with no practical meaning. They were political enemies covenanters would have to defeat in war before the age of Roman and/or Moslem rule would come to an end, and the age of Jewish rule would begin. The Day of the Lord marked the division between the two.

The Messiahs

The typology of Saul. —Basic to the expectations that the age of
the Christians and/or Moslems had come to an end and the age of
Judaism was about to begin was the belief that two messiahs
would be involved in this change of administrations. The first
messiah would be from Ephraim (see Targ PsJ Ex 40:11; Targ SS
4:5; BB 123b; Suk 51a). One poet called him the son of Kish,
identifying him with Saul, the first king to rule Israel before
David. Like Saul, the Messiah, called Nehemiah, would lead the
Samaritans against the enemies who were the Philistines for Saul,
but the Christians and/or Moslems for Nehemiah. Nehemiah
would overpower the enemy and reestablish Jewish rule from
Jerusalem, defeat the Jews and kill the Messiah of Ephraim. Like
the two witnesses identified with the two messiahs of Zechariah
(4:3, 11-14) who prophesied for 1,290 days in Jerusalem (Rev 11:1-
12), the Messiah of Ephraim was killed by the Gentiles and his
body left unburied, Nehemiah for forty days and the two
witnesses for three days. Afterwards, Nehemiah was laid in a
tomb and still later raised from the Dead by Elijah and Menahem.
The two witnesses were raised after three days and bodily
ascended into heaven before the eyes of their enemies. In some
cases the Messiah of David was in hiding[4] for seven years as a
leper, or, as some say, even from the time of David the king or the
creation of the world, undergoing extremely severe tortures so as
to pay for all the accumulated sins recorded against Jews in the
ledger or book used on the Day of Judgment. His suffering was
intended to redeem Israel before his military leadership began (PR
161b). Like the suffering servant of Isaiah, he was despised, not
only by the Gentiles, but also by the Jewish scholars and leaders of
his own day before he put on garments of vengeance and was
exalted as the Messiah. Details varied somewhat among
narratives, but it was always Elijah and Menahem who raised
Nehemiah, and in some cases Nehemiah was commissioned to
announce the good news to Jews all over the world and gather
them together to Jerusalem. He acted as an ambassador to the
Messiah, son of David. This reflects a Jewish reaction to the old
conflict between Judah and the ten tribes of Israel. From the division of the kingdom on, Jews believed they should rule all the
twelve tribes under the leadership of a son of David, and that the
Samaritans should run interference and later be subordinate to

[4]Note the Son of man was hidden from the creation of the world (Enoch 48:6; 62:6-7).

them as they had done before under Saul's leadership. Their eschatology included the ten tribes but only under Jewish administration (see IV Ezra 13:40-48). Even Nehemiah, the Messiah of Ephraim, was expected to restore worship at Jerusalem, not Gerizim, and rule from Jerusalem, not Gibeah or Samaria. During the birth pangs of the Messiah, the Messiah of David would suffer in Rome; Nehemiah would be killed; Jews would fast in the wilderness; and finally the Messiah son of David would appear and the changes of administration would begin. The Day of the Lord would mark the beginning of the war of Gog and Magog, the complete defeat of the Gentiles, the restoration of the temple, and the age of prosperity for the Jews from Jerusalem.

Samaritans and Armilos.—The expectation that the ten northern tribes of Israel would return is as old as Isaiah 27, and it was confirmed as late as the second century A.D. (IV Ezra 13:40-48). During the Middle Ages, however, Jews developed an expectation that the ten northern tribes would not only return to the acceptance of Davidic rule, as Ezekiel predicted, but they would first function as a rescue mission, fighting against the enemies of the Jews in battle. This would take place under the leadership of Nehemiah, the Messiah of Joseph or Ephraim, who would defeat the Romans. Then the Romans, after a short rule of the Israelites in Jerusalem under the leadership of Nehemiah, would kill this Messiah under the direction of the monster Armilos. Still later the Messiah of David, Menahem, would kill Armilos and rule the world from Jerusalem.

Medie al Jews had good imaginations, to be sure, but their theology usually had a typological base. They believed that which would happen in the future is that which already had happened in the past. When and what happened to inspire these hopes? There was no time in the post-Babylonian biblical period when Samaritans actually acted as deliverers of the Jews. What led Jews to think that they ever would? There is one likely situation.

In the seventh century, Persians were ready to make peace with the Romans when some Samaritans sent an envoy to Persia urging them to fight Rome. They even volunteered 50,000 Samaritan and Jewish troops to support the movement.[5] A certain Benjamin from Galilee recruited and financed numerous troops for the movement. Persia agreed and they successfully sacked Jerusalem, killing 90,000 Christians, according to Jewish reports, and 3,000

---

[5]Graetz, *History* III, 19-20.

according to Persian records.[6] Levi suggested that Jews thought of Benjamin as the Messiah of Joseph[7] and later Roman king Heraclius as Armilos.[8] The apocalyptic imagination did not need more than an initial germ to create an eschatological narrative. This germ may have come from the seventh century and reflects Jewish expectations of Samaritan support. It also indicates hostility to Persia afterwards with Haf-zi-bah appearing to kill the Persian king Shiroi after he had killed Nehemiah. Jews were not finally discouraged when their favorable conditions were ephemeral. The true Messiah was the son of David who would defeat Heraclius = Armilos = Rome = the Christians.

Later generations evidently developed a detailed eschatological theory based on the seventh century historical event. In the future a much larger contingent of Samaritans would come and fight for them, and two Messiahs became the expected norm. Involved with this whole picture was the expectation of the resurrection together with the judgment.

The human messiahs. —The messiahs were not just cultic leaders or roving teachers; they were redeemers who suffered for Israel; and they were military leaders who destroyed Gentiles in war before they became kings ruling from Jerusalem (Targ PsJ Gen 3:15; 35:21; 49:1; Ex 40:9;Num 23:21; 24:17-20; Targ Ps 61:7; 72:8; Targ SS 7:4, 14; Targ Lam 2:12; 4:22; Targ Esther 1:1).[9] Messiahs were not just vague religious symbols of the future. They were real men, like Alroy, Abu Issa, Serenus, Ephraim,Obadiah, Bar Cochba, David el David, and others who actually gathered troops, claimed to have performed miracles, and fought real battles with real political and military opponents. After their movements failed, they were ridiculed as false messiahs, but they first convinced Jews that they were real messiahs to be identified with normal Jewish eschatological expectations. Those who ridiculed them did not accuse them of being false because they were human beings and political leaders rather than messiahs, but they had not been or could not be *successful* in their political and military messianic leadership.

[6]I. Levi, "L'Apocalypse de Zorobabel et le Roi de Perse Sirois," *REJ* 69 (1918), 112.

[7]*Ibid.,* 114.

[8]*Ibid.,* 71 (1920), 60-61.

[9]S.H. Levey, *The Messiah: An Aramaic Interpretation* (Cincinnati, 1971), XIX, concurs: "The Messiah will pronounce doom upon the enemies of Israel, will mete out reward and punishment in truth and justice, and will serve as an ideal king ruling the entire world."

The Time of the End

Daniel and Jeremiah's prophecy. — The pro-Hasmonean Jew who believed that the Maccabean victory over the Greeks was the true fulfillment of Jeremiah's promise was faced with the problem that it came hundreds of years after Jeremiah had promised (Jer 25:11; II Chron 36:21). He solved the problem by making the figures concur with the facts, as had probably been done before.[10] Jeremiah may have prophesied "seven years" which was changed to ten times seven years to agree with the actual seventy years that transpired between the captivity and the restoration under Joshua and Zerubbabel (Hag 1:1; Zech 1:12). After the temple had been cleansed, the author explained that Jeremiah really intended seventy *weeks of years* (Dan 9:2, 24). After Daniel was accepted as scripture, this method of adjusting figures in prophecy to concur with convictions was an accepted methodology. This allowed later covenanters who considered themselves to be "captives" to make numerous transfers and reinterpretations. Not only could years be changed to weeks of years, but on the basis of Ps 90:4, days could be changed to thousands of years. The "fourth beast" (Dan 7:7-11) could also be identified with Rome rather than Greece. Other factors were added to the possibilities, such as the nine months of a pregnancy, the seventy years spent in Babylon, the four hundred years' captivity in Egypt, and the six days of creation. The NT seer calculated in terms of millennia, on the basis that there were six days of "work" and one day of "rest." The Messiah was to come one of the last days of the week of seven thousand years. He would conquer the world and rule during that millennium before the thousand years of "rest" with Israel ruling the world and no enemies to interfere.

Revelation and the millennia. — According to one calendar, Jesus began his ministry at the beginning of the sixth millennium.[11] According to the seer, the "dragon" would be bound in the abyss throughout one millennium (Rev 20:1-2). During that same time the Messiah would rule for a thousand years (Rev 20:4-6). The next millennium would begin with the resurrection of the dead, the release of the dragon (Satan), and the war of Gog and Magog (Rev 20:5, 7-9). Then the dragon (devil), the beast, and the false prophet would soon be thrown into the lake of fire. The next event

[10]For a justification of this theory about Daniel see the Anchor Bible no. 36, *To The Hebrews* (Garden City, 1972), 42-48.
[11]A.H. Silver, *Messianic Speculation*. 6, 16-19.

would be the judgment (Rev 20:11-13) with all the wicked thrown into the lake of fire (Rev 20:14-15; 21:7-8). Then, during the same millennium, apparently, there was to be the new heaven, earth, and Jerusalem where the righteous elect would live in the Garden of Eden. The next does not say, but it may have been at this point that the thousand years of Sabbath "rest" began when the righteous should rule for ages and ages (Rev 21:1-22:5). It is not certain which two days of the week the two millennia specified by the seer represent, but the author clearly was calculating on the basis of the seven thousand year week as many medieval apocalyptists did.

Medieval calculators.—The eighty-fifth jubilee cycle coincided with four hundred years after the fall of Jerusalem (A.D. 468) and was anticipated as the time for the deliverance of Israel. Some medieval Jews specified the exact year when the "captivity" would be over. One popular prediction was

"nine hundred and ninety years   תשע מאות ותשעין שנה
the salvation of the Lord."   תשועה לה'

This meant 990 years *after* the fall of Jerusalem, which was A.D. 1060—just a jubilee before the end of the fifth millennium.

Other calculators predicted A.D. 960. Halevy promised that in the year תת"ץ (A.D. 1130) the enemy would be crouched (תרחץ). Maimonides said A.D. 1210 would be the time of redemption. Alharizi predicted (probably after the fact of Saladin's victory at the Horns of the Hittim) that God would use Moslems to drive out the Christians in A.D. 1190. Abulafia prophesied A.D. 1288 and Nahmonides, A.D. 1359. Rabbi Hiyya offered several possibilities—A.D. 1290; 1340-1358; 1448-1468; and 2240. Gabirol calculated A.D. 1464.

When someone promised redemption on a certain date there were almost always some Jews who would believe and act on the prediction, even at the risk of life and possessions, but since there were many variables and no controls, there was never any real certainty that the calculation reached was the right one. Cautious counsellors told which signs Jews should anticipate ("Signs of the Messiah" and Mt 24:4-21, 29-31), but were careful to warn against false prophets (Mt 24:4-6, 11, 23-26) insisting that no one knows the exact time (Mt 24:36-44; 25:13). This uncertainty left most Jews looking for a prophet and asking, "When will these things take place" (Mt 24:3)? "When will the son of David come?" There was much anxiety, impatience, and lamentation as years passed without redemption. Ibn Ezra said:

> Yes, generations pass and go, but the people of God will
> stand in its pain (Lam 1:12).
> A thousand years of marvel (Dan 12:6) will pass. With
> deep anguish
> he says, *If you will redeem, redeem; if you will not
> redeem, tell me* (Ruth 4:4).

Rabbi Zerah asked:

> How long will you keep still and gaze at sin and wicked-
> ness and not have mercy on Jerusalem and the cities of
> Judah with whom you are angry?

Halevy complained:

> When will my head be raised? When will there be an
> acceptable time to seek him?
> When, O my Rock, will I arise and once again beseech him
> in your jealousy for your name, for your city, and
> for your people?

In poetry and prayer Jews complained of their lot and begged
the Lord to act to destroy the Gentiles, gather the scattered flock
of Israel, rebuild Jerusalem, construct the temple, send the
Messiah, restore the promised land, and bring near the day of
redemption. From the time of Jesus to the time of Nahmonides
covenanters never stopped asking, "When will the close of the age
arrive?"

Redemption in history. —Saadia Gaon said there were three
enslavements: 1) the enslavement in Egypt, 2) the enslavement in
Babylon, and 3) the current enslavement to Rome. In the past
there had always been a redemption after each enslavement, and
medieval Jews looked forward to the third redemption from the
third enslavement. Jews compared the former redemption with the
redemption still to come (PR 162a). The former redemptions were
followed by the inheritance of the promised land. In the future the
Jews expected to inherit not only Palestine but all the land then
controlled by Moslems and Christians. This would involve all of
Europe, North Africa, the Arabian Peninsula, and all the land as
far as India.

Redemption literature in the OT. —Redemption literature is that
literature which was composed in anticipation of a future
redemption. During the Babylonian captivity, Jewish prophets

composed Ezekiel, II Isaiah, and Zechariah. Saadia probably
assumed that Daniel was also related to this redemption, since he
did not isolate the Greek enslavement as something separate.
Rabbis were probably correct in considering the Song of Songs to
be an apocalyptic document. It makes little sense to evaluate the
document as an irreligious, sensuous love song, as some have
done. What girl would be flattered to be described as one whose
hair is like a flock of goats moving down the slopes of Gilead (4:1;
6:5); whose teeth are like a flock of shorn ewes (4:2; 6:6); whose
cheeks are like halves of a pomegranate (4:3; 6:7); whose neck is
like a tower of David (4:4; 7:4); and whose breasts are like two
fawns (4:5)? Would a lover say his sweetheart had a navel like a
rounded bowl (7:2), a belly like a heap of wheat (7:2), eyes like
pools of Heshbon (7:4), a nose like the tower of Lebanon (7:4), a
head like Mount Carmel, and breasts like towers (8:10)? This does
not flatter a woman, but by implication, the promised land is
made the object of a passionate love. For those who had ears to
hear, the song, which the nationalist Rabbi Akiba called the "holy
of holies," is a national anthem to be sung in a foreign land,
looking forward to the consumation of "marriage." In other affectionate contexts, the following geographic locations are
mentioned: Sharon (2:1), Jerusalem (3:4; 5:8, 16; 8:4), Lebanon
(3:9; 4:8), Zion (3:11), Amana (4:8), and Hermon (4:8). Other
terms like wheat, pomegranates, vineyards, flocks, and spices call
attention to produce from the promised land. All of these terms
are fitting in a love song whose object is the promised land rather
than a human bride. As a national anthem sung by exiles, the Song
of Songs also should be considered redemption literature, and the
medieval rabbis considered it so.

Redemption literature in the NT. —In the NT, the gospels are
concentrated on Jesus announcing that the time is fulfilled and the
anticipated redemption has arrived. The expected kingdom has
arrived. This seems like a type of redemption literature.

Hebrews is a homily based on the conviction that the readers
were in the same position as the Hebrews at the border of Canaan.
By typological reasoning, if they would not yield to temptation,
they would soon enter this promised rest. Throughout the book
the author compared his readers to the ancient Hebrews and the
anticipated redemption to previous redemptions. This is redemption literature.

Like other apocalyptic literature the Book of Revelation is
redemption literature, and certain epistles also have as their basic

message some counsel for those expecting the end and whose eschatological expectations provided problems for the ongoing community. This literature is similar to medieval or pre-Christian redemption literature in purpose and form. Therefore it can best be understood in relationship to other similar literature and other redemptions whose purpose and identification are clearly expressed.

Redemption in the New Testament

Early Christian world view.—The Christian who has been accustomed to think of eschatology in terms of existential experience or in some philosophical concept of time or history will have found the eschatology of medieval Judaism quite a different kind of religion, but those familiar with the NT will have recognized many similar terms and concepts—the suffering Messiah, the treasury of merits theology, salvation, redemption, judgment, the war of Gog and Magog, Gehinnom, the Garden of Eden, the new Jerusalem coming down from heaven, the theology of the wilderness, anxiety for the end of the age, hostility to Rome and the Gentiles, the chosen people, repentance, forgiveness of sins, exodus typologies, and many others. These were not new inventions, but there was, for the most part, a direct continuity with the OT and the same meanings were given in the intertestamental literature, first century apocalypticism, like IV Ezra and II Baruch, early medieval literature, and literature composed at the close of the Crusader period. The messianic role of Bar Cochba in the second century was very similar to that of Alroy in the twelfth century. Medieval messiahs were redeemers who were to suffer, lead troops in war, and then rule the world from Jerusalem as successors to David. The end they expected was the end of the Moslem and/or Christian rule over Palestine, Persia, and the entire European and Mediterranean world. They wanted an end to the Jewish diaspora. After the end had come, they expected history to continue in a new age, under a new administration—namely theirs. This international, political shift of powers was called salvation, deliverance, or redemption. Redemption and salvation were not exactly synonyms. Redemption was the judicial, theological act that had to take place in relationship to God, the treasury of merits, and sabbatical eschatology before salvation was possible. Salvation was the result that effected the Jews directly in practical, political, economic, and international affairs. There was a sequential relationship chronologically between "this world," ruled by Roman or Byzantine Christians and/or Moslems and the same geographical territory to be ruled by the Jews, called "the world to come." Heaven and earth were believed to exist at the same time and to be interrelated. The activity of the Lord and his angels in heaven influenced the success or failure of armies on earth.

The religious world was in direct continuity with that of the OT, differing only in necessary historical and geographical realities of existence, reflecting the corresponding cultural and linguistic influences. Between OT times and medieval Jewish times Christianity came into existence in the same land of Palestine, and the NT was composed, employing many of the same expressions and thought forms as pre-Christian and medieval Jews in relationship to a Jewish messiah. It seems rather normal under the circumstances to examine some of these eschatological concepts in the NT against the religious and political aspirations of other Jews to understand the meaning of this movement and the proper interpretation of the literature of the NT.

Redemption.—The servant of II Isaiah and the Messiah of Ephraim in medieval redemption literature were believed to have suffered extensively and then died to cancel Israel's debt of sin. Medieval Jews believed the sufferings of the Messiah were judged by a different scale (see PR 159a) from the suffering of other Jews, so that one messiah could be given enough credit for his suffering to compensate for all the previous sins of all other Jews of all time.

After the death of the Messiah, Jesus, Christians understood his suffering and death to be that which was necessary to obtain God's judgment of "not guilty" and receive their needed redemption (ἀπολύτρωσεως), the forgiveness of sins (Rom 3:22-24; I Cor 1:29-30; Eph 1:4-7; Col 1:14). It was not through the blood of bulls and goats given on the Day of Atonement, but through the blood of Jesus (Heb 9:11-12, 15; Eph 1:4-7) that they might receive the promised inheritance. Jesus had died to redeem covenanters and become a down payment (ἀρραβών) of their inheritance for redemption (Eph 1:14; Titus 2:14). Those who had been sealed or baptized were prepared for the day of redemption that was still to come (Eph 4:30). When the prophetess Anna saw Jesus at his birth she began to speak "to all who expected the redemption of Jerusalem" (Lk 2:38). After Jesus' death some Jews were sad, because they had hoped Jesus was "the one who was about to redeem Israel" (Lk 24:21). Like medieval covenanters, early Christians were told that the appearance of the Son of Man coming with the clouds was their sign that their redemption was coming near (Lk 21:38).

Redemption in relationship to the forgiveness of sins, Jerusalem, Israel, the inheritance, and the Son of man seems to be in the same contexts as redemption in medieval Jewish literature, and there is no obvious internal reason for thinking that the eschatological goals would not have been political, national, and earthly, just as they were in pre-Christian Jewish literature and in redemption literature.

Messianic Secret

Medieval messiahs. —Maimonides warned the Jews in Yemen to suppress the man in their midst who was claiming that he was a messiah, before the Gentiles learned about the movement he was leading and punished the whole Jewish community very severely. To illustrate the possibilities, he told of other aspiring messiahs who had organized followers and led armies who had been soundly defeated. The Jews were heavily taxed, and made to live in very restricted conditions. When the king of Persia learned of Alroy's movement he threatened the Jewish community with annihilation if they did not stop him. These messianic movements had as their goal the overthrow of the existing regime, which intended subversion did not make governments in power happy.

First century messiahs. —Josephus told of many messiahs in NT times and earlier who led armies that finally resulted in the show down at Jerusalem (A.D. 66-70). During the same period Jesus began to organize a movement that led to his crucifixion between two insurrectionists as "king of the Jews." His movement involved recruiting twelve officers to assist him. These were to be assigned as judges over the twelve tribes of Israel when the Messiah came into his glory. He sent his apostles out to get support for his movement, promising rewards for supporters but severe punishment for those who would not cooperate. During his program planning he sometimes lived a rather fugitive existence with "no place to lay his head." Herod's spies were trailing him to keep a threatening political force from getting out of hand. Like medieval Jews, he met with thousands of Jews, on a hill away from the cities where they tried to make him king. He told followers that the time of the captivity was over; the time of their redemption had come; the kingdom of God was about to be introduced. When Peter declared that Jesus was the Messiah, Jesus warned him not to tell anyone. The parables he told about the kingdom of God were sometimes subversion parables of seeds growing secretly, leaven working in a loaf, or binding the strong man; and sometimes they were like lightning warfare in which the Son of Man would come like a thief in the night or like lightning flashing from one end of heaven to the other. He worked frequently with rich tax collectors, urging them to give large amounts of money to finance the movement. Those who questioned his authority asked him to perform miracles. He had been closely allied with John the baptist who had been beheaded for his conflict with Herod. He was called by the royal titles—Son of God, Son of man, Messiah, Lord, and King. The political kingdom of Solomon was called the "kingdom of the Lord," and Solomon was called the Lord's son. Jesus had as his primary goal the formation of the kingdom of God with himself as the Son of God in the ruling position. The guards at Gethsemane had weapons, and the Romans came out to capture Jesus with an armed force. He lived in a very tense period when zealots were always looking for a leader to help them to overthrow the Romans. He was able to muster a large following among a group of people who were religiously convinced that it was not God's will that the Romans be in political control of the promised land. None of his followers either betrayed or denied him until it seemed unlikely to them that he would lead a military movement at that particular feast. When he was crucified, some Jews were sad that their hopes in him as the one who was about to redeem Israel had failed. The political, nationalistic, traditional Jewish hopes and implications associated with Jesus are too many and striking to believe that he had very different meanings for all of these concepts and still gained a large following in the midst of rebellious times. The redemption literature of the Middle Ages and the pre-Christian Jewish literature are so closely related to NT literature that it is unreasonable to think that they are unrelated in thought form. The study of this literature obligates the NT scholar to study the NT again from this perspective.

597

INDEX OF SUBJECTS

599

606

608

Rechab, Yehonadab ben 515
Redeemed 41, 64, 66, 67, 80, 166, 306, 307,
    315, 316, 331, 332, 333, 334, 340, 355,
    416, 443, 446, 468, 572
Redeemer 7, 22, 45, 115, 141, 151, 168, 171,
    175, 190. 215, 218, 222, 224, 227, 229,
    230, 236, 238, 243, 246, 247, 270, 280,
    387, 324, 329, 346, 388, 406, 447, 516
Redeemers 8, 586
Redeeming 233
Redeems 63, 70, 285
Redemption ii, 1, 3, 6, 14, 19, 23, 40, 42,
    46, 54, 59, 62, 63, 65, 74, 79, 81, 82,
    84, 120, 130, 133, 134, 142, 143, 144,
    145, 148, 150, 153, 157, 158, 159, 163,
    164, 165, 167, 169, 170, 172, 186, 202,
    203, 204, 208, 212, 213, 220, 223, 225,
    226, 231, 233, 234, 240, 242, 243, 249,
    280, 283, 284, 287, 288, 291, 301, 309,
    312, 322, 329, 333, 342, 343, 344, 354,
    407, 419, 420, 427, 448, 458, 487, 488,
    490, 498, 499, 502, 504, 507, 511, 514,
    517, 550, 579, 588, 589, 590, 591, 592,
    593
Redemption Literature 570, 571, 575
Redemption, Midrashim of iv
Redemption, Promise of 422
Redemptions 90, 573
Refined 47, 48
Refuge 248, 259, 284, 316
Refugees 50, 125, 237, 281
Reign 104, 395
Remnant 207, 236, 254, 414, 499, 501
Renew 53, 208, 223, 234, 268
Renewal 521
Repent 48, 119, 283, 383, 467, 482, 510
Repentance 40, 45, 109, 110, 154, 159, 166,
    236, 245, 315, 319, 323, 326, 328, 343,
    514, 551, 556, 591
Repentant 322, 554
Repenting 111
Repents 544
Rescue 233, 556
Resh Lakish 323, 551
Resistance 94, 317
Responsa 27, 570
Response 417
Rest 5, 23, 31, 32, 103, 154, 155, 156, 209,
    212, 235, 249, 271, 315, 328, 443, 470,
    519, 557, 587, 588, 590
Rest, Millennia of 140
Resting Places 219
Restoration 235, 237, 247
Resurrection 10, 26, 52, 120, 123, 126, 127,
    130, 134, 140, 141, 143, 144, 150, 153,
    154, 156, 157, 158, 159, 176, 277, 507,
    508, 521, 579, 581, 582, 586
Return 224, 229
Reveal 163, 164, 269, 402, 438, 476, 508,
    532, 539, 540, 564
Revealed 107, 108, 119, 123, 127, 129, 138,
    140, 145, 151, 153, 169, 170, 255, 262,
    275, 288, 290, 293, 297, 301, 322, 332,
    333, 341, 346, 357, 376, 388, 389, 409,
    416, 419, 420, 425, 436, 478, 494, 501,
    516, 520, 528, 582
Revealer 135
Reveals 299
Revelation 1, 140, 178, 260, 443, 570, 587
Revelation of Messiah 582
Revenge 200
Reviles 215

Revive 150, 459, 473, 503, 504
Revolt 22, 69, 174, 175, 398, 472
Revolution 102, 482, 538
Revolutionaries 174
Reward 38, 41, 42, 48, 52, 65, 66, 111, 154,
    187, 221, 314, 323, 343, 392, 452, 526,
    554, 577, 586
Rewarded 79, 207, 273
Rewarding 250
Rewards 593
Righteous 47, 52, 65, 67, 98, 102, 126, 128,
    133, 155, 158, 200, 237, 244, 266, 294,
    314, 317, 321, 322, 325, 330, 343, 364,
    371, 425, 434, 439, 440, 452, 472, 475,
    482, 489, 507, 509, 519, 522, 530, 545,
    546, 548, 551, 553, 556, 557, 558, 559,
    562, 563, 564, 566, 567, 581, 588
Righteous Deeds 344, 533
Righteous Messiah 76, 77
Righteous Ones 66, 102, 111, 132, 341, 444,
    490, 501, 502, 523, 532, 560
Righteousness 3, 61, 65, 69, 78, 92, 130,
    195, 196, 217, 234, 251, 282, 303, 314,
    316, 435, 470, 483, 514, 516, 518, 532,
    534, 556, 568, 577
Righteousness, Teacher of 196
River Gozen 514
River Sambation 403
Riyah 421
Rock 589
Roman 18, 102, 109, 174, 258, 313, 318, 418,
    480, 482, 483, 572, 581, 586
Roman Christianity 418
Roman Christians 25, 26, 27, 305, 388, 442,
    493, 512, 592
Roman Empire 176, 571
Roman-Arabian Captivity 44
Romania 176
Romans 9, 19, 20, 24, 26, 28, 45, 46, 63,
    107, 115, 121, 132, 178, 198, 217, 219,
    220, 242, 269, 319, 329, 330, 339, 387,
    401, 412, 413, 459, 471, 477, 483, 562,
    583, 585, 594
Romanus 419, 420
Romatros 379
Romulus 351, 400
Rosh Hamaim 365
Rufus 174
Ruin 174, 517
Rule 96, 104, 110, 121, 128, 129, 132, 159,
    172, 213, 234, 238, 240, 246, 249, 254,
    268, 275, 291, 293, 305, 327, 335, 339,
    342, 384, 390, 393, 395, 400, 405, 417,
    419, 420, 422, 445, 468, 470, 471, 474,
    505, 513, 538, 540, 571, 581, 582, 588,
    591
Rule, Moslem 417
Ruled 149, 341, 459
Ruler 175, 320, 330, 485, 583
Rulers 315, 424, 579
Rulership 147
Rules 294
Ruling 466
Russian Jews 177

Saba 541
Sabatian Messianic Movement 385
Sabbath 4, 5, 6, 10, 14, 64, 103, 212, 283,
    471, 479, 511, 555, 556, 557, 561, 564
Sabbath Rest 235, 271, 588
Sabbath Year 117
Sabbath Years 378

617

INDEX OF BIBLICAL REFERENCES

620

629